The Cambridge Handbook of Social Representations

A social representations approach offers an empirical utility for addressing myriad social concerns such as social order, ecological sustainability, national identity, racism, religious communities, the public understanding of science, health and social marketing. The core aspects of social representations theory have been debated over many years and some still remain widely misunderstood. This handbook provides an overview of these core aspects and brings together theoretical strands and developments in the theory, some of which have become pillars in the social sciences in their own right. Academics and students in the social sciences working with concepts and methods such as social identity, discursive psychology, positioning theory, semiotics, attitudes, risk perception and social values will find this an invaluable resource.

GORDON SAMMUT is Lecturer in the Department of Psychology at the University of Malta.

ELENI ANDREOULI is Lecturer in the Department of Psychology at the Open University.

GEORGE GASKELL is Professor of Social Psychology at the London School of Economics and Political Science.

JAAN VALSINER is Niels Bohr Professor of Cultural Psychology in the Department of Communication and Psychology at Aalborg University, Denmark.

The Cambridge Handbook of Social Representations

Edited by
Gordon Sammut
Eleni Andreouli
George Gaskell
Jaan Valsiner

CAMBRIDGE UNIVERSITY PRESS

CAMBRIDGE
UNIVERSITY PRESS

University Printing House, Cambridge CB2 8BS, United Kingdom

Cambridge University Press is part of the University of Cambridge.

It furthers the University's mission by disseminating knowledge in the pursuit of education, learning and research at the highest international levels of excellence.

www.cambridge.org
Information on this title: www.cambridge.org/9781316635681

© Cambridge University Press 2015

This publication is in copyright. Subject to statutory exception and to the provisions of relevant collective licensing agreements, no reproduction of any part may take place without the written permission of Cambridge University Press.

First published 2015
First paperback edition 2016

A catalogue record for this publication is available from the British Library

ISBN 978-1-107-04200-1 Hardback
ISBN 978-1-316-63568-1 Paperback

Cambridge University Press has no responsibility for the persistence or accuracy of URLs for external or third-party internet websites referred to in this publication, and does not guarantee that any content on such websites is, or will remain, accurate or appropriate.

Contents

List of figures	page viii
List of tables	x
List of contributors	xi
Preface	xiii

Part I. Foundations

1 Social representations: a revolutionary paradigm?   3
   GORDON SAMMUT, ELENI ANDREOULI, GEORGE GASKELL
   AND JAAN VALSINER

2 Representation in action   12
   WOLFGANG WAGNER

3 Social representations and societal psychology   29
   CLAUDIA ABREU LOPES AND GEORGE GASKELL

4 On (social) representations and the iconoclastic impetus   43
   MARTIN W. BAUER

5 Researching social representations   64
   UWE FLICK, JULIET FOSTER AND SABINE CAILLAUD

Part II. Conceptual developments

6 Central core theory   83
   PASCAL MOLINER AND JEAN-CLAUDE ABRIC

7 Attitudes, social representations and points of view   96
   GORDON SAMMUT

8 Communication and the microgenetic construction of
   knowledge   113
   CHARIS PSALTIS

9 Image, social imaginary and social representations   128
   ANGELA ARRUDA

10	Collective remembering as a process of social representation BRADY WAGONER	143
11	Cognitive polyphasia, knowledge encounters and public spheres SANDRA JOVCHELOVITCH AND JACQUELINE PRIEGO-HERNÁNDEZ	163
12	Making community: diversity, movement and interdependence CAROLINE HOWARTH, FLORA CORNISH AND ALEX GILLESPIE	179

Part III. New directions

13	Social representations and social construction: the evolutionary perspective of installation theory SAADI LAHLOU	193
14	From representations to representing: on social representations and discursive-rhetorical psychology STEPHEN GIBSON	210
15	Positioning theory and social representations ROM HARRÉ AND FATHALI MOGHADDAM	224
16	Social semiotics and social representations GIUSEPPE VELTRI	234
17	Identity process theory GLYNIS BREAKWELL	250

Part IV. Applications

18	Representations of world history JAMES H. LIU AND CHRIS G. SIBLEY	269
19	Social order and political legitimacy CHRISTIAN STAERKLÉ	280
20	Social representations of sustainability: researching time, institution, conflict and communication PAULA CASTRO	295
21	Social representations of national identity in culturally diverse societies ELENI ANDREOULI AND XENIA CHRYSSOCHOOU	309

22	The essentialized refugee: representations of racialized 'Others' MARTHA AUGOUSTINOS, SCOTT HANSON-EASEY AND CLEMENCE DUE	323
23	Exploring stability and change through social representations: towards an understanding of religious communities MOHAMMAD SARTAWI	341
24	Of worlds and objects: scientific knowledge and its publics NICOLE KRONBERGER	358
25	The self-control ethos HELENE JOFFE	369
26	Social representations of infectious diseases VÉRONIQUE EICHER AND ADRIAN BANGERTER	385
27	Social change, social marketing and social representations MARY ANNE LAURI	397
	References	411
	Index	471

Figures

1.1	The Toblerone model of social representations (after Bauer and Gaskell, 1999)	page 7
2.1	Mediation effect of self-identity for low ambivalence (bold beta coefficients, adj. R2 = 0.21) and for high ambivalence respondents (italic, adj. R2 = 0.29) (after Castro *et al.*, 2009)	16
2.2	Eight days' thermostat settings for 'valve' theory (upper) and 'control' theory (lower) subjects (schematic redrawing according to Kempton, 1986)	21
3.1	Coleman's macro–micro model	34
4.1	The basic unit of analysis and attribution of representations	53
4.2	The Toblerone model of social representations (after Bauer and Gaskell, 1999). From Bauer, M. W., & Gaskell, G. (1999). Towards a paradigm for research on social representations. *Journal for the Theory of Social Behaviour*, 29(2), 163–186. Copyright © 1999 by John Wiley & Sons, Inc. Reprinted by permission of John Wiley & Sons, Inc.	55
4.3	The irregular 'wind rose' model of social representations (Bauer and Gaskell, 2008). From Bauer, M. W., & Gaskell, G. (2008). Social representations theory: a progressive research programme for social psychology, *Journal for the Theory of Social Behaviour*, 38(4), 335–354. Copyright © 2008 by John Wiley & Sons, Inc. Reprinted by permission of John Wiley & Sons, Inc.	55
5.1	Alceste analysis of Bali climate conference	75
7.1	Point of view	107
7.2	A nested model of social behaviour: social representations, points of view, and attitudes (adapted from Bauer and Gaskell, 1999 and based on Heider's (1946) balance of reciprocity in the cognitive organization of attitudes)	109
14.1	Physical representation of Chamberlain's waving gesture by A13 (corresponding to lines 5–6 in the extract), with Chamberlain's original gesture (30 September 1938; from www.youtube.com/watch?v=FO725Hbzfls)	219
15.1	The positioning triangle	231

16.1	A representation of the different ways of conceiving the denotation–connotation–object relationships (adapted from Eco, 1973)	237
16.2	Recursive social significations underlying anchoring and objectification	245
27.1	Adjectives used to describe donors and non-donors	404
27.2	Representations of the human body	405
27.3	Number of organs transplanted from 1988 to 2005 (source: A. Bugeja, Transplant Coordinator, Malta, personal communication, 12.05.2007)	409

Tables

6.1	Formal properties of central and peripheral elements	*page* 85
6.2	Expressive properties of central and peripheral elements	87
6.3	Psycho-social properties of the central and peripheral systems	88
6.4	Changes or transformations of social representations	89
11.1	Cognitive polyphasia: dimensions, constituents and levels of contradiction	172
11.2	Varieties of cognitive polyphasia: knowledge encounters and cognitive outcomes	175
16.1	A summary of the differences regarding connotative meanings within the structural semiotic paradigm and between the latter and interpretative approach	241
27.1	Campaign messages for groups with different social representations of the body	406
27.2	Perceptions of organ donation after the campaign	409

Contributors

CLAUDIA ABREU LOPES, University of Cambridge

JEAN-CLAUDE ABRIC, University of Aix

ELENI ANDREOULI, The Open University

ANGELA ARRUDA, Universidade Federal do Rio de Janeiro

MARTHA AUGOUSTINOS, University of Adelaide

ADRIAN BANGERTER, University of Neuchatel

MARTIN W. BAUER, London School of Economics and Political Science

GLYNIS BREAKWELL, University of Bath

SABINE CAILLAUD, Paris One Research Program

PAULA CASTRO, Lisbon University Institute, ISCTE-IUL

XENIA CHRYSSOCHOOU, Panteion University

FLORA CORNISH, London School of Economics and Political Science

CLEMENCE DUE, University of Adelaide

VÉRONIQUE EICHER, University of Lausanne

UWE FLICK, Free University Berlin

JULIET FOSTER, University of Cambridge

GEORGE GASKELL, London School of Economics and Political Science

STEPHEN GIBSON, York St John University

ALEX GILLESPIE, London School of Economics and Political Science

SCOTT HANSON-EASEY, University of Adelaide

ROM HARRÉ, Georgetown University

CAROLINE HOWARTH, London School of Economics and Political Science

HELENE JOFFE, University College London

SANDRA JOVCHELOVITCH, London School of Economics and Political Science

NICOLE KRONBERGER, Johannes Kepler University, Linz

SAADI LAHLOU, London School of Economics and Political Science

MARY ANNE LAURI, University of Malta

JAMES H. LIU, Victoria University of Wellington

FATHALI MOGHADDAM, Georgetown University

PASCAL MOLINER, University of Montpellier

JACQUELINE PRIEGO-HERNÁNDEZ, London School of Economics and Political Science

CHARIS PSALTIS, University of Cyprus

GORDON SAMMUT, University of Malta

MOHAMMAD SARTAWI, Gulf University for Science and Technology

CHRIS G. SIBLEY, Victoria University of Wellington

CHRISTIAN STAERKLÉ, University of Lausanne

JAAN VALSINER, Aalborg University

GIUSEPPE VELTRI, University of Leicester

BRADY WAGONER, Aalborg University

WOLFGANG WAGNER, Johannes Kepler University, Linz

Preface

This handbook aims to take stock and to look forward at key theoretical, methodological and applied desiderata of the theory of social representations. It is designed to appeal to psychologists and social theorists, as well as scholars and students working in cognate disciplines including cultural studies, sociology, anthropology, political science, philosophy, communication studies and linguistics whose interests focus on the ordinary knowledge in the life-world.

In 1968 Gordon Allport wrote:

> the modern social psychologist is haunted by the question: How can the individual be both a cause and a consequence of society. How can his nature depend indisputably upon the prior existence of cultural designs and upon his role in a pre-determined social structure, while at the same time he is clearly a unique person, both selecting and rejecting influences from his cultural surroundings, and in turn creating new cultural forms for the guidance of future generations? (Allport, 1968, p. 8)

Towards the end of 'The historical background of modern social psychology', Allport sets out the challenge for social psychology: the burning issues of war and peace, education, population control and effective democracy, are all in need of assistance. But he suggests that such assistance is unlikely to come from 'small gem-like researches, however exquisite their perfection'. Will, he asks, the current preoccupation with methods and miniature models lead to theory and application? He goes on: 'integrative theories are not easy to come by: like all behavioural science social psychology rests ultimately upon broad meta-theories concerning the nature of man and the nature of society'. Allport contrasts the 'high level conceptualisations' of the likes of Machiavelli, Bentham and Compte with the contemporary non-theoretical orientation of the empiricists. He hoped that the tide might turn (Allport, 1968, p. 69).

The turning of the tide is evidenced in this handbook, which brings together forty authors whose research is inspired by the theory of social representations. This theory traces its origins back to Durkheim's notion of collective representations. Since its inception in Moscovici's (1961/1976) writings, it has adopted a societal level of explanation to account for the fact that human behaviour, however assessed from the outside, is sensible within a cultural context that validates and legitimates such behaviour. The theory of social representations has thus served to advance the sociocultural agenda by highlighting how human behaviour is sensible within the context of its production. Consequently, it has provided sociocultural theorists with a framework for studying and understanding sense-making processes in different sociocultural contexts.

The theory of social representations has come to stand as the foremost psychological theory for the study of common sense. Over the past fifty years it has stimulated much research that has addressed these concerns and charted its implications on varied psychological behaviour such as communication (Moscovici, 1961/1976), social cohesion (Duveen, 2008), social cognition (Augoustinos, Walker and Donaghue, 2005), identity (Moloney and Walker, 2007), dialogicality (Marková, 2003), discourse (Wagner and Hayes, 2005), and others. And while much sociocultural research draws inspiration from the theory of social representations, publications in the field remain dispersed in innumerable journals and volumes that have researched these concerns and advanced our understanding of psychological phenomena in their context of production.

The theory of social representations takes a societal or sociocultural perspective. Sociocultural characteristics have featured in the psychology agenda since the beginnings of the discipline. Indeed, Wundt's (1916) concern with 'folk psychology' balanced the remit of study for the discipline by including concerns with mental events that originate in community life alongside concerns with physiology and the biological basis of human behaviour. Wundt thus included within psychology's remit concerns with language and cognate phenomena such as customs, religion, myth and magic (Farr, 1996). The quest for understanding human behaviour in its situational and cultural contingencies is, therefore, not new. However, in recent years the discipline has witnessed a concerted effort on the part of sociocultural psychologists who have sought to emphasize the fact that environmental, social and cultural conditions constitute an invariable condition for the very existence of psychological phenomena (Valsiner and Rosa, 2007; Valsiner, 2012).

In essence, human behaviour differs widely across behavioural conditions. The fact of individual differences in behavioural outcomes is well known and has received considerable scholarly attention. In response to a similar stimulus, an individual may respond in a certain way while another individual may respond in a totally different manner due to their personal inclinations. Human behaviour, however, differs even more widely than this. It differs due to social and cultural conditions that determine how a thing is perceived (Moscovici, 1984b), what construal of that thing is brought to bear in describing and understanding that behaviour (Ross and Nisbett, 1991), and what repertoire of behavioural outcomes is plausible and legitimate as a course of action for that individual in a given society (Wagner and Hayes, 2005). In this complex determination of behaviour, social and cultural conditions characterize psychological phenomena. Sociocultural psychology has drawn our attention to the fact that social and cultural conditions give rise to particular psychological phenomena that manifest within contexts which shape their emergence as well as ontogenetic progression. Understanding human behaviour in its manifold complexity, therefore, requires more than an appreciation of individual differences. It further requires sensitivity to those extra-individual conditions that also determine behavioural outcomes. A consequence of this added focus is that assumptions of universality and standardization across cultural conditions are challenged. Sociocultural differences require a particular and specific focus on cultural elements that give rise to intercultural differences in the manifestation of psychological phenomena.

This handbook brings together various theoretical strands and developments that have emerged from the theory of social representations, some of which have become pillars in social psychology in their own right and have stimulated further inquiry in their turn. It also extends the social scientific agenda beyond that of the theory of social representations and into equally relevant concepts and domains of inquiry such as social identity, discursive psychology, positioning theory, semiotics and others.

The chapters provide an overview of the core aspects of the theory that have been debated over the years, some of which remain widely misunderstood, and provide an up-to-date account of developments such that further productive inquiry can be stimulated. Finally, the handbook will serve as an invaluable tool in the teaching of the theory of social representations. The theory has gained popularity over the years and routinely features in both undergraduate and postgraduate social psychology curricula in many countries. This handbook matches theoretical aspirations with real-world empirical concerns of interest to those of a sociocultural persuasion.

The handbook is divided into four parts. The first part, 'Foundations', deals with foundational issues and with the core concepts and debates within social representations theory. The second part, 'Conceptual developments', elaborates further notions and concepts that have become part of the social representations approach to sociocultural psychology. The third part, 'New directions', reviews some of the major social psychological theories that have furthered the theory of social representations and advanced the sociocultural agenda. The final part, 'Applications', presents empirical studies that have been undertaken in diverse fields and which demonstrate the breadth of application and the utility of a social representations approach.

GORDON SAMMUT, ELENI ANDREOULI,
GEORGE GASKELL AND JAAN VALSINER

PART I

Foundations

The first part of this handbook addresses a number of foundational concerns that can be traced back to the origins of social representations theory in Moscovici's (1961/1976) study *La Psychanalyse, son image et son public*. Since its inception, social representations theory has contended with a number of conceptual and empirical issues that have drawn the interest and criticism of scholars in equal measure. The lack of conceptual clarity has enabled both a theoretical and an empirical eclecticism to arise over the years, and arguably this has enabled the theory to thrive and to address myriad social and psychological issues in its later developments. Fifty years later, this handbook revisits these foundational concerns in order to take stock of the contributions that have shaped the theory's development and to elucidate the characteristic contribution that social representations theory has made to social and cultural psychology in the understanding and explanation of social and psychological phenomena.

The five chapters of this opening part of the book disambiguate certain notions that have proven thorny over the years, such as the scope of action in social representations and the theory's relevance in the study and explanation of human behaviour. They also address the merits and concerns of theorizing and conceptualizing 'representations' and the 'social'. In doing so, they are intended to help the reader to understand what analytical and explanatory levels the theory is suited to address, and to identify the sort of phenomena that the theory has served to investigate. Finally, this part of the book aims to provide the reader with a blueprint for further developments and applications. It presents a wide-ranging discussion of empirical methods in order to provide social representations scholars and researchers with the required toolkit for an enquiry into social affairs and human conduct.

1 Social representations: a revolutionary paradigm?

Gordon Sammut, Eleni Andreouli, George Gaskell and Jaan Valsiner

Against the prevailing view that progress in science is characterized by the progressive accumulation of knowledge, Thomas Kuhn's *Structure of Scientific Revolutions* of 1962 introduced the idea of revolutionary paradigm shifts. For Kuhn, everyday science is normal science in which scientists are engaged in problem solving activities set in the context of a widely accepted paradigm that constitutes a broad acceptance of a fundamental theoretical framework, an agreement on researchable phenomena and on the appropriate methodology. But, on occasions normal science throws up vexing issues and anomalous results. In response, some scientists carry on regardless, while others begin to lose confidence in the paradigm and look to other options, namely rival paradigms. As more and more scientists switch allegiance to the rival paradigm, the revolution gathers pace, supported by the indoctrination of students through lectures, academic papers and textbooks. In response to critics, including Lakatos who suggested that his depiction reduced scientific progress to mob psychology, Kuhn offered a set of criteria that contributed to the apparent 'gestalt switch' from the old to the new paradigm. But that is another story, as indeed is Kuhn's claim that the social sciences are pre-paradigmatic – in other words, that the only consensus is that there is no consensus.

Yet, consider this paragraph from a leading theorist of social psychology, Michael Billig (1991, pp. 57–58):

> One of the most important recent developments in European social psychology has been the emergence of the concept of social representations. The emergence of a new concept does not always indicate the formulation of a new idea. Sometimes in social psychology a concept is created to describe a novelty of experimental procedure, and sometimes to accord scientific pretentions to a well-known truism. By contrast, what has characterized the concept of social representations has been the intellectual ambition of its adherents. They have announced an intellectual revolution to shift social psychology to the traditions of European social science. Serge Moscovici, who has been both the Marx and Lenin of this revolutionary movement, has advocated a fundamental reorientation of social psychology around the concept of social representations. This revolution, if successful, will affect both pure and applied social psychology. In fact, the whole discipline will become more applied in the sense that the emphasis will be shifted from laboratory studies, which seek to isolate variables in the abstract, towards being a social science, which examines socially shared

> beliefs, or social representations, in their actual context. According to Moscovici, this reorientation would transform the discipline into an 'anthropological and a historical science'. (1984, p. 948)

Even without Kuhn's blessing, this statement points to social representations as a paradigm shift – a change in the intellectual agenda and scope of the discipline of social psychology; a more catholic approach to research methods, and a movement towards the study of social phenomena in context (Branco and Valsiner, 1997). Psychology is in dire need of a transformation in its methodology in order for it to live up to science – a new science of the processes of human being (Valsiner, 2014).

In this introduction we explore the origins of social representations theory, the theory's foundational concepts, and recent developments in theorizing and researching social representations. There is a great intellectual richness in this realm of knowledge. Since Moscovici's original work, the field has been an arena for interdisciplinary scholarship.

Locating the social representations approach

For a long time the discipline of psychology has had as its central focus the study of human behaviour. The research agenda fashioned by the early behaviourists is somewhat obsolete nowadays, but the quest for explaining human behaviour still permeates the discipline. The notion that all it takes for human beings to behave in one way or another is positive or negative reinforcement, is by and large accepted as a simplistic explanation of human behaviour. Interestingly, the core concept of 'behaviour' is taken for granted in that tradition; questions about whether non-observed human acts of conduct (e.g. a person's decision to act in a socially non-approved way being inhibited by his/her moral norms) can qualify as 'behaviour' have not been asked, nor answered. Human conduct is replete with such inhibited (= non-occurring) 'behaviours' – hence the behaviourist track misses many relevant psychological phenomena.

This paradox – the indeterminacy of what is 'behaviour'? – is not new (see also Chapter 2 in this volume). Early critics of the behaviourist approach are nowadays cited as classical authors due to the impetus they provided the discipline in their search for alternative explanations of human conduct. Most notably, the Gestaltists rejected behaviourist explanations and introduced the idea that the human mind imposes meaning on sensory stimuli. Consequently, in advancing explanations for human behaviour it is necessary to consider cognitive processes that lead to the perception of a stimulus. Cognitive processing determines which stimuli are attended to, how they are perceived, and how that information is translated into behaviour. The historical outcome of this criticism was that the study of cognition took centre stage over the study of behaviour in defining the psychological agenda. Characteristic explanations of human conduct today typically investigate an extensive list of independent variables (i.e. stimuli) that determine, when they all come together in characteristic ways, certain behavioural responses (i.e. dependent variables).

The Gestaltists' critique of behaviourism (Asch, 1952/1987) provided the foundations for the cognitive approach to psychology which dominates the discipline today. Yet it was not the only critique to be levelled at the behaviourist approach to psychology. Nor was the influence of some of the Gestaltists' core ideas limited to the cognitive school. Other critiques levelled at the behaviourist approach were sociocultural or sociopolitical in nature (e.g. Berger and Luckmann, 1966; Harré and Secord, 1972; Potter and Wetherell, 1987; Billig, 1987). In essence, these criticisms were based on three core tenets. Firstly, how human beings interpret events and understand their social and physical surroundings depends fundamentally on the cultural and political context in which they are embedded. Secondly, human beings are agentic; their actions are not merely behavioural responses, but rather, human action is volitional, purposive and meaningful. Thirdly, humans are inherently social. That is, their psychological activity is oriented towards others in a systemic way. When people come together they do not merely aggregate; they form social groups (Lewin, 1936) within which they function in line with the group's norms, purposes and goals.

The social representations approach, like the Gestalist, social constructionist, discursive, rhetorical and sociocultural approaches to psychology, is faithful to these core tenets. Further, it adds a component to the understanding of human behaviour by way of social representations. In Moscovici's (1984b) own diagrammatic formulation, social representations frame S-R responses in that a stimulus is understood as a certain stimulus warranting a certain response according to a social representation that describes the event in an intelligible way for the human subject, given the conditions in which they find themselves (Wagner, 1993). This notion has led to the social representations approach emerging as a countervailing paradigm in psychology (Farr, 1996). According to Himmelweit (1990), it presents a molar view of human activity that is temporally extended in space and time, as opposed to the molecular view of considering human behaviour in discrete terms. In other words, for a given stimulus to elicit a given response, a social representation must associate that particular stimulus with a particular response in an intelligible way for the human subject. To give an example, for somebody to call the police when hearing a gunshot, a social representation of law and order prohibiting the use of guns is required. In certain cultural contexts, or indeed in certain situations, a different social representation might be at play that would lead to a different behavioural outcome. For instance, one might respond very differently to hearing a gunshot at a military parade. The difference between the two situations that leads to an expected difference in behavioural responses is the intelligibility of the social situation from the respondent's point of view. The social representations approach thus brings about a focus on meaning-making processes and the intelligibility of situations in understanding human psychological activity.

Rationale and origins

The roots of the social representations approach can be traced to Durkheim's distinction between individual representations and collective representations (Durkheim 1924/1974). Durkheim discarded the former in favour of the latter in his efforts to understand collective ways of life that determined custom and practice in particular societies. The distinction remained in Moscovici's (1961/1976) original postulation of social representations in his investigation of the meanings of psychoanalysis in France. Moscovici argued, however, that it was more pertinent to speak of social rather than collective representations, due to the plurality of representations that exist in contemporary public spheres (Jovchelovitch, 2007; also Chapter 11 in this volume). This condition is termed *cognitive polyphasia* and refers to the coexistence of different and potentially incommensurable representations within the same public, or indeed, the same individual. Collective representations in the Durkheimian sense are hegemonic. Moscovici noted that different social representations of psychoanalysis circulated in the same public sphere in France. He went on to distinguish between *hegemonic* representations that are similar to collective representations in that they are shared by all members of a highly structured group; *emancipated* representations that are characteristic of subgroups who create their own versions of reality; and *polemical* representations that are marked by controversy (Moscovici, 1988). The central idea here is that a social group develops some intelligible understanding of certain aspects of reality, which comes to inform the various perspectives of the members of that group. Individual members of the group thus come to see the world around them, or certain salient social events, in group-characteristic ways. The meaning of things in our environment is thus not a given of the things themselves. Rather, it is 'represented' as a forged understanding between social subjects oriented to the same social phenomenon.

Meaning-making is therefore an imperative concern in the social representations approach. Social representations have been defined as systems of values, ideas and practices that serve to establish social order and facilitate communication (Moscovici, 1973). They arise in an effort to make the unfamiliar familiar (Moscovici, 1984b). In this way they enable the achievement of a shared social reality. On the one hand, they conventionalize objects, persons and events by placing them in a familiar context. On the other hand, they serve to guide meaningful social interaction (Sammut and Howarth, 2014). The social representations approach has thus become a primary method for studying common sense in different social and cultural groups. Rather than judging a group's ways by the normative code of one's own sociocultural group, researchers adopt the social representations approach to gain an insight into the system of knowledge (common sense) that justifies certain human practices.

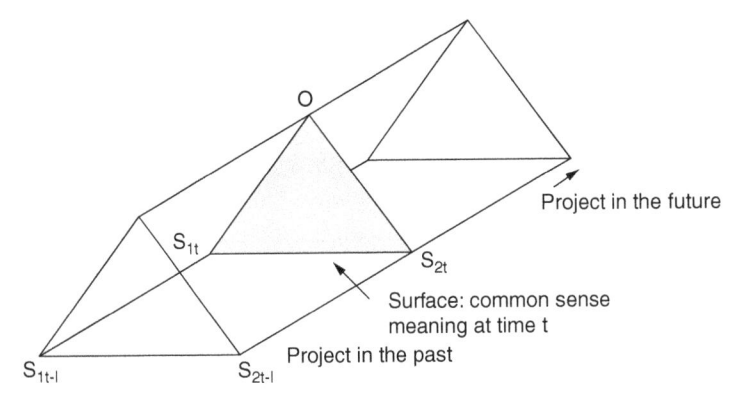

Figure 1.1 *The Toblerone model of social representations (after Bauer and Gaskell, 1999).*

A formal model

As interest in social representations grew through the 1990s, challenges were voiced about the vagueness of the concept – what is the precise definition of a social representation and what are the appropriate methods for studying them?

Bauer and Gaskell (1999) identify three defining characteristics of representations: the cultivation in communications systems; structured contents that serve various functions for the communications systems; and their embodiment in different modes and mediums. In social milieus, systems of communication (representations) evolve and circulate. This is referred to as the process of symbolic cultivation. Representations are embodied in one or more of four modes: habitual behaviour, individual cognition, informal communication and formal communication.

The minimal system involved in representation is the triad: two persons (subject 1 and subject 2) who share a concern with an object (O). The triangle of mediation [S-O-S] is the basic unit for the elaboration of meaning. Meaning is not an individual or private affair, but always implies the 'other'. While individually cognized, in form, function and content, the presence of the 'other' is always implicated on the basis of past social experience. To this triangle of mediation a time dimension, capturing the past and the future, is added to denote the project (P) linking the two subjects and the object. The project links S1 and S2 through mutual interests, goals and activities. Within this project the common-sense meaning of the object is an emergent property similar to a socialized form of the Lewinian life space (Lewin, 1952). The basic unit of analysis is now S-O-P-S and is depicted as a Toblerone (see Figure 1.1).

The elongated triangle, the shape of the Swiss chocolate bar, depicts the triangular relations in the context of time. In this way, a representation is a time gestalt of 'inter-objectivity'. A section through the Toblerone at any particular time is a surface that denotes the common-sense meaning (the representation) of that object at that time. The Toblerone model is at the heart of Bauer and Gaskell's (2002) analysis of the 'biotechnology movement' – a social psychology of new technology drawing upon twenty-five years of societal assimilation and accommodation to the science of life.

A final extension of the formal model is the differentiation of social groups (wind rose model) (Bauer and Gaskell, 2008; see also Chapter 4 in this volume). Groups are not static; they evolve over time – growing, dividing and declining. Thus over time it is likely that various triangles of mediation emerge and coexist in the wider social system, characterized at different times by conflict, cooperation or indifference.

In this vein, a social system is a pack of Toblerones with O as the link between different representations – the common referent. A section through the Toblerone pack denotes the different common senses that exist in different social groups. The elongation of the triangles denotes how representations change over time. Equally, over time O may change due to its own dynamics [material process], or in response to common senses [representations].

This concept of triangles of mediation brings into focus social milieus or natural groups formed around different projects. As Moscovici (1961/1976) shows, the meaning of an object (psychoanalysis) appeared in different forms in the different French milieus. In this sense common projects, we-cognitions, collective memories and actions, define a functioning social group.

Social representations are systems of knowledge, or forms of common sense, that human subjects draw upon in order to make sense of the world around them and to act towards it in meaningful ways. Social representations, therefore, are social inasmuch as they are never idiosyncratic. If they were, they would be incomprehensible to others. According to Wagner and Hayes (2005), what marks 'social' representations is that their meaning is holomorphic, that is, for a given social group the meaning attributed to a certain object or event is consistent.

Communication

Communication plays a critical role in the production and circulation of social representations, as ideas concerning social objects and events circulate in public and are incorporated in social representations. Chryssides and colleagues (2009) have drawn a useful distinction between 'social representation' and 'social re-presentation' to address some ambiguity concerning the term. The former refers to the content described in a social representation by which an object or event is identified as a matter of fact, object or event for a particular social group. The latter refers to a process of contestation by which newer meanings are proposed in a process of re-presentation that serves to change aspects of the content of a given social representation. The distinction is one of product and process. The latter is essentially a communicative exercise of meaning-making among members of a social group. Communication guides both the production and the evolution of social representations over time (Sammut, Tsirogianni and Wagoner, 2012).

Moscovici (1984a) has identified two processes that serve the production of new social representations. *Anchoring* refers to a process of classification by which the new and unfamiliar is placed within a familiar frame of reference. The meaning of a new object or event is thus anchored to an existing social representation. *Objectification* is a process of externalization by which the meaning of an object or event is projected in the world through images or propositions. New concepts, ideas or events can be objectified in intelligible ways for the purpose of facilitating meaning-making. For example, images of scientists inoculating tomatoes have served to objectify biotechnology and genetically modified organisms (GMOs) for certain publics (Wagner and Kronberger, 2001).

Communication thus plays a central role in the production of new social representations to make sense of new things and events that enter everyday life. It also plays a central role in how social representations circulate in public. In his study of the social representations of psychoanalysis in France, Moscovici (1961/1976) identified three communicative strategies that perpetuated the social representations of distinct groups. *Propaganda* is a centralized and ideological form of communication that perpetuates a social reality defined for a group in political terms. *Propagation* is a communicative exercise founded on belief that is dictated by a central authority. *Diffusion* is the least circumscribed communicative genre and it allows for a diversity of opinions based on scepticism and the questioning of consensus. Different groups may be more or less open to alternative constructions of the object or event in question by other individuals and groups. Consequently, they adopt characteristic patterns of communication that serve to perpetuate their own versions.

The role of communication in the perpetuation of social representations highlights two important issues that have received scholarly attention over the years. Firstly, with the integration of new ideas into existing social representations, the content and form of social representations may change over time. Central Nucleus Theory has distinguished between the *core* and *periphery* components of social representations. The core of a social representation is its central component and defines the social representation as well as its reason for existence. The peripheral component of a social representation consists of beliefs, ideas and stereotypes that serve to make the social representation relevant and applicable to a particular milieu. Peripheral ideas are amenable to change and they help in making the social representation adaptable to changing social realities (Abric, 2001; see also Chapter 6 in this volume). Sammut, Tsirogianni and Wagoner (2012) propose that communication enables social representations to evolve over time in the manner of an epidemiological time series. As such, a historical focus may make manifest the core and peripheral elements of a social representation over the course of time. In this light, understanding social representations may necessitate exploring the historical trajectory of a representational project. Through *collective remembering* the past exercises an influence on present social relations via the content available in social representations in circulation at a given historical epoch (see Chapter 10 in this volume).

This brings us to the second focal point concerning the role of communication, that is, intergroup and interpersonal relations. Duveen (2008) has argued that communicative strategies serve not only to perpetuate social representations, but also serve to forge affiliative ties among group members. He has stated that propaganda serves to develop *solidarity* between group members. Such groups come to share a political commitment and are distinguishable from out-group members who do not share the same ideology. Propagation serves in developing *communion*. Founded on belief, the social representation serves to mark out-group members, i.e. those who do not similarly believe, or those whose political ideology is incompatible with the group's beliefs. Lastly, diffusion serves in developing *sympathy*. This is characterized by the voluntary association of individuals who stand in contrast to dogmatic out-groups. One way that these affiliative bonds are put in place is through *alternative representations* (Gillespie, 2008). This term refers to that component of a social representation that describes what others who do not subscribe to the same social representation are like. Alternative representations, such as, for example, that a particular out-group may be closed-minded or ignorant, serve to put in place *semantic barriers* that limit dialogue with out-group members (Gillespie, 2008). This may often be perceived as a shortcoming in political agendas that seek reconciliation between different groups. However, such strategies remain highly effective in protecting a representation's core, ensuring its survival over time, perpetuating the affiliative bonds and social capital among group members that is already in place (Sammut, Andreouli and Sartawi, 2012), and strengthening the social identification of members with the group.

A final issue that the role of communication has put on the social representations agenda concerns socialization. Duveen and Lloyd (1990) argue that social representations are evoked in all forms of social interaction through the social identities asserted in individuals' activities. They refer to this as the *microgenetic* process of social representations (see also Chapter 8 in this volume). It occurs firstly in the ways in which individuals construct their own understanding of the situation and locate themselves and others as social actors in social relations. Secondly, in instances of discord, the negotiation of *social identities* becomes explicit and identifiable in social interaction in a microgenetic process that serves to negotiate a shared frame of reference. Social representations, according to Duveen and Lloyd, furnish the resources for such negotiation.

New directions

Over the last fifty years the social representations approach has flourished and this has led to numerous refinements and developments in understanding myriad social-psychological phenomena. It has also attracted much criticism over thorny issues such as the role of cognition (Parker, 1987), the notion of what is shared in social representations (Verheggen and Baerveldt, 2007), the ambiguity of the terms and concepts utilized (Jahoda, 1988; Bauer and Gaskell, 1999), as well as the meaning of the term 'social' (Harré, 1988). Much of this criticism remains relevant today. Arguably, this has helped to develop rather than dismantle the social representations approach, as scholars have sought to refine their definitions, resolve inconsistencies and reconcile certain notions with other schools of thought. Many of these ingredients are present in the chapters of this handbook. Some issues are still debated, such as the difference between social representations and attitudes, the difference between individual representations and social representations, the impact of diversity in contemporary public spheres, and the way to define social groups and communities. Rather than avoid these questions, the contributors below critically engage with these debates and propose ways of addressing the issues with the objective of strengthening the pragmatic potential of the social representations approach.

Much has been achieved since Moscovici's (1961/1976) original study concerning the social representations of psychoanalysis in France. The social representations approach has developed into a coherent framework for the study of the evolution, structure and functions of common sense in its variability across sociocultural and sociopolitical contexts. The concept of social representations has come to serve the task of querying of mentalities and corollary issues that arise in the diversity of human behaviours across myriad contexts. More recently, it seeks to understand how this diversity is reconciled in social relations. Whether this effectively constitutes a paradigmatic shift is certainly debatable. Yet the social representations approach stands as a pillar among other approaches that have overcome the simplistic reductionism of behaviourism. Furthermore, it adds a critical focus to the prevailing information-processing and nomothetic approaches to psychology. Robert Farr's assessment of social representations theory is that it offers a conceptualization of human action that is context and culture specific, furnishing accounts of behaviour as it occurs *in situ* (Farr, 1996). It is now recognized in many scholarly communities as a rival paradigm in social psychology. The revolution is gathering pace.

2 Representation in action

Wolfgang Wagner

Behaviour and action

Of ducks and men

My office window opens on to a large pond where ducks, swans, coots and the occasional bird-loving person with an interest in feeding them can be observed. As soon as a bird lover approaches the rim of the pond and opens a paper bag, a lot of birds start eagerly moving in the direction of the rustling sound produced by the bag. Once there, both the birds and the man or woman providing dry bread appear to be happily united in a pattern of animal and human behaviour. I find this pattern of human behaviour and the complementary waterfowl behaviour quite instructive: first, it illustrates the conceptual difference between behaviour and action; second, it highlights a widely distributed – but in my opinion wrong – belief of attitude and intention 'causing' behaviour; and third, it is a nice example of how behaviours happen in concert. Each of these points will be discussed in the sections that follow.

The term 'behaviour' is obviously an observer term applied to an organism's activity that we do not or cannot deeply empathize with. On the other hand, if a person describes what he or she is doing or has done, the person will say that he or she 'acted'. Hence, 'action' is an actor's term or a term used in talk about another person one can empathize with. This concurs with a host of experimental findings in attribution theory where the perspective of actors makes them explain their behaviour by external, situational factors in contrast to internal, personality-related causes, as observers tend to do. The actor has a more intimate knowledge of the reasons relating to his or her behaviour, while observers are deprived of this knowledge.

Consequently, in the case of our university pond, we would talk about the ducks as behaving. The persons' feeding of the waterfowl will be imagined as an action. The crucial difference is the justification an actor – if asked for – can provide for his or her actions that, even with a considerable stretch of imagination, birds cannot provide. Birds cannot account for their behaviour in symbolic terms; people can.

In the rest of this chapter I will discuss behaviour and action and their articulation with beliefs and social representations. I will reject the common-sensical idea of behaviour being caused by beliefs that is so often invoked in theory and implemented in empirical studies. Instead of the idea of a contingent causation of behaviour, I suggest a view where action is part and parcel of a social representation as can be seen in their microgenesis, the fact that actions attain meaning only in the long run, and that representations come to bear on patterns of cooperating individuals and interacting collectives. Finally, overt action takes primacy as the only psychological event that links directly to material reality.

The paradox of overt behaviour in psychology

There are two types of behaviour that play a conceptual role in psychology: verbal behaviour as in talking and writing; and bodily or overt behaviour that involves posture, change in body position, arm and leg movements, locomotion, and so on. In what follows I will call the latter kind of behaviour 'overt', although language use or verbal behaviour are also overt since they do require mouth movements and the production of acoustic stimuli.

Given the centrality of overt behaviour in everyday life and considering the label of a field such as behavioural science, it is rather paradoxical that the vast majority of research in social and behavioural sciences is almost exclusively done with verbal data. Virtually all studies about behaviours and activities employ questionnaires, probing respondents' memory or attitudes for past or imagined behaviours. These studies take verbal responses as a proxy of the overt behaviour being addressed in the questionnaire item. Rarely do researchers verify whether their assumption is justified, that is, if verbal recall corresponds with the respondents' real overt behaviour as manifested in the past. Be it as it may, the dominant methodology of social, behavioural and psychological sciences creates the impression that verbal behaviour is all you need to research overt behaviour.

I can think of two reasons for omitting overt behaviour from research designs: first, it is far more economical to restrict data collection to questionnaires and interviews than it is designing an observational study for a lengthy time period. This 'economy argument' may well hold a kernel of truth if there were no serious consequences of this deficit in data collection; but then it is hard to understand how we can maintain a 'behavioural science'.

The second reason is the 'irrelevance argument': couldn't it be that overt behaviour per se is rather irrelevant for the symbolic 'truths' of our local worlds being addressed by social sciences? The irrelevance argument could be invoked if the principal conveyer of meanings were only words, either spoken or written, and not, for example, the hand gesture used to usher a person to a seat. According to this argument, language should be able to represent and carry everything that overt action can convey in a reliable and veridical way. If this were the case one could safely judge persons by their words instead of by their deeds; but is this assumption warranted?

The 'irrelevance argument' does indeed receive some support from studies that have engaged in time-consuming observation of overt behaviours, albeit not a support that the researchers intended. For example, Barker (1968) and colleagues worked on their theory of 'behaviour settings' by observing the behaviour of people at different locations in a small town for almost twenty years. They did this in order to identify the stable behaviour patterns typical of certain locations such as at shops, markets, the church, pubs and so on. Now, if I tell you, the reader, the results, don't hold your breath: indeed, what was found, was not far from what one could have inferred from talking to a local informant. The researcher took the position of an observer similar to the one watching the ducks on our pond instead of recognizing the competence of the inhabitants in mastering their environment and everyday life, that is, the actors' representation of the environment and the associated behaviours. In everyday life people's behaviour in different situations, locations and times has an unstrained and smooth oneness that resists easy conceptual decomposition. Any culturally competent informant can recognize how people's engagement with their environment is reflected in the social and cultural world; and vice versa, the particular forms of the human environment would not exist without the collective activity of the protagonists, a point that Barker and colleagues dismissed. Thus, there could be some truth in the argument that overt behaviour is not a privileged data source when it comes to exploring social worlds. This is in spite of a daily life where people constantly have to take action in the service of their social standing; that is, where they are under the rule of what I call the everyday 'pragmatic imperative' (Wagner and Hayes, 2005, p. 78).

Behaviour as a consequence of belief and attitude

Attitudes causing behaviour

It is part of common sense that our everyday behaviour is guided by what we know about the world and by how we think we can achieve a goal. This common sense has been 'scientifically' framed in the Theory of Self-Efficacy (Bandura, 1977). The most basic assumption of this theory is that what people achieve by doing is better predicted by what they believe they are able to achieve than by objective factors because the individual already anticipates these factors in his or her planning: people who regard themselves as highly efficacious produce their own future, rather than simply foretell it (Bandura, 1986). In more mundane words, people will reach any goal that they strongly desire, if they possess – and know they possess – the required capabilities and where no objective obstacle prevents them from homing in on this goal.

More explicitly this view of the mind–behaviour link is formulated in the so-called 'Theory of Planned Behaviour' (Ajzen, 1991). This theory holds that first there is a deliberate cognitive process where humans plan an action by following their attitudes, their beliefs about whether they may be able to control future behaviour or not, and their subjective norms regarding proper behaviour in the given situation. These factors result in a behavioural intention, which in turn causes the planned behaviour to be executed. The successful action then consumes the intention.

There is mixed empirical support for this theory, particularly for the role subjective norms, that is social beliefs, play in determining behaviour. In particular, studies have shown that social norms only have a significant impact on intention formation if the source of the norms, the referent others, pertain to the same group as the actor. In other words, the influence of norms on behaviour is conditioned by group identification and occurs primarily with in-group norms (Terry and Hogg, 1996). This finding fits with the tenets of Social Identity and Self-Categorization Theory, which state that persons will assimilate into their in-group's behavioural tendencies (Hogg, 2006).

Irrespective of these details, the Theory of Planned Behaviour postulates a causal chain from mental states, attitudes, norms and behavioural beliefs to behavioural intentions, which determine subsequent behaviours. In the language of psychological experimentation, the mental elements preceding behaviour are independent variables and the observable behaviour is the dependent variable. Let's keep this in mind for when we come back to this assumption and a concomitant form of theorizing later in this chapter.

Representations 'informing' behaviour

As with other psychological approaches, social representations theory has a say over how behaviour comes about and is being shaped. In an experiment designed as a zero-sum game, Faucheux and Moscovici (1968) manipulated the expectations of experimental subjects about their alleged game opponents. One half of the participants was told that they were going to play against a 'random' programme, while the second half was supposedly playing against 'nature'. The terms were not explained any further, with the effect that the test participants had to rely on their representations of 'random' and 'nature'. In actual fact the gaming behaviour of the opponents in both cases was the same and controlled by a computer program. The dependent variable in this experiment was the cooperative or exploitative moves during the game.

The results revealed a marked influence of the representation that the initial manipulation had evoked. Subjects who believed that they were playing against 'nature' had the idea of a relatively good-natured and predictable opponent. The 'random' participants felt they were not able to predict the opposing moves which would have allowed them to estimate the chance of winning. Consequently, the participants in the 'nature' condition reported that they understood the logic of the payment table much better than subjects in the 'random' condition and hence they successfully maximized their gains. The authors concluded that either activating the representation of a predictable and thus controllable opponent, nature, or the opposite, chance, obviously determined the participants' gaming behaviour. Hence, the idea that representations are separate from, and guide, behaviour is at the cradle

```
                      Self-identity
         0.45       ↗            ↘    0.41
         0.34                         0.40

    Intention ─────────────────────→ Behaviour
                    0.11 n.s.
                     0.28
```

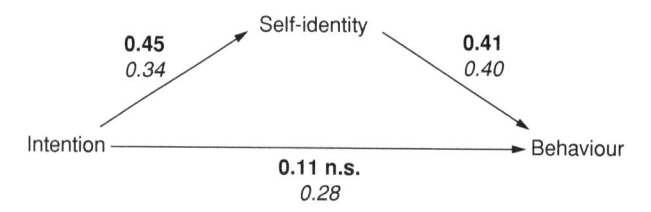

Figure 2.1 *Mediation effect of self-identity for low ambivalence (bold beta coefficients, adj. $R2 = 0.21$) and for high ambivalence respondents (italic, adj. $R2 = 0.29$) (after Castro et al., 2009).*

of social representations theory: this is necessarily implied if social representations enter as independent and behaviours as dependent variables in ANOVA-style experiments.

One of the contemporary societal problems that receives growing attention is ecological behaviour. In such studies the social psychologist's interest usually is to find links between normative stimuli and the corresponding pro-ecological behaviour.

A study by Castro and colleagues (2009) is framed in terms of an attitude–intention–behaviour model but it may also serve as an example of the social representation–behaviour link. The authors' relevant results comprise three variables that were collected as responses to questionnaire items: the intention to collect and separate metal cans, the respondent's self-identity subscribing to an ecological ideology or not, and self-reported recycling behaviour. The sample was divided in two groups: high and low ambivalent respondents in the sense of simultaneously maintaining, or not, contradictory attitudes about metal can recycling. In the present context, the authors' concept of 'self-identity' can be likened to a representation: if self-identity is high, then the respondent subscribes to a pro-ecological representation; with a low self-identity, the respondent does not maintain a positive ecological orientation. An analysis of how self-identity moderates the regression of behaviour on intention for low and high ambivalent respondents reveals an interesting finding (Figure 2.1). It shows that low ambivalent respondents stand by their self-identity exhibiting a high relationship between self-identity and action, while immediate intentions have no significant influence on behaviour. In other words, with low ambivalence, behaviour corresponds strongly with the degree of self-identified pro-ecological behaviour if there are no interfering 'second thoughts' about the costs of recycling.

The issue of metal can recycling is particularly suited to illustrating a significant positive representation–behaviour relationship. First, recycling metal cans is a complex behaviour that involves collecting empty cans in one's house, compacting them to save space, keeping them separate from the usual waste, and finally transporting them to a collection point. Such behaviour involves costs and is not a one-off affair. Additionally, at the time of the study recycling behaviour was a highly contentious issue that involved law-making and public deliberation. These latter factors are important ingredients of social representations that primarily come into being with conflict and debate.

An elaborate study on littering is a bit different. In fact, this is one of the few studies where actual overt behaviour in real-world settings played a role: the researchers observed littering behaviour in a central public space at their university and they were interested in interventions to reduce littering by students. The authors conclude 'that a representational account was inadequate for explaining the pattern of attitudes and behaviour regarding littering' (Liu and Sibley, 2004, p. 381). More predictive of cleanliness behaviour were situational changes such as mounted ashtrays. Measures of the representation–action link were general and specific items that assessed locally relevant attitudes and behaviour on one hand and the observed active dropping of litter on the other.

As admirable as the design of this study is, in my opinion it provides a less than ideal example for illustrating representations and associated behaviours. First, in contrast to the 'metal can study', it involved a behaviour that could have been 'just so', meaning that littering means just dropping a piece of wrapping paper or a cigarette butt and certainly not a reasoned action like recycling metal cans. Second, dropping litter at a site that is part of an architectural ensemble of buildings where cleaning staff is part of maintenance, is not the same as throwing litter away in open nature. Third, it can be assumed that littering probably was neither a contentious issue at the authors' institution nor a societal problem at the time of the study. Consequently, we might not expect too strong a relationship between representations of cleanliness and actual littering.

Irrespective of the particular results of the afore-reported studies in the field of social representations theory, the common theorizing is that behaviours somehow follow from pre-existing representations. While somewhat different in their argument from Bandura, Ajzen and followers, the present authors leave the exact theoretical status of the relationship between representations and behaviour unclear. The design of the studies appears to imply some kind of temporal sequence between mental representation and overt behaviour, but whether this temporal sequence is to be interpreted as causal is not clarified.

Critique of the conventional belief–behaviour articulation

This supposed causal 'belief–(intention–)behaviour' mechanism has been criticized as oversimplifying the structure of rational systems. Smedslund (1985), for example, likens the belief–behaviour relationship to a cultural logic that has nothing to do with a contingent causal relationship. Even though we can and do design experimental studies where beliefs are the independent and behaviours the dependent variables, a significant effect of belief on behaviour does not indicate causality but just illustrates a culturally implied relationship between belief and behaviour. That is, in contrast to textbooks of psychological methods maintaining that strictly designed experiments allow causal inferences (e.g. Bröder, 2011), whether a causal conclusion can be drawn depends on the character of the stimulus material and the psychological system under investigation. Smedslund (1978) showed that experiments 'confirming' Bandura's 'self-efficacy theory' do just reveal 'necessarily true cultural psychologies' akin to common sense. Others, using variants of this argumentation, have critically discussed causality assumptions in rational systems in a similar vein (Brandtstädter, 1982; Greve, 2001; Holzkamp, 1986).

Following this lead I expanded Smedslund's (1978) argument to the field of social representations theory where, rhetorically, behaviour is tightly linked to representations but is not a causal effect of mental states (Wagner, 1994a). Himmelweit (1990, p. 30) roughly makes this point when she states: 'a social representation worth studying is one that makes a noticeable difference to the reactions of those accepting the representation compared with their beliefs and conduct before such acceptance'.

Despite this rhetoric, though, some experimental studies inspired by social representations theory speak of representations as 'steering', 'controlling', 'influencing' and 'guiding' behaviour and action (e.g. Echebarria Echabe, Guede and Castro, 1994; Faucheux and Moscovici, 1968; Thommen, Amann and von Cranach, 1988). These and other empirical studies subscribe to an 'intentional causality' either explicitly or implicitly by designing studies according to the idea of causal research: they first assess a belief as part of a representation, give it the status of an independent variable X, and subsequently 'observe' a verbal proxy of behaviour as the dependent variable Y. The rationale for this design is that the dependent behaviour is a causal consequence of the belief or representation. Hence, the underlying assumption is that 'Thinking X makes or causes the subject to do Y.' The rhetoric of social representations 'guiding' behaviour appears just as a thin semantic disguise of thinking in 'causalities'.

The non-contingent, quasi-logical relationship between belief and action can be indirectly illustrated by research on the validity of self-reports and volitional behaviour: in a word-list learning experiment on the validity of subjects' self-reports, Eagle (1967) asked one group of subjects to use a rote learning technique and the other group to use associative techniques. The associative technique was known to be superior to rote learning for the given task. After the learning phase the subjects reported which learning technique they actually had used. The results showed that performance depended only on what the subjects had reported. If they had reported using the rote technique, they had learned fewer words than when they reported having used the association technique. This effect was independent of the instructions given by the experimenter. Apart from the author's intention to show that people report correctly about what they think and do, this experiment also makes the point that subjects in fact did what they thought or believed to be the best thing to do. Believing that the associative technique was the best thing to do immediately obliged the subjects to do exactly this. It was logical to do what they considered best; their doing was not contingently caused by their belief but necessary and rational under the precondition of their beliefs.

Other research on volitional behaviour or self-determination consistently shows that what people actually do depends significantly more upon what they believe and intend to do than upon objective situational determinants. Experiments on eating, heterosexual affiliation behaviour and others revealed that effect sizes of volitional control factors are unusually high to a degree that virtually never can be observed in experiments with situational independent variables (Howard and Conway, 1986). This provides evidence to the point that representations, beliefs, volition and action are integrated with each other beyond contingency. In a nutshell, *any behaviour in an event where the actor possesses an a priori representation of the situation, is culturally necessary and not causally contingent on the representation.*

Let me give a quick example just in case any readers ask for an illustration of causality at this point. A contingent causal relationship would be, if a toddler's distressful crying triggered an adult to respond with protective behaviour (e.g. Boukydis and Burgess, 1982), notwithstanding any cultural variation of the extent and form of the adult's response. Given the adult possessed a representation of 'babies-needing-help', the causal link in this example is between the 'crying' stimulus and the adult's behaviour and not between the representation and the protective action; rather, the protective action is part and parcel of the representation.

None of the aforementioned arguments about cultural logics and excessive effect sizes provide empirical evidence for our position that behaviours are an integral part of representations; neither is this an empirical problem. The arguments are brought forward to justify a conceptual frame that is better suited to depict the position of behaviour in representations than the loose language used in some contemporary research.

The place of behaviour in social representations theory

Primacy of action in the genesis of representations

In the foregoing section I criticized the view of assigning social representations the status of 'independent' mental structures influencing 'dependent' behaviours. In fact, the 'independent–dependent' dichotomy is misleading and distracts from the fact that in social representations research the sequence of the two concepts does not denote temporal order. Whether overt or verbal behaviours – responding to questionnaire items – is first in a study is entirely up to the research design and not to some intrinsic temporal or logical necessity. Indeed, in the case of representations being formed by individuals in small groups – their microgenesis – overt behaviour may frequently precede the 'mental movement'.

In an ethnographic study of primary school classes, Kasanen, Räty and Snellman (2001) provide evidence for the role of action in microgenesis. They observed teachers modifying the seating order in a class based on their conception of 'educability'. A new seating order required the pupils to obey and to reconstruct the representation of their position in the class's pecking and educability order. Their coping with these changes consisted in overt actions, in conversations among themselves and in disputes with the teacher. The result of this activity had a bearing on a new representation contingent on the changed situation. Obviously, the teacher's modifications not only influenced seating order but also changed the behavioural space available to the pupils, which in turn changed their representations.

Similar observations of the development of children's gender representations, their interaction with toys and conversations with others of the same or opposite sex confirm the deep integration of overt behaviour and thinking in the microgenesis of gender-role beliefs (Lloyd and Duveen, 1992), as does research on forced behavioural compliance and subsequent changes in the mental part of representations (Renard *et al.*, 2007). Because the social world exists before and initially independent of an individual, he or she inadvertently has to interact with the existing objects and issues in order to get a 'feeling' for the world's constitution and repetitive collaborative patterns. This is just like the pupils in a rearranged classroom. The imposed pattern, finally, will be called a new social representation.

These studies provide an illustration of group members coming to terms with challenges to the received way of seeing the world. This requires pupils, for example, to negotiate a new class structure by way of a trial that first is anchored in established ways. As the pupils change their actions and reflect the forced situational changes in conversation and deliberation, it can be assumed that they have developed a social representation that renders the novel as part of their common sense. The change, however, does not come about by contemplation but by collective deliberation and activity. This places action at the root of a new representation and makes it its integral part; in other words, 'belief is part of the action' (Douglas, 1982, p. 200).

Dynamic patterns in behaviour and discourse

To illustrate my critique of the dominant way of thinking about the belief–behaviour relationship a bit further, let us look at an investigation of vernacular beliefs about home heat control (Kempton, 1986). In this research, conducted within the tenets of cognitive anthropology, the author identifies two cultural models for the functioning of thermostat-regulated heating systems: the valve model and the cybernetic model. The former models furnaces as continuously adjustable to temperature demands. This implies that a room will heat fast with the lever turned high. The latter model pictures the lever technically correctly as a thermostat by means of which the desired temperature is preset and a control circuit does all further regulation. The two models imply crucially different behaviours: Kempton investigated these behaviours by recording switch settings, room temperature and furnace activity in different homes for several weeks. The result confirmed – not surprisingly – that the type of heat-control belief corresponds to subjects' control action: believers in the cybernetic model preset the temperature and believers in the valve model used the thermostat as a lever according to their belief that heating can be accelerated by high lever settings (Figure 2.2).

It seems that Kempton's research is striking evidence for the common-sense idea that beliefs determine behaviour or that representations guide action: beliefs and behaviours were assessed independently and their relationship observed. However,

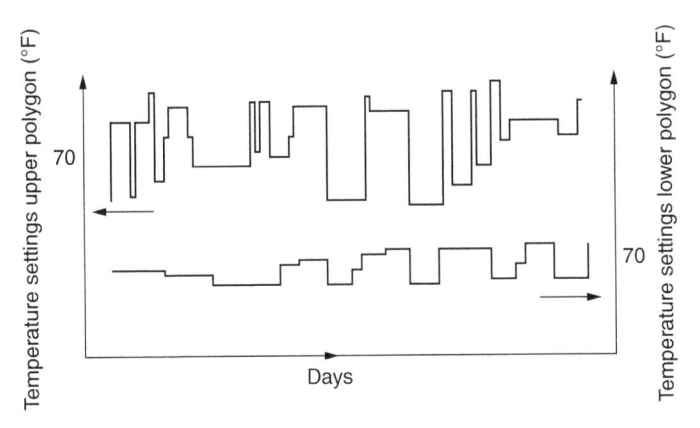

Figure 2.2 *Eight days' thermostat settings for 'valve' theory (upper) and 'control' theory (lower) subjects (schematic redrawing according to Kempton, 1986).*

even a cursory inspection of the patterns in Figure 2.2 makes it clear that no single up or down movement of the lever can sensibly be predicted by the underlying folk model. Rather, the relationship between representations and action only becomes visible in the long run of extended activity. Also in Faucheux and Moscovici's (1968) study of 'gaming against chance and nature', it was not the gamers' single moves that reflected the two different representations, but the entire series of moves. Only when seen 'from afar' does a series of events and social actions exhibit a structure and form that is not shown by a 'snapshot' (Wagner, 1994a).

According to this understanding, social representations can be conceptualized as 'dynamic units' within volatile talk and other activity. Traditional units of analysis, such as a belief or an attitude, are conceived of as rigid, locally integrated mental entities with clear boundaries and whose definition is based on properties inherent to the unit itself. Dynamic units may be fuzzy and they are based on observing a stable pattern of correlation across the elements composing the unit. Their meaning cannot be separated from the context of observation: units are not defined unless within a specific context and thereby impart sense to the environment (Mandelblit and Zachar, 1998; Wagner, Mecha, and do Rosário Carvalho, 2008).

The entirety of interactions and formal and informal talk shows a pattern of correlation across actors and across time. This pattern acquires its meaning from the context within which it is performed. The emergent meaning creates the social objects such as the particular phenomenology of psychotherapeutic clients, their afflictions and the therapists' actions (Thommen *et al.*, 1988), 'heated homes' (Kempton, 1986) or the meaning of genetic engineering for their daily life (e.g. Gaskell *et al.*, 2001). These 'objects' exist at particular points in time, at particular places, and are the outcome of actions and interactions over time.

Social objects emerge as a dynamic unit in the visible pattern of correlated behaviours across actors and situations because 'individuals or collectives to some extent see [them] as an extension of their behaviour and because, for them, it exists only because of the means and methods that allow them to understand the object' (Moscovici, 2008, p. 8). Equally, just as the objects are a result and part of behaviours, so the behaviours are an extension, and indeed part of the representation. The representation endows the behaviour with meaning, as 'there is no definite break between the outside world and the world of the individual' (ibid.). Actors with their reasons and agenda do what they do not because they want to realize some implicit representation but because they want to achieve something concrete; *people represent social objects in and through action*.

The foster-parents of mentally handicapped people in Jodelet's (1989/1991) seminal study took pains to keep their crockery and clothing separate from that of their guests when washing. This behaviour corresponded to a deep-seated belief in contagion and sympathetic magic that things in contact will spread impurity and transmit mental illness. These people represented mental illness in a comprehensive way where their verbal responses to the researcher's enquiry and their everyday behaviours were just two expressions of the same thing: the 'madness' of their guests.

Cooperational meaning in interaction

The diversity of activities that unfold in a group's daily life can be overwhelming for the uninitiated observer. There are behaviours related to agriculture and gardening, building and construction, production and commerce, and a lot of others in all walks of daily life that serve a reproductive purpose. Any occasional observer easily understands these behaviours if he or she has some idea of the activity's aim and perhaps the technology involved. On the other hand there are behaviours the purpose and details of which are puzzling to an uninitiated observer. Most often these are related to ritual and religion, be it birth, coming of age, marriage, death or worship. Although comprised of overt behaviours, these activities do not easily disclose their aims and details except as a gross hunch. Observers may guess the reasons and occasions for them, but their concrete enactment escapes superficial observation. In contrast to the former group of activities, the latter carry a significant symbolic burden.

Imagine Gosh, an Indian tourist uninitiated into local Austrian culture, seeing a carpenter in his workshop struggling to move a plank to a work bench. As Gosh is a helpful person, he will consider helping the carpenter to move the plank and prevent it from falling. In virtually no culture would Gosh have to overcome any symbolic obstacle, as the aim and mechanics of the activity are evident to everybody. Besides the eventual rules of proximity or of spontaneous versus requested helping, Gosh and the carpenter are free to cooperate on this particular problem.

Now imagine Gosh observing a Catholic mass in a small French village. He will see the attendees put their fingers in a small bowl with water and wetting their forehead and coat in a crosslike fashion. Being a helpful person, as we already know, he might consider helping a worshipper to wipe off the water from her clothing, but being also a bright person, he will hesitate, and rightly so. Our traveller is observing a foreign ritual, and he will be far from initiated enough to cooperate correctly with the other attendees on this occasion.

Gosh's position in the two situations is completely different. In his interaction with the Austrian carpenter he shares an understanding of effort, body strength and the mechanics of balance and gravitation due to the fact that he is a human being. The meaning of the joint action is crystal clear and the symbolic burden minimal; both interactants easily share the meaning of their cooperation. Cooperational meaning in the case of a church ritual carries a high symbolic burden. Thus, cultural strangers cannot cooperate with locals on these things, besides the fact that they also lack the requisite group membership.

A study accompanying an arts project in an ethnically mixed community in London shows how participants enact representations in confrontation with outsiders. The lay artists appeared as active producers of their identity and the representation others were supposed to form of them: 'Cultural identities are always inherently oppositional as they rest on our simultaneous psychological needs to belong, to develop common understanding *and* to develop a sense of difference, of agency and of having a unique identity' (Howarth *et al.*, 2013). The participants' art actively reconstructed the representation of their ethnic group in the context of, and inspired by, the dominant 'white' British culture. By ironically including bits and pieces of the majority's stereotypes in their art, the artists established 'cooperational meaning' with their audience.

The cooperational meaning of potential interactions between people has two important consequences. First, representations must be conceived as overarching structures across interacting people, and second, representations must be comprised of one's own behavioural meaning as well as that of others. This is a characteristic of all situations where people interact with objects, other people and with institutions. The success of mundane interactions is guaranteed either by the similar or complementary actions of those involved, depending on whether they are facing each other as equals or are acting from different hierarchical positions. For example, interaction within a hierarchy conditions complementary behaviour patterns in both the superior and the subordinate actor. Although different, the patterns of action of those involved in the hierarchy complement each other in such a way that they create, or rather confirm, the social reality of dominance and subordination.

An inevitable consequence of the aforesaid is that actors must not only be aware of their own available courses of action, but also have some general representation of perception, judgements and the courses of action open to potential co-actors, even though they will never take on their counterpart's role. Hence, cooperational meaning is comprised of a person's own action rules as well as the rules underlying the actions of potential co-actors. We refer to this quality as the 'holomorphic' – that is, encompassing – character of representations (Wagner and Hayes, 2005).

The meaning of representational action, thus, lies in the fact that others will accept the actor's justification of an action if pressed to do so. In analogy to Habermas' (1985) criterion of discursive truth, we may want to call 'cooperational truth' an event where an *inter*action by one or more persons is not questioned among the interactants. Its execution is warranted in the meaning system that is being implied by the entirety of the interaction.

Mutual representational behaviour

It is a well-established fact that there is a mutual relationship between people's membership in groups and their tendency to broadly subscribe to their in-group's norms, beliefs, ideology and representational system (Abrams, 1992; Duveen, 2008; Terry and Hogg, 1996). People prefer to talk to similar others and consequently tend to affiliate with groups whose members share representations which are similar to their own, a tendency that has been referred to as homogamy (Griffitt and Veitch, 1974; Wagner and Hayes, 2005, p. 256). Likewise, individuals adapt their own norms and beliefs to the norms and beliefs of significant others who are often members of the same groups. It is clear that such commonalities among people in groups bolster individuals' self-esteem, tighten social relationships and increase group efficiency (Gonzales *et al.*, 1983).

Research on crowd behaviour has shown participants in demonstrations and riots to adapt ever so quickly to the norms of an active minority. This happens even if the majority of participants is only loosely organised at the beginning. They quickly unite when the initial majority encounters 'unjustified' resistance or is assaulted by outsiders, in many cases the police. In situations of perceived unjustified resistance, feelings of solidarity and belongingness go hand in hand with violent actions against the assailants (Reicher, 1984; Reicher, 1996). This illustrates the tight integration of identity and belonging, the situated sharing of norms, beliefs and representations in communal and coordinated activity.

In such situations, the two antagonistic groups, the protesters and the police in the so-called 'Battle of Westminster' for example (Reicher, 1996), are jointly responsible for the development of the confrontation: the police by impeding perceived rights of the protesters and by staging aggressive moves by mounted police units, and the protesters by merging into a compact block and by resisting the police's orders. Processes where the behaviours of one group's members are antagonistically related to the behaviours of an opposite group are called 'hetero-referential' relationships (Sen, 2012).

Antagonism of this kind is usually fuelled by simultaneous claims for a geographic area, for resources, and for political and religious supremacy as in many long-lasting conflicts around the world. There, the representational and ideological system of both groups develops in the long history of the conflict where, on and off, ideologues take up the other group's past 'wrong-doings' to justify estrangement and dehumanization of the Other in the service of securing their power and their group's dominance. Besides buttressing one's own identity, hetero-reference 'ensures' that the other group feels the need to respond (Sen and Wagner, 2005).

Social structures characterized by hetero-reference are not only determined by the group members' representations and ideologies but also simultaneously by their inadvertently antagonistic and mutually hurting behaviours. Hence, intergroup relationships are characterized first, by the group members being aware of themselves forming a group with an identity and repertoire of norms and behaviours, and second, by their being *grosso modo* also aware of the others' representations, even though this stereotype may sometimes be exaggerated (Wagner, Holtz, and Kashima, 2009): *one's social identity is reflected in the others' stereotype*.

Tajfel (1978) already acknowledged that in-groups are defined in relation to out-groups (also Turner *et al.*, 1987). Since this insight can be found at the cradle of group formation, it connects us to the mundane and above all more peaceful interpersonal encounters mentioned in the last section. That is, people act towards relevant objects, persons and institutions in a way that considers the kind of behaviour to be expected by their fellows. Co-actors comprehend and derive meaning from actions and interactions, if the representation being enacted follows a shared framework, which, in turn, brings us to the processes of objectification and social construction.

The production of social facts in the collective 'concert of interaction' implicitly endows the facts and 'representations in interaction' with validity since they are the circular evidence for the 'truth' of the social representations. Representations in action 'remodel... and reconstitute... the elements of the environment in which the behaviour takes place'. Representations must be seen as the meaning in concerted behaviours by integrating them into a network of relations in which it is bound up with its object (Moscovici, 1961/2008, p. 9). Hence, representations are objectified when the actors recognize the objects as evident and true. That is, when 'justifying the evidence comes to an end; but the end is not certain propositions striking us immediately as true, i.e. it is not a kind of *seeing* on our part; it is our *acting*, which lies at the bottom of the language-game' (Wittgenstein, 1994, paragraph 204). Our acting, being the very way we do things, co-constructs our world and simultaneously is the evidence for its 'truth' (Wagner, 1996).

Representations that count as action

It is standard in less democratic states to prosecute people if they openly confess to an ideology different from the official doctrine. There are abundant examples of this tendency that at times can also be found in democratically governed countries. Why do regimes persecute so-called dissidents? Usually dissidents are people who publicly voice opinions that deviate from what the regime considers tolerable. The emphasis here is on 'voicing' – that is, verbal and not overt behaviour such as throwing tomatoes at power holders or placing bombs. One could expect that rulers are interested in stifling actions and overt behaviours that are directed against their rule and that could potentially endanger the regime's supremacy. However, in the majority of cases dissidents do little more than utter their opinion without any hostile overt action being implied.

Now it could be that power holders are afraid of dissidents finding enough followers and initiating a revolt that might eventually topple them. Imprisonment or other oppressive means would then be meant to discourage potential followers before a movement reaches a critical mass. While such an interest is comprehensible from the point of view of power holders, including democratic ones, there may also be a symbolic aspect involved in stifling 'deviating' opinions, particularly in democratic societies.

The historical case of an author expressing 'clandestine joy' in the wake of a killing by the Red Army Faction (RAF) in Germany is an interesting example. On 7 April 1977 members of the RAF shot the German general Federal Prosecutor Siegfried Buback. About two weeks later a critical 'obituary' appeared in a student periodical that had been written by an anonymous member of a militant students' organization at the University of Goettingen. The text of the obituary expressed understanding for the deed as well as a critique and rejection of RAF's use of violent action.

State and law representatives reacted severely to one paragraph in the obituary reading:

> My immediate reaction, my 'stupefaction' after the shooting of Buback is quickly described: I could not, and didn't want to (and still don't want to) conceal my secret joy. I've frequently heard this guy agitate. I know he played a prominent role in the persecution, criminalization, torturing of leftists.[1]

The signatories, distributors, editors, of this obituary and magazine faced criminal prosecution on the grounds of being sympathizers, of supporting the RAF and of being hidden terrorists themselves (Bahn, 2003). Later, some of the initially harsh sentences were reduced or rescinded. Only the anonymous author, calling himself Mescalero, managed to escape unscathed.[2]

What is it that makes the above paragraph in the 'obituary' so dangerous that German authorities reacted with such conspicuous force? Certainly it was not that the author could be considered being on the brink of joining RAF, because he rejected their methods in the remainder of the text. Given his rejection of violence, the authorities were most likely not trying to stifle an expected violent action by the author, but rather to silence a person who symbolically violated their 'prescribed' anti-terrorist lament; his symbolism counted as overt aggression. More recently, in cases of Muslim fundamentalist terrorism, for example, the authorities in the United States and Europe have condemned with comparable rigour voices that do not clearly denounce the attacks and who do not share in the nationally 'prescribed' lament.

This and abundant similar examples illustrate the fact that ideology, representation and belief may have the same significance as overt behaviour. It is not necessary for a person to enact his or her beliefs overtly; holding 'wrong' beliefs or not joining

---

1 Buback – ein Nachruf, retrieved 03.10.2012, www.staff.uni-mainz.de/franz/vda/proj1968/ueberreg/doku/mescale.htm
2 Göttinger Mescalero, retrieved 01.10.2012 from http://de.wikipedia.org/wiki/Göttinger_Mescalero

in the chorus of 'national lament' is action enough to be considered conspicuous and defiant.

The case of dissidents and their persecution should ring a bell with social representations theorists. One of the central tenets of social representations theory is 'that the subject and the object are not basically heterogeneous in their common field' (Moscovici, 1961/2008). In the same way as the message of the mock-obituary in the aforementioned example is perceived as implying a (subjective) 'terrorist representation in action' on the part of the author and the simultaneous (objective) terrorist behaviour from an outside perspective, so social representations cannot be thought of as mere mental constructs. Rather, they require an appreciation of the entangled action.

Conclusion

In this chapter I have rejected a basic assumptions of common sense and some psychological research: behaviour and belief are integral to representations and not something that can be conceptualized separately. Representations exist in action as well as in belief and discourse. They are holomorphic in order to allow for concerted interaction, anticipation of others' actions, and the constitution of meaning in cooperation. While a representation's different aspects are not contingently articulated but rather are linked by their overarching meaning, they always have a contingent causal impact on their surroundings: a cry for help is contingent on others' effective help and representing waterfowl in winter as needing fodder is contingent on the birds' survival. Hence, what can be treated as separate entities and contingent issues are not beliefs and behaviours but rather representational action and its material and social consequences.

The precise nature and theoretical significance of social representations' articulation with what is usually called the outside reality has been the topic of a lively debate between the 'Enactivists' (Verheggen and Baerveldt, 2007) and 'Social Representationists' (Chryssides et al., 2009). This cannot be outlined here, suffice it to say that in my opinion the theoretical construct of representations being 'shared' and the driving force in actors' jointly effectuating an outcome is a more useful account for social psychological research than the Radical Constructivists' neurological individualism. 'If one considers social representations to be at the intersection of the individual and the collectivity, they are neither wholly idiosyncratic phenomena, nor marked by some form of agreement within a social group . . . they are shared' (Chryssides et al., 2009, p. 90).

The integral nature of representations observed at the individual level and assessed through interviews, and the meaning of interactions of people in groups, assessed by observing behaviour patterns over time, are the most important achievements of social representations theory. Due to its overarching character, the concept of social representations allows for an effortless transition from the individual level to the collective level: on the one hand we have individuals with their motivations, beliefs, knowledge and affiliation preferences that entail a person's actions; on the other hand, individuals in concert enact social representations, the pattern of which constitutes what we call social reality. Thus, the two conceptual levels are linked by action because bodily action is the only instance where representations are in 'full contact' with hard facts. That is why *representation is in action*.

3 Social representations and societal psychology

Claudia Abreu Lopes and George Gaskell

The ambition of societal psychology is the study of social phenomena and cultural forces that both shape, and in turn are shaped by, people's outlooks and actions. As we will outline in this chapter, the theory of social representations can play a foundational role in societal psychology and, at the same time, the theory itself can be enriched by taking a societal perspective.

Social representations are a socio-evolutionary development of the concept of collective or common consciousness, defined by Durkheim (1894) as the beliefs, norms and values common to all members of a society that constitute the basis of social integration. In arguing that these social facts are *sui generis*, exercising a coercive power above and beyond the minds of individuals, Durkheim outlined a project for sociology that excluded reference to psychological constructs.

For Moscovici (1973) the static nature of collective representations was not adequate to address the flux of conditions in modern societies confronted by scientific, political and social change and also by a plurality of social groups and the plethora of beliefs and value positions. He proposed that social representations are systems of values, ideas and practices which give order and meaning to the material and social world, with which members of a community exchange views, and make sense of their world and their individual and group history. As such social representations are like Eco's contractual realism; 'faced with a reality of sorts, a community engages in discussion until it finds a negotiated ("contractual") solution' (Eco, 2000).

This definition positions the phenomenon of social representations, in terms of origins and functions, at both the individual and group level. The inclusion of the interplay between micro and macro levels is a consistent theme in developments and elaborations of the theory. For example Duveen's (2001) microgenetic process of social gender identity formation (see also Moscovici *et al.*, 2013); Jovchelovitch's (2007) notion of social representations operating in a space between the individual and society, and the public sphere; and Bauer and Gaskell's (1999) Toblerone model of social representations combining actors in natural groups with a common project and objects of representation. In these and in many other studies we see attempts to combine levels of analysis in theoretical speculation and empirical research. However, there is a lack of clarity as to the role of social representations in the evolving relations between the macro and micro levels. Before characterizing social representations in a macro–micro analytic framework, a clarification concerning the micro level is required.

Methodological individualism, attributed to Weber (1922), holds that the social scientific analysis of phenomena must be rooted in an account of the intentional states that motivate individual actors. Of particular relevance to our current concerns, methodological individualism calls for rigour in the specification of hypotheses deduced from the macro level about the consequences at the micro level.

In analytic sociology, methodological individualism accepts the stipulation of precision in the specification of macro to micro mechanisms, but as seen in the work of network analysts, the sovereign individual is replaced by the actor in a social context – for example, in a network of strong and weak ties (Granovetter, 1973). This approach shifts the focus of attention away from the isolated individual (unqualified individualism) to the person acting in concert with others. This is the position of social representations theory, in which the individual thinks and acts in an intersubjective context, much in the same way as is elaborated by the symbolic interactionists (cf. G. H. Mead (1934)).

Consider the contrast between attitude and social representational research. In much attitude theory and research, attitude formation and change is modelled in terms of information processing. By contrast, social representations theory assumes that changes in representations – whether these are in the form of attitudes, values or identities – are the outcome of interpersonal process (formal and informal communications).

The difference between the two approaches is illustrated in a classic study by Kurt Lewin (1958) on changing food habits. In this research one condition modelled a mass-media campaign informing the isolated individual about the need to serve the family with less attractive cuts of meat and how these could be cooked; the second condition used group discussion based on an agenda along the same lines as the simulated mass-media message. The former condition led to minimal attitude and behaviour change; the latter to far more. Why? According to Lewin (1958), there are group dynamic processes that unfreeze normative positions and promote the participants to entertain other ways of thinking and of behaving. The group decision – a public commitment to change – consolidates commitment to the new behaviour, creating in effect a new normative position. It is for this reason that methodological intersubjectivism seems an appropriate term to adopt in social psychology. It reminds us to retain rigour and precision and to focus our attention at the micro level on the socially interconnected actor whose norms, values, common sense and decisions are the outcome of symbolic interaction.

A notable contribution to the debate on levels of analysis in social psychology is seen in the work of Doise (1986a), which was published at a time when social psychology was embroiled in a crisis of confidence. At stake was a heated debate over the nature of the discipline. In the 1970s the established paradigm prescribed experimental research to test hypotheses, laboratory studies with university students as subjects, and manipulations that often involved deception.

This paradigm was subject to challenge on both sides of the Atlantic. In the United States there was criticism of the 'fun and games' theatrical approach (Ring, 1967), concerns about external validity and the possibility of generalizations from both students and the laboratory context, and evidence of biases due to experimenter effects. Orne's (1962) essay 'On the social psychology of the psychological experiment' illustrated how the discipline had become almost autopoietic.

In Europe, the critique of the paradigm took on a quasi-political dimension as Tajfel, Moscovici and others made a commitment to establishing a distinctively European approach to the discipline with the establishment of a European Association of Social Psychology.

How did the experiment become such a dominant feature of social psychology? Farr's (1996) history of the discipline describes what he terms the 'individualisation of the social' – the study of the individual abstracted from the social context. This emerged as social psychology and sections of sociology strove to create distinctive and mutually exclusive academic disciplines. Durkheim's project for sociology was the identification of 'social facts' that would constitute the causal mechanisms of what might otherwise be considered the outcome of individual decisions, for example suicide. For Durkheim (1894), suicide was the predictable outcome of societal structures and forces. In social psychology, Allport (1954) championed methodological individualism. In this there was room for nothing beyond the mind of the sovereign individual. The group, in contrast to Lewin's (1952) conception of group dynamics as a field of forces, was for Allport (1954) an epi-phenomenon.

Doise (1980) enters the debate with some challenging questions: Is experimentation desirable in social psychology? What are the links between social psychology, psychology and sociology? Is social psychology fundamentally reductionist; does it aim to explain social phenomena in terms of non-social factors? Doise's (1980, 1986a) consideration of these questions led him to argue that, on the basis of the current literature, experimentation is not necessarily reductionist. He identified four levels of analysis that characterized social psychological theory and research as follows:

1. Intrapersonal: how the actor processes information in the perception of others and in attitude change – cf. Festinger's (1957) cognitive dissonance theory and other consistency theories.
2. Interpersonal and situational: how the behaviour of the others affects the actor – cf. Sherif (1936) on norm formation.
3. Positional: how the other's social status or group membership affects the actor – cf. Milgram (1963) on obedience to the 'voice of science'.
4. Ideological: how belief systems, ideologies or shared values determine the actor's outlook and choices – cf. Lerner's (1980) Just World Hypothesis.

With these examples Doise (1986a) argues that social psychology has never been exclusively individualistic (level 1); the other levels can be found in the theorizing and research of prominent social psychologists. For him, each level is legitimate and can make a contribution to the understanding of social psychological phenomena. However, the over-reliance on level 1 explanations restricts the scope of social psychological enquiry to the sovereign and autonomous individual without reference to group membership, social status, ethnicity, nationality and so on. At the centre of Doise's (1986a) levels of analysis is a project for social psychology that takes account of the social context in the explanation of behaviour by investigating, where appropriate, any of the four levels. He also retains a commitment to experimentation as a key means to test causal hypotheses, noting the virtues of the field experiment as outlined in Campbell and Stanley's (1963) concepts of internal and external validity.

Doise (1986a) recognized serious epistemological problems concerning the articulation between levels. As he puts it, 'some way of articulating these levels needs to be invented because social processes can only occur via processes in the individual' and 'the contributions of the individual are affected by the social structure which generates and guides individual activities' (p. 4). He went further to assert that the articulation of levels of analysis should be a topic of research in its own right (p. vii).

In a consideration of Doise's four levels of analysis and their relevance to social representations, Wagner and Hayes (2005) argue that the phenomena to be explained in social psychology, for example Lerner's 'just world hypothesis', and the level of explanation of the phenomenon are most often at the micro, the individual level. They further suggest that the level of analysis of the phenomenon to be explained is not given consideration in Doise's formulation. This leads them to distinguish between three levels of aggregation that apply to both the phenomenon and its level of explanation: intrapersonal (the subjective world), situative (transient changes in the environment) and sociocultural (enduring features of the environment).

Conceptual homogeneous explanations imply concordance of levels of complexity of the explanation (the explanans) and the phenomenon to be explained (the explanadum). Theories from psychology and social psychology lie in the intrapersonal and situative levels while sociocultural explanations call for sociological, economic and socio-anthropological theories.

When the explanans and the explanadum are situated at different levels, theoretical causes linking the two imply some form of reductionism. Micro reductive explanations use concepts of a lower level to explain higher level phenomena. By contrast, a macro-reductionist approach alludes to situative and sociocultural contexts to account for intra-individual phenomena.

Wagner and Hayes (2005) map the theory of social representations into this macro–micro theorizing. From a top-down perspective, social representations mediate the transition from macro contexts to individual mental constructs. Conceptualized as projections of sociostructural and cultural conditions shared across social groups, social representations offer an interim explanatory step to link macro and micro levels of aggregation. From a bottom-up perspective, the individual and the sociocultural levels are linked through socially embedded discursive processes that generate and transform social representations.

From both Doise (1986a) and Wagner and Hayes (2005) we may draw a rough line between the micro and the macro analysis of social phenomena. Micro analysis employs a bottom-up approach, putting individuals at the centre of social reality, whereas macro analysis relies on a top-down approach, starting from groups and societies to contextualize human action. Micro theories refer to psychological processes. For example, relative deprivation theory (Runciman, 1966) explains how the perceived economic situation depends on the subjective positioning in relation to others. Macro theories, in turn, rely on social forces and institutions that constrain collective behaviour. One example is anomie theory (Merton, 1938), which explains deviant behaviour based on the concordance of socially determined materialistic goals and the instrumental ways that are available to individuals to achieve these goals. When societal pressures to achieve material goals clash with limited ways to achieve them, a state of anomie arises facilitating deviant behaviour.

In this example, micro and macro theories may be intuitively combined: relative deprivation can be the motivational force that fosters deviant behaviour among individuals from anomic societies.

This type of micro–macro theory is not common in social thinking albeit sociological theories imply certain assumptions about psychological processes – usually in terms of rational choice and action (Opp, 2011).

Bridging the individual and societal levels using social mechanisms

It is an ambitious task to test hypotheses that combine psychological (micro) and sociological (macro) mechanisms integrated through adequate linkages. Within sociology, methodological individualism postulates that the ultimate unit of analysis of social phenomena is a purposive individual and as such 'social science explanations should always include explicit references to the causes and consequences of their actions' (Hedström and Swedberg, 1998, p. 12). Rather than reducing social science to the study of individual processes or attributing an outstanding place to psychology, methodological individualism advocates that psychological theories should not be disregarded when it comes to explaining higher order phenomena such as collective behaviour.

Contemporary analytical sociology (Hedström and Bearman, 2009) also elaborates on the idea that social facts can be better addressed through the combination of micro and macro theories linked together into a coherent framework. This is redolent of Merton's notion of middle-range theories that explain a class of events instead of isolated social facts. The most cited example is the self-fulfilling prophecy (Merton, 1957), which explains how a false definition of a situation may cause the expected situation to be brought about. If a person expects something to happen, he/she will behave in accordance with his/her expectations, contributing to the definition of the situation and unintentionally generating the anticipated outcome. This theory has been applied to educational, organizational and economic contexts. For example,

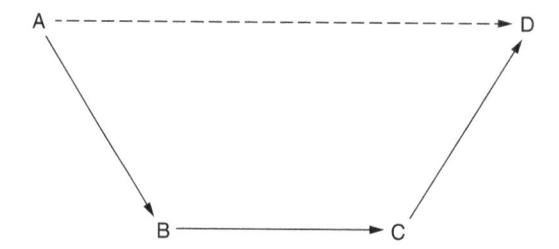

Figure 3.1 *Coleman's macro–micro model.*

economic growth of a nation may be brought about by consumers' confidence in the overall state of the economy. Higher confidence will generate more spending, effectively boosting the economy in a virtuous cycle (Katona, 1975).

Micro and macro linkages are articulated through social mechanisms, defined as 'plausible hypotheses, or sets of plausible hypotheses, that could be the explanation of some social phenomena, the explanation being in terms of interactions between individuals, or individuals and some social aggregate' (Schelling, 1978, p. 32). A social mechanism is expected to be found inside a black-box when one moves beyond mere associations between variables to explanations for the observed association. In this perspective, a theory may encapsulate several social mechanisms or several theories may be summed up in one single mechanism. Research hypotheses should explicitly make reference to social mechanisms and statistical testing serves to decide between alternative mechanisms, or parts of mechanisms, providing an assessment of the underlying theory.

Social mechanisms combine explanations across different levels of analysis. Coleman (1986) proposed a macro–micro typology that conceptualizes social action through the integration of different social perspectives defined at different levels. The rationale for this model is that effects at the macro level can be explained by how macro-states at one point influence the behaviour of individual actors, and how individual actions generate new macro-states at a later point in time (Hedström and Ylikoski, 2010). Figure 3.1 depicts 'Coleman's boat' and represents three possible mechanisms.

In this figure, A refers to the normative environment (actions of others or environmental or social conditions); B refers to individual norms, beliefs, desires, opportunities or habits; C refers to individual actions; and D refers to emergent social outcomes (aggregation networks, extent of action or typical beliefs). Elements A and D are macro-level variables whereas B and C are micro-level variables. The association A→B is conceptualized only in descriptive terms and strictly speaking can only be captured by a correlation. The explanation of the association implies the formulation of the social mechanism that explains how A leads to D. The arrows between A, B, C and D describe associations between those variables that can be explained by three different partial mechanisms comprising an overall social mechanism: contextual, psychological and transformational mechanism.

Type I (macro–micro) is a contextual mechanism that explains how macro-level conditions (e.g. culture or economic forces) affect the behaviour of individuals. Situational mechanisms have been studied extensively in political and cultural psychology.

Type II (micro) is an individual mechanism that evokes beliefs, attitudes, desires and opportunities as antecedents of action. It is called an action-formation mechanism. Social and cognitive psychology occupy this niche of research.

Type III (micro–macro) describes how isolated individual actions generate collective outcomes – intended or not – and is called a transformational mechanism. Among the social sciences, the discipline most attuned to the study of transformational mechanisms is economics. In its simplest form, a transformational mechanism may refer to the direct extrapolation from the individual to the aggregate. The market is the prime example of the outcome of a transformational mechanism: the decisions and actions of millions of people (C) appear to be coordinated to create an economic system characterized by order (D). Adam Smith (1776) looked upon this system as if an invisible hand was in command of all operations. This metaphor encapsulates a transformational mechanism (or multiple transformational mechanisms). Katona's (1975) efforts to predict economic behaviour at the macro-level based on consumers' decisions constitute a remarkable example of theory seeking transformational mechanisms.

In sociology, the issue of how individual norms and preferences translate into culture may also be approached by transformational mechanisms. However, the interplay between individuals and culture tends to be studied in only one direction, emphasizing how culture influences behaviour (Adamopoulos, 2008). One possible explanation is that available conceptual models do not offer methodological guidelines for studying the interaction between individuals and culture (Vijver and Leung, 2000). By considering the different levels of phenomena covered by several theories within the social sciences and the possible integration among them, the social mechanisms approach takes a step further towards a unified and multidisciplinary approach of the social sciences.

Social mechanisms in social psychology and sociology

A notable example of theorizing in social psychology that combines macro- and micro-level analysis is Sherif and Sherif's (1956) classic contribution of realistic group conflict theory. This was further developed in Tajfel's (1981) social identity theory, which brought new insights into micro-level processes. Realistic group conflict theory set out to explain the roots of intergroup conflict. At the macro level the social structure involves groups of people brought together with particular goals and aspirations.

The contextual mechanism arises from the nature of the relations between societal groups, which are characterized on a continuum from positive interdependence –

working with compatible aspirations towards common goals – to negative interdependence – in conflict for power, influence or any other scarce resource. According to Sherif (1956), intergroup attitudes – positive and negative – are a consequence of the nature of group interdependence. Two types of negative interdependence are identified. Those in which the groups are of equal status and those where one group dominates the other. These create the conditions for micro-level processes. Where the groups are of different status, the higher status group seeks to rationalize its dominant status in self-justificatory accounts of the inequality. In situations where the groups are of equal status, in each, group micro-processes cultivate over-evaluation of the in-group and derogation of the out-group. The transformational mechanism is that in-group over-evaluation and out-group derogation sets the scene and justification for intergroup conflict. To militate against intergroup conflict, Sherif and Sherif (1956) show that the imposition of superordinate goals that necessitate intergroup cooperation shifts the micro-processes towards positive group interdependence and positive intergroup attitudes.

Tajfel (1981) and colleagues challenged the 'realistic conflict' hypothesis. In a series of ingenious experiments social identity theory posited and empirically demonstrated that the mere categorization of in-group and out-group, with no apparent utilitarian basis (the transformational mechanism), is sufficient to induce the syndrome of in-group over-evaluation and out-group derogation at the micro level. In social identity theory this process is the result of the drive for a positive social identity, which is acquired through group membership and favourable social comparison against other groups – so-called positive group distinctiveness. We need to believe that the group to which we belong is special and a good way of achieving this idea is to believe that one's own group is superior to the other group on relevant attributes. But, social identity theory leaves open the question as to why in pluralistic societies some intergroup categorizations are simply irrelevant, while others lead to the micro-level generation of hostile intergroup perceptions.

In sociology, social mechanisms are illustrated by the example of Merton's theory of anomie and social structure (Merton, 1957). This theory was formulated at three different levels of analysis: societal, positional and intra-individual. Some authors (e.g. Messner, 1988) assert that the theory comprises two distinct and apparently independent theories: the theory of social organization and the theory of deviant motivation. Each one refers to different partial mechanisms, as will be explained below.

In the theory of social organization, Merton describes a strong social structure as one in which the 'social structure allows individuals to reach the cultural approved goals through the normative means' (Messner, 1988, p. 37). Contrasting with a strong social structure, a strained social structure is more prone to deviant behaviour. In Coleman's (1986) scheme (Figure 3.1), element A is the type of social structure (strong vs strained) and element D is the rate of deviant behaviour in lower classes in a given society. The theory predicts that a strained social structure is associated with a higher prevalence of deviant behaviour in lower classes. This macro-level association is formulated only in descriptive terms.

The Type I mechanism (contextual) considers that in a strained social structure, individuals in disadvantaged positions aspire for goals imposed socially (e.g. material success) that are not available by normative means (e.g. a well-paid job). As the opportunities to achieve materialistic goals are restricted by social structure, individuals who perceive that their way to material success is blocked compared to individuals in more comfortable positions feel relatively deprived. This contextual mechanism corresponds to the theory of social organization (Merton, 1957).

The Type II mechanism (psychological) explains how in strained societies individuals violate norms and engage in deviant behaviour. In societies where materialistic goals are more valued than the means that individuals use to pursue them, the 'end justifies the means' principle prevails. Individuals who feel deprived opt for non-normative means to achieve material success, such as dishonest behaviour. This mechanism corresponds to the theory of deviant motivation (Merton, 1938).

The Type III mechanism (transformational) explains how collective deviant behaviour spreads especially among the lower classes. Pressures to break social norms or rules are experienced differently across the social structure. Individuals from lower classes are more likely to feel relatively deprived due to feelings of frustration linked to perceptions of restricted opportunities for social achievement and mobility.

In this context an anomic state is installed in lower classes as social norms lose their power and deviant behaviour is more likely to occur, explaining social class dependent patterns of deviant behaviour.

The transformational mechanism in Merton's theory of anomie and social structure consists of a simplistic extrapolation from the micro level to the macro level using an additive rule: a higher motivation for deviant behaviour in individuals from anomic societies or groups is associated with higher rates of criminal behaviour in these groups or societies.

The actions of individuals in concert may generate unexpected outcomes. The collective outcomes are not always directly inferred from behavioural rules, values or motivations. In particular, if individual actions or choices are influenced by the actions or choices of other individuals, they create systems of interaction and interdependence. For example, Flache and Macy (1996) showed how strong friendship ties between friends lead to less cooperation in groups. A high drive for approval at the micro level discourages overt criticism between friends and the subsequent failure to regulate the actions of individuals when they engage in non-cooperative behaviour.

The study of aggregation patterns has been applied to traffic, marriage, job mobility, language development and markets, and all these examples warn us that it is not possible to predict the behaviour of the aggregate only by looking at individual motivations, intentions and actions.

Thomas Schelling (1971, 1978) has inspired approaches to collective behaviour that take aggregation rules into account. With his classic example of patterns of segregation in residential areas based on preferences of residents, Schelling (1971)) explains patterns of mobility of residents in areas with mixed ethnicities.

The preference for belonging to the majority ethnic group, yet with some degree of tolerance in terms of ethical diversity, explains how residents gradually leave a neighborhood of mixed ethnicities. When residents from a different ethnicity gradually join the neighbourhood, those from a different ethnicity will become less represented. At a certain tipping point, when residents of the other ethnicity outnumber residents from the same ethnicity, residents will be motivated to leave the neighbourhood, thus creating a dynamic of segregation.

An application to economic morality

Inspired by the Merton's theory of anomie and social structure (Merton, 1957), a social mechanism for consumer fraud was advanced and tested using micro and macro data from twenty-seven countries from the European Social Survey and the European Values Survey (Lopes, 2012).

Consumer fraud is a type of dishonest consumer behaviour involving material gains for the person who performs it and clear negative consequences for a company or the state via the acquisition, consumption and disposition of goods, services or ideas. Consumer fraud can assume two forms – active and passive – depending on whether the consumer initiated the behaviour or merely took advantage of a situation faced (Muncy and Vitell, 1992). An example of 'active fraud' is insurance fraud. An example of 'passive fraud' is keeping extra change from a shop assistant. Other examples of fraud are income tax evasion, paying cash-in-hand to circumvent taxes, falsely claiming social security benefits, bribing public officials and buying on credit with no intention of paying. Although not all dishonest practices are necessarily illegal, some cross the boundaries of legality.

The social mechanism derives from the idea that the emergence of unfair practices in the marketplace is facilitated by the transition to neoliberal markets if such transitions are not accompanied by a concomitant evolution of social institutions. This constitutes the macro-level association that can be explained using theories from the intrapersonal, interpersonal, intergroup and societal levels.

The thesis defended by Roland (2004) and Messner and Rosenfeld (2010) posits that rapid economic development promotes the disembeddedness of the market with social institutions (family, education, religious and political). This scenario leads to an overemphasis on materialistic values in society. Because sanctions for immoral behaviour are usually imposed by non-economic institutions, as non-economic institutions lose power, moral restraints to dishonest behaviour will be lifted in a new economic order. In this view, rapid economic development may be accompanied by a cornucopia of opportunities for unethical behaviour that encompass neoliberal markets (Karstedt and Farrall, 2006). An overemphasis on materialistic values coupled with opportunities to behave dishonestly triggers dishonest practices (both from business and consumers), configuring a state of market anomie (Karstedt and Farrall, 2006) characterized by distrust in the economy and in economic agents, fear of being victimized, and cynical attitudes towards the law.

A general level of perception of corruption among the public sector may also lead to changes in economic morality, in other words, the perception of the fairness of the economy works (Karstedt and Farrall, 2007). Corruption in the public sector is associated with lower judicial/legal effectiveness (Kaufman, 2004). By relaxing legal barriers, law compliance regarding fraud diminishes. Fraudulent behaviour will be more common in all sectors, and perceptions of the unfairness of the economy will be fostered in society. Thus, there is higher acceptance of fraudulent practices in countries with higher levels of corruption, because economic morality is poor and law is not effectively enforced.

Besides the rapid transition to neoliberal policies and a higher level of corruption, a high level of social inequality may also have an impact on the perception of fairness of the economy. The 'inequality trap' (Uslaner, 2008) suggests that in unequal societies individuals trust less in others and distrust generates corruption and fraud.

The common denominator of the effect of macro-level factors (disembeddedness of the market with social institutions, corruption in the public sector and social inequalities) is the syndrome of market anomie that may arise by impacting economic morality. This is an example of a Type I mechanism for consumer fraud (macro–micro). But not all individuals hold this constellation of negative feelings towards the market to the same degree, and those who feel victimized by unethical business practices are more likely to experience anomie. Market anomie sets the stage for dishonest practices by impacting individual morality and attitudes towards dishonest behaviour. A Type II mechanism (micro–micro) is needed to explain individual differences in dishonest behaviour.

Relative deprivation fuels illegitimate ways (such as dishonest/criminal behaviour) of achieving material success. Lower-class individuals are more likely to feel relatively deprived, especially in unequal societies (Merton, 1957). Social inequalities signal a strained social structure with deep boundaries between social classes. This psychological mechanism is particularly suited to societies where consumer fraud is uncommon, as it applies to behaviour of a deviant nature (Merton, 1938). Relative deprivation offers an account for the emergence of fraudulent behaviour, especially in societies where social norms dictate its deviance. The perceived legitimacy of governments and regulations is maximized in egalitarian societies and transparent and accountable governments help to hamper fraud and corruption.

In societies where consumer fraud is widespread, social norms of behaving dishonestly dictate practices in the marketplace. To explain the process of expansion of fraudulent behaviour, a critical mass mechanism (Schelling, 1978) explains that consumer fraud may be self-sustained once the number of fraudsters passes a certain tipping point. As individuals perceive that more individuals are engaging in fraud, the more the likelihood that they will also commit fraud.

Firstly, this may be explained by the power of social norms to impel individuals to adopt the behaviour of the majority, especially if this behaviour can bring material gains. Secondly as more people are engaged in fraud, so the perception of the effectiveness of the law is weaker. Thirdly, as more people engage in fraud, so the feeling of moral obligation and the expected societal return of behaving according to the law loses its effect. This may happen only if a certain threshold for the number of people committing fraud is achieved and above which the economic and social costs of one additional fraud act is negligible. Consequently, as more people are perceived to be engaging in fraud after a certain threshold, so the more people will be pushed into fraud and the higher the perception of widespread fraud that in turn will generate even more fraud.

Relative deprivation and social conformism offer an account for the motivation of dishonest practices. Opportunity and psychological characteristics, such as human values (Schwartz, 1992), and perception of moral obligation (Beck and Ajzen, 1991) determine the extent to which motivation materializes in dishonest behaviour. If people believe that others are doing the same, then subjective obstacles for initiation behaviour such as damage of social image or fear of being caught loose power. Neutralization processes in the form of 'everybody does it' (Gabor, 1994) and 'business is unfair' legitimate and help individuals to integrate dishonest behaviour and determine its continuation.

Critical mass models (Schelling, 1971) that describe how a collective process is generated and evolves over time before and after reaching a tipping point explain a wide range of phenomena in social sciences and may bring explanatory power to the social mechanism of economic morality presented before. Adding a temporal dimension to economic morality, a micro–macro link potentially explains how isolated and deviant actions become more frequent. When a sufficient number in the population engages in fraudulent behaviour a norm emerges that impels other individuals to comply. By systematizing the models underlying collective phenomena, Schelling's work offers an important contribution to the social mechanism approach.

The aggregation rules implicated in micro–macro explanations may be mapped on to the transformational mechanism of the 'Coleman boat' (the Type III mechanism in Figure 3.1). However, in social psychology, theories focussing on micro–macro links are under-represented despite their relevance to the formation of norms and group behaviour based on social influence and communication processes.

Social representations as social mechanisms

Coleman's (1986) boat directs our attention to four related foci in the analysis of social phenomena: the macro level, the contextual mechanism, the micro level, and the transformational mechanism. In what follows we outline what these mean in practice for social representations theorists.

The macro level: societal challenges

The macro level captures the social context that motivates or inspires a specific research question. The context may be politics, health, education, the environment, science and technology, the media or any other area of occasional significance to the everyday life of sections of the public. We do not wish to imply that such contexts are unified fields. Rather, they are likely to be a heterogeneous collection of a number of actors and institutions promoting different visions of social progress and differing means to achieve such ends.

The contextual mechanism

These contexts will at times appear to be stable and at other times to be subject to development, evolution and change, spurred by competing interest groups, new political ideologies, fashion, unexpected and disruptive external events or new discoveries in science and technology. At times of stability, the social context is akin to Thomas Kuhn's (1962) normal science; it is taken for granted without question. By contrast, in times of change the taken-for-granted is challenged; it is called into question. Think of climate change, the depletion of non-renewable sources of energy, the failure of banks, questions about the risks of immunisation and developments in the life sciences such as GM food and human embryonic stem cell research. By bringing into focus cleavages of values, such issues constitute a challenge to the taken-for-granted. In the public sphere the alternative positions are aired and debated as interested parties attempt to secure support for their position. While the wider public may be onlookers, only a few may be isolated from the controversy.

The micro level: intersubjective representations

It is at this level that we see much of the theorizing in social representations theory. The research question posed is how the public understand and make sense of the challenge to the social context. How does the novel and unfamiliar come into common sense? In social representations theory concepts such as anchoring and objectification, core and periphery, and cognitive polyphasia have been elaborated to describe and explain the process of the intersubjective transformation of the unfamiliar to the familiar. Here again, this process does not necessarily lead to homogeneity (the same representation). Different groups within the wider public generate their own understandings on the basis of their past, current or future life projects. As such, contemporary societies are characterized by a diversity of representations about the same issue or object.

The transformational mechanism

The transformational mechanism captures the ways in which the outcome of micro-level processes impinge on the macro – the social – context. Hence, if the social representation is the independent variable, then the transformational mechanism is the dependent variable. Responses to the way in which a particular challenge is understood (the social representation) might follow one of Piaget's genetic epistemological positions – assimilation or accommodation. The former constitutes the acceptance of the 'new' within current practices; the latter involves changing current practices in order to deal with the challenge. A third option is resistance – personal and/or social mobilization to challenge the challenge; and a fourth is to follow the example of the ostrich with its head in the sand – ignorance is bliss.

Towards a societal psychology

In essence we are proposing an ambitious agenda and methodology for a societal psychology based upon the theory of social representations. The objective is a study of social phenomena that combines macro-level and micro-level analyses. Returning to Doise (1986a), this is not to suggest that the study of the micro level or experimentation should be abandoned. Rather, it is to suggest that we need a balance in our research efforts. Social representations theory has led to many significant developments in the understanding of the micro level. It is now timely to consider taking this a step further; using these insights to research societal phenomena. Now, it is appreciated that researchers in the field may not have the time or the resources to mount studies that cover the macro and micro levels and their linking social mechanisms. It is also appreciated that the methodology will, on occasions, call for multidisciplinary research teams bringing together social psychologists with experts in, for example, political science, sociology and anthropology.

But it has to be recognized that societal issues are multifaceted and few can be understood with a solely social psychological approach. If social psychology does not rise to this challenge, then the other social sciences will, as noted by Moscovici (1990), develop their own varieties of social psychology.

Social representations theory must go beyond the micro level to embrace the social context that gives rise to micro-level phenomena and then speculate on the transformational mechanisms that capture how the micro level contributes to changing the macro level – the social context. In other words, social representations theory needs to expand its aspirations to become a theory of social change.

4 On (social) representations and the iconoclastic impetus

Martin W. Bauer

This chapter explores the notion of 'representation' from the point of view of societal psychology (see Himmelweit and Gaskell, 1990). It builds on previous discussions seeking to clarify the problematic carried forward by Farr (1987), Wagner (1996), Marková and Jovchelovitch (2008) and Howarth, Kalampalikis and Castro (2011). The argument develops in four steps expanding on two previous statements (Bauer and Gaskell, 2008 and 1999):

- The periodic sense of representations in crisis;
- Some particular 'representations' in the social sciences: scientific, statistical, political and mental, but not artistic;
- Recapitulating ideas for a theoretical paradigm of 'social representations';
- Rehearsing the implications for research into modern mentalities.

Why worry about representations: the iconoclastic impetus

In 2012 the *Economist*, a weekly magazine which is not known for any religious orientation beyond markets, commemorated a curious event.[1] In June 1913 Russian gunboats resolved a theological conflict on Mount Athos in Greece by brute force. An 'onomatoclastic' abbot had called in imperial help against his 'onomatodoxian' monks who repeated the 'Names of God' to unleash mystical powers. This conflict, which in the Orthodox world is known as the 'Imiaslavic controversy' (see Bulgakov, 1931/2012) centres on the issue of whether a word is more than just a *flatus voci* (Latin for a vocal fart). These events are historically contemporaneous with Ferdinand de Saussure's lectures in Geneva where he stressed the conventional link between the material signifier (the spoken, written or depicted 'horse') and the signified general idea (a four-legged riding animal) as the foundation of modern semiotics in a context of social psychology (Saussure, 1916/1960; Harris, 1987).

These events of 1913, recalled one hundred years later, point to old preoccupations about modalities of representations. The foundation narrative takes the following lines: Moses, who led the people of Israel out of Egyptian slavery, climbed up Mount Sinai, and when he came back there was upheaval. Aaron, who

---

[1] War and theology – in the name of the Name, *Economist*, 22 December 2012, 46–48.

'represented' Moses as acting leader of the people in the meantime, had made concessions and the people regressed to venerating their old Golden Calf. An irate Moses reprimanded Aaron and the people of Israel and angrily destroyed the symbol of slavery. This was the exemplary act of biblical iconoclasm, presenting a violent act of liberation from false representations.

Why destroy the Golden Calf? Deference to idols is an act of infidelity, a transgression. The Bible tells of the Covenant of Freedom that was received on the mountain top and which stated clearly that God first and foremost is jealous and does not tolerate competition; deference should be to the one and only (hence monotheism); and secondly, to make this easier, God forbids the making of 'graven images of things in heaven or on earth' that could distract from the one and only (the iconoclastic impetus). This event leaves the Jewish tradition with a strong premonition of two lingering dangers of visualization and representations: infidelity and cognitive error (see Halbertal and Marglit, 1992), and a struggle with visual art (Julius, 2001). Islam inherited the iconoclastic ban of images of Allah, the prophet, and all human figures. Iconoclastic art is thus bent towards the ornamental and abstract to avoid infringement of the commandments.

Christianity inherited the iconoclastic impetus with ambivalence that manifests itself in historical waves of iconoclasm. In the Eastern Church this came to a peak in the controversies of the eighth and ninth centuries, when images of Christ were destroyed. The conflict between iconoclasts and iconophiles was resolved in favour of the latter, when in 843 CE the 'Triumph of Orthodoxy' council put icons back into religious practice. Eastern Christianity has since had a regulated practice of two-dimensional depictions of Christ, Maria, prophets, angels and apostles. In this context visual art became a mystical pursuit. In the West, the problem of representation came to a crunch in the Reformation of the sixteenth century, when the iconoclastic impetus resurged in the stripping of altars and the destruction of relics and religious art of all kinds (Duffy, 1992). Sacred spaces were not to represent anything except in the modality of words; *in extremis* even the sounds of music were considered distractive and potentially iconolatrous.[2]

In contrast, the historical defense of images counted on three lines of argument. First, modalities of representations such as pictures, movements or sounds were helpful for instructing the people as memory props and as illustrations of more abstract points. This didactic defence is traceable to Greco-Roman rhetoric, which states that to aid memory we should use vivid images: not many, but beautiful, grotesque or ridiculous ones (*imagines agentes*; see Yates, 1966). This was recognized by the fourth century and reinforced in the sixteenth century. The Catholic Counter-Reformation defended representations with baroque exaltation in all modalities such as carved, sculptured, pictured, sounded, and with colours

---

[2] Clearly this is a heroic simplification of historical events. These issues gave rise to complex crisscrossings among different trends of the Reformation; and theological conflicts mixed with earthly concerns for the nationalization of the church's property (see MacCulloch, 2003; Wandel, 1994; Eire, 1986). The language used is the language of the victors: rejecters of images see themselves as correct and the others as 'iconodules'; while 'iconoclast' is the polemical term used by 'iconophiles' for the erring others.

and even smells and public processions. All the senses should be mobilized for the higher realm by the rhythms and textures of locations that reminded the community of the physical presence of Christ and the saints.

Second, the veneration of images was an aesthetic act of resistance to Islamic expansion in early medieval times. In the Mediterranean world, the military success of the new creed seemed to strongly indicate Allah's favour and defeat was easily blamed and internalized as punishment for the idolatrous practices of Christianity. The call for a return to 'purity' seemed only rational for some; for others it was a concession too many to the victors. Icons were thus in popular demand to mark identity and difference to Islam, and victorious Islam was rather tolerant of visual practices once firmly in power.

Finally, the controversy of the ninth century highlighted a third argument: the 'power-charged contemplation of icons' (MacCulloch, 2013, p. 107) offered an alternative route to salvation. Meditating and contemplating icons had the power to change lives; an aesthetic effect we still expect from exceptional works of art. Sloterdijk (2012) cites the poet Rilke to make this point: upon seeing Apollo in the Louvre, 'you have to change your life'. The iconoclastic authorities sought to monopolize the liturgy in the *Hagia Sophia* in Constantinople, presided over by clerics, as the only spiritual highway. While the iconophiles, led by wandering monks, offered icons as the democratic pathway open everywhere. Icons could be kept in the house or carried on the road by everyone (for all this, see MacCulloch, 2013, p. 107 ff.).

Why start this chapter with a potted history of an undoubtedly complex problem: that of iconoclasm and the defence of religious images? It is important to remind ourselves of this heritage, which seems fully present in current concerns about 'representations'. A sense of crisis that has been building up is felt in both politics and the arts (see Behnke, 1992). The postmodern dismissal of all representations as ideological (Woolgar, 1989), defences that are to stem a return of behaviourism by the back door (Jovchelovitch, 1996), and various claims to revival of the iconic (Redner, 1994; Latour and Weibel, 2002) are underpinned by new-old arguments. We might profit from this history for our current understanding of sensitivities over 'social representations'.

The argument is that in researching 'social representations', social psychology is entangled in the legacy of monotheistic, in other words Judeo-Christian-Muslim, worries about symbolic activity – about the risks and dangers of 'imagination' and 'making images'. Social representations theory manages these anxieties by embracing this history rather than enacting it in the conduct of social research.

The monotheistic foundation story and its reception cultivate a sense of suspicion against 'representations'. Halbertal and Margalit (1992, p. 112 ff.) reconstruct this history as the chain of criticisms that moves from debunking folk idolatry (biblical) to the religious enlightenment of philosophical theology (medieval), to the secular critique of all religion (enlightenment), and finally to the modern critique of collective delusions and mass ideology (nineteenth and twentieth century). Endorsing representations is risky to freedom, salvation and effective action. In this legacy, representations distort, mislead and create a false focus of attention and deference which in religious terms is blasphemy or fetishism, and in secular terms delusion or ideology. The policing of this risk is historically both a call for the powers that be, as in the case of Mount Athos in 1913, as well as for the revolt against such powers (as in the Russian Revolution of 1917; or see the Reverend Gilles Fraser and his recent comments on protests in Turkey and in London).[3] The critical notion of 'fetishism' also derives from this concern over misplaced deference. A fetish is an object that is attributed powers which it does not 'really' have. An amulet is just an ornamented stone, and nothing more. Fetishism is a pagan practice, which, according to Christian missionaries, needs to be denounced and left behind. This is a powerful frame of mind: the quest for Progress. Recent discussions of this history, however, argue that the attribution of powers to material objects is an anthropological constant rather than a historical residue that can be left behind (see Boehme, 2006; Ellen, 1988). Modern life, supposedly beyond the fetish, is cluttered with objects invested with powers. Enthusiasm for new technology and luxury goods is driven by a process of valuing objects far beyond their substance; 'buying a lifestyle' is empowering goods far beyond a piece of metal, cloth or leather.

The legacy of a *via media*: neither conflation nor separation of symbol and reality

The solution of the iconoclastic controversy in Christianity seems to hinge on avoiding certain solutions to the problem of the 'incarnation', in other words, the problem is how to think of Christ as God and human body, messenger and message, abstract and concrete, absent and present, signifier and signified.

The dogma of the Trinity, established in the fifth century, claimed the unity of Father, Son and Holy Spirit, or in a modern language, the three modalities of God, to resolve the paradox of the simultaneous godliness and humanity of Christ. In the Chalcedonian Creed of 451 CE we find the paradoxical formulation about unity in diversity: 'We teach... one and the same Christ, Son, Lord, Only begotten, known in two natures, without confusion, without change, without division, without separation'. In doing so the clerics contrasted and highlighted two heterodoxies[4] while steering clear of both. On the one hand, the Diaphysites (two natures/bodies) stressed the human nature of Christ, ordinary flesh and blood while being God only by casual association (e.g. Nestorians). This resonates with an arbitrary link between signifier (Christ) and signified (God), no divine kinship. On the other hand, Miaphysites (one nature/body) stressed the godly nature of Christ. This comes in two versions. One stream believed Christ equals God in identity and no difference; Christ's human nature was negligent, like a drop of vinegar in the sea. The Gnostic tradition claimed that Christ could not and therefore did not die a humanly painful death but a stooge died instead (i.e. Docetism); the Gnostics ridiculed the common belief in Christ's crucifixion and cultivated a

---

3 Reverend Gilles Fraser, Are you an iconodule or iconoclast?, *Guardian*, 15 June 2013, 53.
4 These pre-Chalcedon creeds survive as Oriental or Coptic, Ethiopian and Syrian Orthodoxy, currently under existential pressure, but historically protected by Islam.

hermetic-esoteric knowledge of this falsehood that was propagated by a dark power (Gnostic dualism: Jonas, 1934/2001). This position also resonates in a fixed identity between signifier (Christ) and signified (God); an identity that is confused by appearances of duality among the multitudes, but is known by the few.

The dogma of the Trinity upholds a third way between these two positions by adding the concern for the mediating 'spirit' and by holding to 'similarity' and 'analogy', neither difference nor identity between signified and signifier. The triadic solution comprises the sign, the object and the abstract and mediating interpretans (according to Peirce; see Eco, 1985, p. 76 ff.). In the image, the object is described as such and such, as if it were such and such (Goodman, 1976, p. 28 ff.). Now, we also say the image frames the object. This compromise is unstable and oscillates the interpretation of the symbol between a leaning towards embodiment (the concrete action on the object) or towards transcendence (the abstract interpretans) without ever giving in totally. This might throw light on the cryptic prediction of Charles Taylor (2006, p. 609 ff.) on the various forms of resistance to the 'excarnation' of rationality; the historical trend leads away from the abstract-individual-calculus to the embodied-social actor; it appears salvation does not rest in Dr Strangelove and Strategic Bomber Command but in the bloody suffering *Die Hard* – Hollywood seems to pick up this trend.

The iconoclastic controversies needed to come to terms with representations, not least because of the unwavering popular demand for images. Because Christ was also human, he could be represented on wood blocks, but with certain care. The question was what were people doing when venerating the physical icons? Were people venerating God in the painted icon? – this would amount to an untenable miaphysite error, because there is an obvious difference between the woodwork and God. Were people venerating the painting as coloured woodwork only? – this was useless and at worst amounted to a diaphysite blasphemy (see Bulgakov, 1931/2012 for the theological intricacies of this). People were venerating God, but *through* the icons, and the motion 'through' needed guidance by the spirit.

The moral of the story is that the discussions over 'representation' in psychology and beyond remain within this tradition of quarrelling over the semiotic problem, *without confusion (identity) and without arbitrary separation (difference)* between signifier and signified, the act of representing and the represented object, and thus sustaining an aversion for settling on either extreme. In this tradition, social representations theory supports an ontological commitment to what is 'represented', it retains as much onomatopoeic-mimesis as it is semiotic-arbitrary. This debate extends into the secular social sciences: thus, what is a social representation?

Different meanings of 'representation'

The dictionary meaning of the term 'representation' is ambivalent and manifold. Some usages have found massive elaboration under attributes such as 'scientific', 'statistical', 'political' and 'mental'.

Scientific representation is discussed in relation to how models represent a target reality fittingly. For example, Frigg (2002) argues that for scientific models three features are required: (a) a formal system of symbols and relations, (b) an actor purpose, and (c) a physical-substantive embedding. Structural isomorphism between model and target reality is not sufficient to show how models represent, because there are models without a similarity to reality. Without substantive assumptions a model will have only abstract relations; a physics theory without physics, economics without an economy, a computer without a mind. However, how models represent real-world targets remains full of 'mystery': how does a non-verbal object, the physical design, for example a computer, represent another non-verbal target object, for example the brain/mind. The supposition seems to be that 'to represent' refers to different relations between symbol system and target, the specification of which is a wide open field of enquiry. Frigg (2010, p. 121 ff.) later argues that it might be useful to distinguish p-representations from t-representations, the latter implying the former. T-representation refers to the relation between the model and the real-world target, which is prototypically explored by one-to-one 'mapping'. P-representation is the narrative element of the model, the import of fictional characteristics which allows the observer to be surprised and carried beyond the formalism; it specifies the relation between the model and life-world.

Statistical representation is a well-trodden territory (e.g. Kish, 1965). Sampling theory deals with the logic of observing a part and making valid inferences about the whole. In terms of persuasion, we are dealing with a synecdoche, a rhetorical trope for which the felicitous conditions are very well specified: the quality of the sample determines whether or not the trope is persuasive. A population is represented, the sample is more or less representative, and representativeness is achieved by procedure; drawing randomized units that provide an unbiased sample and error controlled estimates of parameters of the whole. The language used for this is rich and includes population, sampling frame, stratification, cluster, weighting and random selection. Another set of well-defined terms specifies the 'representativeness' in terms of sources of errors such as coverage, sampling, non-response and measurement. A key insight of statistical sampling is that good design matters more than sample size. Doubling the sample size reduces error only by square-root of 2, which is a huge effort with little returns; hence 'big' is not better. Statistical sampling is a powerful tool of social research that runs the risk of over-application.

Political representation is the activity of making citizens' voices, opinions and perspectives 'present' in the policy-making processes; it makes present what would otherwise be absent (Dovi, 2011). This involves a representing party, a represented constituency, opinions and perspectives that are represented, and a setting where this takes place. However, there are different fashions of how this 'presence' is achieved and each concept holds those who act as 'representatives' to different standards. One tension concerns the role and autonomy of representatives: to act as 'delegates' who embody the preferences as instructed or as 'trustees' who contribute to the deliberations to their best judgement. Political representation can vary on four dimensions (Pitkin, 1967). Formally it involves procedures of becoming authorized and accountable; these may be democratic but need not be. Symbolically, those represented relate to the representative with degrees of acceptance. Descriptively, the representative is more or less similar in culture and attitude as his or her constituents. On substance, the interests of the constituency are more or less served. Political scientists observe how the significance of these four dimensions changes with political contexts, for example democratic formalism trumped other concerns during the Cold War when it provided a model for propaganda. Researchers are also concerned with the design of well-functioning deliberations, with how voices are raised or marginalized in the process, and whether 'representative democracy' might be a contradiction in terms: representatives assume a degree of independence from the represented which does not seem to be democratic (Dovi, 2011).

Mental representation brings us to psychology, cognitive science and the philosophy of mind. It is a key concept in constructing computer models of 'mind'; representations are mental models upon which 'cognition' operates. Mental objects have semantic properties, that is, they have propositional content 'x is y', a referent, and thus they are true or false (see Pitt, 2013). In addition, humans display attitudinal relations to these true or false mental objects. We say that chocolate must be represented in our minds if it is chocolate that we desire. Chocolate is the intentional content of the mental representation, and desiring or despising it is the propositional attitude we take to it. Mental representations are about things, they have intentionality, but they are also about objects that have no correspondence in reality, such as fairies and unicorns. Much attention is paid to misrepresentations of existing things, and to the unreality of representations to which we exhibit attitudes. These processes are modelled in computer programmes of brains (computer models of the mind), and in so doing we are led to believe that brains might think and desire something. We therefore lose sight of the rest of the body and other people supporting or challenging this event. Thus we easily commit the *mereological fallacy* of attributing a capacity exhibited by the whole to some of the parts, to a part which might be necessary but not sufficient for realizing the activity. It is an easy confusion of language to argue neurologically about psychological phenomena: for example the amygdala part of the brain might be involved in experiencing 'a dangerous animal', but it is more than odd to say that the 'brain represents the animal'; the predicate 'represent' is adequate only for the entire organism and not solely for the brain (Bennett and Hacker, 2003).

I have not dealt with representation in the arts (e.g. Goodman, 1976), which seems to me a dauntingly vast territory to explore here as well. However the point of this review is not completeness, nor is it a quest for the true meaning underlying all these different meanings of 'representations'. Rather it seems more useful to explore a *family resemblance* among different usages. This might reveal a set of features (F_R), and each usage makes use of a different subset of these features ($fR_{mental} \subset F_R$), any two uses covering a subset of features, but the common ground of all uses, conjunction [$fR_{science}$, $fR_{political}$ .... fR_{mental}] = 0], is an empty set. There is thus no prototypical usage of the term 'representation'; at most there is something close to a common concern: the iconoclastic impetus. In the sociology of knowledge this is also known as a 'boundary object' (see Riesch, 2010): the same term is used by collaborators with partially overlapping meanings for purposes of tentative cooperation; the term links separated parties with a boundary. This is a liberating position within which to work on 'social representations'. Social psychology adds to the burgeoning concert of 'representation' players, to a concert where traditional iconoclastic worries and anxieties may be contained.

The paradigmatic formulation of social representations theory

The conceptual contribution of the theory of social representations to social psychology at large is to highlight and to guide the analysis of social groups as a serious pretend play involving the 'as if' of common sense, mentalities and vernacular knowledge. Representation means naming things, an act that makes use of common places rooted in social interaction. This defines an ample, powerful and critical ambition of real-world social-psychological research.

Everyday mentality is controversial and often identified derogatively as just 'common sense' or 'popular delusions'. These derogative terms inherit the age-old tensions between episteme and doxa, knowledge and opinion or belief, science and non-science, between dignified and less dignified knowledge. The theory of social representations enters this debate decidedly on one side; it sides with doxa, belief and common sense. The theory of social representations defends the dignity of these notions against the onslaught from enlightenment notions of popular prejudice, nineteenth-century middle-class angst over crowds and mass delusions, Marxist analysis of ideology and 'false consciousness', and existentialist debunking of 'bad faith'.

Social representations theory inherits relaxedness about the pretend play of 'as if' and 'as such'. The 'as if' and the 'as such' of representations are not so disturbing to the analyst that he or she would be immediately drawn to cry foul and to debunk the fictional element of these representations. The theory of social representations steers us towards care and circumspection in that respect. The iconoclastic impetus is suspended, tamed or sublimated.[5]

The iconoclastic impetus is tamed because social representations theory rejects the dilemma of mimetic identity or convention, of iconicity or arbitrary association between signifier and signified. The theory of social representations stands in a tradition of a triadic solution to sharp dilemmas, of avoiding the fallacy of the excluded third (Boyes, 2000). It rejects the Either/Or in favour of the Neither/Nor. On the semiotic issue the theory of social representations retains an ontological investment despite the doubling up of reality in representations and without recollapsing it in either identity (fundamentalist) or an arbitrary regress of symbols onto

---

5 The historical acceptance of this inheritance of taming the iconoclastic impetus is here more alluded to than really analyzed. This historical work still needs to be done.

symbols (constructivism). The 'as if' reality of social representations are not tested on fact; instead, they are tested on practical social functions (Wagner and Hayes, 2005).

Harré (1984) positioned this effort within a wider tradition of 'socialising the mind', in elective affinities with an understanding of Wittgenstein's language games: as there is no private language, but only established rules of using words to buy into, there is also no private representation of the world. Social representations are shared by members of the group in analogy to language: it is a commons, a distributed resource without any one individual being in command of it all. In the 1970s social psychologists from both sides of the Atlantic tried to stem a 'crisis of the discipline' by redefining a more valid social psychology – Hegelian, reflective, real-world, multi-method; this in contrast to the then dominant approach – individualistic, Cartesian, busy-productive, experimental of mainly undergraduate student behaviour (Moscovici and Maková, 2006). Forty years on, it seems that the latter style of work still wins the day, though recently engaging in some soul searching over lack of replicated evidence, and the socially biased evidence base; the credit-seeking sophomore student continues to populate most busy-body studies (Arnett, 2008).

The theory of social representations continues to make an enormous difference to the analysis of social innovations and new technologies. Formulated in the 1960s against the then dominating and still ongoing notion of 'diffusion of innovation' (Rogers, 1962), social representations theory considers the adoption of innovation as a creative process of transformation and appropriation. The serial reproduction of ideas or designs is no encoding-decoding, identity preserving communication process on the high fidelity (hifi) model. Where the diffusion model only considers adoption rates and quality decay, the theory of social representations highlights the transformation of ideas and redesigns in social circulation. The theory of social representations therefore continues to make a critical difference over hifi models of communication in science communication and innovation studies. One could even consider social representations theory as a theory of resistance against technocratic dreams (Bauer, 2013 and 2015).

The theory of social representations is a logical function with several arguments

'Representing' is an activity, a constituting and constructing of a relation either by mental act or by investing in ink blots on paper or in matter such as building a skyscraper: we are building a relation: *'x represents y'*. And designing, thinking and symbol use are brought about by moving human bodies; hence *'x represents y for actor'*.

The target object 'y' is said to exist or not to exist independent of human actors. But even if the object is found, it is still 'made' in a certain fashion by the means used to represent it. We tend to find stars as 'sets of molecules' or 'angels in the sky'. The means 'x' (molecules or angels) of representation vary in two ways: first they employ concepts, words, sentences, thoughts, pictures and images, or sound and music. Different modalities have a different logic of constituting the relation '*x represents y for actor by modes m...*', something that is well explored with language, spoken or written, but less clear for images and pictures or for sound and music (Hondrich, 1995). Second, representations also vary on modalities along a set of genres, '*x represents y for actor by mode and in modality*', for example Churchill is represented as the victorious knight on a horse (knight genre in sculpture mode). In all cases, fact and fiction are curiously mixed up in the act of representing (a noema, intentionality, actuality or aboutness) and in a certain moment in time (kairos). One feels an acute sense of category mistake if somebody declares that 'they do not read fiction because it is not true'; our sense is that fiction entails fact; our sense of fact seems poor without fiction. One might further worry about the possibility of two or more representations equally fitting the target reality; fitting but logically inconsistent world-makings (see Kung, 1993, contrasting the notions of 'world-making' and of 'constitution'). Or we might consider the case that the representation anticipates what will become efficient reality, guiding the actions that bring it about. Utopian social engineering seems to follow this path (Bloch, 1953/1986).

However, we might not worry about 'reality fitting'. We might worry less about semantic truth value and more about the pragmatic value of representations. Suspending the fact–fiction distinction and the truth value problem for the moment, we might ask: what do representations do for the actors and how do they do it? That is the task of societal psychology: to elucidate the content structure and the social functions of current common sense, in other words, to empirically and comparatively clarify the mentalities of everyday life. Jodelet (1989b) has aptly identified the study of social representations as the anthropology of the present rather than of faraway places.

The paradigmatic definition of 'social representations' as developed in previous writings (Bauer and Gaskell, 1999 and 2008) highlights five elements, which I will briefly rehearse:

- Subject–Object–Project communication systems
- Modes of representation (multi-methods)
- Modalities of representations (multi-level)
- The time scape – temporal extensions
- Some methodological implications

The purpose of this paradigm was not normative, but an attempt to define the specific contributions of the theory of social representations for the purposes of social psychological research. The paradigmatic description of social representations theory recognizes social representations (SR) as a logical function with several arguments:

$$SR = f\left(object_{12}, subject_1 - subject_2, project_{12}, genre_x, time_{12}\right).$$

$$SR = f\left[x \text{ relates to Y, by actors, mode and modality, kairos}\right].$$

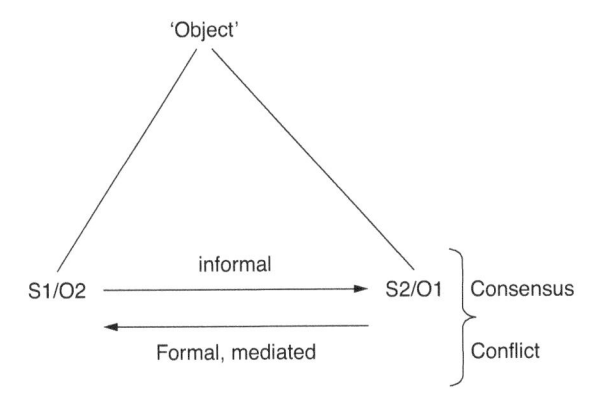

```
                    'Object'
                      /\
                     /  \
                    /    \
                   /      \
                  /        \
                 /          \
                /  informal  \
         S1/O2 ─────────────→ S2/O1  ⎫ Consensus
               ←─────────────         ⎬
                Formal, mediated      ⎭ Conflict
```

Figure 4.1 *The basic unit of analysis and attribution of representations.*

Talking of an argument with several functions suggests that talking of social representations means that, in studying social representations of X, we should clarify the subjects involved, in other words, the social group that is constituted by the joint intentionality of a project$_{12}$; the object$_{12}$ Y that emerges as the 'as if' in that interaction,[6] and the genres of communication and the sense of timing, the kairos, that defines the form of social integration (Duveen, 2008).

Social representations theory guides the analysis of communication systems

Social representations theory adopts the basic unit of analysis, self-other-in-relation-to-common object, which has been postulated for social psychology with mixed success in the past. The analytic unit and the target of entity attribution is thus the dialogue between subjects, a unit of communication. The mentality manifests itself in this conviviality, though this conviviality is not free of conflict. Figure 4.1 depicts this idea schematically in the Subject S_1 who is 'other O_2' to subject S_2, who in turn is 'other O_1'. The object arises from this interaction as a pretend play 'as if' with both factual as well as fictional elements. The interaction can be informal face-to-face or mediated by formal communication involving attention to media genres of mass circulation at a distance. The diversity of perspectives of subjects gives a dynamic tension to this basic triangle (Marková, 2003; Farr, 1997; Moscovici, 1984).

Social representations therefore need to be observed both in people's minds, as semi-privately introspected and verbally or behaviourally expressed, and as circulating sign vehicles in society and between people (see Farr, 1981). Our symbolic

---

[6] On the important difference between 'actuality' and 'reality', I refer to the classic book by Berger and Luckmann (1966). The authors struggled with the English translation of the German distinction between 'Wirklichkeit' and 'Realitaet'. According to Luckmann, the title of this book should have been the 'social construction of actuality' (English translation of 'Wirklichkeit') and not 'the social construction of reality' as this created much misunderstanding about their argument (personal communication, 2006).

environment constrains and scaffolds common sense and practical activity; we are dragging along in a continuous stream of mass media, physical artefacts and designed symbols.

Social representations exhibit structural features and serve many functions

The theory of social representations cultivates two structural intuitions: the features of core–periphery, and the distinction between reified and consensual elements. Reification is often synonym to 'natural' and 'essential' and therefore deemed to be given, fixed and unchangeable. The consensual is deemed open to change. We can expect that social representations in real life have this duality of structures; some notions are peripheral and negotiable, that is, the consensual, while others are more central and are not negotiable, that is, the more reified and essential in the 'nature of things'. But we might also observe peripheral elements that are naturalized as ecology, and central elements that are negotiable in social representation. These distinctions are flexible and fungible.

The structural build-up of mentality serves pragmatic functions to guide – what to do next – and to justify action – why to do it. Social representations serve attitudinal, attributional, identity presentation and collective memory functions in social integration, or in the language more common in the literature, social representations constrain, select and enable particular attitudes, attributions, identity and collective memory; they frame particular actions.[7]

Our research on the public perception of new technology, in particular biotechnology, in a comparative manner, has given rise to the formulation of this paradigm and its developments from the Toblerone model to the wind rose model and the waterwheel model.

These subsequent developments involve both the suggestive use of metaphor and the drawing of schematic images to stress different points.

The Toblerone model in Figure 4.2 is basically an elongated triangle. This elaborates the basic triad of communication (subject–subject–object) into a temporal extension as projected by shared intentionality. New technologies come with a vision of the future which changes in time. The figure shows a slice in the Toblerone as the mentality, project or common sense at a particular time (Kairos) that is derivative of the past $project_{t-1}$ and in transition to the future $project_{t+1}$. These notions are reminiscent of Lewin's depictions of the psychological field-at-a-given-time with its extensions into the past and into the future with variable complexity (Lewin, 1952). The Toblerone model absorbs two further notions beyond that of the basic triangle: those of $project_{12}$ and $time_{12}$ in addition to the $subject_{12}$-$object_{12}$.

---

7 It appears that the social movement literature has developed an entirely parallel language game that explores the pragmatic function of symbolic activity and social imagination under the heading of 'framing collective action' (see Benford and Snow, 2000). It seems a future task for SRT researchers to engage that literature in some detail (for an attempt, see Bauer, 2015).

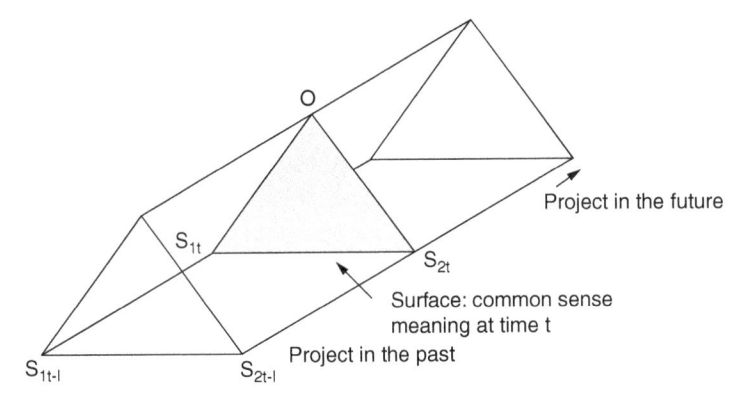

Figure 4.2 *The Toblerone model of social representations (after Bauer and Gaskell, 1999).*

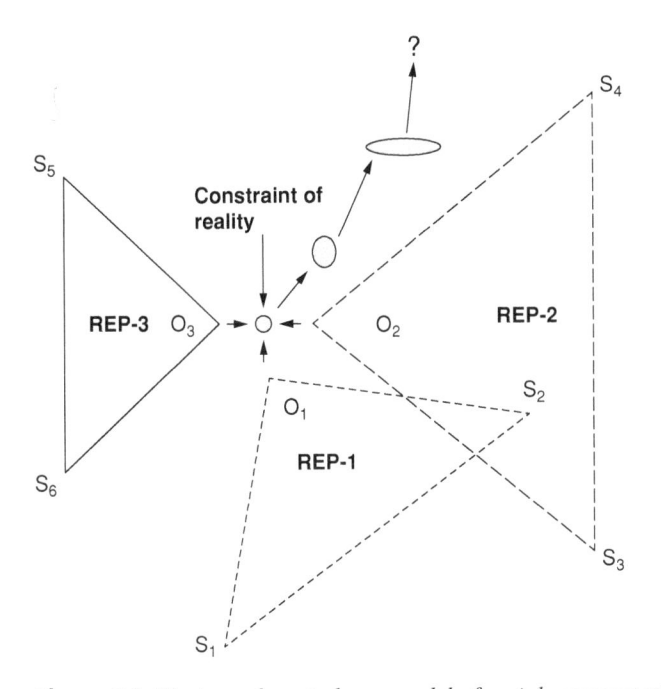

Figure 4.3 *The irregular wind rose model of social representations (Bauer and Gaskell, 2008).*

However, in empirical research the particular features, structural and functional, of social representations only come to light in comparative research, and thus we need to extend the model to a set of triangles that are held together by a 'linking pin' at the centre, that is, the common reference of discourse to which all refer (though in their specific 'as if' pretend play). Hence we come to the wind rose model of several triangles linked by a central pin as shown in Figure 4.3. This extension incorporates the basic reality of us/them intergroup behaviour that defines the functions of social representations. A particular representation of 'food' as 'organic, not genetically engineered and sustainable' is traded against other representations of food as 'industrial, genetically modified and unsustainable'. The fact that these different representations of food have unequal power to determine the history of food production is reflected in the relative size of the triangles linked together in common reference. The reality of food stuffs we eat is the outcome of the intergroup behaviour of actors who sustain and propagate different notions of what we all should eat. The wind rose model absorbs the fact that some discourses share elements, hence the overlapping triangles. Also, a particular subject might juggle several representations in 'polyphasia', as if they spoke several languages without confusion; however, the representations might not be of equal weight when tested under stress. The theory of social representations develops the notion of 'cognitive polyphasia' in contrast to cognitive dissonance on how people handle contradictory mind frames (Jovchelovitch, 2007).

Thus the wind rose image is a model of intergroup contexts. Social representations do not stand in isolation, but in the middle of social polemics and competitions, they evolve in demarcating identities, and through resistance to the machination of dominant stances. Hence, one of the key functions of social representations is the preservation of autonomy by enabling resistance against undue influences.

Finally, by repeating the move from triangle to elongated triangle, we reach something that looks ideally like a waterwheel; several elongated triangles rotate around a central hinge, as does the waterwheel that propels the steam boat on the river. The 'waterwheel' model depicts an evolving reality in the central pin that is put under tension by the rotating segments. The model is converging with that of evolving ontologies, otherwise called 'sausage ontologies' (see Kung, 1993), each constituting a more or less demarcated action space with its projections and time dimension. The waterwheel is a rather too regular model for this, as we must expect the segments to be irregular, contorted and converging with and diverging from each other. Mentalities and mind frames tend to fuse in social interaction (meta-frames), and they also tend to differentiate over time (frame splitting). This becomes impossible to visualize on paper; it requires rather animated computer graphics. A model for comparative social representations research is emerging which incorporates multiple elongated, triangular units of communication, different 'as if' objects projected into an open future, competing with other representations and actors, and in doing so defining a co-evolving reality as the linking pin and common reference.

The key point of the theory of social representations is preserved through all these models, the iconoclastic impetus is muted: social representations theory remains agnostic with regard to the ultimate dignity of any of these 'as if' pretend plays. The key point is functional analysis of representations for action; the iconoclastic suspicion is suspended, though not abolished. Iconoclasm remains a possibility, but it is not the main theoretical preoccupation. The theory of social representations left behind notions of teleological development from mythos to logos, from mythical, to dogmatic and to scientific knowledge, stages of societal development, or notions of social maturity. It can recognize, however, that such notions of historical telos are part of the claim-making among social actors and their representations of reality.

Research and practical implications of this paradigm

All this has methodological implications, as has been suggested in a previous formulation (Bauer and Gaskell, 1999). I will briefly rehearse and update: content and process, mode and modalities of representations, natural social milieus, within milieu cultivation, longitudinal designs, historical crossings, and the disinterested research attitude.

The added value of these implications is illustrated in the conduct of a large international project 'Biotechnology and the Public' (Bauer and Gaskell, 2002). At the time, the theory of social representations served us as a strategic dispositive to guide data collection and stimulate conceptual discussions, and at the same time to fend off any inclination of social researchers to reify common sense in the latest questionnaire-based survey data: public opinion is more than what the latest survey depicts. As the Toblerone model kept reminding us: 'we ain't there yet'.

Methodological implications for the research design

The preceding discussion leads to several implications for the design of social representations studies in order for it to live up to the ambitions of the concept. A set of criteria is proposed to provide a guideline for our own empirical research and that of our colleagues. This will also allow us to identify social representations studies by 'family resemblances', both by common inspiration and origin or by elected affinities. There are many studies of real-life phenomena which do not use the term 'social representation', but are entirely within its remit and ambition (while on the other hand there might be others which use the term, but hardly serve the label). An ordering of the key questions will define the approach by comparison with other research programmes of social psychology and the social sciences and allow both to identify the elected affinities as well as the false positives. And if Devereux was correct, then the clarification of methods is a way to manage anxieties of the researcher, in our case the worries that might persist in dealing with 'representations' (Giami, 2001).

Modes of representations: multi-level analysis

Social groupings are more or less institutionalized, are organized and have taken historical shape. The elaboration of different levels of representation in habitual behaviour, individual *cognition, informal and formal communication* corresponds to the degree of institutionalization. New groups show less formality than older ones; but informality and simple habits do not disappear with formality. This multi-levelled reality requires a multi-method approach to compare the various levels simultaneously: questionnaires and interviews might reconstruct and monitor individual cognition; transcripts of group interviews the informal group dialogues; and document and mass-media analysis cover formal communication. Established canons of discourse and content analysis can characterize the contents of representations comparatively across different levels.

The primary requirement is multi-method design, combining spontaneous interview data with written and documented data. Triangulation of different levels is central; however, not to validate claims (similarly Flick, 1992), but to determine core and peripheral elements through the comparison of levels and data, and to determine the functions of representations in different contexts. Differences between data and levels of analysis will refer us back to the research process: thus reflexivity becomes an integral part of the conduct of research.

Modalities of representations: multi-method analysis

A feature of social representations is that we have to expect them to be invested in all possible modalities: in *speech and conversation, scripture and texts, images, sounds, and movement, even smell and taste*. This is clearly a call for diversification, as most research in social psychology is focussed on the spoken or written word, as in conversational interviews or questionnaires. Computerized experiments might also use movements such as keystrokes and decision speed as key indicators of mentality, but such micro-activities are notoriously uninformative and a disappointing data source with which to explore the contents of mentality (see Baumeister, Vobs and Funder, 2008). Movement without knowledge of the invested intentionality is vague and ambiguous in meaning. The social researcher clearly needs to be open and able to deal with many of these modalities of 'representations', in combination of mixed-method. One of the difficulties lies in the implicit hierarchy of data dignity mapped on to these modalities. The iconoclastic tradition has also left a preference for the word over the visual, and even a preference for action/movement over the word and image (i.e. revealed preferences), when it comes to constructing data streams that give access to mentalities. Many researchers suspect that images hide more than they reveal, while words seem to be open and transparent. A close inspection reveals this as a curious prejudice. The most reliable source of data seems to be the observable behaviour that can be registered in the legacy of 'behavioural science'. However, the theory of social representations makes us query these assumptions, as much as we recognize that implicit data hierarchies are part of the historical struggle over worrisome 'representations'.

Segmentation of 'natural' groups

The problem of social segmentation for comparative research brings us to the differentiation of groups as carriers of representations. Social representations theory is primarily interested in natural groups that exhibit self-reference, and less in statistical aggregates, however defined.

Let us consider the classical study *La psychanalyse, son image et son public* (Moscovici, 1961/1976): what suggested at the time the differentiation of an urban-liberal, a milieu-Catholic, and a party-communist segmentation of the French public? The question can only be answered by historical witnesses. We start with speculations: the segmentation refers to milieus of 'Weltanschauung'. The world is and feels a different place for secular liberals, Catholics and communists shortly after World War II. As a consequence, the three milieus take very different positions towards 'psychoanalysis' and its model of the human psyche. This difference is grounded in different ways of seeing and experiencing the world, how it works, and the role of human action. But the three representations of psychoanalytic knowledge can be typified and contrasted. The result makes the segmentation plausible *ex-post facto*.

Segmentation, however, is a problem at the design stage of research. We need heuristics to determine relevant groups for particular topics, in order not to follow blindly the default of much social research to segment according to income, age and sex. The multiculturalism of formerly homogeneous modern societies may be diagnostic. To what extent are old distinctions of social class, language, religion or urban–rural still relevant life-worlds? For international comparisons we may continue to consider 'political nation-states' as self-referential units. A heuristic might also be whether a group commands a mass medium edited by-and-for-itself. These are not necessarily costly TV or radio stations, but events such as newsletters, pamphlets, musical subcultures or social media networks may be relevant formal media.

Furthermore we should clarify how far functional differentiation of operations in law, business, art, religion and science (Luhmann, 1984) segment into social groupings of the 'natural' type. Is this a conceptual or an empirical problem? According to system theory, functional differentiation historically replaces social hierarchy in a globalizing context. Is this replacement complete or partial?

We need a diagnostic eye to gauge whether current statistical or functional aggregates carry the potential for self-reference. Observed groups can become self-referential groups-in-and-for-themselves. Social representations theory needs sociological imagination to observe the historical trends.

Sender–reception studies within each collective

Our analysis of social groups as communication units leads to a further implication. The study of psychoanalysis in France has shown that representations are embedded in a production–reception system of ideas; and these communication systems need to be introduced as variable into the research design. The notions of diffusion, propagation and propaganda are types of production–reception based on particular speaker–audience relations. The list might not be exhaustive and might include other systems such as rumours or advertising.

We need to consider groups as communication systems with informal and formal communication arrangements involving a mix of mass media of circulation and contact, with processes of worldview cultivation, agenda setting, framing or spiral of silence (see McQuail and Windahl, 1993). Mass-media systems express different sender–receiver relationships which can be typified and compared. What is the audience's view of the producers: trust, mistrust, ridicule, familiarity? And what are the producers' views of the audience: condescendence; elitism; patronizing? The focus of such an analysis is, unlike in audience research, not the divergence of receptions of a single media event (e.g. of soap operas) but the typification of production–reception relations in different groups: the medium from-and-for the group is the embodied representation. Diffusion, propagation and propaganda are a special case, some may still be relevant, others may be discovered. This is an empirical problem and offers scope for innovation in the theory of social representations.

In researching social representations we are not only interested in the autonomy of audiences vis-à-vis certain media messages, the resistant decoding, but in the active mobilization of messages and images for the projects of groups, the resistant encoding. This process generates the representation of particular groups which is the focus of social representations studies. Insights into ownership and influence in the mass-media markets are relevant for such studies.

Content and process

'Content matters' is a slogan of the social representations programme. The discussion of social representations has in the past and will in the future invest time and effort to describe content. The methodical developments focus on the differentiation between core and periphery, the analysis of anchors in naming, classification and free associations, and the inventory of images, pictures and metaphors which objectify the abstract issues involved. Processes of communication influence these contents. Diffusion, propagation and propaganda are not content-neutral. The presumption is that the 'stickiness' of contents of representations are as important as their generation, and essential to understand their impact on action.

Here the theory of social representations contrasts with the narrow attitude paradigm of social psychology. Mini-theories on attitude formation, resistance and change are formalized in general terms, thereby abstracting from different attitude objects and contexts. The problematic starting point is the assumption that any attitude's context is formally equivalent. However, the relationship between attitude and behaviour is not the same whether it relates to drug consumption or the purchase of hair sprays.

Time structures and longitudinal-sequential data

Social representations are structures with a medium-range life cycle; they have some stability over time with a rate of change somewhere between the elusiveness of conscious cognitions and the *longue durée* of collective mentalities. Only a long-term research design is therefore adequate to observe changes in social representation.

Furthermore, a functional analysis of representations, in line with the above distinction of structure and functions, requires us to describe representations and their consequences over a longer time period. Interviews and documentary analysis need to be repeated and extended over time. Data collection should span several time points to assess the internal and external consequences of contents.

Using the Toblerone or the waterwheel model, a social representations research design would include several elongated triads, for example by studying the elaboration of genetics in several social contexts over twenty-five years. This would suggest that studies of the 'social representation of X' tend to take on the scale of a research programme rather than single study. However, this ambition should only provide a horizon, and not discourage any smaller scale studies.

Cross-overs of cultural trajectories

Another implication is mainly diagnostic of the relevance of social representations for a particular research context. Which situations are likely to be productive for the study of social representations? A common view in the community is that these are situations of novelty and sociocultural challenges as they are likely to occur in fault lines of cultures with different historical trajectories. In other words, the theory of social representations is indicated at points in time and space where different social groups cross paths.

Social representations are in evidence when one group resists the machinations of another in an intergroup us/them context; or in contexts where groups cope collectively with a natural threat or catastrophe of some sort. Different groups have different historical trajectories; as they cross paths, sensitivities are high. 'Crossing paths' means something becomes a common focus of attention for the different groups. Social representations are best studied when 'new' concerns arise for different groups. The origin of the concern could be one of the groups involved. Group A putting an object, idea or problem into the world, and the differential reactions and elaborations of this issue by groups B to K is precisely the stuff of social representations.

These meetings of cultures constitute an uneasy situation: in the extreme of violence, the migration of large groups of refugees, the less problematic but no less significant encounters of different visions of the future on 'nuclear power' or 'genetic inheritance'. In these situations, traditions bring existing symbolic resources to bear to resist, assimilate and accommodate each other, while changing themselves and the challenge in the process.

The 'melancholic' attitude

The theory of social representations requires stepping back from intervention into social affairs; it requires an attitude towards the object of study which could be characterized as 'live and let live': disengaged observation of mentalities with the iconoclastic impetus tamed and sublimated. This attitude preconditions a particular sensitivity and the holding of judgement, which would otherwise be flushed out by the fervour of the researcher's own mission.

An example of how the mission can cloud the analysis is the linear hifi model of communication and diffusion (Rogers, 1962). The difference between source intention and reception is attributed to audience resistance, channel problems or sender incompetence. Resistance is supposed to be controlled efficiently by competent management of messages and channels; it has nothing to contribute to the process. Here the researcher is on a mission, and not concerned with studying representations of the audiences in their own terms, but only with a view to increasing the efficiency of the sender in changing the audience in set direction. The theory of social representations took issue with this manipulative take on communication from the start.

This attitude of social representations theory has some affinity with the melancholia as *mal du siècle* as analyzed by Lepenies (1969/1972): the melancholic, and those who think they are, relegate themselves to a disengaged position of sensitive observation and reflection on the situation with a (self-)imposed action block. Abstaining from engagement is instrumental for a particular sensitivity towards the world.

Melancholia is conditioned (a) by over-stimulation in situations of chaos and civil war, which motivates a search for ideas radically different from the status quo; utopia compensates for the present desperation with a future in remote space and time; this vision includes the eradication of melancholia as a problematic state. Or (b) melancholia is conditioned by chronic under-stimulation which is historically characteristic of persons who are capable but excluded from power. Both situations are characterized by imposed inaction that leads to a particular colour of sensitive experience of the world. Historical examples are those of the French aristocrats of the Salon conversations who are excluded from the court life at Versailles and instead of engaging warfare write up moralistic observations; or the German romantic bourgeois with no prospect for political power, instead exploring 'Innerlichkeit und Natur'; or the Marxists disillusioned by Stalinism after the Russian Revolution and instead engaging in 'Kulturkritik' far removed from the direct action of the day.

This is not to suggest that social representations theory is a melancholic pursuit without 'relevance'. On the contrary, there may be many studies which can inform the social engineer intending to ameliorate a social problem. Disinterested analysis of notions of mental illness, of the environment, of health and illness, of popular science are indispensable entry points for re-constructive intervention without being intended as interventions themselves. One might even argue that the theory of social representations would be a better ground for social engineering than many traditional experimental studies of attitude and attitude change strategies explicitly designed to create change.

In social representations research the researcher is methodically disengaged from social engineering; but paradoxically, the revolutionary among his or her audience may be better served by the results obtained from this disengaged attitude. Though impact is not the purpose of the theory of social representations, it might well be one of its unintended consequences.

Conclusion

We have asked ourselves where the curious suspicion about representations comes from, and have traced it in the iconoclastic impetus of monotheistic religious traditions. In that very tradition, representations are defended as didactic memory props, as tactics of popular resistance, and as non-elitist practices of life.

The theory of social representations is part of a family of disciplines in the social sciences that elaborate on the term 'representations'. While all usages might share the motive of iconoclastic suspicion, social representations theory in particular seems to sustain a third way of neither/nor between total identity and utter difference of symbol and referent; it remains suspended in an uneasy compromise 'without confusion and without separation' of symbol and reality and thus retains an ontological commitment to what is represented.

The paradigm of the theory of social representations is best defined as a logical function of several arguments: X is represented as Y by a purposeful actor using modes and modalities at a certain time. In the context of comparative research, this leads to the Toblerone and waterwheel model, where actual mentalities are compared over time, and different actualities define an intergroup context. The methodological implications of the theory of social representations include considerations of mode and modalities of representations, natural social milieus, within milieu symbolic cultivation, content and process, longitudinal research designs, diagnostic moments of historical crossings, and the disinterested attitude where the iconoclastic impetus is suspended and sublimated. Considering the entanglement of secular social representations in the iconoclastic suspicion, how might mentalities and common sense be understood by researchers who work in cultural contexts of Asia or Africa without such iconoclastic suspicions? Has the iconoclastic suspicion gone global or are there functional equivalences in different traditions? These might be questions to address in the future.

5 Researching social representations

Uwe Flick, Juliet Foster and Sabine Caillaud

The issue of methods in social representations theory has proved contentious for some time, although we would argue that the focus of this discussion has shifted in recent years. During the 1980s and 1990s much criticism centred on the supposed lack of focus on methods in early considerations of social representations, and an alleged methodological polytheism (Jahoda, 1988): some critics suggested that an 'anything goes' attitude to methods would only serve to weaken the theory, and argued that researchers needed greater guidance as to how to 'do' social representations research. Many of these concerns have been discussed at some length elsewhere (see, for example, Flick and Foster, 2008): as a theory, and not a method, the social representations approach aims to examine the ways in which individuals within social groups make sense of the world around them, and how these understandings change, develop, interact and so on. The methods that can be used in order to examine these research questions will, as in any social science research, vary, and must be considered carefully on each occasion in order to ensure that the most appropriate methods are used. Indeed, it could even be argued that there are different ways of defining social representations within the developing theory, and different aspects of representations on which to focus, and so multiplicity in methods and analysis is not only inevitable, but preferable (Bauer and Gaskell, 1999). This chapter illustrates this point.

Similarly, more work has now discussed the issue of approaching methods in social representations theory in more depth, providing the researcher with more guidance (see, for example, Bauer and Gaskell, 1999; Breakwell and Canter, 1993; Wagner and Hayes, 2005). However, concerns now focus more on problematic aspects of the use of particular kinds of methods, rather than on a lack of relevant discussion. For example, social representations studies continue to take both qualitative and quantitative approaches: should this be an issue of concern, or something to be encouraged? Another issue concerns the role of the researcher in social representations studies. Later in this chapter we hope to address these issues, among others, in more depth.

Levels of analysis: relating theory to method

Many studies now routinely consider the way that representations develop and circulate at different levels: Duveen and Lloyd (1990) argued that representations need to be considered at the three interrelated levels of ontogenesis, sociogenesis and microgenesis, and consideration of the implications of this methodologically is important. Ontogenetic processes refer to the way that representations become active for the individual, as he or she 'grows' into existing representations within society. This is a common consideration in social developmental studies, and a strong focus in this area has been on representations of gender (e.g. Duveen, 2001a; Duveen and Psaltis, 2008). Longitudinal studies might have particular relevance in the study of the development of representations in relation to particular identities: indeed, given the importance of development and change in the process of representation, there is wider scope for longitudinal studies in general (Bauer and Gaskell, 1999). Few studies take a longitudinal approach, although there are some notable exceptions (e.g. Brondi *et al.*, 2012). Sociogenetic processes refer to the ways in which representations circulate and are active at the broader level of society, and how they develop, change and interact with one another. A common way of attempting to access representations at this level is to engage in documentary analysis of some kind, perhaps including official policy documents, or the media. This approach is also often combined with an attempt to consider the more microgenetic processes within social representations, that is, the way in which representations are evoked and discussed at the interactional level, between individuals within a social group: interviews are often employed here, although there is also scope for other methods, including ethnography and experiments. These levels of analysis also relate to wider discussion of the aims of social psychological research, such as those discussed by Doise (1986a) (see Chapter 3 in this volume for more consideration of this issue).

In this chapter we seek to examine some of the important questions that relate to methods and analysis in social representations research. We hope to do this through a close consideration of different methods that have been used and the various issues pertaining to social representations that relate to these. The first section will focus on qualitative analysis; although some of us (Flick and Foster, 2008) have argued elsewhere that this is particularly suited to social representations work, we then want to broaden this debate to include quantitative analysis and consider the advantages of this as well. Finally, we will discuss mixed methods research, and the importance of triangulation.

It should be noted that we would like to avoid the common assumption that particular methods can be designated 'qualitative' or 'quantitative' all too easily. We would, instead, prefer to argue that an approach, and a form of analysis, can be either qualitative or quantitative or mixed method. It is not the case that the interview, for example, is a qualitative method: the questions may, of course, be more or less structured, and the analysis may be more qualitative or quantitative, depending on the research questions. While we will include examples of particular methods in the different sections that follow, this important point should be borne in mind.

Qualitative analysis

Although there were some qualitative aspects to Moscovici's (1961/1976) first study using social representations theory, Herzlich's (1973) work on representations of health and illness is usually seen as the first purely qualitative study using social representations theory. In it, she analyzes individual semi-structured interviews to examine the representations held by individuals in both urban and rural areas of France. In this early study we see many aspects that will recur in social representations studies that employ qualitative analysis in the future: individuals are asked what they think, the researcher analyzes their responses, compares them for similarities and differences, and suggests the presence of different themes, or representations, of health and of illness.[1] In this section, on qualitative analysis, we will firstly consider methods that rely on asking participants for responses, before moving on to consider other possible methods that might examine social representations from a qualitative perspective. We will also consider the all-important process of analyzing the data qualitatively.

Asking people what they think

At the heart of social representations theory is the idea that common sense has a value and a purpose, and that it is all too often denigrated in comparison with scientific understanding (Moscovici, 1984). In many ways, then, it is not surprising that one of the main methods that has been used qualitatively in social representations studies is the interview: if we value lay understandings about a topic, then it makes sense to ask an individual, or a group, what they think about that topic. This runs counter to some approaches within psychology, in which the research participant is seen as being less capable than the omniscient expert researcher (Spears, 1997). A wide variety of interviews have been employed in social representations studies, including individual interviews, as in Herzlich (1973), discussed above. Narrative interviews have also been very successfully employed: as Jovchelovitch and Bauer (2000) point out, there is a close relationship theoretically between the concepts of the narrative and of social representations, so this is not surprising. Some studies (e.g. Foster, 2007) draw on aspects of the narrative interview to examine social representations as participants tell their own stories: this is particularly useful where there is any sense of change or development, as in cases of illness or the development of identity. However, this might not always be the most appropriate interview format for studying other representations, and indeed the traditional structure of the 'narrative interview' (Flick, 2014) might prove too stringent for social representations studies: the suggestion, for example, that the researcher should not ask 'why' questions in the main body of the interview could be seen as limiting if we want to engage seriously with how representations influence our action, and

---

1 Herzlich (1973) found three different representations of health ('health-in-a-vacuum', health as equilibrium and reserve of health) and three different representations of illness (illness as destructive, illness as liberator, illness as an occupation).

interaction, and provide us with a template for understanding and approaching the world. In a similar vein, but avoiding some of these disadvantages, is the episodic interview (Flick, 2007, 2014), which has been used extensively by Flick (e.g. Flick and Röhnsch, 2007 or Flick et al., 2012). Here the idea is to combine narratives of situations (episodes) with questions (e.g. about subjective concepts, causes and consequences of a phenomenon) in one interview. For example, most people remember their first day at school or a situation in which they decided whether to leave school or to continue attending. Such situations can be recounted in short narratives. At the same time these people will have a concept of what a good teacher is or what defines success and failure in school. While those concepts may be built on or influenced by the above situations, concepts can only be presented in answers to questions and not in narratives. The episodic interview combines both approaches in moving back and forth between stimulating situation narratives and question/answer sequences.

It has also been argued (Lunt and Livingstone, 1996) that the socially shared aspects of social representations make group interviews particularly useful. The individual interview might be less sensitive to capturing interactional aspects of representations which are socially shared and maintained, as well as contested and challenged. However, what constitutes a group is important. Bauer and Gaskell (1999) employed focus groups as part of their study of representations of biotechnology: they make the distinction between strong groups, who share a common goal, project and identity, and weaker groups, who might share aspects of a representation through some (but not all) aspects of a shared project. They use the example of mothers of young children, who share the project of raising healthy children, and so might share representations of genetically modified foods as a result of this. Careful consideration of segmentation in this way is an important part of methods in social representations: much of social science research divides participants by age, ethnicity, gender, socioeconomic status, and so on, yet there is no a priori reason to assume that all white female middle-class thirty-somethings will share a representation of a particular object (Foster, 2011). The social representations researcher needs to consider common projects and identities much more subtly so as to avoid imposing a structure on to a representation that might stem from existing assumptions (see also Gillespie, Howarth and Cornish, 2012).

However, it is also possible to find ways of bringing a lack of consensus to the fore in focus group interviews, either through deliberately including participants who hold diverse views (and therefore do *not* share a common project or identity) or through the researcher playing 'Devil's advocate' by introducing aspects of representations that go against those being evoked and discussed by the group. This strategy was used to good effect in Arthi's (2012) work on representations of mental illness amongst the Tamil community in Singapore: most participants did not volunteer information regarding spirit possession unless it was introduced by the researcher as a controversial topic, but resulting discussion was often highly informative, and revealed more belief in paranormal explanations for experiences/behaviour labelled as mental illness.

Using the moderator/interviewer in this way can also bring to the fore taken-for-granted aspects of consensual representations, in other words the things that a group may not mention, as they are accepted as matters of fact, or ontological reality (Marková, 1996). This touches on the wider issue of the role of the researcher in social representations studies, by no means limited to qualitative analysis in social representations research: later in the chapter the importance of understanding the process of the choice and interpretation of quantitative analysis, and the researcher's role within this, will also be stressed. However, it has frequently been assumed that qualitative analysis requires closer attention to reflexivity, given the researcher's particular role in the elicitation and subsequent analysis of data. This is perhaps debatable, but it is certainly the case that designing a project, developing an interview guide and then analyzing the resulting data involves the researcher's own perspectives to a significant degree (Hodgetts *et al.*, 2010). The researcher must be able to recognize how he/she is embedded in a network of representations, and to bear these in mind while approaching those of others. Presenting oneself to participants as a 'learner' keen to understand their perspectives and ideas can work well in some cases (again, see Foster's (2007) study of mental health service clients' understandings of mental health problems) but this may not always be appropriate. In some cases, researchers may be considered to be 'insiders', or positioned in a particular way by participants, which may affect their responses: Rose (2003) found in a review of studies looking at attitudes towards electro-convulsive therapy that much greater satisfaction was reported if clinicians asked the questions, while research conducted by service user organizations or independent researchers engendered much more ambivalence and dissatisfaction. This could be even more relevant in interview situations when the participant is face to face with the interviewer and aspects of his/her identity are particularly salient.

Another significant issue is whether the researcher can (or should) have any role in changing the situation which is being researched. This is complicated, since social representations theory explicitly moves away from the idea of one 'correct' version of understanding, and the notion that any other understandings are therefore faulty and in need of correction. Bauer and Gaskell (1999) suggest that the researcher's role should be, for the most part, disinterested. However, it is also clear that there is a potential for social representations researchers to engage more critically with representations, working with communities to challenge stigma (Campbell and Jovchelovitch, 2000; Howarth, Foster and Dorrer, 2004).

Moving beyond what people say

Qualitative analysis of interviews of different kinds can clearly be useful in social representations studies. However, there may be limitations to this from a representational point of view. In many places, different theorists discuss the ways in which representations are not merely present in people's heads, nor only manifest in what they say (e.g. Moscovici, 1984). Instead, representations are present in actions and interactions within daily life, and are also evident in the ways in which we organize our lives, our institutions, our rituals and so on (ibid.). If we rely purely on self-report and discussion in the form of interview data, are we easily able to access this representational level? There are two possible responses to this problem: firstly, we can address the way we approach interview data, and secondly, we can move beyond interviews. In the case of the former, we must remember that interviews should not only be used as a way of accessing what people say, but also of accessing how they think, what they fail to say, what they cannot say, and so on. Analysis, which will be discussed later in this section, must move beyond the 'facts' of what is being said and we must employ our skills as researchers to enable this (Condor, 1997), or we risk what Bauer, Gaskell and Allum (2000) have referred to as 'empiricism by proxy'.

There has been interesting discussion of representations that are not always conscious (Joffe, 1999, 2003), questioning whether all aspects of a representation are accessible to research participants. A paradigmatic (and much quoted) example of this comes from Jodelet's (1989/1991) study of representations of madness in a French community in which psychiatric patients live as 'lodgers' with local families: here, although the family participants overtly rejected the idea that mental illness was contagious in any way, they organized their lives around rituals of separation to avoid contact between bodily fluids. As in Joffe's (1999) work, the need to construct some aspects of representation as 'Other' in order to protect the Self (and therefore not see oneself as being vulnerable to mental illness, HIV, etc.) was paramount. However, it is also possible that participants may be fully conscious of aspects of their representations of a particular issue, but not prepared to mention these overtly, however creative the researcher is in his/her attempts to elicit them. This could be the case if we consider representations which might be stigmatizing of particular issues or groups: social desirability bias or a fear of seeming discriminatory might mean that some participants refrain from saying what they privately believe and might even publicly demonstrate in other settings.

It is for these reasons that finding other ways of collecting data which can be qualitatively analyzed is important. Ethnographic work has been particularly fruitful in social representations studies: again, returning to Jodelet's (1989/1991) study, an ethnographic approach that combined informal discussions and observations of the community with detailed analysis of documentary material, and semi-structured interviews, provided a very rich set of data from which to examine the ways in which the foster families, professionals and lodgers interacted in different places (homes, public spaces and so on) and the way that the entire community was organized. This allows for a close consideration of the ways that representations are enacted and communicated and developed both in non-verbal communication and also in institutional practice. Other social representations studies have also taken an ethnographic approach: in Foster's (2007) study, using this approach not only allowed access to some of these less linguistic and more non-conscious aspects of representations of mental ill-health, but also allowed for a greater understanding of settings which are often hidden from the general public (here, three mental health services). Participant observation can also allow for greater rapport building with participants, and can allow the researcher to generate hypotheses and theories about what they observe, which can then be discussed with participants and altered as necessary. In cases where participants may have problems expressing themselves verbally, or problems concentrating for longer periods (for example, because of age, illness or medication), this method has further advantages.

Documentary analysis can form an important part of ethnography, but is also a useful stand-alone method in social representations study. The analysis of media representations has been particularly common for some time, with studies not only focussing on the text of articles, but also on pictures and on moving images in television and in film (Rose, 2000).

However, to return to the point made at the very start of this chapter, the most important aspect relating to the use of any of these methods is the way in which the resulting data are analyzed. Interviews, observations and documents can all be analyzed quantitatively if that is best suited to the research questions, and ways of approaching this will be discussed below. However, the qualitative analysis of such data also needs discussion. In recent years a number of high-profile papers have been published that seek to clarify the process of qualitative analysis, especially thematic analysis (e.g. Attride-Stirling, 2001; Braun and Clarke, 2006); a wide variety of textbooks now also detail the process of coding and analysis in more depth (e.g. Flick, 2014; Sullivan, Gibson and Riley, 2012). These works have been enormously important in providing researchers with a stage-by-stage guide to how to approach analysis, something which had perhaps been previously portrayed as a rather mystical and opaque process. Elsewhere we have commented on the utility of thematic analysis in social representations research (Flick and Foster, 2008): a close consideration of the themes in any data (and the relationship between them) is an important step in considering the representations of any issue. However, Provencher (2011b) has warned against fetishism when it comes to thematic analysis in social representations studies: she argues that we should not be lulled into assuming that following a number of different stages of coding will automatically lead to understanding the social representations of a particular concept. She points out the importance of *sociological imagination* in moving beyond the basic themes that might be considered in any data if we are truly to consider social representations. In this way, we need to be able to make links, consider absence as well as presence (Gervais, Morant and Penn, 1999), suggest why such patterns might be in evidence, and develop hypotheses about social understanding in action and interaction. It is also the case that thematic analysis might not be sufficient, or relevant, in all cases. As we discuss above, focus groups are particularly useful for considering the communicative practices involved in the development and maintenance of social representations, and a form of analysis that can take this interaction into consideration, such as analysis from a more dialogical perspective, may be more appropriate (see Marková *et al.*, 2007, and Caillaud and Kalampalikis, 2013, for comprehensive discussion of this). Barbour (2014) and Halkier (2010) suggest integrating a conversation analysis approach to analyzing how things are said in a focus group and in particular to analyze how the interaction evolves, how turn-taking is organized in the group and what this reveals about group dynamics. Developing this approach allows Lunt and Livingstone's (1996) idea – that focus groups can reveal how social representations are constructed and changed in interactions – to be put into practical terms.

Of course, advocating use of one's sociological imagination should not be equated with an 'anything goes' attitude, since the researcher must remain grounded in the data and aware of the different ways in which the quality of the analysis (and overall research) can be maintained. We return to this in the final part of this chapter, but before that, let us move on to consider quantitative analysis of data and its relationship with social representations research.

Quantitative methods

We will use the notion 'quantitative methods' for analytical tools based on statistical inferences. They can be used to analyze both quantitative and qualitative data. These tools are inviting: they provide a procedure and give the analysis a 'scientific aspect'. However the efficiency of statistical software – where using one command gives results – should not blind us and we should avoid using these procedures as a 'black box'.

We must keep in mind some of the assumptions of the social representations approach when choosing an appropriate tool. First, society thinks (Moscovici, 2001) and thinking always implies dialogicality (Billig *et al.*, 1988; Marková, 2000). In this sense, social representations are not fully consensual: debate is necessary, tensions exist and consensus only makes sense as 'functional consensus' (Wagner, 1994b). This is a consensus based upon a common language and a common argumentative level of immediate social interaction (Voelklein and Howarth, 2005). Therefore, it may not make sense to calculate means and compare them when using a social representations approach, and the standard deviation may be more useful.

However, we do not want to reject all social representations studies that employ means calculations. For example, sometimes people prefer a consensus (even a feeble one) to dissent (Moscovici, 1994), making the mean informative. Obviously this statistical description alone does not provide an interpretation as to *why* a feeble consensus exists and the researcher still has to give meaning to the result he/she observes (but this is another problem).

The start of every quantitative analysis is a data table: however, methods differ as to how this table is regarded and approached. Reflexivity implies knowing what the software does (and does not do). 'Knowing how it works' enables the researcher to choose the procedure appropriate both to the data and to the theoretical approach. Our aim here is not to give an exhaustive overview of 'relevant' quantitative methods but to outline, using some examples, how the same methods can be used differently according to the approach. However, the examples will demonstrate that the relevance of the methods lies in their ability to throw light on tensions structuring the social representations of an object.

Factor analysis and different ways to use it

Factor analysis is a set of techniques for determining how variables are linked together and/or are linked to individuals and/or to variables describing these individuals and/or to the context of data production. Factor analysis does not take into account means and variance, but outlines similarities and differences. Despite some differences, all the techniques follow a common general procedure. From a data table (with lines and ranges), two scatter plots are constructed: one represents the lines, while the other represents the ranges. These two scatter plots are projected on to a succession of orthogonal axes so that the largest proportion of the overall variance is explained. Each factor explains a proportion of variance: the first one explains the largest; the second will explain the next largest one that is not explained by the first factor; and so on. Some variables load most highly on each factor. So the factors differentiate the variables that are opposed to one another. Factor analysis allows us to make some assumptions about the tensions organizing social thinking.

Beyond these generalities, the different techniques (Principal Component Analysis, Correspondence Factor Analysis, Multiple Factor Analysis, etc.) differ through the table used as the point of departure. For example, principal component analysis uses a table which crosses individuals with quantitative variables (e.g. their age or their weight or their attitudes measured by a Likert scale). Correspondence factor analysis, in contrast, uses a table where qualitative variables are crossed (a contingency table, indicating frequencies). Therefore in this method, we lose the individuals but we have the link between different variables. Finally, multiple factor analysis, the most complex procedure, uses tables which cross qualitative and quantitative variables and individuals. Factor analysis offers some important opportunities: for example, factorial scores can be used as a new variable to compare individuals or groups. Moreover some additional variables can be projected in a second stage on the factor plane.

Organizing principles of individual differences

Doise, Clémence and Lorenzi-Cioldi (1993) propose a specific approach to social representations and highlight which method fits each step of the research procedure. Probably the most famous study is that on human rights (Doise, Spini and Clémence, 1999): here, the authors make the assumption that objectification is defined as common views about a given social issue. Moreover, differences in individual positioning are organized and the variations between individuals are anchored in cultural symbolic realities, social psychological experiences and beliefs. Campbell, Muncer and Coyle (1992) used a similar procedure without referring to the notion of 'organizing principles'. They examine social representations of aggression and suggest that women subscribe to an expressive model of aggression (focussed on intrapsychic determinants of aggression and loss of self-control) whereas men subscribe to an instrumental model of aggression (aggression as an attempt to gain control over a situation). To test this hypothesis, a questionnaire with bipolar items was administered to men and women. Each item could be answered using an instrumental or an expressive model of aggression. Factor analysis was conducted on the answers to these items. The first factor refers to the dichotomy instrumental/expressive; the second factor is defined by items differentiating private and public aggression. Finally, the third factor appears to be a guilt factor. The analysis therefore reveals some principles organizing social representations of aggression, which can be interpreted as tensions structuring the discourse on aggression. Having conducted and interpreted the factor analysis, the authors search for any link with gender (note that gender is not introduced in the factor analysis) and validate their hypothesis. However, at this stage, gender differences are not explained; they are only observed.

Outlining the role of context

Factor analysis can be used to follow an aim other than looking for organizing principles of individual differences. Some experimental studies using the central core approach analyze their data using factor analysis (Flament, Guimelli and Abric, 2006; Lo Monaco and Guimelli, 2011). Their aim is not to highlight the central nucleus but to show that the same social representation inspires different discourses in various contexts.[2] In this way, the hypothesis that these answers are organized through a one-dimensional structure is tested. Using principal component analysis, it means that a horseshoe phenomenon (or Guttman effect) exists. This phenomenon, which is not at all systematic, is observed when the two axes explain more than 90 per cent of the variance. The first axis often opposed extremes conditions (also called a size effect) and the second axes opposed the extreme cases and the intermediate cases. Graphically, the scatter plot has a parabolic form (like a horseshoe).

To illustrate this effect, we will use the results presented by Lo Monaco and Guimelli (2011). This experimental study concerns social representations of wine in the French context. Despite its cultural aspect, a social debate around wine (healthy and socially positive versus dangerous) exists. The interviewer first asked the respondent if he consumes wine, before identifying himself as a consumer or a non-consumer. So, four experimental conditions of data collections are used: a non-consumer asking a consumer, a non-consumer asking a non-consumer, and so on. Then, subjects were asked to rate ten propositions concerning various aspects

---

2 This is relevant for the central nucleus approach, which postulates that the central core of the social representation is stable.

of wine. A principal component analysis was conducted (on a table linking the context of data production and items)[3] and shows a horseshoe phenomenon.

One of the factors opposes non-consumer and consumer and shows that their answers are more extreme when the interviewer shares the same identity. Also some aspects of social representations are 'masked' or 'un-masked' depending on the context. For example, non-consumers rated wine as more dangerous when the interviewer presented himself as a non-consumer too. If the interviewer presented himself as a consumer, these aspects were 'masked'. This echoes the earlier discussion on the role of the interviewer. Therefore, we are tempted to say that here factor analysis is used to access *organizing principles of contextual positions*.

Hierarchical analysis and the Alceste method

The social representations approach also often employs hierarchical cluster analysis. Comparing this procedure to factor analysis, we suggest – even if this is a simplification – that cluster analysis only looks at the data table in one way, comparing the lines or comparing the ranges. As with factor analysis, different methods can be employed. Hierarchical cluster analysis can be ascendant: the first stage is to measure the proximity or the similarity between the variables (usually the squared Euclidean distance). Then, the variables are grouped together to form a cluster: the two variables having the shortest distance are grouped together, and then the next variable having the shortest distance with this cluster is associated. An ascendant hierarchical cluster analysis was conducted for example by Doise, Spini and Clémence (1999) in their study of representations of human rights to group together articles for which similar responses' patterns were observed.

Another procedure is descending hierarchical cluster analysis. Here, at the beginning all the variables are in the same class and they are then divided into different classes: the variable with the highest distance is retrieved, then the second one and so on. In fact, these two methods differ in the way the variables are considered at the beginning: a whole that has to be divided in classes or, alternatively, elements which should be grouped together into clusters. But both methods finally reveal a dendogram.

The Alceste method

The Alceste method is based on a descendant hierarchical cluster analysis and is often used in social representations research (Klein and Licata, 2003; Lahlou, 2001; Kalampalikis, 2003). Alceste is a method of statistical lexical analysis which seeks 'to investigate statistical similarities and dissimilarities of words in order to identify repetitive language patterns' (Kronberger and Wagner, 2003). First, the text is decomposed into groups of words or phrases called elementary contextual units

---

3 Note that the PCA is not conducted on the table linking individuals and items but experimental conditions and items. This is coherent with the experimental approach: answers are considered as dependent from the conditions, not from the individuals.

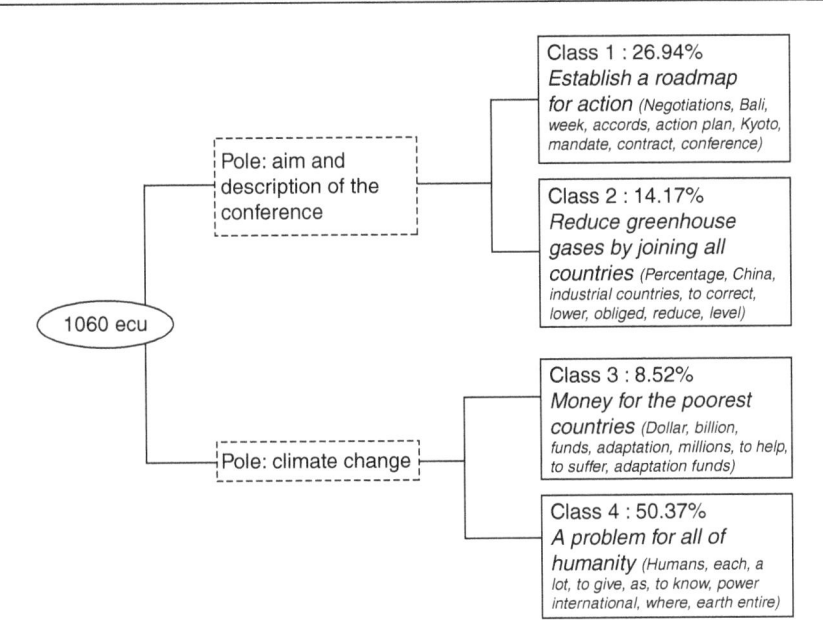

```
                                    ┌─────────────────────────────┐
                                    │ Class 1 : 26.94%            │
                                    │ Establish a roadmap         │
                                    │ for action (Negotiations, Bali,│
                                    │ week, accords, action plan, Kyoto,│
            ┌───────────────────┐   │ mandate, contract, conference)│
            │ Pole: aim and     │───┤                             │
            │ description of the│   ├─────────────────────────────┤
            │ conference        │   │ Class 2 : 14.17%            │
            └───────────────────┘   │ Reduce greenhouse           │
                                    │ gases by joining all        │
    ┌─────────┐                     │ countries (Percentage, China,│
    │1060 ecu │                     │ industrial countries, to correct,│
    └─────────┘                     │ lower, obliged, reduce, level)│
                                    └─────────────────────────────┘
                                    ┌─────────────────────────────┐
                                    │ Class 3 : 8.52%             │
                                    │ Money for the poorest       │
                                    │ countries (Dollar, billion, │
            ┌───────────────────┐   │ funds, adaptation, millions, to help,│
            │Pole: climate change│──┤ to suffer, adaptation funds)│
            └───────────────────┘   ├─────────────────────────────┤
                                    │ Class 4 : 50.37%            │
                                    │ A problem for all of        │
                                    │ humanity (Humans, each, a   │
                                    │ lot, to give, as, to know, power│
                                    │ international, where, earth entire)│
                                    └─────────────────────────────┘
```

Figure 5.1 *Alceste analysis of Bali climate conference.*

(ECUs) and the software reduces the words to their root (plurals, conjugations, etc.). Next, a contingency table indicates the presence versus absence of each reduced form in each ECU. Then a descendant hierarchical cluster analysis is performed on the table. The result is a hierarchy of classes, of 'lexical universes' present in the corpus. The link with illustrative variables is calculated afterwards (for example: who is speaking? when was a discourse held? etc.). When interpreting the classes of words obtained, we must remember that they stem from the same text but were divided because of differences between them. These differences lead the interpretation.

In fact, the Alceste method is not, initially, interested in the meaning of words. The method looks only for the organization of the discourse and therefore enables the researcher to study pragmatic aspects of social representations (Moscovici and Kalampalikis, 2005). Combined with a more semantic analysis, this method enhances the interpretation of the data.

Caillaud, Kalampalikis and Flick (2012) used the Alceste method in this way in a study of social representations of the Bali climate conference in French and German media. The different classes were interpreted as 'references spaces and anchoring categories'. We will take as an example only the German results.

The corpus was divided into four classes as shown in Figure 5.1. The titles are proposed by the researchers themselves to designate the classes. The most representative words of each class are in brackets.

Classes 1 and 2 refer to political discourses about the conference itself. In class 1, the discourse is concrete and local (the aim of the conference) whereas in class 2 the discourse refers to a more global aim (to reduce greenhouse gas production).

Class 3 and 4 both refer to climate change and its consequences for humanity. Again, the opposition between concrete and general perspectives structures the discourse (all humanity versus poor countries).

In this sense, in Germany, the conference is anchored in political and human categories linking both global and local dimensions.

Also, this procedure searches for tensions organizing the discourse about an object by paying attention to the co-text (which words are often associated together). The Alceste method also enables the researcher to take into account the context of discourse (Moscovici, 1994). Klein and Licata (2003) analyzed the speeches from Patrice Lumumba during the decolonization of Congo using the Alceste method. They consider some illustrative variables (e.g. political and historical context, audience). The results were interpreted with reference to the historical context and the authors show how the speeches of Patrice Lumumba contribute to the social change.

Despite a growing interest in Structural Equation Modelling (SEM) in social psychology, only a few studies using social representations try to use this method. SEM can be used in two ways: to test the relationships between different variables; or to test the relationships between observed variables (what we measure) and latent variables (what we want to measure). Friestad, Rise and Roysamb (1999) use SEM to show that social representations about smoking mediate the effect of smoker status on attitudes towards smoking restrictions. Alternatively, Carugati, Selleri and Scappini (1994) propose using SEM to underline the way social representations are structured (how different concepts are linked together in common sense and forms theories). Once more, the same methodological tool is used in quite different ways. However, we can question why SEM is not used as widely by social representations studies as it is more generally in social psychology to try to 'make sense of absence'. Perhaps the implicit idea of SEM to test 'causal relationships' does not fit well with the epistemological assumptions of social representations: for example, does the smoker status cause the social representations, or do social representations of smoking cause smoking behaviours and lead to smoker status? Social representations theory turns to a dialogical relationship between identity and social representations (Marková, 2007) which go beyond causality. Nevertheless, we can hypothesize that some relevant use of SEM will be developed in future research. This seems plausible especially as SEM offers numerous possibilities and only tests causality if inputs variables refer to an experimental design.

The quantitative methods we have presented here share the same perspective. They propose some answers to the following research questions: What tensions structure the data? What is opposed? What is similar? What goes together? How does the context structure the data? There is no doubt that these questions are relevant within social representations theory. However, the different examples we have presented also outline the importance of interpretation of the results and also of the data (as relevant indicators for the social representations in the focus of the concrete study). Moreover, we show how the same method can be used to follow different aims. Ultimately, these are only tools we have to use with reflexivity to enhance our understanding of social phenomena.

Triangulation and mixed methods in the study of social representations

As mentioned at several points in this chapter, studying social representations often needs more than one methodological approach due to the complexity of the phenomenon. Two major methodological concepts (and discussions) are relevant in such multi-method approaches.

Triangulation

Triangulation was introduced to social research by Denzin (1978). It refers to combining several approaches in the study of a phenomenon or of several aspects of it (e.g. knowledge and practices as parts of a social representation of an issue). The original idea of cross-validating results by a triangulation of methods was initially criticized (see Flick 1992 as an overview) and soon replaced by the aim of seeing the phenomenon from different angles and thus elucidating its diversity or complexity. Denzin mentioned triangulation on four levels: of different *researchers*, of various sorts of *data*, of different *theories* and methodological triangulation – the combination of two (or more) independent methods (*between methods triangulation*), which can also consist of two qualitative methods. The alternative is *within methods triangulation* when several approaches are combined in one method (see the episodic interview discussed above as an example for this). Triangulation refers to combining several perspectives in a systematic way (Flick, 1992) and thus goes beyond confirming results. Often triangulation produces complementary results, highlighting different aspects of a phenomenon and differences between what people say and what they do, for example. In studying social representations, triangulation can be fruitful in various ways.

If social representations of a phenomenon include the views of various groups, then we may need to use several methods for studying it. To examine a phenomenon like the utilization of professional healthcare by homeless adolescents, for example, we can first interview the adolescents using the episodic or narrative interview. To understand the processes and barriers influencing whether the adolescents use services or are reached by these institutions more fully, it may be necessary to integrate service providers' views on the phenomenon. For this purpose, expert interviews (about the target group, needs, barriers, cooperation of services, etc.) should be a second methodological approach. If the processes being examined (health problems and use of services) also call for the study of practices and discourses in the target group (homeless adolescents and their peers in open spaces), then an ethnographic approach using participant observation may be necessary. Thus the methodological triangulation in this example (see Flick, 2011a; Flick and Röhnsch, 2007) addresses three levels of the phenomenon (adolescents' knowledge, their practices, and expert knowledge) with three methods. A theoretical triangulation complements methodological triangulation, in this example, when the perspective of social representations is complemented by the theoretical approach of 'social problems work' (Holstein and Miller, 1993) focussing on the practices of identification and classification of social problems in the interaction (or lack of it) between clients and service providers (see Flick, 2011a). Thus, triangulation – in this example of multiple qualitative methods – can open a more comprehensive empirical approach to studying the social representation of a complex phenomenon. The triangulation of several theoretical perspectives can provide a more comprehensive theoretical ground for combining these methods. Of course the methodological triangulation can also include qualitative and quantitative methods.

Mixed methods

In recent decades a discussion about using mixed methods has developed and attracted much attention (see e.g. Creswell and Piano Clark, 2010 and the *Journal of Mixed Methods Research*). This discussion has a strong focus on combining quantitative and qualitative methods and thus fits into this chapter in that it brings together both the approaches we discussed separately earlier. However, this approach has a number of limitations (see Flick, 2011a). First, its focus is on (only) combining qualitative and quantitative methods and not, for example, on combining several qualitative methods. Secondly, we see a concentration on methods and lack of concern for their theoretical backgrounds and potential differences. Thirdly the use of the concept of 'paradigms' for describing qualitative and quantitative research neglects differences in the ways qualitative research is done in different contexts (say narrative research and ethnography). As we argue elsewhere in more detail (see Flick *et al.*, 2012), a mixed methods approach of combining quantitative and qualitative research can be integrated in a more complex approach of triangulation to a complex phenomenon. In a study of the social representations of sleeping problems of nursing home residents and their treatment, we applied a systematic approach by focussing on an in-depth case study. Two sources of quantitative data (assessment of residents' status and medication prescribed by physicians) and several contextualized qualitative approaches – one that focusses on physicians' interpretive patterns concerning their prescription practices, and another that looks at nursing staff and nursing home residents' attitudes toward sleep medication – were triangulated. Here, the quantitative approaches demonstrate first the relevance of the problem (sleeping problems in their frequency, distribution and link to other medical problems) and how often medications are prescribed for treating them. The qualitative approaches showed the representations of the problem held by staff and residents. The combination of approaches revealed that physicians' statements in interviews, for example, made us expect a much higher prescription rate than became evident in analyzing the actual prescription rates. Thus the triangulation showed differences between the levels of knowledge and practices as two levels of the social representation of this phenomenon.

This example shows, as do several others, that triangulation is a substantial addition to the methodologies for studying social representations. In particular, using the concept to address several levels of social representations – such as knowledge and practices or states and processes – allows us to draw a fuller picture of an issue and its representations. By linking several approaches, which also means linking several types of data, and in assuming that these approaches are indicators for the social representations under study, a specific form of interpretation is possible – of the data and of the findings produced by the combination of methods.

Concluding remarks

This chapter has shown that a range of qualitative and quantitative methods are available for empirical studies of social representations, and that they can be used as stand-alone methods or in combination. All of these methods have to be considered for their appropriateness to the issue being studied. None has been designed exclusively for studying social representations. For all, then, a number of decisions have to be taken by the researchers: How far can data collected with each method be seen as an indicator of the representations that shall be studied? How far can differences between certain subgroups in the study be seen as an indicator of a *social* representation? Data as well as statistical or other forms of results cannot per se be equated with a social representation. This link is a theoretical inference and thus an interpretation which the researchers have to draw. Which method should be used and whether methods should be combined (and which methods) should be decided with respect to the phenomenon under study. Whose representations and which levels of the social representation of a phenomenon will be studied are the relevant points of reference for methodological decisions, rather than a general preference for qualitative or quantitative research or for combining both. In the end all methods and their theoretical backgrounds are tools for making empirical research fruitful for understanding social representations.

Inevitably, this chapter has not been a comprehensive discussion of all possible methods, but as the selection of methods presented shows, the toolkit for empirically studying social representations is substantial. This should allow researchers to find the 'right' method for the issue they want to study within the framework of social representations. However, the more methods are available and prove successful in the study of social representations, the more researchers face the need to take the decision regarding a method that is appropriate both for the issue and for the approach of social representations. This brings the general question of the indication of methods back into focus: how should researchers decide which methods to use (see Flick, 2014, for qualitative research, Flick, 2011a, ch. 6, for quantitative and qualitative research, and Flick, 2007, for triangulation studies)? This is even more relevant in a field like social representations, which is not tied to any specific methodological approach, but within which basically all methods in psychology and the social sciences have been used in one way or another, as Breakwell and Canter (1993) have already stated. In this sense, our chapter has provided an orientation to the variety of methodological approaches to social representations research by discussing prominent examples.

PART II

Conceptual developments

The second part of this handbook expands on the contribution of the first section by extending the discussion and elaborating on the conceptual issues that mark social representations theory in two directions. Firstly, what follows presents the major theoretical developments of social representations theory that have ensued Moscovici's original formulation. Social representations theory today has come to include a conceptualization of the structural forms of social representations, of how these intermingle in diversified public spheres, and of the specific role played by communication in their formation and circulation. Secondly, social representations theory has developed in parallel with other sociocultural and psychological notions that similarly serve in the understanding of social psychological phenomena. The reader is thus presented with detailed explanations of concepts and mechanisms such as attitudes, identities, communities, remembering and the imaginary. These have been incorporated into social representations theory to provide an overarching and holistic framework for the study of human conduct in everyday life.

The seven chapters presented in this part of the book reflect the scholarly engagement that social representations theorists have undertaken over the years. The progress made in associated disciplines and theories in the social sciences has led to more nuanced understandings of various social and psychological phenomena. In themselves, social representations do not exist in a vacuum, but are fashioned out of the identity projects that individuals undertake in community with others, drawing on their constructed histories, their imagination of social issues and events, the characteristic perspectives they adopt in communication, and the frameworks that legitimize their views in social relations. This section provides the reader with a deeper understanding of the dynamics that inhere in the production, negotiation and circulation of social representations and the relations these bear with associated sociocultural and psychological phenomena. Taken together, this provides the reader with a detailed articulation of how the theory complements other prevalent frameworks that have furthered our understanding of the processes and dynamics that characterize human conduct.

6 Central core theory

Pascal Moliner and Jean-Claude Abric

Central Core Theory (Abric, 1976, 1987, 1994a), also known as Central Nucleus Theory from the original French expression '*noyau central*', is a structure theory of social representations. It is based on the premise that, regardless of social object, any social representation is organized in a dual system. The main function of this dual system is to maintain the stability of the representation within the group which conveys it. In other words, the system stabilizes the meanings that group members associate with the representation's object. This stabilization depends on the ability of the system to preserve the consensus within the group while allowing for some individual divergences.

In the first part of this chapter we will show that since the earliest formulations of social representations theory, representations have been considered as structures. We will specifically examine how Moscovici's (1961/1976) epistemological orientations converged with those of several of his contemporaries who pioneered social cognition research (Asch, 1946; Heider, 1946, 1958; Festinger, 1957; Rosenberg and Hovland, 1960). We will then proceed to look at how Moscovici integrated the idea of structure into his theory, mainly via the notion of dimensional representation and the concepts of field and figurative schema.

In the second part of the chapter we present the different propositions of central core theory. We will show how the concept of core derives from that of figurative schema, but also how it differs from it. Further, we will explain how the successive formulations of central core theory (Abric, 1976, 1993, 1994) attempted to clarify the structural approach to representations from a simple dichotomy between central and peripheral elements to the introduction of the notion of dynamically interacting central and peripheral systems. In this section the central and peripheral systems will be described according to their formal, expressive and psycho-social properties.

The third part of the chapter is devoted to the consequences of central core theory for the comprehension and study of social representations dynamics. Indeed, interactions between the central and peripheral systems form a single principle which can simultaneously account for both the stability and the dynamics of representations. However, central core theory also offers a conceptual framework which has

---

Jean-Claude Abric died a few weeks after the end of this work. He was very happy to participate in this project and he would have been proud to see his name in this handbook.

largely contributed to the evolution of comparative (diachronic and synchronic) research on social representations.

The fourth part of this chapter presents the major methodologies developed in the framework of central core theory, from the Challenging Method or 'méthode de Mise en Cause' (Moliner, 1989), and its variations, to the Test of Independence from Context or 'Test d'Indépendance au Contexte' (Lo Monaco et al., 2008).

Finally, we conclude with a discussion of one of the most recent developments in central core theory: Matrix Core Theory or 'théorie du Noyau Matrice' (Moliner and Martos, 2005; Moliner, 2007). This new formulation, in line with Moscovici's and Abric's proposals, propounds to redefine the functions of the central system, placing particular emphasis on the symbolic and psycho-linguistic properties of central elements.

Social representations as cognitive structures

When, in 1946, Solomon Asch published his first works, he suggested the idea that certain cognitions might play a specific role in the impressions we build of others. At the same time, with Cognitive Balance Theory, Heider (1946) suggests that people tend to maintain consistency in patterns of their liking and disliking of one another and of inanimate objects. A little later, Festinger (1957) assumed the existence of a cognitive coherence principle inducing individuals to seek a certain balance between the various self-cognitions available to them. For Festinger, any incoherence between those cognitions would generate a state of dissonance which would trigger a rationalization effort aiming to reinstate coherence into the subject's cognitive environment. Around the same time, Heider (1958) laid the foundation for his attribution theory by identifying and distinguishing between internal and external causalities. Lastly, with their tri-component model, Rosenberg and Hovland (1960) aimed to describe attitudes according to three interrelated dimensions (cognitive, affective and behavioural). It became obvious to all those pioneers of social cognition that our knowledge about the social environment is organized in structured sets. This very organization is the reason why such knowledge is abundant and easily accessible.

From these early to more contemporary works on social cognition, the theory of social representations adopted the same epistemic stance. For Moscovici (1961/1976), social representations are organized in three dimensions, which are also elements of their analysis or comparison (information, field and attitude). These dimensions are related to each other, since, for example, the field refers to the organization and the prioritization of the information contained in the representation. In the same vein, the group's attitude towards the representation's object guides the selection of information, its organization and its prioritization. In other words, according to Moscovici (1976, p. 27), 'the representation is an organized body of knowledge'. More precisely, a social representation can be described as a set of elements between which individuals establish connections. In that perspective, social representations are cognitive structures.

Table 6.1 *Formal properties of central and peripheral elements*

Central elements	Peripheral elements
Few	Numerous
Significant consensus among group members	Many differences among group members
Stable over time	Varying, unstable

This structural design of representations is also the basis for another theoretical proposal made by Moscovici, that of 'figurative nucleus'. One of the main processes involved in the construction of social representations is that of objectification. This is a cognitive process which allows the abstract to be made concrete. The first stage of this operation is perceptive selection, during which individuals retain some information at the expense of other information. This filtering allows for the selection of only those elements deemed consistent with the values of the group. Individuals then perform a decontextualization of the information, during which it is disconnected from its original context and subsequently naturalized. Finally, the selected information will be recombined into a 'figurative nucleus, or *core*' – in other words, a reduced and streamlined set of objectified notions which will provide a solid basis for apprehending objects and for legitimizing the more concrete meaning which is now given them. Thus, the figurative core will constitute the embryo of a social representation, especially because it provides individuals language and naming categories with which to organize knowledge about the object. For example, the neologisms 'complexed' and 'repressed', which appeared in France in the 1970s, are rooted in the emergence of the social representations of psychoanalysis pervading 1960s French society. It appears, therefore, that for Moscovici, the role of the figurative core is a dynamic one concerned mainly with the process of social representation in its emergence phase.

Central elements and peripheral elements

The notion of central core stems directly from that of figurative schema, but it focusses more on the contents of stabilized representations. In its original formulation, central core theory (Abric, 1976, 1993) proposed to consider the representation as a hierarchical set of beliefs including peripheral elements organized around a core. Formally, the core is made up of a limited number of beliefs, which gather significant consensus within the group and are remarkably stable over time. Conversely, peripheral beliefs are numerous, unevenly shared among the group, and change over time (see Table 6.1).

The core performs three structuring functions:

– *A meaning function*. The core generates or modulates the meaning of all the other elements of the representation, and ultimately, its overall meaning. Here, the core elements are assumed to have a similar role as that of the 'central traits' suggested by Asch (1946) in his studies on perception. For this author, the impression we form of a person is organized around specific traits, which modulate the signification of the other traits attributed to this person. For example, attributing the trait 'cold' or 'warm' to someone influences the other traits that we may attribute to that person. Ultimately, the difference between our overall impression of a 'warm' and 'meticulous' person and that of a 'cold' and 'meticulous' person is due to the 'warm–cold' polarity, which modulates the signification of the trait 'meticulous'. In the first case, we picture thoroughness inspired by goodwill, whereas in the second case, we fear that, behind the thoroughness, a certain darkness lies.

– *An organizational function.* The core determines the nature of the connections linking the elements of the representation. In fact, this function derives from the first one: assuming that central elements can modulate the signification of peripheral ones leads to the understanding that the connections between two peripheral elements are ultimately dependent upon the central elements to give them meaning.

– *A stabilization function.* The core is both the most stable and the most resistant part of a representation. This function results from the combination of the two previous ones and the consensual nature of the central elements. Indeed, central beliefs are widely shared, giving meaning to other elements in the representation and determining their organization. Consequently, the modification of these beliefs generates significant cognitive and psycho-social costs. On the cognitive level, any change in central beliefs leads to an overall change in the representation's meaning. On the psycho-social level, changes may pose a significant dislocation risk to the consensus among the group, and therefore to the social connection. For all the above reasons, the theory makes the assumption that there will be strong resistance to any change in central beliefs.

The peripheral elements are characterized by two properties:

– On the one hand, they are beliefs that refer to concrete and individualized experiences. While they evidently depend upon core elements, they reflect the experience of individuals. For example, in the representation of the Enterprise world (Moliner, 1993, 1996), the notion of 'hierarchy' is considered central. In that respect, any company is thought of as a hierarchical organization. However, the experience of hierarchy varies from one individual to the other. To some, it is expressed through the figure of a 'boss'; to others, through that of a 'steering committee' or of a 'board of directors'. A consequence of this is some variation in the degree of sharedness of peripheral elements. Some of them are more shared than others.

– On the other hand, the beliefs are conditional (Flament, 1994). For example, continuing with the representation of the world of Enterprise, the notion of 'profit' is also considered central. But the profit a company makes is rarely visible in its rawest form. Most often, it is noticeable only via indicators such as advertising done by the company, the degree of luxury of its premises, the investments

Table 6.2 *Expressive properties of central and peripheral elements*

Central elements	Peripheral elements
General characteristics of the object, elements of definition.	Specific cases.
Abstract elements.	Concrete and contextualized elements.
Unconditional beliefs, non-negotiable.	Conditional beliefs.

it makes, and so on. As a result, depending on the situation, individuals will consider a company is actually profitable if it advertises a lot, or if its offices are posh, or if it makes major investments, etc.

In terms of expression (see Table 6.2), it is generally assumed that central elements have an abstract nature (Moliner, 1988), do not depend on context (Abric, 1994) or constitute elements of object definition (Flament, 1994). Furthermore, individuals associate element characteristics with the object in a 'non-negotiable' way (Moscovici, 1993a). Instead, peripheral elements rather express specific, contextualized experiences, which individuals associate conditionally with the representation's object.[1]

The experimental validation of core theory (Moliner, 1988, 1989) provided an important clarification about central elements. Indeed, it was shown that they maintain a symbolic link to the representation's object. Thus, any mention of this object implicitly or explicitly refers to its representation's central elements, while any mention of the central elements refers to the object. For example, if we are told of an activity that it is 'rewarding' and 'transitional', we are unable to determine what this activity is, or what the relationship between the two adjectives may be. However, if we are also told that this activity leads to a 'diploma', we can now infer that we are probably talking about 'studying', and the link between the above adjectives becomes clearer. Drawn from research on the representation of Studies (Moliner, 1996), this example accurately illustrates the notion of a symbolic link between a social object and the central elements of this object's social representation. But it also shows the organizational function of the central elements.

Stability and dynamics of representations

In its original formulation, central core theory was introduced as a particularly effective conceptual tool to describe the structure of social representations, regardless of their contents. However, it remained relatively unconcerned with the evolution of representations. It was under the impetus of the works of Claude Flament that the theory integrated the notion of 'system' (Abric, 1993, 1994a). As seen

---

1 Marková (2003) suggested that we can make a distinction between knowledge-based and belief-based social representations. The former could be more flexible whereas the latter more rigid representations. Core theory makes no difference between belief, opinion and information, but it would be intersting to examine the links between beliefs and central elements.

Table 6.3 *Psycho-social properties of the central and peripheral systems*

Central system	Peripheral system
Related to the group's values, norms and history.	Related to group members' individual experiences.
Ensures the sustainability of the representation.	Absorbs contradictions and changes.
Contributes to the group's homogeneity.	Allows for the group's heterogeneity.

previously, a system is defined as a set of interacting elements aiming to perform a function or produce a result. For Flament (1989), central core theory must not only describe the structure of representations, but also provide explanations for their stability and dynamics. From that point on, representations were considered 'dual-systems' (Abric, 1994a, p. 27), consisting of a 'central system' and a 'peripheral system' (see Table 6.3). The main function of a dual system is to ensure the stability of the meanings assigned by group members to a social object. To that effect, the central system and the peripheral system perform specific functions:

– The central system's function is to manage the meanings associated with the object and to strengthen them into non-negotiable beliefs. This is why it is composed of elements with high consensus, connected to each other and directly related to the group's values, norms and history.
– The peripheral system's essential function is to protect the central system. Due to the properties of its component elements (contextualized and conditional beliefs), it allows individuals to integrate potential contradictions by making them more bearable, that is, singular and contextualized. Similarly, the peripheral system allows for the integration of new information without the need to transform central system elements.

In fact, the central system's stabilizing role cannot be conceived without the peripheral system's protecting role, which allows the integration of newness, singularity or contradiction. The two systems are mutually dependent; they 'work well as an entity in which each part has a specific role, remaining complementary to one another' (Abric, 1994, p. 79). Thus we understand why 'social representations are both stable and unstable, rigid and flexible', and at the same time 'consensual but also marked by strong interindividual differences' (Abric, 1994, p. 73).

However, in certain circumstances some elements may move from one system to another. This will sometimes trigger a transformation of the representation. Since the beginning of the 1980s various studies have examined this question (on this subject, see Moliner, 2001). The perspective on this research can now offer a fairly complete description of the dynamics of social representation (see Table 6.4). The starting point of these dynamics is generally located in the social group's environment, where (technological, economic, ecological, etc.) changes will occur. These changes then compel individuals to adopt new behaviours within an adaptation

Table 6.4 *Changes or transformations of social representations*

Peripheral changes of social representations	Transformations of social representations
Emergence of new elements or disappearance of older peripheral elements.	Emergence of new elements or disappearance of older central elements.
Stability of the central system.	Modification of the central system.
Stability of the meanings associated with the object.	Changes in the meanings associated with the object.

objective. For example, in a study carried out in the south of France, Guimelli (1988) showed that the spread of a myxomatosis outbreak finally led hunters to include game-preserving measures in their hunting practices so that reproduction (and hunting!) could be maintained. Hence, the adoption of new behaviours within a group may impact social representations – provided, however, that the environmental changes and the adaptive behaviours they induce are perceived by individuals as 'irreversible' (Flament, 1994). Two cases are observed:

- The adoption of new behaviours does not come into conflict with the representation's central elements, or contradictions can be absorbed by the peripheral system. In this case, minor (peripheral) changes in the social representation can be identified.
- Or, the adoption of new behaviours does come into conflict with the representation's central elements. These contradictions cannot be absorbed by the peripheral system. In this scenario, profound transformations of the social representation are observed.

It should be pointed out that peripheral changes in a representation may progressively lead to the transformation of this representation. This is essentially what happens when peripheral beliefs gradually spread within the group to eventually become very consensual. Sometimes called 'soft transformations', these changes may progressively lead to the transformation of the central system, which is then enriched with new elements. In many ways, we can assume that this is the most common mode of evolution of social representations. For instance, in the representation of hunting (Guimelli, 1988), the peripheral notion 'territory management' became progressively central since the generalization of new practices intended to preserve game in hunting areas.

Thus we see that according to this conceptualization, the transformation of a representation necessarily involves that of its central system. Therefore, central core theory appears as a particularly useful tool for the study of the dynamics of social representations. While it offers an explanation for the stability and change of a representation, it also provides, at the same time, criteria with which to estimate the intensity of a representation's evolution. These criteria are obviously related to the central elements. In the strict sense of the theory, two representations are considered equivalent if their central elements are identical. But social representations are not isolated from each other and two representations could have more or less common central elements. Sometimes the peripheral elements of one representation belong to the core of another representation. These different cases of 'embedding' or 'reciprocity' (Abric, 2002) occur when the social objects of representation are linked, such as Work and Unemployement (Milland, 2001), or Money and Bank (Abric, 2002). Thus, whenever we need to compare social representations, the identification of central elements is of major interest.

Methodology developments

Two main types of method were developed within the framework of central core theory. *Exploratory methods* are aimed at detecting central elements, and *corroborative methods* are designed to identify these elements. Each type was developed from the basis of an initial method, to which many variations were added over time.[2]

Exploratory methods: free association and hierarchical evocation

In 1992 Vergès proposed the use of verbal association techniques for gathering the contents of social representations. His idea was that it was possible to explore, with only one method, the content and structure of a representation. Indeed, he thought that since central core theory was primarily a theory of meaning, the study of a representation had to explore the meanings that individuals assign to an object. Hence, collecting those meanings through free verbal associations seemed like a logical way to proceed, especially since, on a technical level, this method offers great flexibility. In practice, the first step consists in asking the individuals questioned to name all the words and expressions that come to their minds when prompted by an inductor word designating the object of the representation under study. A corpus of data is then obtained, on which various lexico-metric analyses can be performed (number of different words, frequency of each word, etc.), as well as theme content analysis (themes and dimensions by which the corpus can be arranged.) It must be pointed out that several current pieces of software greatly facilitate this type of analysis. Alceste and Iramuteq, especially, can be mentioned for their ability to perform correspondence factor analysis and hierarchical classification analysis on such datasets. Thus, free association proves to be an extremely flexible technique for exploring the contents of a social representation. However, in order to explore the structure one must combine data collection with an expertise phase carried out by the respondents themselves.

---

2 In this chapter we will only examine each initial method type and its main variation. For more details, see Abric (2003) and Moliner, Rateau and Cohen-Scali (2002).

The hierarchical evocation technique meets this requirement. It comprises asking respondents about the importance they attach to each of the associations they produce. This is generally achieved by having subjects arrange their own production by order of importance. Thus, for each corpus term, its occurrence frequency in the population surveyed and its average rank of importance can be known. It can then be inferred that the terms showing the highest occurrence frequencies and the highest average ranks of importance point to potential core elements of the representation. However, at this stage only hypotheses can be made. Indeed, while the free association technique allows us to detect frequent and important elements in the subjects' production, it does not inform us on the 'non-negotiable' character of these elements. For example, when asked about friendship, most individuals bring up the notion of shared opinions: 'When people are friends, they share many opinions.' However, most of the individuals surveyed agree that people can be friends *and* hold different opinions (Moliner, 1988, 1989). In other words, knowing the frequency and importance of a discursive element does not allow us to assert that this element refers to a central belief. This is why verbal association and hierarchical evocation methods should be considered exploratory methods.

Corroborative methods: challenging method and test of independence from context

According to the theory, the central elements of a representation are features which individuals consider inseparable from the object. Hence, an object cannot be seen as such by individuals if one of its features is inconsistent with a central element of the representation. Would you say of an animal that it is a bird, if you were told that it has no feathers? Obviously you would not, because you believe feathers are an inseparable feature of birds! This process of refutation of the object can serve as an indicator of centrality: it is generated only when central elements are challenged. Conversely, peripheral elements allow for contradiction. Their challenging will not constitute a risk for the representation, nor lead to a refutation process of the object. The mechanism of the Challenging or 'Mise en Cause' Technique (Moliner, 1988, 1994) is therefore based on a double negation principle: if the negation of an element leads to the negation of the object, then it is a central element of the representation. Operationally, the challenging technique is implemented in two successive steps. First, a representation content-gathering step is performed on the basis of the methods described above, and second, an estimation step is performed during which individuals are invited to judge whether or not an object X may be considered the representation's object *if it does not exhibit* the characteristics previously identified. Two scenarios can occur for each element. Either the subjects concede that object X can be the representation's object in spite of the challenging of the element; the element is then deemed peripheral. Or, the subjects do not see object X as the representation's object when it is challenged; then it is a central element of the representation.

In practice, a questionnaire is put together which uses generic and imprecise terms to ambiguously introduce the object studied. For example, to suggest the idea of work, the term 'activity' is used; for that of company, 'organization', and so on. The questionnaire is introduced with a question such as: 'Would you say of an activity that it is work, if...?' The question is then followed by the list of characteristics collected previously and now presented in their negative form. For example, for work, 'this activity is not compensated', 'this activity is not fulfilling', and so on. Each such challenge is associated with a response scale allowing subjects to indicate their agreement from a totally positive end to a totally negative end. The data is then analyzed, and any characteristic which receives a negative agreement response rate statistically equivalent to 100 per cent is considered a central element of the representation's object. Therefore, if almost all the respondents consider that an activity which is not compensated is *not* work, it can be inferred that, for these individuals, compensation constitutes a central characteristic of the representation of work.

The challenging technique is a great tool for identifying the central elements of a representation. However, for various reasons (groundwork issues, demographic characteristics, etc.) it cannot always be implemented. Since 2008 a reliable alternative exists: the Test of Independence from Context or 'Test d'Indépendance au Context' (TIC) (Lo Monaco et al., 2008). This new technique is based on another theoretical property of central elements: their non-contextual nature (see Table 6.2). In other words, central elements correspond to characteristics which are always present within the object of the representation, whereas peripheral elements correspond to characteristics which may be absent from the object of the representation. Using the above bird example again, we could say that all birds have feathers, but that some birds do not fly. Thus, testing the systematic and non-contextual nature of the association between an object and its characteristics enables us to identify the central elements of the representation. TIC advocates suggest that it be implemented with a question such as: 'In your opinion, does a bird, in all cases, have feathers?' When a positive response rate statistically equivalent to 100 per cent is obtained, the element tested is considered part of the core of the representation.

From central core to matrix core?

Central core theory has proven one of the most effective conceptual tools available to study social representations to date. Yet, its figurative model roots (Moscovici, 1976) raise several questions about the generation function of the central elements' meaning.

The first question is found in research on the social representation of psychoanalysis. In this foundational research, Moscovici (1976) identified four key notions (the unconscious, the conscious, repression and complex) forming the figurative model of the representation. He pointed out, however, that while these notions have 'indicative value', they have no 'real specific meaning' (ibid., p. 241). Concerning the word 'complex', he also added: 'None of the people surveyed was able to say what they meant by the word "complex".' The elements of the figurative model therefore seem relatively devoid of specific meaning. For Moscovici, this very characteristic is precisely what allows them to be associated with many other terms and also to become symbols of the representation's object; 'devoid of any precision, the complex is a source of symbolic accuracy' (ibid., p. 244). In other words, if the figurative model elements constitute the premises of the core elements, we must admit that, in the genesis of a social representation, they gradually acquire their own meaning, allowing them later to generate the overall meaning of this social representation.

The second question paradoxically originates from research based on the challenging method (Moliner, 1988, 1994). Indeed, to explain the results achieved with this method, the symbolic value of central elements is used. The properties of the figurative model elements therefore become references. In other words, the results obtained with the challenging method can be explained without referring to the meaning generation function of the core elements.

The third question is brought up by the many results evidencing the associative capability of central elements (Guimelli, 1993; Rouquette and Rateau, 1998). These studies indeed show that it is much easier for subjects to make out verbal associations from central elements than from peripheral ones. This can only be explained by either the polysemy of central elements or their lack of meaning. In the first case, it is conceivable that they may assume a meaning generation function, but in the second one, it is unclear how they could do so.

With the proposals of Bataille (2002), this discussion has gained a unique perspective. For this author, central elements are, in fact, polysemous (think back to the example of hierarchy in the social representation of Enterprise world), and their meaning is specified by peripheral elements. This view is reminiscent of Flament's (1994, p. 85), which propounds that 'the core's operation can only be understood in terms of ongoing dialectic with the periphery'. In other words, peripheral elements, because they are concrete and contextualized, may modulate the meaning of central elements, which are abstract and symbolic. Core elements may then allow individuals to define the object of the representation in common terms, giving the illusion of consensus but likely fostering interpretations which vary with contexts and individual experiences. For example, while we all agree that 'salary' is crucial to defining the activity 'work', we may refer to vastly different realities forged in individuals' experiences when we refer to the word 'salary'. In short, according to Bataille, central elements are meaning receivers, not meaning generators.

In a series of experiments (Moliner and Martos, 2005), we effectively showed that in the social representations of Studies and of Group, peripheral elements did in fact exhibit the most stable meanings. The meaning of central elements proved variable, depending on their association with other elements. This result, which modulates the proposals of central core theory, led us to suggest the notion of *matrix core*, which we feel may provide answers to the questions above while preserving the essential tenets of the theory. Our proposal articulates three points concerning the functions of the core in social representations:

- According to us, the core's primary function is one of *denotation*, relying on the symbolic properties of central elements. The core may in fact provide verbal labels allowing individuals to summon or recognize the object of the representation without the help of lengthy speeches or in-depth analyses. The crucial point here might be that the verbal labels' indicative ability matters more than their intrinsic meaning. Central elements could in fact be signs allowing individuals to determine which opinion world they situate their discourse in. For example, if we say that someone has complexes, we indicate that we are using the repertoire (the representation) of psychoanalysis, much more so than if we only spoke of *problems*.
- The core's second function is one of *aggregation*, directly linked to the significant semantic potential of central elements. In fact, while relatively vague in terms of their own signification, these elements could allow individuals to gather, under a sole term, a variety of contextualized experiences. For example, the association 'work/salary' effectively suggests a certain type of work (denotation function), but the term 'salary' can refer to very disparate realities (money, exchange for something else, taxed or not, etc.). In other words, central elements may be language and perception categories – collective ones, for sure – designed to outline facts and direct the observation of concrete events' (Moscovici, 1976, p. 240).
- A result of the previous two functions, the core's third function is one of *federation*. Offering only vague element definitions, the core may function as a common matrix enabling the summoning of the representation's object while authorizing the cohabitation of various individual experiences. Thus, members of a given group could rely on an emotional framework which would generate consensus and integrate individual differences. Indeed, in the same manner that one need not know all the words of a language in order to use it, it is not necessary for all the members of a given group to adhere to all the core elements of a social representation. Several studies on consensus in social representations offer empirical evidence of this phenomenon (Flament, 1996, 1999). Generally, in studies on social representations, finding 100 per cent-consensus items is quite rare, even if the population surveyed is very homogeneous. On the other hand, when looking at the entire set of central elements of a social representation and examining individual responses to these items in a given population, one realizes that 100 per cent of the subjects adhere to either one or the other subset of the core. This means, therefore, that it is always possible for two individuals to agree on a common definition for the object, even if it remains minimal or if it refers to different experiences.

In summary, the *matrix core* would allow the denotation of a representation's object, the aggregation, in one whole set, of disparate experience, and the federation of group members around seemingly consensual opinions on this object. These hypotheses do not challenge central core theory. Rather, they are developments which enable us to remove the contradictions we pointed out concerning the meaning generation function of central elements. Furthermore, they shed light on the dialectics at work at the heart of social representations theory, which have to do with the relationships between beliefs, individuals and social groups.

Conclusion

Nearly forty years after its initial formulation, core theory remains a useful conceptual tool for studying the structure and dynamics of social representations. It was instrumental in the development of many original research methods which have pushed our field forward. Finally, as this chapter has shown, core theory is a living theory that has evolved and is still evolving. But one aspect of it remains poorly understood, and we discuss its prospects in our conclusion. Indeed, in the late 1990s many studies began to focus on the relationship between social representations and sociocognitive processes (for an overview, see Rateau *et al.*, 2011). This development has led to a major challenge for the theory of social representations, as it attempts to identify the layered connections between social representations and processes of social cognition (categorization, stereotyping, social comparison, attribution, etc.). As it happens, much of this research was performed within the framework of core theory – probably because it allows for an experimental approach to social representations, which is not the least of its qualities.

7 Attitudes, social representations and points of view

Gordon Sammut

Over the years numerous scholars have pointed to problems that are inherent to the clash of beliefs, ideas and perspectives in contemporary pluralistic societies. The scholarly efforts directed towards the clash of beliefs have aimed at understanding and identifying ways to reconcile divergences and promote cooperative relations between human beings (see Giddens, 1991; Huntington, 1996; Benhabib, 2002; Moghaddam, 2008). In social psychology, the problem of clashing beliefs struggling for recognition has been put firmly on the agenda by Moscovici (1961/1976, 1985a, 1985b, 2000). The problem, as Moscovici (1985b) articulates it, is to understand how a minority can see things as it does and how it can think as it does. In contexts of cultural diversity, intergroup relations are embedded within interpersonal relations. Individuals encounter each other as individuals, but their relations are framed by their relative group relations (Sherif and Hovland, 1961). In such circumstances, understanding how individuals relate with one another is an imperative concern. How do individuals orientate themselves in what appears to be a plurality of perspectives? Why do they adopt one perspective and not another? And in adopting a certain perspective, how do they then treat others who hold a different perspective?

The concept that social psychology has put forth in studying the manner by which individuals orientate themselves towards objects in their environment is the attitude, along with its collective counterpart – public opinion. These, however, have come to overlook the requirement to understand individual relations in a way that includes a reference to the social framework which validates some perspective over others in a given public sphere (Gaskell, 2001). As Asch (1952/1987) succinctly claims, 'to act in the social field requires a knowledge of social facts' (p. 139). Individuals participate in public life and orientate themselves to others and to objects in their environment by adopting mutually meaningful outlooks towards social objects and events that others recognize as legitimate and sensible. Neither attitude nor public opinion include such a reference to social knowledge.

An alternative way for understanding such individual orientations was proposed by Asch (1952/1987) in the notion of the *point of view*. This chapter reconciles this notion with the theory of social representations to propose a nested model of social behaviour that includes reference to societal dynamics, situational circumstances of orienting oneself amidst a plurality of views, as well as sociocognitive

This chapter draws on material presented in a doctoral thesis by the author. See Sammut (2010).

inclinations that individuals demonstrate in social relations. In this conception, the ingredients for a 'synthetic approach' (Moscovici, 1963) come together, including a focus on 'the organization of mind', which Moscovici (1963) highlights as the last necessary concern for an integrated social psychological science. As this chapter demonstrates, the inclusion of this focus in the study of social behaviour enables the discipline to address the concern of clashing views, as noted above, and understand the degrees to which alternative perspectives are afforded a legitimate place in social dialogue or dismissed without a hearing.

Attitudes

The pervasiveness of the 'attitude' concept in social psychology and the social sciences at large has been extensively documented (Moscovici, 1963; McGuire, 1985, 1986; Zaller and Feldman, 1992; Farr, 1996; Gaskell, 2001; Howarth, 2006a). The study of attitudes spans the historical development of the discipline (McGuire, 1986). Moscovici (1963) observes that for a long time social psychology was considered to be the science of attitudes. In spite of its popularity, however, the conceptual meaning of attitude has a chequered history. Attitude has gone from being a social concept in its origin, to becoming an individual, asocial and apolitical concept at present (Howarth, 2006a). The general influence of individualism on the social sciences (Graumann, 1986), and the influence of cognitivism on social psychology in particular (Farr, 1996), have redefined attitudes as an individual's evaluation of an attitude object (see Fishbein, 1967). A contemporary definition of attitudes, and the one that this chapter adopts, is that the concept represents evaluations individuals hold towards elements (i.e. attitude objects) in their environment (Aronson, Wilson and Akert, 2005). The purpose this serves in the social sciences is that of an independent variable that can be measured efficiently and concisely towards predicting behaviour. As an empirical concept, its popularity is largely unparalleled.

Attitudes are held to be cognitively based if they are based on information and facts, affectively based if they are emotive and value-laden, and behaviourally based if they stem from people's observations of behaviour towards an attitude object. Moreover, people's attitudes can be explicit if consciously endorsed, or implicit if held unconsciously (Aronson, Wilson and Akert, 2005). This conception of attitudes gives rise to various problematic issues concerning their nature and the circumstances that condition their activation. Attitudes are conceived as inherent dispositions (Tesser, 1993). In this way, they are reified as continuing states that mark an individual's stable sense of self over time (i.e. personality-based). On the other hand, attitudes are held to be malleable in the face of changing circumstances as well as social influence (Sammut and Bauer, 2011). As such, they are conceived as context dependent and to reflect only an individual's orientation towards an attitude object at a particular point in time.

Naturally, these conceptions of attitudes have attracted much critique over the years (see Asch, 1952/1987; Sherif, Sherif, and Nebergall, 1965; Farr, 1990; Billig,

1991; Gaskell, 2001; Howarth, 2006a), and various scholars have sought to address the attitude's primary shortcoming of overlooking the 'social' in its conceptualization. As some scholars have pointed out (Farr, 1990, 1996; Fraser and Gaskell, 1990; Fraser, 1994; Gaskell, 2001), the theory of social representations has come to serve as a countervailing force to individualistic theories like 'attitude', by foregrounding the social rather than the individual (Gaskell, 2001). However, most theorists retain the fact that the two concepts are incommensurable due to their differing underlying epistemologies (Farr, 1994; Howarth, 2006a). While attitude is clearly a cognitive attribute of the individual even in its aggregate form – namely, public opinion – social representations are held to be intrinsically social. They are conceptualized as existing across minds rather than inside individual minds (Wagner *et al.*, 1999; Wagner and Hayes, 2005; Wagner, Mecha and do Rosário Carvalho, 2008). According to this conception, the individual extends into the social as a relational unit in a *systemic* network of social meaning. In this tradition, rather than being two sides of the same coin, the individual–social dichotomy is a false dichotomy to begin with, as the individual is ontologically part of the social firmament.

Theoretical usage of concepts, however, cannot escape reification and for this reason problems persist in reconciling the dual focus of the social and the individual contemporarily. Gaskell (2001) has outlined this as the challenge that can reinvigorate the discipline. Traditionally, researchers either study the social field as a collective by looking at things such as social representations and discourses, but failing to locate the individual within these wider polemics. Alternatively, they study individual orientations, possibly even in aggregate, but fail to account for the wider social meaning that legitimates individuals' evaluations (see Harré, 1984). The gap between the two remains a ubiquitous challenge.

Overlooking the processes of social legitimation served by systems of knowledge handicaps an adequate explanation of social behaviour. This handicap is characteristic of attitude scaling and has long been identified in this tradition, as Thurstone (1967a) notes:

> It is quite conceivable that two men may have the same degree or intensity of affect favourable toward a psychological object and that their attitudes would be described in this sense as identical but that they have arrived at their similar attitudes by entirely different routes. It is even possible that their factual associations about the psychological object might be entirely different and that their overt actions would take quite different forms which have one thing in common, namely, that they are about equally favourable toward the object. (p. 21)

Thurstone goes on to provide the example of an atheist and a pious believer both expressing similar attitudes to a statement such as 'Going to church will not do anyone any harm.' According to Likert (1967), whose simple attitude scale has, according to Allport (1967), enabled the discipline to better measure than define attitudes, and whose widespread use across the social sciences is perpetuous, this state of conceptualization is unsatisfactory since the measure should be in such way that 'persons with different points of view, so far as the particular attitude is concerned, will respond to it differentially' (p. 90). For this reason, Likert (1967) claims that attitude scales, like intelligence tests, should be standardized for cultural groups, and one devised for one group should not be applicable for another. Likert's suggestions have, however, gone largely unheeded in the measurement of public opinion.

The divide between the 'social' and the 'individual' is ontological as much as it is epistemological and involves different levels of explanation (Wagner and Hayes, 2005). The social pertains to the collective life of human beings and applies to processes that take shape at this collective level, such as ideologies and discourse. The individual pertains to the human being as a single specimen and applies to processes that take place at this level, such as cognition and perception. The gap between the two is well explicated by Harré (1984) in his distinction of aggregates from collectives. While aggregates bring together individual specimens, collectives exist independently of individual cognition. Social behaviour, however, retains elements of both. Insofar as it involves an element of positioning relative to other, equally agentic beings, then such behaviour can be deemed social. And insofar as such interpersonal relations involve an element of perception and interpretation, then such behaviour can be deemed personal and cognitive. Alternatively, one could characterize this demarcation as between the intrapersonal and the interpersonal spheres of psychological activity (Kruglanski, 1989).

This characteristic dichotomy of social behaviour has confounded explanations on either side. Attitude thus serves to understand an individual's inclination towards some social object on the basis of characteristics of that individual, including affect, behavioural tendencies, cognition and external influences. Put simply, an attitude represents an individual's sum total evaluation of an attitude object (Aronson, Wilson and Akert, 2005). It does not, however, provide an explanation for why individuals resort to certain courses of action given a certain stimulus. For instance, two individuals may be equally appalled by some event, but their individual responses may vary as a function of the different cultural conditions in which they are embedded. Social representations, on the other hand, describe context-rational behaviour that is deemed reasonable in certain circumstances. They describe how for a certain social group, a particular course of action is reasonable given certain conditions. Social representations do not, however, explain why such context-rational behaviour may be adopted by some individuals but not by similar others facing the same circumstances. Not all individuals react in the same way to similar events, even within the same cultural context. In other words, neither attitudes nor social representations are useful for a situational explanation of social behaviour, that is, for an explanation of why a certain individual acts in a certain way at a certain point in time to a certain stimulus.

Our everyday understanding of relating individuals serves as a useful guide in gaining some further understanding. In everyday language we use attitude to mean opinion (how one thinks) or orientation (one's mental posture). What we commonly mean by an attitude is one's mental outlook, rather than the narrower meaning of a cognitive evaluation of an attitude object that reflects that mental outlook. Furthermore, etymologically, what we often want to capture in accounting for social behaviour is not common sense either (i.e. a social representation), but a *perspective*[1] that is rooted in common sense. This chapter proposes the point of view as an intervening concept that can bridge the gap between the intrapersonal and the interpersonal, that is, the individual–social spheres of psychological activity. This, as detailed hereunder, provides a transitive explanation of the social as the context in which a particular perspective is located, which perspective is itself sociocognitive, and which relates to other perspectives on the basis of its own inherent cognitive and affective structure – attitude being one such component.

The fact of culture and the social attitude

The aim to counterbalance the individualization of 'attitude' in social psychology is not exclusive to European forms of social psychology. Even before the advent of societal forms of social psychology (Himmelweit and Gaskell, 1990) such as social representations theory (Moscovici, 1961/1976), social constructionism (Berger and Luckmann, 1966) and discourse analysis (Potter and Wetherell, 1987), Asch (1952/1987) took issue with 'attitude' as a purely individualistic construct and

---

[1] 'Perspective' is etymologically similar to 'point of view', denoting a view of something that is acquired by virtue of looking at it. As such, this represents a phenomenal view, one that is perceived (or experienced). Having a point of view denotes that a subject stands in relation with an object such that the object can be perceived by the subject phenomenally. Having a point of view enables the subject to develop a perspective on the object. In psychological terms, the two concepts can largely be used synonymously, as both terms represent an individual's perception of an object that accrues by virtue of their point of view relative to the object. Yet, given their current usage in psychology, we prefer the term 'point of view' to 'perspective' for the present purposes, due to the fact that perspectives can be construed in purely individualistic and cognitive terms. Inasmuch as a perspective refers to an individual's phenomenal perception of an event or object, it constitutes the specific image of what the individual 'sees' (i.e. perceives) of the object. The reference to point of view adds two elements to this conception that are somewhat given in routine interaction, that is, it establishes the individual's perspective as (a) relational and (b) relative. Inasmuch as a perspective is a property of a person, i.e. an image of an object that is somebody's own perception of it, then it represents a cognition (perspective) in social terms by linking the person perceiving with the object perceived. It marks an individual's *view* of *something*. Additionally, the point of view establishes that perspectival view as one point amongst others, one that is relative to the perceiving subject. By implication, other subjects will hold different views inasmuch as they occupy different points relative to the object. They orient themselves to the same object from some other *point*. Furthermore, in the course of communication subjects can articulate their perspective to the object with reference to other points of view that reveal features of the object which do not transpire in their own perspective. This marks the interpenetration of views. As an example, we do not all have to get injured after crashing a motorbike at high speed before we develop a perspective of motorbikes as dangerous when ridden at high speed. The implications of the term 'point of view' thus refer explicitly to these sociocognitive processes. These enable human subjects to position themselves in relation to objects in their surroundings on the basis of their own perspectives and experiences as well as those of others that lie outside their own perceptive and experiential realm, but that stand in systemic relations with their own.

drawing on Sumner's notion of *mores*,[2] went on to postulate the notion of point of view to develop a social psychology that in understanding the complexity of social behaviour, accounts for the social as much as it does the individual.

In line with more recent scholars such as Farr (1991) and Billig (1987, 1991), according to Asch, measuring attitudes does not provide any insight into societal processes, factors or conditions. For Asch, material and social conditions are far more than objects of reflection. They bear significant consequences on how individuals relate with the world they inhabit: 'the surroundings do not look quite the same to one who believes in reincarnation and to one who has studied the principles of genetics' (Asch, 1952/1987, p. 365). This has clear implications for how we conceptualize individuals, for, as Asch explains: '[h]ead-hunting, polygamy, Mohammedanism are not simply traits of individuals like height or colour vision. They are properties of individuals in so far as the individuals are members of a given society' (ibid., p. 16). Asch goes on to give another example of how social behaviour is rooted in social facts having historical direction:

> It is not enough to say that some societies observe rules of cleanliness and others do not. It would be more consequential to ask whether one can as readily teach one group to adopt the habits of cleanliness as another to surrender them; whether one can as readily convert an American community to curing illness by sorcery as persuade a primitive group to adopt modern medical practices. (ibid., p. 382)

One notes that in this early conception, attitudes are not regarded as inherent and stable dispositions marking some individual's personality. Rather, they are conceived as context-dependent variables that accrue in social circumstances. Attitudes, Asch argues, join central processes in the individual with central processes in society. They orient individuals by ordering the data of social surroundings, and their function 'is to be found in the effects it exerts upon current experiences and the appraisal of new conditions. Generally an attitude functions as an orientation to and context for current events' (ibid., p. 582). Attitudes do this on the basis of social knowledge that orders meaning in the world:

> Only if the knowledge exists that there are germs and viruses that produce disease will it be meaningful to have an attitude about the right of the state to compel children to be vaccinated against smallpox regardless of the wishes of their parents. If, instead, the available data contain such entities as spirits and the belief that they produce illness, medical problems will be solved by medicine men and there will be different attitudes towards vaccination and hygiene. In order that the burning of witches make sense it is necessary to have as part of the intellectual climate the propositions that there are devils and that persons can be in league with them. In each of these instances a particular factual definition of the given situation is the necessary condition for conviction and action. (ibid., p. 564)

It is worth again bearing in mind that Asch's conception of attitudes differs from its predominant conceptualization as an evaluation of an attitude object today. On

---

2 Mores are the customs and habitual practices of a community that reflect moral standards that a community accepts and follows.

the one hand, as in Asch's works, attitudes transpire as a discursive display of social circumstances. Its contemporary usage, on the other hand, marks the attitude as a stable attribute of an individual regardless of social circumstances. The social, in this latter conception, does not feature as a discursive condition of the production of attitudes, but as an extrinsic variable of influence (i.e. social norms), among other variables of influence, on the intrinsic disposition individuals hold towards elements in the environment. The social constitutes normative standards that influence an individual's evaluation of something on the basis of what others seem to also be doing. For Asch, however, attitudes are social due to the fact that they 'arise in view of and in response to perceived conditions of mutual dependence' (ibid., p. 576). They form part of what Asch describes as 'the mutually shared field' (ibid., p. 577), that is, a phenomenal field that for subjects in relation constitutes reality.

Asch argues that humans experience their surroundings in an experientially objective manner. Individuals do not experience their perceptions of the world as cognitive products of their internal physiological processes, they experience objects in terms of properties attributed to objects themselves. In this way, the biological basis of human cognition orients human subjects to a phenomenal inter-objectivity (Latour, 1996; Sammut, Daanen and Sartawi, 2010; Sammut, Daanen and Moghaddam, 2013). The presence of others affects human subjects by bringing within their psychological sphere the thoughts, emotions and purposes of others, bringing them into relations of mutual dependence. It is not simply that individual action is mutually oriented and elicits in another a similarly oriented response. Mutuality is a systemic condition that refers to an *interpenetration of views* that forms the basis of social interaction. It is not the awareness of others' evaluations of an attitude object that influences one's attitude on the basis of normative influence (Sammut and Bauer, 2011). Rather, it is that others' orientations towards a social object, alongside one's own, define the object systemically for a particular social group. As Asch explains, humans do not live in their own space, in their own time, and in their own systems of cause and effect. They live in a shared space, in shared time, and in shared systems of causality. When humans interrelate, they do so on the basis of this inter-objective, open field that surrounds them and which stands in similar relation to all of them. One necessary requirement for studying attitudes, therefore, is that human actions and experiences, being in relations of interdependence, be studied systemically, in terms of the units of which they form part.

In outlining his theory of social attitudes, Asch then goes on to call for a specification of the individual's frame of reference, which is concerned with the centre of gravity of a person's outlook, how wide or narrow it might be, whether it is oriented to a future project or a present situation, and what the place of the individual's assertions might be in the context of his outlook (Asch, 1952/1987, p. 559). This does not equate with the contemporary conceptualization of attitudes however, despite the fact that in its contemporary usage attitude bears the overtones of individual disposition. The contemporary definition of attitude lacks a concern with the social, as detailed above. On the other hand, neither do social representations include a specification of an individual's personal outlook. Asch's proposal for addressing these issues is the 'point of view', which constitutes an individual's perspective towards a social object or event, oriented towards others' perspectives, in terms of which individuals act meaningfully in their everyday social relations. It is by means of this operation that alignments and oppositions arise in the social order.

Points of view, according to Asch, allow individuals to engage in psychological processes of far-reaching importance. They enable individuals to engage in social checks to verify the nature of their surroundings. They also enable individuals to participate in a mutually shared psychological field, where the actions and orientations of others have a bearing on their own. In a systemic and relational context, each subject's point of view is mutually intelligible. A subject is able to adopt a perspective and interrelate with others on the basis of it, because others can comprehend one's point of view even if they can disagree with it. As Asch argues, social action requires a unique organization between participants who stand on common ground, oriented towards one another and to the same environment, and that their acts *interpenetrate* and regulate each other.

On the basis of social interaction we are able to derive the reasonable grounds for divergences, based on differences in perspectives. We realize that certain points of view and certain experiences are our own, but we do not maintain that we are in singular relation with the environment. We turn to the thoughts of others for confirmation of our relations, because we understand that they can illuminate us with some perspective that is inaccessible from our point of view. Social relations are enabled by means of the critical capacity of human subjects to take the perspective of the other. As Asch argues, I am able to understand my own action as it appears to another, and to view the action of another as if it were my own. Furthermore, divergences in perspectives are considered as more than brute differences. We are able to understand that one perspective may be capable of correcting another distorted view by appeal to a deeper-lying unity of shared action, feeling and thought.

To sum up Asch's postulation, the mutual relations in which human subjects engage extend and deepen their individual psychological field and form a systemic, psychosocial, phenomenal field that enables the interpenetration of views. In a clash between divergent views, individuals are induced to take a stand and view their actions as others view them, and conversely to view the actions of others as their own. In this way, limitations of individual thinking are transcended by inclusion of the thoughts of others. Individuals become open to more alternatives than their own unaided individual cognition makes possible. This knowledge, that our understanding can be in disagreement with that of others, is of high significance. It makes evident to us the possibility of error as an intellectual fact, and prepares the way for entertaining errors in our own view. In consequence, individuals become able to deliberately approve one view and dismiss another on the basis of a process of social validation, by appeal to a common frame of reference that serves to provide 'logical' proof for one's own thinking.

Social representations

Since Moscovici's (1961/1976) pioneering study on the social representations of psychoanalysis in France, the study of social representations has proceeded along a number of lines. This has been permitted as a result of an eclectic definition of social representations. Social representations have been variously described as a concept, a conceptual framework, a theory and an approach (Allansdottir, Jovchelovitch and Stathopoulou, 1993; Bauer and Gaskell, 1999; Carugati, Selleri and Scappini, 1994; De Rosa, 1993). Moreover, a further distinction is applicable to the term 'social representation'. Used as a verb, 'social representation' refers to a *process* of representing 'socially', while as a noun, it refers to some *product*, a representation, whose content it is possible to study (Chryssides *et al.*, 2009).

Social representations are the outcomes of processes of communication that represent reality for a given people, and once in existence they constitute social reality *sui generis* (Moscovici, 2000). Social representations as phenomena pertain to 'a world that, although belonging to each of us, transcends all of us. They are a "potential space" of common fabrication, where each person goes beyond the realm of individuality to enter another-yet fundamentally related-realm: the realm of public life' (Jovchelovitch, 1995, p. 94). Moreover, 'More than consensual beliefs, social representations are therefore organizing principles varied in nature, which do not necessarily consist of shared beliefs, as they may result in different or even opposed positions taken by individuals in relation to common reference points' (Doise, Clémence and Lorenzi-Cioldi, 1993, p. 4).

In public life, each individual is uniquely positioned in relation to others in the process of social representation, on the basis of the point of view that they adopt. While individuals within a social group share a holomorphic frame of reference, they will not hold the same positioning within the social representation (Clémence, 2001; Doise, 2001; Wagner and Hayes, 2005). Clémence defines social positioning as 'the process by which people take up position about a network of significations' (2001, p. 83). This is corollary to Asch's notion of adopting a point of view. Divergent positions are expressed by individuals who attempt to define the phenomenon from their points of view, as Sartre (1943/2003) has pointed out, using a framework of normative rules based on ideas, values and beliefs characteristic of their group for the elaboration of meaning. The frame of reference must be shared by individuals if they are to interrelate at all. While positioning may be idiosyncratic (an individual's point of view may be unique), it cannot be idiomorphic, as others would be unable to relate meaningfully to the frame of reference that legitimizes the actor's point of view (Wagner and Hayes, 2005). Diversity within the social field means that individuals position themselves differently, engaging with the phenomenon from a particular point of view relative to other agents, who are similarly engaged in the process of social representation (Clémence, 2001; Liu and László, 2007). Social positioning in terms of adopting a point of view in social relations is not only the expression of an opinion (Thurstone, 1967a), it is a way of processing information to align our thinking with what society thinks (Clémence, 2001).

This account of social representations is consequential for the theory of social representations. It serves to demarcate social representations as systemic and collective phenomena (Harré, 1984), settling the issue of how social representations differ from individual representations. In social interaction, individuals stand in relation with others and objects in their environment, that is, they position themselves relative to elements in their environment. By virtue of the positions they adopt, they come to occupy a point in social space and time that grants them a particular view, or perspective, of the object. In doing so, they bring to bear their own idiosyncratic inclinations towards the object (i.e. beliefs, cognitions, attitudes, individual representations) and fashion their perception and interpretation of it. Together, these serve to articulate their points of view, on the basis of which they interrelate with others who hold similar or different points of view. In this clash of beliefs, some alternatives they incorporate into their own perspectives through an interpenetration of views, and some others they reject.

The totality of the various discursive points of view that provide different objectifications of the element in question, in Sartre's terms revealing different aspects of the phenomenon, emerges as a systemic product in its own right, that is, a social representation. It is in this way that social representations exist across rather than inside individual minds. They include the conglomeration of diverse points of view that define the object in multifarious ways for a certain public at some particular point in time. This systemic characteristic of social representations provides the conditions for cognitive polyphasia (Arthi, Provencher and Wagner, 2012) – the plural, and at times contradictory, composite of coexisting objectifications in the same public.

The conceptualization of points of view/social representations in these mutual terms thus overcomes the Cartesian individual–social dichotomy (Marková, 1982) as well as resolves the challenge of retaining this dualistic focus contemporarily (Gaskell, 2001). In these terms, the point of view provides an explicit focus on an individual's frame of reference as embedded in a network of social relations. As detailed hereunder, this conception presents a model of social behaviour as drawing on intrapersonal dispositions like attitudes, to articulate an interpersonal explanation of social behaviour *in situ* (Sammut and Gaskell, 2012), given a systemic network of social meaning that grants that behaviour legitimacy and meaning in others' views. The social–individual dichotomy is resolved through a systemic conception of social representations, where the social is not treated as an extraneous influence but as a systemic condition of production. On the other hand, intrapersonal characteristics like attitudes are retained as cognitive features that bias one's inclination towards an event, object, or other, to formulate a point of view towards it. At this junction, the intrapersonal gains interpersonal moment and becomes participative in societal structures like social representations. Accordingly, individuals cannot be held to position themselves relative to social representations in social intercourse. In formulating and articulating a point of view, they position themselves *within* social representations, relative to others and objects in their social environments.

The point of view is thus that feature of social cognition that achieves positioning – an act that accrues by virtue of holding, articulating and defending some point of view. Were an individual to hold a different set of intrapersonal inclinations relative to the object, such as a different attitude, her point of view would change accordingly. In turn, a social representation changes inasmuch as individuals either come to occupy previously non-existent positions relative to the object, from which they articulate new points of view revealing some new aspect of the phenomenon, or if they cease to occupy certain previously legitimated positions relative to the object, they go on to make that point of view redundant. This process of changing points of view in its systemic totality marks the evolution of social representations over time (see Sammut, Tsirogianni and Wagoner, 2012).

Modelling the point of view

Social representations are social insofar as they retain a sense of the collective existing across individual minds, and they are representations insofar as they are phenomena representing reality[3] and constituting the real.[4] This conception of the social representation is found in Bauer and Gaskell's (1999) Toblerone model that postulates social representations as elaborated by a collective in an inter-objective space. This is similar to Asch's (1952/1987) conception of the shared phenomenal field. For Bauer and Gaskell, representations can be formally characterized as the relation between three elements: subjects, or carriers of the representation (S); an object that is represented, which may be a concrete entity or an abstract idea (O); and a project, or pragmatic context in which the representation is meaningful (P). Subjects, object, and project form a *system of mutual constitution*. This enables an understanding of how 'in the object, the project of the subjects is represented; or how in the subjects the object appears in relation to a project; or how the project links the subjects and object' (Bauer and Gaskell, 1999, p. 168).

Bauer and Gaskell argue that social representations, unlike mental representations that require a single individual, involve a minimal triad of two persons (subject 1 and subject 2) concerned with an object (O), constituting a triangle of mediation (S_1-O-S_2) that is the basic unit for the elaboration of meaning across time. This formulation is similar to Heider's (1946) account of the balance of reciprocity in the cognitive organization of attitudes between three entities. The links between any two entities in this formulation represent attitudes, which are balanced systemically in their reciprocal relations, or within what may be held to be a social representation. In this formulation, the angle that is the subject's perspective, oriented towards another subject's perspective and the object in question, represents an aspect of

---

3 The noumenon, or object-in-itself.
4 The phenomenon for a given community.

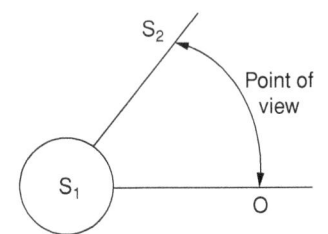

Figure 7.1 *Point of view.*

the phenomenon in Sartre's terms, that is, the subject's point of view. This point of view is constitutive of the subject's attitudes towards the object and the other (Figure 7.1).

Bauer and Gaskell argue that a final extension to their model concerns the differentiation of social groups. Over time, they argue, various triangles of mediation emerge and coexist to form a larger social system. This leads to the 'Toblerone pack' model, where O is the linking pin of different representations, their common referent being the brute fact. More recently, the authors have proposed a 'wind rose' model of social representations that denotes different representations in different communities at different points in time (Bauer and Gaskell, 2008). The surface of each triangle, which is a section through the Toblerone pack, denotes the different common senses that prevail in different social groups at the same time, while the elongation of the triangles denotes the evolution of common sense (Sammut, Tsirogianni and Wagoner, 2012) in the various groups.

The extension of the Toblerone model to a Toblerone pack model, a wind rose model or a waterwheel model (see Chapter 4 in this volume) is required to model divergent points of view pertaining to different social representations (i.e. when the object is the linking pin between two different social representations (S_1-S_2-O, O-S_3-S_4))[5] that come into contact in some public sphere. In relations between points of view based on different social representations individuals engage in processes of social re-presentation (Chryssides *et al.*, 2009) on the basis of which they seek to comprehend alien perspectives and make the unfamiliar familiar (Moscovici, 2000). Until a new social representation is forged to provide a frame of reference that enables alternative perspectives to be understood in their own legitimacy, they will be incomprehensible from any point of view embedded in another social representation. In such cases, an individual's perspective would impede one from seeing the potentiality of another perspective in its legitimacy, or, to put it another way, as a result of the way I see it, I cannot see how it can be seen differently. In the event of an encounter with an alternative perspective that draws on a different

---

5 Angles of view in different triangles, such as S_1 and S_3, not only characterize divergent perspectives, but also represent perspectives which draw on different meanings of the same object. In this case, the object is not the same to the two subjects in question; it is a wholly different phenomenon for the two groups S_1-S_2 and S_3-S_4.

rationality, the alternative point of view may appear abhorrent or bizarre (Asch, 1952/1987; Giddens, 1991; Benhabib, 2002).

A nested model of social behaviour

So what are the consequences of conceptualizing points of view and social representations in this manner? Asch suggests that it is necessary to describe their main lines of organization and their degree of structurization; insofar as attitudes are part of wider systems, they cannot be understood in their own terms alone. It is also necessary, according to Asch, to understand the directions of individuals' outlooks, and the cleavages that may exist between different outlooks. In this way we can understand an attitude's place and function in the general scheme of social behaviour, how it takes shape and changes in a medium of already functioning views, and how a change in part leads to a change in whole.

The cause of behaviour, as Moscovici (1984) argues, lies with the individual's interpretation of things in a particular situation, in which individual perception is mediated by a social representation that describes how things are and prescribes what behaviours ought to follow. Whether the individual follows through, or otherwise, is a function of the individual as well as extraneous influences in his or her environment. The two come together in an individual's point of view: his or her actual perception of the event in a given situation and given the individual's own inclinations (i.e. attitudes) and environmental factors. Behaviour follows by virtue of the point of view, in response to certain conditions or events that occur to the individual. Causality, as outlined in Moscovici's model, is still located in the interplay between a stimulus and a response, but resides at the situational level of explanation.

At this point we are therefore in a position to outline a nested model of social behaviour that includes attitudes, points of view and social representations (Figure 7.2). The model is nested due to the fact that underlying concepts are necessarily implicated in overarching ones, that is, attitudes are necessarily implicated in points of view (in terms of the person's characteristics); and points of view are necessarily implicated in social representations (in terms of social positioning). Neither social representations theory nor attitudes on their own provide a situational explanation of social behaviour. Social representations theory provides a societal-level explanation. It describes societal prescriptions that bear on the way people interpret events and what they will hold to be legitimate courses of action. Attitudes, on the other hand, provide a personal-level explanation of social behaviour, outlining the individual's evaluation of an attitude object that bears on their inclination to act in a particular way. Whether, in a given situation, individuals do act in a given way depends on their point of view at the time and in the situation, given the conditions they find themselves in.

To illustrate, the culture of honour prevailing in certain societies provides a suitable hypothetical example. Whether two individuals to whom the same

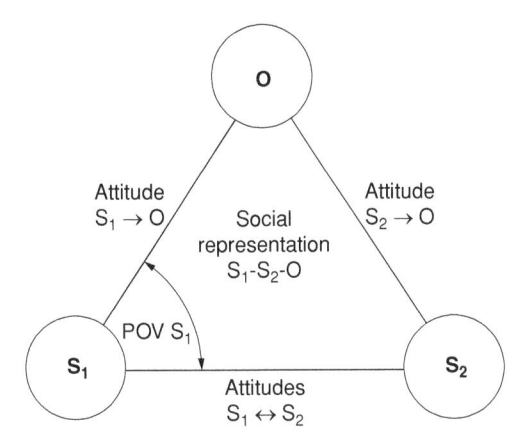

Figure 7.2 *A nested model of social behaviour: social representations, points of view, and attitudes (adapted from Bauer and Gaskell, 1999, and based on Heider's (1946) balance of reciprocity in the cognitive organization of attitudes).*

dishonourable event happens, for example a daughter falling pregnant out of wedlock, behave in the same way may be due to different attitudes they may hold towards the attitude object. For example, one might evaluate the event more harshly than another. Such would be a characteristic explanation of behaviour as a function of attitudes. Yet two individuals may hold the same evaluation of the attitude object that is dishonourable, but still act differently. They may be equally appalled by the event, and equally inclined to punish whom they regard as the perpetrator. In such a situation, therefore, the attitude variable is constant. Their actual behaviours, however, may differ due to the fact that different societal prescriptions bear on the interpretation of the event and the legitimacy of the ensuing behaviour. In one group, for instance, it might be reasonable to attack the perpetrator whereas in another it may only be reasonable to request maintenance payments. Such would be a characteristic social representations explanation. However, behaviour differs even more widely than this. Two individuals, with similar attitudes and in the same social setting, may nevertheless opt to do very different things when faced with the same event. One might opt to save face and lose the offspring, whereas another may opt to lose face and save the offspring. This is because while the experience of the event may be similar to both, the way the two *see* the event may differ. One might adopt a certain point of view in relation to the event and the community, whereas another might take a different standpoint. If we are to truly understand social behaviour, then aside from knowing what social representations prescribe and what evaluations people may hold, we also need situational-level explanations that account for the individual's situational reality given certain events.

The present characterization of 'point of view' provides this missing link. At each level, however, one needs to pay due consideration to characteristics particular to that level as well as adopt an epistemology suitable to that same level. The manner by which we can come to understand attitudes may be different from the manner by which we can come to understand points of view, which might be different in turn from the manner by which we can come to understand social representations. The analogy with water is apt in this case. Water may be understood at the molecular level: H_2O. That understanding however is different from the way we understand masses of water, such as seas and oceans. Neither understanding however is adequate for an explanation of tides and currents. While the latter are implicated in the existence of oceans, and while physically the molecular structure is none other than H_2O, at each level a different understanding of water is required despite the fact that the phenomenon in its materiality remains the same.

Conclusion

The assimilation of Asch's conception of social attitudes within the social psychology of attitudes as it stands today is largely impossible due to the individualization and cognitivization of the concept (see Farr, 1996; Graumann, 1986). This stems largely from discrepant epistemological assumptions between the two. Yet, Asch's approach and the social representations paradigm share an underlying epistemological base, and their assumptions derive largely from common roots (Marková, 1982; Farr, 1996). Reconciling the two, as proposed above, in a formulation of points of view based on social representations, presents social psychology with new challenges and requires of it new explanations, such as: How can we come to understand individuals' outlooks towards the social phenomena they face? Why do different individuals adopt different points of view when they orientate themselves towards the same social phenomenon? How is it that certain different points of view may appear sensible while others may appear nonsensical? What happens in encounters between divergent points of view, when these draw on the same worldview? What happens when they do not? And conversely, what happens in encounters between similar points of view when these draw on similar world views? And what happens when they do not? These questions present themselves as new and worthy challenges for the social representations programme on the one hand, and for social cognition on the other hand, as well as for the discipline of social psychology in general. The linchpin between the two is the point of view concept, which provides a specification for the location of the individual *within* a social representation.

Points of view draw on systems of knowledge that are legitimated in public spheres, which public spheres may themselves be marked by a multiplicity of knowledge systems that coexist within them. In this state of affairs, typical of cosmopolitan publics, encounters between different points of view may represent more fundamental encounters between distinct world views. Interpersonal relations in these publics instantiate intercultural relations. On the other hand, points of view may draw on systems of knowledge that are not legitimated in a given public sphere. Such alien points of view present a twofold empirical concern: (1) the requirement to study the alien point of view from the outside, as it seeks to negotiate its version in the context of a discrepant system of social representations; (2) the requirement to study the reception and encounter with the alien point of view from the inside, as it is received by individuals for whom this version is out of the ordinary. Clearly, understanding social behaviour on these bases requires a deeper appreciation than mere evaluative judgements, as not only dispositions but also perceptions and common sense bear distinctly on social behaviour.

This chapter has introduced a conceptualization of the point of view concept. The overarching contribution of this, to the social sciences in general and the discipline of social psychology in particular, is the formulation of a concept that effectively bridges the gap between the social and the psychological. It does this by retaining a dual focus on overarching social structures and underlying psychological processes that is achieved in a nested model of social behaviour. Such a concept enables researchers to gain a fuller understanding of the individual in terms of the individual's social-psychological characteristics, and of human relations in their social-psychological complexity. Formulated at the situational level, the point of view is able to provide an explanation of social behaviour as it takes place *in situ* (Sammut and Gaskell, 2012). Empirically, if one wants to understand some particular aspect of social reality, then the model outlined helps in recognizing what to look for as well as outline where (i.e. at which level) to look for it.

In the course of research, the discovery of certain points of view might warrant detailed investigation into their characteristics. This clearly overlaps with a social representations study, but such extended inquiry aims to understand how some individuals or groups are positioning themselves in some particular way, given a particular social representation and given particular other points of view (i.e. contrasting ones) that exist towards the object. This is the study of points of view at the situational level that looks at orientations, the justifications provided for them, and the cognitive characteristics that typify them. A full understanding at this level requires an understanding of the argumentative structure that legitimates that position as well as an appreciation of the relational aspects of relating to someone else's position, both manifestly in social relations and introspectively in social cognition. At this level, the distinction between different types of points of view is a useful one (see Sammut and Gaskell, 2010). This in itself can be discerned from accounts or assessed through self-categorization (Sammut, 2012, 2013). The study of the points of view of some regarding some object, as they relate with others, aims at understanding (1) how the object exists for the subjects being studied, (2) who is the other in relation to whom the subject/s position themselves in social affairs, (3) the argumentative content of a point of view, and (4) its sociocognitive structure. Together, these fulfil Moscovici's (1963) call for studying closed-mindedness and investigating the organization of mind in achieving an integrated social psychological science.

A concrete example illustrates this point more fully. Moscovici's own *La Psychanalyse, son image et son public* (first published in 1961) can be held as an example in mapping the social representation of psychoanalysis in France at the time from the liberal, the Catholic and the communist points of view. Another of the few empirical works to claim an explicit enquiry into points of view is Moghaddam's 2006 work: *From the Terrorists' Point of View: what they experience and why they come to destroy*. This book illustrates the fact that a given social representation in a given public does not prescribe any specific behaviour, but legitimates certain action sequences (Wagner, 1993). Given a certain stimulus, some are compelled to take up arms and sacrifice themselves to the cause while others are not. A social representations inquiry would investigate the sense-making of matters such as war, foreign policy, the West, Islam, and so on, in a given public. One finding of such an inquiry might be the plausibility of martyrdom or suicide bombing. This, however, in and of itself provides no information as to the reasons why certain people resort to such behaviours amidst a myriad of alternative and equally plausible positions that they are able to take within the same social representation. Why do some individuals advocate diplomacy whereas others advocate armed conflict, given the same struggle? For instance, the divergent perspectives between Hamas and Fatah in the Palestinian struggle against Israel at present bear testimony to this. What changes between the two factions is not the struggle itself, nor the representations of the other, but the point of view on how the issue may or may not be resolved.

The point here is that what might be changing across these identified groups is not a representation of the object per se, but a preference for particular relations with that object. These preferences are justified by reasons; justifications are reasonable given the social representation. The study of points of view inquires into these reasons and answers the question of *what* points of view people are taking towards the object given the social representation, and *why*.

8 Communication and the microgenetic construction of knowledge

Charis Psaltis

> I've always said that social psychology was responsible for the study of communication and ideological phenomena and I think that when studying representations, we are actually studying communication.
>
> Serge Moscovici, 1995

Moscovici's words in the epigraph to this chapter suggest that the study of social representations involves the study of communication, and this is in itself one of the main aims of social psychology. This chapter focusses on a discussion of the microgenetic construction of knowledge, which will hopefully clarify the role of communication in social representations processes and will provide an exploration of the dynamics of social representations – a rather overlooked topic in social representations theory. I will start with a short genealogy of the notion of microgenesis in social developmental psychology and will then focus on how microgenesis has been conceptualized by Duveen and Lloyd (1990) in the context of a *genetic social psychology*. A specific line of research on the microgenesis of knowledge from this theoretical perspective is then presented (Duveen and Psaltis, 2008; Leman and Duveen, 1999, Psaltis and Duveen, 2006, 2007; Psaltis, Duveen and Perret-Clermont, 2009), and the implications of the findings are discussed for the theoretical notion of cognitive polyphasia and an understanding of culture and heterogeneity from a social representations perspective.

Microgenesis: the genealogy of a powerful idea

The origins of the idea of microgenesis can be traced back to the 1920s and the work on *Aktualgenese* by Sander, Krueger and Werner (Catán, 1986; Valsiner and Van Der Veer, 2000; Wagoner, 2009b). They studied the evolution of percepts over time through the operation of lawfully organized mental activity. Werner was actually the first to use the term 'microgenesis' in the English language, in 1956. For Werner, it referred to 'any human activity such as perceiving, thinking, acting, etc. as an *unfolding process*, and this unfolding or "microgenesis", whether it takes seconds or hours or days, occurs in developmental sequence' (Werner, 1956, p. 347). Vygotsky was clearly influenced by Werner's work in the

1920s. He argued for the creation of a new methodology, or general psychology, that was sufficiently developed to deal with the phenomena studied. In his case, the method is simultaneously prerequisite and product, the tool and the result of the study (Vygotsky, 1978, p. 65), so that theory and method become intertwined.

It was argued that what both Werner and Vygotsky, as well Vygotsky's student Luria, had in common was the use of the microgenetic method and experimentation as an imaginative means for constructing small-scale, living models of large-scale developmental processes (Catán, 1986, p. 258). A further historical development of the notion of microgenesis in the context of the United States after the 1950s imbued it with 'non-developmental explanatory systems' (Valsiner and Van Der Veer, 2000, p. 312) that represented a more general trend in psychology of losing interest in the study of psychological processes and treating the outcomes of these processes as if they themselves constituted explanations. For example, Flavell and Draguns (1957), who reviewed the previous work on *Aktualgenese*, proposed a rather simplistic and impoverished sense of microgenesis that lacked the conceptual tools for grasping construction, tension, novelty and the idea of holistic reorganization of the forms in its process. Piagetian theory underwent a similar impoverished and non-developmental translation by Flavell (Valsiner and Van Der Veer, 2000) with its introduction in the United States.

Microgenesis has been studied more recently in the United States by Siegler (1995; Siegler and Crowley, 1991). In this work the non-developmental question of locating *when* particular cognitive strategies emerge is still detectable, but there is an interesting change towards an understanding of the interdependence between the social and cognitive experiences in training sessions. This illuminates the sociogenetic nature of experimentation among children, as was the case with Vygotsky's method of *double stimulation*. Furthermore, it broadens the focus of the study of change by exploring the path, rate, breadth, variability and sources of change. A precursor of this work could be found in the Piagetian microgenetic work of Inhelder and colleagues (1974) in Geneva, where they focussed on an exploration of the functional conditions of the construction of cognitive structures and their integration. By using children who would use 'primitive' (e.g. non-conserving) responses, they were able to observe acquisition processes at work and the different transitions and dynamics of progress (Catán, 1986).

In parallel with Inhelder and his work in Geneva, a group of social developmental psychologists started exploring microgenetic issues in the context of experimental time spanning a single interactive episode and expanding to subsequent immediate and delayed post-tests. This research programme was initiated by Willem Doise and his colleagues Gabriel Mugny and Anne-Nelly Perret-Clermont (Doise, Mugny and Perret-Clermont, 1975; Doise and Mugny, 1984; Perret-Clermont, 1980), and made use of Piaget's classic experimental investigations as problems for pairs of children. The research was able to focus on the consequences of social interaction for children's cognitive development (Duveen and Psaltis, 2008; Psaltis and Zapiti, 2014; Psaltis, 2005b).

In their designs, Doise and his colleagues tried to integrate experimental rigour, offering analyses at the aggregate level while at the same time introducing microgenetic concerns (cf. Wagoner, 2009a). They took a clear sociogenetic, social constructivist stance, claiming that social interaction leads to cognitive development. To explain their findings they introduced the notion of *sociocognitive conflict* as the crucial mechanism for cognitive development, that is, the conflict of perspectives in social interaction. They argued that sociocognitive conflict could be resolved either in an epistemic/constructivist way or in a relational way that amounted to compliance, a superficial form of change that did not amount to true change since it did not entail cognitive reconstruction (Doise, Mugny and Pérez, 1998). But again, this distinction, while theoretically important, was really a post hoc interpretation that did not result from direct observation of interaction or meaning-making processes (Duveen and Psaltis, 2008). Still, on the whole this work was important not only because of its concern with microgenetic issues in the context of communication, but also because of the links it made with Moscovici's (1976) model of social influence, taking as it did a clear sociogenetic and social constructivist view of development premised on the triadic subject-object-other epistemological framework (Zittoun et al., 2007), which could be expanded to the study of the microgenesis of social representations (Duveen, 2002).

In fact when the word 'microgenesis' was first invoked in the context of social representations theory by Duveen and Lloyd (1990), the kind of changes studied experimentally by Doise and Mugny (1984) were described as 'ontogenetic transformations in the development of social representations in individual subjects' (Duveen and Lloyd, 1990, p. 9). In this chapter I argue that what the children in Piagetian experiments are doing is reconstructing the reified universe of mathematics, physics and logic in the same way that Moscovici (1961/1976) was exploring the reconstruction of the reified scientific field of psychoanalysis in the common sense of everyday people. This resonates with the rationale used by Moscovici (1998/2000) himself when he explicated the influence of Piaget on the formation of social representations theory (see also Duveen, 2001a). As Moscovici (1998/2000, p. 208) admits:

> I read the *Child's Conception of the World* (1926/1929) a little later than I should have done as I was already nearly 30. However, after I had read it I was in a state of shock. I had a great opportunity. Thanks to that reading and to others of Piaget's writings, my thinking liberated itself from the innumerable constraining notions with respect both to the methods of research and to the significant questions that our science addressed.

The vision that Moscovici formed on the basis of that reading was of turning social psychology into an anthropology of the common sense of our modern societies using the same methods that Piaget had used with children. The main commonality between the two theorists, according to Duveen (2001a), is their concern for genesis and structure and in particular with how knowledge/representation is transformed from one structure to another.

Microgenesis in the context of social representations theory

Duveen and Lloyd (1990) argue that a genetic perspective is implied in the conception of social representations in the sense that the structure of any particular social representation is a construction and thus the outcome of some developmental process. Three types of transformation, associated with social representations as a process, are proposed. There is the process of sociogenesis, which concerns the construction and transformation of the social representations of social groups regarding specific objects; ontogenesis, which concerns the development of individuals in relation to social representations; and microgenesis, which concerns the evocation and (re)construction of social representations in social interaction (Duveen and Lloyd, 1990).

People communicate in social interaction and thus social representations are *evoked* through the social identities asserted in the activity of individuals. As Duveen (2001a) has convincingly argued, social identity from the perspective of social representations theory appears as a function of social representations. It concerns both the process of identification as well as the process of being identified, and can be construed as a point or position in the symbolic field of culture. Representations always imply a process of identity formation in which identities are internalized and which results in the emergence of social actors or agents. Finally, they provide ways of organizing meanings so as to sustain a sense of stability (Duveen, 2001a).

Thus a process of negotiation and *(re)construction* of both social representations and identities is taking place in social interaction. From the genetic point of view, microgenesis holds a privileged and central position as it is the motor for the ontogenesis and sociogenesis of social representations (Duveen and Lloyd, 1990). Microgenesis is defined as 'the genetic process in all social interaction in which particular social identities and the social representations on which they are based are elaborated and negotiated' (Duveen and Lloyd, 1990, p. 8).

Compared to the definitions of microgenesis discussed earlier, this definition bears close resemblance to the social constructivist work of the 'social Genevans' as the emphasis is on change as a form of construction through sociocognitive conflict in social interaction. However, it is unique in that it implicates social identity and social representations in this process. The idea of social representations being evoked in social interaction in this context is also new. According to this perspective, the *evocation* of social representations in social interaction occurs in the ways in which individuals construct an understanding of the situation and *position* themselves and their interlocutors as social subjects in the field of social representations. This process can run smoothly along the lines of the 'taken for granted', but it can also lead to ruptures (see Zittoun et al., 2003). Duveen and Lloyd (1990) describe these different paths of change or no change eloquently:

> In many circumstances, of course, there will be a mutuality in the understandings constructed by different participants which will obviate the need for any explicit specifications or negotiation of social identities, though one can still describe

the course of such social interactions as the negotiation of social identities in the same sense as one speaks of a ship negotiating a channel. But where the mutuality of understanding cannot be taken for granted, or where an assumed mutuality breaks down, the negotiation of social identities becomes an explicit and identifiable feature of social interaction. In these circumstances the negotiation of social identities may involve the coordination of different points of view and the resolution of conflicts. In every social interaction there is a microgenetic process in which social identities are negotiated and shared frames of reference established, processes for which social representations provide the resources. (p. 8)

In the process of microgenesis the pragmatic aspects of language play a crucial role. Moscovici (1994), in a somewhat self-critical remark, states that in his early work that focussed on the way representations are shaped and diffused in ordinary communication, he privileged questions of meaning and content at the expense of the study of the pragmatic aspects of communication. As he characteristically said: 'Yes, the time has come to loosen the link with semantic communication, which is too exclusive, and take more interest in pragmatic communication' (p. 165). In this work Moscovici convincingly argues that what we effectively transmit in a statement in social interaction is underdetermined by the implemented semantic content, and in this respect what we communicate about a representation is only partially conveyed by the meaning of a sentence. As possible starting points for the study of pragmatics, Moscovici (1994) makes reference to floating representations in communication as 'taken for granted presuppositions buried under the layers of words and images' (p. 168) that float in the heads of real people and orient communication, going unnoticed until a rupture takes place in the form of a violation of customs and habitual ways of 'what has to be'. Ruptures are therefore opportunities to thematize a social representation and explicitly make it a topic of discussion (see Marková, 2003; Gillespie, 2008).

The importance of the implicit aspect of communicative expectations was the hallmark of work on the microgenesis of knowledge initiated in the early 1990s by Anne-Nelly Perret-Clermont in Neuchâtel in the educational context that followed the work of the 'social Genevans'. Known as the second generation of research on social interaction and cognitive development, this work focussed on the communicative demands of the task situation (Perret-Clermont et al., 1991; Schubauer-Leoni and Grossen, 1993; Perret-Clermont, 1994), and particularly on the pragmatics of communication between adult and child in the testing situation, emphasizing the forms of experimental or didactic contracts that exist in the way pupils differentially relate to experimenters and teachers in a testing situation on a single task. An important point to keep in mind here is the *partially* shared nature of representations that makes ruptures possible, but more importantly that makes communication itself possible. If we completely shared views, then there would be no need to communicate, and if we had nothing in common, then the process of communication would not be possible (Jovchelovitch, 2007; Moscovici, 1994; Gillespie, 2008). In this sense, generativity of social representations is premised on difference. But at the same time, microgenesis of a social representation implies reorganization towards a holistic structure with a certain coherence, since the basic function of social representations is to make the unfamiliar familiar. As Moscovici (1988) made clear:

> When a representation emerges, it is startling to see how it grows out of a seeming repetition of clichés, an exchange of tautological terms as they occur in conversations, and a visualisation of fuzzy images relating to strange objects. And yet it combines all these heterogeneous elements into one whole and endows the new thing with a novel and even cohesive appearance. The key to its method of production lies in the anchoring and objectivation process. (p. 244)

It should be stressed that anchoring, for Moscovici (1994), refers to 'the link between generating sense and communicating' (p. 164) and should be read in the light of communication. In particular, he makes the insightful comment that when interlocutors keep a constructive ambiguity or a false consensus between them, it is because they actively avoid anchoring the social representation of what is being discussed, letting it float on purpose so as to avoid a 'real dissensus'. In this sense, successful anchoring of a social representation would amount to thematizing and making explicit what is implicit and taken for granted – the presuppositions at the basis of their reasoning in relation to the issue at hand.

Microgenesis of knowledge in the third generation of research on social interaction and cognitive development

In the last ten years an emerging body of research in Cambridge has expanded our understanding of the microgenesis of representations. In the social developmental work of the late Gerard Duveen, one can recognize the long-term project of building a genetic social psychology that has as its aim the study of the articulation between the microgenesis, ontogenesis and sociogenesis of social representations (see Jovchelovitch, 2010; Castorina, 2010; Leman, 2010). The social developmental approach propounded by Duveen takes the social-psychological subject as the unit of analysis and provides both theoretical insights on the ontogenesis of social representations of gender (Duveen, 1993; Lloyd and Duveen, 1992) and the relations between social representations and identities (Duveen, 1997, 2001a and 2001b), as well as empirical evidence for the microgenesis of social representations and the importance of distinctions between varieties of communication or social interaction and their links with forms of learning and cognitive development (Duveen, 2002; Duveen and Psaltis, 2008; Leman and Duveen, 1999; Psaltis and Duveen, 2006, 2007; Psaltis, Duveen, and Perret-Clermont, 2009).

Gerard Duveen and colleagues' (see Moscovici, Jovchelovitch and Wagoner, 2013) later work on the social interaction of children and their moral and cognitive development was to provide, for Duveen, an exciting and important research field.

Through the study of varying forms of communication, it offered the contours of a model of transition from pre-operational to operational thought in children that could be extended to a more general model of the role of social relations and communication forms (Duveen, 2002; cf. Castorina, 2010; Leman, 2010; Jovchelovitch, 2010) in the transition from representations of belief to representations of knowledge.[1]

In this work the experimental microgenetic paradigm of the 'social Genevans' is applied in order to explore how children age 6–7 years interact under conditions where an asymmetry of gender status is crossed with an asymmetry of knowledge on cognitive tasks (Psaltis and Duveen, 2006; Psaltis and Duveen, 2007; Psaltis, Duveen and Perret-Clermont, 2009; Psaltis, 2011a; Psaltis and Zapiti, 2014). This work explores the effects of such criss-crossings of asymmetries on conversation types and on the change of the representation of the conservation of liquids and the village task (for reviews and commentaries of this work, see Castorina, 2010; Jovchelovitch, 2010; Leman, 2010; Ferrari, 2007; Martin, 2007; Maynard, 2009; Nicolopoulou and Weintraub, 2009; Simao, 2003; Sorsana and Trognon, 2011; Psaltis, Duveen, and Perret-Clermont, 2009; Psaltis, 2011b).

In this work one can clearly see the interplay between two processes of representation: the process of evoking social representations of gender and the process of evoking the social representation of the cognitive task, which is of course also an opportunity for the reconstruction of knowledge of both representations in social interaction. The work expands Moscovici's (1961/2008) insight in *Psychoanalysis* when he distinguished between the 'logical system and the normative metasystem' (p. 166), as well as Doise's plea to articulate the four levels of analysis in social developmental psychology (Doise, 1986a; see also Chapter 3, this volume). One operationalization of the interplay between the two systems came from Doise (1990), who argued that the study of social representations should highlight the social regulations which the normative meta-system of social representations exerts over the cognitive system, in order to explain under what conditions social positioning activates specific ways of cognitive functioning. Doise and Mugny specifically introduced the notion of *social marking*[2] as working in tandem with sociocognitive conflict, forming a twofold mechanism of cognitive development (Doise and Hanselmann, 1990). Social marking refers to 'the correspondences

---

1 Moscovici's (1998/2000, p. 136) distinction is between (a) social representations 'whose kernel consists of beliefs which are generally more homogeneous, affective, impermeable to experience or contradiction, and leave little scope for individual variations', and (b) social representations founded on knowledge 'which are more fluid, pragmatic, amenable to the proof of success or failure, and leave a certain latitude to language, experience, and even to the critical faculties of individuals'.

2 An example of social marking from Doise and Mugny (1984, pp. 69–72) is in an experimental condition where original non-conservers distributed fruit juice to two children who 'had worked equally hard and therefore merited the same amount of juice to drink'. In the control situation, without marking, the aim was only to establish an equality between two quantities of liquid in the classical transformations. It was found that the socially marked condition produced significantly more correct solutions than the unmarked one and this was explained as the result of conflict between the equality norm and the inequality perception of the non-conserver.

which may exist between, on the one hand, the social relations presiding over the interactions of persons actually or symbolically present in a given situation and, on the other hand, the cognitive relations bearing on certain properties of the objects through which these social relations materialise' (Doise, 1989, p. 395). More recently, Doise, Mugny and Pérez (1998) specified Doise's definition of social regulations by forging more explicit links between the social psychology of influence (Moscovici, 1984; Pérez and Mugny, 1996) and the findings from the first generation of studies. Here, a broad conception of social regulations (implying both social marking and modalities of resolution) and an articulation of how these contribute to cognitive progress – on the condition that they are used to orient a sociocognitive conflict – is provided. Moreover, it is concluded that the resolution of conflict depends largely on the nature of the sources of this influence. Those of higher status tend to induce a more relational regulation of the conflict, that is to say, a socially explicit re-establishment of consensus (imitation in developmental studies, compliance in social influence). Sources of an equal status (developmental studies) or inferior status, minorities or out-groups (studies of influence) induce a more constructivist process.

The importance of introducing the notion of social marking by Doise and his colleagues is that of finding a notion that makes the link between the 'logical system and the normative metasystem', but it would appear as a mechanism that is 'too good to be true', to use the same words that Moscovici (1990, p. 179) uses when he raises doubts about Vygotsky's notion of internalization. What disturbs Moscovici is that Vygotsky's formula suggests a direct relationship between social practices and individual functioning. In Vygotsky's work there is no reference to any structures or processes mediating between the inter-psychological and the intra-psychological. What is missing in Vygotsky's notion of internalization as well as Doise's notion of social marking, even if we accept that social marking does work in tandem with sociocognitive conflict, is the dynamics emanating from group belongingness and social identities of the interlocutors as they relate to positioning and resistance (Duveen, 1993, 2001) during the actual unfolding in microgenetic time of a social interaction. This would be closer to Moscovici's original argument about how the cognitive system is regulated by the normative meta-system in natural thought, where he evokes dynamics of group belongingness:

> We have in other words, ordinary operational relations on the one hand, and normative relations that check, test and direct them on the other. Normative values and principles are by definition, organized. This means that relations between the logical terms are directional, and that the relationship between A and B is not the same as that between B and A ... If we look for the criteria defining permitted combinations and forbidden combinations we find that the former are associated, either directly or indirectly, with the subject's group, whilst the latter are associated with another group. (Moscovici, 1961/2008, p. 167)

The way that social representations are striving for the whole is captured by Duveen when he argues that the stability of particular forms of identity is linked to the stability of the network of social influences which sustain a particular representation since, as the balance of influence processes changes (Duveen, 2007, 2008), so does the predominant representation and consequently the patterns of identity which are a function of that representation. In this way identity can be considered as an asymmetry in a relationship, which constrains what can be communicated through it, 'both in the sense of what it becomes possible to communicate and in the sense of what becomes incommunicable and potentially a point of resistance, or communicable only on condition of a reworking of that identity' (Duveen, 2001a; see Cornish and Gillespie, 2010).

Take as an example the kind of social interactions we observed in some of our work with Duveen between conservers and non-conservers (Psaltis and Duveen, 2006, 2007; Psaltis, 2005a and b). From the perspective of the Piagetian epistemic subject, it could be argued that what we see in such social interactions is the different qualities of the two forms of understanding (conservation and non-conservation). The form of understanding that conservers entertain is closer to what Piaget (1941/1952) and Smith (1993) described as necessary knowledge in that it has an implicational character of the following nature: since nothing was added or taken away from the two glasses then the amount of water necessarily needs to be the same in the transformation and the original glass (Psaltis, 2005b). The fact that one glass looks taller is thus irrelevant to the amount of water in the glass. Indeed the two dimensions of the glasses compensate for each other since one is taller but the other is wider. Moreover, if we reverse our operations then we will end up where we started with the two original glasses having an equal amount of water. On the contrary, the non-conserving position is centred on one dimension of the glasses (either height or width) and thus is of a different quality from the previous description in that it is less elaborate and less flexible. A non-conserver would usually support his or her position with a simple justification that the glass is taller or wider. It is therefore less decentred compared to the conserving representation in that it lacks coordination in a coherent explanation of the two contrasting perspectives on the object.

But of course the interacting children are not merely epistemic subjects, but social psychological subjects (Duveen, 1997), and 'operativity' cannot be understood outside the context of its usage (Psaltis, Duveen and Perret-Clermont, 2009). The children, to isolate one social group membership, are either male or female working with other males or females. Social gender identities, as a function of social representations of gender, structure the situation through the evocation of social representations of gender when the children socially represent the task. When the children are asserting an argument, this can serve as the signifier for positioning both children within the interaction, with one being placed in the role of tutor or expert and the other that of tutee or novice. In the field of gender, starting with a justification and then making an assertion can take a completely different meaning and lead to a completely different microgenetic path as the interaction unfolds, from starting an argument with an assertion and then proceeding with its justification. This is because positioning as an expert can either be consistent with or conflict with expectations or habitual ways of positioning the gendered self derived from presuppositions of social representations of gender – the same 'presuppositions buried under the layers of words and images' discussed by Moscovici earlier (Moscovici, 1994, p. 168). A girl positioned as a novice by a boy asserting himself as an expert may find this situation all too familiar, while a boy who finds himself positioned as a novice by a girl may find that this conflicts with his expectations of an expression of a certain dominant masculinity. Indeed, this is exactly what we find with the well-established 'Fm effect'[3] (Leman and Duveen, 1999; Psaltis, 2005a, 2005b, 2011a; Psaltis and Duveen, 2006, 2007; Psaltis, Duveen and Perret-Clermont, 2009; Zapiti and Psaltis, 2012; Zapiti, 2012; Zittoun et al., 2003; Psaltis and Zapiti, 2014). We consistently find that the conflicting nature of gender status and knowledge asymmetries in dyadic interaction of female expert-male novice (Fm) creates a more balanced communication between the interlocutors. Such communication is linked with more flexible and novel forms of knowledge, interiorization of operations and in-depth understanding of the object under discussion. As Jovchelovitch vividly commented on the 'Fm effect' in Duveen (2002, p. 148), 'what the girls are doing is they are bringing the boys an apple, and when the boys bite into it, it becomes new knowledge for them'. This effect resonates quite well with the Vygotskian method of 'double stimulation' and the Piagetian notion of groping since it is like the boy is reaching a distant 'object' (regaining his dominant gender position) through the means of an intermediary (constructing novel conservation arguments). In the process of communication he discovers how to use the intermediary object (conserving arguments) as a means to attain his end, and then incorporates this action into his already existing schemata of representing the conservation of liquids.

Another innovation of the third generation of studies is the introduction of a more molar level of analysis of unfolding communication in microgenetic time by distinguishing different types of conversation or interaction types (Psaltis, Duveen and Perret-Clermont, 2009; Psaltis, 2005b; Psaltis and Duveen, 2006, 2007; Duveen and Psaltis, 2008). For example, in the conservation of liquids task, the following conversation types were identified:

1. *Non-conserving.* In a minority of cases the non-conserving child was able to persuade their conserving partner to agree on a joint response of non-conservation.
2. *No resistance.* Conversations which began with an assertion of conservation by the conserving child to which the non-conserving child offered no resistance.
3. *Resistance.* Conversations where the non-conserver offered an argument in support of their position at least once during the interaction.

---

3 In this series of experiments four different pair types were employed. For example, in Psaltis and Duveen (2006) in the conservation of liquids task in Mm dyads, male conservers worked with male non-conservers, in Mf dyads male conservers worked with female non-conservers, in Ff dyads female conservers worked with female non-conservers, and in Fm dyads female non-conservers worked with male non-conservers.

4. *Explicit recognition.* Conversations in which the non-conserving child gave some explicit indication that they had grasped the idea of conservation, often by giving a conservation argument themselves.

The coding of interaction at this molar level of analysis provided a clearer and stronger pattern of relationships between this feature of the interaction and the outcome for the original non-conservers in the post-test. Progress in the post-test was observed for almost every child who participated in an explicit recognition conversation (Psaltis and Duveen, 2006), but never for those from non-conserving conversations. And while about half the children from No Resistance and Resistance interactions made progress in the post-test, they did so without producing any novelty in the post-test. Novelty was almost exclusively observed in the post-tests of children who had participated in Explicit Recognition (Psaltis and Duveen, 2006). Explicit recognition therefore is the conversation type which is uniquely associated with the type of interaction which stimulates reflection and leads to an authentic transformation in the representation.

In this conversation type there is explicit recognition of conservation by the original non-conserver, but the kind of intersubjectivity implied by the fact that non-conserving children changed their stance during the interaction suggests that recognition takes a clearly relational nature having to do with how the non-conserver is being identified by the conserver. From the perspective of the non-conserver, there is a validation by the conserver of a *change* in their subjective point of view at the meta-level culminating in joint agreement as a form of mutual recognition, which Rommetveit (1984) calls an intersubjectivity of a temporarily shared world where both interlocutors know that the other knows the same thing that they know themselves. Such a conversation type is characterized by a form of recognition of the original non-conserver as a *thinking subject* (Psaltis and Duveen, 2007), or an autonomous agent who on reflection can take responsibility to *change* their mind. But for this to be done, it also has to coordinate with the other's point of view and thus the influence taking place here is *bi-directional*. On the contrary, in Incorrect Answer and No Resistance, there appears to be at play a form of *instrumental recognition* where one of the partners is relegated by the other to an object that either just fills in the slots offered by the other or is not taken into account at all. Influence here is uni-directional. Finally, resistance seems to be a form of categorical recognition where there is a limit to the unidirectional influence that can be achieved by the other due to his or her social category membership.

Implications of the third generation of research for social representations theory: towards a genetic social psychology

The first and most important implication of the reviewed work concerns the epistemology of social representations. Moscovici stated after Duveen's untimely death that his work 'had been able to raise fundamental epistemological questions and to propose some elements of answer on which we must reflect further' (Moscovici, 2010, p. 2.4; Moscovici, Jovchelovitch and Wagoner, 2013). What the work on the third generation of research achieves is to offer a *unified* epistemological framework of genetic social psychology allowing one to reflect on both the microgenesis of social representations and on the microgenesis of cognitive development. Contrary to what has been suggested recently (Marková, 2010), that Duveen's 'studies on child development are mainly influenced by Piaget's epistemology while his sociocultural studies owe a great deal to Serge Moscovici', Duveen thought both with and against Piaget and Moscovici throughout his work (Moscovici, Jovchelovitch and Wagoner, 2013; Jovchelovitch, 2010; Castorina, 2010) and certainly did not split his work into sociocultural and developmental; nor did he apply different epistemologies to the two lines of research. On the contrary he was very clear on the ways that Piagetian constructivism could be reworked into a social constructivism so that it converges with the theory of social representations (see Duveen, 2002, 2007; Duveen and Psaltis, 2007; Psaltis, Duveen and Perret-Clermont, 2009). At the same time, in the same work he was also very clear about what ways social representations theory could benefit from Piagetian insights and particularly the distinction Piaget (1932) made between relations of constraint and relations of cooperation. For example, Duveen considered Moscovici's distinction between social representations based on knowledge and social representations based on belief as limited because it does not include any clear discussion of the functional aspects of these representations, of the modalities through which they circulate or are communicated, or the ways in which they serve to structure different types of social groups or are structured by different types of social relations (Duveen, 2007, p. 547). Drawing on the Piagetian distinction, Duveen (2002) proposed that we could distinguish between two realms, the realm of belief that is based on social relations of constraint (an asymmetrical social relation) and is related to compliance, and the realm of knowledge that is based on a social relation of cooperation (symmetrical social relation) that is conducive to innovation and conversion. The move from the realm of belief to the realm of knowledge, he argued, can be achieved if doubt is introduced through sociocognitive conflict, and the way this sociocognitive conflict is resolved is similar to the conversation types that we identified in our work (Psaltis and Duveen, 2006, 2008). From this model, Jovchelovitch (see Duveen, 2002, p. 151) suggested that:

> You can work very comfortably towards other social situations in putting questions about how traditions are established based on the criss-crossing between symmetric and asymmetric relationships. And instead of the apple being offered by a girl, today you have thousands of apples being brought to you by different people who come with different belief systems and introduce doubt into our taken for granted.

To this remark Duveen replied: 'That's exactly what I would think. This model is established through the concrete example of what happens between children but it is not just a description of this situation. It expresses something more general' (ibid., p. 152).

An example of the application of these ideas to the more general processes of societal/sociogenetic change through processes of communication is attempted by Psaltis (2012c), in which I explore the reduction of prejudice through intergroup contact between Greek Cypriots and Turkish Cypriots in the context of the post-conflict and divided society of Cyprus. In this work I show how the absence of contact or the presence of negative quality communication which is not based on mutual respect directly relates to adherence to the official narratives of the conflict in both communities, that in turn directly relate to feelings of anxiety, threat, distrust and prejudice. From the present theoretical framework this is expected, since official narratives are characterised by their partial and ethnocentric nature – functioning as closed systems characterised by being homogeneous, affective and impermeable to experience or contradiction – and leave little scope for individual variation, similar to ecclesiastical 'dogma', a fine example of what Moscovici (1988, 2000) called social representations based on belief. As such, they are based on social relations of unilateral respect, fail to promote true dialogue and reflection (Psaltis and Duveen, 2006, 2007; Duveen and Psaltis, 2008; Psaltis, 2012a), and claim a hegemonic role in society. Their resistance to change comes from their isolation from alternative representations or from the way dialogue with alternative representations is undermined by varying semantic barriers (Moscovici, 1961/1976; Gillespie, 2008) that inoculate against change.

Cognitive polyphasia and social relations

Another theoretical notion that microgenetic research can help clarify is that of cognitive polyphasia (see Chapter 11, this volume). In one sense it could be described as the case where both interlocutors agree to disagree and learn to live with dissonance. However, another form of cognitive polyphasia could be extracted from the example I gave earlier of an interaction between a conserver and a non-conserver. As Duveen (20001a, p. 176) argued on the basis of the distinction between social relations of constraint and social relations of cooperation, 'Piaget himself might have moved towards a notion of cognitive polyphasia. But he remained a committed monophasic.' It is possible at some point in a social interaction for a person to construct a flexible operational structure in relation to a specific topic, problem, or task that is logically coherent. But communication around these objects can of course take place in different settings, with different individuals, or different groups with considerable variation in their structure, aims and functions. In this respect, the person will evoke and possibly reconstruct his representation in this different context, and it is possible that in this second context the form and content of this representation will be different to the one reached earlier. As long as the form of representation constructed serves different goals, more epistemic in the first one but more dominated by concerns of group belongingness in the second one, the persons will have in their 'toolbox' two ways to react with different people or groups to the same object without the need to exhibit unitary behaviour across situations. As long as s/he is not required to confront the two contexts simultaneously, s/he can continue in this cognitive polyphasia of applying varying logics indefinitely. In particular 'developmental' tasks the pressure towards a more 'scientific' point of view is over-determined since the chances of meeting a person with the same representation of conservation of liquids as that of the conserver is indeed high (e.g. adults, teacher, books), even if this is not really a scientific representation of the task.[4] It is in this sense that Duveen and Lloyd (1990) argued that microgenesis and ontogenesis do not always lead to sociogenesis. The non-conserving children are unlikely to form a group that would make it their life's project to convince society through a mass-media campaign of the non-conservation of liquids. But this is not the case with tasks and problems such as discussing preferences or attitudes towards immigration or minority rights, for example, when the issues are a matter of ideological contest and struggle in the public sphere between adults. Discussions between adults on these issues, it would seem, are more likely to entail at least the possibility of a transition between microgenesis to ontogenesis and sociogenesis. From the work cited earlier, for example in Cyprus (Psaltis, 2012c; Makriyianni and Psaltis, 2007), we can see how bi-communal civil society organizations[5] dealing with history teaching take joint collective action to produce educational material for both communities that will facilitate decentring from ethnocentric narratives at the societal level, premised on communicative forms based on mutual respect that facilitate all three types of genetic change.

Avoiding the reification of culture

Another field of application of the findings from the third generation of research was apparent in Duveen's discussion of the notion of culture as viewed through the lenses of social representations (see Psaltis, 2012a) when he discussed hegemonic, polemical and emancipated representations (Moscovici, 1988). In the last paper he wrote, Duveen (2008) expanded on this thinking, revisiting the second part of the original work of Moscovici (1961/1976) on psychoanalysis, making a call for heterogeneity in social psychology. He argued that we need to recognize that there is an intimate relation between the values and attitudes of a group and the characteristic patterns of communication which sustain it (Duveen, 2008). In particular, he likened *diffusion* to a form of communication with a specific form of *affiliative bonds* linking the members of this group of people who are engaged in sceptical the exchange of ideas as a form of *sympathy* where the out-group become

---

4 A more correct scientific representation of the task would be that the two glasses (pre-transformation and transformation) actually do not have the same amount of water since some droplets are always left without the experimenter's will in the pre-transformation glass.
5 An example of such an NGO is the intercommunal Association for Historical Dialogue and Research.

the dogmatics. *Propagation*, which is based on belief, sets limits to the intellectual curiosity of individuals since it is established by a central authority. The affiliative bonds linking the members of this group of people is *communion* and the out-group(s) are characterized either by their lack of belief or by their adherence to alternative beliefs (Gillespie, 2008). Finally, *propaganda* draws together people who share a specific political commitment and who envisage an appropriate form of political organization where the centre dominates by defining realities, and these people form affiliative bonds of *solidarity*. The out-group(s) are defined either by their lack of commitment to this ideology, or by their commitment to a different ideology (Psaltis, 2012a).

Conclusion

The fundamental question of modernity that brought Piaget and Vygotsky to the study of varying forms of knowledge is still with us today in the twenty-first century, and due to postmodernity and globalization, more so than ever. Amidst the financial crisis and the questioning of multiculturalism as a way of managing diversity (Psaltis, 2012a), these latest developments in social representations offer a way to navigate the theory away from the cultural relativism of 'everything goes', or reducing social representations to a simple descriptive enterprise, towards enhancing the critical potential of social representations theory (Howarth, 2006c). These kinds of distinction, made earlier in relation to the quality of social relationships as they implicate questions of power and status asymmetries, could be applied in an array of social arenas to develop a critical perspective in relation to politics, education, minority rights, racism, fundamentalism and nationalism.

9 Image, social imaginary and social representations

Angela Arruda

The early outlines of contemporary theories of the imaginary in the social sciences date back to the end of the nineteenth century and the beginning of the twentieth century (Wunenburger, 2003). Since then, and despite its late appearance in social psychology, the notion of 'imaginary' has gained prominence in various disciplines such as history (Duby, 1978; Le Goff, 1988/2005), psychoanalysis (Lacan, 1973), anthropology (Durand, 1992), philosophy (Castoriadis, 1975; Taylor, 2004), and sociology (Maffesoli, 1993). Le Goff (1988/2003), in his study of the Middle Ages (published in English as *The Medieval Imagination*, 1985), further claims that the 'history of imagination' – *imaginaire* in French has – emerged as a new sub-discipline for history.

The 'imaginary' is a complex notion. It refers to an adjective – such as 'an imaginary friend' – as well as a noun – such as 'an urban imaginary'. While being well established in the humanities in France (besides the above mentioned, see also Bachelard, 1949/2002; Morin, 1956/1985; Wunenburger, 2003, among others) and Latin America[1] (Carvalho, 1990; Canclini, 1997; Baeza, 2011; Silva, 2007, among others), it is often translated into English as 'imagination', which has increased its opacity for the English-speaking reader.[2]

The imaginary may be considered as the mental activity of producing iconic or linguistic images. The social imaginary, on the other hand, refers to a network of significations, collectively shared, that each society makes use of to think about itself (Castoriadis, 1975). In the social scientific literature the imaginary has been variably defined (Barbier, 1994; Augras, 2000; Le Goff, 2005), and unlike social representations theory, there is no single specific theory. Some authors consider it as a set of myths (Durand, 1992), others emphasize the affect it may arouse (Baczko, 1991; Maffesoli, 1993), and others still focus on the representations which express it (Le Goff, 2003) or the presence of memories in its composition (de Alba, 2007; de Rosa, 2002; Banchs, Agudo and Astorga, 2007). Consequently, the imaginary

---

1 Discussions about national identity in Latin American countries often refer to the imaginary. The arrival of colonizers initiated the creation of an imaginary 'new world', described as a paradise on earth (O'Gorman, 1992; Souza, 1986). Each nation, as an imagined community (Anderson, 1983), invented successive narratives about its origin, its heroes and glories (Thiesse, 1999), according to the successive political/cultural national projects (Carvalho, 1990).
2 In English the translation of the noun into 'imaginary' sounds strange to many and therefore the noun persists as 'imagination', which increases the confusion. The acceptance of imaginary as a noun is recent; see the Canadian philosopher Charles Taylor (2004).

is easy to identify but difficult to define, and its multiple definitions reinforce its vagueness.

The imaginary permeates reality but also includes what cannot be said in words. As Geertz (1980) famously argued: 'the real is as imagined as the imaginary' (p. 136). It can both incorporate representations and provide elements to their constitution. While imagination is considered as an individual figurative capacity, the imaginary which interests us presently, that is, the social imaginary, may refer to both the process of creating as well as the set of images, models and beliefs individuals inherit from participation in society that related to a period of time (the Middle Age imaginary: Duby, 1978; Le Goff, 1988), a situation (urban imaginaries: Silva, 2007; Canclini, 1997), or society itself (the imaginary institution of a society: Castoriadis, 1975).

Castoriadis (1975) has advanced the study of the imaginary. In his works, it refers to image, that is, to form, but not only. According to him, the imaginary may be both individual and collective. Two key concepts in his theory are the radical imaginary and the social imaginary. The radical imaginary is a constant creative flow of affects, desires and representations which yield the emergence of forms, figures and symbols. It is the root of all creation. It constitutes the basis of the unconscious and is a constituent of the psyche. The social imaginary, on the other hand, is the continuous creation of social imaginary significations. These are imaginary because their meaning is a creation, with no correspondence whatsoever to rational or real elements (such as language, for example). They are social because they are instituted and shared by an impersonal, anonymous collective: no individual would be able to make them up. They form a web of significations carried on and embodied by a given society (Castoriadis, 1997).

The imaginary appears in social representations research in multiple ways and at multiple levels. It may be detected in different kinds of images and transpires under different methodologies. It may be expressed by means of the images that a social representation creates through the processes of anchoring and objectifying,[3] which associate imaging and imagination. On the one hand, this is an imaging process: it produces an image that is not a copy of the object. On the other hand, to create images is an exercise of imagination intended to find meaning for the unfamiliar (Jodelet, 1984a). The production of meaning is thus a creative process: imaginative solutions to the difficulties associated with understanding the unfamiliar. The social imaginary may be one of the sources for this production, inasmuch as it provides the background for anchoring the unfamiliar. The example of Columbus describing the new lands to the king of Spain as a paradise on earth illustrates the influence

---

[3] Anchoring and objectification are two important processes in the elaboration of a social representation. Anchoring is giving meaning to a new object by means of including it among the previous stock of notions of a group/subject. This movement towards stabilization of an uncertain, unfamiliar object corresponds to anchoring it to a firm territory. Both the object and this territory are modified in this operation. Objectification is the process of giving concreteness to this object, selecting its main features and recomposing them in a scheme or figure so that it gains a more accessible structure and becomes tangible as an object. This may also happen by means of figures of speech, such as metaphors, etc.

of a medieval imaginary still existing when he reaches America (Souza, 1986; O'Gorman, 1992). At the same time, the social representation that results from this process may become part of a previously existing social imaginary.

The imaging dimension in a social representation thus comprises the ensemble of figurative elements and images (iconic, linguistic, etc.) existing within it, including those intervening in the processes of elaboration of the social representation. Moreover, the imaginary is also part of the dynamics of social representation, whenever it is part of the movement of redefining (signification: anchoring) and of redesigning (figuration: objectifying) the object. This changes the group's/subject's previous stock of significations at the same time.

This chapter discusses the theory and studies that have related images with the social imaginary and social representations. Firstly it reviews the theoretical relations between imaging, the imaginary and social representations theory. Secondly it reviews social representations research that has included an explicit concern with the imaginary. Finally it proposes some methodological techniques that may serve for studying the imaginary and incorporating this focus in the investigation of social representations.

The imaging dimension of social representations

The dimensions of social representations formulated by Moscovici in 1961 – attitude, information and field of representation – permeate the whole process of elaboration of social representations. Fifty years later, however, they might need some updating. Some of us prefer to think in terms of an affective dimension, which goes beyond the evaluative compound in a social representation (Banchs, 1996; Arruda, 2003; Campos and Rouquette, 2003, among others). This interferes in every step of such elaboration: the anchoring ground to be adopted, the elements to compose the figurative scheme, and the structure of the central core. As for the field of representation that includes the images and models articulated, encompassing the network of meanings contained in a social representation, this is considered as part of the imaging dimension of a social representation. A social representation is a complex network of meanings intertwined and interrelated with images among which some will be objectified. Figures thus belong in this network.

The imaging dimension has proven relevant in research undertaken by different authors since the 1970s, and has also become the focus of some recent discussions among social representations scholars (Arruda and de Alba, 2007; see also *Papers on Social Representations* special issue on imaginary and social representations, 2014). The imaging dimension in social representations implies the social imaginary as studied in sciences such as history, anthropology and sociology, as previously noted. These sciences are interested in the relations between social structures and the imaginaries, that is, how imaginaries influence social conducts and vice versa. Le Goff (1988) explains the inextricable relation with representations from a historical point of view: the lives of individuals and groups in society are not limited to material, tangible realities. They include and are also explained by the representations subjects have made about history, about their own place and the role of society. This imaginary is part of such representations. And the history of the imaginary is a territory of the history of representations. Imaging and representing are the way to access certain imagination processes.

Figuration and production of meaning in social representations

Figuration is an important part of the process of representing socially. It is the process already described by Durkheim (1912/1968) in his analysis of totemism and it is also seen as one of the ways of human thinking. It is a key support to make sense of the unfamiliar, synthesizing it verbally or iconically. Wagner and Hayes (2005) associate the process which gives concreteness to the abstract – objectification – and the construction of metaphors. Objectification, in the movement to give the unfamiliar a more precise format, to eliminate its vagueness, is a cut-and-paste of those elements that the group/person can manage into a new object.

Consistent with Lakoff and Johnson (1980), Wagner and Hayes assume that a source domain would provide the ground for objectifying the target domain – the unfamiliar focus of interest. Objectification may come in the shape of a metaphor, a scheme, or an iconic illustration of an unintelligible target domain. Examples of objects studied by the social representations approach are the fertilization process (Wagner, Elejabarrieta and Lahnsteiner, 1995), biotechnology and genetic engineering (Wagner and Kronberger, 2001; Wagner, Kronberger and Seifert, 2002), among others.

In the study of the social representations of the fertilization process, fertilization assumed the sexual role metaphor: the sperm and the ovum are portrayed as the active and passive actors of fertilization. Their activities and characteristics (the target domain to be understood) are projected on to the sex-role stereotypically active behaviour of men respectively to the passive behaviour of women (the source domain in terms of which the target is understood) (Wagner and Kronberger, 2001). This metaphor enlightens such a complex process as fertilization, drawing upon the current idea of sexual roles and gender asymmetry which is part of our daily experience. To produce a metaphor is an exercise of imagination which (not consciously) highlights certain parts of the object and recombines them into an effective analogy.

For these authors, the mechanics of metaphor building is the process of construction of the social representation. The production of meaning is a dynamic operation which comprises both anchoring and objectification, oriented by the choices (not conscious) of the subjects. At the same time, image building may activate or contribute to create something new, such as genetically modified food. The image of the engineered tomato draws upon the experience and the visual information of inoculation into the human body, such as in vaccination (Wagner and Kronberger, 2001).

For Moliner (1996), to objectify (see footnote 3 above) means to encourage the production of images, because concrete objects are perceptible and thus reproducible in the form of images. Lay thinking is based on analogy; the search for similarity between objects. Imagery would be very important as it allows for more immediate analogy, based on perceptive resemblance (ibid., p. 110). Moliner quotes McLuhan to say that images condense and concentrate huge regions of experience in a small surface. The elaboration of a mental image requires figurative traits with which to coincide. Social representations are in the origin of visual images. Likewise, social representations will determine how these visual images will be interpreted and included in what Moliner calls social image: a sort of collective opinion. The social representation is a process which, once finalized, has a social image as its product.

For these authors, the object must be somehow synthesized and figurated. Imaging processes function as a sort of illustrated editing of the object by individuals and groups (Wagner and Hayes, 2005). For Wagner, its rewording comes out as a metaphor, an analogy, which is at the same time an image of the object. For Moliner, the process happens thanks to similarities between aspects of the object and figurative traits of perceptible objects. Perception, then, is a main resource in the elaboration processes of social representations, according to this author. Wagner deals with verbal or visual metaphors, and, therefore, with analogy as well, but the symbolic dimension of social representations is more developed in his work. Both authors indicate how figuration (iconic or verbal) is at the core of the dynamics of social representations building.

Both refer to similarities and dynamics, but with different approaches to the metamorphosis of a new object. Both give credit to experience as part of the ground in which the inspiration for processing the new will be found. For Wagner and Hayes (2005, p. 205), this is not an analytical process. There is no investigation of the 'suitability' of the attributes of an object in a categorization. Instead, the available concepts and their features apply to the new. The result comes up before any analysis takes place. Moliner refers to the filliation of social image (the result of the representational process) to visual image, and reminds us that the image touches us because it recalls previous perceptive experiences. The relevance of perception gives his argument a stronger cognitive perspective.

These authors deal with the weaving of images in the network of meanings that constitute the social representation. In both cases, some cognitive work is due in this elaboration, with more or less use of imagination. Either way, it appears that the gestalt of the object and of the ground or domain it will take root in is relevant for the success of this operation, even though Moliner insists on the similarity of figurative traits. Let us consider that the movement of finding the coincidences or similarities between the novelty and the familiar, be it a conscious effort or a spontaneous movement, is dealing not only with iconic or linguistic images, but also with social configurations at the same time. For example, a woman of the rural area of Brazil answering a question on mental health explained that, when we have some 'nerve problem' we start to cry, we fall apart, just like what happens to our home if the beams split open: the house falls down (Arruda, 1993). This is not a metaphor simply because of the analogies nerves–beams and mental balance–house. The social ingredient is also brought to the fore, as well as the affective dimension: the house/home is the place where we should feel safe, protected. It is a space of social relations – with others who live there and with society in general, from which it hopefully gives us a certain distance. The social-affective element may come from experience and contains a strong affective charge. The imaginary of our individualistic society figures home as the sacred place of privacy and quietness in contrast with the bustling day-to-day in public space. Analogies thus carry an affective orientation; perhaps this is the dynamo for the metaphorical expression, which may be a sort of unconscious association. Analogies serve to make the unfamiliar familiar, and rely on the imaginary to achieve this.

The power of the imaginary and the affective dimension

An old social imaginary frequently functions as the source of inspiration for anchoring and objectification processes, as we will see. This imaginary, as Castoriadis would say, allows for the creation of new operative significations: 'it is operative in the practice and in the doing of the society considered as a meaning that organizes human behaviour and social relations, independently of its existence "for the consciousness" of that society' (Castoriadis, 1975, p. 141). Indeed, this imaginary will perform its function from within the representation: once the meaning of the novelty is established, it will orient behaviour accordingly. The literature about slave liberation in the nineteenth century helped people understand the collective fear and prejudice triggered by Afro-descendents in Brazil. From that moment on, black and poor became synonymous with miserable and dangerous (Valladares, 2000). That was a first anchoring of those newly arrived to society. Today, in a context of increasing urban violence and drugs commerce, the collective fear of the 'dangerous classes' has shifted to the youth living in the *favelas* (Valladares, 2000). The success of the *funk* produced therein increased their visibility (Arruda *et al.*, 2010). At present, young males with a modest aspect are identified as *funk* fans and suspected of selling drugs or stealing. They objectify danger, concentrating the vagueness of fear into one specific character and one image. The old transversal representation was updated by the arrival of a new character on the urban scene. The treatment these young men receive from the rest of the population and from the police confirms the successful anchoring and objectification, proving how effective an imaginary can be (Arruda *et al.*, 2010). In such cases, its power relies on the affective dimension and underlies the affective reaction which produces rejection, discrimination and violence.

The imaginary can be the dynamo of the social representation. Lively ideas, suggestive words, image ideas, contain an explosive affective charge, which appeals to imagination, and when the image appears, action follows (Moscovici, 1981a).

The relation of this image to beliefs, secular feelings and memories influences this mobilizing effect. Baczko (1991) points out the power of the imaginary to upheave crowds. It expresses the affective dimension, linked to deeply held beliefs, values and expectations that drive human beings. It also shows the need for new institutionalities to be crowned with figures that fix these institutions into a social imaginary, making explicit how affect interferes with this process: if an 'emotional anchoring' happens, then the venture will be successful. Incidentally, this is one of the bases of propaganda. The importance of creating new imaginaries to back up political-cultural projects is well known. Making sense is not only rational. According to Castoriadis, man is not a rational animal; rationality is but a piece in the immense realm of his madness.

The intensive use of lively images as in publicity (Barthes, 1957), politics and social movements (Baczko, 1991) reaffirms the relation between the imaginary and the affective dimension. Affect can be intensively mobilized by and can mobilize images. This confirms the power images can exert.

The imaginary as knowledge

Knowledge is not constituted solely by reason. After studying the epistemology of science, Bachelard (1949/2002) embraced this perspective. Scientific imagination was based on myths and archetypes, archaic images living in the collective unconscious, which would inspire scientists in need of symbols to represent highly abstract entities such as the forces of physics. Abstract thought needs to be supported by concrete thought – figuration, analogy, metaphors – in order to elaborate knowledge. This also happens in the process of objectification, as previously described. What seems confused, unfamiliar and abstract gains concreteness through figuration: verbal, iconic or other.

Wunenburger states: 'The imaginary may thus appear as a pathway that allows us to think there where knowledge is failing' (2003, p. 70). He illustrates this: the manifestations of natural phenomena were expressed by concrete characters, identified by proper nouns – objectified. For the ancient coastal-dwelling Greeks, the rainbow's arc was most often seen spanning the distance between cloud and sea, and so the goddess Iris was believed to replenish the rain clouds with water from the sea. For some ancient poets, the rainbow itself was called 'iris'. Iris would originally be the personification of the rainbow.[4]

For Wunenburger, thinking, in contact with the spontaneous forces of life, first produces metaphors. Facing such forces thus may produce 'thought which justifies the possibility of acting there where physical and biological laws do not reach' (Moscovici, 1992, p. 307), thought which expands the possible world in order to conceive a startling, excessive event or change. This means a way of transforming

---

4 Source: *Dictionary of Greek and Roman biography and mythology*, www.theoi.com/Pontios/Iris.html

and representing things that escapes from the normal, a way which has its own causal chain: magical thinking, which coexists with the so-called rational and points out the existence of a kind of thought which pierces the boundary of the impossible, bypassing the concern about separating perception and the imaginary.

Objectification brings about in lay knowledge the same transformation that happens in science: it gives fluidity a form that helps coping with the object. The creation of a new knowledge draws upon memory and invention, whether in lay or scientific imagination. It is a powerful cognitive device.

Social representations research with/on images

The following sections do not attempt to bring a state-of-the-art overview but rather a brief overview of the work with images in the social representations field. If, as Castoriadis (1975, 1997) claims, in order to exist everything must exist in the imagination, then converting strangeness into familiarity may be considered as an imagining operation. This brings to a specific symbolic universe a new social imaginary signification, unknown until then. Hence social representations contribute to the instituting process, which is part of the imaginary institution of society. Finding meaning, or making sense, is a continuous human activity in the pursuit of understanding the novel/renewing the old. Social representations have a part to play here. In this sense, they are part of the imaginary institution of society, as defined by Castoriadis (1975, 1997), part of a process of imagination. On the other hand, the imaginary itself may also be part of the social representation, either through the influence of a context to which those who represent something belong, or as a provider of images, since it contains all the social imaginary significations of a society. In this case, it will help the processes of anchoring and objectification.

Early work with images in the field of social representations confirmed two of social representations theory's assumptions: the imaging dimension of social representations and the web of significations which constitutes a social representation. This web was clearly expressed by the whole field of representation: the elaboration of articulated images, models, values that compose a representation. It also related to the general web of meanings – the magma – that characterize a culture and society (Castoriadis, 1975).

Jodelet (1982) inaugurated systematic research with/on iconic images in the social representations field. This first study was mainly based on research with drawings produced by respondents, which increased participants' construction of meaning from the images given or produced. Following a critique against the simplification produced by cognitivism about space, she went on to describe space not only as physical and geographic but also as a place of human experience, practices, attachment and identity: 'space represents and is represented' (ibid., p. 150). Representations of the city are social representations because they are collectively shared and consensually reflect the significance that social, cultural and historical characteristics of the city add to the geographic frame. Jodelet renewed the concept and the methodology of 'cognitive maps' when she considered them as social representations,[5] calling them 'mental maps'. In her original research with Milgram, participants sketched the map of Paris, identified places on photos and answered questions about the city. Paris boundaries were the first element they drew, frequently depicted as the walls of the Farmers-General – the old city walls removed in the nineteenth century – and often represented by the boulevard Périphérique. The Seine was the second element that organized the sketch of the city, although it was sketched as flowing down a straighter course. The third element was Ile de la Cité and Notre Dame, confirming the relationship between the city's history and its representation, since the historical heart of the city coincides with the nucleus of its representation (De Alba, 2011). We may conclude that these elements relate to a city that lives in the imaginary of its residents: surrounded by its history (the old city wall); divided into north and south by a river that becomes straighter than the Seine; and proud of its admirable historical heart.

These aspects are real and imaginary at the same time. They are social imaginary significations of Paris. Maps express a collective imaginary which modifies experienced space, through the work of memory, into feelings of belonging and pride, into a projection of desire. This indicates the inextricable relation between 'reality' and the imaginary and the ways in which mental maps expose this relation. In drawings, spontaneity brings to the fore aspects which might not appear in verbal communication: the presence of an iconic imagination.

De Rosa (1987, 1994) developed an extensive research programme on the social representations of madness by children and teenagers. She asked them to draw a mad person and to draw like a mad person. Three main categories concentrated the images resulting from the drawings: (1) magical-fantastic representations – madness as a creative opportunity (objectified as an artist, an eccentric) and as monstrous, diabolical (a devil, a mutilated person); (2) deviance, ranging from violence to the breaking of norms (a terrorist with a bomb, a person undressing on the street); (3) medicalized representations (someone in a wheelchair, a person subject to hallucinations).

These images were very similar to those portraying madness in past centuries: 'They provided evidence of the figurative nucleus and archaic symbolic dimensions inherent in madness' (Duveen and De Rosa, 1992, p. 102). Apparently, these images have remained in the collective imaginary throughout the last four or five centuries and contradicted the verbal answers of the children and adolescents. These long-lasting elements indicate the existence of a transversal representation (Arruda, forthcoming) of madness, whose central core, designed by the imaginary, has remained practically untouched.

---

5 Tolman's definition of cognitive maps comes from his study of rats that run through a maze, which led him to conclude that the animals elaborated 'a tentative, cognitive-like map of the environment... indicating routes and paths and environmental relationships, which finally determines what responses, if any, the animal will finally release' (Tolman, 1948, p. 193). Cognitive maps are mental representations of physical locations produced by men and animals. They convey the most salient features identified by them.

These initial works point to the interest of the images produced by participants as a means to attain their social representations and show how deep the graphic representation can go. Following Jodelet's contribution, some authors have adopted the social representations approach of space in order to study cities such as Mexico (de Alba, 2002, 2004, 2007) and Vichy (Haas, 2002, 2004). These researchers have associated memory, identity, affects and space. Symbols of both history and modernity inhabit the cartographic imaginary of the city. Real and imaginary maps intertwine to form the urban experience in which each inhabitant is layered, makes decisions and operates a constantly changing space (de Alba, 2002). Omitting places or the historical/political past appears either as a result of their assimilation to the daily practice of the inhabitants (in Mexico), or as denial of a shameful past (in Vichy). In both cases a selection and reassembling of characteristics creates social imaginary significations in a web that institutes the city. This result produces a new imaginary institution for each of them.

Other researches have followed different paths. The use of visual productions such as photography, publicity and others, has also been explored. Transiting from science to common sense is a significant development in Wagner's work. With his colleagues, he has studied what happens when new scientific facts such as biotechnology have consequences in our daily lives, as in the case of engineered food (Wagner and Kronberger, 2001; Wagner, Kronberger and Seifert, 2002), objectified by the images of big tomatoes being inoculated by a person dressed in white. He and his colleagues have contributed to elicit the social processes underlying the elaboration of imaginary understandings and the dynamics of social representations. He calls it the theory of symbolic coping, which values the power of 'everyday imaginations'. It gives 'the concept of images and related beliefs a dynamic character allowing [on one hand] everyday imaginations to be replaced by popularized scientific understanding within a short time' (Wagner, Kronberger and Seifert, 2002, p. 341). On the other hand, it 'allows for a backlash in the sense that "menacing imaginations" might supersede popularized scientific accounts again, should political controversy re-emerge' (ibid.). Finally, this theory 'makes a case in favor of everyday imaginations as being functionally equivalent to scientifically informed knowledge' (ibid.). It sheds light into processes existing in other kinds of social representations.

Wagner and collaborators have also studied relevant social issues with the help of photos and images relating to the Muslim and Hindu conflict in India (Sen and Wagner, 2005), proving the author's concern about taking into account the interplay of diverse forces which explore images in the hunt of the public's support. This has come to constitute a trend of social representations research related to cultural and political facts, as in the next example.

During the institution of a newly occupied territory – Brazil in the sixteenth century – the medieval imaginary still present in the colonizers' minds (Holanda, 1994) helped to anchor that strange new world (Arruda, 1998). Historians confirmed that the newly found land was easily compared to paradise on earth (Holanda, 1994). This powerful image would institute the character of the noble savage two centuries later in Europe, a product of the political and cultural European context, thus testifying to the creative force of the social imaginary. Transversal representations may cross long periods and become part of an imaginary. In Brazil, exuberant wild nature was the general image-idea used to objectify the new land. Updated each time there was a change of the national project, the renewed representation had to find a new anchoring. At present, the old transversal representation has lost some of its strength. In recent research, wild nature was drawn/objectified in sketch maps mainly in the Amazon forest, the farthest frontier of virgin forest, the last corner of an untouched paradise (Arruda, 1998, 2007).

An example of the latest production with images is Moloney's research (Moloney and Walker, 2007) on how refugees and asylum seekers are portrayed by editorial cartoons, considering the construction of identity as resourced by social representations. The cartooning characteristics reveal typification and prejudice hidden by humour. However, the power to create identity lies not in the caricature itself, but rather in the prescriptive power of representation when inequitable communicative processes exist and the identity of the groups is imposed. Highlighting this asymmetrical construction was the author's concern and the aim of this research. The images were analyzed and revealed the existence of the social imaginary signification of these groups in this society.

A further example also investigates social representations and identity, this time in relation to racism. Howarth (2007, 2011) is interested in forms of resistance to racism and changing dominant representations. In her research she uses a multi-methodological approach with children in which visual methods proved to be very useful, as they also allow researchers to study the participants' image: analysis of a television series and drawings are some of these methods. The most original aspect of her work, however, is the use of workshops in which art (photography, painting, weaving) is used as a means of subverting stereotypes, encouraging narrative and self-reflection. These workshops provided an ideal context to explore the value and limitations of visual methods, besides the social psychological benefit they could bring to the children and adolescents who participated. Visual methods powerfully demonstrate that identity is both restricted by and liberated by its visibility. Another contribution of this programme of research, actually action research, is its multi-sensorial approach as a possible stimulus for imagination and for the change of social representations, as well as the inspiration for the use of similar methods in other social representations/imaginary researches that would allow for the study of images in another form than oral or graphic.

It is worth noting that social representations research generally shows the imaginary as a backdrop. It is rarely conceptualized or supported by any specific reference or author. A group of researchers undertook a series of studies on Latin American imaginaries from 2001 to 2005 (Arruda and de Alba, 2007).[6] Their common interest was social thought regarding Latin American countries. They faced a double

---

6 This project was supported by the Laboratory of European Social Psychology/Maison de Sciences de l'Homme. The Brazilian research was supported by FAPESP and Fundação Carlos Chagas.

challenge: working with images to achieve this goal, trying to find relations with the imaginary. They used images produced by different sources, such as respondents' drawings, films, literature and history. Their idea was to work empirically with the imaginaries as a dimension of the representational universe, using different forms and methods: mental maps of Brazil (Arruda, 2007), Mexico (Guerrero, 2007) and the city of Mexico (de Alba, 2007); drawings of the school in Brazil (Prado de Sousa, 2007), the imaginary conveyed by narratives of the inhabitants of a Venezuelan rural community (Banchs, Agudo and Astorga, 2007); and by the political polarization in Venezuela of graffiti, photos and slogans of Chavez's supporters, and the opposition produced of each other and of themselves (Lozada, 2007). The imaginary of Brazil in American and European films (Amancio, 2007), and the imaginary of Brazil and Mexico in Bernano's and Artaud's writings were also studied (Jodelet, 2007). Some of these studies tried to find points of contact with Castoriadis' philosophy, which considers that each nation has its own symbolic universe, its own magma of social imaginary significations.

Some methods for researching social representations and the imaginary

Most of the work undertaken in the social sciences is based on two languages: iconic and linguistic. Sound, film and photo research is still at an early stage. Due to space limitations, only two kinds of production with iconic images related to social representations and the imaginary will be discussed here: drawings/maps and moving images.

The methodology of mental maps in social representations studies consists of maps to be drawn by participants: maps about preferences, familiar places, economic and cultural differences, among others, are drawn and explained by respondents. In research about the city, the respondent's urban experience is explored by means of sketches of their itineraries and of known places in the city. Participants may be asked to comment on photos of specific places. Identification questions are also asked.

The search for more spontaneous answers, so as to allow for the expression of the imaginary dimension, nevertheless, has its limitations. The lack of drawing skills generally reduces the possibility of accurate expression. The explanation by the respondent about what she/he intended to draw and why, which may be a narrative about that production, is very important in order to avoid 'over-interpretation' by the researcher.

The drawings go through a qualitative analysis to identify general aspects such as their structure and organization. The next step is a detailed analysis of images and answers. A protocol of analysis of the images is elaborated. The analysis may include: (1) semiotic, hermeneutic and/or other approaches for images – grids of analysis may be helpful; (2) discourse analysis software, content analysis for textual answers; and (3) statistical analysis of precoded answers. This methodology can be adapted to other kinds of drawings in social representations research. The challenge of analyzing images should stimulate researchers to try different alternatives.

Studies using these methods have led to some conclusions. First, drawings allow for a greater spontaneity and reveal more in-depth information when compared to verbal answers. Second, the interest of diversified methodologies to study the imaginary and social representations. Third, drawings contribute to the study of the figurative aspect of social representations providing a sharper view of the field of representation and of objectified elements. Fourth, drawings display traces of archaic, utopian, mythical, fantastical and affective elements (Arruda and de Alba, 2007). The iconographic code is capable of revealing the most archaic dimensions of social representations (De Rosa, 2011).

When it comes to moving images (film, soap opears, etc.), the choice to identify the director, the public, and the characteristics of what will be studied comes before the methodological choices. In order to see these productions in their context, it is important to survey audience polls as well as critiques. These may influence the reception and the development of the plot.

Television novels with many chapters may be studied as a whole or for a specific period (number of months/chapters). In any case the whole story should be known by the researcher. The overall analysis should consider the main features of the material: its objective, time and place, genre, plot, etc. The written script, technical, dramatic and aesthetic resources should be observed, identifying different moments and solutions in the material. These convey social imaginary significations.

The amount of material to consider and the level of detail in the analysis depend on the researcher's objective. This may determine universes of different extension to be studied, as well as different densities of exploration: extensive or intensive. The interest for specific aspects in a film, such as the social representations of a female character, or the influence of an urban imaginary, will require different choices. The same will happen if the goal is to study a television novel.

For an in-depth exploration, the scene can be the unit of analysis. That means the filming technique/angle, the actors/characters, actions, affects and the soundtrack may be registered and categorized. The verbal material may go through a content/discourse analysis. The images – visual context, body language, movement, light, colours – and the soundtrack contribute to the intensity and tone of the affective dimension.

In films and plays, scenes may be timed and analyzed one by one. For an exhaustive work, the time of specific aspects may also be measured: the presence of certain characters, or of two or more characters together, and so on. This multilayered analysis, however, risks scattering results and loosing sight of the whole. The different foci of work must be put in relation by the researcher.

For a larger amount of material, the researcher may choose a more extensive methodology. If she/he thinks a content analysis would help, it is advisable to (1) go through part of the material and make synopses of sequences of scenes, list characters and/or other item/s; and (2) find categories in this organized material and apply them to the whole material. If the images are to be considered as such, the researcher will also have to find a way to choose them according to her/his objective: the movement of sequences; the relation between action and soundtrack; the rhythm of the piece studied; the interplay between certain characters.

There is no formula for working with images. Creativity and open-mindness will be required from the researcher.

Conclusion

The imaginary is part of the imaging dimension of social representations in different ways. Since imaging is a dimension of social representations and since every social representation's elaboration appeals to imagination in order to proceed to anchor and objectify, creation is at play in this movement. This movement in itself may lead to a cognitive polyphasia (see Arthi, Provencher and Wagner, 2012) as another rationality is requested to fill in the blank in one's knowledge. The blank will disappear so as to let a social representation come true. Those two intertwined processes appeal to procedures and images regardless of their strict pertinence to the characteristics or to the organization of what is being represented. They embody the dynamics of social representations, creating a new figure or scheme, be it visual or linguistic. This could be, on the social psychological level, part of the instituting process Castoriadis describes for a society as it comes to be part of a group's stock of ideas and practices.

The solid ground in which to anchor the novelty may be an imaginary – archaic, futuristic, urban and so on. The process of constructing an image, giving the social representation a figure, may, in turn, integrate an imaginary already existing. For instance, the social representation of the city of Mexico finds in a contemporary urban imaginary a category that helps to translate it (the metropolis with its traffic jams, its violence, its charm), and at the same time embodies a specific urban imaginary, that which belongs to the Mexican capital (with a glorious native past under the city ground). These are close relations.

The ongoing research on social representations and images confirms some of the premises of the theory's epistemological project: the creative and dynamic aspect of social representations is reinforced by the interplay with the imaginary, and the coexistence of different rationalities imply the non-hierarchy among different kinds of knowledge when it comes to interpret the unfamiliar. The imaginary as an ensemble of ideas, representations and beliefs – a web of significations instituted by an anonymous collective – constitutes a resource for creativity as it gives an answer where none could be found otherwise. Therefore, in order to better understand the process of elaboration of many social representations, identifying the presence of an imaginary is requisite. It may require a good knowledge of the multiple contexts of the person/group who represents – historical, political and situational – so as to have access to the modes of inspiration for coping with the novel in that group, contributing to the dialogue between experience and the unknown. There is probably more to say about imaginaries in our research than we think, but we do not always find that link. The imaginary adds complexity to the elaboration of a social representation. It is part of the dynamics of transversal representations in interplay with other social representations: it makes explicit the resilience of old beliefs as well as the influence of new technologies of communication, giving an idea of the thought orientation of a group in certain situations and of the extension of its symbolic alternatives, as some of the examples in this chapter have shown. Memory and identity are two important *liaisons* that can bring these imaginaries to participate in instituting a new social representation.

To conclude, the ongoing research in social representations shows a wide range of interests, objects and methods for the use of images. As for the methods, I hope this chapter has made a contribution, but such good research practice requires continued development. In my view, it is time to gather the existing experience in the field, and this chapter has aimed to advance such a contribution. It is also the time for a discussion about the imaging dimension of social representations, which puts social representations theory – and social psychology – in line with the recognized and growing importance given to images in thinking, communication, social influence, education, politics, consumerism, visual technologies and many other domains of human activity.

10 Collective remembering as a process of social representation

Brady Wagoner

Social representations are carriers of collective memory; through them past experience shapes the present. Thus, social representations ensure for social groups a degree of continuity through time. This is done by flexibly using the past to meet the demands of the present and move towards a future desirable to the group. This notion is different from the traditional understanding of memory in psychology (now being widely questioned) and everyday discourse as a thing put into storage (whether that be in the brain, the 'long-term memory store' or digitally inscribed on a computer hard disk), which is later taken out in roughly the same form it was put in. While this model may have been useful to conceptualize issues like retention capacity, it is inadequate for exploring the functional and social dimensions of memory (see Brockmeier, 2010; Wagoner, 2012). In contrast, memory from the standpoint of social representations is actively engaged, socially and materially situated, reconstructive and oriented to the future.

This chapter explores parallels between research on collective memory and social representations. First, it reviews the two approaches' shared heritage in the classical studies of Maurice Halbwachs, Frederic Bartlett and Lev Vygotsky, which were all, in their own way, inspired by Durkheim. This review will help to explain what it means to say memory is social and provide a background against which to compare it with social representations. Second, this chapter outlines a number of different modalities through which collective remembering operates (viz. through the body, language and the organization of space). Third, it applies these theories to two classic studies in social representations research: Moscovici's (1961/2008) *Psychoanalysis* and Jodelet's (1989/1991) *Madness and Social Representations*. This will help to further exemplify concepts from collective memory research, see these studies with new eyes and derive novel ideas for the study of collective remembering.

Memory after Durkheim

Emile Durkheim was a key forerunner for both social representations theory and social approaches to memory. From him comes the core insight that the mind is social in origin and therefore must be explained in its distinctly social dimensions. In *The Elementary Forms of Religious Life*, Durkheim (1912) demonstrates how the categories of space, time and causality emerge from social organization. For example, Australian tribes understand space as a circle that has the same shape as their camp; thus, the concept of space mirrors the social-geographic relations of the settlement. In this example and others the divisions of society are externalized and transformed into symbolic objects, which in turn function to hold the group together through a shared framework. Moreover, as society changes so too do the categories of thought. The influence of Durkheim's approach on the sociology and social psychology of memory cannot be underestimated. In what follows we will explore how it was taken up by Halbwachs, Bartlett and Vygotsky.

Halbwachs and the social frameworks of memory

Halbwachs was a close follower of Durkheim's approach, having worked directly with the group of French sociologists organized around his journal *L'Année Sociologique*. In Halbwachs' celebrated *Les Cadres sociaux de la mémoire* (*The Social Frameworks of Memory*, abbreviated and translated as *On Collective Memory*), he sets out to show that memory only becomes possible through participation in social life, using the same line of argument made by Durkheim with regard to the categories of thought: 'It is in society that people normally acquire their memories. It is also in society that they recall, recognize, and localize their memories' (Halbwachs, 1925/1992, p. 38). In his account, a purely individual memory is an illusion, thus attempts to explain memory by recourse to the brain miss the point. For even in the most personal states of consciousness, such as dreaming, where it seems we are entirely removed from society, our thoughts are still immersed in society through language (an irreducibly social product), which aids us in interpreting the strange images that appear to us in this state. Thus, social forces are always at work in remembering. The task of the researcher is to explore how society conditions memory.

Halbwachs is more specific than Durkheim in his analysis of society's influence on memory. Where Durkheim speaks of society in general terms, Halbwachs prefers to discuss the memory of different social groups, such as the family, class and religious group. Every social group provides its members with a particular 'social framework' through which they experience and recall the world. These social frameworks are active even when the individual is alone:

> In reality, we are never alone. Other men need not be physically present, since we always carry with us and in us a number of distinct persons. I arrive for the first time in London and take walks with different companions. An architect directs my attention to the character and arrangement of city buildings. A historian tells me why a certain street, house, or other spot is historically noteworthy. A painter alerts me to the colors in the parks, the lines of the palaces and churches, and the play of light and shadow on the walls and façades of Westminister and on the Thames. A businessman takes me into the public thoroughfares, to the shops, bookstores, and department stores. (Halbwachs, 1950/1980, p. 23)

Social frameworks are first of all the other people that we interact with. It is with them that we orient to the world, discuss what we have experienced and are reminded of important events. This is close to Marková's (2003) argument that social representations always imply a triadic relation between self, other and object. Moreover, like social representations, social frameworks can also be understood at a more symbolic level as a series of condensed images of the past and a structure to give them order and meaning. This comes very close to Moscovici's characterization of social representations as being comprised of image and symbol, figure and field, or objectification and anchoring.

Halbwachs (1925/1992) gives the example of how a family creates a condensed image of itself through expressions like 'in our family we have long life spans', 'we are proud' or 'we do not strive to get rich' (p. 59). These statements then bestow a physical and moral quality to the group, which is passed on to its members, and functions to hold the group together more cohesively. In a similar way, Durkheim (1912) described how a totem, a group's externalization of their social order, functions as a point around which the group orients itself. A family's collective memories centre on vivid images that concretely express an abstract evaluation of the group and its members. These vivid memory images tend to condense many episodes and elements from different periods into a composite image, which becomes a prototype, model and example for the group. In contrast to contemporary discussions of memory in psychology, Halbwachs does not consider these 'distorted' or 'false' memories, but as a highly effective and efficient way of retaining the general idea of the family's past.

Composite images are one important mechanism through which individuals localize their memory in relation to social frameworks; however, as in social representations theory, Halbwachs also gives central place to the role of language. '[One] cannot in fact think about the events of one's past without discoursing upon them. But to discourse upon something means to connect within a single system of ideas our opinions as well as those of our circle' (Halbwachs, 1925/1992, p. 53). It is through language that we name and categorize our experiences, and thereby attach them to a larger system of thought, a network of relations and meanings. For example, the very names of our family members remain surrounded by a certain aura and set of associations, long after our family members pass away. They are indexes or symbols of the group's taken-for-granted understanding of itself and the world.

In modern societies, individuals are members of a number of different social groups and as such remember through a variety of social frameworks. This is similar to Moscovici's (1961/2008) notion of 'cognitive polyphasia', in which multiple frameworks of thought coexist within the same society or even the same individual (see also Arthi, Provencher and Wagner, 2012). These frameworks do not remain isolated from one another but rather co-develop through communication between them. Halbwachs describes how an individual's act of remembering involves moving between different social frameworks. Because of the unique combination of frameworks and the contrasts between them, the individual has the illusion that his or her memory is wholly personal. In fact, individuality emerges from one's positions in society. Halbwachs can be critiqued for often overemphasizing the social determination of individual processes, as if the individual were a kind of automaton of the group. His insight that individuals move between social frameworks in remembering suggests that we should pay more attention to the actual thought processes of the individual who remembers. This was the analytic focus of the Cambridge psychologist Frederic Bartlett, to whom we now turn.

Bartlett and reconstructive remembering

Bartlett's book *Remembering: A Study in Experimental And Social Psychology* remains the classic psychological work on the subject. The title of the book is noteworthy in two respects. First, he is very explicit that he does not intend to study 'the memory', a self-contained mental faculty, as Ebbinghaus (1885/1913) had done; but rather 'remembering' as an everyday activity involving a number of different social and psychological processes. Second, his approach highlights the importance of distinctly social processes in remembering, and in that way it is similar to Halbwachs. Bartlett, however, is critical of Halbwachs' metaphor that the group itself has memories. Instead, he is clear that remembering is done *in* a group, not *by* a group. The two thinkers also differ in that Halbwachs tended to emphasize the characteristics of different social frameworks at the expense of how individuals combine them, whereas Bartlett focussed on how social meanings and relationships enter into individuals' remembering. His approach involves the complex interplay between an individual's interests, prior experience, group membership and social setting.

In Bartlett's scheme, psychological processes must always be socially situated: 'The individual who is considered in psychological theory, in fact, is never an individual pure and simple. The statements made about him always have reference to a particular set of conditions. The individual with whom we deal may be the-individual-in-the-laboratory, or – and in social psychology this is always the case – the-individual-in-a-given-social-group' (Bartlett, 1923, p. 11). Moreover, the group is itself given properties that are irreducible to the individuals in them. As such, a study of the individual-in-the-group means understanding individual psychological processes in relation to the 'customs, traditions, institutions, technical secrets, formulated and unformulated ideals and numerous other facts which are literally properties of groups, as the direct determinates of social action' (Bartlett, 1932, p. 254). He goes on to say: 'They are correctly regarded as group properties, because they come into being only as the group is formed, and if the group disintegrates they pass away' (p. 254). Durkheim and Halbwachs would certainly have approved.

Bartlett's early 'experiments on remembering' were actually first conceived as a psychological contribution to the anthropological process of conventionalization. Conventionalization refers to the process by which foreign cultural elements are transformed in the direction of the recipient group's customs and traditions. This was a major area of investigation for his anthropology mentors at Cambridge, Alfred Cort Haddon and W. H. R. Rivers, who looked at how decorative art forms or cultural practices were assimilated into a receiving culture, causing it to change. Bartlett investigated this process experimentally by having his subjects repeatedly reproduce a variety of stories and images, many of which came from foreign cultures. Most famously, he gave the Native American story *War of the Ghosts* to his English students and colleagues and had them repeatedly reproduce it at increasing time delays. In the reproductions, 'hunting seals' became 'fishing', 'canoes' became 'boats', the proper names changed, supernatural elements were rationalized away, and so on. In short, his participants were 'making the unfamiliar familiar'.

Moscovici is directly drawing on Bartlett's work when he argues that the primary function of social representations is 'to make something unfamiliar, or unfamiliarity itself, familiar' (1984b, p. 25). Bartlett's focus on the *transformation* of material as it moves from one group to another is also clearly in line with Moscovici's (1976, 1990) call for a 'genetic social psychology', which studies the construction and reconstruction of representations either through 'Bartlett's way' (in sociogenesis) or 'Vygotsky's way' (in ontogeny). This emphasis on transformation shifts the focus of representation's research from Durkheim's hegemonic approach to a much more dynamic perspective that highlights the generative exchange that takes place between different social groups in contemporary society. Finally, Moscovici explicitly acknowledges Bartlett's influence in articulating the process of objectification whereby abstract ideas are made into concrete images and projected into the world as real (see Moscovici and Marková, 1996). In his study of perception, Bartlett (1932) noted how his subjects added to images concrete details that made them conform to a conventional representation. For example, in a perception experiment one subject called a design a 'pick-axe' and gave it pointed prongs, while another called it a 'turf-cutter' and rounded the blade (p. 20).

From the results of his experiments, Bartlett (1932) famously argued: 'Remembering is not the re-excitation of innumerable fixed, lifeless and fragmentary traces. It is an imaginative reconstruction or construction, built out of the relation of our attitude towards a whole active mass of organized past reactions or experience, and to a little outstanding detail which commonly appears in image or in language form' (p. 213). The 'active mass of organized past reactions or experience' is elsewhere given the name 'schema' (see Wagoner, 2013a). Instead of the retention of distinct memory images, Bartlett argued that the most basic level of remembering involves a generalized pattern of response and experience (i.e., schema), as one finds with habits and bodily skills. When an event is remembered, such as going to a restaurant, we tend to blend what is usually the case with what happened during the particular event in question. The first and last occurrences of going to a restaurant will exert a greater influence on the general pattern and a greater number of specific elements will be remembered for them in comparison to events between them. Thus, our memory for specific events in a particular setting tends to form a U-shape graph, where time is on the X axis.

Remembering is reconstructive because it involves this generalization of experience into conventional forms (e.g. normal restaurant activities) but also by bringing together experiences coming from diverse sources in an act of remembering (Wagoner, 2013b). This latter meaning of reconstruction is often missed in contemporary discussions. Bartlett (1935, p. 224) gives the example of an enthusiastic journalist's account of a cricket match: 'To describe the batting of one man he finds it necessary to refer to a sonata of Beethoven; the bowling of another reminds him of a piece of beautifully wrought rhythmic prose written by Cardinal Newman.' In this way, the individual welds together different domains of experience in remembering a particular episode, an insight similar to Halbwachs' idea that we move between different social frameworks in remembering. In an earlier work, Bartlett (1923) used this more radical notion of (re)construction to describe how social groups construct new cultural forms, out of elements coming from different sources, in order to move towards a group's 'prospect'. More recently, social representations theorists have called it a group's 'project' (Bauer and Gaskell, 1999). The concept is important in that it highlights the fact that individuals and groups are not simply determined by their past but creatively use it in their striving towards the future.

Vygotsky and mediated memory

Central to Vygotsky's theory is Durkheim's idea that concepts (e.g. space, time and causality) are social in origin. Vygotsky extends this insight to describe 'the general genetic law of cultural development' as a process in which higher psychological functions (e.g. attention, thought and voluntary memory) begin as actual relations between people (intermentally). These social relations later reappear on the intramental plane, where they take on a new function. For example, language is a distinctly social product that is first used to coordinate social action between people, but with its internalization it comes to fundamentally transform the process of thought in the developing child (Vygotsky, 1987; Vygotsky and Luria, 1994). Like Bartlett, Vygotsky focusses on individual memory but situates it within the mnemonic traditions and resources of different societies. He explicitly uses the example of mnemonic technologies to substantiate his claim that higher mental functions have social-cultural origins, though it should be said that he never rejects the notion of memory trace (as Bartlett had done); rather, he relegates it to lower psychological processes. He believed purely individual psychological processes could not explain the dramatic increases in memory seen in both ontogeny and sociogenesis. Instead, psychologists would have to look to the development of different cultural tools and strategies in remembering.

Vygotsky gives the example of making knots on a rope as a mnemonic device, a common practice in pre-literate societies around the world. The kind, colour and placement of a knot had particular meaning for those in the society concerned. Tying a knot as a conscious attempt to remember involves creating a meaningful 'sign' in the environment, which then acts back on its creator in the future. Mnemonic signs have been around at least since humans began making marks on surfaces (Donald,

1991). Today we construct such signs when we make a note in the calendar, bring back a souvenir (literally translated from French as 'to remember') from a vacation, or leave out a letter in order to remember to mail it. In each case, we deliberately transform our environment to regulate our own memory (cf. with recent work on inter-objectivity; Sammut, Daanen and Moghaddam, 2013). For Vygotsky, this constituted what was distinctly human about memory:

> The very essence of human memory is that human beings actively remember with the help of signs ... human beings actively manipulate their relation to the environment, and through the environment they change their own behaviour, subjugating it to their control ... the very essence of civilization consists in the fact that we deliberately build monuments so as not to forget. In the knotted handkerchief and the monument we see the most profound, most characteristic and most important feature, which distinguishes human from animal memory. (quoted from Bakhurst, 1990, p. 210)

This framework was applied in a famous study done by Leontiev under Vygotsky's supervision. They had children remember lists of words but in one condition, meant to approximate the 'cultural line of development', they provided children with picture cards to help them remember – for example, using a picture of a sled to help remember the word 'horse'. However, for the picture cards to be useful, the children must be able to turn them into meaningful signs that stimulate their memory for the target word. They find little difference between with and without picture-card conditions for children aged 4 to 5 years, and thus 'natural' and 'cultural' memory. However, between the years of 5 and 12 children's performance increases dramatically in the with picture condition when compared to the without picture condition. From 12 years of age performance on the two conditions begin to converge again, such that the graph approximates a parallelogram. Vygotsky (1987) argued that the convergence was indicative of children's increasing use of internal signs (such as inner speech and mental imagery) such that the external signs became redundant.

Vygotsky's focus on the construct of signs in the environment and on how we think and remember through social tools is clearly compatible with social representations theory's notion that people respond to an environment of their own construction. However, Moscovici (1990) points out that it is difficult to generate a distinctly social psychology out of Vygotsky's approach, as he does not provide any mediating structures (e.g. forms of social relation, social positions, etc.) between social practices and individual functioning. As a result, the direct relationship between the two levels in Vygotsky's 'general genetic law of cultural development' seems 'too good to be true' (p. 179). Following these criticisms, Duveen (1997) has argued that we need to explore the ways in which the process of internalization of sign systems is structured by social representations. For example, Duveen investigates how representations of gender are a mediating link in children's development of knowledge (see Moscovici, Jovchelovitch and Wagoner, 2013). His framework thus brings together the insights of Halbwachs on institutional structures, Bartlett on knowledge reconstruction, and Vygotsky on the development of higher mental functions. Applying this framework to social memory, we can say that a person's tools of remembering are developed from and connected to his or her social position in society; memory and position dynamically change in relation to one another.

Modalities of remembering

In the last section, we saw how Halbwachs, Bartlett and Vygotsky all describe ways in which memory involves distinctively social processes using theoretical constructs akin to those found in social representations theory. Each theorist, however, develops a distinct approach with particular points of emphasis: Halbwachs describes the dynamics of different social groups' social frameworks; Bartlett mainly highlights where social processes enter into an individual's constructive remembering; and Vygotsky analyzes the role played by various mnemonic technologies. In this section, our analysis shifts from these particular theories to a classification of different modalities through which remembering occurs. The three modalities given below (i.e., the body, language and place) should not be considered exhaustive but rather as particularly central to how individuals and societies remember. It should also be noted that any particular act of remembering can simultaneously involve different modalities.

The body remembers

The concept of 'embodiment' has become a buzzword in contemporary social science, but its implications for the study of remembering have remained underdeveloped. Psychological studies of memory have traditionally focussed purely on cognitive processes removed from everyday activity in real (social) environments. Since the 1980s psychologists have increasingly recognized the importance of incorporating the body and the environment in their investigations; however, the two are often analyzed in separation and then said to 'interact'. The analytic focus should be the body in action within a particular environment, which is socialculturally constituted. This conception can be seen in one strand of the theory of social representations, where the body is the vehicle through which representations are performed in social practices (e.g. Jodelet, 1989/1991). In this sense, social representations may not even be available to conscious reflection; they are transmitted through participation in stable social practices, where they become incorporated into one's body. This understanding of social representations comes close to Bourdieu's (1990) theory of practice, which also builds on Durkheim's approach but focusses mainly on how social inequalities are reproduced in society. In both approaches, embodied social memory has less to do with cognitively representing the past than with its retention through the re-presentation in social practices.

With regard to the body's role in social remembering, Durkheim is once again a forerunner. Durkheim (1912) described how 'primitive' societies commemorate the mythical past in bodily rituals where participants must themselves perform the heroic events of the group's past. The events are literally *re-presented*, rather than narrated as if the performer were separate from them. Ritual performance of this kind does not allow for the kind of variations nor critical distance that one finds in normal language use (see below); thus, body rituals are a very effective medium for transmitting tradition intact from one generation to the next. Durkheim's nephew and collaborator, Marcel Mauss, further advanced his uncle's insight (in more mundane context) in a famous paper entitled 'Techniques of the Body' (1934). He argued that societies socialize their members to walk, swim, sit and so on in particular normative ways. Mauss gives the example of his generation's particular technique of swimming, whereby one swallowed water and spat it out again as if one were a kind of steamboat (p. 256). Some body techniques that we take for granted, like spitting, are never developed in certain societies, while others, like resting in a squat position, have been lost to us as a result of our life in furnished industrial environments. These socialized body postures are not in themselves representational, but they become so when they are linked to different social practices and identities, where they can function as indexes of social representations of, for example, gender. In the process of body socialization, adults correct children's postures physically or with expressions like 'girls don't sit like that' or 'sit like a man'. Social representations of what it means to be a man or woman become incorporated into one's body and performed without reflection. To change one's gender later in life, requires not only a sex change, but also a resocialization of one's body (Garfinkel, 1984).

Connerton (1989) has recently argued that practices *incorporated* into the body are central to 'how society remembers', but have been neglected by social scientists because of the dominant focus on *inscription* (i.e. written texts). To make his argument he begins with the example of the French Revolution, in which many deliberate efforts were made to tear down the existing social order, that is, to erase social memory. Perhaps the most dramatic statement of this was the trial and execution of Louis XVI. This was not simply a regicide – that had been done before, though in private. It was a public ritual to put an end to the institution of royalty, to destroy both the king's physical and representative body, thereby denaturalizing the existing social order. Social representations of kingship had up to this time been objectified in ritual performances. Before the revolution, the sacred nature of the king's body was vividly conferred in the coronation ceremony, where a bishop of the church crowned the king, anointed him with holy oil and announced his rule 'by the grace of god' (Connerton, 1989, p. 9). This ritual bestowed on the king a sacred status, such that the enemies of royalty would also be the enemies of religion and God. At this time a society without religion had never been seen. As Durkheim (1912) argued, it is precisely through sacred beliefs and rituals that society is preserved. What the revolution did was to replace one set of beliefs and rituals with another, a religion with a philosophy. The trial of Louis XVI designated the institution of royalty a great injustice and the execution literally severed the sacred head of the institution.

At a more mundane level, the revolutionaries invented new styles of clothing, which all estates of society were to wear. The pre-revolutionary clothing objectified the social hierarchy of estates. The new clothing was a deliberately created body practice to erase memory from the earlier social order, to denaturalize it. This was accomplished by doing away with overt signs of privilege and encouraging the underclasses to transgress previous rules and dominate the street. The transgression of norms was further facilitated in that the revolutionaries' clothing had the added feature of carnival flare, which like all carnivals was meant to suspend rank, privilege, norms and prohibitions. Thus, the revolutionaries effectively anchored social interactions within a perpetual carnival. In the new clothing, as well as the king's trial and execution, we find an intervention at the level of bodily practices in order to transform social memory, to anchor social relations to the ideals of revolution (i.e., equality, fraternity and solidarity). The transformation of social memory often requires a deliberate act, because there is inertia to our embodied social practices, which function largely without reflexivity.

Language: from orality to literacy

Most research in the psychology of memory is undoubtedly done through the medium of language, though the role it plays in psychological processes is not typically analyzed explicitly. From the review of Halbwachs, Bartlett and Vygotsky, we have already seen the important role played by language: human memory owes its origin to communication with others in society and the act of remembering is itself mediated through language (or 'vocalization', in Bartlett's terms). The theory of social representations is also distinct, as a psychological theory, in its inclusion of communication and language in its analysis of social psychological processes: it analyzes how different forms of communication lead to different psychological outcomes, and how language is used to name and categorize experience, thereby anchoring the new in the old. We might add to this that as the media of communication changes in a society so do social psychological processes. Several studies have, for example, analyzed the shifts in mentality as societies transition from orality to literacy (see e.g. Goody, 1986; Luria, 1976). This section offers a brief account of how changes in communication technology have affected collective remembering. This is not a relationship of technological determinism but one in which multiple social and cultural factors play a part.

In oral societies stories and myths are a primary means of passing on the group's knowledge and memory from one generation to the next. The meaning of memory within this context was very different from that of written societies. For example, the pre-Socratic Greeks only used the word 'mneme' in specific contexts, such as to describe the activity of bards who told epic poems at festivals, which could last several days and thus required a prodigious memory. These epic poems would begin by evoking the goddess Mnemosyne or her daughters, the muses, in order to bring memory to the performer. Both the *Iliad* and *Odyssey* begin in this way. Thus, memory at this time was not seen as something individual and internal to the speaker but rather as divinely inspired from the outside. Similarly, anthropologists have noted that memories are sometimes conceptualized as dead ancestors by illiterate groups (see e.g. Vitebsky, 1993).

The pre-literate concept of memory also differs in that remembering involves the speaker's adaptation of the story to audience and circumstance at each telling; as such, the story evolves over time and several versions of the 'same' story result. Performance involves creatively filling in gaps in memory (also aptly demonstrated by Bartlett's studies). However, storytellers would say that they are producing the same story, because without a written text to compare their version they must rely on the standard of spoken memory and from this perspective the story is the same. The arrival of literacy changes oral traditions by introducing a fixed standard to which storytellers refer back to between performances. As the tools of memory change so does its conceptualization: Memory comes to be understood in literate societies as a place were some fixed information is stored. Furthermore, in literate cultures a process of *canon* formation can ensue, whereby particular texts become central measures, models and rules within a group, which are referred back in the discussions of each successive generation (Assman, 2011).

In short, in pre-literate oral societies innovations tend to occur in the retellings of stories, whereas in literate societies innovations occur through a reinterpretation and extension of fixed texts that can be easily referred back to. The kind of dialogue with tradition found in literate societies leads to recognition of the differences between past and present. This can open up a historical dimension, although it should be noted that this is not a *necessary* outcome of literacy; many societies, such as ancient that of Egypt, had the technical means of preserving the past but did not develop a historical consciousness (Assman, 2011). Literacy can also encourage a more critical attitude towards a group's knowledge and what Bartlett (1923) called 'social constructiveness', the intentional welding together of ideas coming from diverse sources into a new cultural form. These become possible because written texts can be put next to each other and compared, so that inconsistencies as well as possibilities for synthesis can be literally seen. With oral societies the recognition of inconsistencies and syntheses will tend to remain local discoveries and thus not have the accumulative impact that one finds when they are solidified in written texts.

Thus, writing can transform collective memory from a more 'hegemonic' representation (à la Durkheim) to become conflicted and negotiated within a public sphere: Moscovici (1988) has argued that representations in modern society are frequently 'emancipated' (when there is a free exchange of ideas between different social groups) or 'polemic' (when there is social conflict between antagonistic groups, creating mutually exclusive relations between them). Modern society is characterized by a multiplicity of different social groups in extensive contact with one another. As such, groups develop both their own social representations as well as representations of other groups' representations (i.e. 'alternative representations'). From this situation, the need arises to regulate the influence of other groups' ideas through 'semantic barriers' (see Gillespie, 2008). Similarly, Wertsch (2002) has argued from the standpoint of collective memory that a group's representation of its own history can be 'dialogical' (where alternative accounts are explicitly brought into dialogue with ones own) or 'monological' (where alternative accounts are only implicitly acknowledged and immediately silenced). There is no definitive and impartial interpretation of the past which we can consult to obtain the 'true' historical causes of conflicts. We have inevitably to deal with different and even opposing ways of (re)constructing the past attached to different social frameworks. Social groups typically invent tactics to block other group's interpretations, but there is also the possibility of encouraging dialogue and reflexivity on one's own constructions through, for example, a more critical teaching of history (Egan, 1997; Rosa and Blanco, 2007).

Space, image and monument

Collective memory is not only carried in bodies, language and text but also in space/place. The theory of social represntations implicitly acknowledges this in the idea that human environments are invested with social meanings and values, which become the constructed external stimuli that people act on (Moscovici, 1984; see also the section on Vygotsky above). This idea runs counter to stimulus–response models of the behaviourists as well as input–output models of cognitive psychology, in which the environment is conceptualized as already given and seen to directly cause the individual organism's response. In contrast to this, social representations theory conceptualizes the environment as being constructed (in both the symbolic and material sense) by social groups embedded within a cultural tradition. In relation to collective remembering, we can say that a group's memories become objectified in the environment. For example, a square retains the aura of protest long after any conflicts have taken place there, and may be used as the scene for protests over new issues, thereby implicitly linking new struggles to the old. Thus, places become part of a group's collective resources for anchoring new ideas. This section considers work that explores the relationship between memory and place.

The power of place was already recognized and cultivated in ancient Greece with the art of memory. To improve one's memory one imagined a familiar place (such as a street or a building) and situated striking symbolic images of the things to be remembered in the discrete loci of it. To remember the items, one simply walked through one's mind reading off the images as one passed. The art of memory went through a number of transformations within the western tradition (Yates, 1966), from its cultivation as part of rhetoric in the ancient world, through the function of aiding memory for virtues and vices in the medieval Christian world (e.g. Dante's *Divine Comedy* presents heaven and hell as spatially organized memory systems into which symbolic images of rewards for virtues and punishments for vices are placed). In the Renaissance, 'memory theatres' were planned to spatially organize all existing knowledge (i.e. cosmic truths, not scientific facts), thereby bringing the mind (microcosm) directly into contact with the universe (macrocosm).

Shakespeare's Globe theatre was originally designed to perform this function. More recently, Nora (1989) extended the tradition to a programmatic level (den Boer, 2010), exploring the different memory sites (*lieux de mémoire*) that the French nation has constructed to retain its past, such as archives, libraries, festivals, the Pantheon and the Arc de Triomphe. All of these memory places (from ancient Greece to Nora) can be thought of as collectively constructed sign systems, in Vygotsky's sense, which once created act back on individuals socialized into the culture from which they come. Moreover, these places can be used to anchor new knowledge – for example, the meaning of a new play is set against the backdrop of a spatially organized network of meanings objectified in earlier performances taking place on the same stage.

Nora (1989) famously contrasted the artificially constructed places of memory (*lieux de mémoire*) to spontaneous remembering embedded in daily life customs and rituals, the environments of memory (*milieux de mémoire*). The latter was the main focus of Halbwachs (1950/1980), who gave a central role to the environment in sustaining a group's 'social framework'. This can be seen in both the spatial language he uses to develop his theory (e.g. 'localization', 'framework', 'implacement', etc.) and in his attention to the role played by material spaces and objects in providing a material and symbolic anchor for memories. The materiality of memory can be demonstrated by the family house, which is filled with memorabilia of the family's history (e.g. furniture, arrangements, photos and objects from trips) and is divided into spaces that family members associate with different activities and occasions. These objects and spaces act as a scaffold for both the group's bodily and cognitive memory. At a more general level, cities serve to scaffold a community's memory: 'The great majority may well be more sensitive to a certain street being torn up, or a certain building or home being razed, than to the gravest national, political, or religious events... Not only homes and walls persist through the centuries, but also that *whole portion of the group in continuous contact with them, its life merged with things*' (Halbwachs, 1950/1980, p. 131, emphasis added). As Halbwachs notes, many social divisions are objectified and sustained through the organization of space. A social class inhabits particular neighbourhoods of a city: historically the upper class has lived on the side of the city from which the wind blows, so that they would not be exposed to the city's smells, which the working class got on the other side. Moreover, city inhabitants develop social representations of neighbourhoods, which can be difficult to overcome even if the reality on the ground is different (Milgram, 1977, 1984).

The French Revolution again provides an illustrative case study of an attempt on the part of the revolutionaries to transform the structure of society, here through the reorganization of space. During the revolution churches and houses of the rich were targeted as insults to republican morals. Bell towers were threatened with destruction because 'their height above other buildings seems to contradict the principles of equality' (quoted from Bevan, 2006, p. 22). A new architecture was even developed in which the different 'estates' of society were to live in the same buildings as one another, though on different floors. The pantheon in Paris was transformed into a symbol of enlightenment by burying key figures there and by inserting scientific symbols, whereas it was originally intended as a grandiose religious symbol. Such monuments can be seen as objectifications of a community's values, which at a later point can serve to anchor new ideas. As Vygotsky noted, monuments are deliberately constructed signs in the environment that stimulate successive generations to remember. Conversely, their destruction transforms a group's relation to the past, and has often been deliberately used to reconstruct a group's history. For example, after Mosques were destroyed in the Yugoslav wars, Serbian leaders confidently announced that Muslims had never been a part of the society (Bevan, 2006).

The classics through the lens of memory

This last section aims to apply some of the ideas discussed above to the classic studies in social representations to foreground processes of collective remembering in them. Moscovici's (1961/2008) *Psychoanalysis* and Jodelet's (1989/1991) *Madness and Social Representations* are two foundational texts, which represent two rather different understandings of social representations. According to Harré (1998), Moscovici's work understood social representations as a property of a person that is shared among members of a group, whereas Jodelet's work focussed on joint practices of a group, which stand above any one individual; in short, social representations can be seen as 'transcendent' or 'immanent' to practice. For our purposes, the difference is useful in that each study emphasizes different aspects of collective memory: Moscovici explores text-mediated discourse, while Jodelet attends closely to body memory and the organization of space. I will discuss each study in turn.

Moscovici's study of psychoanalysis

Moscovici (1961/1976) sets out to re-evaluate common-sense thinking and to explore how expert ideas (in this case, psychoanalysis) are transformed into public forms of knowledge. In bringing back the 'lost' concept of 'social representation' (advocated by Durkheim, Halbwachs and others), he hoped to also revitalize a societal focus in social psychology. However, the focus on processes of transformation (i.e. a 'genetic social psychology' – Moscovici, 1990) leads him away from Durkheim's hegemonic look at representations and towards Bartlett's attention to the change of culture as it moves between different groups and societies. Modern societies are characterized by differentiation into different social groups, which are in continuous and constructive communication with one another through various kinds of mass media. In this situation, individuals and groups not only remember but also respond to others' memories, which can come into conflict with their own. Cultural strategies must thus be developed to block the influence of other ways of thinking, so as to manage the heterogeneity of the social world and one's identity in it (Gillespie, 2008). These dynamics occur mainly at the level of discourse; as such, Moscovici's study is a textual analysis of questionnaires, interviews and the press.

Moscovici's study illustrates that the new (i.e. psychoanalysis) is constructively understood in terms of the old. In his words, 'Memory tends to predominate over logic, the past over the present, the response over the stimuli and the image over the "reality"' (Moscovici, 1981b, p. 189). Collective remembering thus operates as a kind of background condition for understanding (cf. Bartlett's schema – Wagoner, 2013a), which is dynamically carried forward to interpret the new. Psychoanalysis is linked to (or anchored in) the more familiar activities of conversation and confession. This is similar to linguists' notion of metaphorical mapping, whereby one object is seen in terms of another. For example, the common metaphor 'argument is war' foregrounds conflicting aspects of the phenomenon whereas the unconventional metaphor 'argument is dance' highlights harmonious qualities (Lakoff and Johnson, 1980). The new psychoanalytic description of mind is metaphorically connected to how individuals relate to themselves through the imaginary dimension of *depth*. Already existing and exchangeable antinomies (e.g. hidden–visible, voluntary–involuntary, authentic–false) are used to give shape to the psychoanalytic notions of conscious and unconscious mind. The two terms are then seen as pitted against one another causing 'repression', and leading to 'complexes'. This concrete idea image serves as a model for individuals (cf. Halbwachs' description of a family's memory) to relate to psychoanalysis. However, in this model the central and unifying concept of the libido is left out.

In the second part of *Psychoanalysis*, Moscovici reports on how the liberal, Catholic and communist presses communicate psychoanalysis. Each group uses psychoanalysis as a tool to advance its own 'prospect' or 'project'. It is here that we see the 'cultural battle' over the meaning of psychoanalysis as each group sharpens and manipulates the tool for its purposes. The past drawn upon to situate the unfamiliar is specific to each group. The Catholic and communist presses, in particular, use the canonical models of their group to measure and evaluate the new. These do not speak directly about psychoanalysis but they still set the framework through which it can be understood. For Catholics, confession is one of the most important social rituals. They see psychoanalysis as similar but different to it and thus psychoanalysis is accepted as a supplement to, rather than a replacement of, confession. At the same time, the sexual and aggressive image of man is rejected for its incompatibility with church doctrine. The communist press, in contrast, entirely rejects psychoanalysis, slotting it into the bad side of its dichotomized worldview. This is accomplished through a linguistic device in which psychoanalysis is always prefixed with American, irrational, pseudo-science, bourgeois and individualist (i.e. the group's negative categories), whereas the opposite set of positive categories is applied to communism. As Halbwachs noted, these networks of categories make up a group's social framework and can be used to assert its individuality against others.

Moscovici's study shows how societies retain a multitude of ways of knowing (i.e. cognitive polyphasia) within their tradition that can be used for understanding the unfamiliar. They are brought forward in time through their continued use, and may not even be recognized as past. These ways of knowing can be considered collective memory in that they bring past ideas forward by flexibly using them to move towards the future; it is an adaptation and selection of tradition to meet current demands. It is also interesting to note that the patterned consumption and distribution of media is done as a function of group membership. A social framework, Halbwachs argued, emerges and is sustained by processes of communication within a group. Memory is intimately linked to one's membership in different groups and the processes of communication that take place in them. Thus, memory and knowledge cannot be separated from identity.

Jodelet's study of madness

Jodelet's (1989/1991) study was conducted in a village in central France, where mental patients have been fostered out to families since 1900. At the most general level, the study explores how communities handle otherness, in this case the mentally ill, or *bredin* (loonies), as the locals call them. As the doors of the asylum are opened up introducing the mentally ill into society, so symbolic barriers are constructed in their place to keep them at a distance and thereby retain continuity with the past. The mentally ill are 'tolerated' but not integrated into the community. This dynamic results from the dual considerations of economy and fear. On the one hand, the *bredin* provide a fertile economic basis for the community, as locals are both paid for keeping them and can extract labour from them, while on the other hand they are seen as a potential danger. Fear is overcome by the development of customs and norms, which separate the mentally ill from locals and limit the possibilities for contact and mixture between the two. The dynamics of simultaneous profit and exclusion in many ways resemble practices towards African-Americans in the United States (Wacquant, 2002), substantiating Jodelet's claim that the study provides knowledge about how communities deal with otherness in general. Social remembering can be seen in the study, at the broadest level, in the various embodied customs and practices developed in order to maintain the social order through time. More specifically, it can be analyzed in three ways: (1) how the community draws on its collective memory in order to situate otherness; (2) how knowledge about mental illness is transmitted between generations; and (3) how places and objects are used to objectify the exclusion of the mentally ill.

First, Jodelet points out how the deep-seated resources of collective memory are employed to orient to the mentally ill. She uses the metaphor of 'impregnation' to analyze the need for separation; at base, it can be understood as a magical fear of symbolic contagion through body contact and the mixing of bodily fluids – blood, sweat and semen. It is magical in that locals are well aware that medically mental illness is not contagious, but symbolically the boundary must be kept. Thus, the existing social order is retained primarily through an embodied feeling rather than a cognition. Modern and archaic beliefs coexist (in a relation of cognitive polyphasia); the latter still remains a part of embodied collective memory. The clothing worn by the mentally ill is washed in different water than the families', and the mentally ill are made to use different dishes and cutlery. The power of body fluids, especially blood, is itself a deep and ancient part of the group's collective memory (p. 286 ff.). For example, the church's doctrine of Transubstantiation (the conversion of bread and wine into Christ's body and blood); traditional beliefs about the medicinal properties of blood (including the removal of 'bad' blood); the notion of royal blood ('blue blood') which was also seen to have 'healing powers'; the racial sense of having pure blood (e.g. Africans are seen to be less dangerous than the Maghreb because the skin of the former is black and their blood is thus purer than the latter). There is also a traditional belief in a close connection between blood and smell; it is thus highly significant that one of the primary means of differentiating *bredin* from locals is smell.

Second, common-sense knowledge of how to identify different kinds of mentally ill and deal with them is passed on in exchanges among locals. This is how the linguistic categories for understanding mental illness are transmitted from one generation to the next. The communication is so extensive that Jodelet says it was as if the locals were all speaking with a single voice in her interviews. Identification of kinds of mental illness borrows from a figurative model of tripart division between brain, body and nerves. As in Moscovici's aforementioned study, this idea-image is something between a percept and a concept, taking on characteristics of both. In deciding whether to take lodgers, locals seek out extensive advice from peers (Jodelet, 1989/1991, p. 110 ff.). This communication serves to pass on the community's categories for the mentally ill as well as techniques and habits of managing them. What begins as recipes for handling the lodgers transforms into rules and normative conventions. The more experience locals have with lodgers, the more likely they are to use a normative language of laws, rules and principles in dealing with the mentally ill. Thus, transmission of knowledge is initiated to get advice, used in practice and becomes hardened into a formal rule. Deviations from the rule are considered 'taboo', as they threaten to fuse locals and lodgers by opening up the symbolic boundary between the two.

Third, separation and exclusion is further objectified and carried forward in the community's memory through the organization of space. In public, regions are set aside for the mentally ill:

> At the dance a lodger is allowed to watch but not to take part. When films are shown at the local hall, the darkness proves to be a cause for reticence and the patients are consigned to a corner whose seating is separated from that of the public. In church, where once they were grouped together in a special area close to the side door, they are now perfectly free to sit wherever they please. Although the priest, once attacked as a 'revolutionary' for opposing these segregatory measures, has been unable to gain them access to seats traditionally reserved for certain families, some of them are, at least, allowed to approach the altar. (Jodelet, 1989/1991, p. 61)

Local cafes likewise have special rooms set aside for the mentally ill which others do not enter. Special pots of coffee are reserved for the mentally ill that are inferior to those given to the locals. Even in death they are buried in a separate area of the cemetery with uniform crosses as one finds in a military cemetery. In private homes, the lodgers are often made to live in outhouses separate from the family and those that have a room in the home are frequently 'locked out' of the family's living spaces. There is also an exclusion from family activities such as having dinner, watching television or playing with the children. All of these practices function to maintain the social order, which involves keeping a rigid barrier between locals and lodgers. The symbolization of space becomes a key mechanism of solidifying collective memory of community divisions and dominance. Locals, in fact, use the notion of 'placement' in its double sense of a designated geosocial space and placement in a hierarchy of social relationships, asserting their rightful authority over the mentally ill. The role ascribed to places (e.g. special rooms and regions) and objects (e.g. coffee pot and cutlery) in creating a material scaffold for a community's memory is clearly fitting with Vygotsky's idea that we fashion our environment to regulate ourselves and others, as well as more recent work on interobjectivity (Sammut et al., 2013).

Conclusion

The theoretical relationship between collective remembering and social representations remains complex. This is partly due to the open and heterogeneous nature of both fields of research, particularly memory studies. As this chapter has shown, the two fields share a common heritage as well as many key ideas and concerns. Even so, there has been little cross-referencing in more recent approaches, with some notable exceptions (e.g. Liu and Hilton, 2005). This may be partly the result of the different emphases of the two approaches: the transmission and reconstruction of the past is the primary object of memory studies and only a secondary concern in the theory of social representations. Nonetheless, when social representations theorists ask questions about how a collective relates to its past and transmits its knowledge through time, it is very squarely operating within the field of memory studies (Olick and Robbins, 1998). In the remaining space, I will offer some suggestions for how the two fields of research might be brought into closer contact around issues that concern them both, and at the same time point to their practical usefulness in exploring contemporary social questions.

First, collective remembering is expressed and communicated in some material medium. The medium used will put different constraints on the transmission and accessibility to reflection of the group's social representations of its tradition. Above, we saw how the body is very effective at transmitting representations intact from one generation to the next, as it does not generally afford self-reflection, at least in comparison to representations carried through language. Even more, a person may hold a different representation at a conscious reflective level than they do at the level of body habits and affect, as we saw in people's ideas about the contagiousness of mental illness in Jodelet's study. Language itself takes on different characteristics for transmitting the past when it is written/recorded. In literate cultures traditions of commentary often develop, where ideas begin to accumulate much faster through time. Like writing, material objects and places leave durable traces, but they tend to relate more directly to a collective's bodily habits. They also remain powerful objectifications from a particular time, which must be either destroyed or significantly altered to change their meaning in the present. For example, the landscape of the Nazi Party rally grounds in Nuremberg was a powerful fascist symbol, which officials tried to temper in the post-war period by stripping away swastikas, letting the buildings degenerate and turning the space into a public park; despite these efforts, the site remains controversial to this day (Macdonald, 2006).

The different media through which the past gnaws into the present serve as a reservoir of resources to anchor new ideas, which brings us to the second point. Representations of the past provide groups with a clarification of the present and an orientation to the future. For example, as Americans increasingly came to favour intervention in Iraq in 1991, they tended to anchor the issue within a World War II analogy over a Vietnam analogy (Shuman and Rieger, 1992). The past may be selected and shaped in this way, or simply fabricated to support a group's prospect; the latter strategy has been analyzed under the rubric of 'the invention of tradition' (Hobsbawn and Ranger, 1983/2010). All this points to the fact that the way the past is represented has direct implications for how a group moves towards its future. As such, groups will often try to impose their own way of representing the past onto other groups. This symbolic struggle has real consequences. Majority groups will generally have control over public spaces (such as monuments) and official history, while minority groups will often be forced to communicate their representation through other avenues, such as graffiti or new media. For instance, new media not only provided protestors a network to organize the 2011 Egyptian revolution, but also kept alive and diffused the memory of state brutality on a Facebook page called 'We are all Khaled Said'. Said was a political activist savagely killed in front of his house by two police officers; an image of his mangled face is now recognizable to any Egyptian and has been used in post-revolution graffiti as a powerful symbol and reminder of the revolutionary cause.

The conflict of memories between different social groups reminds us that there is no neutral way of representing the past; remembering is always done *from* a social position and *with* cultural tools, such as language, images and narrative. These tools help us to cope with the unavoidable ambiguity of the past. Nevertheless, one can distinguish between more and less critical approaches in doing this. Social scientists can guide the public to reflect on the way they represent the past by making the processes of its construction explicit. Denaturalizing accounts may be an important first step in encouraging dialogue between two groups that have become entrenched through polemically held representations of their histories. The teaching of history, construction of monuments or collective rituals can all be done in such a way as to open up a dialogue between different ways of representing the past. However, we should not forget that one of the primary functions of collective remembering, as a process of social representation, is to create a sense of identification and solidarity within the social group. To what extent reflection and dialogue, regarding a group's memory, interferes with these identity functions remains an open question.

11 Cognitive polyphasia, knowledge encounters and public spheres

Sandra Jovchelovitch and Jacqueline Priego-Hernández

The encounter of ideas, beliefs and representations is integral to the history of human cultures and all public spheres are created in communicative spaces where people exchange views and practices about the world. The history of all cultures is made of cultural borrowings (Said, 1978) because since times immemorial ideas have travelled and mixed, exposing human communities to the thoughts, perspectives and preconceptions of unfamiliar others. The unfamiliar has never been too far away and is a central motivation in the production of knowledge. Today, increasing world-wide interconnectivity and novel mass media of communication make this process more visible than ever and accentuate questions about what happens when different systems of knowing travel and meet in public spheres. Is the world becoming too homogeneous as more powerful representational systems displace others? Is heterogeneity in social life enabling a rich and diverse public sphere? Or is the confluence of differences producing fragmentation and exclusion? How do we treat what is unfamiliar and different? And how do these issues affect our social representations and ways of thinking about our social worlds?

Addressing these questions requires understanding how social representations are formed and interact in public spheres. This was a central problem in Moscovici's original study on the reception of psychoanalysis in France. Its design and execution constitute a paradigmatic example of how to explore social representations as phenomena of the public sphere. This study showed that as psychoanalysis moved between different communities through multiple modalities of communication it became a public entity, an object of discussion, contestation, and ultimately widespread knowledge. Apprehending how the plurality inherent in human public spheres shapes knowledge outcomes and the structure of representational fields is at the core of studies of social representations. Different people, in different contexts and historical periods within and across cultures, produce different representations, symbols and narratives about what is real. Mapping out these variations has been central to sociocultural approaches to cognition (Cole, Engestrom and Vasquez, 1997).

In this chapter we address these issues by examining the interrelations between social representations and public spheres through the notions of knowledge encounters and cognitive polyphasia. Research and interest on cognitive polyphasia has evolved and proliferated in the last decade, but much remains to be done to systematize and clarify the concept. We know that there is dynamic coexistence between different systems of knowledge, but we have little systematization of *how* these processes take place. To address this gap, we will proceed in three steps. The first part of the chapter presents theories of the public sphere and how its contemporary transformations shed light on the dynamics of social representations. The second part introduces the notion of cognitive polyphasia, reviews the origins of the concept and places its conceptual resources in the wider programme of situated cognition and communicative rationality, which are central to social representations. Drawing on evidence from social and developmental psychology and related disciplines, we argue that cognitive polyphasia is a basic property of all sociocognitive functioning. In the third part of the chapter we outline the model of knowledge encounters and its relations to styles of communication and processes of recognition. We review research on the communicative processes underlying cognitive polyphasia and provide a synthesis of the various typologies identified by researchers in this area. We draw on these contributions to develop the concept and cast further light on *how* communicative processes in knowledge encounters determine the cognitive outcomes of polyphasic systems. In doing so, we offer a model that unpacks the communicative dynamics of cognitive polyphasia and explains its variety. Throughout the chapter we present the concepts focussing primarily on research in the fields of health and community.

The social psychology of public spheres

We define public spheres as open spaces where communal life is jointly experienced and becomes known to all (Jovchelovitch, 2007). Public spheres comprise political, spatial and social psychological dimensions: (1) *politically*, they are arenas for institutionalized debate and the exercise of critical public opinion, which are controlled neither by the state nor by the interests of markets and the economy. They express a realm of critical judgement in which civil society discusses and scrutinizes the action of states and markets (Habermas, 1989; Calhoun, 1992); (2) *spatially*, public spheres involve cities, neighbourhoods, parks, public markets, streets and any other environment, natural and built, that is accessible to all and enables people to come together. Think about a park in London, an art gallery in New York and a square in a small rural community in Peru; think of the festivals of the Yanomami in the Amazon forest and the Grand Bazaars of Istanbul: these are all public places where people come together mediated by the natural and/or built environment, which operate as enablers of physical circulation and communication; (3) *psychosocially*, public spheres are spaces of mediation and communication, where self and other come together in a variety of forms to create identity, representations and imaginations. Consider intergroup relations, the dynamics of social identity and social representation, impression and expression in the life of the self, how meaning is constructed and communicated across cultural and socioeconomic divisions; think about feelings of belonging and rituals of community life; consider collective behaviour in protest movements and riots:

these psychological phenomena are intrinsic to, made possible by, and formative of, public spheres.

Drawing on the work of Arendt (1958), Habermas (1989) and Mead (1934), Jovchelovitch (1995, 2000, 2007) developed a social psychological theory of the public sphere that focusses on three interrelated phenomena: plurality, perspective and communicative acts. Arendt's theory of public life foregrounds the inseparable link between the phenomena of plurality and perspective. We are plural because we are many and no individual is like another. Bridging different perspectives through speech and action is the basis of a life uniquely human and it is in public that the human condition comes to the fore.

Plurality and perspective introduce the question of how to handle differences, which is central to the work of Habermas and his theory of the public sphere. This becomes a key concern if members of a community are to build togetherness and act in concert. Self and other can settle differences in many ways, including the use of authority, force and even violence, as when self has total power to force its position and disregard the perspective of the other (more is discussed later in the chapter). In Habermas' theory, it is mutuality in communication and the use of reasons that provide the normative and practical requirements for settling differences and finding a way of acting in concert. They are the basis of all possible sociality and indispensable if people are to live together. To talk and to argue are practical requirements for the efficacy of action; without communication, joint action usually goes wrong (Gillespie and Richardson, 2011) and people get hurt psychologically and physically (Reader, Flin and Cuthbertson, 2007).

Mead's notion of the communicative act completes the conceptual framework of a social psychology of public spheres. The communicative act, as the basic unit of analysis for understanding human psychological life, is concomitant to the human condition of plurality and prerequisite for settling the differences embedded in human publics. Communication does not seek to efface difference and conflict because these can be generative; indeed tension and asymmetry fuel communication and drive dialogical acts. The communicative act dynamically bridges difference, elucidates conflict, creates and clarifies meanings and gradually stabilizes what Mead (1934) called the *generalized other*, a shared societal framework that provides the background horizon for thinking and behaviour. Mead's concept of the generalized other helps to conceive of public spheres as co-constructed common ground that is created and at the same time creates collective and social representations (Durkheim, 1898/1996; Farr, 1996; Moscovici, 1989).

Unpacking the communicative constitution of the public sphere enables us to grasp how it relates to the constitution of social representations. Here we can already see how both concepts use the interrelations between self, alter and object as the starting point for studying individual and social life.

Social representations and public spheres

Communication between self, alter and object is the basic architecture and unit of analysis for a substantively *social* social psychology, for public spheres and, as it has been extensively pointed out, for social representations (Bauer and Gaskell, 1999; Chapter 20 in this volume; Marková, 2003; Moscovici, 1984; for a discussion of the public sphere as space for the production of social solidarity, see Calhoun, 2002). For example, authoritarian public spheres hold a top-down asymmetrical architecture where the relations of self to alter impose, prescribe and force whereas democratic public spheres seek, at least in principle, symmetric architectures of mutuality and reciprocal recognition. We know however that lack of recognition and reciprocity are to be found everywhere and most certainly in so-called democratic societies.

Different modalities of self–alter–object communication establish different representational fields, making social representations heterogeneous and diverse phenomena. This was widely discussed in the second part of Moscovici's original study on the reception of psychoanalysis in France. Propagation, propaganda and diffusion were identified as the forms of communication that led to different ways of knowing psychoanalysis. Catholics, communists and liberal professionals displayed different styles of communication when talking, discussing and writing about psychoanalysis. These different ways of re-presenting selves, others and world shape the cognitive organization of social representations and explain the variation of knowledge systems.

Today new architectures of community and representation are unsettling public spheres and the boundaries of social representations, making the latter less likely to remain as collective and widely shared as Durkheim (1898/1996) first proposed. A focus on creative processes is changing public spheres and the internal structure of social representations. As intercultural groups come face to face connected by the World Wide Web and massive displacements of people and goods, so sociocognitive systems become more open to multiple fields of signification and practice. The result is detraditionalization in the public sphere (Giddens, 1991) and transition from collective to social representations (Jovchelovitch, 2007), a process in which individuals and groups rely less on consensual frameworks established by cultural traditions collectively upheld and more on decentralized and culturally diverse sources of legitimation for thinking and action.

In this type of public sphere a new global civil society is emerging, connecting local diasporic communities to multiple public spheres and directing representations to both local and global issues. The network society suggested by Castells (2002, 2008) organizes its public spheres on the basis of communication networks that bypass traditional institutions and media. These new networks spread in multiple directions and diversified flows, decentralized and poly-located in the new technological means available to young and unconventional political actors. New flows of public opinion, new time–space combinations and new social actors make public spheres polyphonic and polyglot, altering top-down vectors of social influence, the content and structure of social representations and thus public life itself.

Moving from the very personal to larger societal structures and back, the intense regime of knowledge encounters we all experience today is changing how public spheres think and relate to internal and external others. Things become less taken for granted and more open to contestation and debate. Importantly, plurality of social representations does not mean that public spheres accept and grant equal value to all. Some social representations are more valid than others because they are better aligned with local common sense and cultural traditions or because they are held by less powerful social actors. Certain social groups are thus able to impose their interests, meanings and projects over those of groups with less material and symbolic power (Howarth, 2001). There can also be a sharp increase in the displacement and even destruction of specific systems of knowledge. Scientific thinking, for instance, occupies the highest rung, while other ways of sense-making are left at the bottom and measured against allegedly more rational criteria. Correspondingly, the more legitimized a form of knowledge is, the more likely it is to be institutionalized and, by this means, the less likely it is to be challenged.

As can be seen, increased meeting points of social representation, which we define as knowledge encounters, not only have an impact on social cognition but also put into sharp evidence the plight of those whose representations, practices and ways of life do not hold the same power to be heard and recognized. When asymmetries in power enter the equation, the very plurality of the public sphere is under question and with it, the predicament of invisible, discriminated and excluded social representations.

Cognitive polyphasia: diversity in representational fields

A central aim of Moscovici's original study (1961/1976) was to rehabilitate common sense (Jovchelovitch, 2008) and demonstrate that ordinary people, not only intellectuals and scientists, are able to think rationally (Moscovici and Marková, 2000, p. 228). Leaving behind the traditional dichotomy between 'logical and non-logical, rational and affective and social and non-social' (Moscovici, 1961/2008, p. 163), he set himself the task of unpacking the characteristics of natural, everyday thought, without using science as the privileged model for comparison.

The study found that when people talked about psychoanalysis different rationalities were displayed, each of them with contextual functions and value in their own right. Differing modes of thinking were determined by the engagement with the social object in question, the communicative goals (influencing the other, uncovering facts, etc.), and the relationship between the person and the given milieu to which she belongs. It was not a matter of finding one logical system that would 'evolve' and become more developed, but rather of coexistence of multiple logical systems.

The finding that representational fields contain multiple ways of thinking gave origin to the concept of *cognitive polyphasia*, a state in which different ways of reasoning coexist in the same group and even in the same individual. Cognitive polyphasia was introduced by Moscovici as a hypothesis understood as:

> the same group and, mutatis mutandis, the same individual are capable of employing different logical registers in the domains which they approach with

> different perspectives, information and values ... [T]he dynamic coexistence – interference or specialization – of the distinct modalities of knowledge, corresponding to definite relations between man and his environment, determines a state of cognitive polyphasia. (Moscovici, 1961/2008, p. 180)

Cognitive polyphasia enabled Moscovici to address an important debate relating to the development of cognition and its relations to culture and rationality. For Piaget and Durkheim, who were central influences on Moscovici's thinking, the development of cognition implicated a series of successive stages through which 'lower' forms of thinking are displaced by 'higher' forms. In their studies, children and so-called 'primitive' peoples displayed lower forms whereas adults in 'advanced' societies displayed higher forms (Durkheim and Mauss, 1905/1963; Piaget, 1995). Moscovici's findings provided counter-evidence for this theory of displacement, showing that cognition does not evolve linearly but it is rather malleable and context-sensitive. Thought sustains contradictions in the minds of both children and adults in all cultures, including of course, western culture. This view distanced Moscovici from the cold logic of a purely epistemic subject (Duveen, 2013) and further challenged the Cartesian idea of an autonomous thinker in possession of a single logic and unified reason.

The concept opened the way for researchers interested in the dynamics of cognitive systems and how these relate to communication and situation. The emphasis shifted from final equilibrium to process, from knowledge as given to knowledge as a social encounter that is continuously developing (Jovchelovitch, 2012). States of cognitive polyphasia show that knowledge is incomplete because it is embedded in processes of social exchange and adaptation. This may take us away from the exactitude of formal logic but provides a more realistic view of human cognition, reuniting the epistemic and the social psychological subject.

Since its initial formulation, research on cognitive polyphasia has expanded considerably and corroboration of the phenomenon comes from different disciplines and areas of psychology. Joint work by anthropologists and psychologists, involving both field and experimental evidence, shows that different types of representations/explanations coexist; there is no displacement of one type of thinking by another but coexistence of different conceptions (Astuti and Harris, 2008; Harris, 2011). In developmental and cognitive psychology, researchers have experimentally demonstrated the coexistence of different beliefs and modalities of reasoning in the minds of both children and adults (Legare and Gelman, 2008; Rosengren and Gutiérrez, 2011). Research shows that scientific and religious explanations coexist, are treated as compatible and combined in various ways to explain problems and to fulfil people's deeper need for meaning (Evans and Lane, 2011).

Cognitive polyphasia is systematically reported in discourses and practices associated with a number of different domains. In the field of health there is solid evidence that everyday understandings of health and illness draw interchangeably from different types of knowledge. These understandings operate as a pool of resources to guide health behaviours depending on the situation. Both in western

(Gervais and Jovchelovitch, 1998a, 1998b; Provencher, 2011b) and non-western contexts (Arthi, 2012; de-Graft Aikins, 2002; Legare and Gelman, 2008; Wagner *et al.*, 2000) groups and individuals, children and adults, mix and match representations to act and make sense of health and illness. Among the Chinese community in England, traditional Chinese thinking coexists with biomedical approaches, with alternative behaviours deployed depending on ailment and situation (Jovchelovitch and Gervais, 1999). In Ghana, representations of diabetes comprise common sense, religion and science and are heavily mediated by the realm of emotions (de-Graft Aikins, 2003, 2012). Both in rural and urban areas people use different treatments simultaneously and display 'healer shopping' behaviours to deal with the condition as well as identity, emotions and spiritual needs (de-Graft Aikins, 2005).

Cognitive polyphasia, self and community

Cognitively polyphasic systems have been found to correspond to a multivoiced self, whose multiple positionings mediate the production and use of social representations (Renedo, 2010). Divergent logics are inherent in representational fields because people display multiple identities and inhabit multiple life worlds (Wagner *et al.*, 1999), which need engagement and sense-making. This internal flexibility of human identity has been widely demonstrated (Wetherell, 2009). This is as much the case for lay communities as it is for professional cohorts; health professionals and other specialists move constantly between identities, institutional discourses and systems of local knowledge (Castro and Batel, 2009; Morant, 2006; Renedo and Jovchelovitch, 2007). Constant movement enables individuals and communities to make sense of complexity and respond to different situations of social life. When Israeli-Jewish parents, for example, report a simultaneous preference for peace and for their sons to serve in the armed forces, the cognitive and emotional tension between these two representations may be thought impossible to sustain. But recent research shows that no discomfort with the tension is evident; rather, parents use diametrically opposed emotional and social logics to cope with the difficulty of the situation and to confirm both parental love and commitment to a national project (Friling, 2012).

In this sense cognitive polyphasia elucidates a central aspect of social representations: the intertwining of social representations, identity and community. The idea of cognition as free from contradiction, sustained only by one type of logic, derives from the assumption that cognition is free from identity and community and that external environments do not shape the development of cognitive structures. From this perspective, cognition of the world develops from within the subject's individual mind and mirrors the external world outside the individual person (see Marková, 2012 for a review of this problem). However, sociocultural contexts are not external to cognition but rather one of its constitutive foundations, requiring understanding and proper characterization.

Sociocultural approaches to representation have elucidated how the culture and societal configuration of a community shapes the formation of thought and social thinking (Cole, 1996; Tomasello, 1999; Valsiner, 2000; Vygotsky, 1978). This work shows that social cognition is an evolved adaptation that changes historically in conjunction with the diversification of society and culture. As societies develop different languages and spheres of thinking and action, so representations both assimilate and accommodate this diversity. We suggest that polyphasia is an outcome of this process, an evolved cognitive property of human thought whose evolutionary foundations may lie in its connections with sociality and cooperation. Acting as a resource in everyday cognitive functioning, it may have enabled ancestors to read the intentions and thinking of both competing and collaborative social groups, to communicate across vantage points and to coordinate action (Franks and Jovchelovitch, in progress).

Cognitive polyphasia allows specialized sets of representations to coexist in human thought, thereby empowering individuals and communities to make sense and cope with plurality and make full use of the diversity of the human symbolic landscape. It enables people to use knowledge from different spheres and logical registers to make sense of contested, challenging and culturally diverse issues. For instance, wearing a condom can be highly contested in rural Catholic communities in Mexico, but in many health centres the image of the Virgin of Guadalupe hangs on the wall right next to a sexual health campaign advertisement bearing the slogan 'wear a condom' (Priego-Hernández, 2011). In the health care context, both religion and medical knowledge seem necessary. Incompatible as they might be, they are held together and used effectively in everyday life.

Our recent research on underground sociabilities in the *favelas* of Rio de Janeiro (Jovchelovitch and Priego-Hernández, 2013) found further evidence of cognitive polyphasia in the system of social representations held by favela dwellers about the city, themselves and their religious practices. Our findings show that favela dwellers respond to urban segregation by developing two different sets of representations and behaviours, one for the favela and one for the city. In favela logic, these contrasting representations do not compete: both are necessary to master the crossings between two worlds and are used as a resource for coping with barriers and navigating the different areas of the city. In this case, polyphasia is a sense-making strategy for thinking in a divided society, an emotional tool for coping with discrimination and a pragmatic mechanism for handling exclusion.

The evidence we reviewed above substantiates the view that states of cognitive polyphasia are a pervasive feature of representational fields. Combining and mixing different sources, registers and rationalities is a cognitive strategy regularly deployed by individuals and communities. States of cognitive polyphasia evince the relations between social representations, identity and culture and confirm the internal plurality of human sociocognitive systems. The concept challenges decontextualized views of individual and social thinking, adding weight to the understanding of cognition as situated and relational. Cognitive polyphasia is a resource, a cognitive asset for dealing with variability and complexity in intergroup relations, contexts and cultures.

Cognitive polyphasia is now widely confirmed (Marková, 2008a). However, one area where further research is needed is on *how* exactly different representations coexist and relate in representational fields. Whereas we know that states of cognitive polyphasia presuppose coexistence, we still need to know more about the specific dynamics of this coexistence, that is, to grasp the communicative processes that hold different representations together. In the next section we introduce the model of knowledge encounters and review developments that focus on identifying the communicative processes operating in cognitive polyphasia. We provide a synthesis of the various typologies described and offer a model for understanding the different varieties of cognitive polyphasia.

Knowledge encounters and varieties of cognitive polyphasia

Jovchelovitch (2007) defined a knowledge encounter as 'the meeting between two or more representational systems, expressing different subjective, intersubjective and objective worlds' (p. 129). Conceptually, the notion of knowledge encounters captures the *point* (in terms of time and physical or imaginary space) at which representational systems, which interdependently circulate and influence each other, meet and engage in communicative activity (Priego-Hernández, 2011). In this sense, any knowledge encounter is an instantiation of a communicative act. Focussing on the dynamic transformation of representational fields as they meet and communicate in public spheres takes us back to Moscovici's original call in his study of psychoanalysis. There he explicitly pointed to the avenue of study opened up by cognitive polyphasia: 'the analysis of transformations – equilibrium and evolution – of these modalities of knowledge' (1961/2008, p. 191). Studying knowledge encounters enables us to address this call.

Levels and dimensions of coexistence

Encounters between knowledge systems can be understood at the macro level between groups and at the micro level between individuals and within the self (Priego Hernández, 2011). Examples of the macro level include encounters between health professionals and lay health services' users, or between the colonizing and the colonized in the colonial experience. At the micro level, encounters occur between individual selves who, despite belonging to the same group (for example, environmental activists or a political party), have access to different stocks of knowledge. Even if a group is cohesive, its representations are dynamic.

Table 11.1 *Cognitive polyphasia: dimensions, constituents and levels of contradiction*

Dimensions	Constituents	Levels of contradiction
Content	Semantic/Symbolic	What an object means
Process	Logic/Reasoning	How people think
Emotion	Affective	What people feel

Equally, knowledge encounters happen within the self, for it is as a psychological structure comprising multiple others (Bakhtin, 1984; Hermans and Kempen, 1993).

A state of cognitive polyphasia can be generated by different dimensions of representational fields: contents, processes and emotions (see Table 11.1). There are polyphasic states based on the coexistence of contradictory contents, involving the semantic aspect of representations. This is a widely described type of cognitive polyphasia: when an individual, group or community holds opposing views, ideas and meanings about the same social object. For example, mental illness can be considered to be both a disease and a curse from the ancestors. In this case, a sociocognitive system is polyphasic because it contains plural representations about *what* something *means*. Other prevalent states of polyphasia refer to the coexistence of contradictory processes, involving the logical aspect of representations. In this polyphasic state, the representational field is dominated by differences in *how* distinct reasonings are brought together when thinking about a social object/situation. For instance, scientific and religious explanations are widely used to explain death (Harris, 2011). Emotions are powerful components of representations (Jodelet, 1989/1991; Joffe, 1999) and essential to determine the type of communication obtained in knowledge encounters. In this state of polyphasia contradictory affects coexist in representational fields, expressing differences in what people *feel* about a social object/situation.

Arguably content, process and emotion are inseparable aspects of social cognition and states of cognitive polyphasia involve the coexistence of opposing and contradictory elements of all these dimensions. However, for diagnostic purposes it is useful to analyze the dynamic of the knowledge encounter and to establish which dimensions of polyphasia are salient and operative in the social representations at hand. This is so in particular if a programme of practical intervention is envisaged. For instance, in health and community development it is essential to identify how contradictory emotions underlie the manifest content of representations. Fear of contamination and deep-seated emotions related to otherizing have been found at the heart of social representations of AIDS, madness and handicap (Jodelet, 1989/1991; Joffe, 1999; Rose, 1997; Farr and Marková, 1995), usually coexisting with manifest medical knowledge and acceptance of the ill other. As long as this contradictory dynamic is not made explicit and worked through, health campaigns will fail (Campbell, 2003).

Modalities of coexistence and cognitive outcomes

The coexistence of contradictory contents, processes and emotions is a fact of human cognition; indeed, we argued above that this coexistence, in the form of cognitive polyphasia, is a basic property of all cognitive functioning. However, states of cognitive polyphasia can vary depending on the communicative dynamics that establish how the knowledge of the other is perceived and treated in the knowledge encounter. Is the knowledge of the other recognized, internalized or shared? Is it rejected, supressed or dismissed? These are central questions for identifying how coexistence is worked through in the knowledge encounter.

We suggest that recognition or denial of the knowledge of the other is the fundamental criterion determining the cognitive outcomes of a knowledge encounter and therefore varieties of cognitive polyphasia. Recognition of the knowledge of the other is a central foundation underpinning the argumentative styles and genres of communication that shape cognitive outcomes. Research in social psychology, communication and linguistics has identified a number of communicative genres and argumentative styles that illustrate how recognition is played out in knowledge encounters. They all refer to how interlocutors treat – or recognize – the knowledge of the other.

Non-recognition of the knowledge of the other generates a univocal discourse that is coercive and seeks to impose its own perspective, in contrast to polyvocality, which recognizes the existence of multiple perspectives and is non-imposing (Linell, 2009). Similarly, when facing alternative representations, actors can adopt argumentative styles that act either as semantic barriers or as semantic promoters of the perspective of the other (Gillespie, 2008). This is compatible with processes of consensualization and reification in encounters between different spheres of knowledge (Batel and Castro, 2009). These argumentative strategies operate in similar ways, as arguably semantic barriers reify the representations held by others through rigid oppositions and stigmatization. These are strategies regularly found when experts discuss the knowledge of local communities, where we find monologizing practices that seek imposition of representations, or transformative dialogue in which interlocutors negotiate balance in terms of power (Aveling, 2011). In knowledge encounters, proponents of different knowledges rarely, if ever, meet in symmetrical terms. Some systems of thinking and knowing have more power than others to establish their authority, legitimacy and veracity, while others are seen as ignorance (Sammut and Sartawi, 2012).

Argumentative styles form the basis of wider communicative genres. For example, persuasion and argumentation (Marková, 2007a, 2008b) involve polyvocality, semantic promoters and consensualization which seek some form of shared view, or consensus. This is equally the case in propagation and diffusion but not in propaganda, where the knowledge of self seeks to colonize the whole representational process irrespective of the other. Moscovici's psycho-social analysis of propaganda (1961/1976) and Marková's (2012) discussion of political confession as a communicative genre exemplify well a case where the position and knowledge of the other is denied and even destroyed.

In Table 11.2 we provide a summary of the overall discussion and the various terminologies used in the literature. This is a tentative classification that aims to stabilize the terms of this field of study and develop conceptual resources that clarify how styles of communication in knowledge encounters lead to different varieties of cognitive polyphasia. As with all classifications, this one should not be considered exhaustive.

We suggest three varieties of cognitive polyphasia, each defined by a specific modality of coexistence and cognitive outcome:

1. *Selective prevalence*. Distinct systems of knowledge are held together and retrieved separately at different points in time/space; here we can use the metaphor of multiple drawers, were different knowledges are kept and drawn upon to respond to different contexts and fulfil different functions.
2. *Hybridization*. Multiple systems of knowledge are drawn upon simultaneously and interpenetrate generating a single mixed representational field.
3. *Displacement*. One system of knowledge is favoured over other parallel systems leading to the displacement of alternative representations from a representational field.

Selective prevalence involves recognition of multiple knowledges, which are used alternatively depending on situations and which aspects of phenomena are considered. In this type of cognitive polyphasia different knowledge systems live side by side retaining their content, logic and emotional load. Knowledges are preserved in interdependent relation and tension is maintained and stabilized through practices that make it functional and useful in everyday life, such as healer shopping in Africa and a combination of biomedical and complementary treatments in the West. This, we suggest, is the most explored variety of cognitive polyphasia, and likely the most widespread, enabling different knowledges to live side by side as a pool of resources used by individuals and communities to deal with the complexity of everyday life.

Hybridization (García Canclini, 1995/2001) entails exchanges and complex interactions in which knowledge is produced from previously held knowledges. Representations are not just combined or applied simultaneously, but amalgamate and create a new form of knowing. In such encounters there is recognition of other knowledges and interaction that enables the integration of contradiction. Religious syncretism in Latin America is an instance of hybridization, corroborated in our own research on subterranean sociabilities in the favela communities of Rio de Janeiro, where we found a hybrid form of religious belief called 'mixed' by favela residents. Combining Catholic, Afro-religious, evangelical and Kardecist traditions, this hybrid belief is pragmatic and seeks to accommodate spiritual and cultural needs while remaining compatible to the favela way of life. For example, while the theological tenets of Evangelism are embraced by some favela dwellers, values and practices requiring austerity and simple demeanour are at odds with the needs of

Table 11.2 *Varieties of cognitive polyphasia: knowledge encounters and cognitive outcomes*

Knowledge Encounters	Recognition of the other	Non-recognition of the other	Level of analysis
Argumentative styles	Transformative Consensus	Monologizing (Aveling, 2011) Reification (Batel and Castro, 2008)	Individuals (children and adults) and collectives (groups, communities)
	Semantic promoters	Semantic barriers (Gillespie, 2008)	
	Multi-perspective/ polyvocality Non-imposing	Single perspective/ one-voiced (univocal) Imposition of response (coerciveness) (Linell, 2009)	
	Thematization	Conventionalization (Mouro and Castro, 2012)	
Genres of communication	Persuasion Argumentation	Propaganda Political confession (Marková, 2007a, 2008b, 2012)	
	Propagation Diffusion	Propaganda (1961/2008)	
Cognitive outcomes: varieties of cognitive polyphasia	Selective prevalence	Displacement	Individuals and collectives
	Hybridization		
	Separation	Pluralism (Arthi, 2012)	Individuals
Empirical and theoretical support	Mixed representations		Individuals and collectives
	Hybrid representations (Gervais and Jovchelovitch, 1998a)		
	Hybridization (cognitive polyphasia)	Segregation/destruction (monological cognition) (Jovchelovitch, 2007)	Individuals and collectives

(*cont.*)

Table 11.2 (cont.)

Knowledge Encounters	Recognition of the other	Non-recognition of the other	Level of analysis
	Target-dependent thinking Integrative thinking		Individuals
	Synthetic thinking Integrative thinking (Legare et al., 2012)		
	Polyphasic	Non-polyphasic (Mouro and Castro, 2012)	Individuals
	Hybridity	Coercive supplantation (Priego Hernández, 2011)	Individuals and collectives
	Dynamic coexistence		
	Cognitive polyphasia	Cognitive monophasia (Provencher, 2011b)	Individuals
	Open point of view		
	Bounded point of view	Closed point of view (Sammut and Gaskell, 2010)	Collectives
	Cognitive polyphasia (Renedo, 2010; Wagner et al., 2000)	Cognitive closure (Kruglanski et al., 2006; Webster and Kruglanski, 1997) Cognitive dissonance (Festinger, 1957)	Individuals and collectives
Diagnostic instantiations	Democratic political systems Healer shopping Tokenistic participation		Individuals and collectives
	International policy Syncretism	Totalitarian regimes Intolerance to contradiction Asymmetric doctor/patient relations Racial discrimination	Individuals and collectives (political sphere, health and illness, social development, social identities)

conviviality, joy and fiesta of favela inhabitants. Enjoying dancing in their everyday lives is possible if evangelical principles are combined with Afro-Caribbean religious practices, which include, and even encourage, corporal expression of emotions. In this way, favela dwellers draw on different sources to which they ascribe similar functional value. This example foregrounds the hybridization of different phases of the same type of rationality (religion, in this case) that produces a new way of sense-making that favela dwellers call '*mistura*' (mixture).

In displacement there is lack of mutual recognition and exclusion of the knowledge of the other. Displacement in the knowledge encounter was discussed in Paulo Freire's (1973/2010) classic paper on extension or communication, where interlocutors seek to 'extend' their knowledge to other interlocutors. This can be found at the heart of development initiatives based on the traditional north–south divide, where the 'transfer' of knowledge, economic policy and political systems from the developed north to the underdeveloped south is the main directive. For example, in encounters between health staff and indigenous adolescent service users, doctors and nurses expressed their own knowledge towards service users and regarded it as legitimate and worthy of authoritative remarks (Priego-Hernández, 2011). These policies and practices undermined local knowledge and social identities, compromising autonomy and pointing to the disadvantaged symbolic and concrete position of participants, who had little opportunity to challenge the impositions.

Displacement can also operate at the individual level, when the individual faces the challenge of dealing with contradictory knowledges and oppositions. The management of contradiction is mediated by culture. We assume that non-western public spheres experience contradiction and the coexistence of opposites in a different way to western public spheres, because the separation between domains and modalities of thought and knowledge are more typical of western thinking and its social organization. We suggest that this is the case in processes of cognitive dissonance (Festinger, 1957), which are widely studied in social psychology.

Cognitive dissonance requires the displacement of contradictory knowledge in order to restore equilibrium to the self. We speculate that this is a cognitive operation which is tied up in western values and historical principles of reasoning, such as the law of non-contradiction. However, as we have already discussed above, social and cultural psychologists find evidence of contradictory coexistence in a variety of cultural contexts, including the western context. We therefore suggest that cognitive dissonance is one possible outcome of cognitive polyphasia, in other words one among various other ways of coping with and responding to the dynamic coexistence of ideas, modalities of reasoning and emotions that inhabit sociocognitive systems in all public spheres. Juxtaposing cognitive dissonance and cognitive polyphasia opens up a fascinating avenue of research for social and cultural psychologists.

Conclusion

In this chapter we have revisited the interrelations between social representations and public spheres through the notions of knowledge encounters and cognitive polyphasia. We put forward a social psychological theory of the public sphere and examined how its contemporary transformations shed light on the dynamics of social representations. We have reviewed work on cognitive polyphasia and placed its conceptual resources in the wider programme of situated cognition and communicative rationality, arguing that polyphasia is a basic property of sociocognitive functioning in all public spheres. Central to what we have sought to achieve in this chapter is the understanding that the architecture of self–alter–object is at the basis of public life and knowledge construction, imprinting the dynamics of communicative situations in all cognitive systems.

Cognitive polyphasia expresses the diversity of knowledge that is typical of the human symbolic landscape and the flexibility and resourcefulness of cognitive functioning. It can also express unequal relations of power and asymmetries that exclude and denigrate systems of thinking and knowing of vulnerable and historically excluded populations. We have brought together for the first time, to the best of our knowledge, a typology of cognitive polyphasia that encompasses different modalities of coexistence of systems of knowledge and the various terminologies produced by research undertaken in this area. Cognitive dissonance, we suggest, is one among other possible varieties of cognitive polyphasia.

The bases for understanding cognitive polyphasia and its varieties are processes of recognition between the self and other. Ultimately, this takes us back to Moscovici's fundamental insight formulated in the conceptual spine of social representations theory: cognition is a sociocultural construct and all representational fields are grounded on the complexity and realization of the human experience they simultaneously build and reveal.

12 Making community: diversity, movement and interdependence

Caroline Howarth, Flora Cornish and Alex Gillespie

Using the concept of 'social representations', Moscovici established that contemporary knowledge systems are not uniform or universal, as Durkheim's collective representations had conceptualized them. Modern societies are characterized by the coexistence of a diversity of views held by a diversity of groups. The concept of social representations thus unsettled understandings of the social as being characterized by homogeneity, shared beliefs or cohesive identities. Research within the social representations tradition has also demonstrated that social knowledge is not afloat in the ether, only loosely connected to people, but rather is systematically related to particular social locations, situations, roles and identities – in a word, communities. The word *community* rests on the idea of 'common' – what is shared. This sense of commonality seems to have less traction in complex, diverse contemporary societies. But how should we conceptualize communities in a world of diverse social actors with varying degrees of interconnection, commonality and difference? Moscovici advanced the understanding of social knowledge beyond collective representations and stable knowledge systems, with a focus on the recognition of differences and the consequences of such diversity. How should we understand communities today, if not by reference to the idea of uniformity or collectivity? How might we (re)conceptualize communities, in a world of multiple and competing representations, without returning to a universalizing concept of collective representations?

Under contemporary postmodern or altermodern conditions, the diversification of society continues apace. It is anticipated that contemporary workers will change their jobs thirty-eight times across their careers. In 1950 there were 25 million international arrivals each year; in 2010 there were 1000 million (Urry, 2007). World cities such as London and New York attract immigrants from every continent, such that one third of Londoners and New Yorkers were born abroad. For some, this diversification is interpreted as threatening community and solidarity, with explicit calls to work towards greater 'cohesion' or 'integration' (Andreouli, 2010). Diversification is not the only story, however. As much as societies are diversifying, there is also communication, interpenetration, mutuality and civic solidarity among these diverse groups (Sammut, 2011; Howarth, 2011). For instance, London's diverse city dwellers have become proud of their diversity, espousing inclusive, multicultural identities (Massey, 2007). Overtly cosmopolitan identities (Gilroy, 2004; Beck, 2006) emerge. Coalitions and partnerships between diverse groups are formed. Increasingly, we live in a network society (Castells, 2004) and have relational responsibilities (Gergen, 2009). Community itself does not disappear; nor is it simply replaced by networks or intersectional identities. Community still has meaning in how people develop a sense of belonging, knowledge systems and possibilities for participation. We see this most vividly in what people do, in social movements and in social protest. Hence diverse groups are knitted together through the need to be heard, to collaborate, or through sharing the experience of crossing boundaries from one community to another. Furthermore, communities are not passively related to social knowledge, do not passively take on or pass on knowledge, but rather are active, creating, arguing, counterposing, transforming, re-presenting their knowledge against the knowledge of other communities. Communities appear fluid, contested and often contradictory. To understand the significance of community in today's complex societies, we need a nuanced and flexible set of conceptual tools. A conceptually rich starting point for this endeavour is social representations theory.

The concept of community is at the heart of social representations theory (Howarth, 2001). Moscovici's (1961/1976) original study showed how urban liberals, Catholics and communists in Paris 'digested' or made sense of psychoanalysis in different ways, each group producing and supporting a distinctive form of communication – propaganda, propagation and diffusion – in their transmission of representations of psychoanalysis. For instance, within communist communications, representations of psychoanalysis merged with stereotypes of American decadent culture and western imperialism in order to reject it as a pseudo-science. They thereby defend distinctions between in-group and out-group identities and affirm commitment to the communist community. By contrast, propagation was used in the Catholic community as a means of accommodating specific aspects of psychoanalysis within existing religious principles and so uses representations of psychoanalysis to preserve the authority of the Catholic community. Diffusion occurred within liberal communities as a means of generating public debate. Liberal professionals would claim a certain sceptical distance to psychoanalysis and so characterize other communities as dogmatic.

Thus the different ways of representing psychoanalysis coincide with the construction and defence of community identities and the relationship between community and social representations seems straightforward, at least in this study. Some fifty years later, has anything changed? Would we still find the same communities of Catholics, communists and liberals in present-day Paris, as Bauer and Gaskell (1999) have also asked? What is the relationship between community and social representations in our conditions of postmodernity or altermodernity? The simple answer could be that 'community 1' possesses 'social representation 1' and 'community 2' possesses 'social representation 2' and so on, and that we simply have a lot more communities and corresponding sets of social representations today. However this leads to the problematic assumption that there is a simple and circular relationship between social representations and community (Wagner and Hayes, 2005). We suggest that a one-to-one correspondence between 'a community' and 'a social representation' is not a plausible account of the relation between communities and social representations in contemporary societies. For a researcher today, this brings an array of complexities. Are (shared) social representations encountered in the field evidence of 'community'? Or, are they more a product of the relationship between researcher and the participants in that specific context (and the differences of culture, identity and politics that this brings)? Do social representations 'belong' to the particular research context; can they be seen to be representations of community x (and possibly contrasted with representations of community y)? For instance, could we compare the representations of secularism found in France and India, or between Muslims and Hindus in India (as Sen, Wagner and Howarth, 2014, do)? A comparative researcher will no doubt find differences across different research contexts, but does this constitute different and coherent communities? Clearly there are many different ways to approach this and signal the inherent problems involved in imposing the notion of community when doing social research (Gillespie, Howarth and Cornish, 2012). In this chapter we argue that we cannot assume that representations are 'the social "glue" that bind communities together' (Tsirogianni and Andreouli, 2011). Communities, as the representations that sustain them, are multiple, polyphonic and fluid. Given this, we need to explore the ways in which the relation between community and social representations has changed under these complex conditions.

In what follows we explore the contemporary nature of community through three themes. Each theme disrupts the idea of commonness or sameness in our understanding of social groupings. The first two problematize the easy definition of community by reference to social categories, exploring, first, the diversity within contemporary communities, and second, the movements of individuals and groups between communities. In the third, we come to an alternative conceptualization of what it is that stabilizes social groupings, namely interdependence around activities. The three themes draw on social representations research to illustrate and develop our argument.

From community cohesion to community diversity

As we have seen, Moscovici (1961/1976) introduced the concept of social representations to grapple with the fact that contemporary societies can no longer be characterized as single, homogeneous communities (with collective, stable representations), but rather, contemporary society has become more differentiated, with multiple communities, sustaining a diverse range of practices and representations (Howarth, 2001). How many communities are there today? This is not a question one could ever answer, but it opens our minds to the staggering number of communities that comprise contemporary society. There are geographical communities, professional communities and communities brought together by political projects, not to mention the multitude of online communities, some of which are even based on being anonymous (Donath, 1998). This proliferation of communities has provided the social-material basis for the proliferation of diverse social representations, and accordingly, social representations have become as varied as the communities which support them. Hence part of understanding the theory of social representations is to understand the changing psychology of community.

Social representations theory helps to develop an analysis of community with difference or alterity at its heart (Marková, 2003; Jovchelovitch, 2008), as representations, and the communities that sustain them, contain the battle of ideas (Moscovici, 1998; Howarth, 2006a). This connects to the need to promote 'a cosmopolitan outlook' (Beck, 2006) 'based on 'dialogical imagination which acknowledges the presence and legitimacy of alternative ways of thinking' (Tsirogianni and Andreouli, 2011; Gillespie, 2006). In a similar way to Bakhtin's and Herman's concepts of the dialogical nature of self that highlights the polyphony of positions, narratives and projects within any one self (Renedo, 2010; Hammack, 2008), we also need to emphasize the polyphonic and fundamentally de-essentalized nature of communities today. In social research, however, we sometimes assume certain social categories of belonging – Catholics and Protestants in Northern Ireland, ethnic minority communities, gay communities, student communities; we sometimes assume they share social representations – when often these groups of people may not experience themselves as belonging to a community at all (Bauer and Gaskell, 1999; Gillespie, Kadianaki and O'Sullivan-Lago, 2012). When we look within any one community, what we see is a polyphony of community identities, practices and projects (Crossley, 1996). A good example of this is Gervais and Jovchelovitch's (1998b) study of the British-born Chinese community, which shows the interconnections between the hybridity of cultural and generational identities and food, familial and health practices.

Following this example (Gervais and Jovchelovitch, 1998b), we need to disrupt the ways in which we assume and impose community as a homogeneous form on our research participants. Rather, we need to ask: What are the different ways by which community is defined and contested? Following the example discussed above, for whom? When and in what contexts and social activities is community made meaningful? For instance, Stephens (2007) explores the diverse ways in which community is claimed for different strategic purposes. In this way, one can be described as a member of different communities, but these communities become salient only when there is something to be done. It is a rhetorical and political, action-oriented process to affirm one sort of community membership over another. Claiming membership of a particular community legitimizes particular kinds of claims, actions and representations, as we see here:

> across the fields of sexuality, ethnicity, neighbourhood life, work or religion it is possible that one person at different times may claim identity as a member of the gay community (to take responsibility for encouraging condom use), the Jewish community (to decry the desecration of a cemetery as happened in New Zealand recently), the Beachhaven neighbourhood community (when invited by researchers to consider one's 'sense of place'), the Maori community (to be

concerned about provision of health services) and the academic community (to claim certain freedoms of speech). Each of these representations of community offers certain social obligations, opportunities or calls to practice which are related only to the specific field of activity. (Stephens, 2007, p. 111)

Hence there are diverse ways in which community may be mobilized in different contexts and relationships, even by the same individuals. A classic study of the shifting ways in which community is defended and practised is Jodelet's *Madness and Social Representations* (1989/1991). Here patients diagnosed as mentally ill lived as lodgers in a community. On the face of it 'lodgers' and other community members were integrated, sharing homes, mealtimes and social activities. With detailed, extensive observation, Jodelet found that the community had developed implicit social rituals that demarcated 'the mad' from 'the sane' and so served to preserve ideological constructions of madness, otherness, contagion and danger. Here we can see how 'community' is mobilized through the struggle of social representations to protect identities, to defend positions and to separate one from the other. Clearly there are times when we do claim community and affirm a sense of belonging, identity and fate and also times when we impose community on to groups of others, asserting that they hold certain (and strange) values, practices and identities in common. These really need to be seen as two sides of the same coin, two ways in which community is defined, claimed, projected and rejected.

This is very clearly seen in a study of representations of community in Brixton, a multicultural area in south London (Howarth, 2002b, 2006a). For some, Brixton is defined by an impressively multicultural market, cosmopolitan identities and aspirations; it is a place where people have the 'ability to mingle with other people' or 'to have inter-racial relationships' (respondents in Howarth, 2000). It is an exemplar of successful diversity within community. For others, this diversity breeds division, distrust and hostility, as it is 'always going to be an area full of racism' (ibid.). This illustrates how social representations can be used to co-construct community and difference. That is, through attaching certain meanings and evaluations to the representation, people locate themselves as members of the community, or they distance themselves from the community by denigrating Brixton. Proclaiming community can be about asserting common identities as much as asserting incompatible cultures and beliefs.

Community could be seen simply as a matter of identity (Howarth, 2001) and just as we acknowledge the multiplicity and intersectionality of identities today (Gergen, 1991; Moghaddam, 2012), so we can see that communities are also much more diverse. But to always equate identity with community (at any historical point) is simplistic; clearly there are times when community and identity are conceptually interchangeable, but there are other times when communities are brought together by people who may *not* in fact identify as one but who do act together in a joint project, as we shall see below. Shared or overlapping identities can be part of community, but to identify as a group does not always lead to acting as a group. Many participants in the Brixton study identified themselves as being 'from Brixton', but this did not always equate to acting as a cohesive group with shared beliefs and aspirations. For many, divisions and differences across the neighbourhood meant that despite a shared identity, they could not be seen as a community.

Communities as well as individuals are capable of assuming the role of the other (Mead, 1934). Hence in defining community we are also making claims about 'other' communities, whose difference marks what we have in common. In demarcating 'other' communities we are also asserting a sense of difference and commonality, as identities are a matter of negotiation, connection, imagination and resistance (Duveen, 2001a; see also Chapter 11 in this volume). And yet this is not so clear cut; it is not just about being 'from Brixton' or not; being black or white, English or Muslim. Simple binary categorizations are rarely reflected in everyday encounters today (Howarth, 2009). The participants in the Brixton study (as for Stephens (2007) above) are members of many intersecting communities – as they move from different contexts, different attachments to Brixton and other communities become salient or diminish – and within this community itself there is an almost irrepressible hybridity and diversity, as their quotes indicate. Young people in Brixton are not alone in this, however, and nor are the mixed-heritage, bicultural diaspora who experience the constant interplay of different communities of belonging or 'acculturation in movement' (Howarth et al., 2013; Bhatia, 2002). We all mobilize community in different social activities, and this can be particularly clear when we move from one context to another.

From located communities to people moving through communities

Social science has, until recently, been a-mobile (Urry, 2007). People, groups and communities were conceptualized at best developmentally, but rarely in terms of mobility. Theory has not kept up with practice. Urry (2007) subscribes to the estimate that in 1800 people in the United States travelled an average of 50 meters a day, while now they travel an average of 50,000 meters per day (see Nakicenovic, 1995). Taking seriously the extent of mobility in contemporary society requires reconceptualizing the relation between individual and community (Gillespie, 2013). Instead of people being 'in' a community, as if trapped, we have to conceptualize them as 'moving through' communities. This in turn has consequences for the relation between community and social representation. Specifically, we suggest, taking mobility seriously can aid the conceptualization of cognitive polyphasia.

Cognitive polyphasia refers to people participating in multiple and seemingly contradictory social representations (see Chapter 11 in this volume; Provencher, 2011b; Gillespie, 2008). Taken at a cognitive level, it is a puzzle why people oscillate between seemingly inconsistent points of view. However, if representations are rooted in communities, and we allow for the fact that people move in social space, moving through communities, thus participating in multiple and sometimes quite discrepant social representations, then we have a simple explanation for cognitive polyphasia. Our social world is not only heterogeneous, but people move through this heterogeneity, being socialized into diverse, and sometimes seemingly incompatible, communities. Thus in so far as contemporary society is differentiated in such a way that it sustains divergent social representations, then it should be no surprise to find individuals who have been socialized into these divergent social representations, thus giving rise to cognitive polyphasia. Indeed, cognitive polyphasia is a powerful adaptation enabling people to move about within contemporary heterogeneous societies.

One of the classic studies of cognitive polyphasia was reported by Wagner and colleagues (Wagner et al., 1999; Wagner et al., 2000). Their examination of beliefs about mental illness in northern India showed that many middle-class Indian professionals subscribed to both traditional and psychiatric representations. When talking about traditional beliefs one woman said: 'I have some faith [in traditional healers] and at the same time I don't believe in them.' How could these middle-class Indians subscribe to beliefs which might seem logically incompatible? To explain this, we need to return to consider the material communities which these participants were embedded in. On the one hand, they all had extended families, many with grandparents and links to rural villages. On the other hand, many were university-educated, having professional jobs and working for large corporations. Thus, on a daily basis, in moving from home to work and back, these participants were moving through communities, one traditional and the other modern and international. The so-called contradictory representations which they espoused were not contradictory in terms of daily practices – the polyphasia was adaptive, enabling them to function in two different communities.

The movement through communities is particularly acute for immigrants (Kadianaki, 2010). Immigrants often make repeated trips between their country of origin and new home, thus engaging in traffic, which maintains participation in two quite different communities (Gillespie, Kadianaki and O'Sullivan-Lago, 2012). Movements between the 'home' and 'host' communities can, however, occur on a more local level. Research by Aveling and Gillespie (2008) examined second-generation Turkish adolescents in London, who moved between a regular British school during the week and a Turkish school during the weekends. Their analysis, which focusses on the dialogical positioning of these young Turks, shows that they sometimes position themselves as Turkish while at other times they position themselves as British. A common tendency was to espouse a Turkish identity while enacting a more British identity, such as rapping about being proud to be Turkish. Again there is what might appear to some to be contradictory representations at work. One could look for contradictions in what these youths say and do. However, this would be to overlook a more important fact, namely that they are adapting to contradictory environments. They have to adapt to British schools, but they also have to go home and fit in with their immediate and extended Turkish families. To not be cognitive polyphasic would, arguably, be non-adaptive and lead to uncertain cultural identities (Howarth et al., 2014). It could lead to marginalization and a narrowing of social participation (Berry, 2011; Howarth, Andreouli and Kessi, 2014). Thus again we find that cognitive polyphasia at the representational level can be made comprehensible by considering not only the way in which representations are bound into communities, but also crucially the way in which people move about the social world, moving between communities, and adapting to multiple communities.

What is important to stress is that this emphasis on mobility does not undermine the concepts of either community or location; rather, it enriches them. Locations are different and communities are distributed in space. People moving between locations and communities certainly make these locations and communities porous; but it is because these locations and communities are different that people are shaped by their mobility. What we have seen thus far is that communities are defined from multiple positions, and this can give rise to a struggle over the meaning of community, that we are all members of multiple communities and it is adaptive to draw on seemingly incompatible representations in moving through the different communities we identify with. Despite such diversity, people no doubt continue to associate together. They live, work and communicate together in meaningful communities. If sameness or commonality is not the basis for community, then what holds communities together?

From community as commonality to community as interdependence

Traditionally, communities have been defined by commonality or sameness. Despite controversies over the most appropriate way of delineating a community – as a 'community of place', a 'community of identity' or a 'community of interest' (e.g. Mayo, 2000) – each of these definitions relies at its root on the assumption that communities are defined by members' sameness, whether it is in living in the same area, subscribing to the same identity or sharing a common interest. Yet, it is also evident that, in practice, people with different locations, identities and even interests do manage to work together to constitute a form of collective life together. While some of the time *commonality* or even identity may be the basis for community, at other times, we suggest, *interdependence of different actors around a common activity* or project is a profound basis for community.

Bringing attention to the pragmatic aspect of collective knowledge construction, Bauer and Gaskell (1999) introduce the concept of the 'project' as the engine of social representation. A project is an activity in which people have an interest, such as the education of their children or building the reputation of their company. Knowledge is never disinterested or neutral, but its construction is motivated by people's interest in their joint project. Relationships – of the sort that may constitute a community – build up through people's joint activity around a project. Bauer and Gaskell use this idea to guide thinking about how to 'segment' the social world into meaningful groups for the purpose of research, particularly for sampling. They criticize 'taxonomic' ways of segmenting society (e.g. by gender, age, ethnicity, etc.), arguing that often these categories are not meaningful social groupings in the sense of either representing sites of mutual identification or of shared knowledge. They suggest, instead, a consideration of 'social milieux', that is, meaningful social groups defined by having mutual interests or mutual projects.

There is an ambiguity here, however, and it is expressed in the ambiguity of the word *mutual*. This word can mean 'held in common by two or more parties' (*OED*) (i.e. a single thing is shared) or 'a feeling or action experienced or done by each of two or more parties towards the other' (i.e. each side expresses something towards the other, where there are two feelings or actions, which might be different). 'Mutual interest' can mean that we have the same interest (e.g. two parents both interested in their children's wellbeing and achievement at school), or different interests in each other's activities in relation to a common object/project (e.g. teachers' and parents' interests in bringing off successful education). We suggest that, even when people's interests are not exactly the same, or where they do not subscribe to a shared identity, a meaningful community may be forged around their collective practice. So, while traditionally employees might be considered members of one community and employers another, they may be constituted as a single community of interdependent though unequal actors through their mutual interest in pulling off a successful project.

For example, we have argued that a community development project working to empower marginalized sex workers to tackle HIV/AIDS constitutes a 'project community' which brings together a diverse array of actors with a diverse array of sometimes conflicting interests (e.g. 'beneficiaries', local leaders who stand to lose power, development practitioners striving to implement policy, international donors) (Cornish and Ghosh, 2007). Despite their differences, these groups do comprise a meaningful social milieu, each group contributing a different part of the social representation of the project and all sharing (in different ways) in the project of bringing off a funded community development project. Despite different and at times conflicting interests, the different groups succeed in communicating together, making events happen together, assisting each other, enjoying social events together. In sum, they constitute a community, even if it is a community with fractures, divisions and diverse identities. Durkheim's (1893) distinction between organic and mechanistic solidarity is helpful here. Mechanistic solidarity, according to Durkheim, was characteristic of 'traditional' societies, where solidarity was based on the similarity of people's experiences and roles (e.g. all peasant farmers). Organic solidarity, characteristic of 'modern', complex societies, is based on *interdependence* rather than commonality. The wish for community 'cohesion' and the assumption that communities must be made up of homogeneous individuals fail to incorporate the interdependence of different perspectives in our complex societies. If we had to be the same to get along together, or simply identify as one, then our diverse societies would fall apart. Indeed, pressures for diverse groups to assimilate into normative practices often meet with intense resistance and a strengthening of separatist, identity politics (Wagner *et al.*, 2012).

We have argued for the role of joint practice in holding together a diverse, complex array of people in our study of the Occupy movement as it emerged in its encampment in the churchyard of St Paul's in London (Cornish *et al.*, 2014). Participants in the movement were a diverse array of people, including students, seasoned activists, professionals and homeless people, among others. They represented diverse causes, from economic reform to internet freedom, environmental responsibility, arms dealing and more. Indeed, they were frequently criticized for not articulating a central demand. Yet, somehow, a sense of meaningful collectivity emerged. This happened, we argue, through participation in the joint practice of organizing an encampment together and creating a process for making decisions together. The Occupiers had a project of creating a safe and effective encampment, and only a vague sense of a shared dissatisfaction with the political and economic system. The project of living together and of forging critiques was enough to sustain a community – at least for some months. As winter temperatures dropped, eviction by police became a possibility and the challenges of collective decision-making mounted, for many, the encampment became unsustainable. The practice of living together was not, in this instance, a sufficient project to maintain a visible and active community after eviction. Projects have a pragmatic nature: they are sustained by their connection to the satisfaction of interests. For practice to work as a community-building function, it needs to be a motivating practice, satisfying interests among its diverse constituencies.

Conclusion: conventions and transformations

The postmodern turn of the late twentieth century drew attention to the breakdown of traditional communities and boundaries, the fluidity of people's identities and their freedom to rewrite their own identities. Gergen (1991) vividly described how 'an open slate emerges on which persons may inscribe, erase, and rewrite their identities as the ever-shifting, ever-expanding, and incoherent network of relationships invites or permits' (p. 228). Similarly, we have argued that communities are increasingly diverse, mobile and connected through different interests. As a consequence there has been an explicit turn towards community cohesion as a stabilizing remedy to all current concerns, from worries over the rise of far-right and 'home-grown' terrorist attacks to conflicting moral conventions (Moghaddam, 2012), and from concerns over economic prosperity to those of social inclusion. For instance, the European Committee for Social Cohesion has asserted that 'the question is how to manage diversity so that it becomes a source of mutual enrichment rather than a factor of division and conflict' (2004, p. 3; quoted in Sammut, 2011). Cohesion becomes the antidote to the threat of diversity (Tsirogianni and Andreouli, 2011).

If we look to social representations theory and research, however, we see something quite different: cohesion and diversity, location and mobility, distinct identities and collective projects all go hand in hand. Social representations, born of our diverse times, rest on the dialectical pull towards developing common cultures, shared practices and congruent identities while also fostering subjective understandings and unique perspectives (Farr, 1991; Howarth, 2010). Cohesion without diversity would take us back to a past that can no longer exist, where located, stable and unchanging communities produce collective representations and uniform identities – or to a totalitarian future of hegemonic representations and assimilationist ambitions. Insisting on commonality, uniformity and a rigid sense of community without diversity may in fact promote resistance and destructive tensions, as Wagner and colleagues (2012) demonstrate in relation to current social and legal restrictions on religious attire. Nevertheless, insisting on diversity without community may lead to fragmentation, psychological uncertainty and social isolation (Jovchelovitch, 2007). Therefore, we need to examine how communities develop through a sense of difference and distinction as well as commonality and sharedness. Psychologically speaking, community does not emerge and does not survive without the recognition of diversity.

Hence we need to be careful not to overstate this 'vertigo of unlimited multiplicity' (Gergen, 1991); the lives of people in communities, as evident in this chapter, are not wildly open, incoherent or fluid. Amidst such compelling diversity, people have attachments and stakes in specific communities. Many of these are products of broader historical commitments to particular interests and identities. People inherit and produce knowledge and perspectives from their embodied locations in specific communities. They stabilize the complexity of communities around themselves through shared discourse and common practice as 'the knowledge of the community is practical knowledge' (Crossley, 1996, p. 94). Counter to a postmodern position which suggests free-floating and freely ascribed identities, we have emphasized that our identities and knowledge are pinned down, constrained in a way, by the concrete community relations in which we move and act. When we examine social representations in everyday interactions, we see that we have, and also need, community.

We suggest that social representations theory is useful here in that it demands a focus on how community, and competing versions of community, are produced and made valid through people's interactions, identities and corresponding systems of knowledge exchange and social action (Howarth, 2001). Patterson and colleagues (2011) draw on Shotter's argument for a dynamic and ongoing socially constructed notion of community, in which people are not simply members of a category but creatively participate in the reproduction and evolution of the group's collective lives:

> to live in a community which one senses as being one's own ... one must be more than just an accountable reproducer of it. One must in a real sense also play a part in its creative sustaining of itself as a 'living tradition'. One must feel able to fashion one's own 'position', within the 'argument' or 'arguments' to do with both constituting and reconstituting the tradition. (pp. 162–163)

This chapter began by asking how we might (re)conceptualize communities, in a world of multiple and competing positions, traditions and representations, without returning to a universalizing concept of collective representations. To debate what communities 'really' are, as 'things-in-themselves', is to fail to be alive to the fact that communities 'really' are historical. The defining feature of pre-modern communities may well have been homogeneity and similarity (but see Pigg, 1996 and Cohen, 1995). But today the situation is different. Communities are no longer isolated in either space or time. There is traffic of ideas, values, images, practices, artefacts and bodies. Communities of difference defy any rigid demands for conformity or sameness. Communities of location have become porous. Communities of practice are in ascendance, where people gather around sometimes transient goals. These goals, however, often entail other communities. Accordingly, future research needs to conceptualize these phenomena not so much in terms of representations or communities but, rather, in terms of the project (Bauer and Gaskell, 1999, 2008) or social activity being examined. Projects, or social activities, as conceptual concepts integrate potentially diverse groups and representations into an interrelated whole. So, for example, if we are interested in representations of education, then we would need to examine the interacting views of parents, children and teachers around a common object, as well as the representations of educational policy circulating in media and political debate.

Contemporary communities are, in a self-reflective sense, communities amongst other communities. Being in a community means taking a position vis-à-vis alternative communities. Any community today must acknowledge this plurality and justify itself in relation to it. Contemporary communities are not simply given; they are not 'social facts' in a Durkheimian sense. Being in a community, that is, being in some form of social interrelation or collective positioning vis-à-vis other communities, means being in a community which represents itself as a community amongst communities. In turn, this means that contemporary communities come with a politics of recognition – seeing one's community from the standpoint of other communities and a recognition of (constructed and evolving) difference. In parallel to the increasing differentiation and integration of communities, it may be that communities increasingly imply this politics of recognition. Hence communities are not found but are made, stated, contested, defended, transformed. These processes ultimately rest on the tensions inherent in social re-presentation, tensions which simultaneously conventionalize and transform communities – and so invite new possibilities for how we live and research communities in the future.

PART III

New directions

In the third part of this handbook we consider new directions in the elaboration of the theory of social representations, following the discussion of foundations and conceptual developments in parts I and II. The theory of social representations has been developed with the agenda of redefining the study of social knowledge through an emphasis on communicative processes and social relationships. It has sought to overcome the individual–social dichotomy by building an overarching framework of social thought. It is not surprising that such an ambitious project has had close affinity with other theoretical traditions and has been embraced by theorists across the social sciences. Over the last fifty years much scholarly work has sought to integrate the theory of social representations with other theoretical frameworks from psychology and the social sciences. Part III brings together some of these theoretical developments.

The five chapters that follow advance the theory of social representations by drawing useful insights from other theoretical traditions, such as evolution theory, discourse psychology and semiotics. Together, the chapters discuss some of the central tenets of the theory of social representations, such as anchoring, objectification and communication, and seek to answer some of the 'big questions' that the theory has posed, such as the relationship between the individual and society and the interaction between micro and macro processes of social construction. The chapters make unique contributions to the theory of social representations by elaborating on the roles of language, rhetoric, identity and institutions in processes of social representation, and by creating new avenues for research and scholarship in the field. Part III of the handbook will be of interest to scholars of social representations who are interested in new theoretical developments in the field, as well as scholars working outside the field who have a theoretical interest the broader areas of language, identity and social construction.

13 Social representations and social construction: the evolutionary perspective of installation theory

Saadi Lahlou

How do societies reproduce? Berger and Luckmann (1966) popularized the idea of a continuous reconstruction of society; they showed the importance of education of individual members in this reproductive reconstruction. Societies are enacted and reproduced by human behaviour, through practice.

Societies are not static; new objects are constructed, new phenomena occur. Tony Giddens' structuration theory highlighted the two sides of this continuous reconstruction: while individual behaviour results from societal structure, human action also reproduces (that is, sustains *and modifies*) the structure (Giddens, 1984).

In this reproduction process through which successive generations reproduce and gradually modify society, representations play an important role. Earlier, Moscovici had shown in his seminal work on psychoanalysis (1961/1976) how the process of social construction operates on the psychological level. He discovered the mechanism by which new social 'objects' emerge: anchoring their representation in previous cultural notions, through debate between stakeholders, until they become reified 'social representations' which in turn may serve as anchors for future cultural innovations.

This chapter focusses on the specific role social representations plays in the larger chicken and egg societal evolution outlined above. It does so via a pragmatic perspective (installation theory), which attempts to explain the phenomenon but also to provide the tools for regulators and change agents. The first part of the chapter provides a framework – *installation theory* – to describe how societies scaffold, shape and control individual behaviour and the specific role of social representations in that framework. Human behaviour is determined at three levels: affordances of the environment; embodied competences in actors; social influence and rules by other actors and institutions. An *installation* will be defined as a socially constructed system with three such layers, which guides a specific activity by suggesting scaffolding and constraining what society members can/should do in a

The research for this chapter benefitted from a CNRS DRA grant (programme CADEN, UMR 8037/8177, from a EURIAS fellowship at the Paris Institute for Advanced Studies, and from funding from the French state managed by the Agence Nationale de la Recherche (programme 'Investissements d'avenir', ANR-11-LABX-0027-01 Labex RFIEA+).

specific situation (Lahlou, 2008, 2011a). Installation theory is a theory for nudging (Thaler and Sunstein, 2008).

The second part of the chapter addresses the issue of social (re)construction in social representations. It provides a formal definition of social representations as a *set* of individual representations *installed* in human populations. This definition enables a consideration of their transformation within an evolutionary perspective. The section then makes explicit the genetic relation of social representations to the objects they represent, physical or not. It introduces the notion of *dual selection*, where the pairs (representations, objects) are selected for fitness both in the symbolic realm of ideas – by thought experiments and controversies – and in the material arena of the world of action – by empirical trials.

Installation theory

Modern conceptions of societies as being continuously reconstructed echo older views pointing at how the social frames the individual (Durkheim, 1895/1992, 1912). That societies reproduce themselves across successive generations of humans has been both well described by the functionalist approach since Talcott Parsons (1951) and criticized (Bourdieu and Passeron, 1990). These conceptions also point at the crucial function of individual behaviour in the reconstruction of the system, in pattern maintenance as well as in innovation: while framed by the social system, social reconstruction happens at the point of delivery, at least partly, through the proxy of individuals themselves as they act.

Describing the evolution of societies is difficult, because the phenomenon is complex in the sense that there are many feedback loops between different parts of the global system (Bertalanffy, 1968). A purely functionalist, ahistoric analysis in not sufficient because evolution is path-dependant: the 'causes' of the present observable state may have disappeared in the past. For example, the current shape of 'bottles' is only partly determined by function; they also bear the trace of what was technically easy to make long time ago with the techniques then available. The same goes for political regimes, for example; this accounts for some peculiarities such as democratic royalties. For the sake of simplicity, let us separate the analysis of-the-system-as-is from the analysis of its genesis and evolution, even though they must be combined in a second stage. The evolutionary aspects will be addressed in second section below. In the current section we will consider the systems in their homeostatic properties, focussing on how they reproduce rather than on how they change. I will present an analytical framework to describe complex social systems such as societies or organizations, namely *installation theory*. Since addressing the issue at social or structural levels tends to occult the concrete aspects of how reproduction occurs *in practice*, I will analyze the problem from the perspective of individual actors in order to show how their behaviours are determined in the world of action.

The world as a series of local installations that guide human behaviour

Jakob von Uexküll described how living organisms interact with the world as they perceive it, their *Umwelt* (self-centred environment) (Uexküll, 1965). For example, take the tick (*Tixus ixodes*). The sweat of mammals contains butyric acid. When sensing butyric acid, the tick drops from the branches where it lives and hopefully falls on some hairy hot skin into which it then dips its head to suck out blood. Because mammals are hairy, the tick can have a firm grip on its prey. Because they have hot blood, a simple temperature sensor can guide the tick as to where to dig its head to access blood. When the tick has missed its prey, it tries to climb, driven by positive phototropism. Because the sun is above the branches, and because the branches are finite, the tick ends its climb at the edge of a branch; and there it clings until it smells butyric acid and restarts its foraging cycle (which may be a long wait).[1] The tick can therefore be described as a simple but efficient interpretive system that makes sense of some features of its environment in order to take actions that are relevant for its existence.

As organisms adapt to their environment, through biological evolution and individual experience, so they embody systems of sensors and interpretation that foster adaptive responses to the situations they encounter. Through this phylogenetic and ontogenetic construction of a given organism, objects in the environment become 'carriers of significance' for this organism; they are interpreted by the organism as connotations for activity. Seen from the tick's perspective, a mammal is some kind of feeding *installation* which displays various affordances (Gibson, 1966, 1982, 1986), for example advertising food availability (butyric acid), sitting (hair), serving (hot soft skin) and so on.

For us humans, a fruit would naturally carry the connotation of eating. But we have also been trained to make sense of complex artefacts such as restaurants, which offer human-friendly equivalents of what the tick perceives in mammals: neon-lit signs, chairs, trays and so on. A restaurant is a man-made installation; it scaffolds a specific project (here, eating). It is usable by humans because they have incorporated the interpretive system that enables them to use the restaurant: a representation of the 'restaurant'. These representations are culturally constructed; they are not innate, like the tick's, but have a similar function in enabling us to interpret the environment in order to come up with adapted responses.

We all house individually our own representation of a 'restaurant' and these individual representations have enough similarities to enable us to communicate. These 'shared' (we will come back to this thorny point in section two) representations of our life-world are what we call 'social representations'. Individual representations of a given object are similar because they are produced by exposure to similar environments and experience, and because humans communicate and exchange information. The need to cooperate in society forces humans to reach some degree

---

[1] Uexküll reported that ticks at the Zoological Institute of Rostock remained alive for eighteen years without eating.

of consensus about how they interpret phenomena and construct objects (Lahlou, 2001).

Humans are specific in their exceptional capacity to learn, and also to modify their environmental niche. In fact, while simple organisms like the tick have to rely on biological evolution to adapt to their environment, humans actively modify their environment (and their interpretive system) to suit their needs; for example, they create restaurants and representations of restaurants. This cultural niche construction (Laland, Odling-Smee and Feldman, 2001), in which organisms modify the environment that will in turn have effects on their life-world as a species (Lewontin, 2001), is not specific to humans, but it is especially developed in our species. It can be considered as the essence of cultural development: new generations build upon the experience of previous generations stored in the environment through a 'ratchet' effect (Tomasello, 1999).

What characterizes human installations is that they are *designed* with a specific purpose: they support a project of activity. Humans make installations for all kinds of activities. Some are apparently simple, such as chairs (installations for sitting); some are more complex, such as intensive care units (installations catering for patients with critical health conditions). In fact, from the cradle to the grave, humans continuously use installations (a cradle is an installation, and a grave too, and so are schools, factories, beds, homes, etc.). This perspective is consistent with the spirit and approach of ecological psychology, although our own framework here is much looser and less sophisticated – a trade-off for practical application. Barker's 'behavioural settings', in other words 'stable, extra-individual units with great coercive power over the behaviour that occurs within them' (Barker, 1968, p. 17), address the same phenomena we call 'installations'.

As Uexküll showed, organisms operate by linking their environment to their interpretive system, thereby activating a functional loop producing adapted activity. In a functional perspective, we cannot separate the analysis of the perception from the action. Neither can we separate the analysis of the representation from the analysis of its object. The meaning of an object is *what can be done with it*; the world of action is the ultimate arena for the survival of social objects.

I will now detail the nature of installations and clarify how representations are a part of *every* installation.

The three layers of installations

In human societies the determinants of human behaviour are distributed: they lie in the subject (motives, goals, preferences, habits, etc.) and also in the context (artefacts, rules, other people). From an operational perspective, for practitioners who want to understand, predict or influence human behaviour, the world can be considered as a series of local *installations*.

Installation must be understood here in the artistic sense of assembling patterns in space and time to modify the way we experience this situation. To paraphrase Stanley Milgram's phrase about the *situation* he created in his 'obedience experiment' (Milgram, 1963): the *installation* carries 'a momentum of its own' (Milgram, 1974, p. 9).

The installation of the world guides subjects into their activity track at three levels: physical, psychological and social.

Physical layer

The physical level refers to the material properties of objects. It provides affordances (Gibson, 1982, 1986) for activity, that is, which activities can be supported by the objects. For example, chairs afford sitting; buses afford transportation. One can only do what is afforded by the environment. This layer of installation is distributed in the physical environment by nature, construction of infrastructure and various mechanisms of supply and procurement, for example the market.

The physical layer of *hat* is the collection of hats existing in the world: your hat, my son's baseball cap and so on. Hats come in millions, in different shapes and colours, but all share some essential protection and signalling functions as some device we wear on the head.

The physical layer of *democracy* is less obvious. Democracy is reified mostly in the form of processes and practices, for example in delegating decision-making. Physical installations of democracy include parliament, electoral registers, voting booths, but also 'elections', 'debates' and other control and reporting systems which are observable compound phenomena involving physical objects and people.

This first, physical, level of determination affords a tree of possible behaviours. But not everything that is possible will be realized; for example, I could be wearing this hat on my foot, but I don't.

Psychological layer

This is where psychology comes into play. To take action, subjects must *interpret* situations and other phenomena into some course of action. The subject makes sense of the environment by recognizing some significant pattern. This recognition is not a mere bottom-up process from the environment to the mind. Recognition is oriented and mediated in a complex process that involves memory and motivation (see the effects of priming, for example). More trivially, translating Chinese, playing a partition, diagnosing an illness, are sophisticated examples of how this interpretation process includes complex, feed-forward, top-down loops.

I insist that 'interpretation' should be understood here as more than merely associating ideas. Rather, I take it in the musical or theatrical sense of performing a piece of music or a play. Indeed, interpretation is an embodied experience and activity involving emotion and motion, passion and action. It has a motor aspect (acting) as well as a mental one (understanding).

Interpretation is done with individual representations. Neuro-imaging brought empirical evidence that individual representation does involve emotions (Salzman and Fusi, 2010); for example, fear is part of the evocation of a snake. Individual representations also involve sensori-motor areas in the brain (Barsalou, 2009). When we travel, when we are ill, when we engage in salutations, we engage with our own interpretation of travel, illness, salutation. Symbolic representations cannot be dissociated of a sensori-motor aspect, which connects them to the world of action.

We all house a massive portfolio of individual representations, which we carry around to interpret our life-world. Individual representations involve 'how to act' with objects – for example, a restaurant, a hat or democracy. Individual representations also enable subjects to elaborate and plan behaviour, because they may be instantiated and processed in the physical absence of the phenomenon they represent. This (semi) autonomy of the individual representation from the object it refers to will prove a crucial property in evolution, as we will see in the second part of this chapter.

This psychological layer of installation is *distributed* as individual representations over individual human minds by means of experience, education and exposure to discourse (media, advertising, etc.). Social representations theory (Moscovici, 1961/1976) deals with these constructs, and we will come back to them in more detail below.

The psychological layer of *hat* is comprised of the individual representations we have of hats, which include knowing a hat's shape and function, but also embodied motor know-how, learned through practice, by which we put a hat on and off in various situations, or adjust it, fold it, clean it, and so on. The psychological layer of *democracy* is comprised of the individual representations we have of it, which connect to ideas of governance, justice and so on, as well as to the embodied practices we have learned about, for example how to vote, how to voice our opinion, how to respect other people's opinions in debates, and so on.

Note here that, because there is this psychological layer, an installation as we define it is therefore not entirely external to the actors: part of the installation resides in the actors themselves.[2] An installation cannot 'work' if the user does not have the representations that enable her/him to play her/his part. I don't know how to wear a turban; in many areas people have difficulties with interpreting democracy.

Institutional layer

But again, not everything that is even both possible and imaginable will be realized: a third level of determination, social, will cut off more branches from the tree of possibilities, and here institutions (Hodgson, 2006) come into play. For example, although we could drive on any side of the road, only one is allowed in each country. Because individual actions produce externalities, they are limited by others. Institutions are a social solution to controlling potential abuse or misuse and to minimize social costs (Coase, 1960), which is also called 'negative externalities'.

---

2 We have elsewhere described the phenomenological perspective of actors when they are taken in the situation and induced, without deliberate decision, to interpret it into adopting a specific course of action (Lahlou, 2000).

Institutions set common conventions which enable cooperation (e.g. all must drive on the same side of road, etc.). Many rules are already contained in the normative aspects of representations, but institutions are special in their capacity to enforce behaviour by social pressure or more direct means.

The institutional layer of *hat* may seem minimal, but actually there are many institutions involved in prescribing and enforcing rules about how to make hats, how to wear them, and so on. Professional associations of hat makers and sellers edict precise norms and rules; the international conventions on size are an example. But this can go much further. In 1925, in a ruling by Mustapha Kemal (aka Atatürk), wearing a fez was officially banned by law in Turkey as part of the wider reforms of secularization and westernization. In a speech, Atatürk described the fez as 'a symbol of neglect, bigotry, and hatred of progress and civilization'. The law apparently sentenced those wearing a fez to three months, but in practice hundreds of people were sentenced to years of hard labour and a number of individuals were executed for the reason that wearing the fez was considered an invitation to rebellion. Current controversies around wearing the Islamic veil remind us that the use of head coverings is far from neutral (Wagner *et al.*, 2012).

If we now turn to *democracy*, it is obvious that institutional rules formalized in laws, rules and conventions and reified in various bodies are a crucial layer of construction, guideline and control for this 'object'.

Thus, at a given moment, individual behaviour is determined by this distributed installation: objects installed in the physical environment, interpretive systems installed in humans, and institutions installed in society. Material objects do have their say in social interaction because they enable, scaffold or prevent practice; they are 'actants' (Akrich, Callon and Latour, 2006). While this may seem obvious, social psychology has long neglected material objects. Recent developments in inter-objectivity (Moghaddam, 2003) and the debate started in the field of social representations (Sammut, Daanen and Sartawi, 2010) will hopefully change this situation. Social representations studies so far has mostly focussed on discourse, and objects and behaviour have been somewhat neglected (Wagner, 1994a).

An installation is the *result* of a social construction, but through its scaffolding properties it is also instrumental in the process of reproductive reconstruction of society. For example, 'priority seats' in public transport (for people who are disabled, pregnant or less able to stand) are the reification of social constructs such as courtesy, handicap, and so on, which in turn may reproduce (and modify) these constructs in the same process where they support specific behaviours. Most of these installations are emergent historical productions to which no specific author can be attributed (e.g. a hospital); still, they do carry agency and intentionality because they were designed to solve problems in the world of action (hats: head protection; democracy: governance; etc.). As we will see in conclusion, installation theory is of course intended to help change agents and regulators to improve current installations or design new ones.

We have examined how, in practice, society is continuously scaffolding, shaping and nudging the behaviour of individuals with *installations*. This clarifies the role of social psychology in this framework. But because some determinants of behaviour lie in the context, psychological theories alone cannot explain or predict behaviour. Since some determinants are psychological and social, a social psychological approach is indispensable to analyze the second layer.

A three-layer framework of installation theory is of course very schematic. It is deliberately so to enable a first orientation in the complex sociotechnical systems which regulators and change agents must deal with; it provides a simple checklist for analysis and an agenda for action.

I will now focus on the psychological layer in order to describe how individual representations are distributed over human populations as *social representations*; then I will deal with the evolutionary aspects of representations.

Social representations and their evolution

The first part of this chapter framed a systemic vision of society where individual representations are in one layer, embodied in humans. We will now look at how representations are linked with the other layers, and at how their evolution is connected with them.

Representations and objects

In society, we share the built environment of 'objects' that surround us. This built environment includes simple physical 'objects', phenomena like chairs or apples, but also more complex 'objects' which are experienced as systems, situations or processes: phenomena like hospitals, nations, democracy or justice. These 'objects' are meaningful compounds which humans identify as coherent functional units because they emerge as an installation scaffolding some specific activity. Lorentz, after Uexküll, defined an object as that which moves as a unitary whole (Lorenz, 1935). This is true for physical objects (this is why we would for example identify 'a crowd', 'a bee hive' or 'a suit' as a single unit although they are composed of several parts which 'go together'); but it is also true for more complex objects like a hospital (including the building, equipment, staff, procedures) or justice (courts, lawmen, laws, trials). Because we humans have a more sophisticated nervous system than the tick, we are able to subsume a considerable amount of elementary perception-action loops under a single overarching framework, which we can mobilize to address a specific phenomenon – therefore making a series of specific exploratory strategies and responses readily available to address a given 'object' in its various dimensions. I have showed elsewhere how some partial aspects of the phenomenon can prompt by association the activation of a complete representation of the global phenomenon (e.g. from the visual perception of an apple I will evoke the representation of food and eating), which in turn empowers the subject to process relevant and adapted activity with the object at hand (Lahlou, 1995).

A simple empirical criterion for identifying what humans consider as 'objects' is often the fact that they are designated by a single word or expression (e.g. 'hospital'). In what follows, I will use the term 'object' in that general sense of a phenomenon that is, in practice, considered as one single entity, whatever its nature: purely material, compound of material and other, or whatever ('swimming pool', 'bus', 'fear', 'religion'). Empirically, a list of what are considered as 'objects' by a given society can be found in its encyclopedias and dictionaries.

Because we use objects in daily activity, each of us has a representation of these objects: we all have representations of hats, restaurants, intensive care units, democracy, and so on. Because the representation is designed to interpret the phenomenon, the individual representations of different people tend to have something in common, since they couple with the same 'object'. For example, individual representations of 'apples' – as some edible fruit that grows on trees – tend to be similar among various individuals. In their detail, individual representations will vary: cooks, farmers, grocers and consumers may have developed more specific aspects of their own representation of apples following their own individual experience.

> [A] social representation is not completely shared, it is only partially distributed, just as part of the meaning of words is known to some people and unknown to others. Therefore everyone lacks some item of the knowledge that other speakers possess.
> I can even add that if all people pictured things to themselves in a similar way, they would be nothing but mirrors engaged in specular conversations. In short, they would be a mass of individuals reproduced in thousands of exemplars, not a real society. In real societies, people routinely understand some statements as agreeing with their social representation and others as conflicting with it.
> (Moscovici, 1994, p. 168)

The social division of labour enhances this effect of distributed knowledge which Roqueplo (1990) calls '*savoir décalé*': we do not all need to know everything; what matters is that 'those who act' have an operational representation. But, because we all communicate, usually a large part of the representation is shared, enough at least to enable necessary cooperation about this specific object. This does not mean that representations are consensual (Rose *et al.*, 1995), nor that we would all 'share' *the same* representation (see below). In fact, representations may vary considerably in content within a population, and there is ample literature regarding their diversity and content. Indeed, they may even appear contradictory (Castro, 2006; Jovchelovitch, 2008; Moloney, Hall and Walker, 2005; Provencher, 2011b).

When we study the construction of society, because representations are essential to communication and cooperation, we are interested in the way these representations are created, reproduced and evolve. This is what the theory of social representations is primarily about (Abric, 1987, 1994; Bauer and Gaskell, 1999; Doise, 1986; Flament, 1994; Guimelli, 1994a; Jodelet, 1989a; Lahlou, 1998; Moscovici, 1994). We are also interested in how representations connect with action and practice (including communication and reasoning), since this is a functional role of representation. This has also been studied extensively (Abric, 1994, 2003; Flament, 1994; Guimelli, 1994b; Jodelet, 1983), although less in depth than the way representations are communicated.

Individual representations and social representations

A social representation of a phenomenon (e.g. illness, democracy, etc.) can be seen as the set of its individual representations that are distributed over the members of society. Let us consider social representations as *sets* of individual representations.[3] For example, the social representation of 'hospital' in Britain is the set of the millions of individual representations of 'a hospital' held by the British population.

More technically, in the mathematical theory of sets (Cantor, 1874; Halmos, 1960; Runde, 2005), an *intensional* description defines a set by some properties of its elements (e.g. a rule or semantic description; necessary and sufficient conditions). An *extensional* definition explicitly lists all the individual elements of the set: for example an *intensional* definition of 'dogs' could be 'mammals that bark' – $\{x \in Mammals : x\ barks\}$ – while an *extensional* definition would be 'the physical set of all animals that are called dogs on the planet' – {Rex, Laika, Lassie, etc.}. Social representations, as any set, can therefore be defined in intension or in extension.

Classic social representations theory implicitly takes the intensional approach; it describes the *properties* of the social representation of an object; see, typically, the structural approach developed in Aix by Abric and colleagues (Abric, 2003; Flament, 1981; Guimelli, 1998; Moliner, 1994). Since individual representations are easily observable empirically, these intensional properties are usually inferred by some data extraction and analysis technique from a *sample* of individual representations. For example, the social representation of 'studying' is found (Lheureux, Rateau and Guimelli, 2008) to contain the following cognitive elements: knowledge, investment, diploma, culture, future, work, job, long term, university; this is obtained through questionnaires filled by a sample of students. More generally, social representations are usually studied by analyzing what is common or similar in individual representations or discourses about the object by individual subjects, in a sampled subset from the general population.

Taking an extensional approach means considering a social representation as 'the set of all individual representations of the object'. While this is not practical for description, it is essential to understand how representations disseminate and evolve *as a set*. This also opens the avenue for considering the intensional properties of the social representation as statistical characteristics of the set of the corresponding individual representations, as is implicitly done by all the techniques based on the

---

3 I would include here also individual representations carried by non-human actants such as documents, tools and other artefacts because they contribute to the reproduction process of representations. To what extent material objects stand as a representation of themselves is an interesting issue which I will leave open for discussion.

analysis of samples of individual representations. This clarifies the epistemological status of the notion and provides clean theoretical ground for the classic methods of characterizing the intensional properties of social representations.

There is a difference in *logical type* (Russell, 1908; Whitehead and Russell, 1962) between individual and social representation. This difference is similar to the one between *token* and *type* in logics (you can eat a specific apple, but you cannot eat the Apple type; one individual can have her own individual representations of a hospital, but she does not embody the full social representation of the hospital). Technically, a class (here: social representation) is of a logical type higher than its members (here: individual representation). A class cannot contain itself as a member: a social representation cannot be an individual representation. As sets, social representations have properties that the individual representations do not have.[4]

Among other things, the diversity of their elements (individual representations) enable social representations with evolutionary capacity, like the diversity of a biological species provides room for evolution of that species as a population, as we shall see. Also crucial is that individual representations are not independent of each other; they cross-breed and reproduce as members of the set (there is discussion, controversy, influence, education). Finally, this set of individual representations is linked by the *representation process* to their object, which is another source of interdependency. This is why social representations differ from 'memes' (Dawkins, 1976), and more generally why the theory of social representations is different from the naive approach of 'shared' representations, which considers a set of multiple replicated occurrences of a single representation distributed over a population. This simplistic view misses some crucial points, as noted above.

This last misconception is well described by Harré (1984, p. 930): 'The weight of an army is a distributive property, while its organization is a property of the collective. As far as I can see, the concept of *représentation sociale* is used by the French school as a distributive property of groups.' Let us be fair: this inaccurate distributive interpretation of the theory of social representations is widespread among many users of the theory, and there is a real ambiguity in the core texts regarding the epistemic status of social representations. This has been noted many times (Billig, 1988; Jahoda, 1977; McKinlay and Potter, 1987; Potter and Edwards, 1999; Potter and Litton, 1985; Potter and Wetherell, 1987). The fact that most descriptions of representations are done in intensional mode did nothing to help clarify the issue. I hope it is now clarified. Most important to note is that this formal definition of social representations as sets of individual representations provides solid epistemological ground for all techniques that describe social representations based on surveys on samples of individual representations.

---

4 One must remain careful in using mathematical formalism too exactly here; for one thing, individual representations are a moving target – they are fuzzy and change all the time in number and detail (panta rhei!). The idea that we should consider the set as a type, while useful for the issue of SR, has some technical and metaphysical limitations. See the *Stanford Encyclopedia of Philosophy*, 'Type and Token', for a detailed discussion.

The heart of the matter is that there is no opposition between the individual and the social; of course individual representations are inherently social, since they are socially constructed. Nevertheless, they have some autonomy. Conversely, even though the social is constructed by an aggregate of individuals, it has some autonomy (it will survive even when individual members die) and emergent properties at the level of its logical type (e.g. structure, internal variability, etc.). Individual and social is another type of chicken *and* egg issue.

Considering social representations as sets seemed to raise some surprise when I first proposed it (Lahlou, 2010), so I assume it will take some time to sink in; but it is necessary to take an evolutionary perspective.[5]

The evolution of social representations

Considering social representations as sets enables a better understanding of how they evolve. Their evolution is similar to the evolution of a biological population, by local mutations of individual representations, and adaptation to their ecosystem constituted by the culture and the society, and more specifically to the objects they represent. Dennett considers that 'evolution occurs whenever the following conditions exist: (1) variation: there is a continuing abundance of different elements; (2) heredity or replication: the elements have the capacity to create copies or replicas of themselves; and (3) differential "fitness": the number of copies of an element that are created in a given time varies, depending on interactions between the features of that element and features of the environment in which it persists' (Dennett, 1996, p. 343). These conditions apply to individual representations: they are continuously reproduced through discourse and practice, and this reproduction is subject to some fitness criteria.

Evolution of human societies is a chicken and egg process, as are all evolutionary processes. But it is more complex than natural evolution because it *also* takes place in the symbolic realm, as we show below. This will clarify the relation between layer 1 (physical) and layer 2 (embodied) of installation theory.

Of course representations can to some extent reproduce through discourse. But that is not the only way; practice is another way. Representations and objects follow a co-evolution process: representations are constructed by the practical experience

---

5 In his studies on the 'contagion' of ideas, anthropologist Dan Sperber developed an epidemiological approach to representations. Strangely it is rarely cited in SR literature. What he calls 'cultural representations' is very close to the notion of SR, even though here, too, the distinction of logical type between individual and social representation is unclear.

> Among the mental representations, some – a very small proportion – are communicated, that is to say, bring their user to produce a public representation which in turn leads another individual to construct a mental representation of similar content to the initial representation. Among the representations provided some – a very small proportion – are communicated repeatedly and may even end up being distributed in the whole group, that is to say have a mental version in each of its members. We call cultural representations such representations that are widely distributed within a social group and inhabit this group durably. Cultural representations as defined are a fuzzy subset of the set of mental and public representations housed by a social group. (Sperber, 1996, p. 50, my translation)

people have of objects. For instance, people learn about 'hats' by using hats or by sharing experience with other people who know about hats. Conversely, objects are made (built, constructed) after the pattern of their representation: hats are made after representations of hats, firemen are trained to behave as firemen; democracies are constructed in political debates about democracy, and so on. In other words, social representations serve as templates for constructing the world in practice. This is the reason why representations match with objects: it is not by chance but by design; at least for man-made artefacts, the objects have been designed after their representation.[6]

Let me now draw attention to the fact that objects also come in sets, and that they are also distributed over human populations. For example, we notice that a set of hats is distributed over the population of humans. Most of us own one, sometimes several. There are many democracies as well, each with its specificities. The world is full of such sets of similar objects, just as it is full of sets of similar representations.

Therefore, for each 'object' (hat, democracy, etc.) we usually have three sets to consider: the population of humans; the set of individual representations of the object embodied in humans; the set of observable phenomena that are subsumed by the name of the object (hats, instances of democracy).[7] These sets verify the three Darwinian conditions above where laws of evolution apply. Let us forget here, for a given object, the population of humans who evolve at a different pace, to focus on the set of individual representations (the social representation of the object) and the set of objects themselves. They seem to act as populations, in the sense that they inhabit the same geographical area and are capable of interbreeding (cf. what we saw above, they are taken in a chicken and egg reproduction cycle). But the reproduction cycle appears more complex than for biological species, because while representations can to some extent reproduce among themselves alone (e.g. through oral or other symbolic transmission), material objects do not reproduce by themselves.

Nevertheless, while representations and objects are taken in a chicken and egg process, each form of the object (material, symbolic) is continuously tested for fitness in its own realm. Reified objects endure a 'reality test', that is: Can they survive the confrontation with other objects in the arena of the world of action? Does this device work? Is this hat good protection? Is this democracy sustainable? In this reality arena, only the fitter survive. At the same time, representations undergo 'thought experiments' in the symbolic realm: Is this representation acceptable? Is it compatible with the local culture? Is it (politically, ethically, culturally, etc.) correct? In this symbolic arena, only the fitter survive. Survival here often

---

6 Because representations are constructed from the objects, and vice versa, it becomes ontologically difficult to separate the representation from its object, especially since, from the subject's perspective, 'the representation is what it represents' (Lahlou, 1998). This is a thorny epistemological issue. Asking whether the object and the representation are different is a bit like asking if the chicken and the egg are different; they are different manifestations of a single process.
7 And here, we not only mean governments, but also what people would consider to be an instance of democracy (e.g. an election process).

means that this representation will be used to design objects or action in the real world.

This separate evolution of phenomena and their representation is possible because, as we have seen above, representations have some autonomy from their object. Even though, as seen from the subject's perspective, the representation is what it represents because the subject only has access to her own representation, in fact the individual representation and the phenomenon are located in different places (inside the individual and out there) and therefore can be changed independently. But, in the course of evolution, when a new variant emerges, should the new object *or* the new representation fail the fitness test, they will be eliminated. This is what I mean by a 'dual selection process'. Objects have a dual form, symbolic (representations) and concrete (in the world of action). Instead of a simple trial and error process selecting variants, like in the natural selection of biological organisms (Darwin, 1859), we see here a more complex but also more economical process, where objects are selected twice, in each of their forms (symbolic, concrete), by 'thought experiments' and reality tests. For example, one can imagine making hats of human baby skin – but this solution is not culturally acceptable (it does not fit the psychological layer); one can also try making hats out of spaghetti but the first rainfall will demonstrate they do not fit the physical layer.

This dual selection applies to material objects (hats, cars) as well as to more virtual objects (democracy, education) of which the 'concrete' form emerges in the substance of situations and practices. This clarifies the role of representations in societal evolution. They are the symbolic form of objects in our culture. This symbolic form can be modified and selected for fitness through mental simulation and discourse, in though experiments which are much faster and cheaper than material trial and error in the world of action. Therefore representations enable a much faster and cheaper evolution of the material form, through the 'thought experiment' side of the dual selection mechanism. While this could be done at the level of a single individual representation (and this is sometimes the case in creativity), doing this on populations of representations (social representations) brings the efficiency of distributed evolutionary mechanisms. Social representations are a form of collective intelligence (Lahlou, 2011b), and therefore are irreducibly social.

The role of institutions

Those who tried wearing a fez under the Kemal regime soon enough discovered at their expense that it did not fit the institutional layer at the time – it must have been hard times for fez makers in Turkey.

At a societal level, the co-evolution of objects and representations is monitored by domain-local communities of interest and stakeholders (users, providers, public authorities, etc.) who set the patterns of objects, the rules of practice and more generally what is allowed in the public space. Because these stakeholders know the field, objects, representations and rules are adapted to behaviours. These stakeholders create institutions, which are both sets of rules to be applied to maintain order and foster cooperation, and communities of interest aware that they are playing in the same game. We now see better the evolutionary role of institutions as a social monitoring and control system overlooking the reproduction of objects and practices.

Indeed, embodied knowledge of how to use the affordances is not always sufficient to execute adequate behaviour. Some people might do something wrong and provoke (by ignorance, personal interest, etc.) negative externalities for themselves or others. Institutions are a social answer: they create and enforce rules to control misuse or abuse; they set common conventions enabling cooperation (e.g. all should drive on the same side of the road).

As stated above, many of these rules are already contained in the mental representations, which are by nature normative (Guimelli, 1998). But institutions come with a physical control layer of these norms. They enforce them with special personnel. Also, every loyal member of the community tends to serve as a rule enforcer and bring others back on track. Often these rules are made formal and explicit (regulations, laws, etc.), but they may remain informal rules of good practice, tricks of the trade or traditions. As these rules are the result of compromise between local interests, they vary from place to place.

While installation theory considers for the sake of pragmatic simplicity the institutional layer as separate from the others, we can see that in fact it is deeply entangled with the two other layers, just as the first two were entangled in a chicken and egg genetic process – but space lacks to discuss this here.[8]

As social representations are about the construction of real-world phenomena, which are important stakes for the society members, economic and political factors also intervene which reflect the interests and projects of members (Lahlou, 2008). Because construction is a social process, psycho-social mechanisms intervene. The cognitive content and structure of social representations reflect this historical, path-dependant and psycho-social process by which they were constructed. The co-evolution between artefacts and representations is done under monitoring and control of stakeholder communities, which create and use *institutions* as social and economic instruments to safeguard their interests. Institutions reflect the *rapports de force* between stakeholders, and they evolve as these *rapports de force* themselves evolve.

Social construction is therefore a complex evolutionary process, multilayered and path-dependant, where material objects and their representations evolve as two semi-autonomous sets distributed over – and used by – populations of humans as

---

8 Of course, since institutions are also objects, there are representations of institutions. And individual representations are also constructed by institutions. The distinction between the three layers is a gross pragmatic simplification. Each of the 'layers' is, in its genesis, co-constructed by and/or with others and so there cannot be a clean epistemic cut. Models are not the phenomena, but only a simplified and practical way to deal with them, and in this respect the installation framework is no exception. A trade-off is made here between simplicity and precision.

scaffolding instruments to interpret the world and act upon it. Objects themselves are not passive; they are actants which contribute to the interactions with and between humans. Humans have constructed institutions as social instruments to control the reproduction and evolution of these sets of scaffolding instruments; and these institutions themselves evolve as a result of *rapports de force* between human communities in the installation they build.

Conclusion

This chapter introduced a framework – installation theory – where the determinants of individual behaviours are scaffolded, shaped and constrained at three levels: affordances of the physical environment, individual representations embodied in humans, and institutions in the social world. This installation of the world carries its own momentum, and accounts for the reproduction of societies and their subsystems.

We defined social representations as *sets* of individual representations; they are therefore of a higher logical type than individual representations. This distinction clarifies a series of ambiguities in the theory of social representations. Social representations are sets of entities that reproduce under conditions for fitness, and their evolution follows Darwinian processes. We showed, however, that the evolutionary process of social representations is more complex because they co-evolve with their object, and undergo a dual selection process. Mutation and selection occur simultaneously in two realms: material and symbolic. This is also one of the reasons for the efficiency of social representations as a superiorly efficient distributed process of collective intelligence.

The three layers of installation interact in an entangled chicken and egg manner: material objects and representations co-evolve by trial and error as they reconstruct each other; institutions monitor and control the process according to social *rapports de force*. We have therefore showed how social representations enable societal evolution, in practice and in relation with objects and institutions.

Some theoretical issues are left pending or loosely formalized to some degree, and need further development. Nevertheless, while I believe that a tighter degree of formalism still needs to be reached in the theory of social representations, I would suggest that in this endeavour we should find a trade-off between the enthusiasm of scholarship and the pragmatic value of our models. Simple models are less exact but more practical. One of the reasons for the long-lasting success of the theory of social representations, and of its many uses in policy-making, is precisely that the theory is a bit loose. In this same vein, installation theory is deliberately kept simple.

If we want to change the world, or more modestly one of its sub-domains, then installation theory makes it clear that action limited to a single layer of determination alone – for example a new product or a media campaign – is unlikely to change the behaviours of people in a sustainable manner. We should make sure that appropriate installation in all three layers (physical environment, individuals concerned, and relevant institutions) has been addressed. What is left to us is the strategy of how to create and distribute such installation. For example, we could start by the physical layer by procuring new products, then try to recruit some institutions so they take over the educative part of the installation: changing representations.

More generally, by understanding better the role of social representations, and of the cultural installation, in the social continuous reconstruction of our world, we can better intervene to improve it. As we saw, this cannot be done by social psychologists alone, because there are other layers of determination than psychological; but we also saw that social psychology is an essential part of the picture, and that the symbolic aspects of the dual evolutionary mechanism of society, and especially social representations, are the key to collective intelligence.

14 From representations to representing: on social representations and discursive-rhetorical psychology

Stephen Gibson

This chapter focusses on active processes of representing, and does so by exploring the links between social representations theory, discourse analysis and rhetorical psychology. It is argued that the focus on action in discursive and rhetorical approaches provides a lens through which we might view how social representations are used in specific social settings. Equally, the focus of social representations theorists on the 'sedimentation' of cultural themes provides one possibility through which discursive and rhetorical psychologists might be able to combine a focus on the micro-interactional with the more diffuse cultural-historical processes that partially shape the objects of discourse. The details of such an approach are necessarily preliminary, but in the latter part of the chapter I will provide a brief empirical example in an attempt to sketch out some of the possibilities afforded by a combination of a concern with both historical and micro-interactional processes of social construction.

Social representations theory and discursive-rhetorical psychology have much in common, such as the use of some form of constructionist epistemological metatheory, and the variety of approaches encompassed by these broad umbrella terms. Social representations theory has diversified into distinct traditions such as Abric's (e.g. 2002) structural approach, Marková's (e.g. 2003) dialogical approach, and many others besides (e.g. Wagner and Hayes, 2005; Jovchelovitch, 2007; Howarth, 2006a). Similarly, discursive-rhetorical psychology takes in a range of approaches from Parker's (1992) critical realist approach, to Potter and Edwards's (1992) avowedly relativist discursive psychology (see Edwards, Ashmore and Potter, 1995) and Billig's (1996) rhetorical psychology. Indeed, the term 'discursive-rhetorical psychology' is preferred here precisely in order to capture this breadth, and is intended to afford the potential to draw on the insights of these traditions while

---

This chapter is a development and extension of ideas first presented in 'History in action: The construction of historical analogies in televised debates concerning the Iraq War', published in *Papers on Social Representations* (2012, vol. 21, pp. 13.1–13.35). I am grateful to the London School of Economics and Political Science, publisher of *Papers on Social Representations*, for allowing me to reproduce some material from the earlier paper in the present chapter.

recognizing that there may sometimes be epistemological tensions as a result of any attempt at eclecticism.

Such problems also have the potential to arise in any attempt to suggest a rapprochement between discursive-rhetorical psychology and the theory of social representations. However, with movement on both sides these may not be insurmountable. Indeed, while there is a well-established tradition of critical engagement between the two theories – largely stemming from discourse analytical critiques of the theory of social representations from the mid 1980s onwards (e.g. Billig, 1991, 1993; Gibson and Noret, 2010; Litton and Potter, 1985; McKinlay and Potter, 1987; Potter, 1996a, 1996b; Potter and Billig, 1992; Potter and Litton, 1985; Potter and Edwards, 1999; Potter and Wetherell, 1987, 1998) – both social representations theory and discursive-rhetorical psychology have developed in various ways since the height of these critical encounters. Notably, as Howarth (2006a, p. 68) has argued, in social representations theory there has been greater recognition that social representations 'are not static templates that we pull out of our cognitive schemas' but should instead 'be seen as alive and dynamic – existing only in the relational encounter, in the in-between space we create in dialogue and negotiation with others'. There is thus clearly potential for some level of integration, but this is more likely with some varieties of discursive-rhetorical psychology and social representations theory than with others. Whereas Howarth's approach is close in many respects to forms of discursive-rhetorical psychology which take a broader approach to discourse, others – such as the structural approach – are less amenable. Similarly, approaches to discursive-rhetorical psychology which are aligned more closely with conversation analysis (CA) are less likely to be able to incorporate the level of cultural-historical analysis necessitated by a broader focus on social representations.

For CA-oriented approaches, the question of where discursive resources come from is often simply sidestepped, but it is argued here that these questions are crucial: How do discursive resources become sedimented into the cultural milieu? What is the cultural milieu if not the constant sound of ongoing human interaction? How can a view of reality being constructed anew in each social encounter be sustained in the face of the seeming necessity for some element of temporal continuity (Condor, 1996)?

The initial discursive critique of the theory of social representations emphasized the alternative concept of interpretative repertoires; yet despite the continued use of this concept by some discourse analysis researchers, it has been suggested by proponents of more CA-oriented approaches (e.g. Wooffitt, 2005) that the concept of interpretative repertoire is itself too vague and insufficiently grounded in detailed analysis of interaction. This creates something of a problem, for discursive-rhetorical psychology needs some sort of a theory of cultural reproduction, in a way that it doesn't need a theory of psychology (in the traditional sense).

For discursive-rhetorical psychology, agnosticism on the underlying concept of mind is a necessary and desirable position, but agnosticism on cultural processes is – in my view – simply not an option. Discursive-rhetorical psychology needs to answer the question, 'Where does all this stuff come from?' If interpretative repertoires are no longer seen as adequate to do the job, then other conceptual tools are needed. Social representations may constitute one such tool, but for many they will themselves come with too much theoretical baggage to allow for successful integration with discursive-rhetorical psychology. Trying to find common ground is therefore a challenging task, but one that is potentially made easier if we consider what I take to be the two key problems facing any such attempt to integrate the approaches: the problem of 'sedimentation', and the problem of discourse.

The problem of 'sedimentation'

Discursive-rhetorical psychologists are faced with a problem of explaining the longer-term processes of construction that furnish interaction with the basic building blocks from which social objects are constructed in each separate social encounter. This problem can be illuminated by considering a critique of the use of interview methods in qualitative psychological research. Potter and Hepburn (2005) point out that one of the key problems with interviewing is that the interaction will inevitably be 'flooded' with social scientific categories and priorities. They suggest that

> The social science agenda is bound up with (although goes beyond) the categories that are used. These include the various more or less technical terms and descriptions that appear in interview questions and interview responses. This is a rather complicated topic as it may be quite hard to judge what terms are social scientific and what are not... However, as social representations researchers, Foucaultians and others have argued, everyday talk can involve a range of 'sedimentations' of earlier 'theoretical' notions as the languages of psychoanalysis, Marxism, symbolic interactions and so on become parts of people's everyday conversational currency.
>
> (Potter and Hepburn, 2005, p. 292)

Recent developments in discursive-rhetorical psychology have arguably moved it towards a position where the focus is almost exclusively on the local interactional accomplishment of phenomena, with limited attention to the ways in which the 'sedimentations' referred to by Potter and Hepburn come about. In the absence of such an account of sedimentation in discursive-rhetorical psychology, the analyst is compelled to look elsewhere, and Potter and Hepburn provide two such candidates in social representations theory and Focaultian analysis. Yet if discursive-rhetorical psychologists can point to the problem of sedimentation, why can this not be built into discursive theory and analysis? To fully understand, say, the way in which some stretch of discourse is put together, it is surely necessary to explore both its local interactional accomplishment *and* the extent to which the resources on which it draws have become culturally sedimented and available for mobilization by speakers (Wetherell, 1998). For example, the discursive-rhetorical psychology project of respecifying psychological terms as speakers' resources rather than as objects of investigation themselves with referents 'under the skull' has furnished a great many insights into how psychological business gets done in the course of everyday activities. The counterparts to this microsocial constructionist position, however, are the more broader-brushed constructionist approaches to psychological language developed by authors such as Danziger (1997) and Soyland (1994). For instance, Danziger has traced the historical construction of the psychological domain through the use of particular linguistic categories. It is through this approach that we can begin to appreciate, for example, how many terms that we now take for granted as referring to mental interiority used to refer to external, publically accessible phenomena. One feature of the history of psychological language therefore, is a gradual interiorizing of that which was once physical and observable.

This necessarily demands a form of analysis which moves beyond the focus on local interactional accomplishment. As Elcheroth, Doise and Reicher (2011, p. 755) have recently argued:

> In understanding how particular representations win out, we should look at the ways in which they are sedimented into collective practices and institutional facts. Looking at survey responses is not enough, nor is looking at 'natural' discourse. In any case, ethnographic descriptions of collective rituals and routine practices allow us to broaden the interpretative context for 'speech acts': they help to explain what is communicated by other vehicles than words, and they clarify what words allow people to do together.

Although Elcheroth and colleagues' distinction between the discursive and the non-discursive is perhaps too straightforward, their focus chimes with the more extended conceptualization of 'discourse' afforded by approaches such as semiotics (see, e.g. Hall, 1997), and indeed with those varieties of discursive-rhetorical psychology which incorporate a more ideological-historical level of analysis (e.g. Billig, 1995; Wetherell, 1998). Billig's (1995) analysis of the unnoticed national flags (both literal and metaphorical) providing the banal national framing of everyday activities, is a particularly good example of how the analysis of 'collective rituals and routine practices' (Elcheroth, Doise and Reicher, 2011, p. 755), extending beyond a narrow conceptualization of 'discourse', can provide insights into precisely these processes of sedimentation. This also highlights the extent to which such sedimentations perform identity-work, naturalizing some groups (e.g. 'national' groups), and – moreover – particular versions of those groups. These sedimentations should not be understood as overly constraining – the possibility of contestation is always present (Billig, 1996; Reicher and Hopkins, 2001) – but they furnish social actors with a range of cultural resources on which they can draw.

A fully worked out discursive-rhetorical psychology therefore needs both the focus on local interactional processes and a focus on broader cultural processes. In short, it needs a theory of social representation. Whether some version of the theory of social representations itself could ever successfully be integrated with discursive-rhetorical psychology would, however, require a similar movement on the part of social representations theory towards resolving the problem of discourse.

The problem of discourse

The core of the discursive critique of the theory of social representations (SRT) has been the observation that discursive processes have 'the anomalous position of being at the heart of SRT as the engine for the generation and refinement of representations, and yet being a topic which has received no analytic attention' (Potter and Edwards, 1999, p. 449). Despite the varied responses to this critique from social representations researchers (e.g. de Rosa, 2006; Liu et al., 2010; Marková, 2000; Moscovici, 1985c; Moscovici and Marková, 1998; Räty and Snellman, 1992a, 1992b; Wagner, 1998), there has been acknowledgement in some quarters that 'conflict and argumentation are still under-theorized within social representations theory' (Voelklein and Howarth, 2005, p. 441). Edwards (2006, p. 41) has referred to the terrain of the discursive psychologist as being the 'rich surface of language and social interaction'. There is little doubt that the broad array of approaches captured here under the discursive-rhetorical psychology umbrella have contributed to a radically different way of approaching the subject matter of psychology, and to the extent that psychological phenomena have been recast as fundamentally *social* objects, many have suggested that there is little need to return to the traditional concern with interiority associated with mainstream psychology. However, for social representations theorists, the 'rich surface' in itself is not enough; to understand representational processes, we must extend our theorizing into the twin realms of the social group and individual cognition.[1] Yet the discursive critique has emphasized that we are in no position to make these extensions until we have a firmer grasp on what is going on discursively, and that once we have achieved such a grasp we may find that further extension is in fact unnecessary. An essential element in any attempt at integration is therefore a movement away from traditional conceptions of cognition on the part of the theory of social representations. Indeed, with recent moves towards engaging with dialogicality in social representations theory (e.g. Howarth, 2006a; Marková, 2000, 2003), there are signs that the centrality of cognition may not be as pronounced in some versions of the theory of social representations as has sometimes been the case. By adopting a constructionist position on the relationship between language and cognition, any distinction between social representations theory and discursive-rhetorical psychology arguably becomes more a matter of emphasis than degree. A number of things would follow, one of which would be a clearer focus on representation-as-action, with the analytic focus being drawn towards the way in which representations are

---

1 This rather broad characterization necessarily obscures differences in emphasis between approaches, but all varieties of SRT arguably feature this tripartite concern with cognition, language and groups.

'produced, performed and constructed in precisely the way they are for their role in activities' (Potter and Edwards, 1999, p. 488). Potter and Edwards conceptualize action 'in terms of the enormous range of practical, technical and interpersonal tasks that people perform while living their relationships, doing their jobs, and engaging in varied cultural domains' (ibid.). Such a focus is necessary to ensure that the dynamic conception of social representations espoused at the theoretical level is followed through empirically, and would also dovetail with the methodological techniques afforded by discursive-rhetorical psychology.

Although in one sense the theory of social representations has a long tradition of concern with the functions of social representations (e.g. Lahlou, 2001; Jost and Ignatow, 2001), it has typically not been concerned with the ways in which particular representations are constructed in particular contexts to perform particular actions. Billig's (2008a, 2011, 2013; see also Billig, 2008b) recent work on social psychological writing offers a clue as to how this may have come about. Billig suggests that the focus on the noun *representation* has led to a relative neglect of the active verb form *representing*. Similarly, Voelklein and Howarth (2005, p. 447) have argued that the primary focus of the theory of social representations has been 'on the content and structure of a social representation as opposed to its function and broader societal implications'. They thus suggest that social representations research needs 'to examine what social representations *do* in social and political relations' (ibid., p. 448, emphasis original), in other words, the theory of social representations requires a renewed focus on *action*, and it is here that discursive-rhetorical psychology can make an important contribution.

Social representations of history

To illustrate how these arguments may be used to point the way to a different approach in areas of current research in social representations, I will now consider recent work on social representations of history (e.g. Liu, 1999; Liu *et al.*, 2005, 2009; Madoglou, Melista and Liaris-Hochhaus, 2010; Paez *et al.*, 2008; Pennebaker *et al.*, 2006). Much of this work has adopted large-scale cross-cultural survey methodology to explore which people and events are seen as being the most important in world history. For example, Liu and colleagues (2005, p. 175) asked the following question of over 2,000 participants spread across twelve territories: 'Imagine that you were giving a seminar on world history. What 7 events would you teach as the most important in world history? How positively or negatively do you regard each event?' They found that 41 per cent of all events selected across the sample as a whole involved warfare – far greater than any other type of event. Moreover, they found that in all twelve samples, World War II was identified as the most important event in world history, with World War I being identified as the second most important in all but one (the French sample selected the French Revolution). These studies have been accompanied by a theoretical framework which appears to offer much promise in addressing issues of narrative, discourse and contestation (e.g. Liu and Hilton, 2005; Liu and László, 2007). For example, Liu and Hilton (2005, p. 537) argue that 'history provides us with narratives that tell us who we are, where we came from and where we should be going. It defines a trajectory which helps construct the essence of a group's identity, how it relates to other groups, and ascertains what its options are for facing present challenges.' They go on to suggest that 'while the main events and people that constitute lay representations of history tend to be uncontroversial, their meaning and relevance to current events is often highly contested' (p. 539).

Despite this emphasis on narrative and contestation, it is notable that there is often a striking *under*-emphasis on processes of argumentation and contestation in work adopting this approach. For instance, Liu and Hilton (2005) consider the varying responses of France, Germany and Britain to the 9/11 attacks on the United States:

> That the same challenge elicited such diverse reactions from three allies confronted with the same problem is not difficult to understand in the light of history: Britain's charter sees it as a world policeman with the US just as in 1941 when the two nations combined to defend democracy against Germany, Italy and Japan; France's charter sees it as defending human rights, but as a nation resistant to Anglo-Saxon world hegemony; finally, Germany is in quest of a new charter that will allow it to define a 'normal' role in the world without arousing historically grounded fears of German aggression both at home and abroad.
> (Liu and Hilton, 2005, p. 538)

As broad glosses of the positions of these three states, these characterizations may seem plausible enough, but problems arise when one attempts to unpack them. To use the UK as an example, Liu and Hilton point out that 'Britain' was 'America's principal military ally and dispatched troops [to Afghanistan] almost immediately' (ibid.). Yet it is unclear precisely what type of entity 'Britain' actually is in this formulation. The decision to send troops was taken by political actors, but to what extent does 'Britain' in this instance incorporate the UK population? There is evidence to suggest that the wider public was not generally supportive of the actions taken by the UK government (Miller, 2002), so to suggest that the decision to go to war simply reflects a view of 'Britain' as a 'world policeman' is rather problematic. What view of 'Britain' underscored the opposition to war, and how can this be consonant with the notion of a singular 'charter'? There is, I would suggest, an elision here between government policy and public opinion, and at a more conceptual level between 'Britain' as pertaining to a social identity and 'Britain' as a synecdoche for 'the British government' (Condor, 2006; Gibson and Condor, 2009).

Similarly, at the level of methodology, the continued reliance on survey technologies obscures the constructive and narrative work that generates social representations of history. Where discursive findings are cited, they tend to be used as a point of departure for scale development (e.g. Liu and Sibley, 2009; Sibley *et al.*, 2008). In this respect, studies in this tradition have largely taken processes of construction for granted as underpinning responses to survey measures, without ever really subjecting these constructive processes to analytic scrutiny. Fundamentally, this neglects the constructive work done by survey instruments themselves, a key insight of Potter and Wetherell's (1987) original statement of the discourse-analytic position in social psychology. The arguments outlined above concerning representations and discursive action are therefore particularly applicable to this tradition of work, and as Tileagă (2009, pp. 350–1, emphasis original) has noted, this 'highlights the importance of studying representations of history as situated social action and social practice. A discursive approach suggests treating representations of history not as something "pre-given", but as in need of *constitution*.' In the remainder of this chapter I will briefly sketch an alternative approach to the analysis of social representations of history informed by discursive-rhetorical psychology.

History in action

Rather than exploring what, in abstract terms, are seen as the most important events in world history, we might fruitfully address the issue of what, precisely, such events are important *for*. This leads to a focus on the uses of representations of history – to a focus on history in action.

To flesh out these arguments, I will now turn to an empirical example from a broader project examining a corpus of televised debates collected during the early months of 2003 in the run up to the Iraq war (for a fuller outline of the dataset, see Gibson, 2012a). The data presented below are drawn from an analysis of the use of historical analogies in arguments concerning the Iraq War (Gibson, 2012c; for further analyses derived from this dataset, see Gibson, 2011, 2012b, 2012c; for another discursive analysis of the use of historical analogies in the context of the Iraq war, see Burridge, 2005). The extract is taken from an episode of *Question Time*, a British Broadcasting Corporation (BBC) programme, which was broadcast on 13 February 2003. The format of *Question Time* involves an audience composed of members of the public putting questions on the significant issues of the day to a panel of politicians, journalists and other commentators. It is chaired by David Dimbleby, and at the time the present dataset was collected, was dominated by discussions of Iraq. In the following extract, we see a World War II analogy being mobilized by an audience member, with a panellist, Simon Thomas (a Member of Parliament for the Welsh nationalist Plaid Cymru Party), then contesting it through the invocation of an alternative historical analogy:[2]

---

[2] See the appendix at the end of this chapter for an explanation of the transcription conventions used in the extract.

1	DD	OK and the man in the ((pointing)) second
2		row here °°you sir°°
3	A13	er: u- unfortunately not many people here
4		are of my age (.hh) do they not remember
5		Chamberlain and I bring home a letter (.)
6		of peace for ever [(.)] appeasement took
7		place
8	?	[(°°aha°°)]
9	A13	during the nineteen thirties (.h) and what
10		happened (.h) we had the most dreadful war
11		imaginable (.h) if people'd take notice of
12		[Churchill in the thirties] (.h) that would =
13	ST	[((shakes head))]
14	A13	= not have happened (.h) we'd have saved
15		millions of lives
16	?	you shaking your head for? ((inaudible))
17	ST	because the comparison is with Suez (.) not
18		with in with [the Second World War]
19	?	[((inaudible))]
20	ST	[the comparison is with Suez!]
21	?	[((inaudible))]
22	A13	I'm talking about the
23		[thirty nine forty five war!]
24	ST	[the comparison is with Suez]
25		[not the t- not the Second World War]
26	?	[((inaudible))]
27	A13	I'm >talking about< thirty nine forty five
28	DD	OK dy- may-
29	A13	may I continue
30	DD	Yes
31	A13	ahm (.)
32	DD	and then [you can make your point] which =
33	?	[((inaudible))]
34	DD	= I didn't [quite catch cos] there was no
35		microphone yes!
36	A13	[((laughs))]
37	A13	er we we have two er countries objecting
38		France and Germany (.h) Germany are
39		pacifists we all know why they're pacifists
40		(.h) the French are only fit to ban our
41		beef (.) there's nothing we should do now
42		but get on with the job
43		[and move Hussein out =]
44	?	[((inaudible))]

It is notable here that both historical analogies used in the extract – the Munich agreement of 1938 and the Suez crisis of 1956 – are invoked in ways which assume a shared understanding of the meaning and significance of the analogies. In constructing an analogy between World War II and the Iraq war, A13 uses category entitlement (Edwards and Potter, 1992): 'unfortunately not many people here are

Figure 14.1 *Physical representation of Chamberlain's waving gesture by A13 (corresponding to lines 5–6 in the extract), with Chamberlain's original gesture (30 September 1938; from www.youtube.com/watch?v=FO725Hbzfls, retrieved 11.12.2014).*

of my age' (lines 3–4). He explicitly invokes memory in the question 'do they not remember Chamberlain' (lines 4–5), which, if taken literally, is oxymoronic – in addressing others as being younger than himself, he is positioning those others as specifically *not* having relevant first-hand memories. His reference to *remembering* here can thus be understood as an exhortation to pay heed to a particular collective memory that should not be forgotten. He invokes the figure of Neville Chamberlain and paraphrases his infamous 1938 speech on returning from Munich (lines 5–6: 'I bring home a letter of peace for ever'). This active voicing (note the way in which the first person is used on line 5), coupled with the physical action of raising his hand in imitation of Chamberlain's holding aloft the piece of paper (see Figure 14.1), enables A13 not simply to invoke this event verbally, but to physically recreate it.

This reference to the policy of appeasement is then followed by a rhetorical question (lines 9–10: 'what happened'), which is used to construct a direct linkage between appeasement and 'the most dreadful war imaginable' (lines 10–11). A13 continues by invoking Churchill, and suggesting that had his warnings been heeded, 'millions of lives' would have been saved. The use of extreme case formulations (*most dreadful, millions*; see Pomerantz, 1986) works up the seriousness of the fate that awaits humanity if the mistakes of the past are repeated. It is notable that A13 invokes the failure to recognize the graveness of the situation in the 1930s: 'if people'd take notice of Churchill in the thirties' (lines 11–12). At this point the screen cuts to Simon Thomas, who can be seen shaking his head, and an unidentified member of the audience challenges him to explain this (line 16). This challenge in itself highlights the difficulty of contesting the Munich analogy. Thomas' explanation involves contesting the relevance of World War II as a historical frame for the situation in Iraq, and he instead argues that 'the comparison is with Suez' (lines 17, 20 and 24). This is formulated as a straightforward matter of fact: no hedging or qualification is involved, and there is no attempt to mark the assertion as his opinion. This highlights the extent to which the audience is expected to understand what is meant by the invocation of 'Suez' – no additional information or explanation is required to explain the ways in which the present situation is analogous to the Suez crisis, it is simply treated as a collective memory which will resonate with the audience. Here, then, we have a speaker challenging the analogy between World War II and the Iraq war by invoking a conflict in which military intervention is generally understood to have been a mistake, and which ended in humiliation and the resignation of the then prime minister, Anthony Eden (for a history of the Suez crisis, see Kyle, 2011).

The role of the World War II analogy in A13's argument then becomes clear as he seeks to explain away the objections of France and Germany to military intervention in Iraq. The reference to common knowledge (line 39: 'we all know') to explain German 'pacifism' again involves a more implicit invocation of World War II – albeit one that is perhaps made somewhat less implicit given the invocation of Chamberlain, Churchill and appeasement that preceded it. The crux of his argument is then reached, as he argues for 'get[ting] on with the job' and 'mov[ing] Hussein out' (lines 42–43).

We can understand this exchange as a contest over the most appropriate anchor for the situation in Iraq. This process should be understood as a rhetorical struggle over competing culturally sedimented narratives (Billig, 1991; see also Lowe, 2012): one of British national triumph in the face of initial reluctance to go to war, the other of British national humiliation as a result of undue haste in taking military action. It might be thus suggested that these narratives constitute good examples of social representations in the classical sense: they are consensually held narratives used for making the unfamiliar familiar. The sense-making function of the social representations of World War II and the Suez crisis can be seen quite clearly in the extent to which they are used in trying to frame the way in which the Iraq situation is to be understood. However, the sense-making function is only part of the story. People are not making sense of the Iraq situation in abstract terms, but are instead doing so as part of rhetorical projects aimed at making the case for or against military action. The social representation thus performs a discursive action within the context of its mobilization. This is in accordance with Howarth's (2006a, p. 68) assertion that social representations should 'be seen as alive and dynamic – existing only in the relational encounter, in the in-between space we create in dialogue and negotiation with others'. It is only possible to fully draw out the implications of this, however, if analyses of social representations focus principally on the relational encounter, and for this the analytic tools and perspectives of discursive-rhetorical psychology are indispensable.

Similarly, the suggestion that these social representations of history may be consensually held requires some clarification. One could, of course, conduct a survey to find out what meanings people associated with these events, but – as noted above – this would ride roughshod over the idea that social representations exist 'only in the relational encounter'. Instead, the conceptual and analytic toolkit of discursive-rhetorical psychology can be drawn on to recast our understanding of the nature of consensus. Rather than an empirical question requiring some form of quantified answer to reassure ourselves that a social representation is indeed held by sufficient numbers of people to merit the description of it as being held consensually, we can treat such matters as participants' concerns. This avoids the retreat into cognitivism and methodological individualism associated with a survey-type approach which almost inevitably results in a picture of individuals carrying around social representations in their heads. Edwards (1997, p. 114) reformulates such questions in terms of an approach to shared knowledge in which the analyst explores what participants' 'talk *treats as* shared, and when, and how' (emphasis in original). What is of interest is thus the way in which the speakers in the extract presented above mobilize the competing analogies in ways that treat them as consensual.

This, however, is not enough on its own, and it is here that the need to explore the genealogy of the contents of discourse becomes important. Despite the roots of discursive psychology in (among other things) post-structuralist thought, discursive psychologists have arguably come to pay less attention to this key issue in more recent times. The crystallization of a conventional narrative of World War II as 'the good war' (Terkel, 1984) into a familiar cultural trope – a social representation – is, however, worthy of sustained attention.

In his impressive analysis of the creation of what he terms 'the pleasure culture of war' in British popular culture, Michael Paris (2000, p. 221) has argued that World War II 'has become, for the British people, a never ending story told and retold to remind themselves of a glorious past, in a far less glorious and depressing present'. With the decline of the UK's status as a significant world power following World War II, 'the nation preferred to look back to past military triumphs, in order to convince itself that Britain was still great. And the war which most epitomized the triumph of national spirit and moral certainty was, of course, the Second World War' (pp. 238–9). In this context, the Munich agreement, and the broader policy of appeasement which it represented, has come to be seen as deeply misguided, to say the least.

Despite enjoying widespread support at the time of the Munich agreement, the castigation of appeasement began very shortly afterwards. As Finney (2011, p. 194) has pointed out, this arose in no small part due to the ideological functions of such a critique of appeasement. Finney traces the historiography of appeasement to build a complex picture of how the dominant British image of World War II was developed and sustained. This process was already well underway during the war itself, as writers sought to construct accounts of the origins of the war which fulfilled the functions of both justifying military action, and engendering a sense of national unity. In particular, he points to the way in which the influential text *Guilty Men*, published pseudonymously as 'Cato' by Michael Foot, Frank Owen and Peter Howard in 1940, 'effected closure over other, more complex, explanations of the 1930s, by offering the only account which worked ideologically to provide a national history and present identity in tune with the new realities of the "People's War"' (p. 194). As Finney's argument makes clear, in (re)constructing these processes, we begin to see the relationship between representations of history and representations of identity. By furnishing a particular historical narrative, the conventionalized representation of the Munich agreement made it possible for the British to tell a particular kind of story about who 'we' are (see also Elcheroth, Doise and Reicher, 2011; Liu and Hilton, 2005).

However, this is not to say that such historical narratives are beyond contestation, both in terms of their historical accuracy (see Finney, 2011; Noon, 2004) and in terms of the general lessons that are to be drawn from them. In this latter respect, the Suez crisis arguably fulfils a similar role in the UK as does the Vietnam War in the USA (see e.g. Taylor and Rourke, 1995). The narrative of national humiliation, the 'end of empire' (Kyle, 2011) and subsequent decline can be used to serve as a warning of the perils of military misadventures. As with Finney's analysis of Munich historiography, the concern is not with whether this view of the Suez crisis is accurate or not, but instead should be with the way in which a conventional narrative of the crisis crystallized, and the uses to which this narrative can be put.

Concluding remarks

This chapter has argued that the potential for fruitful rapprochement between the theory of social representations and discursive-rhetorical psychology can be developed by addressing the twin problems of discourse and sedimentation. If social representations theorists are confronted by problems concerning the appropriate incorporation of the discursive realm into their analytic schemas, then discursive-rhetorical psychologists are faced with the problem of explaining the provenance of cultural-discursive resources used by speakers/writers in any concrete setting. To be sure, these problems apply more to some variants of both approaches than to others, and the example outlined here should be seen as merely a preliminary step towards an integrated constructionist position. Nevertheless, the explanatory possibilities of seeking to build on existing attempts to combine micro and macro forms of social constructionism (e.g. Abell and Stokoe, 2001; Wetherell, 1998) are potentially greater than either social representations theory or discursive-rhetorical psychology, in their own right, are able to generate.

There may be reluctance among practitioners within both traditions to accept that in doing the type of work discussed here we are, in fact, studying social representations. It might be that terms such as 'collective memory', 'shared knowledge' or 'interpretative repertoire' are preferred. But we are dealing with the representation of something as socially shared, and there is already a term within social psychology's theoretical lexicon which captures the concept nicely: *social representation*.

Appendix

The transcription conventions (adapted from Hutchby and Wooffitt, 1998, pp. vi–vii) used in the example above are a slightly simplified form of the Jeffersonian transcription conventions (Jefferson, 2004) favoured by conversation analysts and many discursive psychologists, and are particularly useful for capturing the finer details of talk.

(1.0)	The number in parentheses indicates a time gap to the nearest tenth of a second.
(.)	A dot enclosed in parentheses indicates a pause in the talk of less than two-tenths of a second.
[]	Square brackets between adjacent lines of concurrent speech indicate the onset and end of a spate of overlapping talk.
.hh	A dot before an 'h' indicates speaker in-breath. The more h's, the longer the in-breath.
hh	An 'h' indicates an out-breath. The more h's, the longer the breath.
(())	A description enclosed in double parentheses indicates a non-verbal activity. For example, ((pointing)). Alternatively double parentheses may enclose the transcriber's comments on contextual or other features.
-	A dash indicates the sharp cut-off of the prior word or sound.
:	Colons indicate that the speaker has stretched the preceding sound. The more colons the greater the extent of stretching.
!	Exclamation marks are used to indicate an animated or emphatic tone.
that	Underlined fragments indicate speaker emphasis.
° °	Degree signs are used to indicate that the talk they encompass is spoken noticeably quieter than the surrounding talk.
> <	'More than' and 'less than' signs indicate that the talk they encompass was produced noticeably quicker than the surrounding talk.

Speaker identification: DD = David Dimbleby (Host); ST = Simon Thomas MP (on-screen caption: Plaid Cymru). Audience members are identified by the letter 'A' followed by a numeral which indicates the order in which they responded in the programme. Collective audience responses (e.g. applause) are identified by 'Au'. Unidentified speakers are indicated with a '?'.

15 Positioning theory and social representations

Rom Harré and Fathali Moghaddam

On initial assessment it seems that the theory of social representations is 'neutral' with respect to the moral status of the content of representations. Social representations just are. If that were so the study of social representations would be outside the scope of positioning theory analysis. However, it would be a natural extension for a meta-social representation level to identify positions such as rights and duties, relevant forms of 'good' or 'bad', or 'better' or 'worse' social representations. For example, the social representation of Jews as subhuman conspirators inspired grotesquely evil conceptions of people's civic rights and duties. We must recognize that the theory of social representations does engage in positioning in important ways. The focus in social representations research is on collective representations, in the special sense that every person in a collective has more or less the same representation apropos of some matter, trivial or important. This contrasts with the focus on the individual in traditional psychology, leaving open the question of how it is possible for people to act as a group or faction or party. Second, this focus on the collective is associated with the highlighting of the collaborative processes through which shared representations arise.[1] 'Collaborative' does not mean that all the parties involved in the process of meaning construction have equal power. The study of social representations and their role in shaping forms of life necessarily involves attention to power disparities. Along with that must go attention and the issue of motives embedded in a socio-political system. Once this complexity is attended to, the various distributions of rights and duties to act within the collective become important. Who has the right to lead the crowd (*le fol*) and how has that right been established? According to positioning theory, the underlying motive for the prevalence of a shared representation is not to be found in individual minds, but in the characteristics of a socio-political order and the means through which this order is perpetuated. A current case of interest is the seemingly irrational stubbornness with which members of the National Rifle Association in the United States hang on to their interpretation of the 'right to bear arms'.

The work of Denise Jodelet (1989a) revealed the way in which representations of mental illness in rural areas of France profoundly affected the way rights and duties

---

[1] In social psychology we should, though we have not always done so, distinguish between a group as an aggregate where the group exists only by virtue of similarities between the members, and a group as a collective, in which there are real relations between members, for example engaging in a conversation, or even passing on rhino viruses to one another.

were assigned to the people relocated from asylums to farming families. Similarly, Claudine Herzlich (1973) showed how rural and urban social representations of 'being ill' affected the way people self-assigned the right to play the sick role, and how the recognition of that role differed from town to country.

The issue of positioning is deeply embedded in the whole programme of social representations research. Once some body of knowledge has been identified and its content established, that is, a social representation of some matter has been made explicit, the question of how it is to be realized arises – and that requires attention to the way rights and duties are distributed among the people who share the representation. Bringing the pattern of rights and duties to light must be an integral part of the research efforts inspired by the hypothesis that a social representation is shaping the content and form of what people are doing.

The role of language

To appreciate the significance of positioning analyses in any field of psychology one must first reflect on some main features of the relations between language and thought and language and action. Thinking has many forms, but the form that is of paramount importance for most people is thinking as the use of cognitive tools to carry out the tasks of everyday life. The most important cognitive tools are symbols, usually words and other language-like devices such as timetables, and models, maps and other forms of iconic representation. Only recently has it been realized by psychologists that thinking can be communal as well as individual, public as well as private. And this immediately raises questions of morality. Are the uses of these devices freely open to all the competent members of a social group?

The domain of thinking is both intrapersonal and interpersonal. Thinking is not only an individual–personal activity but also a social–public one (Harré and Sammut, 2013). For example, the process of remembering includes conversational as well as introspective activities. Members of a family group or a committee or the golf club reminisce, a terrorist cell make plans, a loving couple discuss the future, each member contributing something to the construction of a version of the past from which that future will spring. Versions of both past and future are communally constructed, and each member takes away with them some personal version of that communal version on which further action is often based. It follows that there are exograms, records of the past outside the brain of a person, as well as engrams, traces of the past incorporated in long-term memory. There are legible material things, such as diaries, photos and monuments. There are the relevant records of the sayings and doings of other people. These are all resources for acts of remembering, often overriding personal recollections. They play their part in thinking about the future.

There are plenty of examples of thinking spanning both the individual–personal and social–public domains. In deciding what to do, a person will spend time on private reflections of the consequences of a plan of action, perhaps attempting to imagine the future in some concrete way. However, often there are public discussions; people go about seeking advice on the best course of action. There are influences from the unstated opinions of others which may show up indirectly in what they do and say. There are informal varieties of the formal decision procedures involving agendas, resolutions, amendments, votes and so on. In all of these activities people draw on shared bodies of knowledge, that is, on social representations.

Clearly interpersonal relations must enter into communal forms of remembering, deciding, problem solving and so on. Among the most important are rights and duties and their distribution among the people involved. What makes such communal assignment of tasks possible? There must be shared bodies of knowledge and opinion, that is, another level of social representations, of the moral orders prevalent in a society.

Vygotsky's principle

According to Vygotsky, all higher order mental processes exist twice; once in the relevant group, influenced by culture and history, and then in the mind of the individual. The development of a human being is dependent as much on interpersonal relations as it is on individual maturation. Here is the famous passage from Vygotsky (1978, p. 57):

> Every function in the child's cultural development appears twice: first, on the social level, and later, on the individual level; first between people (interpsychological) and then inside the child (intrapsychological). This applies equally to voluntary attention, to logical memory, and to the formation of concepts. All the higher functions originate as actual relationships between individuals.

The appropriation of public–social practices as personal–individual skills comes about by a kind of psychological symbiosis. When an activity is in the Zone of Proximal Development (in Vygotsky's rather clumsy phrase), the less skilled member of a dyad tries to accomplish some task (which may involve the meta-task of recognizing the task required in the first place – and who has the duty or the right to that?). If the junior member is unable to carry through the performance correctly and completely, the senior or more skilled member supplements the efforts of the less competent in such a way as to bring the task to a successful conclusion. The junior member copies the contributions of the senior next time the opportunity arises. Thus individual–personal skills are transferred in social–public performances.

Sometimes the contribution of the more skilled member of a group is hands-on showing and guiding, sometimes it is accomplished by words and other signs. Whatever device is employed, one thing is of paramount importance in the unfolding of such an episode: the distribution and acknowledgement of rights and duties among the members. In both communal thought processes and in Vygotskian development the distribution of power in the group is closely tied in with the assignments and appropriations of rights and duties. Here is the core process for the formation of social representations. When the process of appropriation by the junior member of some of the skills and some of the knowledge of the senior member is complete, both junior and senior member *share* a bite-sized bit of the body of knowledge that will finally encompass the culture at large.

Temporality

Not only do the tools of thought and action change with time, but so too do the distributions of rights and duties among a group of people. The individuals involved in communal cognitive activities are the bearers of a complex and labile psychology, some of which can be captured in a discussion of 'selves'. Though the English word *self* does not translate easily into most other languages, for instance into Spanish, nevertheless the concept can be appropriated as a term of art for scientific purposes. We must take account of how the mutability and multiplicity of self tie in with the local repertoire of rights and duties that shape the thought and action of the actors.

Persons are also selves. There seem to be four main items or aspects of personhood that the word is currently used to pick out. There is the *embodied self*, which comes down to the unity and continuity of a person's point of view and of action in the material world, a trajectory in space and time. The embodied self is singular, continuous and self-identical. Then there is the *autobiographical self*, the hero or heroine of all kinds of stories that one tells oneself and, suitably edited, tells to others. Research has shown how widely the autobiographical selves of real people can differ from story to story. Then there is the *social self* or selves, the personal qualities that a person displays in their encounters with others. This 'self' too is multiple. Psychologists use the phrase 'self-concept' to refer to the beliefs that people have about themselves, their skills, their moral qualities, their fears and their life courses. What sort of stories is it proper to tell? What do we have the duty or the right to tell? And what sort of personas are we able to display, within the constraints of a local moral order? Finally, there is the self as an ever-changing cluster of knowledge and skill, within which we find the content of social representations.

What can change? Clearly the embodied self is invariant under the kind of transformations that occur in everyday life. Changing jobs or partners, the birth and death of family members, even moving into a new linguistic community, does not disrupt the continuity of the trajectory of embodied life through space and time. Nevertheless, when memories fade and anticipation of the future dims, the continuity of the self often fades with it. Though a living human body is before us sometimes we are forced to acknowledge it is no longer an embodied self. However, the repertoire of social selves and the stories with which one marshals one's life may and do change, and sometimes in radical ways. Knowledge, belief and skill are also changing.

Persons have rights and duties which are distributed in a variety of ways, depending on many factors, some of which involve the selves comprising the personhood of an individual. Here we encounter the central point of 'positioning theory'. If beliefs about the way rights and duties are taken up and laid down, ascribed and appropriated, refused and defended in the fine grain of the encounters of daily lives are salient to how people live their lives, then the study of the social representation of local moral orders is an indispensable research tool. A key question for psychologists is what each of us knows about the rights and duties inherent in a situation, and what the rights and duties of others might be. Here we encounter social representations of local forms of social order at the heart of positioning practices.

The language angle

Language is the prime instrument of thought and social action. In following up the line of argument of the discussion so far, we must abandon a widely held presupposition of much psychological research, namely the stability and transpersonal intelligibility of language. In so far as there are psychologically significant varieties of language, so there are other dimensions of multiplicity of selves and the bodies of knowledge to which they have access, either individually or socially. In so far as such bodies of knowledge are shared, that is have some degree of common content, they are social representations.

Cultural variety

Since there are many languages, the *senses of self* as unique, independent individuals are likely to vary from culture to culture. For example, there are differences in patterns of self-reflection between users of languages in which pronouns index individuals independently of their social affiliations, and those in which pronouns index the group or category to which a person belongs. Feminists have drawn attention to the role played by the preference for the third person masculine singular in English in inclining the culture towards marginalizing women. In Japanese there are many first person pronominal expressions, the use of which displays the speaker's and the hearer's sense of relative social position. *Watakushi* is used to display higher status than is displayed in the use of *watushi*. There is even a form, *ore*, which can be used for self-reference but which exempts the speaker from the moral commitments of what he might say. (*He* is needed in this account since pronoun use differs between men and women.) Modern urban Japanese speakers largely omit pronouns, reflecting differences in the modern Japanese sense of self from the socially dominated sense of personhood of the past.

Context

Languages are unstable, in the sense that the *significance of utterances* is likely to vary from time to time and situation to situation. For example, there are subtle changes of the word *captain* from its use in ships, teams and planes. Technically, context includes indexicality, the contribution to the meaning of an expression from knowledge of the place, time and person of utterance. For example, the word *here* indexes the content of an utterance with the place of the speaker. This is one of the functions of the first person singular. Then there is historicity, the way a word's current use is loaded with its past history. No one can use the words 'twin towers' now in the kind of generic descriptive way it was used before 9/11. For the purposes of this discussion, the way that social relations partly determine the *moment by moment significance* of utterances will be of paramount importance. For example, take such a simple utterance as 'I am going out; I might be some time.' Think of the way being married sets up social relations between a man and a woman and so informs the significance of utterances such as 'I am going out; I might be some time.' And then think of these words as uttered by Captain Oates on Scott's ill-fated Antarctic expedition.

Positioning theory

Positioning Theory, as we have briefly introduced the approach, is the study of the nature, formation, influence and ways of change of local systems of rights and duties as shared assumptions about them influence small scale interactions. Such shared assumptions are of course social representations of the moral orders in which the actors live. Positioning theory is to be seen in contrast to the older framework of Role Theory. Roles are relatively fixed, often formally defined and long-lasting. Even such phenomena as 'role distance' and 'role strain' presuppose the stability of the roles to which they are related. Positioning theory concerns conventions of speech and action that are labile, contestable and ephemeral.

Conditions of meaningfulness

There are three relevant background conditions for the meaningfulness of a flow of symbolic interactions. The media of such interactions include linguistic performances, but also other symbolic systems. People make use of religious icons, road signs, gestures and so on, in the maintenance of the flow of actions constitutive of a social episode.

First, the revealing of the local repertoire of *admissible social acts and meanings*, in particular the illocutionary force of what is said and done, is a necessary beginning to any psychological research. Illocutionary force is the effective, then and there social significance of what is said or done (Austin, 1961). The same verbal formula, gesture, flag or whatever, may have a variety of meanings depending on who is using it, where and for what. Uttering 'I'm sorry', may, in certain circumstances, be the performance of an apology. It may also, in the UK, be a way of asking someone to repeat what has just been said. It may be a way of expressing incredulity. There are no doubt other uses for the phrase. Here we have a distinct repertoire of social representations of illocutionary force.

But secondly, we must always ask: Who has the right or the duty to use these words in these ways? Does the contemporary leader of a nation have the duty, or even the right to apologize to the descendants of once persecuted citizens for what was done by a different citizenry of the past with different social representations of humanity? This question can be addressed by reference to the implicit pattern of the *distribution of rights and duties* to make use of items from the local repertoires of the illocutionary forces of various signs and utterances. Each distribution is a position. A mother has the right to discipline her child in whatever way law and custom allow, but a visiting neighbour does not. 'Nice little girls say "Thank you"' is only available, properly, to the parent. Catholics have a duty to confess their sins individually, while Protestants do not. Positions have this in common with roles, that they pre-exist the people who occupy them, as part of the common knowledge of a community, family, sports team and so on. These examples introduce a deeper feature of social representations – the way that a body of knowledge exists in a community rather than in any individual psyche. How does the existence of a public record of a body of knowledge affect its modes and domains of application? For example, the relevant may be recorded in a book which is consulted from time to time to manage local social events, and then put away and forgotten until the next time such a ceremony is required. This observation opens up a facet of life that ought to be of interest to those using the idea of social representations to develop their research programs.

Thirdly, every episode of human interaction is shaped by one or more *story lines* which are usually taken for granted by those taking part in the episode. The study of origins and plots of the story-lines of a culture is the work of narratology. There are strong connections, too, to autobiographical psychology (the study of how, why and when people 'tell their lives' and to whom). A train journey may be told as a 'heroic quest', and what would have been complaints about lateness according to one story-line become obstacles to be bravely overcome. A solicitous remark can be construed as caring according to one story-line, but as an act of condescension according to another (Davies and Harré, 1990).

The positioning 'triangle'

The three background conditions mutually determine one another. Presumptions about rights and duties are involved in fixing the moment-by-moment meanings of speaking and acting, while both are influenced by and influence the taken-for-granted story-lines that are unfolding in an episode. Challenges to the propriety, effectiveness and morality of the way a strip of life is emerging can be directed to

```
                    Position(s)
                       /\
                      /  \
                     /    \
                    /      \
     Illocutionary force(s) ——————— Story-line(s)
```

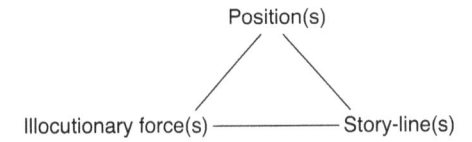

Figure 15.1 *The positioning triangle.*

any one of the three aspects. We can represent this mutuality schematically (see Figure 15.1).

Each such triangle is accompanied by shadowy alternatives, into which it can modulate or which can sometimes exist as competing and simultaneous readings of events.

There is a possible fourth vertex, the physical positions and stances of the actors, for example doctor standing, patient lying; Hitler and Mussolini in Chapman's film in which each tries to elevate his barber's chair above the other; studies of layout of furniture in offices. These gambits are also framed by positioning.

Positioning analysis

Some examples will illustrate the value of using positioning theory to analyze the underlying structure of presuppositions that influence the unfolding of an episode. The research examples we provide demonstrate how positioning analysis has been extended from interpersonal positioning to the levels of intrapersonal and intergroup positioning.

The traditional approach of examining interpersonal positioning, with a focus on how language can influence conflict, is well represented by studies in Moghaddam and Harré (2010). In some cases the main tactic for preventing conflict is for the parties involved to keep talking, because as long as the talk continues there will not be military conflict. Just this kind of situation was examined by Moghaddam, Hanley and Harré (2003) in their analysis of discussions between Dr Henry Kissinger (Assistant to the United States President for National Security Affairs, and later Secretary of State) and the leaders of China (Mao Zedong, Chairman of the Communist Party of the People's Republic of China) and Russia (Leonid I. Brezhnev, General Secretary of the Central Committee of the Communist Party of the Soviet Union). These conversations took place between 1971 and 1976 in the context of the Cold War. Despite the intense rivalry between his country and China and Russia, and despite the ongoing war in Vietnam, Kissinger presented himself as an 'honest friend', having 'frank' conversations with 'chums', and separately Mao and Brezhnev supported this positioning and the dialogue was continued, avoiding an escalation of local military conflicts into global wars.

Positioning analysis has also been extended to the intrapersonal level of private discourse, when a person intentionally or unintentionally positions the self in stories told to the self. For example, Harré and Moghaddam (2008) explored how a person can struggle with her/his own conscience, and with self-imposed duties that in some cases are only known to oneself. Tan and Moghaddam (1995) examined intrapersonal ('reflexive') positioning across cultures, and pointed out cross-cultural similarities and differences. For example, consider how cultural differences in religious beliefs can result in people saying to themselves 'You have to work harder. If you fail, you only have yourself to blame' in one context, and 'You have to pray harder, if you fail it means God did not accept your prayers' in another context. Tan and Moghaddam (1995) also found similarities across cultures, focussing on how both Islamic Sufis and American transcendentalists attempted to arrive at an authentic 'true' self by stripping away all that is not essential and 'real' about the self.

In some cases the positioning of oneself within the self is intended to prepare the self for presentation to others, with exhortations such as 'Come on, you can do it' taking place privately to motivate the self for a particular type of self-presentation, such as a student project presented in front of a class. In other cases, the positioning of oneself is intended solely for review by the self, such as when a person keeps a private diary intended to be read only by oneself. Diaries, 'notes to oneself' and reminders used to help us remember things are all examples of conversations with the self (see examples in Harré and Moghaddam, 2012).

Another way in which this research has been extended is through the application of positioning analysis to better understand intergroup relations. A study of this kind involved rivalries over intellectual patent rights between native people in South America and a scientist and his group of western backers (Moghaddam and Ginsberg, 2003). This unlikely intergroup rivalry arose because a young western scientist came back to the United States from his travels in Ecuador with the claim that he had discovered a 'new variety of plant' with beneficial healing powers. He applied and received a patent for this discovery from the United States Patent and Trademark Office (USPTO). However, the news of this patent resulted in fierce opposition from a number of groups of native peoples in South America, and the international media helped spread an alternative story-line: the *Ayahuasca*, a plant known and used by various South American groups for at least hundreds of years had been stolen by westerners, who were now attempting (through the US patent) to force indigenous people to pay for the use of their 'own' plant. The outcome of this intergroup competition was the revocation of the US patent – the natives won this fight at least. In essence, their right to use the plant in their traditional ways was judged to trump the right of western scientists to patent the plant for drug development and research.

Conclusion

The advent of positioning theory as a development of Vygotsky's conception of the person in an ocean of language, in intimate interaction with others in the construction of a flow of public and social cognition, opens up all sorts of insights and research opportunities, making the interpretation of the idea of 'social representations' as public knowledge corpora meaningful. Moving beyond the overly restrictive frame of role theory, it offers a conceptual system within which to follow the unfolding of episodes of everyday life the orderliness of which ought to be a matter for astonishment and so food for explanation. Here the joint use of positioning theory and social representations is a powerful tool.

16 Social semiotics and social representations

Giuseppe Veltri

Communication processes play a fundamental role in the genesis of social representations. This chapter explores the concept of multiple levels of signification in the theory of social representations through two semiotic concepts, denotation and connotation, to elaborate the processes of 'anchoring' and 'objectification'. These two processes are described in terms of their outcomes: 'making the unfamiliar familiar' in the case of anchoring, or 'saturation of reality' in the case of objectification. However, before discussing the theory of social representations and semiotics, it is necessary to state that the concept of multiple levels of signification is not foreign to psychological theories. Denotation and connotation, and their distinction in semiotics, are a formal way of considering this multi-layered signification. The idea of multiple levels of signification goes beyond a simple expression–content relationship about the way signs and symbols are conceived and how they ostensibly work in the process of human signification and interpretation.

The process of 'multiple significations' has an important place in both the psychological and sociological literatures. Concepts such as 'symbol' and 'sign' have been part of the discipline of psychology since its emergence, and they still play a crucial role in several social psychological theories. The social nature of signs and symbols and the processes of social signification were considered in early sociology and social psychology, for example in Emile Durkheim's (1912) analysis of shared cultural symbols. Thus, from the outset the conceptualization of a process of social signification was not confined to a simple expression–content relationship, but rather entailed the idea that there are multiple levels of signification that perform different epistemic, communicative and social functions. For example, the psychologist F. C. Bartlett (1925) highlighted the need to distinguish between signs and symbols, stressing the multiple significations that characterize the latter as one of the most important social functions of symbols. Other traditions in psychology have also valued the concept of multiple significations. Several psychologists, in rather different contexts, have developed the notion of asymmetrical signification. According to Salvatore and Venuleo (2008), the asymmetrical and symmetrical aspects of signification play a crucial role in Freud's (1923/1962) structural model of the unconscious structure of the mind. In particular, the role of affective semiosis, by contrast to paradigmatic thought, is considered an essential feature of the meaning-making process, as highlighted by other psychoanalysts such as Fornari (1979) and Matte Blanco (1975).

From the perspective of the psychological study of language, the role of multiple signification and connotative meanings is at the core of the three main theories regarding the production of metaphors: Ortony's model (1979) of the 'salience imbalanced'; Gentner and Clement's (1988) model of the 'transposal of structure'; and Tourangeau and Sternberg's (1981, 1982) model of the 'interaction between domains'. However, it is in the sociocultural tradition of psychology that social signification plays its most fundamental role. In the work of Valsiner (2007) and Rosa (2007), culture is essentially seen as a form of semiotic mediation, and these authors borrow heavily from the semiotic tradition, and in particular from the work of Charles Peirce and the successive interpretative semiotics school. For example, for Valsiner (2007) the role of semiosis is at the centre of human experience and he introduces the notions of 'field, node and promoter signs' in his account of the structural features of signs and symbols. It is only in the work of these sociocultural psychologists that semiotics and the theory of social representations have been discussed together.

Social representations

The theory of social representations (Moscovici, 2000) is, above all, a social psychological theory of the social origin of the relationships between knowledge, representations and contexts (Jovchelovitch, 2007), in which the role of communication is central for the production of representations, and particularly for the second part of Moscovici's original work on psychoanalysis (see the recent English translation of 2008). Yet, the idea of multiple significations was not conceptualized directly in the theory, in spite of the frequent indirect references to this, or to processes that might imply this. In fact, signification is often described in terms of a simple expression–content relationship. The role of social signification is referred to very frequently in the theory of social representations, in particular in terms of the process of anchoring and objectification; however, these processes remain as obscure elements – the 'black boxes' of social signification – that require greater clarification.

Many studies applying the theory of social representations deal with processes of communication and instances of social signification in the public sphere and yet include references to the notions of signs and symbols that are heterogeneous and unsystematic. There are several disciplines with their own conceptualizations from which the notion of multiple levels of signification might be discussed in the context of the theory of social representations; semiotics is one of these. The advantage of semiotics is that its intellectual trajectory has many points of theoretical convergence (particularly in the case of socio- and cultural semiotics) with a social theory of the relationships between knowledge, representations and contexts. At the same time, semiotics can provide a set of concepts – such as the distinction between denotative and connotative meanings – with explanatory power. Moreover, opening the 'black box' of signification helps us to understand a number of sociocultural phenomena that have become marginal in the theory of social representations (for examples of this debate, see Semin, 1985; Potter and Litton, 1985; Moscovici, 1985c; Billig, 1993; Marková, 2003).

As mentioned above, the symbolic functions of transforming the unfamiliar into the familiar, and the processes of anchoring and objectification, lie at the core of the theory of social representations. These two symbolic transformations and acts of signification are crucial for the genesis of social representations, and yet they have been the subject of much debate. They are obviously in need of clearer conceptualization.

The aim of the discussion that follows is thus to explore the points of convergence between the theory of social representations and semiotics in order to accommodate both the communicative and the contextual knowledge functions of social representations through the idea of multiple and layered signification. It is precisely this idea of multiple and layered signification, which lies at the core of the distinction between denotative and connotative meanings. Focussing on the role of denotation and connotation also means that any type of sign (e.g. linguistic or not) can play a role in the process of anchoring and objectification.

Denotation and connotation in semiotics and social semiotics

The technical term *semiotics* originated in the fourth century BCE and was used to refer to the medical practice of interpreting symptoms. Etymologically derived from the Greek *sémeion* (sign), the use of this term referred to the recognition of symptoms as signs, and thus of something to be interpreted (*Encyclopedia of Semiotics*). The broader, modern use of the term denotes the discipline stemming from the works of the Swiss linguist Ferdinand de Saussure and of the American logician Charles Sanders Peirce. For Saussure, concerned primarily with linguistics, 'semiology' was to be a 'science' of signs;[1] Peirce defined 'semiotic' as a 'formal doctrine of signs', or logic (Peirce, 1955, p. 98). Semiotics today refers to the study of signs in both the Peircean (cognitive-interpretative) and Saussurean (structuralist) traditions, and many contemporary semioticians see the two approaches as complementary rather than oppositional.[2]

Denotation and connotation are two concepts that have been developed and discussed in a range of theories in semiotics and linguistics. However, they first

---

[1] One of the most famous definitions of semiotics is that of Ferdinand de Saussure (1959, p. 16): 'A science that studies the life of signs within society is conceivable ... I shall call it semiology.'
[2] According to Eco (1976), a general semiotic theory should include not only a theory of how codes may establish rules for systems of signification but also a theory of how signs may be produced and interpreted. A theory of codes may clarify aspects of 'signification', while a theory of sign production may clarify aspects of 'communication'.

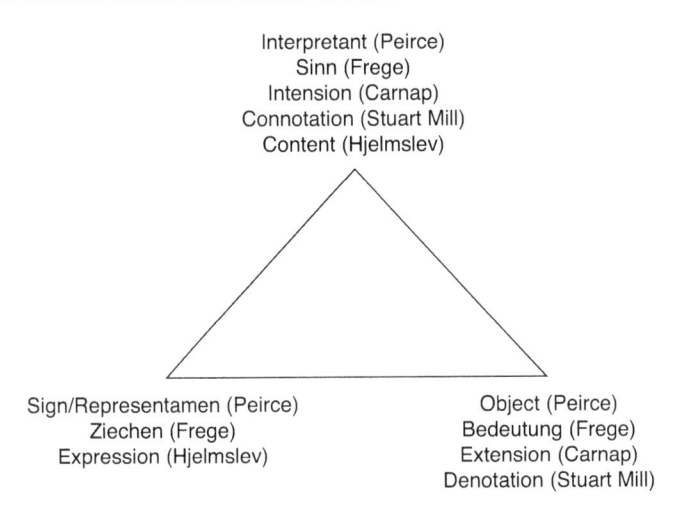

```
           Interpretant (Peirce)
              Sinn (Frege)
           Intension (Carnap)
         Connotation (Stuart Mill)
            Content (Hjelmslev)
                   /\
                  /  \
                 /    \
                /      \
               /        \
              /          \
             /            \
            /_____\
Sign/Representamen (Peirce)      Object (Peirce)
     Ziechen (Frege)             Bedeutung (Frege)
  Expression (Hjelmslev)         Extension (Carnap)
                                 Denotation (Stuart Mill)
```

Figure 16.1 *A representation of the different ways of conceiving the denotation–connotation–object relationships (adapted from Eco, 1973).*

appeared in the writings of logicians and philosophers. In logic, denotation is usually identified as the extension of a word, while connotation is considered as the intension of a word. The extension of a word is the object, or the set of objects, to which that word can be attributed and therefore points to the 'extra-linguistic world'. For example, all objects that have two wheels and pedals are attributed the word *bicycle*. Conversely, the intension is a set of properties that determine whether an object does or does not belong to a given extension (Orecchioni-Kerbrat, 1983). In Ockam, Mill, Frege and Carnap, the two levels of signification are more or less defined in this way – although they are not always referred to specifically as denotation and connotation. The first person to use the term *connotation* consistently was John Stuart Mill.[3] Hence, although the terminology varies considerably from one author to another, it is reasonable to make conceptual analogies. According to Eco (1973), both dyadic and triadic relationships between denotation and connotation and their object can be represented by the famous triangle schema (Figure 16.1).

From the philosophical-logical tradition to linguistics and semiotics, the conceptualization of denotation and connotation changes considerably. While in the first tradition connotative meanings include practically the whole area of meaning, because they are opposed to denotation, in the second tradition connotation is one aspect of meaning. Even with Sapir (1921/1970), we find the linguistic/semiotics approach to denotation and connotation. Sapir discusses the connotative affective value of words that are attached to a word's meaning and that vary from individual to individual, and from time to time. However, Bloomfield (1933) was the first to use the term *connotation* in linguistics. In a chapter on meaning, he divides meanings into 'normal or core' and 'marginal or translated', considering the latter

---

[3] John Stuart Mill, The Collected Works of John Stuart Mill, vol. VIII, *A System of Logic Ratiocinative and Inductive*, Part II, ed. John M. Robson (1843; New York: Liberty Fund, 2006).

as a language's capacity for plasticity. Hence, Bloomfield created the conceptual distinction between a more stable core meaning (denotation) and a more fluid connotative meaning. His focus on connotation is strongly related to what we might describe as style: the accents, grammatical forms and lexicons of individuals have connotative meanings about their social class. This focus on connotative languages greatly influenced Hjelmslev, who was well versed in Bloomfield's theory (for an extensive discussion of such influences, see Garza-Cuarón, 1991).

The precursor: Hjelmslev

Moving from the antecedents in linguistics to semiotics, it is with Hjelmslev that connotation and denotation first became a semiotic notion. Hence, the origin of the denotation–connotation distinction in semiotics is rooted within the structuralist tradition that stemmed from the work of Saussure (1959).

Hjelmslev, whose aim was to develop a formal theory of the study of languages under the name of 'glossematics', introduces the role of 'connotators' to describe the 'particles' of supplementary meaning to the denotative one. The semiotic distinction in the tradition of Hjelmslev concerns a denotation that is a relation between the expression and the content of a sign, and a connotation that relates two signs (i.e. two units of expression and content) in a particular way. According to Hjelmslev (1943), connotation is a particular configuration of languages, opposed, in this respect, not only to denotation, but also to meta-language. According to his definitions, a connotative language is a language, that is, a system of signs, whose expression plane is another language, or the inversion of a meta-language, which is a form of language used for the description or analysis of another language. Contrary to both connotative and meta-languages, denotative language is a language in which none of its planes form another language. Thus, denotation is a relation that serves to connect the expression and the content of a sign, whereas connotation and meta-language both relate two separate signs, each with its own expression and content.

Apart from the definitions, Hjelmslev also gives examples of connotations, such as different styles, genres, dialects, national languages, voices, and so on. In analyzing these and other examples, it becomes apparent that semiotic connotations reside in the choice of a particular expression to stand for a given content, chosen from a set of alternatives, or of a particular variant to realize the expression invariant (Sonesson, 1989). Thus, what is important to connotation, according to Hjelmslev, are not the particular contents, or kinds of contents, conveyed, but the formal relationships that they presuppose. Hjelmslev assigns the study of the 'social and sacral' values usually conveyed by the languages of connotation to the theory of 'substance'.

From Hjelmslev, who conceptualizes connotative meanings in terms of style and indirect sense, and who therefore focusses on the language of connotations, there is an initial disjunction within the structuralist semiotics approach. Barthes, Greimas and, to a certain extent, Eco developed Hjelmslev's ideas in rather different ways. They were interested in connotations at the level of 'lexemes' (Barthes and Greimas) and of encyclopedic connotations (Eco). Therefore, connotative meanings are no longer an issue of style but are to be considered as connotative semantic marks or added meanings.

The semiotics of Barthes and Greimas

Barthes (1968), who greatly diffused Hjelmslev's distinction of denotative and connotative meanings, shifts to the study of 'ideological connotations' with an emphasis on communication processes. For Barthes, connotative semiotics is an instrument for understanding and explaining the 'ideological naturalization of myths' (Barthes, 1957). Barthes focussed on communication processes that reveal the signification structure's underlying myths. In a departure from Hjelmslev's model, Barthes argues that the orders of signification known as denotation and connotation combine to produce ideology – which has been described as a 'third order' of signification: myth. In summary, Barthes retains a structural approach. According to his concept of connotation, in semiotic systems (not limited to natural language) there are some signifiers – the 'connotators' – that in a fluid manner stand as symbolic or connotative meanings. The set of 'connotators' constitutes 'rhetoric' while the set of connotative meanings constitute 'ideology'.

Greimas (1970) does not place the notions of denotation and connotation at the centre of his semiotic enquiry, which focusses on the narrative structures of texts. However, it contributes to the debate by reorganizing Barthes' intuition and making a clear distinction between the study of connotative languages related to discourses and the study of connotation of concepts related to lexemes (Greimas and Cortes, 1979). Connotative meanings are, in essence, given by 'classemes', particles of contextual meaning that complement a more stable semantic core. The context of these classemes is culture. According to Greimas (1990), the connotative structure of a language is a manifestation of the 'cultural universe of common sense' of a given society. The idea is to study connotative structures of cultural objects in order to gain insights about how they are represented by a given culture and thus to gain information about a culture itself. The role of socio-semiotics assumes the shape of a meta-analysis of meanings in society, and those meanings become the instrument with which to investigate society itself. Among the common notions used in this domain of research, Greimas (1990), Lotman (1990) and others consider crucial the 'connotative projections' that a society gives to a cultural object. The focus of attention is the social life of signs, with the intention of considering the social and cultural context of the process of sense-making. It is important to note that both Barthes' and Greimas' theories of denotation and connotation fall firmly within the structuralist approach to semiotics. These notions are therefore viewed synchronically, as code-based, and there is an emphasis on seeking regularities.

The interpretative approach: Charles Peirce

Beyond the structuralist approach, there have been attempts to apply the notions of denotation and connotation within an interpretative semiotic approach based on the work of Charles Peirce (see Peirce et al., 1960). Peirce developed a complex formal theory of interpretative-cognitive semiotics (for a complete discussion of Peirce's ideas in the domain of cultural psychology, see Rosa, 2007). At the core of Peirce's formal doctrine of signs lies the idea of the sign as a triadic relationship, never reducible to a relationship of pairs, between the object, the sign and the interpretant (Figure 16.1). The starting point is the object, understood in a wider sense as the external reality. The object, therefore, is the first engine of semiosis. Although Peirce's terminology is not always univocally interpretable, very often he defines the object as 'dynamic', referring to the thing in itself, the object in the external reality. In order to be aware of and to understand external objects, we need signs. The sign is therefore the fulcrum of semiosis because it mediates between the object and the interpretant. However, to play this role the sign has to 'spotlight' the object, highlighting certain aspects, grasping some qualities and constituting a fundamental idea. The object is 'lit' by the interpretation based on a hypothesis about it. Here Peirce makes another distinction between two components of the sign: the 'representamen' and the 'immediate object'. For Peirce, a sign can also be thought of as the merging of signifier (representamen) and signified (immediate object). If the 'dynamic object' is the external object in itself, the 'immediate object' is the meaning or 'the object as the sign represents it' (Peirce, 1960, p. 536). However, according to Peirce the only way to delimit the content of a sign is to use an 'interpretant', which is another sign that adds greater meaning to the initial sign. Hence, in theory the 'immediate object' is the set of all possible interpretants of a sign, therefore our knowledge will always be partial (in the sense of being asyntonic), and it will never capture the full 'essence' of meaning. The very same reasoning indicates that semiosis is potentially infinite because the use of interpretants is potentially infinite. According to Peirce, the 'infinite regression of interpretants' is also triadic in nature: it includes an 'immediate interpretant' (the sign's initial effect on the mind of the interpreter), a 'dynamic interpretant' (the 'real' effect produced in the mind of the interpreter) and the 'final interpretant', the interpretation that halts, although only temporarily, the process of semiosis.

From this perspective the focus shifts from semantics to pragmatics, hence emphasis is placed on the processes and creations of 'sense' rather than on analyzing structures and codes. The core concept changes from the notion of code, crucial in the structural perspective, to that of interpretation. The most exhaustive discussion of the notion of connotation within a Peircean framework is that of Bonfantini (1987). Bonfantini defines the interpretative approach as compared to the structuralist approach as being characterized by three main tensions: systematic semiotics vs. semiosis; synchronic vs. diachronic analysis; codes vs. interpretants; and more generally, representation vs. interpretation. According to Bonfantini, the structuralist approach to connotation runs the risk of being little more than taxonomic work, useful only to order semiotic phenomena. While he recognizes the value of Hjelmslev's intuition about the notion of connotation, he also recognizes the danger of seeing denotation and connotation as abstract, almost metaphysical, properties. Bonfantini introduced two important ideas about connotations from a

Table 16.1 *A summary of the differences regarding connotative meanings within the structural semiotic paradigm and between the latter and interpretative approach*

	Connotative languages	Connotations
Object	Indirect senses (styles, etc.)	1. Semantic marks 2. Added meanings
Shared	It presupposes a denotative code	
Specific features	• Phrastic dimension (discourses) • Connotators in the plane of expression and content	Lexical dimension Connotation starts from the content plane of denotation
	Structuralist	*Interpretative*
Analytical categories	Synchronic Code-based Systematic Semiotics	Diachronic Interpretant Semiosis
Emphasis	Regularity	Variance

pragmatic point of view. The first is that connotations should be seen as part of the communicative act of individuals rather than the simple outcome of a connotative code excluded from the communication flow. The second point is that communicative acts are characterized by 'communicative games'. Communicative games are constituted by the combined presence of several factors: sociocultural position in society; the participants in the communication process; the time, the place and 'perceptual situation'; the uttered texts; the relevant texts in the communicative game; and the non-linguistic actions. These points give an idea of the complexity of a communicative game from a pragmatic point of view. Connotative attribution and interpretation are thought of as being in the aforementioned frame. In the interpretative approach, the idea of connotation as a semantic property or fixed added meaning is discarded completely. The determination of denotations and connotation become entirely fluid in a communicative game depending on its aims and context; they are the components of semiosis. To summarise, there are two main useful ideas from this perspective: first, denotation and connotation are not considered as static meanings in a cultural code but as stages in a process of semiosis, hence as meanings that are active during interpretation depending on the nature and context of communicative games; second, the idea of considering denotation and connotation as 'interpretants', in Peirce's terms.

In the upper part of Table 16.1 we can see a summary of the differences in conceptualizing connotations in the two structuralist approaches based on the distinction between connotative languages and connotations that refers to the first part of this section. In the lower part of the table the differences between the structuralist and the interpretative approaches in terms of analytical categories and emphasis are summarised.

Eco (1976, 1984, 1990, 2000) has considered the tension between connotations as a code and as an act of pragmatic semiosis. He arrives at a 'hybrid' theory that includes both structuralist and interpretative elements. A necessary premise is that Eco starts his discussion of connotations similarly to Barthes and Greimas, as 'classemes', but goes on to consider them as added meanings (signifieds) (Eco, 1990, 2000). As mentioned above, he tries to combine the interpretative approach characterized by semiosis with the structural notion of 'encyclopedia' (Eco, 1984, p. 109), where the encyclopedia is the set of all possible interpretations. This notion acts as a postulate in the sense that it is impossible to describe entirely, and it works as a regulative hypothesis because when an actor communicates he or she also selects portions of encyclopedia to establish certain semiotic competences as a starting point. The encyclopedia entails semantic instructions and routines attached to context, in other words, 'scripts'. Within Eco's semantic model of scripts in encyclopedic form, giving a sign means sending packets of semantic information activated according to scripts related to contexts, circumstances and interpretative mechanisms. Connotative properties manifest themselves as added meanings that are constituted on the basis of a denotative or a previous code. In this model, rhetorical figures are interpreted thanks to inferences that activate 'semiotic correlations' based on pre-existing denotative codes. In this model, context is crucial and so is the diachronic dimension (interpretative approach) of the fluctuations of denotations and connotations. Eco clearly states that connotations can be seen as a 'phenomenon of system or process', preferring the interpretative approach offered by Bonfantini. However, he also highlights the fact that some connotations are rather more stable in a semiotic community, in other words the encyclopedia is being constantly reshaped by interpretations while also experiencing temporary and unstable equilibriums. The synchronic–diachronic tension is often associated with that of an individual–collective. Connotations born as individual acts or from the interpretation of small groups can become temporarily collective through social influence. To conclude, Eco is convinced of the necessity to consider both the synchronic and the diachronic aspects of denotations and connotations, because 'the unstable equilibrium of this coexistence is not (theoretically) syncretic because our knowledge proceeds on this happily unstable equilibrium' (Eco, 2000, p. 218).

Regardless of the two different structuralist approaches or interpretative takes on connotations, the role of contexts is crucial. The problem of context becomes one of style for connotative languages and one of social and cultural contexts in terms of connotations as added meanings. In the latter case, social and cultural contexts are at the core of social semiotics as envisioned by Greimas and Cortes (1979) and Hodge and Kress (1988). Greimas and Cortes summarised four main research directions: the study of societal attitudes towards its signs, for example the work of Lotman (1990) and Foucault (2006); the study of the degree of verification that a given society attributes to discourses; the study of social discourses and of connotative meanings; the investigation of communication strategies determined by connotations. Fabbri (1998) suggested a further direction for research in social semiotics that focusses on connotations: to pursue a cultural ontology of connotative meanings and the analysis of communication strategies of a connotative nature.

This section has summarised the different approaches to the notions of denotation and connotation within the two main traditions of semiotics, the structuralist and the interpretative/pragmatic, and has highlighted the theoretical tensions between the two. The last part has explored Eco's semantic encyclopedic model that aims to combine the two approaches. In the following core sections of this chapter I will discuss how denotation and connotation can be applied to social representations theory by enriching the notions of anchoring and objectification and adding a distinctive communicative dimension to these processes.

The cultural (semiotic) process of anchoring and objectification

The core idea of this chapter is that anchoring and objectification can be formulated as the outcome of the processes of recursive social semiosis within and between social groups in the public sphere. As a consequence, it proposes a social and communicative description of the dynamics of multiple levels of signification in the public sphere that is largely unaccounted for in the theory of social representations. The outcome of these processes of semiosis is the establishment of denotative and connotative meanings of a social object. Denotative and connotative meanings are the constituents of the different representations that are negotiated in the public sphere. This way of conceptualizing anchoring and objectification brings together the structural and the interpretative approaches of semiotics, both the diachronic and synchronic dimensions of signification. Social groups inhabit different structural semiotic conditions because of their different social positioning, but it is through 'communicative games' (Bonfantini, 1987) that a social object takes on a temporarily stable social meaning. Anchoring and objectification are thus the outcome of communicative games performed by social groups in the public sphere that reach temporarily stable social meanings, and the latter feed into potential new communicative games.

Denotative meanings are the first and most basic codification of the meaning of a social object. From the social representations perspective, denotations are established by groups that have sufficient power and authority to introduce them to the semantic field, or 'semiosphere' (Lotman, 1990), of a given culture. As mentioned before, Moscovici identifies two main loci of knowledge production, distinguishing between first-hand and second-hand knowledge. The former is the result of the formation of scientific knowledge. We might argue that denotative meanings capable of defining the semantic field are produced by groups that have significant amounts of authority, power and prestige, often seen as esoteric in the mastery of their own knowledge. Scientific knowledge is the best, but not the only, example of this. In this context, the main difference between denotation and connotation is that they imply different epistemic roles for actors in the process of establishing or proposing denotative or connotative meaning. Denotations are the outcome of making something intelligible, of defining something that was previously unrepresentable. The role of naming, although in theory available to everyone, is in fact restricted to certain groups within society. Scientists represent a powerful group that is able to introduce new descriptions of reality; they forge denotations from their perceived epistemic position as knowledge-seekers. This is not to say that such groups do not experience intra-group dynamics that influence the way in which they establish shared meanings, in particular through conflicts and debates. However, such dynamics do not usually involve society at large, and only enter the public sphere when controversies escalate.

Connotations follow a different social dynamic due to their epistemic function and the epistemic position of the actors involved: experts present connotations as claims (for example, that in the future nanotechnology will lead to cures for all diseases (Gaskell *et al.*, 2005)), but there are other actors competing in this domain, such as critical scientists, politicians, the media and NGOs. Such connotative meanings are produced through claims, narratives, analogies, symbols, metaphors and other symbolic forms such as myths and recurrent themes. Hence, denotation and connotation play different roles once they enter the public sphere, and they operate in different ways.

Connotations are an additional level of signification. They establish a semiotic domain as the outcome of a semiotic (or interpreting) community. According to Eco (1976), a semiotic community is characterized by the decoding of symbols through a semiotic domain of its value systems and ideological, ethical, religious positions. Hence, a semiotic community is defined by shared cultural codes and common semiotic resources that might not be directly evident and accessible to outsiders. Connotative meanings are 'contextualizers' because they entail specific symbolic repertoires.

Connotative meanings include meta-cognitive knowledge about the limits to the validity of a particular social representation (Wagner, 1995). They are also embedded in the socially constructed world from the point of view of different groups, who are differentiated by the nature of their position and activity towards a particular social object. Here I refer to the notion of semiotic position as formulated by Vygotsky (1962).[4] In the introduction to this chapter I made reference to the social functions of symbols as conceived by the social psychologist Bartlett (1925). In his conceptualization, a clear double function emerges in social psychological terms: the function of facilitating intergroup communication and at the same time expressing in-group social identity (Rommetveit, 1984).

Recursive semiosis

The signification processes that involve denotative and connotative meanings lead to anchoring and objectification in terms of recursive semiosis processes

---

4 According to Vygotsky, the nature of what is said to be our 'inner' lives is explored, and it is argued that they are neither so private, nor so inner, nor so systematic and logical as has been assumed. Instead, people's higher mental processes originate in their feelings of how, semiotically, they are 'positioned' in relation to others around them.

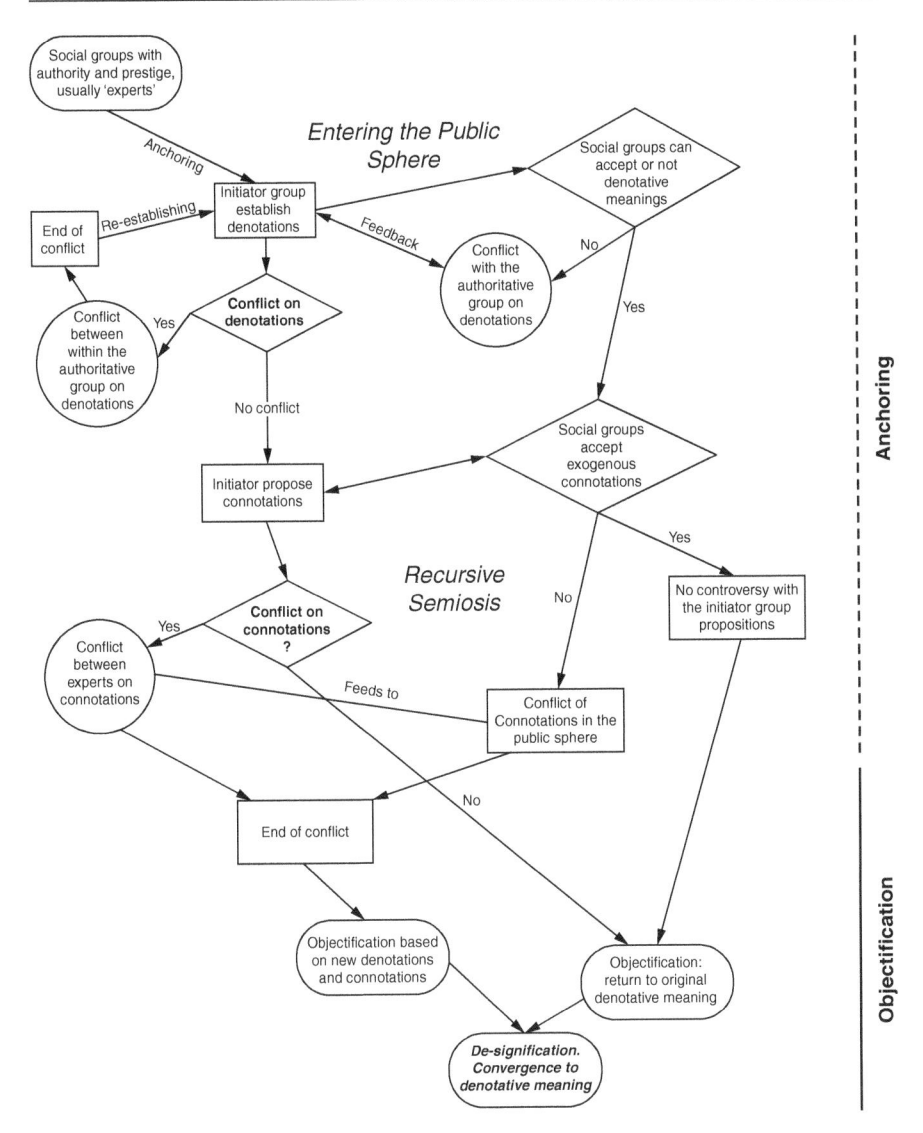

Figure 16.2 *Recursive social significations underlying anchoring and objectification.*

within and among social groups in the public sphere. A recursive semiosis is a process of signification in which a previous semiosis becomes a base (a new representamen) for a subsequent semiosis, therefore adding a developmental dimension (Rosa, 2007). Thus, anchoring and objectification are unpacked in a series of reiteration of signification processes, as summarized in Figure 16.2.

The starting point of the anchoring and objectification of a social object is in the activity of an authoritative social group that alters a society's semantic field by introducing a new social object and naming it. In other words, they establish its denotative meaning. The most straightforward examples come from the role performed by scientists when introducing notions such as 'genes' and 'dark matter', but also from other powerful groups such as economists arguing about 'inflation', 'GDP', and so on.

Authoritative groups are not immune to intra-group conflicts in the process of establishing the denotative meaning of a new social object. For example, at the earliest stages of constructing nanotechnology as a social object, scientists debated its definition extensively (e.g. the Smalley–Drexler debate).[5] This can happen before or in tandem with the introduction of the new social object to the public sphere. Once a stable consensus is reached, or the pretence of one for the benefit of out-groups, the authoritative group disseminates the new social object into the public domain where they also add connotative meanings to its denotative meanings. Such connotative meanings express goals, interests and cultural repertoires of rhetorical forms and myths, given by the social and cultural position of the proposing authoritative group. One possible conflict-free outcome is when other social groups adopt both denotative and connotative meanings of the new social object proposed by the initiating authoritative group. However, conflict might arise at both the denotative and connotative levels. The authoritative group's definition may be contested; consider the definition of an embryo for scientists as compared to lay people with religious beliefs.[6] The recursive semiosis that leads to the re-establishment of a denotative meaning is resignification.

Connotative meanings are potentially even more conflict-prone because they are vested with contextual signification given by the societal position of each social group. In other words, connotative meanings are really the act of interpretation of new social objects that take on board contextual knowledge, values and attitudes. In connotative meanings, signification refers to both a semiotic and a political ordering of sense. In the first mode, what is significant is a symbolic property; in the second, what is significant becomes the product of the assertion of a political will. Hence, it is guided by a project (Bauer and Gaskell, 2008) or a worldview (Wildavsky, 1987).

Conflicts and tensions are viewed as important in the formation of social representations and in the semiosphere through Lotman's conception of the structural heterogeneity of semiospheres (Lotman, 1990), which is the basis for dialogue and therefore also the basis for creating meanings and novelty. In particular, as previously argued by Raudsepp (2005), the notion of 'semiosphere' by Lotman (1990) is a useful notion for regarding the theory of social representations. The semiosphere represents all semiotic resources of a semiotic subject (society/culture/groups). According to Raudsepp (2005, pp. 458–459), we can consider it in terms of the

---

5 R. Smalley, 'Of chemistry, love and nanobots', *Scientific American*, 285 (2001), 76–77; R. Smalley, 'Smalley responds', *Chemical and Engineering News,* 81 (2003), 39–40; R. Smalley, 'Smalley concludes', *Chemical and Engineering News,* 81 (2003), 41–42; E. Drexler, 'Open letter to Richard Smalley', *Chemical and Engineering News*, 81 (2003), 38–39; E. Drexler, 'Drexler counters', *Chemical and Engineering News*, 81 (2003), 40–41.
6 J. Maienschein, *Whose view of life: embryos, cloning, and stem cells* (Cambridge, MA: Harvard University Press, 2003).

theory of social representations because 'it contains all SRs in their objectified and stabilized form (texts, artefacts, images, meanings, institutions)'.

Once the new social object enters the public domain, other social groups might borrow the authoritative group's denotative meaning but contest their proposed connotative meaning, which is to say that they will contest claims, narrative frames, and so on. Specific to connotative meanings is one particular type of sign: promoter signs. Promoter signs are signs of sufficient abstractness that begin to function as guides to the range of possible constructions of the future (Valsiner, 2007).

Most importantly, connotative meanings are a direct expression of social contexts as discussed in the elaboration of connotation in terms of both structural and interpretative semiotics. The conflict or collision of connotative meanings among social groups in the public sphere is what constitutes the upper limit of the process of anchoring conceptualized in semiotic terms. A conflict of connotative meanings can also emerge within the authoritative group. In that case, social groups in their conflict over 'logonomic control' (Hodge and Kress, 1988, p. 4) can use the internal conflict in the authoritative group. There are many examples of competing connotative meanings of a social object by different social groups. The case of AIDS is an apt example (see Marková, 1992); here different groups integrated medical information into their general theories and systems of beliefs in contrasting ways. The same can be said about new technologies with potential risks (such as biotechnology and GM food (see Wagner and Kronberger, 2001)), food risks and the Hong Kong case of bird flu (Joffe and Lee, 2004).

Two processes characterize the recursive semiosis that stands at the core of anchoring: resignification and counter-signification. These are features of communicative games (Bonfantini, 1987) played by social groups in the social sphere to obtain 'logonomic control'. Here, the contribution of the interpretative school of semiotics is to add a pragmatic and synchronic dimension. This means that what stands for denotative and connotative is fluid and is determined within a communicative game as the game proceeds. Strategic or temporary alliances are formed among social groups; see for example the discursive coalitions between experts and other social actors in the case of the public creationism controversy in the UK (Allgaier, 2012). Resignification stands for a rearranging of the denotative and connotative meanings because of their mutual influence (see the example of red and green biotechnology (Bauer, 2005)). Resignification is the process that answers an important question posed by Bauer and Gaskell about reversing the vector (2008, p. 350): 'how does common sense challenge the source of dignified knowledge?'

Counter-signification is limited to substituting connotative meanings that are expressions of one social group for others that are expressions of another social actor that was adversely signified in the original representation, and therefore imposing a different 'project' (Bauer and Gaskell, 2008). Resistance is also a function of social representations, protecting the group in periods of change while at the same time signalling the need for changes to the agents of innovation (Bauer, 1994). Counter-signification is an important resistance strategy used by individuals and social groups when a new transcendent representation is forced upon an immanent one (Jensen and Wagoner, 2009). Both resignification and counter-signification are dynamics of social meanings in the public sphere because of the intrinsically communicative nature of social representations, as discussed before in the role of the public sphere for the theory of social representations (Jovchelovitch, 2007).

That which constitutes anchoring from a semiotic perspective is the processes of recursive semiosis characterized by either resignification or counter-signification. The outcome is a temporary resolution of conflicts that leads to the process of objectification. After the processes of recursive semiosis reach a precarious equilibrium, objectification comes into play as a phenomenon of designification. The designification stage represents the greatest stability of the representation of a social object. Wherever objectification occurs out of a conflict-free path, or after several conflicts for logonomic control, a set of denotative and connotative meanings are crystallized in what Eco defines as the 'encyclopedia'. At least temporarily, the social object finds stability and its social meaning attains maximum consensus, although new contestations in the forms of new semiosis are always theoretically possible. The price of this consensus is a redefinition of denotative and connotative meaning in which many social meanings are lost, to be replaced by a synthesis that is certainly less rich but also less conflictual. Designification is similar to 'ontologizing', one of the three stages Moscovici (2000) identifies in his description of objectification: personification, figuration and ontologizing. However, it does not involve the problem of establishing what constitutes reality in social representations theory, something that, thus far, has not been sufficiently critiqued. Losing their semiotic richness, a social object becomes a 'familiar background'. Many aspects of social life that were once controversial are now part of a familiar background perceived mainly in denotative terms.

Conflict can reappear only as the result of a direct semiotic act by a social group that advocates conflicting denotative or connotative meanings. Authoritative groups have the power in the future to challenge denotative meanings in society by their epistemic position, and therefore it is not unusual that the 'familiar background' is resignified as something else, thereby initiating a new process of anchoring and objectification.

Conclusions

This chapter has presented a semiotic perspective on the theory of social representations, introducing the semiotic distinction between denotative and connotative meanings. The aim has been to enrich the theoretical description of the anchoring and objectification processes, which are discussed not only in terms of their end results. The proposed theoretical framework explains anchoring and objectification from a communicative perspective that refers to both the structural-synchronic and the interpretative-diachronic semiotic conceptualization of denotative and connotative meanings. These two notions are crucial for understanding the roles of social contexts and epistemic selectivity and their positions in the process of social signification by different societal groups.

The different stages of anchoring and objectification (Figure 16.2) orient the researcher so that he or she can recognize what aspect of interaction needs to be focussed upon. For example, one might concentrate on the establishing of denotative and/or connotative meanings by authoritative groups and their reaching of an internal consensus. Another might focus on the conditions that lead other social groups to adopt (or not adopt) denotative and connotative meanings from authoritative groups. These are just a few examples of how the social representations research agenda might be expanded by opening the 'black box' of signification represented so far by anchoring and objectification.

There is potential for the mutual exchange of concepts and methodologies that can benefit both theoretical domains. The theory of social representations can enrich its formulation of social signification processes while social semiotics might benefit from learning more about the social psychological dynamics underpinning social signification. In conclusion, the dialogue between social/cultural semiotics and social representations theory represents fertile ground for future research.

17 Identity process theory

Glynis Breakwell

This chapter outlines how the theory of social representations and Identity Process Theory (IPT) might be linked in order to understand better the processes of social stability and change. The chapter is founded upon the assumption that it is worthwhile examining how individual identity processes relate to the processes of social representation. In fact, the argument presented basically asserts that it is impossible to understand how individual identities are constructed and maintained without understanding how social representations processes operate. As Howarth (2002a) pointed out, social representations have an important role in identity construction. Moreover, it is proposed that social representations processes themselves are influenced by the thoughts, feelings and actions of individuals as they are motivated by identity processes. To the extent that they are, the theory of social representations is advantaged by being explicitly linked to a theory of identity processes. Since readers of this handbook are likely to be more familiar with the theory of social representations than with IPT, the chapter starts with a brief outline of IPT and in doing so shows how assumptions about social representations are embedded in the fabric of IPT. This is necessary for the arguments about the relationship between IPT and the theory of social representations to be further elaborated.

The central tenets of identity process theory

Identity process theory is a theory of individual identity. It is concerned with the holistic analysis of the total identity of the person. It proposes that this identity will encompass elements that derive from every aspect of the person's experience – social category memberships, interpersonal relationships, social representational exposure, vicarious learning, and so on. It is an attempt to describe the complex dynamic process of personhood that incorporates the personal and the social – the active, subjective conscious self and the objectified, known self. At the core of IPT is the assertion that the individual actively seeks to construct and maintain an identity – and that this process is orderly (in the sense that there appear to be relatively predictable states of identity that are sought).

The central tenets of IPT were first presented as a corpus in 1986 (Breakwell, 1986), though some had been presented earlier (Breakwell, 1978, 1979). IPT has developed significantly since then but the underlying propositions of the theory remain. Before focussing in this chapter upon the relationship between IPT and the theory of social representations, it is worthwhile summarizing these central tenets of IPT incorporating reference to more recent key developments.

Identity is a co-production

IPT proposes that identity is a dynamic product of the interaction of the capacities for memory, consciousness and organized construal that characterize the human biological organism, with the physical and societal structures and influence processes (including social representations) which constitute the social context. Identity is considered to be constantly in development since new experiences continually provoke change. Identity is argued to reside in psychological processes but is manifested through thought, action and affect in the social context. In IPT, identity is seen as a co-production between the individual and the social context. As such, the individual is seen neither as the slave of social construction nor as the dictator of identity construction. However, fundamental to IPT is the assertion that individuals are aware of the status of their identity and seek to achieve its optimization given the constraints imposed societally. What constitutes optimization is something that is considered further later.

The structure of identity

According to IPT, identity can be described and analyzed at two levels, in terms of its structural properties (and, indeed, its actual structure at any one time in any one instantiation) and in terms of the processes entailed in its construction and maintenance. In relation to structural properties, IPT argues that identity has two dimensions: the content dimension and the value dimension.

The content dimension consists of the characteristics which define identity: the elements which, taken as a constellation, mark the individual as unique. It encompasses both those characteristics previously considered the domain of social identity (group memberships, roles, social category labels, etc.) and of personal identity (values, attitudes, cognitive style, etc.).

The distinction between social and personal identity is abandoned in IPT (Breakwell, 1983). Seen across the biography, social identities become personal identity: the dichotomy is purely a temporal artefact. The concern in IPT with the agentic role of the person has sometimes been taken to suggest that the theory is ignoring social identities. This is not correct. Social identities (whether derived from category memberships or representational processes) are elements in the total identity. Since they are, there is no reason not to use IPT to explain how people respond to changes in the group-derived elements of identity. In this, IPT complements Social Identity Theory (SIT) – at least in SIT's original formulation (Tajfel, 1978). In fact, any comprehensive theory of identity should support models of intergroup relations and intra-group dynamics. Indeed, researchers are employing IPT in the context of the analysis of group conflict and societal change (Oren and Bar-Tal, 2014; Chryssochoou, 2014; Lyons, 1996).

When the concept of identity is used it is sensible to be clear whether one is talking about the total identity or specific elements in it. Sometimes researchers talk about individuals having 'multiple identities'. This confuses matters since as soon as you talk about multiple identities it begs the question: how do they relate to each other? They cannot be supposed realistically to exist in a series of hermetically sealed units. Then you have the problem of theorizing the superordinate structure that accommodates these multiple identities. Faced with this conundrum, IPT suggests that it is more productive to think about identity holistically and then look at the way the relationships between the elements which comprise it can be theorized.

IPT outlines the relationships between elements in proposing that the organization of the content dimension of identity can be characterized in terms of: (1) the hierarchical arrangement of elements – the ways in which they are connected; (2) the relative salience of elements – the importance of each in the overall evaluation of identity; and (3) the degree of centrality of each element – the extent to which an element has others dependent upon it. This list of the characteristics of the organization of identity was generated in the 1986 exposition of IPT and has been explored empirically (Vignoles, Chryssochoou and Breakwell, 2000, 2002a, 2002b, 2004). As a result, one organizational characteristic worth adding to the list might be labelled 'resilience' – the overall resistance shown by a particular identity content configuration to change. The actual organization for any particular identity is not deemed to be static and is responsive to the action of the identity processes. Yet it is possible that some identity content configurations (ICC) are more resilient to change than others. It may be that some ICCs provide greater scope for effective coping strategies when faced with demands for change. For instance, an ICC that is very complex, with many elements that have multiple interdependences but without a single central salient element, might offer more varied opportunities for the deployment of coping strategies, for instance through the downgrading of salience for any element that is threatened.

IPT states that each element in the ICC has a value (on a positive–negative continuum) appended to it. Taken together, these values constitute the value dimension of identity. The value dimension of identity is constantly subject to revision not only because the ICC itself changes but because the value of each element can be reappraised as a consequence of changes in social value systems and modifications in the individual's position in relation to such social value systems. Additionally, the value of an element may be changed indirectly, as a consequence of revisions in the value of others in the ICC. There will be ripple effects of evaluation changes across the ICC.

Social representations are not only fundamentally important in establishing the potential universe of elements from which the ICC is constructed; they are also fundamentally important in establishing the value of identity elements. To the extent that social representations can evolve to make sense of any aspect of the social or physical world and the roles of individuals within it, they are the ultimate arbiters and carriers of value. This is one of the reasons that the theory of social representations has a vital part to play in relation to any theory of identity processes.

The processes of identity

IPT claims that the overall structure of identity is regulated by the processes of assimilation–accommodation and evaluation, and these are universal psychological processes. These processes are reactive in the sense that they respond to the changing experiences which impact the individual. They are active in the sense that, in keeping with the identity principles that order their operation, they will motivate the individual to seek changes in the pattern of experiences.

Assimilation and accommodation are two components of the same process. Assimilation refers to the absorption of new components into the ICC and accommodation refers to the adjustment which occurs in the existing ICC in order to locate new elements. IPT originally suggested that assimilation–accommodation could be conceptualized as a memory system and subject to biases in retention and recall that were determined by the identity principles (more on these below). However, the memory system analogy is unhelpful since it fails to capture the creativity and innovation that characterizes the assimilation–accommodation process. Individuals are selective in the acquisition, and deliberate in the interpretation, of new identity elements as well as biased in their assimilation or in the way they accommodate the existing ICC to them. This elaboration of the concept of assimilation–accommodation in IPT owes much to the work in the social representations tradition of Duveen (2001a), which emphasized the creativity, as well as the resistance, in the reactions to social representations that occur when constructing an identity.

The process of evaluation entails the construction of meaning and value for identity elements, new and old. The evaluation process works not only to attach a value to a particular element but also to establish the value of the ICC as a whole. Evaluation is a psychological process, and as such is idiosyncratic and individualized, but it is also constrained substantially by societal messages – often through social representations – about how to value identity elements. These messages are not straightjackets but they are robust guidelines and to ignore them – without recourse to coping strategies – would create instability in the evaluative dimension of identity because these messages are often recurrent and the inconsistencies between the individual's valuation and the societal valuation would be evident, if to no one else than to the individual concerned.

The process of assimilation–accommodation and the process of evaluation interact to determine the changing identity content configuration (ICC) and identity value (IV) over time; with changing patterns of assimilation–accommodation requiring changes in evaluation and, importantly, in a recursive fashion.

The identity principles

IPT proposes that the operation of these identity processes is guided by identity principles which define optimal states for the structure of identity. IPT recognizes that the form of identity structure considered optimal may vary over a lifespan and across cultures. If this is so, then it would predict the identity principles will vary. Whether this is so can only be established empirically. Meanwhile, IPT suggested originally that the identity principles evident from current data were: continuity, distinctiveness, self-efficacy and self-esteem.

Subsequently, various researchers have posited the existence of further identity principles. For example, Markowe (1996) argued for additional principles of *authenticity/integrity* and *affiliation* while studying the 'coming out' process among lesbian women; Vignoles and colleagues (2000) identified possible additional principles of *purpose* and *closeness to others* in interviews with Anglican parish priests; and Jaspal and Cinnirella (2010) suggested a *coherence* principle, based on their research into identity conflict among British Pakistani Muslim gay men. Each of these proposals has a basis in data. The question that must be posed, however, before including any new identity principle within the theory is: how far does it improve the explanatory power of the theory? Does it offer additionality? Some that have been proposed can be argued to be subsets of the four original identity principles. For instance, coherence could be seen as an aspect of continuity. To establish that a coherence principle adds to the explanatory power of the theory, it would be necessary to show that over and above the predictive power of the other principles it can predict how the individual acts, thinks or feels. Showing that a new 'principle' is predictive in isolation does not satisfy this more stringent test for inclusion in the model. Further empirical work is likely to establish yet more principles that do fit into some hierarchy in which all have a role to play in guiding identity processes.

Determining how this hierarchy of principles works will not be easy. Indeed, mapping the actual empirical relationships between the four original identity principles is incomplete. Some early studies showed they co-varied but were not identical in their capacity to predict responses to changes in identity elements (e.g. changes in employment status and political affiliation (Breakwell, Fife-Schaw and Devereux, 1989; Fife-Schaw and Breakwell, 1990)). This work showed that while the four identity principles all connote something which might be called positive self-regard, they are not identical to each other in the way they work to affect the ICC or IV. Any new addition to the list of identity principles should satisfy an equivalent test. Of course, in looking for evidence on the way the identity principles operate, it is important not to confuse the measurement of the desire to achieve a particular state for identity with the measurement of the state itself. Occasionally, this distinction is ignored. It clearly should not be.

IPT states that identity principles will vary in their absolute salience and their relative salience to each other over time and across situations. It is suggested that the salience of an identity principle for the identity processes at any one time will be significantly conditioned by the characteristics of the social context, notably by the social representations which are available. For instance, a social representational environment in which distinctiveness was especially valued would be likely to result in the distinctiveness identity principle emerging as more salient than if the dominant social representations were emphasizing the value of esteem. The salience of the identity principles may vary developmentally. However, though it seems a reasonable hypothesis, there is no empirical evidence yet that this is so. Social representations that signal what is to be valued at different stages of the lifespan may be clues to the way salience of the identity principles changes over a lifetime.

The social context: structures and influence processes

An individual identity is created within a particular social context within a specific historical period. IPT proposes that the social context can be schematically represented along two dimensions concerning, in turn, structure and process. Structurally, the social context is comprised of interpersonal networks, group and social category memberships, and intergroup relationships. The original formulation of IPT used a relatively simple and undifferentiated concept of 'group'. In retrospect this was unfortunate but not unjustified (since IPT is not attempting to theorize the social structure merely to acknowledge that it is the milieu in which identity is developed). Many elements of identity are assimilated initially from the social structures which generate roles that are ascribed or to be adopted.

The second dimension consists of social influence processes which interact to create the multifaceted ideological milieu for identity processes. Social influence processes (education, rhetoric, propaganda, polemic, persuasion, etc.) establish systems of explanation, value and belief, reified in social representations, social norms and social attributions, which offer frameworks for both the content and evaluation dimensions of individual identities. As it has developed, IPT has given increasing attention to the role of social representations in explaining how the content and value of an identity emerge and are sustained. As Augoustinos and Innes (1990) explain, social representations are different from social schema (and other social cognition models) because of the emphasis on their shared nature, their genesis in interaction and their maintenance through communication. As a result, the theory of social representations has the potential to say much more about the dynamics of identity. This is the conclusion that Howarth (2002a) arrived at early and which has influenced IPT researchers.

IPT clearly states identity is not determined in any simplistic way by its social context. There are contradictions and conflicts within the social representational milieu which permit the individual some latitude in formulating the ICC and IV. Additionally, variation in individuals' neuro-physiological and cognitive systems will detract from direct or common impact of social influence processes upon identity development. The individual has agency in creating and maintaining identity. In fact, the panoply of coping strategies that the individual may deploy when faced with change suggest that any notion of raw social determinism should be abandoned.

However, IPT does suggest that changes in the social structures or influence processes will stimulate some change in identity and this will vary according to: (1) their personal relevance; (2) the immediacy of involvement in them; (3) the amount of change demanded; and (4) how negative, in terms of the identity principles, the change is deemed to be. IPT emphasizes that no two individuals might be expected to react in the same way to a shift in social structures or a movement in the social representational environment.

Identity threat

IPT has traditionally focussed upon what individuals think, feel and do when changes in the social context threaten their existing identity (either the ICC or IV). A threat to identity is said to occur when the identity processes (assimilation–accommodation and evaluation) are unable, for some reason, to comply with the principles of continuity, distinctiveness, self-efficacy and self-esteem. The origin of a threat can be internal or external. For instance, it can be considered to originate internally where the individual seeks to alter his or her position in the social matrix in accordance with one identity principle only to discover that this contravenes one of the other identity principles. It can be said to originate externally when a change in the social context, for instance a compulsory change of role or a social revaluation of the role occupied, calls for identity changes incompatible with one or more of the four principles.

Identity threats are argued to be aversive and the individual is predicted to seek to reinstitute a state for identity congruent with the identity principles. The identity principles are tied to affect: when breached, the principles arouse an aversive emotional state. The negative emotion aroused can be considered to be the intermediate motivation driving the actions that bring the identity into a new state that complies with the requirements of the identity principles. This assumption is embedded in the original formulation of IPT, but it is worth making it explicit. When identity processes cannot operate according to the requirements of the identity principles, they trigger an emotional response. Understanding more about the way emotional arousal affects identity maintenance is very important. One reason this would be useful is that objective indicators of emotional arousal could be used as a proxy for the subjective experience of identity threat. If this can be done, the irritating circularity in some of the operationalizations of threat and response to threat could be eliminated.

For an identity threat to evoke action, IPT claims it must gain access to consciousness. It is theoretically possible for someone to be in a position that should, in terms of some abstract assessment, threaten their identity continuity, distinctiveness, efficacy or esteem but for that individual to fail to interpret their position in that way. It is therefore possible to distinguish between occupying a threatening position (defined as threatening, for instance, by an objective independent observer) and subjectively experiencing identity threat and the emotional reaction it entails. Indeed, an essential assumption of IPT is that if the coping strategies that are deployed are effective, occupancy of an objectively threatening position will not thereafter be perceived as a threat. As a consequence, if the deployment of effective coping strategies is very speedy, it could make it very difficult to study threat at all because as soon as it is experienced it could be remediated. Of course, the individual could still report having been threatened – though some coping strategies (e.g. denial) might militate against accurate self-report. Alternatively, threat might be deduced from the mere fact that coping strategies were detected – though not all coping strategies are manifest to the observer (e.g. reconfiguration of ICC or IV saliencies). Empirical definitions of threat are fraught with difficulties.

Coping strategies as change strategies

While IPT originally focussed upon reactions to threatened identities, it should not be thought now to be exclusively concerned with this. Identity is continually reconstructed and is perpetually changing in accordance with the principles that direct identity processes. IPT as a model of identity dynamics is not singularly concerned with threat. It can be applied successfully to the general process of identity construction and maintenance. This is indeed the fundamental argument on which IPT is based. The original focus on threat was driven by a desire to understand what happened when people experienced objectively defined threatening changes. By 'objectively defined' IPT tends to mean socially defined. It was a means of starting to describe the strategies that are deployed to manage identity reconfiguration. These were labelled 'coping strategies'. While 'coping strategies' in the early formulations of IPT were defined in terms of their role in responding to threat, it was quickly accepted that the same strategies are used in the everyday business of identity maintenance (Breakwell, 1988, 1992). It may be time to recognize that coping strategies are generically deployed as part of the activity of the identity processes but that they still operate in accordance with the requirements of the identity principles.

Followed through to its logical conclusion, this would suggest that IPT would propose that any activity, in thought or deed, which has as its goal the maintenance or construction of an identity structure that is compliant with the identity principles can be regarded as a coping strategy. Coping strategies are basically identity change strategies. Of course, in a subset of change contexts this coping activity would be specifically targeted at threat reduction or removal.

The earlier categorization of coping strategies used in IPT would still seem to be viable in that they can operate at a number of different levels: the intra-psychic (with individual behavioural implications), the interpersonal and the group or intergroup (again, with acknowledgement of the inadequacies in the way in which social psychology defines the 'group' concept). For illustrative purposes in this chapter, some of the coping strategies at each level used in response to identity threat are described. Some of same strategies can be used when identity principles are not threatened but change in compliance with them is still required. However, it is clear that a much broader set of coping strategies would need to be hypothesized to cover all types of change in identity.

Intra-psychic-level coping strategies rely upon the process of assimilation–accommodation to either deflect or accept the implications of a threat for identity. Deflection tactics entail the refusal to modify either the content dimension of identity. They include: denial, transient depersonalization, belief in the unreality of the self, fantasy, and reconstrual and reattribution. Acceptance strategies act to modify the identity structure in ways required by the threat. Acceptance is rarely wholesale capitulation to the threat. Mostly it reflects a compromise negotiated between the threat and the needs of identity. Acceptance tactics include anticipatory restructuring, compartmentalization, compromise changes, and, only after these, fundamental changes in the ICC. There is another type of strategy which involves the revision of the salience allotted the four principles guiding the identity processes. Rearranging their priority may shift the emphasis from threatened to unthreatened components of identity. Also at the intra-psychic level, the process of evaluation may revise the value placed upon either the existing or prospective ICC to make the changes mooted more palatable.

Interpersonal-level coping strategies rely upon changing relationships with others in order to cope with the threat. Such strategies include: isolationism, negativism, passing (i.e. achieving a social position fraudulently by acquiring some of the outward trappings of the position) and compliance (i.e. 'playing the role' and conforming to expectations to avoid the worst aspects of the threat).

Group or intergroup coping strategies can operate at a series of different levels and the structure of the groups concerned vary. For instance, individuals can use their membership of multiple groups to insulate against threat – shifting their focus for defining identity between different elements of identity to optimise their position at any one time. Alternatively, they can engender group support for their dilemma, using a group to provide a social and information network or as a context for consciousness-raising or self-help. Indeed, group action may be used to bring about changes in the social structure or in the social representational milieu. The objective of the group action may be to alter the characteristics and/or value of the individual's social position. Such groups, which are called into being in order to aid the threatened, may develop social representations and rhetoric of their own and can become a genuine force for social change. Here we see the identity process origins of participation in social representations processes. We also see how the identity principles will shape the form of the social representation.

These descriptions of the coping strategies at different levels merely illustrate some of the large range that the individual can use to construct and maintain an identity. The coping strategy deployed is determined by an enormously complex interaction between the type of identity change required (and the threat it might involve), the way the broad social context is structured (interpersonally and at the group level), the social representational milieu, the prior identity structure (ICC and IV), the cognitive biases (including preferences for cognitive consistency and engagement with social comparisons) and neuro-physiological capacities characteristic of the individual. Predicting what type of coping strategy will be used is almost impossibly difficult, except where there is good evidence of what other individuals faced with the same or very similar demands for identity change have done in the past. So, for instance, there is a tradition of research on unemployment that would predict how individuals from different backgrounds and age groups will deal with the change of status that losing your job entails.

IPT originally proposed that as long as the constellation of factors which precipitated the deployment of a coping strategy, even one that is suboptimal, is maintained, the individual will persist with that strategy. Where coping strategies fail to achieve their objective, the structure of identity will change in ways that are incompatible with the constraints normally imposed by the identity principles. The individual temporarily loses the power to limit or direct change. In most instances of routine identity maintenance, if the coping strategy is thwarted then another will be implemented. Serial attempts to get to a satisfactory point for identity are the norm rather than the exception. However, the failure of coping strategies in the face of chronic threat may result ultimately in withdrawal, either psychologically, socially, temporally or physically, or in the suppression of self-awareness. These extreme forms of withdrawal, such as amnesia or suicide, cannot be considered coping strategies in themselves, but they can be the ultimate response to threat to identity.

Social representations and personal representations

In describing the central tenets of IPT it has become increasingly clear that social representations have a fundamental role to play in creating and sustaining identities. They provide the raw material from which identity elements are crafted. They provide the medium through which identity is expressed. They provide avenues for influence that allow coping strategies to be conceived and deployed. They translate the physical reality into the social reality in which all identities reside. While their role in identity construction is fundamental, it is not determinist. The individual is agentic, engaging with social representations and social representational processes actively and purposively.

IPT has been elaborated to explore how identity processes influence the individual's engagement with social representations (Breakwell, 2001a, 2001b, 2014). The theory of social representations states that objectification and anchoring are not individual processes. They are processes that normally involve social interaction and the establishment of shared meaning and consensus through communication among people. This does not mean that everyone holds absolutely identical social representations. Breakwell (2001a) distinguished between 'personal representations' and social representations. A personal representation is used to refer to the manifestation of a social representation at the level of the individual. To the extent that a social representation is present in an individual's cognitions, emotions or behaviour, it exists as a personal representation. This is not to suggest that the personal representation is a complete reproduction of the social representation. Quite the opposite; it will be partial and selective. The facets of the social representation that appear in the personal representation will be predictable on the basis of the requirements of identity processes. The individual will prefer to adopt aspects of the social representation that fit the expectations of the identity principles.

Individuals do have scope for selectivity in their adoption of social representations. The range of social representations is complex and dynamic. Moscovici (1961/1976), in moving away from Durkheim's notion of collective representation, emphasized the multiplicity of social representations that exist in modern societies and their capacity for change. It would seem reasonable to assume that, in this complex world of different and changing social representations, any one individual would rarely have access to all of the social representations that are operating and might not have access even to a single social representation in its entirety. Individuals will have different roles in the social process of construction, elaboration and sharing of the representation. Essentially, this is to suggest that each individual is uniquely positioned in relation to the process of social representation and the products of social representation.

The individual and the social representation

Why do some aspects of the social representation find their way into an individual's personal representation and others do not? Breakwell (2001a, 2001b) suggested it might help to think about the individual's relationship to any social representation as being described along a number of dimensions:

1. *Awareness*: individuals will differ in their awareness of the social representation. Exposure to, and thus awareness of, a social representation will be affected by social category memberships and past experience. But awareness will also be determined by the significance of the object of the representation.
2. *Understanding*: individuals will differ in the extent to which they actually understand the social representations of which they are aware. There is ample evidence that individuals are capable of reproducing all or part of a social representation even though they cannot explain how or why its elements fit together and, if challenged, they cannot justify it. Such individuals can be said to 'know' the social representation, this is different from saying that they can understand it. In the same way, a person can know a plane can fly but that does not mean that they understand the aerodynamics that explain its flight.
3. *Acceptance*: individuals will differ in the extent to which they believe or accept a social representation even if they are fully aware of it and understand it.

Typically, people can say: this is what is generally believed but, nevertheless, this is what I believe. The importance of being able to resist wholesale acceptance of the social representation so that it appears individualized should not be underestimated. While seeking identification with others through communality of understandings and interpretations at one level, people also simultaneously seek distinctiveness and differentiation through rejection of the social representation. The personalizing of social representations within personal representations is part of a process of establishing and protecting an identity – a type of coping strategy.

4. *Assimilation*: any aspect of a social representation that is accepted will be assimilated to pre-existent systems of personal representation. Since these differ across individuals, the way in which new social representations are assimilated will be different across individuals. Just as social processes ensure that the new social representation is anchored in prior social representations or in material evidence; at the individual level cognitive and emotional processes ensure that it is anchored in prior personal representations and experiences. In fact, there must be an intimate connection between the social processes of anchoring and objectification and their parallel individual processes. It is individuals using prior knowledge mediated through cognitive and conative (i.e. affective) networks that generate the social communication which ensures that novel events and ideas are interpreted in terms of existing systems of meaning to ensure the anchoring of a social representation. Social exchange can produce understandings which no single participant to the interaction might be able to create but at some level even these emergent representations are limited in some ways by the ability of the individuals involved to anchor and objectify.

5. *Salience*: the salience of a social representation will differ across people and for the same person across time and contexts. The salience of the social representation, for instance, may increase if the community that generates it is important to the individual. Similarly, it may increase if the social representation becomes relevant to the individual's ongoing activity. At the level of the community, if the object for social representation is non-salient it is likely that the social representation will be difficult to elicit, simple, undifferentiated and relatively unconnected with other components of the community's belief system. At the level of the individual, the salience of the social representation will be likely to influence how accurately and completely personal representation mirrors it. There is, however, no empirical evidence on this yet.

It is notable that some of the dimensions which shape the personal representation are potentially non-volitional (for example, awareness and understanding) and others are possibly volitional (for example, acceptance). However, this distinction may be rightly regarded as arbitrary. Even those which appear volitional are largely predisposed by prior social experiences and constrained by identity considerations.

The importance of the type of social representation

In addition, engagement with a social representation will depend upon what type of representation it is. Moscovici (1988) identified three types: hegemonic, emancipated and polemical. The three types of social representation offer differing freedoms for the individual to construct a personal representation. The hegemonic representation supposes little individual variation. The emancipated representation supposes individual variation based upon differential exposure within group contexts. The polemical representation supposes individual variation based upon participation in prevailing intergroup conflict.

It is the scope for personalizing representations which emerges when emancipated or polemical representations prevail about an object; that is one of the necessary conditions for innovation and change. This assertion is not meant to trivialize or ignore the real differentials between individuals in their power to maintain or to proselytize their personal representations. One of the things which this perspective emphasizes is that personal representations will be perpetually under pressure to change from the social representations which surround them. Individuals that are personally powerful (through position, expertise or some other route) are more likely to be able to retain their own personal representations and to be able to influence the development of social representations. In fact, the role of the individual in mediating emancipated and polemical representations remains to be examined empirically.

Any examination of the freedoms available to the individual in deriving a personal representation begins to highlight the need to understand the role of the individual in constructing a social representation. Since a social representation is defined as a set of understandings shared by a number of people then, to the extent that any individuals in the relevant communities demure from the shared understanding, the status of the social representation changes. It may be that the social representation itself changes in content. It may be that it simply changes its adherents (moving from one set of people to another). It may be that it changes its significance – becoming less used and less prominent. The important thing here is that the processes encircling the creation of personal representations also flow back to influence the construction and perpetuation of social representations. The intimacy of their relationship cannot be overestimated.

In passing, it is interesting to speculate about another apparent characteristic of social representations. Some seem to have a greater tendency to attract and retain adherents (what Breakwell, 2014, calls 'stickiness'). It seems stickiness can be acquired in many ways. It can be dependent upon who promulgates the social representation (for instance, if it is emanating from a community that is distrusted, it may have low stickiness). It can be associated with how the social representation is transmitted (some transmission routes are more trusted than others; some are more immediate and have high impact). It can be tied to how far the social representation has already achieved saturation in the particular social environment – for example in terms of the number of people accepting it, the length of time it has been active, the number of channels through which it is communicated, or how many times it has been presented. Additionally, stickiness could be associated with the extent to which the social representation is capable of triggering, or is aligned with, emotional arousal.

It seems likely that the stickiness of a social representation will matter when it comes to the way identity processes can work with it. It would still be possible to assume that the individual interacts with the sticky social representation in a purposive manner and is not just reactive but it seems a logical inevitability that resistance or reactance to it will be lower or less effective. The penetration of the social representation into personal representation and then into identity structure would seem likely to be greater if the stickiness is greater. It may also be linked to its permanency or intransience in the identity structure.

Identity process theory and social representations

Although social representations have been defined at one level as being a widely shared set of beliefs, we have also noted that it is not the case that social representations are accepted and used by individuals in their entirety and sometimes they are not accepted or used at all. The interaction of the individual with the realm of available social representations will depend, among other things, upon the significance they have for identity. IPT (Breakwell, 1990, 1993, 2004, 2010, 2011) argues that the awareness, acceptance, use, assimilation and salience of social representations, and their presence in personal representations, are shaped by the requirements of identity processes that act in accordance with the principles of self-esteem, self-efficacy, distinctiveness and continuity. IPT proposes that individual responses to social representations are linked to the ways in which they may threaten or secure the identity principles. It is notable that the coping strategies that manage identity change that were described earlier, frequently entailed the manipulation of personal representations and their relationship with social representations.

IPT has now generated an extensive series of studies which illustrate that individuals in the same social category or community will accept and use (i.e. reproduce or act in accordance with) a particular social representation to differing degrees depending upon its potential impact upon their identity esteem, continuity, distinctiveness and efficacy (Bonauito, Cano and Breakwell, 1996; Hendy *et al.*, 2006; Timotijevic and Breakwell, 2000; Breakwell and Lyons, 1996; Thrush *et al.*, 1997). Such studies would suggest that polemical social representations are most obviously open to manipulation to generate personal representations that optimise identity benefits. Essentially, these studies show that individuals reject social representations that might threaten important aspects of their identity. However, it is too simplistic to use the term 'rejection' when examining how identity constraints motivate the way a social representation is treated. What often happens is that the social representation is subtly modified in personal use. For instance, it can be re-anchored (linking it to a different prior set of referents) or there is a minor tweak to the objectification (often through use of different exemplars). Castro (2006) and Castro and Gomes (2005) in relation to environmental concerns argued this to be the case. Deaux (2006) noted similar findings in relation to immigrant identity and representational processes.

In effect, individuals who are actively engaged in identity maintenance and development are also perforce engaged in social representation creation and change – perhaps at the margins and unintentionally but inevitably because their use of the social representation in any innovative way will impact at some level upon its substance and meaning. Of course, whether or not their amendment of the social representation gains common acceptance or use is a function of the processes outlined in the theory of social representations itself. The significant point that all the studies have shown is that there is virtually never total consensus upon a social representation. The research illustrates variety among individuals despite the existence of the superordinate social representation. Empirical studies emphasize divergence amidst consensus – that is, the personal representation as well as the social representation. Joffe's (1995) studies of AIDS/HIV and Joffe and colleagues (2011) illustrate the variation across individuals and groups in representations of the illness. Moreover, the divergence is not random. It is ordered, systematic, and, in part, predictable in terms of IPT expectations concerning the desire to achieve and maintain esteem, efficacy, distinctiveness and continuity for individual identity.

This whole analysis can, of course, be turned upon its head. Are social representations that support the identity principles of the majority in a community more likely to be accepted, used and become salient? The answer may seem obvious: social representations that promote a community's esteem, efficacy, distinctiveness and continuity do seem to thrive in that community. Empirically this suggestion is best illustrated in research that examines social representations and identity narratives from a historical perspective (e.g. Liu and László, 2007; Liu and Hilton, 2005). In fact, the body of empirical studies that would support this emanate from virtually every side of social psychology, rather than just via IPT or the social representations research (see e.g. Bandura, 1997, in relation to the significance of efficacy at the collective level).

This leads to a very clear assertion about IPT and the theory of social representations – they offer most when they work together. The theory of social representations assumes that social representations have an impact on individuals and assumes individual actors have a role to play in evolving, promulgating and reproducing the representation. IPT assumes not only that social representations frame the realm of the possible identity content and evaluation, but that the identity principles will determine in part at least the nature of the individual interaction with the social representation. Social representations provide the interpretative framework for identity construction and maintenance. Identity processes navigate the individual through the engagement with social representations.

Understanding more about the interactions of identity processes and social representation processes would be valuable. It is particularly important to explore the role of affect in their relationship. Affective or emotion elements are common in social representations. For instance, in social representations of hazards, fear and anxiety are often an integral part of the narrative attached to the risk. There is a different question, however, and this centres upon the role of affect in the social representation process itself. Affect not as a content component of the representation but as an element in the willingness to participate in developing and communicating the representation. There is every reason to suppose that heightened arousal – whether through fear or joy – may encourage engagement with the social representational process. There is evidence that social representations are used more readily (i.e. reproduced and communicated) when they arouse fear (for example, the social amplification of risk model illustrates this (Pidgeon, Kasperson and Slovic, 2003)).

Moreover, it seems likely that the emotional content of a social representation will be important in determining how it is re-presented in personal representations and thereafter how it impacts upon identity at the individual level. One way the emotional content and tone of the social representation might be important is in the extent to which it parallels the emotional status of the individual identity. Put simply, if the social representation carries a narrative which is anxiety-arousing is the individual more receptive to it if his or her identity is already subject to threat that is generating aversive arousal? There is some evidence in the risk literature that this does happen (Breakwell, 2001c, 2007). The emotional content of a social representation could be an important element in the determination of the awareness, use, acceptance, assimilation and salience it achieves.

A concluding challenge

This chapter has outlined some of the complex relationships between IPT and the theory of social representations very much in terms of theoretical constructs. It has not described empirical studies. It has not addressed the very real methodological challenges of conducting research that examines systematically the relationship between social representations and identity processes (Breakwell and Canter, 1993). This was not the purpose of this chapter. However, it is worth outlining in what contexts it may be particularly profitable to explore the relationship between identity and social representation processes. The first fruitful context would be one where a social representation is clearly changing and the change has a direct negative or positive relevance for the social definition of a particular category of people (for instance, the changes that have occurred in the social representations of bankers or of smokers). Under these circumstances there would be expected to be an implication for the identity of members of that category. The second fruitful context would be one where the individual's relationship to a social representation changes because their objective social status changes (for instance, where an individual migrates and their position with regard to social representations of patriotism may be modified). The third fruitful context would be where an individual is actively engaged in attempts to modify an existing social representation (for example, in attempts to change the social representation of physical disability). In all three contexts there is change. Describing the relationship between identity and social representation processes in phases of manifest change is most likely to result in its better understanding. The important thing is to get the research question clear and make it truly pertinent to the verification and development of the underlying theories.

PART IV

Applications

Part IV of the handbook considers practical applications of the theory of social representations and is a complement to the theoretical and conceptual issues considered in parts I, II and III. Since its inception in the 1950s, the theory of social representations has been applied in many fields, showing that it not only offers insights into our theorization of social knowledge but it is also a tool that can be used to understand and explain social phenomena.

The ten chapters that follow deal with a variety of applications in the wider fields of politics, social memory, immigration, religion, health and illness, the environment, public understanding of science and social marketing. Some of these applications have been closely associated with the development of the theory from the beginning, such as public understanding of science, while others open up new areas of research, such as the study of religion. The studies presented in these chapters adopt a variety of methods, from in-depth interviews and focus groups to statistical modelling and action research. What links these diverse applications together is a focus on the dynamics of stability and social change. The theory of social representations is ideally positioned for the study of such dynamics as it explains how social knowledge becomes normative and habituated *and* how it can be adapted when new social conditions arise and stimulate a process of symbolic coping (Wagner, Kronberger and Seifert, 2002). The chapters also address issues surrounding the politics of knowledge construction, what Moscovici (1998) has called the 'battle of ideas'. Inevitably, this involves considering the intergroup context and the broader ideological and historical context. Finally, the chapters examine processes of identity as well as processes of stigmatization and 'othering' against socially devalued groups. On the whole, in this final part of the handbook readers will find an extensive collection of applications of the theory of social representations that we hope will inspire further work in these and other fields.

18 Representations of world history

James H. Liu and Chris G. Sibley

> People don't make history – Burkhalter thought.
> Peoples do that. Not the individual.
> Henry Kuttner and C. L. Moore, *The Piper's Son* (1945)

As research on social representations continues to proliferate, a question arises from a branch application that feeds back to the tap-root of the theory: what is worth studying as representations? There may be other domain-specific considerations, but in the domain of political psychology, it seems that what is worth studying is simultaneously that which is worth theorizing about. Given that social representations are 'at the crossroads between the individual and society, [at] a space in-between, a medium linking objects, subjects, and activities' (Bauer and Gaskell, 1999, p. 167), legitimacy is a particularly worthy subject. Legitimacy is a form of power that arises from consent (Raven, 1993); as such it is intersubjective and representational at its very core.

Why study social representations of history?

When examined through the lens of the theory of social representations, legitimacy can be considered in narrower terms as political regime legitimacy, and more broadly as societal legitimacy. In both of these contexts, representations of history are important. Across cultures, and over the broad course of the evolution of human societies, a short-list of the major bases of societal legitimacy might include genealogy (embodied by such representations as the divine right of kings and hereditary nobility), religion (including the authority of sacred texts such as the Bible or Koran), science (with ideas about rational utility and methods for ascertaining the truth), social contracts (encompassing theoretical bases for liberal democracy and capitalism), and history. History's contributions to ordering society are not duplicated by any of these other bases of legitimacy, though they intersect with genealogy and religion, particularly where myths of origin are concerned (Malinowski, 1926). Whenever the question is asked 'Why should we do this?', one answer that always has some legitimacy is, 'Because our forefathers did it this way.' History has inherently representational elements, as professional historians led by Hayden White (1987) have argued forcefully. Furthermore, as the epigraph with which we began this chapter succinctly expresses, history is created and maintained through group interaction, by peoples, not by the specific individual.

History provides society with a moving feast of lessons learned and symbolic inspirational figures and stories from the past. According to Liu and Hilton (2005, p. 44),

> History provides us with narratives that tell us who we are, where we came from and where we should be going. It defines a trajectory which helps construct the essence of a group's identity, how it relates to other groups, and ascertains what its options are for facing present challenges. A group's representation of its history will condition its sense of what it was, is, can and should be, and is thus central to the construction of its identity, norms, and values.

They note a broad consensus across the social sciences that history is an essential ingredient in constructing and maintaining the 'imagined community' of nationhood (e.g. Anderson, 1983; Hobsbawm, 1990; Kohl and Fawcett, 1996; Nora, 1989; Reicher and Hopkins, 2001; Wertsch, 2002) that is often canonical in form but also a site for contestation over social memory (Olick and Robbins, 1998) and collective remembering (Halbwachs, 1950/1980; Pennebaker, Paez and Rimé, 1997; see Chapter 10 in this volume).

Nora (1989) points out that in France, history was traditionally produced to furnish the state with a canonical narrative that bolstered its authority. By doing so, it also functioned to erase the social memory of constituent (and potentially dissident) subgroups. He argues further that in contemporary times, industrialization, urbanization, democratization and now immigration and globalization have forced an 'acceleration of history' where the tensions between history as 'an integrated, dictatorial memory... that ceaselessly reinvents tradition, linking the history of its ancestors to the undifferentiated time of heroes, origins, and myth' (p. 8) and social memory as part of the spontaneous life-world of people in society are readily apparent. When the rallying cry of '*liberté, egalité, fraternité!*' is invoked as French people collectively remember the storming of the Bastille on the 14th of July, is there narrative space for citizens who are descendants of Tunisian migrants to wear headscarves as expressions of their identities as Islamic women?

Social representations of history provide both empirical and theoretical tools to examine the confluence and disjuncture between history and social memory; they probe the empirical spaces linking national representations and smaller group narratives that nestle and jostle with one another within and between nations to form identities and shape political action. Studying how ordinary people collectively remember history is becoming a vibrant and growing area in social psychology, providing quantitative studies to complement the fact-based narrative reconstructions of professionals in the discipline of history, and the qualitatively oriented work of scholars in social memory (Olick and Robbins, 1998). Again, the epigraph with which we began cuts to the heart of our point: history is a shared resource; it is created and maintained by peoples, not by the individual.

A theory of social representations of history

Social representations of history contain descriptive components that include important events and people that are frequently configured as elements in a story (or stories). These elements may be more or less shared between the various subgroups of a society, but previous research has indicated that 'While the main events and people that constitute lay representations of history tend to be uncontroversial, their meaning and relevance to current events is often highly contested' (Liu and Hilton, 2005, p. 539). Out of the raw material of events and people, history provides symbolic materials for the construction of social identities and the mobilization of political agendas that imbue these identities with different purposes and different boundaries. These symbolic resources can take the form of social representations encompassing the concept of event schemas (Spellman and Holyoak, 1993; Hilton et al., 1996) and other narrative structures (see László, Ehmann and Imre, 2002) that may include symbolic resources that evoke categorization threat (Wohl and Branscombe, 2005), contain legitimizing myths (Sibley et al., 2008) or ideologies (Sen and Wagner, 2005), heroes and villains that can be invoked as in-group and out-group prototypes (Hanke et al., in press), and sentence structures that imbue description with latent meaning (László, 2008).

For some nations, a combination of these resources come together to form a 'charter' (Hilton and Liu, 2008, following Malinowski, 1926). We define historical charters as an account of the nation's origins and historical mission that can be amended or renegotiated over time to frame a normative and culturally enduring response to new challenges. These charters stabilize national identities, but identity entrepreneurs may attempt to reconfigure them in a way that sets a new group agenda and group vision (Reicher, Haslam and Hopkins, 2005). Groups that consider themselves to be a people or a nation claim a life or essence that goes beyond the lives of individuals to intimations of immortality over time (Sani et al., 2007). For such groups, history is an inevitable component of the narrative used to legitimize the group's claim to sovereign power and territorial self-determination. In many cases, ideologies of history operate in response to value-based threats in order to negate the perceived obligations of the in-group to right past wrongs for the in-group's historical transgressions. Sibley and Liu (2012), for instance, argued that the ideological positioning of history is produced at least partially by the motivation to protect the glorious history of the in-group (and the related perception of the ancestors of one's group as decent, hard-working people who earned what they achieved). Consistent with this premise, they showed that majority group members in New Zealand who were high in authoritarianism tended to increase longitudinally in their level of ideology relating to the negation of history and the depositioning of historical injustices perpetrated against indigenous peoples as being of continued relevance in modern-day society. This is exactly what one would expect given that people high in authoritarianism should be among those most motivated to represent the in-group as having a glorious, pure and legitimate historical origin.

Sani, Bowe, Herrera and colleagues (2007, 2008) have developed a measure of perceived collective continuity with historical and cultural subscales and have demonstrated their connection to self- and group-maintaining constructs such as entitativity and collective and personal self-esteem. A motivation for ethno-cultural continuity has been found further to predict in-group dating behaviours for people from smaller ethnic groups (Gezenstvey-Lamy, Ward and Liu, 2012).

Identity entrepreneurs, such as politicians, mobilize these symbolic resources from history to define category membership in ways that favour their own political agendas and render illegitimate the claims of rivals (Reicher et al., 2005). The resonance of their claims with historical representations may well be a key to their ultimate success or failure, in a more occasionally dynamic way (see Klein and Licata, 2003, for evidence from the political speeches from an African leader) than has been traditionally articulated in the anchoring theory of social representations (Moscovici, 1988). In 1944, from Ahmadnagar fort prison, which was under the British Raj, Jawaharlal Nehru wrote and prophesied in *The Discovery of India*:

> Thus slowly the long panorama of India's history unfolded itself before me, with its ups and downs, its triumphs and defeats. There seemed to me something unique about the continuity of a cultural tradition through five thousand years of history, of invasion and upheaval, a tradition that was widespread among the masses and powerfully influenced by them . . . And this panorama of her past gradually merged into the unhappy present, when India, for all her past greatness and stability, was a slave country, an appendage of Britain, and all over the world terrible and devastating war was raging and brutalizing humanity. But that vision of five thousand years gave me a new perspective, and the burden of the present seemed to grow lighter. The hundred and eighty years of British rule in India were just one of the unhappy interludes in her long story; she would find herself again; already, the last page in this chapter was being written.
> (Nehru, 1946, p. 52)

Nehru's *Discovery of India* is a remarkable cultural history that celebrates the myriad layers of Indian cultural evolution from its Vedic origins to the Mughal Empire as a syncretic whole excepting the British, who 'had wealth and power but felt no responsibility for good government' (p. 281). In chapter 7 Nehru describes the British Raj as 'landlords', their Indian Civil Service as 'the world's most tenacious trade union' and 'caste', and the British East India Company as looters and 'the world's high-water mark for graft'. By contrast, he proclaims the Mughal emperor Babar as a 'Renaissance prince' (p. 259) and his grandson Akbar as having a dream of a united India 'organically fused into one people'. In Nehru's reading of history, it was the British, not the Muslims, who were positioned as the out-group.

Three years later Nehru became the first prime minister of India and spoke thus: 'At the stroke of the midnight hour, when the world sleeps, India will awake to life and freedom. A moment comes, which comes but rarely in history, when we step out from the old to the new, when an age ends, and when the soul of a nation, long suppressed, finds utterance.' History was for Nehru the identity entrepreneur an ineffable source of symbolic power that no material power or utilitarian argument within the British Empire could stop. But other identity entrepreneurs were at work at the same time, leading him to preface his stroke of midnight remark with this qualifier: 'Long years ago we made a tryst with destiny, and now the time comes when we shall redeem our pledge, not wholly or in full measure, but very substantially.' For at the stroke of midnight the British Raj was divided into two nations: India and Pakistan. The All India Muslim League, led by Mohammad Ali Jinnah, had produced an alternative identity vision where Muslims under the Raj formed a separate nation to the Hindu majority (Liu and Khan, 2014).

Communal conflict between Jinnah's Muslim League and Hindu nationalists such as Vinayak Savarkar, who thought India should be a Hindu nation in its entirety, was inevitable. Savarkar (1921–22) defined Hindutva (Hindu nationalism) as 'not a word, but a history', producing a considerably more mythologized account of the past than Nehru that positioned Muslims and not the British as the out-group. Savarkar wrote:

> But as it often happens in history this very undisturbed enjoyment of peace and plenty lulled our Sindhusthan [the 'historical' Indian nation], in a sense of false security and bred a habit of living in the land of dreams. At last she was rudely awakened on the day when Mohammad of Gazni crossed the Indus, the frontier line of Sindhusthan, and invaded her. That day the conflict of life and death began. Nothing makes self-conscious of itself so much as a conflict with non-self. Nothing can weld peoples into a nation and nations into a state as the pressure of a common foe. Hatred separates as well as unites.[1]

Nehru's version of history as a layered syncretism with contributions from multiple sources did not fully carry the day. The bloody separation of the Raj into two states and the subsequent conflict between them are today a huge part of representations of world history according to university students in both India and Pakistan (Liu et al., 2009). This history and its representations are regularly exploited by politicians in new identity projects that provoke further sectarian conflict (Sen and Wagner, 2005). The power of history is anchored in the past but constantly updated, with parts of it made relevant by new events and other parts reconfigured by new ideas, so that fresh challenges to a people are reinscribed on history and as history with each new crisis. Schuman and Rodgers (2004) found that the importance of historical events to do with war and crisis increased in the United States following the 9/11 attacks. This terrorist attack killed 3,000. The partition of India and Pakistan cost a million lives. In social representations of history, it is the founding event of the nation and current events that are collectively most remembered in free recall, creating a U-shape of social memory for history (see Liu et al., 2002; Liu et al., 1999; Liu and Gastardo-Conaco, 2011).

This has left India and Pakistan with a burden of history created by conflict and its continuation. They are not alone in this. Collective remembering appears to thrive

---

1 See Reicher et al. (2005) for discussion of identity entrepreneurs, and Liu and Khan (2014) for analyses specific to pre-Independence India.

on recounting historical conflict. It is not the story of peace and prosperity that is most salient in the collective remembering of world history, but war and politics. Around the world and across twenty-four societies, the most frequent categories of freely recalled events by university students were politics and war, whereas economic and scientific developments were under-represented (Liu *et al.*, 2005; Liu *et al.*, 2009; see also Pennebaker *et al.*, 2006 for alternative data collected using a slightly different method). Liu and László (2007) speculated that perhaps stories of conflict were more interesting to narrate, having a protagonist, an antagonist and a clear plot with an events structure. Paez and Liu (2011) have produced an interdisciplinary literature review summarizing effects of collective remembering on both conflict and peace-making.

Given this focus on war, it has been commented that history is written by the victors; indeed, Winston Churchill once quipped: 'history will be kind to me, for I intend to write it'. His *History of English Speaking Peoples* is not only scholarly; it is an act of identity entrepreneurship written to articulate the long-term bonds between the United States and Britain that arose at a time (1937) when Churchill was out of power and Hitler on the rise. As World War II is the most often nominated event in the free recall of events in world history, and Hitler the most often free-recalled individual in social memory for history (Liu *et al.*, 2005, 2009), Germany has the difficult identity position as the prototypical villain in the greatest historical narrative of all time (see Spellman and Holyoak, 1993 for analogical mapping of this). Hardly a year goes by without a World War II movie or book coming out, none of which lauds Nazi conduct.

Collective remembering of Hitler and the Nazis is one area where there appears to be little in-group favouritism in Germany: Holocaust denial is against the law, World War II concentration camp visits are a part of the educational curriculum for schoolchildren, and service on a kibbutz in Israel may be substituted for mandatory military service. Issues of collective guilt (Branscombe, Slugoski and Kappen, 2004; Doosje *et al.*, 1998) and collective shame (Dresler-Hawke and Liu, 2006) pervade German collective remembering of the Nazi era. Some observers have argued that the creation of the European Union may at least in part be attributed to Germany's desire for a superordinate identity position to transcend the historical guilt and/or shame of its Nazi past (Hein and Selden, 2000).

Silence or denial is more typical of Japan, where selective forgetting of World War II, Korean occupation and the Sino-Japanese War has caused tensions with its East Asian neighbours (Liu and Atsumi, 2008; Atsumi and Suwa, 2009). The political costs of such a stand are considerable. Japanese people as a whole have become a politically a-historical, finding it difficult to narrate a coherent story of the historical trajectory of their national identity without encountering internal or external resistance. As a result of wounds not healed (Hanke *et al.*, 2013), political trust in the region is low and social relations are unbalanced (Liu *et al.*, 2011). Japanese positions in international diplomacy can be undermined by their aggrieved neighbours using historical arguments. One of these neighbours, China, regularly produces historical television dramas where the Japanese are depicted as arch-villains. Several theorists (see Gries, 2004; He, 2007) have argued that the Sino-Japanese War forms an important anchor for resurgent Chinese nationalism after the ideological weakening of Marxism and Maoism as China entered into a market economy.

Measuring and modelling social representations of history

László (2008) and colleagues (e.g. Liu and László, 2007) have argued that social representations in general, and social representations of history in particular, are organized not simply as cognitive categories but as narratives. As such, 'The validity of narrative hinges on its credibility, authenticity, relevance, and coherence, which in turn are dependent on the proper use of narrative features – time, plot, characters, perspective, narrative intentions and evaluation.' Following theorists like Propp (1968), who argued that Russian folk-tales could be decomposed into about thirty moves that all had a basic story structure involving conflict between a protagonist and an antagonist moving to a resolution, László and colleagues (2002) theorized that a narrative structure (or event schema) of 'first defeat, then victory' was missing from Hungarian historical narratives, and was responsible for the low frequency of nominations for the end of Russian occupation in 1989. Similar assertions have been made by Wertsch (2002), who identified a Russian narrative template derived from an in-group favouring summary of their historical experiences in dealing with Napoleon and Hitler's invasions (inviting a purely defensive response of the motherland 'coincidentally' used to justify the post-war occupation of other nations). Narratives bring certain elements of collective remembering into the foreground and relegate others to the background, both at the macro level of structure and at the micro level of sentence constructions in explicit and implicit ways.

Vincze, Toth and László (2007) used sophisticated automated textual analysis methods to identify alternative forms of agency expressed in history textbooks of the Austro-Hungarian Empire. Coding at the micro level from six textbooks, they found that Hungarian texts emphasized more personal agency and Austrian texts emphasized more institutional agency. In this way, 'Hungarian textbooks consider events from an intergroup conflict point of view and tend to personalize history, which facilitates the transmission and strengthening of the Hungarian national identity, while Austrian textbooks reinforce the civic identity of readers' (p. 70).

Thus, social representations of history supply content in the form of event schemas (and narrative structures), legitimizing myths and ideologies, prototypical heroes and villains, and descriptive language pregnant with latent meanings, all of which may be worked into group agendas and group boundaries by political elites seeking to engineer social identity. This content appears capable of inflecting psychological processes such that common laboratory findings like in-group favouritism can be transformed into the complex and more culturally dependent forms described above. And indeed, laboratory and longitudinal survey work in this area indicates that it is those high in authoritarianism and most motivated to maintain collective security and in-group cohesion who are more likely to position history in ways that defend from aspersions that the glorious history of their in-group (Sibley and Liu, 2012).

What social representations of history have added to the more long-standing literature on social memory (Olick and Robbins, 1996) and collective remembering (Halbwachs, 1950/1980) is the use of experimental and survey methods to push theory development and supply quantitative answers to questions that had heretofore been examined using hermeneutical (interpretive) methods (see the quantitative anchoring study of Liu, Sibley and Huang, 2014, demonstrating the resilience of political views in the stable society of New Zealand versus their dynamism in the more politically unsettled society of Taiwan; see also Huang, Liu, and Chang, 2004). These have enabled theorists to answer such questions as 'Are representations of world history universal?', and more precisely, 'What aspects of the representation of world history are universal?'

Social representations of world history have been examined by decomposing the subject of history into two open-ended questions: 'What are the most important events in world history?' and 'Which figures have had the most impact on world history in the last 1,000 years, good or bad?' (Liu *et al.*, 2005, 2009). Questionnaires allowing open-ended (free recall) responses to these questions have been distributed to more than 3,500 university students across twenty-four societies. This decomposition of a complex topic into easy-to-answer questions has the advantage of allowing simple counting procedures to determine the prevalence of particular representations, but also the disadvantage of reducing the salience of eras (like the Roman Empire) marked by causal forces (like the Industrial Revolution or capitalism). By identifying common themes in social representations of history, we can then statistically model the core structure of such themes (the factors or classes of items that fit together). This implies a general narrative structure, such as the organizing of events and peoples into themes relating to heroes and villains, or events relating to progress versus calamities.

Hilton and Liu (2008) summarized the results of this mammoth survey undertaking as follows. (1) Warfare was salient among all samples, with World War II the most frequently named event in twenty-two of twenty-four societies, and World War I the second most nominated event in nineteen societies. The second most frequently nominated category of events was politics, and this often included events involving collective violence or its threat (e.g. the French Revolution and the cold war). Hitler, a brutal war leader, was the most frequently nominated individual in nineteen of twenty-four societies, and others such as Stalin, Napoleon and George Bush Jr were also prominent. (2) There was historical foreshortening, with two-thirds of the most frequently nominated events and 72 per cent of figures occurring in the last 100 years. For historical figures, 90 per cent were from the last 200 years, but this result was influenced by the survey injunction to limit nominations to the last 1,000 years. Otherwise, religious founders would have made a greater impact. (3) Less saliently, but also theoretically important, the pattern of nominations was more Eurocentric than ethnocentric. Events representations for some non-western societies (such as Japan or Singapore) were indistinguishable from those from western culture. Figure nominations were more culturally diverse (with non-westerners such as Gandhi and Mandela prominent) and ethnocentric (with local heroes such as Jose Rizal and Kemal Ataturk making local appearances). The social representation of world history as being a story about politics and war with causal forces emanating from the West in the last 200 or so years appeared so common as to be universal.

However, when Pennebaker and colleagues (2006) used a within-subjects design where the same questions were asked about important events for the last 1,000, 100 and 10 years, somewhat different results were observed. When responding to the 1,000 year prompt, the discovery of the new world, the French Revolution, and the Industrial Revolution were the most frequently named events (the world wars were 4–5), whereas World War I and World War II were most nominated given the 100-year prompt. These differences suggest that the narrative or interpretive context (in this case, the use of time periods) made different aspects of history salient in response to the sequence of prompts. As usual, representational processes are group-based and contextual.

More sophisticated quantitative techniques have been employed in recent years to more directly address whether the pattern of results about representing world history is truly universal. A quantitative survey asking for quantitative evaluations of forty of the most frequently nominated figures and events from the open-ended surveys was administered to more than 6,000 university students in more than thirty societies. For the evaluation of events (Liu *et al.*, 2012) and figures (Hanke *et al.*, in press) as positive or negative, multi-dimensional scaling techniques (using Procrustean rotations) indicated poor fit of data from the individual countries to an overall mean configuration. There was a lack of universal agreement as to the associational meaning of events and figures in world history. Thus, even though the general outline of a story of world history appears to be somewhat consensual, the exact meaning of the specific events and figures configured within them is not. Most interestingly, negative events (historical calamities; see Liu *et al.*, 2012) were more consensual across cultures than were positive events (historical progress and the emergence of human rights), whereas the exact opposite was true for figures (Hanke *et al.*, in press). There was more consensus around the positive evaluation of heroic figures (the most highly rated of whom was Einstein) than on the negative evaluation of villains (the worst of whom was Hitler). While there is no quantitative universality in the ratings of events and figures in world history, there was a significant degree of consensus in the events we as a species want to avoid (wars, environmental disasters, economic depressions) and the people whom we admire (Einstein, Mother Theresa, Gandhi). The picture that emerges is a dynamic of human global society in evolution, historically emanating from western causal influences, but producing different historical trajectories of adaptation depending on the home of one's cultural zone (see Inglehart and Baker, 2000).

Sibley and Liu (2013) outlines a general framework for the study of categories or types of social representations using Latent Class Analysis (LCA) or Latent Profile Analysis (LPA). Hanke and colleagues (2013) have applied this method to explore categorical differences in the structure of social representations of history and their density across cultural regions (see Hagenaars and McCutcheon, 2002, for an overview of statistical details; also Liu and Sibley, 2013), for a primer on LCA in the study of social representations). Using LCA, they have identified four distinct representational profiles that were hypothesized to underlie patterns for evaluating historical figures across cultures. LCA is a form of mixture modelling that builds typologies (termed 'representational profiles') by putting individuals into empirically observed groups of common response using a mathematical model rather than relying on a priori classification. This allows simultaneous identification of a representation (as a pattern of mean scores on items within an empirically determined subgroup) and the people who hold them (for theory about representational profiles, see Sibley and Liu, 2013). In the Hanke and colleagues (2013) study, this involved identifying and classifying respondents into different classes based on similarities and differences in their patterns of ratings of the importance of different events in world history (Liu and Sibley, 2013, provides a detailed primer documenting the use of this method more generally).

Hanke and colleagues (2013) study showed that the two most prevalent profiles in western cultures were secular and religious idealists, who were similar in that they rated Hitler, Saddam, and Osama bin Laden very low, and scientific and democratic/human rights leaders very high. The secular idealists gave lower ratings to their heroes, and especially rated religious founding figures (e.g. Jesus, Buddha, Mohammed) less highly. While 90 per cent of westerners fell into one of these two representational profiles, the remaining 10 per cent rated historical figures in a way that was atypical for members of their culture. In Asian and Islamic societies, two other representational profiles were common: political realists, and historical indifferents. Political realists rated dictators, generals and terrorists less negatively than the idealists and rated communist leaders like Marx and Lenin rather highly. But their ratings of the heroes of science and democracy were quite similar to the idealists' profiles, underlining the general finding that it is at the negative rather than at the positive end where people differ on rating historical figures. People in the developing societies of Asia and the Islamic world, where survival is by no means assured (see Inglehart and Baker, 2000), probably see the world as a place where a Machiavellian attitude towards power is sometimes necessary.

Finally, Islamic societies had many people classified as historical indifferents – that is, most of their ratings hovered around the midpoint (except for Hitler and George Bush Jr, who were perceived equally negatively) – possibly because few of the figures rated in the World History Survey came from the Muslim world. But there was a mixture of all four profiles in each society, though their proportions could be predicted based on a priori knowledge of groups. Historical idealism, a pattern of rating scientists and humanitarians high and dictators and communist ideologues low, warrants the legitimacy of a global society dominated by western values. Secular idealism was common in Asia, whereas Latin America had a less concentrated pattern of the historical idealism of western societies. Mapping the causes of the distribution of representational profiles in global society and tracking longitudinal changes in them is a vibrant topic for future research (Sibley and Liu, 2013).

Concluding comments

History is not simply a relevant topic for the study of social representations, but a critical one. It is critical because the ways in which history is constructed can have profound consequences for how politics are mobilized and how the identity of entire generations of peoples may be shaped. Those historical events and people widely regarded as important across all segments of society constitute important symbolic resources for mobilizing public opinion. They are difficult to ignore in public debate because they carry such widely shared emotional resonance and political legitimacy (see Pennebaker, Paez, and Rimé, 1997; Liu *et al.*, 2005). As Liu, Sibley and Huang (2014) point out, it is difficult to imagine a debate about the war in Iraq, for example, without reference to 9/11, the Vietnam War or World War II.

Social representations of history are a relatively new empirical tool from which to examine dynamics of societal legitimacy for both the nation-state and for global society. Advances have been made in theory, methods, measurement, results and application. Trajectories of the development of human societies from the tribal to the state to the planetary, all have a history that can be told as fuel for the fire of either societal stability or change. Identity entrepreneurs like Nehru and Churchill have long understood that historical narratives are a key means to mobilizing political agendas, but social psychologists are only just beginning to examine how social representations of history can be responsible for producing national and international political cultures, as well as more personalized psychological phenomena like collective guilt.

By recourse to their expertise in psychometrics and experimental manipulation, social psychologists can add uniquely to the widespread interest across the social sciences and humanities about the role of social memory or collective remembering in producing historical accounts that shape the political behaviour of peoples and their political elites.

19 Social order and political legitimacy

Christian Staerklé

In the wake of pioneering research on societal psychology (Himmelweit and Gaskell, 1990) and widespread beliefs (Fraser and Gaskell, 1990), there has been an increase in interest in the representational processes underlying social order and political legitimacy during the last two decades (Doise, 1990; Duveen, 2001a, 2008; Elcheroth, Doise and Reicher, 2011; Gillespie, 2008; Joffe and Staerklé, 2007; Jovchelovitch, 2007; Moscovici, 1988; Sammut, 2011; Staerklé, 2009; Staerklé, Clémence and Spini, 2011; Wagner, Holtz and Kashima, 2009). Even though social representations research specifically addressing social order is scarce, many empirical studies (e.g. Howarth, 2006a; Liu and Hilton, 2005; Sarrasin *et al.*, 2012; Staerklé, Likki and Scheidegger, 2012) speak directly to issues of social order and social change.

The theory of social representations offers many insights into the conditions and processes that uphold or contest social order, especially when understood in conjunction with conversion and minority influence theory (Moscovici, 1980). This chapter outlines a social representations approach to social order from a societal perspective (Doise and Staerklé, 2002; Staerklé, 2011); such an account is necessarily rooted in systems of power and in the analysis of relations within and between social groups (Lorenzi-Cioldi and Clémence, 2001). A first section briefly describes some historical foundations of common social order thinking. I then describe central aspects of the social representations approach to social order and apply the distinction between the three communication modes described by Moscovici (1961/1976) – diffusion, propagation and propaganda – to account for three interrelated systems of legitimation and transformation of social order. In particular, I argue that attempts to stabilize and to challenge social order are shaped by communication processes between minority and majority groups trying to influence each other.

Consensus and conflict in explanations of social order

At the heart of the issue of social order stands the question that has eluded philosophers for centuries: what is the glue that holds a human community together? Why is an organized collective of individuals – a polity – stable and viewed as legitimate by its members? These are the fundamental questions underlying the issue of legitimacy. In its broadest sense, legitimacy refers to 'something' that is in line with the values, norms and beliefs of a collective (Zelditch, 2001). It is one of the oldest topics of political and social theories, in particular the concern with the legitimate forms of governance and hence with political stability. Most theories of legitimacy concur that social order can neither be upheld on the sole basis of power and coercion, nor on the basis of instrumental motives such as self-interest or group-interest. Instead, legitimacy requires some form of consent and voluntary acceptance that institutions, social practices and widely held beliefs are 'right' (see Chapter 16 in this volume). A prime indicator of legitimacy is the situation where even those groups and individuals who would gain from alternative forms of social order still accept existing arrangements and believe in a system that is not necessarily in their best interests (see Jost and Banaji, 1994).

A legitimate social order is based on perceptions, beliefs and values that can be organized as a function of the three classical fields of justice perceptions: distributive, procedural and retributive (see Deutsch, 1985). Distributive justice refers to perceived justice and injustice of the distribution of rewards, and thereby to the level of acceptability of social and economic inequality and the legitimacy of status hierarchies (Ridgeway, 2001). Procedural justice describes the legitimacy of power, reflected in submission and obedience to state authority and its various institutions (executive and legislative government branches, courts) (Tyler, 2001). Retributive justice, finally, accounts for processes of social control, in particular institutional responses to norm transgression, deviance and crime (Garland, 2001; Young, 1999). These types of justice perceptions function as interrelated organizing principles of social order; that is, positionings towards social order are likely to be organized along these justice perceptions. A given social order may, for example, be contested because inequalities are deemed inacceptable (distributive justice), because citizens do no trust their government (procedural justice), or because institutional control and repression are considered excessive (retributive justice).

Commonality and divergence of justice perceptions are central to explanations of social order. Theoretical accounts of social order follow two fundamental explanatory principles: consensus and conflict (Zelditch, 2001). Early perspectives on political legitimacy rooted in Enlightenment thinking have in common that their explanations of political legitimacy rely on shared and often consensual representations of what is 'good' for the society and of the principles guiding community life. Here, the upholding of the common good and the maintenance of a stable society requires citizens to believe in the same values and principles; that is, popular consensus about a society's guiding principles is paramount for social stability. Conversely, belief divergence and lack of consensus is likely to lead to political instability. For Rousseau, for example, legitimacy is based on the voluntary belief by all members of a society in the 'general will'. For Kant, legitimacy is grounded in public rationality and is based on the principle of one correct, rational solution to social order problems that is in the interest of all citizens. Like other consensus accounts, this view presupposes a homogeneous (national) community and similar interests among citizens. The consensuality logic reaches its fullest expression in the functionalist sociology by Talcott Parsons. In this view, a stable society is underpinned by consensual norms and values that all group members are expected to endorse. Any disagreement with common norms is viewed as a threat to the balance and stability of social order. Such a consensualist vision of social order is also found in Durkheim's early conceptualization of collective representations consensually shared among members of a community. The historical legacy of consent theory in contemporary approaches is evidenced in accounts that attribute the source of legitimacy either to a principle of public reason – following Kant – or to a theory of democratic approval – following Rousseau – or a combination of the two.

The shortcoming of consensualist views of social order is that they fail to account for disagreement with existing forms of social order and for conflict between groups supporting different models of social order. The legitimacy of social order can never be taken for granted, because alternative ways to organize society and to define its priorities always exist. This is where the second broad logic of explanations of social order based on conflict comes into play (Zelditch, 2001). Two main features characterize a conflict view of social order. First, it is grounded in the assumption of conflicting interests in a society, in particular between groups defined by low and high positions in the social hierarchy. It thereby explains the circumstances under which discontent gives rise to minority movements claiming rights and promoting new forms of social order. A second feature of a conflict view is that social order is achieved through the control of ideological meaning systems and practices by which relations of power and dominance are justified and upheld (Foucault, 1975). In order to bring citizens to voluntarily believe in the system and thus to achieve legitimacy, the ruling class and associated interest groups need to mask their real interests. This logic is most clearly expressed in Marxian accounts of social order where the concept of false consciousness refers to the idea that people are unaware of the real stakes in a society.

A social representations approach to social order

A social representations approach offers insights regarding the social processes underlying legitimacy and social order. Since their inception, representations have been viewed as specific types of knowledge enabling communication and *organizing social relations* (Doise, 1985, 1990; Moscovici, 1961/1976). The concept of social order and the theory of social representations are therefore intimately intertwined. This link becomes even more apparent when considering change and stability as a key dialectic in both concepts. The interplay between change and stability is at the heart of the theory social representations (Duveen, 2001a), and this interaction is also constitutive of the object of representation, namely social order. The extreme case of a completely frozen social order – as imagined by dark totalitarian and other authoritarian-minded spirits – is an order of total social control where any attempt to change is repressed as a sign of hostility against the rulers. Complete instability, in turn, is found in contexts with rapidly shifting and unpredictable power relations, for example in large-scale revolutions and upheavals. Democratic debates about social order reflect this constant tension between the maintenance of existing social arrangements and demands for social change.

On the level of everyday communication, a similar tension between communication oriented towards stability and towards change can be found. Social representational approaches to social influence have analyzed communication modes in the public sphere that oppose everyday communication oriented towards common understanding, consensuality and stability to strategic communication oriented towards shaping others' thoughts and behaviours (Sammut and Bauer, 2011). Strategic communication thus aims at achieving social change through attempts to persuade others of a given point of view, thereby accepting conflict between representations (see Gillespie, 2008).

Given its double focus on change and stability, a social representations view of social order takes up and articulates elements of both consensus and conflict theories. In line with a conflict view of social order, consent is neither seen as a necessary precondition for social stability nor as a routine outcome of community life. Instead, it has to be actively and strategically produced, eventually leading to hegemonic representations (Augoustinos, 1998). Such a view takes into account the fundamentally contested and dynamic nature of social order in contemporary societies, that is, it is rooted in a social psychology of conflict and influence between groups with unequal power and status (Moscovici, 1980; Duveen, 2001a). The recognition of constant encounters between competing social order representations has led Moscovici to develop the concept of social representations as an alternative to the consensualist notion of Durkheim's collective representation. And recently this approach grounded in the inherent pluralism of societies in late modernity has given rise to new developments in the theory of social representations that deal with the negotiation and the psychological consequences of multiple values and discourses (Gillespie, 2008) and with the role of social representations in intercultural encounters (Sammut and Gaskell, 2010).

In order to engage, formally or informally, in social order debates, citizens must know what is at stake, that is, they must be able to refer to common frames of symbolic reference points which enable democratic discussion and contestation around issues of social order (Doise, Clémence and Lorenzi-Cioldi, 1993). As an example of a widely disseminated frame of reference in social order debates, we can think of the question of priority of rights or duties in models of social order. Some forms of social order prioritize community-based duties of the individual and their subordination to the collective interests of the group, whereas others emphasize individual rights that have fundamental priority over community rights (Finkel and Moghaddam, 2005). Such a distinction thus organizes the representations invoked in public debates about social order.

Recent research has started to explore such frames of reference – organizing principles – underlying lay thinking on social order (Sammut, 2011; Scheidegger and Staerklé, 2011; Staerklé *et al.*, 2012). Illustrating the renewed interest in issues of social order, the Social Order Representations Model (Staerklé, 2009) provides a framework for analyzing the relationship between cognitive processes and social representations associated with social order. It distinguishes four generic social order representations: *moral order*, *free market*, *social diversity* and *structural inequality*. These representations refer to four normative models of social order that are used as common frames of reference in political and everyday debates about the guiding principles of a society. The model assumes that particular belief systems (authoritarianism, work ethic, multiculturalism/racism and egalitarianism/social dominance, respectively) provide legitimacy and thereby sustain each type of social order.

Moreover, the model emphasizes the centrality of difference within representations. Representations of social order are at play in processes of social inclusion and social exclusion, for example when group boundaries are negotiated in debates about welfare rights of immigrants or when antagonisms between social groups ('us vs. them') are strategically put forward by interest groups. The model therefore puts the basic psychological process of social differentiation (Tajfel, 1978) at the centre of the analysis and proposes that two forms of differentiation structure social order thinking: normative differentiation that establishes boundaries between norm-conforming and norm-violating in-group members (in the moral order and free market models), and categorical differentiation that creates boundaries between groups defined by self-declared or ascribed group membership (in the social diversity and structural inequality models) (see the Dual Process Model by Duckitt, 2001, for a similar distinction). The social functions of these two forms of differentiation will be discussed below in the sections on propagation and propaganda forms of communication.

More broadly, a social order analysis emphasizes the centrality of processes of categorization and differentiation in social representations theory and research (see Wagner and Hayes, 2005). In this manner, such an analysis joins the call for the theoretical necessity of *representations of difference* that are able to account for the various ways individuals deal with contemporary pluralism (Gillespie, 2008). In this view, social differentiation helps individuals to subjectively define boundaries between social groups, based on shared and widespread definitions of the cleavages that structure social life (Lamont and Molnar, 2002). Differentiation thereby translates societal value conflicts into a psychological process that opposes positively evaluated groups to negatively evaluated groups and ultimately determines perceived entitlements of social categories. Hence, social categorization and labelling of groups is a social struggle in itself (Bourdieu, 1979/1984; Reicher and Hopkins, 2001) and is in this way part of the legitimization process of social order. Processes of differentiation are also a prominent part of political theories that highlight the regulation of intergroup relations and the key role of perceived and constructed antagonisms between groups in democratic politics (e.g. Mouffe, 1993). These theories converge in the idea that the political process is fundamentally concerned with the regulation of relations between groups representing contrasting norms, values and interests.

In the remainder of this chapter I will show how pluralism of representations and differentiation motives can be linked to the communication and dissemination of social order representations. An extended and adapted approach to the classical distinction between the three modes of communication – diffusion, propagation and propaganda (Moscovici, 1961/1976) – appears useful for such an approach. In Moscovici's original conceptualization, the three modes were each associated with a specific form of knowledge: loose and fluctuating opinions were the typical form of knowledge in the diffusion mode, more firmly held attitudes were put forward in the propagation mode, and rigid stereotypes were the typical communication tools in the propaganda mode.

Duveen (2008) refers to this taxonomy to describe different forms of in-group affiliation defined by these 'communicative genres'. Groups organized through diffusion are bound together in sympathy, those based on propagation are bound in communion, and propaganda groups are characterized by solidarity. The taxonomy has also been taken up in a dialogical perspective of the theory of social representations (e.g. Gillespie, 2008; Sammut and Bauer, 2011; Sammut and Gaskell, 2010). Here, the modes of communication refer to varying degrees of openness to other representations. The diffusion mode is seen as a closed, monological system of communication that does not allow for difference and contestation. The propagation mode entails the possibility of dialogue with other, legitimate representations, but retains the aim of asserting its rightfulness in the face of other representations. The propaganda mode is based on conflict and competition with other representations. Yet, at the same time propaganda may also be meta-logical, as it questions its own veracity and considers that other representations could actually be more right than one's own point of view. Somewhat ironically, then, this conflict-based model is the only communication mode that has the potential to overcome difference and turn the diversity of points of view typical of late modernity into a societal strength. It should be noted, though, that in some analyses the three modes of communication from the *Psychoanalysis* are conflated with the three types of hegemonic, emancipated and polemic representations (Moscovici, 1988). These two taxonomies clearly share important features since they are in many respects structurally similar. Nevertheless, it seems beneficial to keep the two concepts separate, because the former refers to communication modes and the latter to the representational outcomes of communication.

For the purpose of the analysis of social order representations, a more political or ideological use of the taxonomy is put forward by associating the communication modes with processes of influence occurring between groups defined by unequal positions in the social hierarchy: diffusion refers to undifferentiated ('diffuse') influence of dominant, hegemonic representations; propagation describes processes of majority influence and their strategic attempts to construe consent around their ideas; and propaganda is associated with minority influence aimed at resisting majorities and promoting social change. In this view, the three types of influence are interdependent with each other, they may occur simultaneously, and the three of them are required to account for the legitimization and contestation processes of social order. The interplay between modes of communication and intergroup settings gives rise to different models of social influence and emphasizes the dynamic nature of a representational analysis of social order.

Diffusion: emergence and spread of social order beliefs

The diffusion mode accounts for the creation and dissemination of objectified beliefs and values justifying social order. In its original formulation, diffusion describes how information is disseminated in an undifferentiated manner, that is, without clearly identifiable sources or targets of communication. Diffusion is therefore a normalization process that produces terms of reference (Sammut and Bauer, 2011). In a social order account, diffusion disseminates social order representations in society and provides citizens with the 'raw material' through which they are able to make sense of and understand issues of social order. Disseminated social order representations orient citizens' thinking and provide normative signposts through which they can understand and engage in societal debates. They provide cues as to the importance of different values in a society and highlight potential threats to a stable social order based on these values.

The channels of communication of diffusion are either indirect (mass media) or direct (informal, interpersonal discussions). Tabloid and free commuter newspapers, for example, relate various events (elections, natural disasters, international conflicts, economic crises, etc.) without justifying their position or taking up a consistent stance towards them. Rather, information is circulated as a function of opportunistic commercial criteria. Media thereby contribute to the undifferentiated diffusion of multiple opinions and contrasting points of view among the public. Advertisements triggering the activation of ideological values (e.g. through the praise of the individualizing nature of consumer products) also contribute to the diffusion of social order beliefs, as do informal private discussions on social order topics. The dynamics of the cultural distribution of social order beliefs has been analyzed in studies on the emergence and spread of representations (Sperber, 1990). Diffusion thus gives rise to the 'common field' of representations, made up by unquestioned and shared but not consensual reference points which individuals refer to in their debates about social order (Doise, Clémence and Lorenzi-Cioldi, 1993).

Recent survey studies have, for example, analyzed the emergence and development over time of representations of infectious diseases such as avian influenza, that represent a public health threat to social order (Gilles *et al.*, 2013; Mayor *et al.*, 2013). Through the temporal analysis of media coverage of disease outbreaks, this research shows the rise and fall of representations associated with the disease threat and demonstrates that symbolic in-group protection ('othering') occurs during the stage of divergence of representations, characterized by an uncertain symbolic environment (see also Bangerter and Heath, 2004). Other survey research on the impact of 'ideological climates', in turn, has shown how conservative municipalities in Switzerland (assessed with municipality-level results of actual popular referenda over a decade) exert an influence on attitudes towards racial policies, over and above individual-level determinants (Sarrasin *et al.*, 2012).

It is in the diffusion phase that knowledge legitimizing or delegitimizing social order enters the public arena, readily shaped into concrete and socially useful forms by processes of objectification (see Jovchelovitch, 2007). A powerful way to objectify abstract social order values such as freedom, equality or responsibility is to associate them with concrete stereotypes of social groups. Joffe and Staerklé (2007) have shown how the ethic of self-control, a key value of western societies, is objectified into stereotypical images of social categories useful for judging and evaluating people. Through this process, the self-control value is transformed and objectified into antagonistic stereotypes opposing those perceived to be conforming to the value (e.g. 'responsible citizens with high levels of self-control') to those disrespecting and violating the value (e.g. 'lazy, self-indulging scroungers').

Ultimately, the diffusion process may give rise to pervasive large-scale social order narratives and systems of social classification which define historical eras and societies. These historically developed representations of social order may take on the form of 'hegemonic' representations (Moscovici, 1988) towards which citizens positions themselves. The contemporary period can be said to be characterized by two intertwined dominating representational systems, one known as neoliberalism, the other as neoconservatism (Young, 1999). Neoliberalism incorporates individualism and the fundamental creed in the 'sovereign individual', reflecting the centrality of individual achievement, self-control, the freedom of individuals to maximize self-interest and participate in social life according to their own motivations and needs (Augoustinos, 1998). This belief system is at the root of contemporary individualistic societies with their distinctive articulation of individual freedom and liberal submissiveness (Beauvois, 1994). Neoconservatism, in turn, stresses the necessity of norm compliance and enforcement, in particular with respect to harsh punitive treatment of deviant and non-conforming groups and individuals (Garland, 2001). These widespread belief systems incorporate a large array of shared reference points to which citizens and policy-makers alike may refer in their defence of specific conceptions of social order. Both are hegemonic representations: pervasive (but not consensual), colouring all aspects of social life, fluid, and malleable. Diffusion, therefore, implies neither consensus nor submission to hegemonic representations, since citizens may refute or oppose them.

Overall, the diffusion mode provides representational content to social order debates without strong normative pressure to endorse this content. Such normative pressures are, however, implied by propagation and propaganda modes of communication.

Propagation: the majority view and the production of consent

Once social order beliefs have penetrated common sense, they may be strategically invoked by social groups and institutions to provide legitimacy to those types of social order that further their interests. This is the propagation phase that is concerned with the purposeful creation of consent by majority groups that aim to maintain or extend their dominant position in society (see Glasser and Salmon, 1995). Majority groups structure the debate and (re)organize the information according to their norms and values – the 'spin' of political communication. The communication process is framed in such terms as to provide cues for citizens who wish to form an opinion. In contrast to diffusion, propagation is strategic and goal-oriented, as it seeks to persuade others of a specific point of view. The majority group calls upon experts, lobbies and think-tanks to affirm and justify its position. This phase is an attempt to disseminate a consistent way of looking at an issue, with often sophisticated communication strategies destined to impose a representation in order to make it hegemonic and subjectively valid in the eyes of a majority. This process of legitimation also aims to make the unacceptable acceptable, for example through justification (denying that a given situation or behaviour is wrong) and excuse (accepting that a situation or a behaviour is problematic, but denying responsibility for it). Majorities with hegemonic motivations are therefore actively engaged in disseminating representations in order to make them appear normal and to be taken-for-granted.

The production of consent is made possible by some form of ideological machinery that purposefully and strategically attempts to shape mass opinion. Many powerful organisms – political parties and governments, multinational corporations and financial organizations – have a vested interest to fabricate consent around representations that support their cause and provide legitimacy to it. These groups may attempt to impose representations by exerting a strict control on the content and form of public communication (media control) and on the language used therein (e.g. 'job creators' instead of 'wealthy' or 'rich' people, as suggested by the US Republican Party). Through such channels, ideological domination and eventually hegemony of certain representations can be achieved. A historical example of propagation is 'orientalism' (Said, 1978), a communications strategy enacted by western governments and elites in the nineteenth century to set 'us' Europeans apart against all 'those' non-Europeans. The goal of western elites was to justify their colonialist crusades by convincing European populations of the intrinsic superiority of European forms of social order. Traces of orientalism are still found in contemporary representations of democratic and non-democratic countries (Falomir et al., 2005; Staerklé, Clémence and Doise, 1998).

This view of the propagation process as a strategy to impose representations bears some resemblance with the Marxist 'dominant ideology hypothesis' according to which hegemonic and virtually inescapable ideologies are disseminated in society by powerful ruling groups. Yet, citizens are not passive receivers of such attempts to make representations hegemonic (see Augoustinos, 1998). The 'dominant ideology' thesis does not, therefore, imply that all citizens are under the sway of a single dominant worldview; rather, it suggests that citizens are surrounded by a normative environment that exerts pressures to adopt elements of dominant ideologies (for example, in educational and professional settings). Notwithstanding such pressures, citizens may still choose to accept or refute such representations in order to form their own positioning towards social order (Billig, 1991; Moscovici, 1988). Such variability is illustrated in a study on the group-level anchoring of orthodox beliefs showing that neoliberal free-market beliefs were more strongly endorsed by students in business and in law (compared to students in social sciences), especially by those who were confident in their own knowledge of economic issues (Scheidegger and Tuescher, 2010). These findings highlight the anchoring of hegemonic beliefs in specific subgroups and show that subjective certainty reinforces these beliefs.

Propagation may sometimes lead to a highly influential, hegemonic belief system to which members of a given subgroup are firmly committed. In a series of experimental studies on orthodoxy, Deconchy (1990) has demonstrated the protective mechanisms in an 'orthodox' group that defines itself by strong adherence of group norms, for example religious groups. Such groups tend to maintain their beliefs even in the light of overwhelming disconfirming evidence. Deconchy's main hypothesis is that when external challenges make apparent the rational fragility and weakness of a given belief within an orthodox group, the group enacts defensive strategies to protect its foundational beliefs: it reaffirms the normative legitimacy of its beliefs and expresses demands for social and institutional control, in particular in terms of control of group membership. A similar defensive propagation process may be at work when dominant groups defend theories against overwhelming evidence that they do not accurately account for 'real-world' problems. An example of such a desperate attempt to salvage majority domination concerns the stubborn defence by leading economists of the normative idea of individual rationality and self-interest on which most economic theories are based, even in the aftermath of the financial crisis in 2008 that should have shaken up the normative foundations of the capitalist system. Another example concerns the resistance with which the industrial lobby and associated political parties meet the ever-growing evidence of global climate change.

Propagation is thus typically a form of *majority influence* whereby an in-group source of influence exerts pressure to normative conformity by highlighting the symbolic benefits of conformism ('true citizens believe X') and pointing out negative effects of rejecting the majority point of view ('the country is doomed if too many people believe Y'). Classical research on reference groups highlights the impact of positive and negative reference groups, which serve as important points of orientation when citizens form their attitudes towards social order (e.g. Newcomb, 1946; Sherif and Sherif, 1964). Citizens are urged to comply with the majority in order to be accepted as group members by other majority members and to receive social validation of their opinion. Propagation thereby underscores the importance of 'meta-representations', that is, beliefs about what other people believe. This concept is akin to Noelle-Neumann's (1993) spiral of silence theory, which explains political behaviour in terms of what people perceive to be the majority opinion in a given context (see Elcheroth, Doise and Reicher, 2011, for a discussion). From a propagation perspective, such meta-representations are instrumentalized by interest groups ('most people trust in this institution, so should you') in order to persuade citizens to endorse positions consistent with their interests.

In propagation mode, the source of influence positions itself as the majority of a superordinate group or otherwise as the legitimate representative of a social category. It presents itself as defender of the 'real' values of the group, that is, it strategically positions itself as the group's prototype. Thereby, it attempts to persuade others (the general population, a competitor group or minority groups) of the validity of its worldview. 'Majority' is therefore a flexible and ambiguous concept that may shift as a function of the way majorities and minorities are categorized. Claiming that one's position reflects (implicitly or explicitly) a majority position is a strategic and rhetoric construction in itself that aims to provide legitimacy to the source of influence (Stevenson, Condor and Abell, 2007). More generally, the exact content of propagation communication depends on the communicative setting, defined by a categorization process that defines the (majority) identity of the source of influence on the one hand, and the identity of the target group, that is, the audience, on the other (see Klein, Spears and Reicher, 2007).

With respect to the above-mentioned types of differentiation, it could be expected that consent-seeking majority influence in propagation is most effectively served by a process of normative differentiation that establishes boundaries as a function of perceived or constructed conformity with important norms and values (Staerklé, 2009). Through this communicative strategy, value pluralism is made illegitimate, since all group members are expected to endorse the very values advocated by majority groups, and these values provide the unique symbolic referents through which citizens are judged. Social cleavages can therefore be presented as the outcome of deliberate individual actions – for example, in the myth of the lazy poor and the hard-working rich – and the boundaries between categories as permeable (anyone can work hard if they want to).

The stabilizing function of normative differentiation stems from the fact that any deviation by in-group members from such values (e.g. the work ethic, self-reliance, obedience, tolerance) can be constructed as a potential threat to a social order based on these values. As a result, it becomes legitimate to discredit individuals on the basis of perceived norm transgression, which at the same time reinforces the validity of dominant norms. Mitt Romney, for example, during his 2012 US presidential campaign, divided the nation into 'winners' and complaining 'victims'. In his system of differentiation, 47 per cent of the American population was lazily scrounging from the rest of the population, implying that almost half of the population are not as motivated or hard-working as the 'tax-paying' majority. In Gillespie's (2008) terms, normative differentiation by majority groups creates a caricature-like alternative representation of minorities that has a stabilizing function, as it protects the main representation from the challenge of alternatives.

To sum up, propagation in the sense of a social order approach relies on normative differentiation through which dominant majorities take the liberty to judge 'silent' individuals and groups as a function of their own set of norms and values. Propagation is therefore a defensive strategy of protection of dominant belief systems; a stigmatizing strategy that does not shy away of purposefully encouraging exclusion in order to produce consent around issues of social order.

Propaganda: the minority view

The third mode of communication, propaganda, is a destabilizing force for representations since it accounts for resistance to dominant social order representations and thereby makes dissent and social change possible. Compared to majorities, minorities and subordinate groups have fewer resources with which to advance their positions. A different communication strategy is therefore called for, one that asserts more forcefully and with less compromise a given position *in opposition* to dominant majority positions. The propaganda strategy can be associated with minority influence as described in Moscovici's conversion theory (1980). Minorities put forward representations that propose an alternative to dominant social arrangements. The social function of propaganda is to rally in-group members around a coherent position that stands in contrast to a given majority perspective, thereby contesting hegemonic forms of social order (see Klein et al., 2007). Entering into a confrontational relation with majorities, minorities advance firm and unyielding claims in order to achieve social change.

In the symbolic battlefield over the legitimacy of different representations of social order, majorities attempt to maintain their dominant position by resisting minority influence. As long as majorities are able to oppose minority influence attempts, the network of social influence is stable, representations upholding social order become normalized and naturalized, and existing social arrangements are maintained (Duveen, 2001a). Innovative minority positions often trigger defensive reactions by the majority. Gillespie (2008) has argued that alternative representations (promoted by minorities) are isolated from dominant representations through various communicational strategies ('semantic barriers'), for example, rigid ideological opposition and deliberate stigmatization of particular representations or representors (e.g. the mainstream media treatment of minority or protest movements). A similar process has also been shown in minority influence studies where the 'psychologization' of minorities is used as a majority strategy to discredit minorities and thereby undermine their influence attempts (Papastamou, 1983).

This precarious and temporary balance of the intergroup influence system may shift, however, through active attempts by minorities to put forward new or modified social representations of social order (see Howarth, 2006a), that is, through collective action (Reicher, 2004). There are numerous examples of innovative social order representations introduced by minority movements engaging in propaganda strategies, in particular the recognition of rights of women and homosexuals, a greater awareness of environmental issues and more recently anti-globalization and anti-finance movements (see Isin and Wood, 1999). This view of intergroup communication is in line with conflict theories of social order as it acknowledges not only the legitimacy of dissent but also its necessity as a driving force for social change. Minorities contest the legitimacy of a single, hegemonic order valid for all as implied by the consent seeking majority strategies of propagation. Instead, they show that alternative routes exist, based on a confrontational communication strategy that questions the legitimacy of dominant social order representations. In this view, conflict between groups defending opposing perspectives is fundamentally positive – an indispensable relation to achieve social progress and political change.

Research in the minority influence tradition has shown that minorities are able to exert social influence to the extent that the message recipients engage in a process of validation of the message that eventually leads to conversion (Moscovici, 1980). In order to be validated, a minority message needs to provide a clear alternative to prevailing norms, recipients must focus on the message itself rather than on the message bearer, and the message has to be advocated with both consistency and flexibility by the minorities (see Mugny and Pérez, 1991). Minorities need to induce a sociocognitive conflict in order to be taken seriously and to exert influence. The difficulty for minorities is that in order for their influence attempts to be effective, they must manage not only to be perceived as a valid alternative to dominant norms, but also be categorized as a group whose positions are not completely incompatible with prevailing in-group norms. Otherwise, propagation strategies by majorities retain the upper hand as minorities can be portrayed as a simple out-group that may legitimately be discredited due to its unconventional point of view. In short, minorities need to be similar and different at the same time: they need to advocate new norms in order to be differentiated from majority norms, but they also need to strategically redefine representations and systems of categorization such that they are no longer perceived as posing a threat to the identity of the majority group (see also Billig, 1985).

Propaganda also differs from propagation in terms of the most effective differentiation strategy. If normative categorization is the strategy of choice of majorities (because it implies a single normative referent), then minorities need to assert their position and their social identity as a valid alternative that cannot be judged as a simple deviation from majority norms. This can be achieved through categorical differentiation whereby group norms are pitted against each other, as opposed to normative differentiation whereby individuals are categorized as a function of their normative conformity. Put another way, successful propaganda requires a collective strategy (Tajfel, 1978) through which active minorities engage as self-conscious group members in a power struggle based on politicized collective identities (Simon and Klandermans, 2001). This self-categorization as members of a cohesive minority group leads to the hypothesis that the protest function of the propaganda mode of communication is best served by categorical differentiation that creates an opposition between antagonistic minority and majority group norms. In categorical differentiation, intergroup boundaries are represented as impermeable, for example between ethnic minorities and majorities, between protest groups and elites, or between groups with different sexual orientations. This type of categorization is able to induce social change because it gives minorities a clearly defined identity and a 'voice' that provides them with the opportunity to disseminate new norms, thereby introducing an alternative to dominant norms.

The articulation between intergroup influence and the three communication modes is thus a central feature of a social representational account of social order. While there is a sequential logic to the three communication systems (social order beliefs need to be disseminated before they can be strategically defended by majorities and subsequently contested by minorities), the model is also recursive: contesting majority perspectives, minorities put forward new models of social order (propaganda) which, if received favourably, become disseminated (diffusion) and eventually advocated by new majorities (propagation). In other words, formerly minority positions may become majority positions, thereby attesting the dynamic nature of the representational process (Moghaddam, 2006b).

Conclusion

This chapter proposes a social representations approach to social order and political legitimacy rooted in a social psychology of power and inequality. A brief historical overview has evidenced two major explanatory principles of social order based on consensus and conflict. It is argued that a social representations approach combines these two foundations of social order, one whose function is to stabilize social order representations (consent-seeking propagation) and one whose function is to destabilize them (conflict-seeking propaganda). A social order approach to social representations therefore relies on the articulation of processes of minority and majority influence with the three classical communication modes of diffusion, propagation and propaganda.

Diffusion is presented as an undifferentiated and non-strategic system of dissemination of social order representations leading to widespread, diffuse and hegemonic social order representations, thereby creating the normative context in which intergroup power struggles over legitimate social order representations are played out. Propagation is associated with majority influence and described as a defensive strategy of active consent-seeking by self-declared majorities, thereby reflecting stabilizing functions of social order. Propaganda, in turn, is linked to minority influence and thus accounts for social change and to the contestation of dominant social order representations. Various social psychological mechanisms at work within these three modes of communication have been described, in particular normative and categorical differentiation accounting for social stability and social change, respectively. Overall, the chapter has aimed to demonstrate the integrative potential of a social representations approach to social order. Such an approach offers insights for the study of pressing social order issues in contemporary societies, many of which can be analyzed from the perspective of representations of social order and political legitimacy.

20 Social representations of sustainability: researching time, institution, conflict and communication

Paula Castro

The purpose of this chapter is to present and discuss some of the contributions the theory of social representations can offer for a better understanding of the socio-psychological dimensions involved in environmental and ecological protection and sustainability and for advancing research in these areas. The chapter does not aim to be an exhaustive review of existing knowledge about the human dimensions of environmental and sustainability problems and solutions. Instead, its main goal is to formulate some of the substantive contributions the approach of social representations has recently made and can continue to make to the field of *social studies of sustainability*; this is broadly defined as a multidisciplinary field researching the social and psychological dimensions of sustainability and related topics, such as environmental concern, environmental protection and climate change. The chapter will illustrate these contributions by presenting studies explicitly drawing on the social representations approach and clearly expressing what can be gained by resorting to it.

The chapter is structured in three sections. The first part briefly describes the emergence of concern over environmental protection and the naissance of the field of social studies of sustainability. The second part outlines the theoretical contributions that the theory of social representations – as a social-psychological approach – has to offer for advancing research in this field. I propose that drawing on the theory of social representations encourages researchers to take into account four main dimensions: time, institution, conflict and communication. Finally, the empirical illustrations follow.

The emergence of modern environmental concern

The *emergence phase* of modern concerns over environmental and ecological protection dates from the post-war years; at this time 'green' concerns, and the social movements and minority groups battling for them, were very much associated with the values of 'counter-culture' and with criticizing consumerism and over-reliance on technology (Castro, 2006; Douglas and Wildavsky, 1982;

Wynne, 2002). The same period saw the first steps towards international cooperation to deal with environmental problems. For instance, it was in 1948 that the United Nations created the International Union for the Preservation of Nature.

The 1970s saw the start of the second phase of modern environmentalism: the *institutionalization phase*. Steps at this time included the organization of international conferences, the signing of international treaties, the issuing of national legislation and the creation of environmental ministries and green parties. It was also during this decade that the major environmental NGOs were founded. These steps were accompanied by a more generalized and less critical environmental concern, which was visible in many countries around the world (Dunlap, 2008).

During the 1980s and 1990s these trends were consolidated and a *generalization phase* began (Castro and Mouro, 2011). In this period polls showed growing public concern over environmental problems and the notion of 'sustainable development' was forged. It quickly became a reference concept, which helped unify discourses and advance social consensus (Castro, 2012; Uzzell and Räthzel, 2009). In the post-war years 'green' critics had raised objections to 'development' as entailing an excessive consumption of resources; however, when 'development' became qualified as 'sustainable', the resulting expression became acceptable and influential (Uzzell and Räthzel, 2009). Today the omnipresent and conciliatory notion of 'sustainable development' is so broad that even groups with diverging goals can find their interests represented in it.

Within the European Union, sustainable development has been instrumental in providing a rationale for the many environmental laws and directives that have been issued in the last two decades (Castro, 2012). The main focus of the generalization phase among EU member states was – and remains – the attempt to achieve generalized change towards sustainability at a national level, spreading fully-fledged accommodation of and obedience to the sets of new and complex legislations already in place and regulating domestic, industrial and corporate waste management, energy options, water conservation, transport options, biodiversity protection or the management of electric residues.

The social sciences, with social psychology among them, tried to monitor and understand these new trends and transformations as they unfolded. As a result, a multidisciplinary field of studies was created that strived to understand the human and social dimensions of environmental problems and (possible) solutions, and to map public positions in this regard. This field – which I propose to call 'social studies of sustainability' – first endeavoured to study the 'socio-demographic factors associated with environmentalism' and the 'values, beliefs and other social psychological constructs related to environmentalism' (Dietz, Stern and Guagnano, 1998, p. 451). Methodologically, these tasks were initially mostly pursued through questionnaire-based studies.

During the first thirty years the field showed some theoretical and methodological fragmentation, and research questions of a dynamic type – such as how different environmental beliefs reflect intergroup conflict – were incipient or even lacking (Castro, 2006). In more recent years, however, it has expanded in various directions and the core metaphors around which it is organized have also extended. Regarding core metaphors, the trajectory has gone from *environmental concern* to *sustainability* and now to *climate change*. During the first decades, as mentioned above, research was focussed on understanding how people made sense of environmental protection goals, looking for instance at how subscribing to certain types of values (e.g. biospheric values) predicted environmental concern (Dietz, Stern and Guagnano, 1998). In the years that followed studies also began to address in a more systematic way how sense-making was linked to action and how people's ideas, norms and behaviours could be changed in order to achieve sustainability. More recent times have seen a preoccupation with how climate change is understood, represented in the media, and what people are doing or failing to do in order to mitigate its consequences. Cutting across the core metaphors, some applied topics have remained relatively stable over these years. Resource conservation – including recycling, energy and water conservation – biodiversity protection and natural resource management, pollution problems and the use of new and renewable energy sources, green purchasing and transportation options are key topics that have been systematically researched.

Recent overviews characterize the field as continuing to pay too much attention to the individual level of analysis, relying excessively on the premise that achieving social change mainly means remodelling the behaviour of individuals (Uzzell and Räthzel, 2009; Castro, 2012), and offering special attention to sustainability problems that can be solved from the consumption side and not enough consideration to those that can be dealt with through production (Uzzell and Räthzel, 2009). Studies have also given more attention to private-sphere behaviours than to public-sphere behaviours, often forgetting the professional and citizen dimensions of people's intersection with sustainability matters (Castro, 2012). Consequently, research has not always looked at how social change towards sustainability also means remodelling the relations among certain groups involved in the production and transformation of 'green' discourses and proposals (Harré, Brockmeier and Muhlhausler, 1999), and/or between these and certain societal institutions, and has therefore failed to actively stimulate the engagement of the field with policy and decision-makers (Spence and Pidgeon, 2010).

In this context, studies informed by the theory of social representations have made a number of significant contributions, which helped in advancing research towards a less individual and introverted perspective, looking instead at more dynamic questions. I hope to show in a later section that the theory of social representations has the potential to continue to do this. Before that, however, I will very briefly present the central aspects of the theory that fashion and position it as instrumental for contributing to the field of social studies of sustainability by integrating and expanding it.

An outline of the potential contributions of the theory of social representations

In social psychology there are two main types of approach aimed at understanding how people interpret and make sense of the world (Vala and Castro, 2013). The first type offers primacy to social factors and interaction. The second type focusses on cognitive factors and the processing of information. The theory of social representations belongs to the first tradition, the one looking at how social factors and social relations inform sense-making. There are other theories and approaches that look at these same aspects, such as those that focus on social norms. Yet the theory of social representations offers an epistemological specificity: the positioning of the dialogical triangle self–object–alter as the condition of emergence of representations (Moscovici, 1972; Marková, 2008). This epistemological positioning means that the theory of social representations sees relations as the locus of meaning-making, or the locus of interpretation of objects.

Two major consequences follow from the assumption that the ego–alter relation is the locus of meaning-making. First, that there can be no meaning-making outside a culture, and second, that there can be no meaning-making outside a given interactional context. In other words, the two consequences are that all representation is doubly situated: it has a cultural component and a contextual component (Vala and Castro, 2013). Let us look at each in turn.

By highlighting the cultural component, the theory of social representations reminds us that 'we absorb social representations, starting in infancy, together with other elements of our culture and with our mother tongue' (Moscovici and Marková, 2000, p. 253). It therefore recalls that there is no reason to believe that we 'are like Adam on the day of his creation, opening his eyes on animals and other things, deprived of tradition, lacking shared concepts with which to coordinate his sensory impressions' (Moscovici, 1998, p. 215). In other words, the theory of social representations reminds us that when we are born we immediately enter traditions of meaning as well as traditions of meaning-making.

This is equal to reminding us that representations – while speaking of an object – also express the cultural and social forms that exist in a time and a space, rather than expressing timeless and spaceless objects. In turn, because culture is always grounded and actualized in institutions, this amounts to reminding us that 'While representations are often to be located in the minds of men and women, they can just as often be found "in the world" and as such examined separately' (Moscovici, 1998, p. 214). Approaching a culture and its institutions involves looking at its representations in the world, or in time and space, and therefore implies looking at stability. Yet focussing on culture obviously also means acknowledging that institutions evolve and change. So in sum, since no culture exists without both stability and change, research drawing on the theory of social representations needs to include the temporal and the institutional dimensions.

Including the temporal dimension when conducting social studies of sustainability means asking questions that will bring into focus the temporal aspects involved in how people deal with the changes required to implement environmental protection and sustainability goals. In turn, the inclusion of the institutional dimension means acknowledging that some representations enter specific cultural and societal structures, that is, are institutionalized, for instance through laws and regulations. This endows them with a particular power, and calls attention to the fact that some representations are formal, quite stable and institutionally decided. Yet it naturally also calls attention to the fact that not all representations are institutionalized; this therefore brings to the fore the fact that representations are not all equal and undoubtedly do not voice equally well all the groups that a society harbours at a given moment in time (Moscovici, 1988; Jovchelovitch, 2007; Castro, 2012; Howarth, 2006a). This makes conflict – among different representations and different groups – a third dimension, together with the temporal dimension and the institutional dimension, that needs to be considered by studies drawing on the theory of social representations. It also means that, while looking at conflict, it is important to contemplate what type of representation – hegemonic, emancipated or polemic (Moscovici, 1988) – is being discussed.

The second consequence of having the dialogical triangle at the centre of meaning-making is, as mentioned, that there can be no sense-making outside a specific interactional context. By highlighting this aspect, the theory recalls that sense-making orients us towards the specific Other of concrete relationships, not just the generic Other of culture. So it calls attention to what is or may be contingent, informal, context- and relation-specific in representation. Again, this calls for taking the time dimension seriously, as no relations exist outside a project, that is, without a projection into an anticipated future (Bauer and Gaskell, 2008).

The combination of the two aspects – culture and context – brings an actor forward who, in communicating and in thinking, in relating and in musing about relations, is always responding simultaneously to the generic alter of culture and the concrete alter of the interactional context. An actor who, in representing, pays attention to what is happening here and now, but also to what is continuously made present through cultural institutions. In order to understand this actor, the field of social studies of sustainability must look at how communication, language and discourse continuously link the cultural and the contextual, the institutional and the contingent (Castro and Batel, 2008). And therefore communication is a fourth dimension to be taken into account.

In sum, then: a field of social studies of sustainability informed by the approach of social representations needs to examine the four dimensions of time, institution, conflict and communication. A number of recent research programmes explicitly reclaiming their link with the theory of social representations have indeed combined several of these four dimensions. I shall now illustrate how they did this, describing their main assumptions and findings, and showing how they intertwine all or some of the four dimensions in different ways, extracting clear research consequences and results from them. By doing so I shall simultaneously attempt to better substantiate what it concretely means to look at time, institutions, conflict and communication from the theory of social representations perspective. I will divide the next section into two parts, one including studies in which the dimensions of time and institution are particularly relevant, the other aggregating research in which the dimensions of conflict and communication are very evident. In many ways this is an artificial division since the four dimensions are present in most of the studies. However, they are not privileged to the same extent, and this division tries to underline that.

Illustrations from recent research

Time and institution

The first set of studies examines meaning-making in the context of individuals and communities dealing with the new laws for environmental protection, and place in time some of the psycho-social processes these bring about. Laws and regulations therefore constitute the main institutional dimension here approached. This is a very important dimension, since this type of *innovation originating in the legal and policy sphere* is highly central in our era of global commitments (Beck, 2009), many of which are subsequently translated into national laws. In the sustainability domain, this trend is particularly clear. Today, in many countries around the world and assuredly in European Union (EU) member states, there are numerous regulations and laws aimed at promoting social and cultural change towards sustainability (Baker, 2007). The psycho-social processes mobilized for the reception of these laws are also the processes through which people adjust to a certain sociopolitical order and its institutions (Moghaddam, 2008), and therefore are a topic of major relevance for a theory dealing with how representations respond simultaneously to culture and its institutions, as well as with how institutional dimensions affect the specific contexts in which relations occur (Castro, 2012).

This institutional side of environmental change is not always recognized by sociopsychological approaches. For instance, although there are numerous studies examining the influence of environmental norms on change, they rarely acknowledge the fact that many of these are new – or innovative – norms that are, or were, stimulated by new laws. These studies consequently disregard the time and institutional dimensions of these norms and the specific effects they may have on change. Moreover, most approaches to norms not only implicitly assume that norms are co-defined in informal groups in ways largely unconstrained by institutional facts such as state laws (Cialdini and Trost, 1998), but also usually look more at behavioural/individual change and less at social change. This means that they also overlook the fact that the new laws and norms affect different non-voluntary formed groups, like professional and/or expert groups in different ways, and affect some communities and groups more than others (Batel and Castro, 2009; Castro, 2012; Buijs *et al.*, 2012). In this sense, many studies on norms forget that the normative system specific to our time needs to be viewed as including not just informal norms and values (Moghaddam, 2008) but also actual laws and policy commitments

(Castro, 2012). In this way, they also neglect looking at how this happens in the context of intergroup relations, and how it brings about conflict.

In contrast to these trends, some studies have drawn on the theory of social representations to explicitly focus on how new environmental laws and regulations as institutional facts affect representational change in time. These studies have looked namely at how: (1) new legislation on water pollution impacts on social representations of a river over a thirty-year timespan (Brondi et al., 2012); (2) certain factors in time can attenuate conflicts over new protected areas (Hovardas and Korfiatis, 2008); (3) communities living in protected sites respond to the new biodiversity laws and regulations (Mouro and Castro, 2012); (4) impression management concerns may offer an indicator of whether or not new laws have achieved the status of hegemonic norms (Félonneau and Becker, 2008; Bertoldo, Castro and Bousfield, 2013; Fischer et al., 2012). I shall now review these studies.

The study by Brondi and colleagues aimed to explore change and stability in the social representation of the Chiampo River, in Italy, over a thirty-year period (2012, p. 286). The authors assumed that the various components of a representation – like emotions, images and practices – need not change in unison, and they wished to explore how three legislative moments (1. first pollution regulations; 2. some years after their implementation; and 3. when new EU regulations were adopted) caused these components to evolve over the years. The results showed how the images of the river progress and become more positive over time as the river becomes less polluted by force of legislation. Yet they also showed how at point 3 the habitual behaviour continues to be one of avoidance and distrust of the river's water, despite the positive image of the now clear waters. This illustrates how the past is slow to evade its representations and how conflicts may emerge among the different components of the representation, expressing intrapersonal contradictions and cognitive polyphasia (Jovchelovitch, 2007) instrumental in adjusting to social and cultural change. Some of the components can change more quickly, while others take longer and may consequently delay change in other dimensions. As a result, only by keeping the debate alive and involving the public and users concerned can the full process of change be assured, even in the presence of laws (Brondi et al., 2012).

In this same regard, another example illustrates how the inclusion of local groups in resource management in time may work to attenuate the intergroup conflicts arising in law-defined protected areas. In the Dadia Forest Reserve in Greece, following fierce conflicts between park staff and local people, the position of local people shifted towards endorsement of the protected area (Hovardas and Korfiatis, 2008). This can be attributed at least partially to the fact that environmental measures in Dadia have been implemented by local people working as park guards and guides involved in several activities in the reserve (Buijs et al., 2012). Their local embeddedness helped to gradually diffuse a representation among local residents of the reserve as 'pure nature'. Moreover, local minority members were recruited for several years, which allowed their influence to persist over time (Hovardas and Korfiatis, 2008).

Another study examined how local communities living in Natura 2000 protected areas manage some of the dilemmas emerging from conflicts between the new laws for biodiversity conservation and local knowledge and positions (Mouro and Castro, 2012). It showed that the encounter between legal and local knowledge engenders a specific format of cognitive polyphasia, which first offers generic support to the law through conventionalization (*in general I agree with the law*) and only then contests it through thematization (*but, in practice, the law is too strict*). This 'yes, but' type of discursive organization allows community members to support the laws – a cultural and societal imperative – while simultaneously opening space for negotiating their contextual meanings and guaranteeing that the criticisms following the 'but' do not elicit negative social consequences. Here, then, cognitive polyphasia seems to enable the expression of representations which do not seek full-blown polemic, but attempt to maintain cooperation in the context of an ongoing negotiation of meaning. This negotiation offers respect to societal goals (expressed in the laws) while it attempts to revise contextual implementations. In other words, polyphasia seems to be happening in the context of emancipated representations, those which sustain the everyday conflict of interpretations and allow some ambivalence to emerge (Vala et al., 1998).

Another set of studies examining the processes through which people deal with new laws in time departs from the premise that since the law is *equal for all*, successful new laws are those which in time become hegemonic representations associated to hegemonic norms, in other words, 'uniform and coercive across a structured group, like a nation' (Moscovici, 1988, p. 221). Classical examples of hegemonic representations associated with hegemonic norms are the *belief in a just world* (Alves and Correia, 2008) or the *internality norm* (Dubois and Beauvois, 2005). However this is the *ideal format* of the process of accommodation of new laws. The actual process can be much more complex and hybrid while it is evolving in time. One path towards understanding representations associated with new laws while the accommodation process is evolving is examining how people present themselves and judge others (i.e. studying impression management). For example, if agreement with the ideas or behaviours promoted by the laws is seen as a requirement of a positive self-presentation, and disagreement a requirement of a negative self-presentation, then the idea or behaviour can be said to be hegemonic (Gillibert and Cambon, 2003). This has been investigated for conservation ideas and behaviours by Félonneau and Becker (2008) and Bertoldo, Castro and Bousfield (2013). These studies show that expressing sustainable beliefs is now required for a positive self-presentation and refused for a negative self-presentation, demonstrating their positive social value. This signals the hegemonic status of sustainability ideas and norms. But a distance, or gap, is still maintained between what is stated as desirable and what is actually performed, and this can be seen as a sign of an emancipated representation. Yet the normative dimension is highly relevant even for those who do not always perform the behaviours. An interview study across five European countries has shown, for example, that many participants – mostly in Scotland and the Netherlands – spontaneously and specifically classified their own everyday behaviours as 'good' or 'bad', the 'bad' ones being those that violated the implicit norms of energy conservation or local purchasing of fresh products (Fischer et al., 2012). This not only indicates a clear awareness of what is normative; it also shows that participants are offering a self-presentation that both incorporates this awareness and signals that the speaker is already 'punishing' her/himself for violating the norm (by classifying their own behaviour as 'bad').

The same study (Fischer et al., 2012) also corroborates the findings of Brondi and colleagues (2012) mentioned above, by showing that the various components of the representations of energy and climate change – in this case, the normative, the cognitive and the affective components – are not in unison and that this creates inner tensions and cognitive polyphasia (Fischer et al., 2012). In a similar vein, another study shows that tensions may arise at the level of one single component – beliefs – and bring about ambivalence (Castro et al., 2009) as an expression of inner conflict.

On the whole, the set of studies reviewed above shows evidence of how the institutional promotion of change through new laws may open up representational conflicts. The conflicts most clearly brought to the fore here are intrapersonal ones, and are expressed in cognitive polyphasia, conveying the fact that not all components of a representation change in unison or are aligned at a certain point in time and space. It was also shown that for an understanding of these phenomena it is important to take into account that there are (at least) three different types of representations, and to examine how these types change over time.

The next section reviews studies that focus more on how representational conflicts can be linked to intergroup conflicts, and how such conflicts are expressed in communication and discourse.

Conflict and communication

As mentioned previously, it follows from the premises of the theory of social representations deducible from the dialogical triangle that working with the theory means paying simultaneous attention to representations expressing the cultural, which are more homogeneous across context, and to those expressing the contextual, which are more heterogeneous across context since they are more contingent to the position of individuals and groups in the social order and regarding the issues at stake. With regards this second dimension, the theory of social representations has often highlighted how social categories constitute an organizing principle for representational processes (Doise, Clémence and Lorenzi-Cioldi, 1992; Echelroth, Doise and Reicher, 2011). As such, the theory may improve our understanding of how different groups differ with regards to sense-making, and how these differences relate to local conflicts, are negotiated in everyday communication and re-presented in mediated formats. It is thus important at this point to note that the communication in the heading of this section will refer to both interpersonal and mediated communication, the two types emphasized by the theory of social representations.

The studies now to be reviewed make salient: (1) how representations respond to cultural repertoires and contextual demands; (2) the role representational conflicts play in social conflicts over how natural resources should be managed (Buijs *et al.*, 2012), how risk information must be transmitted (Poumadère and Bertoldo, 2010) or which types of agriculture to favour; (3) how conflicts between scientific/expert groups and local groups are expressed in discourse and communication (Selge, Fischer and van der Wal, 2011; Batel and Castro, 2009). Finally, a set of studies demonstrates (4) the usefulness of a central notion of the theory of social representations – anchoring – for analyzing mediated communication about climate change (Caillaud, Kalampalikis and Flick, 2012; Hoijer, 2010; Uzelgun and Castro, 2014).

A first example shows how the heterogeneity of representations about the new biodiversity laws (Mouro, 2011) expresses both cultural repertoires and contextual aspects. Three positions emerged from the analysis of discourses of communities living in Natura 2000 sites; these were simultaneously anchored in general categories – views of nature identified by cultural theory and found around the world (see Dake, 1992; Lima and Castro, 2005) – and local concerns. One view supported the current policy for protecting a nature seen as fragile, in the protected sites as well as everywhere. A second view wanted the elimination of laws as an obstacle to local development and depicted nature as robust and unspoilable by industry or intensive farming. Yet another discourse called for adjusting the law to local specificities to allow for sustainable forms of production in a nature seen as robust, but only up to a point.

Also, drawing on the theory of social representations, a synthesis of various studies about how conflicts regarding natural resource management were linked to different representations was carried out by Buijs and colleagues (2012). One study regards the protection of the wolf in the Scandinavian peninsula where, due to strict protection, a new wolf population can now be found. This expansion has led to heated controversies between social groups – between nature managers and sheep farmers, between conservationists and local residents, between biologists and hunters (Buijs *et al.*, 2012; Figari and Skogen, 2011). The study has shown how both enthusiasts and opponents of the reappearance of wolves shared an admiration for wolves as well as a core representation of the wolf as inextricably tied to the idea of wilderness. Yet a closer look at the more peripheral elements of the representation revealed clear divergences with regard to how enthusiasts and adversaries represented the relationship between wolves and local nature. While farmers and hunters – wolf opponents – saw the natural environment as a landscape for humans' sustainable use (i.e. areas for cultivating, hunting or berry picking), wolf supporters saw this same environment as wilderness, and therefore, aligned with the wolf's nature and needs.

Another example of conflicting representations regards those of agriculture but echoes rather similar themes. Working in France, Michel-Guillou (2012) illustrates how the expression 'sustainable agriculture' can encompass a great heterogeneity of positions and conflicting goals. Those farmers committed to ecological farming view the notion of 'sustainable' as leading to a questioning of the very notion of growth, and they represent sustainable farming as local and based on proximity. Yet there are also farmers that view agriculture as humans' sustainable use of the land, viewing the notion as supporting the possibility to conciliate economic growth with environmental protection.

There are also conflicting representations of risk. Poumadère and Bertoldo (2010) analyzed several cases of conflict between the representations of risk that shape the regulations applying to dangerous facilities, on one hand, and the representations of local communities living in industrial areas, on the other. For local populations, risks are naturalized and, when in risk situations, they do not immediately take in the risk information made available by the facilities in accordance with the regulations. In the same vein, a study of social representations of electricity (Devine-Wright, 2009) clearly taps on intergroup factors. It shows how issues of national identity were a part of people's understanding of electricity and that how they positioned themselves on electricity-related themes was influenced by group membership. For instance, participants from a Scottish town 'articulated their concerns about local impacts of pylon upgrade in the wider spatial and political context of Scottish-English intergroup tensions' (p. 369).

Another set of studies illustrating intergroup conflicts focusses more explicitly on tensions arising from the encounters between scientific and local knowledge (Batel and Castro, 2009; Callaghan, Moloney and Blair, 2012; Selge, Fischer and van de Wal, 2011; see also Buijs *et al.*, 2012). A first example regards the new laws aimed at fostering public participation in environmental decision-making processes. Batel and Castro (2009) examined the conflict between the expert and lay spheres of a Lisbon neighbourhood regarding the transformation of a historic convent. The analyses reveal that experts mostly use a *reification-like* communicative format to re-present the controversy (assuming the existence of only one correct form of thinking and acting), which reiterates their position as 'those who know' and excludes community members from the decision-making process, despite the laws. In turn, community members more often used a *consensualization-like* format, in which arguments assumed the legitimacy of different perspectives and discourses left some possibilities of negotiation open. This study highlights that it is crucial to take into account how specific communication formats express power relations and may accentuate conflicts in order to gain a better understanding of the sociopsychological processes involved in acceptance and resistance to change.

Another example concerns recycled water. Despite its scientific validity as an environmentally sound and sustainable solution to Australia's 'water crisis', asserted as such by the scientific community and the government, the Australian public put up unexpected resistance to recycled water (Callaghan *et al.*, 2012). Callaghan and colleagues (2012) shed some light on this. They show how resistance is not linked to a lack of recognition of the environmental value of water recycling, and that the majority of respondents expressed favourable views towards water recycling for purposes that had no direct contact with the body. But they also demonstrate that when the proximity of the water to the body increased, favourability towards recycled water decreased; by identifying the themata of purity/impurity as underpinning the social understanding of water recycling, they show how unfavourability was linked with concerns about impurity/safety. This use of the themata notion amply demonstrates how people 'employ validity criteria for their background knowledge that are at odds with scientific standards' (Wagner, 2007, p. 19) but find their origins in other types of legitimacy.

The themata concept has also been instrumental for understanding commonsense thinking about global warming. An interview study of London residents (Smith and Joffe, 2013) discerned the themata of self/other, natural/unnatural, and certainty/uncertainty; these same themata were also obtained as objectified via mediated images and symbols of global warming frequent in the media. This corroborates the importance of researching mediated communication. In the field of social studies of sustainability, the theory of social representations has stimulated several recent analyses of the press: about climate change (Caillaud, Kalampalikis and Flick, 2012; Hoijer, 2010; Uzelgun and Castro, 2014) or protected areas (Castro, Mouro and Gouveia, 2012; Hovardas and Stamou, 2006). As mentioned, many of the studies resort to the notion of anchoring as a research tool. In a comparison of how the German and the French media represented the 2007 Bali climate conference, Caillaud, Kalampalikis and Flick (2012) show how in Germany it is anchored on political, moral and human categories. This works to bring climate change 'close to home' as both a global and a local problem. In France, the conference news anchors it to financial and political categories, and to the rich country–poor country divide, placing more emphasis on the global dimension and pushing it further away from 'home'. Another study shows how in Sweden, the media anchors climate change issues on to emotions, for example, by using pictures appealing to compassion like 'sweet and cuddly polar bears and walruses' (Hoijer, 2010, p. 727). Another example is the use of the rhetoric of science in the mainstream Turkish press, which presents it in the form of a disembodied monologue, to establish climate change as a factual threat (Uzelgun and Castro, 2014). The study indicates that one way of achieving this is by anchoring climate change to its impacts on 'sweet' species and polar regions, while representing its threats to human society in a distant future, dissociating it from the actual political context and concrete local action.

In fact, all these studies discuss important possible and plausible impacts that the media depictions may have upon public responses and public opinion. Yet none of them has directly coupled media analysis with reception studies. This is therefore a very fruitful avenue for future research, now that the existing mapping of press depictions is starting to offer a comprehensive view of the topic.

Concluding remarks

The results and conclusions of the studies presented here reiterate what the theory of social representations has been demonstrating in other applied fields: how social change is a complex process unfolding gradually, or in phases, and not an on/off accomplishment (Castro and Batel, 2008; Castro and Mouro, 2011), an idea that has been at the heart of the theory of social representations since its inception (Moscovici, 1972, 1988). Moreover, they again highlight how innovation – in this case legal innovation and normative innovation – produces debate, and how debate can result in both acceptance and resistance to change. This thereby originates psycho-social processes and phenomena of great interest for research but which can only be unveiled if we take into account several levels of analysis, and acknowledges that representational change does not happen without conflict, both intergroup and intrapersonal.

Some of the studies reviewed then focussed on the intrapersonal expression of the phenomena involved in the accommodation of innovation and in the debate innovation produces. We saw examples of how the push for change originates inner conflicts, contradiction, cognitive polyphasia and ambivalence, which may work as forms of resistance to change. And we also saw how the same factors in different conditions may produce acceptance and normative influence that help advance change.

Other studies took a more intergroup perspective, showed how representations are expressions of groups and their conflicting positions, and showed the comprehensive nature of meaning-making and social thought. On the whole, it seems clear from these contributions that the approach of social representations can inspire accrued interest in the institutional support received by innovative sustainability laws and norms – or the lack of them – in the different contexts and institutions to which individuals are committed as citizens or professionals (Castro and Batel, 2008).

Importantly, I believe, the studies here reviewed – both those with a more intrapersonal focus and those using a more intergroup perspective – also reiterate two additional aspects. One is that indeed not all representations are equal. The other is that when innovations enter a society, the representations debate assumes different formats in different phases. Some representations are undoubtedly more coercive, or hegemonic, are incorporated in practices and institutions, go mostly undiscussed and require a lot of effort to be changed. Others generate polemic and are passionately opposed by some groups and fervently defended by others as admitting no compromise; and yet others are renegotiated and resignified in subtle, constant, small, creative ways, sometimes for very long periods of time.

By taking this set of recent studies together, it is possible to discern some major opportunities for future research. I will now highlight four of these opportunities linked to the dimensions of time, institution, conflict and communication structuring this review, as a possible contribution to stimulating new studies.

Regarding time, it seems very important to investigate how the three types of representations may be linked to the cycles of innovation, and what are the social, psychological and psycho-social processes that may in time be more important in making representations change from one type to another. Regarding institution, one aspect meriting more future research is how impression management aspects intertwine with resistance to and acceptance of new laws and norms and the role of possible conflicts between different types of norms (namely, local vs. societal). If this is done by taking into account the fact that the specific contexts and groups in which we present ourselves and judge others affect and influence self-presentation and hetero-judgement, then this is also a way of advancing research on conflict. Moreover, if impression management studies are fashioned so as to examine how language and discourse carry the signs of what is normative (cf. Fischer *et al.*, 2012), and in particular carry the signs of how the speaker excuses her/himself for the violation of normative imperatives, then this is another way of advancing research about communication. Finally, and still in relation to communication, reception studies warrant urgent attention; in particular, how specifically individuals and groups respond to different media presentations of key topics such as climate change, calls for urgent exploration. In my view, researching these aspects can help forge comprehensive and dynamic questions and contribute to devising a more integrated field of social studies of sustainability.

21 Social representations of national identity in culturally diverse societies

Eleni Andreouli and Xenia Chryssochoou

The concept of identity, although quite recent in the social sciences (it was popularized by Erikson in the 1950s; see Gleason, 1983), is one of the few concepts to have been so widely studied and theorized. Psychologists, sociologists, anthropologists, even political philosophers, have used the term to shed light on a variety of sociopolitical phenomena, ranging from belonging to exclusion and from stability and homogeneity to social change and cultural pluralism. As such, identity has acquired an array of conflicting meanings, from essentialist notions which focus on unity and distinctiveness to conceptions which emphasize the fragmentation of the modern subject (Brubaker and Cooper, 2000). The challenge in defining identity stems from the fact that it refers to both an individual's sense of self as well as to an individual's relations with others. It is, in other words, a concept that resists the individual–social dichotomy which has traditionally dominated the social sciences in general, and social psychology in particular. In this chapter we adopt a social representations perspective to theorize identity at the social–individual interface. We focus on national identities which have been particularly problematized in the context of growing cultural diversity within nation-states and are often seen as declining or changing.

The chapter is structured as follows: we start with a brief account of the theory of social representations and then present our main argument of identity as a social representation embedded in strategic projects. Then, in two different sections, we discuss national identity projects in culturally diverse societies with a particular focus on Britain and Greece. We conclude with a brief discussion of the implications of these national identity projects for the integration of migrants.

A brief account of the theory of social representations

The theory of social representations introduced by Serge Moscovici in 1961 has had a major impact on social psychological research. The theory has been used to understand a series of psychological phenomena, such as minority influence (Moscovici, 1976), public understanding of science (Bauer and Gaskell, 2002), cognitive development (Psaltis and Duveen, 2006), intercultural relations and communities (Jovchelovitch, 2007; Howarth et al., 2013), and health and risk

(Joffe, 2003). Other chapters of this book expand on the theory and the domains of social representations, and therefore we will not discuss the theory in much detail here. However, we need to say a few words in order to be able to argue about its relation with identity.

Social representations are common-sense theories about the world and one of their main functions is to domesticate the unknown and the unfamiliar. When people are faced with unfamiliar events, they try to make sense of the situation by incorporating the new elements into their existing knowledge and by presenting them in familiar terms and images. According to Moscovici (1988), this domestication is done via the processes of anchoring and objectification. These processes, working at a level of a meta-system, translate social regulations into peoples' way of thinking. Thus, common-sense knowledge is socially elaborated and shared. It constitutes a kind of 'democratic' knowledge in whose elaboration everybody can potentially contribute depending on the nature and dynamics of intergroup relations. Moscovici discussed social representations as lay systems of meaning that are constructed through communicative processes. As such, they inevitably involve self–other relations and vary according to the dynamics of these relations.

Social representations are considered as both the process and the product of the elaboration of social knowledge, which is not initiated either by the knowing subjects or by the objects to be known, but by their interaction. Social representations express quintessentially the social psychological 'regard' as proposed by Moscovici (1988). According to this view, what differentiates social psychology from the disciplines of psychology and sociology is the way it looks at the relationship between a subject (individual or collective) and an object. What social psychology suggests is that this relationship is mediated through another subject (individual or collective, real or imagined). Thus, in social psychological terms, the relationship between a subject and an object 'becomes a complex triangular one in which each of the terms is fully determined by the other two' (Moscovici, 1972). This relationship between self, other and object/representation forms the unit of analysis in the theory of social representations (Marková, 2003).

The triadic model of knowledge construction has been extended by Bauer and Gaskell (1999, 2008), who have suggested that the subjects of the representational process are linked together in a common vision or purpose. In particular, they argue that self–other relations are relative to a common project, a 'future for us' which defines the object and people's experience (Bauer and Gaskell, 2008, p. 343). It is within this common project that people are able to communicate, agree or disagree about an object. Social representations do not mean that everybody has the same opinion but that the organization of individual knowledge is influenced by common principles that are shared by people in the same culture or community. It is important to have common grounds in order to be able to communicate with each other even if we disagree. The ways that different social milieus interact with each other impact on the types of representations that are produced (Bauer and Gaskell, 2008). For instance, the construction of social representations of nationhood involves various actors. One can think of the lay general public (that is composed of various social groups that may have different interests), the state (which demarcates the national boundaries through immigration and citizenship legislation, for example), as well as the migrants (who may also have different projects and claims to national identity depending on where they come from, their legal status, etc.), as key actors in constructions of nationhood. While each actor may construct different representations based on the projects they are pursuing, it can be said that these diverse versions of the world intersect and overlap at points thereby constructing nationhood as a complex and multifaceted object. It should be noted, however, that power asymmetries influence the degree to which projects become successful as alternative projects may be silenced or 'squashed' by projects produced by more powerful social actors (Foster, 2003).

Overall, the theory of social representations is a way of studying common-sense knowledge which is socially elaborated through communication and social influence. Social representations are determined by the interaction between knowing social subjects and different social objects, a relationship mediated by others in the social environment. They express peoples' worldviews that help them domesticate the unknown, give meaning to their environment and position themselves in it. These social representations guide peoples' practices.

Having discussed social representations as a theory of knowledge in general, we now move on to consider identities as a particular type of social representation. We suggest that seeing identity as a social representation allows us to understand both the content of identities (which draws on existing social representations) and the processes of identity construction and negotiation on an individual and collective level. In order to highlight the relationship between identity and action, we draw particular attention to the notion of identity projects. In the final sections of this chapter we apply these ideas to national identity projects in culturally diverse societies, focussing on Britain and Greece.

Identity as a social representation

The concept of identity has attracted much attention within the field of social representations (e.g. Breakwell, 2011 and Chapter 17 in this volume; Duveen and Lloyd, 1986; Moloney and Walker, 2007; Howarth, 2002a). Contributing to this growing body of research, we argue here that the concept of identity has much to gain if it is conceptualized as a social representation. Although we acknowledge that identity has both individual and social aspects, we make no distinction here between personal and social identity (cf. Tajfel, 1981). The argument we make is that people construct their identity in the context of their culture in order to domesticate their environment and position themselves within it. Macro-societal norms and regulations are translated into self-knowledge with the same processes as those functioning for social representations, and, at a meso-interactional level, everyday encounters and interactions customize further these elements to produce a particular form of knowledge at an individual level, forming the overall notion of the individual self (Chryssochoou, 2013). Thus, it can be said that identity is 'a particular form of social representation that represents the relationship between the individual and others (real or symbolic, individuals or groups)' (Chryssochoou, 2003, p. 227). Identity is intrinsically social since it is socially elaborated and enables people to participate in a given culture. A similar argument has been advanced in relation to the different representations of selfhood, for example, representations based on individualism and representations based on collectivism (Oyserman and Markus, 1998). Identity as a particular form of social representation functions like an organizing principle (Spini and Doise, 1998; Elcheroth, Doise and Reicher, 2011) that allows individuals to position themselves within the representational field and that guides action.

Like the psychoanalytic concepts studied by Moscovici in 1961, identity is not only a scientific concept that explains people's affiliations and sense of belonging, but it is also part of common sense and public debates (Chryssochoou, 2003, 2009a). At an individual or collective level, identity refers to three main questions: 'Who am I/who are we?', 'Who are they?' and 'What is our relationship?' (Chryssochoou, 2003). From this perspective, we see identity as a system of knowledge about oneself, about others and about the social context which is constructed and negotiated within social relations. Identity can refer to societal projects that give meaning and content to social categories as well as to particular configurations of these categories at the individual level. It could also refer to specific position-taking within a social context. We argue that all these aspects can be studied if one looks at identity as a social representation which is constructed, communicated, thematized and debated in the public sphere. As the content of social categories but also the very system of categorization used in a particular social context can be seen as the products of a social representational process of knowledge elaboration (see also Augoustinos, 2001), we argue that identity can be viewed in terms of both its content and processes of construction and elaboration.

In terms of content, identity contains self-knowledge (Chryssochoou, 2003). It provides individuals with both a sense of group membership and access to the group's knowledge systems (Wagner, 1994b). The content of social categories become identity projects that give people a sense of who they are, a perspective on the world and a guideline for action. For instance, representations of gender define what it means to be male or female and what type of conduct is expected of men and women. In this sense, identity provides the symbolic material that enables people to define themselves and others and orient their behaviour accordingly.

Through socialization, identity is both a process of self-knowledge construction and a process of self-positioning. Thus, the particular configuration of different identity elements constituting the self is also the product of processes similar to those of social representations. As with the inclusion of new elements in a social representation via the anchoring process, positioning is an active process and as such, allows for variability and individual agency (Duveen, 2001a; Howarth, 2006a). Moreover, making claims about one's identity and resisting claims made by others are part of identity processes. In other words, like all social representations, identities can be negotiated and transformed – this is particularly evident if we take the example of the politics of identity which seek to change hegemonic social representations of minority identities in order to achieve greater public recognition (cf. Taylor, 1992). Like other types of social knowledge, identity is constructed, affirmed or renegotiated through communicative processes and processes of social influence (Chryssochoou, 2003).

In fact, what we argue is that although people have particular identity configurations at a phenomenological level, these are constructed through the same processes as social representations that aim to domesticate the unknown and unfamiliar. People aim to construct knowledge about themselves that helps them domesticate new and changing environments, that is communicable to others and that inserts them to a common social and symbolic space. The elaboration of this self-knowledge is done socially and involves social influence processes in order to negotiate and convince others about the meaning of self-categories and self-positioning. Thus, inevitably identity expresses, at an individual level, the way society is regulated. In that sense, we argue that it is valuable to consider it as a particular social representation that mediates social relationships.

Because of its key role in mediating social relations and enabling people to engage with their social world (based on the knowledge they have of themselves, of others and the dynamics of their relation), identity is inextricably linked to action and participation. The relationship between identity and action is not new. Early in social psychological research identity was linked to action and intergroup behaviour (Tajfel, 1974; Tajfel and Turner, 1986). We argued earlier that identity is a form of social representation that links individuals to their social worlds; it is the representation that provides people with both a location and a value in relation to other individuals who occupy different identity positions (Duveen and Lloyd, 1986). As such, identity has the power to provide the content of action (identity project) and the position from which one is able to carry on this project. Identity, therefore, makes people social actors by endowing them with various positionings that enable them to participate in social life (Howarth, Andreouli and Kessi, 2014).

Identities have the power to mobilize people towards action. As a social representation, identity expresses the interrelation between knowledge and practice and mobilizes towards the creation of new practices (Elcheroth, Doise and Reicher, 2011). The social elaboration of identities can function as particular calls for mobilization. Identities are strategic and future-oriented (Reicher and Hopkins, 2001; Reicher, 2004). The 'identity battle' takes place in the arena of social influence. For instance, minority claims for public recognition of ethnic or religious identities become political claims and constitute actions to accommodate minorities' vision of the world. On the other hand, (mis)recognition from others, especially from powerful social groups and institutions, constitutes an action towards minorities which can mobilize these groups to achieve fuller recognition.

In the following sections we focus particularly on national identity projects in culturally diverse societies. In an environment where nationhood is changing due to migration movements, people need to reconstruct who they are to incorporate these changes. We are not interested here so much at the content of social representations of nationhood in two different countries. Following the claims made earlier, we will discuss the implications of hegemonic representations promoted either by the state or by the cultural majority for people's identities. To do so, we will first discuss national identities in culturally diverse societies as strategic projects.

National projects in culturally diverse societies

We proposed above that identities can be seen as social representations that domesticate the unfamiliar, provide a position to individuals and customize societal projects at the level of the self. The question with which we are dealing here is how existing identities are influenced by a changing social environment where cultural diversity is prominent. In particular, we are interested in how national identities evolve in a culturally diverse environment.

National identities have been constructed on the founding myths of the different nations. History is crucial for the construction of nations (Hobsbawm and Kertzer, 1992). Myths of origin, national memories and histories, national cultures and symbols, are all tools that enable the construction of the nation. In the famous words of Benedict Anderson, 'the nation is an imagined political community – and imagined as both inherently limited [with specific boundaries] and sovereign' (1983, p. 6), giving nationals a sense of continuity and destiny.

Nationhood emerged around the middle of nineteenth century when sociohistorical factors in Europe brought into existence a sociopolitical organization: the nation-state (Gellner, 1997; Hobsbawm, 1990). This political project was based on the idea of a nation, a group that assembled people around the belief that they shared common origins, a common culture and common goals. In this respect, culture became a political principle which fed the representation that a nation-state was a culturally homogeneous entity (Gellner, 1997). The cultural and the political spheres have been closely intertwined in the building of modern nation-states.

Nations were, and still are, powerful identity providers for their members. Following the social representational processes described before, the sociopolitical organization of the nation-state was translated at a certain historical moment at the level of identity and provided a meaningful purpose and a sense of belonging. National identities are carriers of the project of nationhood and their content is subject to social influence by 'entrepreneurs of identity' (Reicher and Hopkins, 2001). Very often, this project consists of creating a nation-state where a community with a common past can establish a common present and pursue a common future. Nationalism, the driving force for the development of the nation-state, is understood in political theory as 'primarily a political principle, which holds that the political and the national unit should be congruent' (Gellner, 1983, p. 1), meaning that the borders of the state coincide with the borders of the nation.

This project is supported by relevant identities and feeds these identities. To create the identities that would carry this political project, nationalism reifies the nation and essentializes the national character (Chryssochoou, 2004). Over time the identities that carry on the national project become reified, conventionalized and taken for granted. Billig (1995) refers to the idea that the world is naturally divided in bounded and distinct nations as a banal ideology which is habitually reproduced in mundane, everyday routines and talk. Constructing the nation as a distinct and cohesive community of people with essential characteristics has important implications for the criteria for national membership. This membership is important since it determines who can be a recipient of material and symbolic resources and who has decision-making power (through electing and being elected) in this community.

Thus, a political project creates national identity projects. The notion of project points to the political and often strategic construction of national identities (see Condor, 2000; Reicher and Hopkins, 2001). These are not neutral endeavours but are guided by the interests of the groups that produce them (Chryssochoou, 2009a). As noted above, the primary project of representations of nationhood has been to preserve the state institution by constructing and maintaining the image of a coherent, homogeneous and continuous national collectivity whose members have common interests that are paramount.

However, the power of the nation-state has been challenged by globalization and the global movement of people. It is quite common nowadays for people to be dual nationals or to live outside their country of nationality. In the UK, for instance, hundreds of thousands of people become naturalized as British citizens every year (Danzelman, 2010). At the same time, the loss of power of the nation-state and the movement of people challenge the national identities of receiving communities. Another project of social order is presented where cultural diversity needs to be accommodated. Research has shown that the more a nation is represented in ethnic terms by its members, the more these members express anti-immigration views (Pehrson, Vignoles and Brown, 2009). Furthermore, the way ethnic minorities are categorized (as in-group or out-group) has an impact on how they are treated (Wakefield et al., 2011). Cultural diversity raises again the issue of conflict within nations, this time not in class terms but in ethnic terms. The efforts of ethnic minorities to be recognized as legitimate members of the nation are in fact efforts to be recognized as legitimate recipients of material and symbolic resources. Often, the response to claims for recognition is the development of ideological beliefs about the incompatibilities between national and ethnic or religious identities (Chryssochoou and Lyons, 2011).

This changing environment raises questions about how national identities evolve. What is the national project today? What is the context in which ethnic minorities and second-generation immigrants build their identities? How do majorities respond to the changes in what they knew was the 'national project'?

We will now present the hegemonic identity projects of two different countries. The first is the United Kingdom, a country with several nations, with a colonial past in which an empire included subjects of diverse ethnicities and cultural backgrounds that were hierarchically oriented. The second is Greece, a country whose members formed a nation-state at the beginning of the nineteenth century after a liberation war on the basis of common culture, a country whose cohesion was built on commonality and homogeneity and which recently, from being an immigrant-sending country, became an immigrant-receiving one. These countries present two different examples of national identity projects. As we will show, however, despite their differences, they do share some commonalities in how they seek to accommodate or manage cultural change.

National identity projects in the UK and Greece

The UK naturalization context

Britishness has always been a somewhat 'fuzzy' concept (Cohen, 1994). This is partly because it has been constructed on the basis of different ethnic and national groups. The UK consists of four nations (England, Wales, Scotland and Ireland) as well as other ethnic minority communities who have migrated to the UK mainly since the 1950s. Power asymmetries amongst the different nations of the UK (with the English being the dominant group) have often led to the construction of stronger regional identities rather than an overarching British identity. For instance, British identity is said to be much more adopted by the white English and the ethnic minority population of England compared to the rest of the UK population (Stone and Muir, 2007). Also, while in England Britishness is seen as an inclusive identity, in Scotland it is associated with an ethnic conception of Englishness (Kiely, McCrone and Bechhofer, 2005). Britishness is therefore defined differently in different contexts as ethnic, cultural and national groups represent this identity in various ways depending on the configuration of power and the history of intergroup relations.

This section will discuss a particular context for the construction of national identity in the UK, the process of naturalization (that is, the process whereby migrants become citizens of the UK). While social psychological research has mainly studied national identities in terms of lay understandings, we argue that state institutions are very powerful actors in concretizing and enacting social representations about national identity (Andreouli and Howarth, 2013). National identities are political projects which are advanced by state policies and practices. The state can act as an 'identity entrepreneur' (Reicher, 2004) and advance a particular representation of what it means to be a member of the nation.

The British state, in particular, has in recent years engaged in a nation-building project through its citizenship and immigration policy. While the UK has traditionally adopted a rather multicultural approach compared to other western countries (Favell, 2001), multiculturalism as a policy for managing cultural diversity has recently been challenged. The terrorist attacks in New York and London and the racial tensions in the north of England in 2001 have given rise to more assimilatory public policy discourse that emphasizes commonality and sharedness. Several policies emphasizing social cohesion and integration have since been implemented. These policies aim to manage cultural diversity and to avoid future conflicts by advancing a common vision of Britishness among all British citizens (McGhee, 2005). Most prominent among those policies are immigration and citizenship policies. For instance, migrants who wish to stay in the United Kingdom now have to pass a 'Life in the UK' test to show that they are familiar with British culture and with the laws and rules of the country. They also need to go through a citizenship ceremony where they swear their allegiance to the UK and the Queen. On the whole, it can be argued that the British state has initiated a top-down nation-building process that seeks to construct a socially cohesive society based on shared British values. These policies have been heavily criticized for their assimilatory and patronizing connotations (e.g. Alexander, 2007).

As any social identity, this vision of the British nation advanced by the state is associated with a model of social relations (Reicher, 2004); it includes some people but excludes others. This is most evident in 'earned citizenship' and 'managed immigration' policies, which have complemented social cohesion policies in the UK. These policies emphasize duties over the rights of migrants and aim at ensuring that only the right kinds of migrants are able to reside in the UK and naturalize as citizens. An analysis of 'earned citizenship' documents by Andreouli and Howarth (2013) shows that at the heart of these policies lies a distinction between deserving and undeserving migrants. The former are seen as an economic resource while the latter are seen as abusers of British resources, mainly of welfare benefits. This finding is in line with a general deservingness culture that seems to be widespread across Europe; in fact, the least deserving of all 'needy' social groups according to survey studies seem to be the migrants (van Oorschot, 2006). The level of recognition afforded to migrants depends on where they come from (for example, from within the EU or from third world countries) and the level of professional skills they possess. Andreouli and Howarth (2013) argue that this bordering mechanism results in a type of institutionalized positioning of migrants, differentiating between 'elite' and 'non-elite' migrants. The former are educated migrants originating in developed western countries, while the latter are less skilled migrants originating from developing countries. In other words, the British state's national identity project for migrants emphasizes the distinction between the West and the Rest, positioning westerners as closer to Britishness and thus more worthy of Britishness than non-westerners. It follows therefore that representations of national identity constructed and institutionalized by the British state serve political projects. They function to exclude some 'less worthy' migrants while aiming to embrace other 'more worthy' ones. Ideas about similarity and difference and ideas about deservingness and undeservingness overlap to a great extent. Non-western migrants are otherized by both lay representations of Britishness as an ethno-cultural identity (which is inaccessible to 'cultural others') and by reified representations produced and enacted by the British state (Andreouli and Howarth, 2013).

These findings are further corroborated by an interview study with civil servants working within the field of naturalization in the UK. The findings of this study show that an earned citizenship discourse is also employed by many of these officers who represent Britishness as an identity that has to be earned through active contribution to the country, making again a distinction between deserving and undeserving migrants (Andreouli and Dashtipour, 2013). While embracing 'worthy' migrants serves to maintain an image of Britain as an accepting society, the symbolic exclusion of 'unworthy' migrants serves to maintain the purity of the nation against the migrant 'threat'. Again, these data show that non-deserving migrants, who are seen as abusing the welfare state, are commonly seen as culturally and ethnically different or 'other' (Andreouli and Dashtipour, 2013).

It seems overall that a key organizing principle in social representations of Britishness as played out in the UK naturalization context is the distinction between deserving and undeserving migrants (see Staerklé, 2009), which seems to overlap to an extent with the distinction between ethnically similar and ethnically different migrants. This principle is linked to a particular vision of Britishness and orients the positioning of migrants in relation to this identity. People that conform with these criteria of deservingness ('elite', highly skilled migrants who usually originate in developed countries) are accepted or recognized, while groups that violate them ('non-elite' migrants who are less skilled and usually originate in non-developed countries) are excluded from the British nation (see also Joffe and Staerklé, 2007). It can be said therefore that (some) migrants are doubly otherized: institutional-level representations and state policies limit their formal participation in the UK while lay representations limit their 'informal' symbolic right to claim British identity.

It is important to consider how such state-level projects relate to the identity projects of migrants and of other ethnic, cultural or religious minorities. For instance, Kinnvall and Nesbitt-Larking (2011) found that Muslim communities in Europe tend to adopt essentialist identity projects (that enhance intergroup boundaries) when faced with policies of assimilation, whereas they tend to adopt more dialogical identity projects (that allow engagement with other communities) in contexts of multicultural policies. In our own research we found that the recognition (of 'elite') and misrecognition of ('non-elite') migrants have an effect on how migrants construe their place in the UK and their relationship to Britishness: non-white, poorer migrants originating outside the West tend to feel less entitled to identify with the British nation compared to migrants originating in western countries (Andreouli and Howarth, 2013). Such powerful representations of Britishness can also shape individual acculturation processes because they limit the extent to which ethnic minority identities are seen as compatible with British identity. Different migrants (depending on their personal and family histories and the specific relationships that they develop with the communities they are affiliated with) may use different strategies to solve this assumed incompatibility: they may reject one or the other identity, construct new hyphenated or superordinate identities, or compartmentalize the different identities into different domains of life (Andreouli, 2013).

Contemporary Greece

The Greek national identity was constructed at the beginning of the nineteenth century as a project that led to a 'national liberation' war from the Ottoman Empire on the basis of a common religion and language and common ancestors: the ancient Greeks. Thus, national identity in Greece is built on the myth of a cultural, ethnic, religious and linguistic homogeneity of the population. Here we do not aim to present the content of Greek nationhood, however. What we aim to show is that when this founding myth is challenged by cultural diversity, people will strategically reconstruct their identity to incorporate this new element. However, this is not done passively but strategically, in order to keep the social stratification intact and to favour the local populations. This reconstruction does not solely involve national identity but also class identities.

Our research indicates that the myth of national cultural homogeneity is still prominent in the social representations of the nation and is shared by both 'native' Greeks and ethnic Greeks from Voreios Epiros, a region in the south of Albania with a large Greek community. In two different studies (Chryssochoou, 2009b) we asked native Greeks (N = 104) and ethnic Greeks from Voreios Epiros living in Greece (N = 111) and aged between 18 and 70 to give their agreement with seventeen criteria that would make somebody Greek. The structure of the representation of both groups was extremely similar. The factor analysis revealed mainly two factors that concern (a) the civic definition of being Greek (*ius solis* and *ius domicili*) and (b) the common ethno-cultural origin (*ius sanguinis*). Both groups claim that it is right for somebody to be considered Greek on the basis of his/her ethno-cultural origins more than on the basis of a civic definition. In addition, the Greek sample was asked what makes a nation. The analysis revealed three factors. The first factor was based on the commonalities between the members of the group (common customs and habits, common culture, history, language, origins and religion). The second factor concerned resources and the constitution of a state (rights and socioeconomic benefits, territorial power, state constitution). The third factor concerned national independence (independent economic life, independent governance). Agreement was significantly higher with the first ethno-cultural factor. If this is the case, and the national project in Greece is built on the idea of ethno-cultural commonalities and *ius sanguinis*, then how can immigrants and minorities ever pretend to be part of the national group? Is diversity the real threat to the Greek national project, however?

Although the movement of populations from and to Greece is nothing new (and nor is the existence of groups with different cultural characteristics in Greek territory), public discourse emphasizes the fact that Greece started becoming multicultural in the 1990s with the reception of immigrants from former East European countries and in particular with the massive entry of Albanians. Immigrants, however, not only changed the culturally homogeneous image of the country; they also changed social stratification, allowing many Greeks to become bosses (Kasimis and Papadopoulos, 2005). The fact that immigrants have been constrained in low-paid jobs, and literary exploited, has allowed Greek society in general to represent them as a separate body of the workforce that is destined to do 'any job' from agricultural and building work to house-cleaning and taking care of the elderly. It could be said that the 1990s was characterized by patronizing prejudice. It was when immigrants, particularly Albanians, started having horizontal or vertical mobility that Greek society became clearly hostile and displayed antagonistic behaviours. This was illustrated by the hostility displayed towards pupils of Albanian origin who, as the best pupils in their school, were given the honour to carry the Greek flag during school parades. The phenomenon of Greek parents protesting against a non-Greek student carrying the flag during school parades became very common. It can be hypothesized that the issue at stake was not the fact that a cultural symbol was carried by non-members, but the fact that non-members were able to succeed.

In two different quasi-experiments we manipulated the horizontal or vertical mobility (stable status vs. mobility) of a fictitious immigrant in Germany with different ethnic origins (Greek, Italian, Albanian or Bulgarian). When we asked participants, Greek university students, to attribute the stability or mobility of the fictitious target, we observed that for the Bulgarian and even more for the Albanian immigrant, his stability more than his mobility was attributed to his culture of origin. This was true for the horizontal and for the vertical mobility. These findings indicate that the construction of difference in terms of culture is used to justify and legitimize social stratification within the nation-state and to create a hierarchy of cultures that would obstruct mobility for newcomers when at the same time the dream for social mobility would remain alive for natives. The national project needs to change in order to accommodate the different ethnicities. To do so, another representation is used that justifies the new social stratification and gives the opportunity to majority groups to keep their prominent position (Chryssochoou, 2009b; Chryssochoou, 2010).

These representations have consequences for the acculturation patterns and the development of identities. On the one hand, immigrants receive the message that in order to be accepted as part of the national polity they need to assimilate; on the other hand, this strategy is not beneficial for all ethnic groups. Research has shown that Albanians, for instance, do not benefit from their religious assimilation (Grigoropoulou and Chryssochoou, 2011). The origins of the minority and the relation to the receiving population interact with the acculturation strategy. Thus, often immigrants and ethnic minorities receive contradictory messages about which type of identity strategy can be better recognized. In fact, the presumed incompatibility of identities is another representation that aims to block a representation of a nation as cohesive and multicultural at the same time (Chryssochoou and Lyons, 2011). Our research with immigrants (Chryssochoou and Dede, 2013) shows that the identification of Albanian immigrants with their ethnic in-group is independent to their wish to assimilate or to their wish to maintain their culture in Greece. It is not immigrants' strong identification with their ethnic group that interferes with their insertion to the receiving society. In the Greek sample described above, the more participants felt Greek, the more they wished ethnic repatriates from Voreios Epiros to assimilate in the Greek society and at the same time the more they wished that this group maintained their different culture in Albania in order to satisfy the politics of the Greek nation-state. These results support our claim that identities, constructed as social representations, are strategically used in order to sustain political projects.

From this discussion about national identity projects in Greece we can observe that there is a hegemonic representation of the national project based on cultural homogeneity. However, when immigrants follow a strategy of assimilation in order to fit the criteria of commonality, they face another barrier, which is produced from a social representation concerning the social stratification of society and the distribution of resources in a society that ideologically supports meritocracy. Thus, following the presumed content of nationhood based on homogeneity and assimilation does not help migrants since in fact they are not excluded on the basis of their culture but on the basis of their social class. In that, looking at identity as a social representation enables us to understand the interrelations between societal regulations and their expression at the level of the self.

Conclusions

This chapter has argued that identity, and national identity in particular, can be seen as a social representation. This means that, as with other social representations, national identity is collectively elaborated through social interaction and debate in the public sphere. Moreover, different social actors have a stake in the construction of national identity, each with their own interests and projects. The notion of project highlights the politics of identity construction: the fact that every representation of national identity carries within it the agenda of the groups or other social actors that construct it. In this sense, there is always a strategic dimension in the social representational process of national identity construction.

We have argued that national identity projects have historically aimed to construct the nation as a homogeneous group of people, linked together by shared history and ethnic origins. This process has allowed nation-states to function as sovereign polities. In other words, the identity project of creating a sense of nationhood has served the political project of nationalism. However, increasing cultural diversity within nation-states has challenged the assumed homogeneity of distinct nations. In light of this, we have argued that new identity projects, that is, new social representations of national identity, need to be constructed in order to accommodate this growing diversity.

This chapter has specifically explored national identity projects in the UK and Greece from the perspective of the majority. In the UK, we focussed on the state, a powerful actor in shaping representations of the nation. We examined state discourses and practices on immigration and naturalization and found that these are organized around the distinction of deserving and undeserving migrants, which functions to exclude non-western, unskilled migrants and include western, skilled migrants on the basis that the former are a burden while the latter are an economic resource. These practices overlap with lay representations of Britishness which also exclude non-western migrants due to their assumed ethnic and cultural difference. In Greece, majoritarian representations of national identity are also based on cultural homogeneity. Social representations of Greekness are associated with a hierarchical view of cultures which serves to limit the social mobility of migrants and ethnic minorities. In both cases, therefore, cultural diversity is not just seen as problematic in itself; rather, migrants seem to threaten other valued resources of the nation, such as the distribution of state resources (e.g. welfare) or the existing system of social stratification.

In both cases migrants find themselves in a very difficult situation. In Greece, migrants are effectively encouraged to assimilate in order to be socially mobile, but this is made extremely difficult by representations of cultural incompatibility. Similarly, in the UK, under an ostensibly just immigration system which rewards those with the right qualifications, non-western migrants are otherized as potential abusers of the British welfare system. However, these ideas about welfare abuse are intertwined with conceptions of ethnic and cultural difference, leading eventually to a double otherization of non-western migrants.

In both cases social changes lead to the reconstruction of identity projects that differ between minorities and majorities and impact on how identity is elaborated. Social representations of national identities are thus constructed on the basis of political projects that serve the interests of powerful social actors and function to maintain a homogeneous or exclusionary national identity. In times of growing ethnic and cultural diversity within nation-states, this sets hurdles for the acculturation of migrants and the overall participation of ethnic minorities. Such national identity projects may have adverse effects: instead of encouraging the construction of a cohesive national identity, they can ultimately encourage intergroup segregation and limit the participation of minorities in the social and political life of a country.

22 The essentialized refugee: representations of racialized 'Others'

Martha Augoustinos, Scott Hanson-Easey and Clemence Due

The psychological and ideological processes of social categorization, differentiation and identification that adhere to how social groups negotiate and acquire identities for themselves, and those defined as different or 'Other', have been central to research in the social representations tradition (Augoustinos and Riggs, 2007; Chryssochoou, 2004; Duveen, 2001a; Howarth, 2006b; Moloney and Walker, 2007; Philogène, 1999). In this chapter we seek to examine how representations of a new social group that has only recently settled in Australia – humanitarian refugees from Sudan – are represented and communicated in both formal and informal discourse by majority group members. We examine how essentialized traits are attributed to Sudanese refugees that position the group as not only problematic but also necessitating exclusion from Australian society. Our analysis suggests that these essentialized and indeed racialized representations are predicated on simplified representations of the African continent – a 'war-torn', dangerous place from which its displaced people should not be offered refuge due to their inherent social and psychological deficits. We use this very specific social and historical example to suggest that essentialized representations of the 'Other' have become reified and objectified ways of making sense of difference. Despite scientific and political challenges to the validity of essentialized categories such as 'race', such representations have remained resilient in everyday understandings of group difference. As Moscovici's theory of social representations (1984b, 1988) argues, such representations become so entrenched and objectified that their social and political origins become forgotten. People come to view essentialized representations of difference as 'natural' and common-sense ways of perceiving and understanding human variability and social diversity.

Essentialism in psychological research

In recent times in the field of psychology there has been a growing interest in the concept of psychological essentialism (Haslam, Rothschild and Ernst, 2000, 2002; Holtz and Wagner, 2009; Raudsepp and Wagner, 2012; Kashima et al., 2010; Rothbart and Taylor, 1992; Wagner et al., 2010; Yzerbyt, Rocher and

Schadron, 1997). Although lacking precise definition (Haslam *et al.*, 2000), psychological essentialism refers to how and why people believe that social categories are strongly associated with unique and fixed properties, or 'essences' that determine their 'true nature' (Gelman and Wellman, 1991; Haslam *et al.*, 2000; Leyens *et al.*, 2001; Medin and Ortony, 1989). These deeply rooted 'essences' are believed to be naturally reflected in observable physical traits such as skin colour, and moreover, in behavioural predispositions of the group. The nature of essences is theorized to be necessary, natural, often pseudo-biological and stable. Thus, essences, because they come from a deeply rooted and unchangeable place, make membership to a particular category immutable, and members are considered to be homogeneous (Haslam *et al.*, 2000). Moreover, according to Haslam and colleagues (2000), two distinct dimensions constitute essentialist thinking – 'naturalness' and 'reification/entitativity' – and they posit that prejudice may not be as simple as believing in the immutable 'naturalness' of social categories, but may be premised on the 'entitative' nature of such beliefs.

The human predilection towards essentialist thinking has invariably been attributed by social psychologists to what has been theorized to be our inherent limited cognitive capacities. Gordon Allport in *The Nature of Prejudice* (1954), for example, attributed essentialist thought to an imperative for simplifying a complex world and intolerance for ambiguity. In a similar vein, Rothbart and Taylor (1992) have argued that people make 'ontological errors' in their treatment of social categories as 'natural kinds' when they should, instead, be classified as social 'artefacts'. Essentialist thinking is marked by a mistaken tendency to view socially constructed categories such as 'race' as if they were as immutable and inductively rich as 'natural kinds'.

While this emphasis on the limits of human perception and cognition may have some validity, what these explanations for psychological essentialism appear to ignore are the long and entrenched intellectual traces of scientific racism and social Darwinism that solidified essentialist categories of difference such as 'race' into both everyday common-sense and scientific discourse during the twentieth century (Richards, 1997). In psychological research (and indeed in many other disciplines of knowledge), the concept of 'race' continues to be used unproblematically as a 'natural kind' variable in ways that reinforce the commonplace view that it *is* a biological and genetic reality (Tate and Audette, 2001).

The resilience of the construct of 'race', despite increasing scientific evidence to the contrary (see McCann, Augoustinos and LeCouteur, 2004), is reflected by its entrenched use as a common-sense, 'natural' category by which to classify people. In Moscovici's terms (1984b, 1988), 'race' can be seen to have become a reified and objectified reality through which social group differences come to be understood and explained. That is, 'race' has become a social representation. Essentialized categories of difference such as race and gender have a ubiquitous appeal, not only in everyday common-sense understandings but also in the reified universe of scientific knowledge. Group differences, whether physical or cultural, continue to operate as socially meaningful and relevant sense-making practices.

These practices, as we will outline in the following section, typically function to construct identities for disadvantaged minorities that while being founded upon racial categories, nonetheless serve to deny racism and social exclusion.

Refugees from Sudan in Australia

Humanitarian refugees from Sudan constitute one of the newest cultural groups to permanently settle in Australia. Most of this Sudanese diaspora has settled since the humanitarian intake from Sudan was rapidly increased from 2002 onwards in response to the atrocities arising from the country's second civil war between the northern and southern regions. To date, over 20,000 people from Sudan have resettled in Australia and, according to the Department of Immigration and Citizenship (DIAC), Sudan became the humanitarian programme's top 'source country' in the 2002/3 financial year.[1]

Despite their legitimate and government-sanctioned status as refugees, refugees from Sudan have nonetheless been represented as problematic in public discourse. To demonstrate how this is done, we examine data obtained from three naturalistic sources: political discourse, the mainstream newsprint media and commercial talkback radio. The first two sources provide insight into the formal discourse in Australia about refugees from Sudan, while talkback radio provides an opportunity to examine informal everyday conversations of the wider polity. In triangulating these three data sources, our aim is to examine how representations of a new and unfamiliar social group – humanitarian refugees from Sudan – proliferate in everyday formal and informal discourse, or more specifically, what Moscovici has referred to as the 'unceasing babble' of everyday life and social interaction.

The theory of social representations is particularly apposite to explicating the transfer and diffusion of knowledge within and between political, media and social domains, and how common sense emerges from these processes (Moscovici, 1998). However, this is not to say that social representations are hegemonic; rather, the process of representing unfamiliar social groups is concomitantly anchored to pre-existing, social-historical knowledge *and* current sociopolitical processes, practices and contexts (Howarth, 2006c; Joffe, 2003). Hence, social representations should not be characterized as universal and immutable – their pluralistic and dialogical nature has always been core to the theory (e.g. Howarth, 2006c; Moscovici, 1998).

The following analysis focusses on a selection of representational threads in the social environment. Our focus on these representations is premised on our critical interest in the ways that people invoke representational resources for strategic deployment in the social world, and how these representations are anchored to simplified representations of the African continent. Specifically, we examine data

---

[1] Commonwealth of Australia, Sudanese community profile (2007), retrieved 26.05.2008 from www.immi.gov.au/living-in-australia/delivering-assistance/government-programs/settlement-planning/_pdf/community-profile-sudan.pdf

on the reporting of crimes and violence allegedly perpetrated both by and towards refugees from Sudan that were represented in the media in 2007. These incidents culminated in the then immigration minister Kevin Andrews announcing that the Australian government was restricting the refugee intake from Africa, while also expressing concerns about African, and particularly Sudanese, refugees not settling or 'integrating' into Australian society.

It is important to emphasize that the category 'Sudanese' used in our analysis conflates many identities and experiences under one label. In particular, while the term is used in the media to refer to all people from Sudan, most people recently arriving in Australia for whom it is used come from Southern Sudan, fleeing conflict between rebel groups in Southern Sudan and government forces from Northern Sudan (Marlowe, 2010). Indeed, even the label 'Southern Sudanese' is insufficient to capture the experiences of these refugees, with people coming from Sudan having backgrounds in many different ethnic groups and religious and cultural affiliations, including Dinka, Nuer, Nuba and Achole. Thus while we use the more general term 'Sudanese' here to denote the groups in question (following its use in both lay and formal discourse), in reality the refugees referred to through this label are far from a homogeneous group; in fact, this term may subsume many of the tensions which caused these people to seek refuge in the first place.

Representations of refugees from Sudan in political discourse

In August 2007 the Australian government announced that it was reducing the intake of refugees from Africa in general from 70 per cent to 30 per cent. The government attributed the significant reduction in the quota to improved conditions in some African countries such as Sudan and the Congo, and an increased intake from the Middle East. Although this announcement stimulated very little media attention, this changed on 2 October 2007 when the federal minister for immigration, Kevin Andrews, was asked in an interview about better resettlement programmes for refugees and, in particular, about the murder of the Sudanese refugee Liep Gony. He replied that the African refugee quota had been reduced due to fears that 'some groups don't seem to be settling and adjusting into the Australian way of life as quickly as we would hope',[2] and that 'Australia has the right to ensure those who come here are integrating into a socially cohesive community.'[3] We will now analyze two extracts where the minister is asked to justify these claims in news interviews. These extracts are drawn from a larger data corpus of five radio

---

[2] More dogwhistling, *The Australian*, 2009, retrieved 21.04.2009 from http://theaustralian.news.com.au/story/ 0,25197,22526972–16382,00.html; J. Topsfield and D. Rood, Coalition accused of race politics. *The Age*, 2007, retrieved 10.11.2008 from www.theage.com.au/news/national/coalition-accused-of-race-politics/2007/10/03/1191091193835.html

[3] F. Farouque and D. Cooke, Ganging up on Africans, *The Age*, 2007, retrieved 23.09.2008 from www.theage.com.au/news/in-depth/ganging-up-on-africans/2007/10/05/1191091363944.html

interviews and two 'doorstop' interviews conducted with the then minister (see Hanson-Easey and Augoustinos, 2010 for a detailed corpus summary), and are illustrative of Andrews and his government's policy position and justifications for reducing the humanitarian refugee quota from Sudan.

In the first extract Andrews is being questioned by Philip Clarke from 2GB Sydney, who asks whether the 'ability' of 'young men from Sudan', in particular, to settle into Australian society was an influential factor in the decision to reduce the quota.

Extract 1. Minister Andrews' interview with Philip Clarke 2GB Radio, 3 October 2007

22	CLARKE:	Okay.h now() there has been some controversy in
23		the past about African(.2) refugee
24		resettlement (.) and the ability of .hh some
25		particularly ah() young men from the Sud::an
26		(.4)and their ability to-to ah to settle easily
27		into Australian society = was that a
28		factor in this decision?
29		(.3)
30	ANDREWS:	ye = yes it was a factor (.)Philip ah (.5) one of
31		the things which we've been (1.1) ah mindful of
32		over the ah (.)last year(.7) i:s the additional
33		challenges with some (.5) people-from-ah Africa
34		.h(.5)that we know for example if we're talking
35		about the(.)Sudanese(.)and this is not = to
36		demonize them (.2) it's just to .hh face the
37		reality that we've got (.5) they have ah very
38		(.9)low levels of education (.)ah on average
39		we're looking at about grade three level (.3)
40		that's a lot lower than any other group of
41		refugees(1.0) you've got people ah particularly
42		young men in their teens and early twenties (.3)
43		ahh(.)difficult therefore for many of them
44		to(.)get a job = they (.3) tend to drop out of
45		school(.3)a lot earlier and then there's a
46		whole lot of other (.3) cultural
47		issues
48	CLARKE:	hmm
49	ANDREWS:	coming from Africa (.3) compared to
50		modern Australia.

In response to Clarke's question, Andrews picks up on the membership category 'some people from ah Africa', but then shifts to the more specific category 'the Sudanese' (line 35), to which he subsequently attaches numerous social deficits that render this group as especially problematic compared to other refugee groups: 'low levels of education' and 'particularly young men' who 'drop out of school' early and who find it difficult 'to get a job'. The demographic profiling of this group as predominantly 'young men' formulates a descriptive account in which 'the Sudanese' are positioned as facing extreme challenges, and are thus especially vulnerable to unemployment and other social woes, which can threaten the young. Ending his turn (lines 45–47), Andrews employs the vague formulation, 'and then there's a whole lot of other cultural issues'. Without further elaboration, this reference to culture infers that more 'issues' could be invoked to provide further 'evidence', but this is not particularly necessary to advance the point. This effectively raises the issue of culture as a differentiating dimension, without having to go into any explanatory depth. This is an efficient way to infer that there are numerous causal mechanisms tied to the membership category 'Sudanese' which explain this group's (in)ability to resettle in Australia and 'cultural difference' is central to these.

Arguably, the descriptive focus on the group's nationality, and attendant deficits, removes connotations of this group as requiring humanitarian consideration. Ironically, the consequences of their refugee status (i.e. low education) is turned around and attributed as a *reason* for their exclusion. What is conventionally understood as part and parcel of *being* a refugee – pre-arrival deprivation – becomes, through this description, something less to do with seeking refuge in a safe country, and more a reified, relatively stable characteristic that has travelled with these refugees from Sudan. As we will see below, the focus on implied social deficits of refugees from Sudan, associated with their refugee status, culture and history, is a recurring representation in the data we analyzed.

Extract 1 also contains a rhetorical device that has been identified as a central feature of modern racism: a *direct denial of racism* (Van Dijk, 1992*)*. Denials of group denigration and racism, through pre-emptive strategies, work to manage the sorts of challenges that a politician could expect when generalizing characteristics to a group (Van Dijk, 1992). Andrews deploys a pre-emptive defence (disclaimer) on lines 36–37, denying that he is 'demonizing' the Sudanese in any way. This disclaimer serves to avoid a problematic identity for Andrews, mitigating against potential claims of unfair treatment and racism against a refugee group.

The possible claims of 'racism' and 'denigration' here are subtly discredited through their comparison with the 'additional challenges' (lines 32–33) and the 'reality' (line 37) that the Sudanese pose for Andrews and his government. This response, thus, positions Andrews' policy as responsible, measured, and, most importantly, necessitated by the behaviour of the refugees themselves. Potential allegations of racism are hence glossed over as irrational and unrealistic – lacking any real insight into the 'real problem' of resettling young Sudanese men.

In the second extract Andrews is being interviewed by Fran Kelly from ABC Radio National. Kelly is asking Andrews to provide 'evidence' and 'data' for his 'harsh' decision to cut the Sudanese refugee numbers. As we can see, this policy change was not accepted uncritically by journalists, and Andrews faced implicit and explicit accusations that the government was invoking the 'race card' for political gain.

Extract 2. Minister Andrews' interview with Fran Kelly ABC Radio National, 5 October 2007

3	KELLY:	Minister(.)the Courier Mail today had a photo of
4		a Sudanese family on the front page with a splash
5		headline .h (.3)blacklist(.4)government says
6		Sudanese don't fit .hh it's pretty harsh stuff
7		.h what evidence (.)what data do you base your
8		decision(.7) to li- to limit the-Sudanese refugee
9		numbers on(.6)the facts and figures that the last
10		man was asking for.
11	ANDREWS:	[11 lines removed] now .h coming to:o the matter
12		you asked about
13	KELLY:	mmhm
14	ANDREWS:	I get .h ah regular reports from my
15		department (.) hhh provide:d information through
16		.hh various community groups and ethnic
17		organisations from other sources (.)police and
18		oth-otherwise .hh (.)and there's been .h a-a
19		number of matters which have (.)continually being
20		brought to my attention about .h things
21		like the establishment of race based ga:ngs
22		ah .hh altercations between various groups .h
23		disagreement between ah .h various ah c-community
24		originations(.)tensions between families .h ah
25		and a range of other things (.)then on top of
26		that .hh we know when we look at the data .h that
27		.h this is a group that have .h ah (.)
28		special or uniq:ue challenges beyond those of
29		other groups of refugees (.1) for example the
30		average .hh schooling age is .h about four
31		compared to .h seven .h just three or four years
32		ago .h a lot more(.)forty percent have spent time
33		in refugee camps compared to .h just fifteen
34		percent .h in two thousand and two-three .h ah
35		the reading ability is quite low

In extract 2 Andrews attributes a comprehensive list of negative traits and characteristics to the category 'Sudanese refugees', and as such, constructs them as a highly problematic group. The purported establishment of 'race-based gangs' not only constructs refugees from Sudan as a criminal threat to the rest of the community, but also explicitly racializes them. Moreover, 'disagreements between community organizations' and 'tensions between families' constructs the collective as internally dysfunctional, ridden with intra-group conflict and disunity. The minister then proceeds to differentiate them further from other refugees by identifying other 'unique challenges' to the group: their average schooling age and reading ability is lower than that of other refugee groups, and a significant proportion of Sudanese (40 per cent) have spent time in refugee camps. Thus Andrews attributes the purported problems that refugees from Sudan face in settling in Australia to the internal fractures of the group itself, and the severity of their social deprivation associated with their pre-arrival experiences. Again, we see how the refugee status of the Sudanese diaspora (i.e. their pre-arrival deprivation and social dislocation) – the very defining features of their humanitarian refugee status – is turned around and attributed as a *reason* for their exclusion.

Note also how Andrews corroborates his account of the 'evidence' for the quota decision: he claims that the 'reports' (i.e. race-based gangs and troublesome inter-family disputes) have come from a wide range of sources including his department, community groups, the police and even ethnic groups. This formulation of 'various groups' corroborating the information is particularly robust to accusations of prejudice or bias that could be made against Andrews, especially in the light of the government's history of invoking 'the race card' on immigration issues. The police and the minister's department may be criticized in this way – community and ethnic organizations, on the other hand, would not be expected to provide evidence against groups whose interests they are expected to protect.

Although not analyzed here (but see Hanson-Easey and Augoustinos, 2010), Andrews' representation of Sudanese refugees as experiencing serious and protracted integration problems, and the subsequent political action that such an account justifies, was not always taken for granted by interviewers. Indeed this is clearly evident in Kelly's request in extract 2 for the Minister to provide 'evidence' to justify the government's actions. Contrary representations were sometimes used to re-represent refugees from Sudan as suffering short-term, transitional problems, expected from *any* new refugee group, instead of some inhering, and thus more threatening, propensity for crime and social dysfunction. Despite these alternative constructions however, the government continued to draw on objectified representations of Sudanese refugees as socially dysfunctional and ridden with intra-group conflict. As we will see, this was a recurring representation of refugees from Sudan that was purported to be strongly associated with their essentialized 'tribal' nature.

Representations in the newsprint media: the criminalization of refugees from Sudan

The government's decision to cut the Sudanese refugee quota was made in the context of extensive media coverage in 2007, of alleged violence and criminal behaviour associated with Sudanese Australians with a refugee background. These incidents included crimes committed both by and against refugees from Sudan. However, as we demonstrate, the mainstream news media coverage of these events frequently criminalized refugees from Sudan, and constructed them as a 'problem', regardless of whether they were the perpetrators or the victims.

The analysis we now present is drawn from a data corpus of articles that appeared in twelve of the highest circulation newspapers from January 2007 to mid 2010.[4] A

---

4 Australian Press Council, State of the news print media in Australia: a supplement to the 2006 report, 2007, retrieved 20.09.2010 from www.presscouncil.org.au/

search of *Factiva* was conducted for 'Sudan* AND (refugee* OR asylum seeker)', which returned 197 news articles, 105 of which were considered relevant to the issues represented in this chapter.

One news story that received extensive coverage concerned a series of crimes committed by a refugee from Sudan, Hakeem Hakeem, in early 2005. Hakeem was accused of going on a 'rape and crime spree' in which he raped and assaulted four women. These assaults and rapes were committed only several weeks after he had arrived in Australia as a refugee.[5] Hakeem was subsequently sentenced to twenty-four years in jail in January 2007, with a fixed seventeen-year minimum.[6] Extract 3 provides a representative example of the reporting in the mainstream news media of the sentencing of Hakeem, and the subsequent investigation launched by immigration minister Andrews.

Extract 3. C. Dore, *The Australian*, 1 February 2007, 4[7]

```
1   Immigration Minister Kevin Andrews has ordered an
2   investigation into how a troubled Sudanese refugee was
3   allowed to settle in Australia only to embark on a
4   three-day rampage of bloody violence and rape within
5   weeks of arriving.
6   Mr Andrews will also consider deporting Hakeem Hakeem
7   after the 21-year-old has served at least part of his
8   24 years in jail for the drug and alcohol-fuelled
9   frenzy two years ago...
10  The new Immigration Minister said he was at a loss to
11  explain how Hakeem managed to get into Australia.
12  'All I can say is that the information I have been
13  provided with this morning is that in terms of the
14  checks that were made, there was nothing that was shown
15  in those checks that at the time made officials here in
16  Australia wary of allowing him to come to the country,'
17  Mr Andrews said.
18  Mr Andrews added that he had asked his department to
19  investigate the Hakeem case. He also said he was
20  concerned about problems Sudanese refugees were
21  experiencing settling in Australia.
22  'We are talking about people who come from frankly
23  a very violent circumstance,' he said. 'This was a
24  country that has been subject to civil war, there is
25  murder and mayhem, we have got boy soldiers – all of
26  those sorts of things are part of the background of
27  that region, unfortunately, of Africa at the present
28  time. So we are putting in place programs that will
29  help these people.'
30  His comments come a month after *The Australian*
```

---

5 R. Robinson, Putting a face to the refugee row, *Herald Sun*, 6 October 2007, 24.
6 B. Roberts, Rapist refugee gets 17 years cut elderly woman's throat, *Herald Sun*, 31 January 2007, 5.
7 C. Dore, Probe on refugee after attack frenzy, *The Australian*, 1 February 2007, 4.

31 highlighted law and order problems among Sudanese and
32 other African migrants in Melbourne, particularly among
33 young men who had been exposed to extreme violence in
34 their homeland.

Hakeem's identity as a refugee from Sudan is explicitly foregrounded in this article, as is the severity of his crimes. The immigration minister attends to the government's accountability for allowing such a 'troubled' refugee to enter the country, providing assurances that the rigorous checks made by immigration officials did not identify any signs of potential criminality at the time of screening Hakeem. Despite these assurances, Andrews orders the Department of Immigration to investigate how Hakeem could have 'slipped through the system', and analogous to the previous extracts we have analyzed, also expresses concerns about Sudanese refugees in general, claiming that as a group they are experiencing problems settling into the country. More specifically, he attributes these problems to the 'very violent circumstances', from which the Sudanese have come and provides a list of descriptors to emphasize the extremity of the situation: 'civil war', 'murder', 'mayhem' and 'boy soldiers'. Again we see how the very reasons for which Sudanese refugees have been given refugee status are used against them, to homogenize and indeed problematize them as a group. Moreover, Andrews conflates this graphic portrayal of the political problems in the Sudan to the continent Africa in general.

Significantly, the crimes committed by Hakeem are represented not simply as the crimes of an individual, but as symptomatic of 'Sudanese and other African migrants' in general. By attributing 'law and order problems' to African migrants in general, and in particular to young men 'exposed to extreme violence', people granted humanitarian refugee status are primarily constructed as not only 'damaged', but by implication inherently violent and criminal themselves. Indeed, what is tacitly undergirding such a representation is, again, an essentialist theory that posits that by mere association with violence and 'mayhem', these experiences continue to have some causal effect on Sudanese-Australians' dispositions and behaviours, even after they have settled in a country far removed from the dangers from which they have fled. Such an essentialist representation clearly functions to explicate and validate government policy that restricts the refugee intake from places of significant need, such as Sudan.

So-called 'ethnic' violence was also the central focus of media articles that covered the murder of Sudanese teenager Liep Gony on 26 September 2007. Gony was bashed by two men armed with metal poles who left him unconscious near a train station in Noble Park in south-east Melbourne, where he was later found by a friend. Gony died in hospital the next day. While much of the media was scathing of this attack and sympathetic towards Gony's family, the mainstream news media still routinely reported this story within a framework of 'problem' Sudanese refugees. In fact, the Press Council upheld a complaint against *The Australian* to this effect, in which it was argued that the wording of several news and feature articles implied that Gony's death was the result of Sudanese gang violence, rather than the violence of two white Australian men.[8]

The extract that follows is taken from an article published on 29 September, before it was revealed that Gony's attackers were not Sudanese refugees. This extract is representative of initial articles published regarding the murder, which generally attributed Gony's murder to 'ethnic' violence.

Extract 4. H. Lloyd-McDonald, *Herald-Sun*, 29 September 2007[9]

```
1   Men are slaughtered in front of their children, babies
2   are ripped from their mothers' arms and those who dodge
3   the violence walk for days seeking sanctuary, shelter
4   and ultimately peace.
5   This is just another day in the life of a tribal
6   African trying to escape the clutches of a never-ending
7   civil war.
8   Liep Gony, 19, was part of such a shocking history but
9   turned his back on it to start a new, safe life in
10  Noble Park. But Liep will not share the Australian
11  dream like so many other eager immigrants.
12  The TAFE student died in the Alfred hospital yesterday
13  after he was bashed violently with either a piece of
14  wood or steel and left for dead on Wednesday night.
15  Homicide squad detectives are investigating the vicious
16  assault, which began at Noble Park railway station
17  after 9 pm and ended with Liep lying unconscious 200 m
18  away on Mons Parade.
19  His cousins told the *Herald Sun* on Thursday two youths,
20  one a South African, had tried to pick a fight earlier
21  in the night at a nearby skate park.
22  Liep and the two youths had allegedly been in an
23  altercation a week earlier. The area has become an
24  escalating hotspot for youth violence and ethnic
25  tensions, with African, Asian and Polynesian
26  strongholds based along the southeast Melbourne train
27  line.
28  Yesterday, the *Herald Sun* revealed a sickening history
29  of recent violence involving out-of-control youths.
30  Incidents include a bloodied Sudanese man repeatedly
31  biting the face of a policewoman trying to help him
32  and, on a separate patrol, a policeman's nose being
33  broken by a rock at Noble Park railway station.
```

The article begins with a list of acts of extreme violence: 'Men are slaughtered in front of their children, babies are ripped from their mothers' arms' (lines 1–2).

---

8 Australian Press Council (n.d.), Adjudication no. 1409, retrieved 17.09.2010 from www.presscouncil.org.au/pcsite/adj/1409.html
9 H. Lloyd-McDonald, Death finds a way: Liep Gony's family fled war in Sudan, *Herald-Sun*, 29 September 2007, 3.

Although providing a graphic portrayal of the horrors of war, the representations of extreme violence in both this and the previous extract become a parody of the intergroup conflicts in Africa, which are drawn upon relentlessly in simplified media accounts that rarely provide any contextualizing detail. Indeed, these experiences of violence are described as just 'another day in the life of a tribal African', and notably, the category of 'Sudanese' is not used at all in relation to Gony, with references instead to the broader term 'African'. Thus 'Africa' here is made to stand in for 'Sudanese', as if the conflation of these categories were possible. This depicts *all* of 'tribal Africa' as violent and dysfunctional, with the term 'tribal' simultaneously drawing upon discourses of Africa as primitive and backward. Such a construction conflates the many diverse realities of the different African countries into one global experience of violence and dysfunction. The repeated references to 'tribal' Africa and 'ethnic tensions' reflects and reproduces stereotypes of Africa as a troubled, primitive place full of violence and intergroup (tribal) conflict: the entire African continent is reified as a homogenized continent, 'Othered' and arguably *racialized*. As Hawk (1992) argues:

> The word 'African', as it is used in the western press, does not mean anyone who lives on the African continent, but rather people who are black and live on the African continent. It is a colonial label. North Africans and descendants of European settlers are not included in the term. This narrow, racial definition of Africa, structured by the language employed to tell the African story, tells readers and viewers that the continent has a simple, homogeneous culture. (p. 8)

Extract 4 also draws on an interesting contrast structure between the 'Australian dream' that provides hope for a better life to refugees like Gony, and 'tribal' Africa. This binary functions not only to reinforce representations of Africa as 'backward' in contrast to a developed and progressive nation like Australia, but also to locate the violence that has resulted in Gony's death as originating from somewhere other than Australia since violence is outside the Australian 'dream'. Indeed, later we read that in fact the violence enacted upon Gony came from 'ethnic tensions'. Thus violence is constructed as stemming from (and indeed inherent within) the very people for whom Australia is offering refuge.

Last but not least, this extract explicitly constructs the violence that led to the death of Liep Gony as 'ethnic' violence, detailing incidents of violence by refugees from Sudan, regardless of whether or not they are related to the incident in question. Thus Gony's death is turned into another example of 'ethnic tensions', and indeed represents Gony himself as complicit in these tensions by reporting on an altercation in which he was allegedly involved. The extract repeatedly racializes the violence not only through the reference to 'ethnic tensions' but also by explicitly racializing the people supposedly involved in this violence ('African', 'Asian', 'Polynesian'). References to 'hotspots' and 'strongholds' invoke stereotypes of ethnic gangs, thereby further drawing upon discourses of 'ethnic violence' as well as constructing the suburbs in which African Australians live as violent, unsafe and dysfunctional, and therefore as 'Other' to the Australian dream referenced earlier.

While the Sudanese community was widely criminalized in the timeframe surrounding Gony's murder (as seen in extract 4), the same criminalization on the basis of race was not extended to the offenders in question once their identity was made public. Indeed, the racial background of the offenders accused of Gony's murder was rarely mentioned in the mainstream news media (Due, 2010). Thus nominally white Australians are not criminalized in the same way as Sudanese-Australians are, with no conflation of white Australians as a group with criminality.

Despite the diversity of the twelve newspapers we included for analysis, the criminalization of refugees from Sudan was a pervasive representation and continued to be employed in November 2008, over a year after it was revealed that Gony's attackers were white Australians. Thus, the mainstream news media drew upon essentialized representations of *black* Sudanese as embodying a predilection for criminal activity, and as socially deficient. Moreover, implicit in these representations was the construction of Australia as a white nation into which those located as racial 'Others' must attempt to integrate if they are to be accepted as belonging. These discursive practices of 'Othering' and social exclusion were mentioned by Liep Gony's mother, speaking at her son's funeral, when she said: 'He is not an African. He is not a Sudanese refugee. He is an Australian. We are all Australians.'[10]

Representations of refugees from Sudan in talk radio: 'tribalism' and intra-group conflict

Talkback radio plays an increasingly significant role in how news and social issues are communicated to a wider populace. Talkback is a radio format that utilizes call-ins from listeners to speak on topics previously initiated by the host, or on subjects that callers themselves initiate. Since 1967, talkback radio in Australia has been implicitly conceived to have a democratizing role, giving a voice to 'everyday' Australian concerns, opinions and views (Turner, 2009). This format was coined by one of its earlier producers, with the egalitarian tag of 'God's great leveller' (Bodey, 2007, p. 15).

What is of analytical interest in relation to talkback radio is how interactants position and represent Sudanese refugees as problematic to a broader listening audience. Moscovici (1984b) has conceptualized the sorts of representations and everyday ideologies we are interested in here as evolving and reproducing socially: 'in the streets, in cafes, offices, laboratories ... people analyse, comment, concoct spontaneous, unofficial philosophies' (p. 30). Similarly, talkback can be likened to a mass-media variation of chatter between customers in Moscovici's coffee shop. Thus, talkback radio provides an under-utilized source of naturalistic data from which to view interactions that would be near impossible to reconstruct experimentally or within an interview setting.

10 M. Davis and C. Hart, Family's plea to end the racism, *The Australian*, 11 October 2007, 3.

We present two extracts from Bob Francis' night-time talkback show on FIVEaa, an Adelaide-based radio station, on the subject of the stabbing to death of Sudanese teenager Daniel Awak in Adelaide in 2008, to exemplify how refugees from Sudan are represented in informal talk. In the extract 5 the host introduces the topic of the stabbing on the night of the event, which functions as part 'editorial' and part request for callers to ring in with their views. In this way, callers regularly adopt this topic setting as a general thematic guide.

Extract 5. Bob Francis, FIVEaa Radio, 12 November 2008

```
 1 BOB:    ah: whaddya feel about that-ah: th't situation in town
 2         today. There's a teenager is dead now .h a:h another
 3         critically injured after being-stabbed in a wi:ld brawl
 4         between .hh Sudanese migrants in-the city this afternoon.
 5         .h y'know? (0.6) I've he:ard (0.3).h rumours in to:wn. that
 6         families that are coming out from the Sudan .hh living in
 7         Adelaide .h ar. are bringing their their sor-of .h ah-their
 8         trouble with them .h between the Hutus .hand the Tutsi
 9         tribes .h and tho:se situations are festering in our little
10         beautiful town like Adelaide? .hh and this could very well
11         well I don't know we- whether this was related to the- the
12         thing tho afternoon bu- ya'know I thought I'd jus bring
13         it up b'cause it's been brought up by .hh other people
14         around town? and I think .hh if you've got problems .h
15         take'em back to your own bloody country.
```

In this extract the host deploys an account, premised on the assumption that imported tribal tensions between 'the Hutus and the Tutsis'[11] (lines 8–9) are 'festering in our beautiful town' (lines 9–10), and this is posed as a possible explanation for the stabbing. In this way, 'Sudanese migrants' are represented as importers of brutal, genocidal violence implied by the categories 'Hutus' and 'Tutsis'. Adelaide, in juxtaposition, is depicted as a veritable hamlet, a vulnerable 'little beautiful town'. As we have already noted in our analysis of the newspaper reporting of other crimes relating to Sudanese-Australians, here again they are presented as harbingers of violence, predicated on a vivid representation of tribal conflicts. Further, they are tacitly defined as negative human capital, bringing 'festering' trouble with them from 'the Sudan'. Francis' solution is unequivocal: 'if you've got problems take 'em back to your own bloody country' (line 15). In this rhetorical moment – in which it is quite possible the intention is to spark debate at the beginning of the talkback show – the host explicitly positions refugees from Sudan as outsiders who do not normatively belong.

The next extract details an account of a violent incident (not shown in full here) witnessed by a caller. Again we see here how one event is represented as symptomatic of deeper, social problems, generalizable to the broader collective of

---

[11] These ethnic groups were the main protagonists in the Rwandan genocide.

'African' (black) kids. And again, the spectre of race-based gangs and intra-group conflict is invoked.

Extract 6. Bob Francis, FIVEaa Radio

9	BRAD:	u:m now of(0.7)just before we get started I- I'm bu- by no
10		way racist in any way shape or form.
11	BOB:	yep.
12	BRAD:	u:::m .hh but this evening I was I was out and about and I-
13		I h witnessed a young Sudane:se? (0.9) lad (.) get-(0.9)
14		completely (.3) smashed by his own kind,
15		(0.9)
16	BOB:	really?
17		(0.4)
18	BRAD:	u:::m (0.3) ee (0.3) an its I-don't I don't know (0.3)
19		after the young lad was: stabbed and killed in the
20		city .hh is- is- (0.8) the Adel = the South Australian
21		police doing anything this? or [or.
22	BOB:	[.hh well I don't know I-
23		I'd read in the paper or saw something on television the
24		other night and the show:ed (0.4) a:h a group of ah:
25		young .h ah black kids who weren't Aboriginal they were
26		obviously ah um African (.) African kids? .hh [and
27	BRAD:	[yep
28	BOB:	ah they'd set up a:h ga:ngs like the ah .h the Cribs
29		and [what's the other ones called
30	BRAD:	[yeah yep- yep- yep-
31	BOB:	.h and the- they're dressed with red bandannas and blue
32		bandannas .hh and their starting up little gangs an and
33		working out from .h from a:h ah bus stations and all that
34		sort of stuff.
35	BRAD:	[yes
36	BOB:	[.hh and that's not on.
37		(0.3)
38	BRAD:	yeah it's definitely not on [its( )
39	BOB:	[yeah I jus hope that the
40		Police are right on top of that (0.2) right from the
41		beginning?
42		(0.2)
43	BRAD:	well I- I'd- I'd like to say like (0.4) I-I'd welcome any
44		culture int'our into [our country.
45	BOB:	[yeah
46	BRAD:	we we've got a great country? an- and .hh and even our
47		nation anthem says we've got boundless place to share?

Like Andrews in extract 1, the caller here makes a disclaimer (Hewit and Stokes, 1975) that orientates to the possibility that the following account could be heard as motivated by racism, with the utterance 'I'm bu- by no way racist in any way shape or form' (lines 9–10). As the caller begins his narration, he describes a fight he has witnessed and that constitutes the reason for his call, specifically, 'I h witnessed a young Sudane:se? (0.9) lad (.) get-(0.9) completely (.3) <u>smashed</u> by his own kind' (lines 13–14). The metaphor 'completely smashed' glosses the initial description of the event as a dramatic and brutal altercation and 'by his own kind' makes clear that this is an instance of intra-group conflict. That is, conflict occurring between subgroups within a collective; an explanation that is elaborated on by the host, when he contends that the Sudanese are importing their '<u>warring</u> factions from their <u>tribes</u>'. An important upshot of extrematizing the event in this way is how it ultimately represents 'the Sudanese' as ostensibly, and dangerously different. This is no schoolyard fight, and these are not typical adolescents.

The emphasis on the aberrant nature of the violence and, it being an intra-group phenomenon, implies that the event may be generalizable to other incidents concerning refugees from Sudan, something that is subsequently elaborated on. The caller links his narrative with the previous incident involving a Sudanese-Australian youth who 'was stabbed and killed in the city' (line 19). Further, the host orientates to this generalization as he delineates another link to news reportage that discusses the development of gangs of 'young black kids' who were 'obviously African' (but not 'Aboriginal'), who take on names resembling those of American 'colour gangs'. What is striking here, and apposite to our discussion on racialized essentialist representations, is how this account presupposes assumptions of shared causality for two distinct events (the stabbing and the witnessed fight), involving two separate groups of individuals. What enables this presumption of causality is an implicit logic that treats 'the Sudanese' as a homogenized collective who share an essential quality that, in the right context, manifests in violent behaviour.

Finally, what is also of note in this extract is when the caller again makes the claim that he would welcome any culture 'int' our into our country' (line 44), and more generally, invokes sentiments from the 'national anthem' about 'boundless place to share' (line 47). Thus, representing himself, and indeed the nation, as fundamentally egalitarian and tolerant of those depicted as 'Other', works as a disclaimer against a problematic, 'racist' identity, something to which the calls analyzed in the corpus regularly orientate.

Conclusion

In this chapter we have drawn on naturalistic data from three different sources – political discourse, the media and talkback radio – to examine the ways in which refugees from Sudan have been categorized as a social group on racial grounds and as deserving of explanation for their purported socially undesirable and morally accountable behaviour. Examining the dynamic contents and functions of representations that society employs to make sense of such events has been one of the principle tasks of the theory of social representations. Indeed, Moscovici and Hewstone (1983) contend that social representations not only provide the representational building blocks by which individuals within their social collectives construe their social world, but also constitute the basis from which imputations of causality can be made.

This casual accounting tacitly accompanied representations of Sudanese-Australians with racialized references to 'African' history, culture and evocative images of a homogenized 'Africa' pervasively despoiled with 'tribal' violence. Crucially, these explanations do much of the ideological toil in 'Othering' Sudanese-Australians, attributing blame and warranting controversial policy decisions.

What should be stressed, however, is that what engenders these explanations as intelligible, is an essentialist theory that reifies Sudanese-Australians *as* a homogenized racial group with a putative 'culture' that embodies a history of violence and social dysfunction. Thus, clearly, one of the implications of essentialist representational practice is that it can be applied with broad brushstrokes to any individual member of the collective, irrespective of their specific individual circumstances. We can discern, then, how essentialist beliefs can be invoked when an unfamiliar and threatening social group is deemed to warrant interpretation, functioning to contextualize or 'anchor' Sudanese-Australians within the representational meaning systems pertaining to 'Africa' more broadly.

Conceptualizing essentialist beliefs about social groups as ostensibly situated within collectively shared representations is the point of departure between the theory of social representations and other psychological approaches in their respective attempts to theorize and study essentialist practices. Cognitive psychology (e.g. Medin, 1989; Rothbart and Taylor, 1992) has, in general, theorized essentialist thinking as constituting an omnipresent cognitive orientation that endows individuals with cognitive efficiencies and 'rich inductive potential' for perceiving the social world. Moreover, psychological essentialism has also been conceptualized as a component of a 'prejudice-syndrome' (Allport, 1954), an unfortunate cognitive style that lends itself to thinking in concrete terms about inhering dispositional qualities and traits, stemming from a group 'essence'. These approaches, in general, ignore how essentialist representations function as an ideological resource, drawn from the body of collective, everyday knowledge.

There are, however, promising synergies between different research traditions. For example, Yzerbyt, Rocher and Schadron's (1997) theory of 'subjective essentialism', although elaborating at the individual level of analysis, nevertheless explicates the functional role essentialism and stereotyping play outside an individual's perceptive and categorization processes. For them, essentialist beliefs function to rationalize and stabilize current 'social arrangements' (p. 49). Similarly, as we have shown in this chapter, essentialist representations of Sudanese-Australians are oriented to extant social and political contexts, enabling explanations that do much to warrant actions that aim to preserve in-group dominance. Moreover, as Purkhardt (1993) notes, social representations help us to render the world intelligible, and 'achieve this by indicating where to find the effects and how to choose causes; by indicating what must be explained and what constitutes an explanation; and by setting an event in the context of a system of relations with other events' (p. 9).

As we have hopefully elaborated here, essentialist assumptions provide ready-made, common-sense explanations that identify the causes of effects, and these accounts can have serious implications for the social inclusion of minority groups. However, we do not contend that essentialist practices are inherently oppressive in and of themselves. As Verkuyten (2003) argues, essentialist and 'de-essentialist' discourses can be brought to bear for achieving various situated social aims – emancipatory or illiberal. Indeed, we contend that it is not the cognitive process and structure of psychological essentialism that should be the sole focus of future investigations. Rather, the contents of essentialist representations and their functional orientation to rationalizing and justifying the social order should also be examined.

Howarth (2007) has argued that what the theory of social representations 'offers... is an explicit focus on the social dynamics of "race", that is, the collaborative, social, and ideological construction and reconstruction, negotiation, and contestation of representations and practices that *race*' (p. 134). While we have specifically focussed on the reproduction of 'race' and social exclusion, it is important to bear in mind that these practices of reproduction can be and are on occasion disrupted through contestation (e.g. Gony's mother's categorization of her son as an 'Australian' as opposed to an 'African' or 'Sudanese refugee'; or refugee youth from Sudan contesting the label of 'trauma'; see Marlowe, 2007). Social representations are not impervious to change, and for those wanting to enable a more equitable and just society, the examination of current constructions, of what constitutes 'common sense', is key to the development of re-presentations of social reality.

23 Exploring stability and change through social representations: towards an understanding of religious communities

Mohammad Sartawi

This chapter aims to take a closer look at the different ways in which the theory of social representations has been applied and understood with reference to a study conducted on British Muslim communities in London. More specifically, it aims to conceptualize social representations as both a construct that serves to maintain the stability and continuity of a particular social group's identity, norms and practices *and* provide a foundation of knowledge from which social groups can adapt to, and cope with, change.

The dual nature of social representations

Social representations are constituents of culture; they are social knowledge systems that define groups and provide them with the tools to make sense of their environments and navigate their worlds. They instill the world with meaning and are drawn on to make sense of the new and unfamiliar. The strength of a social representations approach in cultural psychology is that it provides a framework to understand the self and identity as socially situated, and hence brings to the fore the relationship between social knowledge, identity, communities and practice. It is necessary to highlight that these particular strengths of the theory stem from its conceptualization of a dual function of social knowledge. On the one hand, social knowledge is not always at the forefront of consciousness, and acts rather as rules and guides that allow us to go about our everyday lives. On the other hand, social representations also provide us with the necessary means to renegotiate and resolve aspects of our beliefs and behaviours that may become problematic. This dual function of social representations, their *prescriptive* and *transformative* functions, makes the theory robust, enabling comprehensive and versatile applications when attempting to understand social phenomena. At the same time, it may be cause for a great deal of confusion when approaching the theory and apprehending its multiple uses and interpretations. Thinking about social representations as social psychological constructs that both provide stability for social groups and inform adaptive and coping processes during times of social change, may help streamline its various understandings and approaches.

Initially, Moscovici (1961/1976) was interested in the way different social milieus in France in the late 1950s made sense of psychoanalysis. He particularly paid attention to the dissemination of psychoanalysis through different media and forms of communication, and the nature of its incorporation into existing belief and knowledge structures of different social groups. The form in which psychoanalysis became incorporated into the common sense of these groups, and the media through which the communication of this knowledge took place, were group-specific, and were a function of specific group interests. One can see from reading his work that social representations at that point was a theory of the dissemination of expert knowledge and its incorporation into common sense, and how this was manifested in group-specific forms of communication and discourse. The main emphasis in the work was on language and communication as a medium through which the negotiation of new knowledge and its reception by groups with specific beliefs, interests and motivations could be apprehended.

Following Moscovici, the theory of social representations has been applied to areas exploring attributions (Augoustinos, 1990), identity (Breakwell, 1986), community knowledge processes (Jovchelovitch, 2007), media and communication (Bauer, 2000), trust (Marková and Gillespie, 2008), racism (Howarth, 2002a), gender (Lloyd and Duveen, 1990) and many others. The methods used in social representations studies have ranged from experimental designs, various statistical methods, surveys, ethnography, discourse analyses, free association, interviews and more (see Breakwell and Canter, 1993). This has had implications for the way the theory is conceptualized and reproduced.

Also, due to the aforementioned dual functionality of social representations, its applications served to further diversify its understanding. Many social representations studies attempt to explore the processes in which new knowledge is incorporated into knowledge systems specific to different groups (e.g. Moscovici, 1961/2008; Bauer and Gaskell, 2002; Gervais, 1997). If the theory of social representations is a theory of common sense, then its utility, according to this approach, lies in its ability to draw out *sense-making mechanisms* of various groups and the *social processes* that facilitate the reception and assimilation of this new knowledge. Group-specific forms of communication, mediation and *representation* of this new knowledge in communicative practices within and across groups become the focus of enquiry through which the researcher can arrive at some sense of group identities (Bauer and Gaskell, 1999). This knowledge is at the forefront of social consciousness. By virtue of employing such verbs as 'negotiated' and 'contested', a sense of confrontation with this new knowledge is implied, a reflexive encounter with the issue of placing a new phenomenon within an established structure of social knowledge (Marková, 2003). There is thus a dialectical relationship between new knowledge and existing systems of knowledge from which these processes emerge.

Other approaches to social representations attempt to conceptualize the relationship between existing, well-established knowledge systems and daily experience of the life-world. Such studies are normally interested in a specific group or community within which a specific phenomenon is located. The focus of enquiry here attempts to conceptualize a relationship between socially constituted knowledge and its constitution of everyday practice (e.g. Bradbury, 1999; Jodelet, 1989/1991; Lloyd and Duveen, 1990). This knowledge is taken for granted and non-reflexively embodied and enacted. This is precisely what makes sociohistorical considerations necessary to make sense of sense-making activities, processes and positionings within a representational field.

The prescriptive function of social representations

Belonging to a social group serves different needs for individuals, such as increased self-worth (Tajfel and Turner, 1986), a sense of shared purpose (Asch, 1952/1987), and joint commitment to shared goals (Tomasello et al., 2005). Social groups provide their members with a sense of security by instilling them with feelings of connection, sharedness and stability. In order for this to occur, groups need to have continuity and must be somewhat consistent in their make-up and character over time. The norms, traditions, and practices of groups maintain its identity and give it this continuity and stability.

> There is an art of memory in every culture which makes us see how the memories lying deep in the unconscious are implemented, with the sui generis force of tradition, to appropriate the new elements, and come back to life. In this *ars memorativa*, memory tends to conventionalize representations or words by removing all that is unfamiliar, so as to reproduce them in conformity with a certain typical form. (Moscovici, 1993b, p. 74)

Social knowledge is largely taken for granted, and its structures and roles are not questioned in everyday activity. It takes the form of social structures that inform and define group identities. They are produced or co-constructed by groups to facilitate interaction with their environments, and are thus a natural way of approaching the world. This 'naturalization' is necessary in order to enable individuals to go about daily life without the need to reflexively engage with the elements involved in such activity. Bourdieu and Nice (1977) call it 'a quasi-perfect correspondence between the objective order and subjective principles of organization [through which] the natural and social order appears as self-evident'. We are, for the most part, unaware of the influence of social forces on our everyday functioning. This in Moscovici's view represents the *I* and the *Me* first conceptualized by James (1890) and later developed and elaborated by Mead (1934); 'one taking into account all that is personal, the other all that is impersonal in the sense of the collective, as we later finely understood by Mead' (Moscovici, 1993b, p. 59). This split is generally recognized by social theorists in one form or another as individual–social/agency–structure dualisms. What Mead, following James, managed to accomplish is the internalization of the social by the individual thereby overcoming this dualism to a degree. In effect, these scholars also established that the internalization of whole structures of social forces that influence our responses to, and even our very perception of, the world around us is the essential characteristic of human psychic development. They also determine how we act on the world around us.

The conceptualization of action that dominates social representations has largely been concerned with language and verbal communication. However, modes of dress, occupation of particular public spaces, physical presence or absence at certain types of social gatherings can all be forms of communicative action. Further, all social practices and interactions tell us something about what a particular group or community may think or believe that we may not apprehend through what they tell us that they think or believe (Jodelet, 1989/1991; Joffe, 1999). They are, in essence, expressions of group-specific forms of social knowledge that *are* social representations. Social representations can therefore be seen as

> a form of practical knowledge connecting a subject to an object [or world of objects]... Qualifying this knowledge as 'practical' refers to the experience from which it is produced, the frameworks and conditions in which it is produced, and above all to the fact that representation is used for acting in the world. (Jodelet, 1989/1991, pp. 43–44)

Through the intersubjective processes outlined by Mead (1934) involving conversations of gestures, adjustment to the responses of others, and perspective-taking, individuals acquire a sense of what it means to be part of a social group and how one becomes a member that expresses a specific group identity. Individuals acquire a sense of what is socially appropriate, 'normal', and unacceptable within the groups to which they belong through the responses of others to their actions, and learn to take the perspective of others in their social groups in evaluating their own behaviour. Identity, in this sense, is performed through habits, practices and modes of behaviour that extend beyond language. Human beings find themselves directly and non-consciously engaged in practices and activities that make sense to them. These norms, codes, and practices maintain the continuity of a group's identity and give it stability over time.

Transformative functions of social representations

Social representations are also characterized by multivocality and dialogicality (Marková, 2003). Moscovici adapted Durkheim's concept of collective representations in order to accommodate for the plurality of knowledge in modern times. A defining feature of social representations is the diversity in the elaboration of a social object as a result of the plurality of social knowledge systems. '[S]ocial representations are, for modern man, no more than one of many ways of understanding' (Moscovici, 1961/2008, p. 5).

> [A] social representation is not completely shared, it is only partially distributed, just as part of the meaning of words is known to some people and unknown to others. Therefore everyone lacks some item of the knowledge that other speakers possess... I can even add that if all people pictured things to themselves in a similar way, they would be nothing but mirrors engaged in specular conversations. In short, they would be a mass of individuals reproduced in thousands of exemplars, not a real society. In real societies, people routinely understand some statements as agreeing with their social representation and others as conflicting with it. (Moscovici, 1994, p. 168)

A defining feature of social representations is the plurality of knowledge, their heterogeneous nature and their constitution by divergent perspectives. The various modes of communication and representational processes (discussed in the literature employing action verbs such as 'contest', 'negotiate', 'co-construct', etc.) are contingent upon and only possible due to this diversity. Employing verbs such as 'elaboration' and 'transformation' implies a process of change, modification, or evolution of representations. Change cannot take place without the necessary presence of something new and different; something that unsettles the stability and taken-for-grantedness of well-established worldviews and ways of going about life (Marková, 2003). Therefore, central to the theory of social representations is the triadic relationship between ego, alter, and object (Moscovici, 1972, p. 52). A representational field is characterized by the engagement of at least two subjects in the elaboration of a social object. Not only is this triadic relationship characteristic of micro-level processes of interaction involving at least two individuals; it also describes intergroup relations as well. This seemingly simple model then represents the structure, function, and process of social representations that connect the individual with the collective, self and society.

'Social' representations, as opposed to Durkheim's 'collective' representations, are only possible if there are alternative ways of thinking and acting. Identifying with both their Britishness and their Muslimness allows British Muslims to draw on both social knowledge systems to give meaning to various objectifications in their social worlds and, consequently, continuously renegotiate their identities (see Sartawi and Sammut, 2012). These processes take place amidst a multiplicity of social knowledge systems where religious, pre-migration, and host society cultures meet. Social representations define a group in relation to other groups, and give its members a particular group identity. Societal positions or perspectives with regards to social representations are internalized, and incompatibilities, conflicts, and tensions are not only played out in society but also within the self. The fluidity and malleability of identity result from multiple social affiliations that lead to different positions with regards to social representations, and are defining features of the contemporary self. At times, the constant confrontation with elements of social knowledge that is taken for granted in moments of contradiction becomes so unsettling that Muslims seek to claim spaces and recreate their home cultures in order to escape these tensions and conflicts.

The theory of social representations provides an appropriate framework for the exploration of the experience of culturally dislocated religious communities, and the position of Muslims in the West is illustrative of the main tenets of the theory with regards to sharedness and consensuality. The plurality of Islamic belief is rooted in the diversity of Islamic diaspora, each with their own historical trajectory that, while differentiated and heterogeneous, still forge an Islamic community that is united under the banner of the *umma* in juxtaposition to non-Muslims. Furthermore, specific aspects of Islamic belief and the way in which they are asserted in relation to socially significant objects is defined by what 'other' (or alter) the group is juxtaposed to. In the case of Muslim diaspora in Europe, taken-for-granted cultural norms and practices are often called into question if they are perceived as being incommensurable with a new host culture. Drawing on various sources of cultural knowledge in order to resolve incommensurability in such instances shows how social representations inform processes of negotiation from a platform of long-established, previously taken-for-granted systems of knowledge (Sartawi and Sammut, 2012). What is prescribed by social representations in terms of understanding and practice becomes evident when the need to accommodate conflicts with other knowledge systems arises.

Social representations and the study of religion

In approaching questions of stability and change in the lives of religious communities, it is necessary to understand how religion functions in the everyday lives of religious groups. Religion can be both a catalyst and an obstacle to change, and is often resorted to by believers to maintain a sense of stability in times of uncertainty. In order to address the question of the relationship between religion and everyday life conceptually, one must look to the existing tools and traditions that have been applied to studying religion and religious life in the social sciences. Despite the fact that psychologists had been interested in religion as a phenomenon when psychology was in its nascence (e.g. James, 1902/1936; Leuba, 1916), sociology and anthropology have been the forerunners in social scientific explorations of religion. Durkheim (1912), Weber (1963), Malinowski (1948) and Geertz (1968; 1976) were among the founding scholars of a social scientific approach to the study and understanding of religion and religious communities. Although William James' classic exploration of religious experience (*The Varieties of Religious Experience*) was first published over a century ago, the field of the psychology of religion as it is now known is relatively much younger. In spite of studies in the field ranging across the sub-disciplines of psychology, even to neuropsychology, there has been much more focus on data and measurement than theory and integration (Paloutzian and Park, 2005). One of the main reasons listed by Emmons and Paloutzian (2003) was that religion was seen as more of a philosophical than scientific area of exploration, almost a 'taboo' for psychology. In the first half of the last century those that offered theories of religion were the grand theorists in psychoanalysis (Freud and Jung), and then only as part of a grander project of theorizing all domains of the psyche and human nature (ibid.). Belzen (1997), in discussing problematic issues within the psychology of religion, notes:

> Even though it has existed for more than a century and counts all 'great psychologists' among its contributors (cf. Wulff 1991), to many, psychology of religion is still an obscurity. Either it is considered to be an impossibility – usually because of theological *a prioris* – or it is regarded to be superfluous – often because of a personal lack of interest and sometimes even animosity towards religion. (p. 7)

In their discussion of multiple definitions of 'religion' and 'spirituality' (sometimes even as opposed to each other) in psychology, Zinnbauer and Pargament (2005) touch on a tendency within the discipline towards dualistic views of the phenomena. On the one hand, there are constructs that reflect inner experiences that are dynamic, personal, open and experiential (e.g. Cardena, Lynn and Krippner, 2000; Taves, 2009). These tend to emerge from a phenomenological approach to reported religious experiences such as 'enlightenment' or 'possession' and attempt to conceptualize them as they are experienced in their totality. On the other hand, the opposing constructs within these dualisms are static, institutionalized, rigid, and based on unquestioned and formalized beliefs (see Belzen, 2010, for a discussion). This is not surprising seeing as the majority of research within the tradition has attempted to reduce religion to its assumed constituting elements in order to quantify and measure them on 'scales' or 'dimensions' in relation to various other psychological constructs such as prejudice (Allport and Ross, 1967), attributions (Spilka and Schmidt, 1983) or personality (Emmons and McCullough, 1999). An example of this is Allport and Ross's (1967) scale of religious orientation, which ranges from extrinsic (utilitarian and close-minded) to intrinsic (selfless and open). Other mainstream psychological approaches to religion have coupled aspects of it to existing traditions in the field in their attempts to establish quantification, association and causality. These have ranged from attempts to uncover relationships between religiousness and prejudice, religiosity and emotion, religion and mental health, and religion and personality traits (see Paloutzian and Park, 2005, for a comprehensive review).

Although anthropological and sociological approaches to the study of religion emphasized its significance as an entire system of social knowledge, their interests lie mainly in structural characteristics and symbolic systems as central foci. This obscures the relationship between the individual and the social. The individual is sidelined in accounts of practice, and it seems as though religious customs and rituals have an existence almost independent of the individuals that embody them (e.g. Bourdieu and Nice, 1977; Geertz, 1968; Malinowski, 1948). At the other end of the spectrum, Hill and Hood (1999) review over a hundred standardized measurement tools for various aspects of religiosity and group them into several clusters covering beliefs, practices, values, commitment, coping and fundamentalism among others. These have a much more individualistic level of analysis and attempt to capture elements of cultural expression at the individual level. They express concerns towards this diversity of approaches to measurement and advocate working towards theoretical integration and synthesis. Other specialists in the field express similar concerns regarding the lack of coherence and theoretical integration in the psychology of religion (Paloutzian and Park, 2005; Belzen, 2010).

The most relevant critique of psychological approaches to religion in relation to this present chapter is that of Belzen (2005, 2010). With regards to the psychology of religion, Belzen (2005)) notes that much of the work in the sub-discipline loses sight of its proclaimed object (religion) for individual-based psychic phenomenon that are in some way linked to religion. As such, the sub-discipline has less to say about religion and its impact on the everyday worlds of its followers and more to say about how various reductive constructs in mainstream psychology manifest themselves in relation to religion. For over a decade, Belzen (1997, 1999a, 1999b, 2005, 2010) has been advocating an interdisciplinary cultural approach to the study of religion. He believes that, despite the merits that other more established traditions within the sub-discipline may have, a cultural psychological approach will overcome problematic assumptions and diverse motivations that many psychological research programmes on religion are founded upon. Further, it serves to counterbalance a prevailing tendency to reduce higher-level psychic phenomena such as religion, and social knowledge and interaction, to individual-level processes such as attributions, motivations, personality dimensions or mental disorders (see Hill and Gibson, 2008). Belzen's larger project is based on his firm belief that we cannot claim to be carrying out psychological studies of religion qua religion unless we go beyond the walls of laboratories, bypassing psychometric measures, and immerse ourselves in the sites of religions where those who consider themselves religious become the focus of enquiry (Belzen, 2010).

Investigating Islam in terms of conceptualizations of religion as involving universal psychic processes that emerge in all religious phenomena is very limiting. For many Muslims around the world, religion and culture are inseparable and reproduce themselves through custom and ritual in different ways across the diverse social groups to which they belong (Bourdieu and Nice, 1977; Bourdieu, 1990). For Geertz (1968), the shape or form Islam takes is an attempt to reconcile its structure and content with existing beliefs and traditions in such a way that it continues to exist and develop as part of the fabric of society. This gave rise, he argued, to a fundamentalist orthodoxy in a diverse and multi-societal Morocco and a pragmatic, compromising comprehensiveness in a post-Hindu/Buddhist Indonesia. Therefore, despite the function of religion and the needs it serves, the way that it is shaped and the meanings that are invested in it are culturally variable and differentially experienced. Further, Asad rejects universalist conceptions of religion 'not only because its constituent elements are historically specific, but because that definition is itself the historical product of discursive processes' (Asad, 1993, p. 29). Although Asad's stance is more radical in that he denies any possibility of arriving at a universal definition of religion, he does highlight the fact that the social sciences, much like religion, are rooted in historical process and traditions that maintain themselves and that cannot be easily escaped. In addition, they share similar concerns with regards to nomothetic readings of religion.

It was such limitations that initially dissatisfied Moscovici with existing traditions in psychology and other social sciences. Psychology was, in his view, reductive and individualizing, and the other social sciences, such as sociology, too deindividuating and impersonal (Moscovici, 1961/2008). What Moscovici managed to achieve with social representations was to place them in the space between self and other, structure and agency, the prescriptive and the transformative, the old and the new, knowledge and behaviour, the individual and the social.

> [The theory] sought to a) describe the content of social representations in terms of different dimensions (information, attitude, and field of representation) and its modes of elaboration (information dispersion, inference pressure, focalisation); b) analyse the processes of formation of representations (objectification, anchoring); c) delineate natural thinking and its logical properties (formalism, informal repetition, analogy and cognitive polyphasia); and d) explore the functions of representations (the orientation of behaviour and communication). (Jodelet, 2008, p. 418)

Religion is one area of social knowledge and beliefs that serves to both prescribe everyday behaviour and inform processes of coping and adaptation in times of change or when facing the unfamiliar. Rather than thinking of religion as a social representation, thinking of it more as a molder, producer and collection of social representations can serve efforts to understand it more effectively. On the one hand, social representations are invoked, produced and recreated at times when new phenomena enter various publics and need to be incorporated into existing social knowledge systems. Various groups take different positions with regards to a given phenomenon and attempt to make sense of it in terms of their specific sociohistorical and cultural roots. On the other hand, social representations are also enacted in everyday life-worlds and prescribe the way members of various social groups approach and experience their environments. The former approach views social representations as transformative processes of consciously re-presenting while the latter sees them as embodied in everyday activity, social norms and preferences. It is specifically this dual conception that makes social representations an appropriate framework for a cultural psychological exploration of the phenomena related to social knowledge, beliefs and everyday practices such as religion. Further, it emphasizes the centrality of individuals in their relation to the social knowledge systems that inform their sense-making processes while giving importance to the ways in which knowledge and beliefs shape their thoughts and behaviours.

London's British Muslim community

The original purpose of the study presented here was to explore the experience of British Muslims in everyday settings and understand the implications that being both Muslim and British had on intrapersonal, interpersonal and intergroup processes within the fabric of life in London. The bulk of the data gathered consisted of field notes from a twelve-month ethnography in which the researcher was a covert participant observer in three of London's largest mosques. The researcher took on voluntary work at the mosques and occupied positions as assistant chef at one mosque, personal assistant to the imams at another and archiving administrator at the third. The field notes were mostly recorded after exiting the field and then arranged chronologically to form a corpus of text. This was coded using a computer-assisted data analysis software following a grounded thematic analysis procedure and interpreted keeping in mind intrapersonal, interpersonal and intergroup processes. The participants were Muslims from various ethnicities and of all ages; however, females were under-represented due to the difficulty of access that resulted from the researcher being male. A portion of the data, however, was gathered from female participants in the researcher's role as assistant to the imam.

The data show that social representations have an adaptive function which serves individual and community needs to respond to change. They also show that social representations have a stabilizing function, which allows communities to recreate cultures and norms and feel secure within the bounds of the familiar in an unfamiliar environment. This dual function of social representations, along with its emphasis on bridging the individual and the social when theorizing social knowledge and beliefs, uniquely positions the theory as a tool for exploring the everyday life of religious communities.

Islam and its prescriptions

Ethnic affiliations were very salient within the Muslim community. Visual cues were explicit indicators at times. These were not restricted to skin tone or colour. Many made an effort to dress as Muslims from particular ethnic backgrounds and accentuate their belonging to particular backgrounds, differentiating themselves from others (see Doise, Deschamps and Meyers, 1978). The Muslims at one mosque often dressed in a *djellaba* or a *burnous*, which were long full-body dresses, often with a hood sewn into the back. They would also wear a *kufi*, or a knitted skull-cap. They would trim their beards short as well. The women also wore colourful *djellabas* and *hijabs*. In another mosque, most of the attendees dressed in a way that was typically influenced by Arabian Gulf clothing. They would wear a *thob*, also a long full-body dress with a collar rather than a hood. These were often shortened to above the ankles to avoid having them trail on the ground and bring dirt into the mosque. Their beards were long and bushy, and they would often trim their mustaches. Most of the women covered themselves in black *abayas* or loose cloaks, and wore black *hijabs*. At the third mosque the men would generally wear *salwar kameez*, which is a two-piece type of clothing consisting of a *salwar*, or loose cotton or wool trousers, and a *kameez*, or long (usually knee-length) shirts. They also wore coloured caps or *taqiyas* and let their beards grow long while trimming their mustaches. The women wore loose black garments from head to toe, and *burkas* were quite common. There were also differences across ethnicities when it came to ritual and practice. Alongside the customary dates, Algerians generally broke their Ramadan fast with bananas and milk flavored with fruit syrup. South Asians press their palms together during supplication, as opposed to Arabs, who would hold both hands out with palms facing up. South Asians resembled Hindus in the way they pressed their palms together when supplicating, and this was one clear example of how Islamic cultures are infused with pre-Islamic ones, as Geertz (1968) famously observed.

The taken-for-grantedness of social representations becomes more evident when there are ruptures or contradictions in a particular representational field that unsettle them and force participants to reconsider what they know or believe. An excerpt from the researcher's notes reads as follows:

> The most frequent requests for ruqya [exorcism] came from African Muslims. This was perhaps due to the fusion of traditional African beliefs and customs with Islam over generations. They seemed to attribute any evil, difficulty, or misfortune to the operation of spirits or black magic. This corresponded to the concept of Jin and those who work with Jin in Islam. Despite the fact that most Muslims believe in Jin, their presence and operation in human life is widely disbelieved. The Africans wanted the imam to bless them or perform an exorcism to counter the effects of such spirits/magic. Today, a man seemingly desperate came into my office and sat down. He told me that he believes that his daughter was under the effects of evil spirits. He said she was always a good girl, but as of late she had become rebellious and stubborn. She had made new friends that the parents did not approve of and wanted to spend all her time with them and none with her family.

A conversation with this participant revealed that sudden changes in character or behaviour in his native culture were thought to result from spiritual possession. This belief was thought to be based in Islam; however, it was common across other ethnicities in his country of origin as well. The case presented may very well have been a typical 'coming of age' instance of teenage development. When presented with this view by the imams of the mosque, the man completely changed his understanding of the situation. Prescriptive social knowledge can be both constructive in framing our understanding of objects and phenomena in the world around us, and functional in prescribing cultural habits and practices (see Moscovici, 1993b). Whereas he was convinced that his interpretation of the situation was Islamic, alternative views from the imams led him to entertain the idea that in other cultures that may or may not be Muslim, his daughter's behaviour can be seen as typical of a stage of development for a teenage girl. What the man took for granted as the only way to understand his daughter's behaviour was re-evaluated by drawing on other systems of knowledge that he had now come in contact with.

Several instances of Muslims from South Asian backgrounds wanting to change the names they had given to their new-born children are documented in the data. They seemed to think that this was unacceptable in Islam specifically because the names referred to Islamic figures or concepts. The imams (usually from Arabic backgrounds), who were often consulted as to the permissibility of name-changing, found this strange. In Islam, there is no rule prohibiting the changing of a name, and as Arabs this was taken for granted in their cultures. The understanding of what a name represented and its relation to religion that was once taken for granted by the following participant was renegotiated in light of how it was represented by other Muslims.

> A woman called because she had been praying for a girl and promising that if God granted her wish she would name her Paradise [Fardous in Arabic]. Because the name was difficult to work with here in the UK, she was constantly having to spell it out, and it was making things complicated as spellings varied in different documents she was trying to acquire. Therefore she was constantly reapplying to have documents reissued with consistent transliterations of the name. She asked if she could change it, or whether God would be displeased with her. She was terrified at the thought. She wanted the imam's assurance that violating her oath would not anger Allah and cause misfortune to befall her.[1]

These excerpts and descriptions of modes of dress and practice reflect aspects of religious expression that are usually not questioned. They prescribe behaviour without being consciously apprehended for the most part. Although these beliefs and practices may not be Islamic per se, they do form part of Islamic representations in various cultures. In fact, participants were usually shocked to learn that what they hold as Islamic beliefs and expressions come from regional cultures and not Islamic doctrine. This serves to illustrate the point that studying religion as text or scholarly interpretation tells us little about what is believed and practised by Muslim communities (see Marranci, 2009).

Islamic communities in transformation

The previous section explored how and when prescriptive aspects of social representations are expressed, and when they are called into question and reflected upon by British Muslims. This section explores how various forms of social knowledge and representational systems are drawn upon in processes of *re-presentation*. One particular excerpt from the data shows how practices from what was considered by participants as British culture could be interpreted from an Islamic perspective or perspectives. This followed a call to the mosque from a Muslim man who was upset by a fellow Muslim's wearing of a poppy. The caller accused the poppy-wearer of being an infidel whose loyalties were not exclusively Islamic. The imam's reaction is noted as follows:

> Sheikh Ahmed agreed that the wearing of poppies in remembrance of a national army is not very Islamic, and giving advice and guidance to people who are not aware of this is necessary, however to call someone kafir [infidel] after s/he has done the shahada (declaration of belief) is also non-Islamic. 'In front of us, and in the eyes of Allah, he is a Muslim and we must treat him as a Muslim.' Also there was no issue with expressing national pride and appreciation for the land and state that he came from.

1 Cited in Sartawi and Sammut (2012).

In this excerpt representations of the poppy, of being a British Muslim and being an infidel are all being brought into contestation and negotiation from varying perspectives. The two divergent Islamic perspectives represented here, one that is exclusive and the other that is more open, reflect how being British and being Muslim may be negotiated by members of Muslim communities in the UK. On the one hand this may entail rejecting all that is exclusively British and therefore seen as un-Islamic, and on the other accommodating British cultural practices and incorporating them into a British Muslim identity.

At times, cultural practices that are not questioned in one's native culture suddenly become problematic in a different cultural context. Even their interpretation from an Islamic perspective may come to represent something different. Representations of self-presentation in terms of dress and appearance took on different meanings depending on when and where they were located. At a multi-faith event held by British Muslim community representatives, a scholar commented on the appearance of a white, Scottish Muslim attendee. He was dressed in clothes typical of a South Asian orthodox Muslim.

> 'He shouldn't dress like this. It is only cause for fitna [provocation]. The Prophet encouraged the growing of beards, but not dressing in this way, particularly in a culture where this would be provocative. For some brothers, maybe it's because of their culture. This brother is just trying to make a statement.'

Even Islamic rituals and their validity were sometimes questioned. In his attempt to honour martyred Muslims in ongoing conflicts in different parts of the world and ask for God's blessings and forgiveness, the imam of one mosque suggested a funeral prayer in the absence of the deceased.

> [T]he imam suggested that we perform a funeral prayer mourning the lives of all Muslims who died as martyrs in conflict zones around the world, including Iraq, Afghanistan, and anywhere else. There was outrage. A man shouted loudly that this was unacceptable and inappropriate. It was a bidaa (innovation), and this was something frowned upon in Islam. The Prophet said 'all innovation is misguidance', and the interpretations of what he meant have varied. However, many Salafi and Wahhabi schools agree that ANY innovation with regards to religion is misguidance, and leads to hell.

Being in a distant land far away from the plight of Muslim brothers in the Middle East, the imam opted for a variation of the funeral prayer that did not require the presence of the corpses of the deceased in order to be conducted. The representation of the funeral prayer was undergoing transformation in a British context that was resisted by another Islamic perspective. This was not uncommon with regards to Islamic rituals and interpretations of doctrine in a UK context. These social representations in transformation were not only observed in particular isolated instances, but a more longitudinal transformation was observed over time and across generations. In one mosque where the majority of the attendees were first-generation Muslim immigrants, an excerpt from the field notes reads:

> Many teenagers and schoolchildren hung around. They were probably off school and enjoyed meeting each other in the mosque. There was plenty of jesting and laughter, and the mood in the air was blissful and negligent of the distrust or concern exhibited by police surveillance, the seeming resentment displayed by non-Muslims trying to go about their business and having to make their way through the crowd, or the demands of the weekday on their time.

This particular mosque and Muslim community was located within a larger community of non-Muslim British residents. The separation observed here between Muslim and non-Muslim communities was very clear. Although they travelled the same routes and often passed each other in the streets, they hardly interacted save for some calls to the mosque to turn the 'music' (the recital of the Quran over the microphone) down. The attendees only frequented predominantly Muslim streets and shopped at Muslim-owned establishments. At another mosque where the majority of attendees were British-born, there was more of an effort to establish historical continuity and identification with a British geographical and cultural context. A former director of this latter mosque recalled the construction of the latest annex:

> He said that over 100 years ago it was full of slaughterhouses, and that during the digging for the construction they had found some bovine remains. He had requested that the contractors working on the new project bring him any remains (horns and such) to keep. As if this wasn't surprising enough, the contractors were even more surprised when they actually did find remains. He took them back to his office and now wants to write a piece on the history of the land. He thought that this would help weave the present state of the land and the Muslim presence into the history of the area, reflecting a sense of continuity and rooting Muslims into the sociohistorical landscape.

Social representations are transformative in that they transform objects of knowledge into familiar and actionable objectifications in negotiations with others or within the self. At the same time, they are constituted by a constellation of familiarized and domesticated objectifications and actionable meanings, and prescribe the way in which we act upon and relate to them, enabling us to navigate our environments. Understanding how social representations function in the latter form requires the application of observational methods. When the meanings invested in social representations are no longer actionable, as in moments of rupture and contradiction, individuals need to reconstitute them so that they can just be nonconsciously in their everyday worlds. They need to transform the problematic objects that are implicated in these contradictions into familiar actionable objectifications anchored into group specific forms of social and cultural knowledge. This provides them with a sense of belonging to a stable, historically continuous group identity. Over time, as is reflected in the preceding excerpt, a new source of identification is formed that brings elements of several knowledge systems together and roots communities in a particular geographical location fusing their histories with that of other communities in the same local context.

Social representations, their dual functions and British Muslims

First-generation British Muslims were generally preoccupied with papers and passports, employment and the general challenges of settling down physically, legally, economically, and culturally. In fact, they were less likely than those born in the UK to report feeling that there is more religious discrimination today than there was five years ago, and less likely to think there was less discrimination (Communities and Local Government and National Centre for Social Research, 2010). First-generation British Muslims seek refuge in mosque mini-societies and the communities that surround them based on ethnic and Islamic affiliations to preserve their beliefs and practices and avoid contradictions. Acculturation studies have shown that first-generation immigrants are more concerned with native cultural retention, which is more strongly related to identity change than it is to their orientation towards the host culture (Phinney, 2003). Also, first-generation South Asian British Muslims were found to prefer separation as an acculturation strategy (Anwar, 2005; Shaw, 1988). Their children are born into these worlds that are characterized by attempts to maintain tradition in a culturally different host environment. These pockets of localized traditional cultures are British-born Muslims' first point of contact with Islam. It is the Islam of their parents that embodies their traditions while attempting to incorporate a British everyday lifeworld. The parents in the study attempted to contain their children within these communities and shelter them from the world of dislocation and contradictions encountered by first-generation British Muslims. In the researcher's conversations with some of the children, they would tell him that they were only permitted to watch Islamic channels on television, and that all of their friends were Muslim. These British-born Muslim children grew up to hold particular representations of their parents, just as Bilal (below) held a certain view of this new generation of British Muslims. This juxtaposition of traditionalism and lack of exposure to openness, doubt, and questioning was a very compelling inter-generational dynamic that was observed.

While first-generation British Muslims face the challenges of cultural dislocation and an othering host society that treats them with suspicion, second-generation Muslims are born into a world of cultural juxtapositions.

> Bilal said something today that I found to be quite profound. He said that for the older generations, Islam was an 'emotional thing'. They would adhere to certain practices and follow Islamic law the way they were told blindly. They did this out of fear, guilt, or to avoid shame. The new generation that was brought up here learn to question things. They need to be convinced and 'have a reason for everything'. This coupled with the way that Islam is forced upon them by their parents in a black-and-white, don't-ask-just-do fashion presents Islam in a bad light. That's why they were more likely to abandon Islam as a way of life and take on western values and ideas. 'It's much easier anyway.' They were raised and educated to doubt and question everything. 'Here people decide what is truth, there [the Islamic world] Allah is truth.'

Whereas first-generation British Muslims constantly experience contradiction and renegotiation as moments of rupture and breakdown, British-born Muslims have internalized it as a condition of life. This could explain why second-generation British Muslims may have turned to more antisocial forms of Islamic interpretations in the past (see Esposito, 1984; Kepel, 2006; Roy, 2004; Herriot, 2007). The continuous experience of breakdown and rupture created a need to renegotiate entire cultural knowledge systems. Transformative aspects of social knowledge (contestation, negotiation) are at play in the minutiae of everyday life. Every representation that is consciously encountered and reflected upon is a micro-level renegotiation of meaning of an entire social system. The 'social object' that these groups attempted to come to terms with was (and still is) an entirely new social system (a new Islam in a non-Muslim world) manifested in the little breakdowns of the everyday life of individuals. It is precisely this objectification of Islam and the need to reconstruct its doctrines in the face of identity threat and exclusion that historically caused a turn to forms of Islamic scholarship that were designed specifically to emancipate their followers. Islam is no longer an embodied system of cultural meanings, codes and practices and becomes an object in itself. Islam is objectified and reflected upon and, in these cases, such interpretations were a powerful and empowering rebellion against the forces of exclusion, discrimination and erosion of values experienced by Muslim communities (Roy, 2004; Wiktorowicz, 2005).

Concluding remarks

As this chapter reveals, apprehending the dual function of social representations is pivotal in studying social knowledge, communities and everyday common sense in relation to religion. Both the dynamic and fluid aspects of social knowledge, along with the institutionalized and unquestioned, are necessarily related. Not only is there a need to understand how Islam is constructed in textual symbolic resources that Muslims draw on to understand Islam and how to be Muslim, but also what daily experience of being Muslim and actually doing Islam is about in the phenomenal experience of British Muslims. In attempting to understand what being Muslim means to British Muslims, one can gain a better picture of the elements implicated in the moments of rupture and contradiction that they experience. The collective experience of such moments on a daily basis may serve up some explanations as to how and why British Muslims experience their religion and behave the way they do.

An approach that focusses on the everyday life of religious communities needs to take into account the relationship between religion itself, societal factors and embodied culture in everyday practices, and how these elements come to bear on social psychological processes within the community. This chapter has argued that it is necessary to study Islam and Muslim communities from a cultural psychological perspective. This was particularly important for the research cited here, as it uncovers the relationship between the social, cultural and prescriptive aspects of

Islam and the social and political contexts which inform identity processes. Identity negotiations observed in this study show just how the multiplicity and flux of identities in contemporary British life are tempered with the continuity and stability of Islamic prescription. In addition, a large part of what makes us who we are is defined by how we behave, and a focus on prescriptive social representations offers unique insights into identity research. They constitute that part of social identity that is stable, continuous, and more resistant to change. Traditional social representations research engages social representations but does not adequately grapple with situated practices in everyday settings (with few exceptions, such as Jodelet, 1989/1991). The function of social representations in the lives of individuals and communities in the experience of both change and continuity simultaneously is only beginning to be explored and provides promising new avenues for the development of the theory of social representations and its applications.

24 Of worlds and objects: scientific knowledge and its publics

Nicole Kronberger

Science and technology in modern societies

Social knowledge is built up from two resources: on the one hand, from direct experience; on the other hand, from knowledge that we accept as being true without having direct experience (Moscovici, 2001). This latter kind of knowledge is particularly relevant for everyday understandings of scientific and technological issues. For 'knowing' that much of our physical appearance is determined by our genes, that smoking causes cancer or that radioactivity is dangerous, we depend on socially mediated 'second-hand' knowledge.

In modern societies there are manifold ambivalent dependencies between science and its wider context. Social, economic, political and ideological contexts frame the production of scientific knowledge, and science and technology influence the lives of everyday people. For the public, in 'risk societies', the dependency on experts detecting danger steadily increases (Beck, 1986/1992). 'Perceiving' smog, the greenhouse effect or nitrate in water, and classifying such issues as dangerous or not, fundamentally depends on experts' judgements. At the same time, science and technology, more than ever, are met with high expectations to provide solutions to important human and societal problems. Ironically, in a context of secularization, science has even become a *moral* authority for guiding and legitimizing political decisions (Wagner and Hayes, 2005). However, scientific authority and expertise are not unchallenged; as important controversies over techno-scientific projects such as nuclear energy or biotechnology have illustrated, the publics of modern societies do not uncritically trust in expert judgement (Nowotny, 2010). Rather, different actors make their voices heard, calling for experts' accountability and challenging scientific conceptions by local and contextualized views (Irwin and Wynne, 1996).

This chapter sets out to discuss issues pertaining to the science–society relationship with a special emphasis on the social representations approach. After summarizing some of the important insights of early social representations work, I will discuss both the processes and the nature and functions of common-sense thinking. Finally, the chapter will address both newer theoretical developments (such as, for example, work on 'collective symbolic coping') and challenges for future research.

The relationship between science (which in this contribution shall be defined very broadly, including the techno-sciences, humanities and social sciences) and society has raised the interest of various academic disciplines. While there is no coherent paradigm to the interdisciplinary study of science in society (Wynne, 1995), a historical perspective helps identify trends in conceptualizing the relationship. Bauer, Allum and Miller (2007) describe three broad paradigms that have had varying prominence over time, with each 'diagnosing' different problems and envisaging different solutions. From the 1960s onwards a view emerged that identified a lack of public knowledge as the core problem (the *scientific literacy* paradigm). Research in this tradition focussed on the ways in which everyday people 'misunderstand' science and the solution to the problem was seen in educating the public. Increasingly the view was complemented with the idea that laypeople are not positive enough about science; under the label of *public understanding of science*, from the mid 1980s both laypeople's knowledge and attitudes were addressed. A central assumption in this paradigm was that better knowledge about science would increase people's enthusiasm about it. Interventions addressing the public included both elements of science education and 'selling' science. A more radical change in interpretation of the often troubled relationship between science and society occurred in the 1990s when criticisms of a 'deficit model' of the public (e.g. Wynne, 1982) were voiced. Rather than blaming the public for not being literate or positive enough about science, attention shifted to the (potentially problematic) ways experts deal with techno-scientific issues. In what Bauer and colleagues call the *science and society* paradigm, the problem increasingly was located in a lack of public trust; in response to such a diagnosis new forms of public participation and engagement were called for.

Although the paradigms evolved over time, none of the interpretations has disappeared; the question of how to conceptualize the relationship between science and common sense remains 'contested territory' (Bauer, 2009). While the paradigms show considerable agreement in stating a tendency for common sense to differ from scientific representation, controversies on the meaning of such divergence are ongoing.

It is this historical contextualization that makes the theory of social representations so noteworthy. In the book *La Psychanalyse, son image et son public*, first published in 1961, Serge Moscovici addressed the question of how scientific knowledge becomes integrated into everyday thinking. In contrast to the zeitgeist of the time, he did not follow the predominant 'deficit model', which focussed on identifying 'errors' and 'misunderstandings' in lay reasoning. Rather, his work was guided by a view Bauer and Gaskell (1999) call the *'creative reconstruction model.'* In this view, science and common sense are seen as two separate systems in their own right. The question is not so much how 'biased' one way of understanding is compared to the other. Rather, the interest lies in what logics the systems follow and what functions they fulfil. By conceptualizing scientific developments as potential challenges to the worldviews of different social groups, the theory of social representations also moved away from opposing science with a monolithic public.

Instead, the theory stressed the importance of distinguishing a variety of 'publics' that creatively reconstruct scientific news from a socially grounded perspective (for a similar view, see Irwin and Wynne, 1996).

In his book, Moscovici addressed the example of psychoanalysis, exploring how the new development was integrated into the common sense of French society in the 1950s. An important aspect is Moscovici's illustration of how different social groups select, stress and neglect different aspects of the new. While some ideas become integrated into a group's worldview, others do not. Thereby, the *meaning* of the scientific notions can change significantly. Moscovici, for example, investigated the ways in which communist, Catholic and more general newspapers communicated psychoanalysis. While the communist press thoroughly opposed to the new by classifying it as a US – and thus imperialistic – approach, in the Catholic press some aspects of psychoanalysis were accepted due to a resonance with the concept and practices of confession. Other aspects, such as psychoanalysis's theorizing on sexuality, were ignored or rejected by this medium. In the newspapers with a broader readership, the ideas of psychoanalysis were less rebutted but presented as a new option, without attempts to mobilize readers for or against the development. Obviously, the different milieus interpreted the new development against their group's background, identity and values, resulting in various degrees of resistance to the idea (Bauer and Gaskell, 2008). As the worldviews of the groups were threatened to different degrees, so the responses differed as well. Moscovici labelled the type of communication prevailing in the communist format *propaganda*, *propagation* in the Catholic press, and *diffusion* in the more general press. Everyday knowledge combines affective, evaluative, imaginative and ideological aspects with parts of scientific theory into a patchwork of meaning (Moscovici, 1998).

In modern societies, science and technology provide multiple stimuli that demand creative reconstruction in the life-worlds of different groups. It often irritates experts that some risks, for example, are downplayed or ignored by groups of the public, while others seem to evoke a level of concern that appears exaggerated from a scientific point of view. The theory of social representations, in contrast, highlights that sense-making activities hardly consist of disinterested information processing, but rather of collective efforts of giving the new a place in what is a group's familiar world. Although such social constructionist claims are hardly as revolutionary today as they were when Moscovici published his study in 1961, the theory still provides an interesting framework for addressing the relationship between science and common sense.

Processes of social representation

Rather than being a theory in the strict sense, the theory of social representations constitutes a 'framework to study psychosocial phenomena in modern societies' (Wagner, Duveen *et al.*, 1999, p. 95). In fact the theory has been criticized for being too vague for explaining lay thinking; the approach certainly frustrates those who expect clear predictions on phenomena related to the science–society relationship (Joffe, 2003). However, the social representations framework has not ceased to inspire work on the relationships between different universes of knowledge. It is particularly helpful in pointing to a number of processes that play a role in constituting common sense.

Thus, theorizing within the social representations framework does not conceptualize common sense as a matter of individual reasoning. In situations in which people are ambivalent or confronted with something new and unknown, they seek out the advice of friends, spouse, children or peers; they expose themselves to trusted media influence and listen to (some) professionals' advice. Sense-making of the unfamiliar is a genuinely social process in which the individual is both influenced by others and influences those around them. As such, the theory of social representations is a social constructionist approach concerned with the social forces at work in shaping the understanding of new phenomena within different groups. Communication and discourse play an important role, and group affiliation determines what is relevant and what is not. In the context of technologies and associated risks, for example, there certainly are material circumstances that pose more or less danger; however, it is the expert and lay conceptions of these circumstances that constitute what exactly is understood to be threatening. The focus therefore is neither on 'real' threat, nor on 'biased' thinking, but rather on the *social meaning* attributed to the new technology. Moscovici highlights the interdependence of the social and the individual in the construction of knowledge. In this way, the 'social' is not confined to immediate social interaction; the focus is on the individual embedded in society, history and culture. Common-sense understandings, furthermore, are understood as being flexible rather than static in nature, since taken-for-granted forms of interpretation and everyday routines may be challenged by events such as natural disasters, scientific breakthroughs or cultural encounters. Social groups do not live in isolation; their understandings are continuously challenged by the representations of other groups (Bauer and Gaskell, 2008; Wagner and Hayes, 2005).

Social representations basically are sense-making activities that aim to appropriate the novel and unfamiliar in order to make it intelligible and communicable, on the one hand, and to maintain a group's identity and worldview, on the other (Wagner, Duveen *et al.*, 1999). They are knowledge systems that depend on the introduction of the 'strange' and the 'new': 'the purpose of all representations is to make something unfamiliar, or unfamiliarity itself, familiar' (Moscovici, 1984b, p. 37). Moscovici distinguishes two interdependent processes of familiarization: anchoring and objectification. *Anchoring* is the process of classifying, categorizing and naming the unknown. By giving a name to the unfamiliar, it is linked to a multitude of references, out of which it takes a shape that is familiar and understandable. Such integration of the unfamiliar into existing knowledge imposes order on the world; anchoring has a stabilizing effect (Marková, 2000). But anchoring the unknown is also linked to social values, and thereby becomes integrated into an existing moral order. Classifying the unknown as something of a specific kind implies evaluation according to the criteria of good and bad, normal and abnormal: 'Neutrality is forbidden by the very logic of the system, where each object and being must have a positive or a negative value' (Moscovici, 1984b, p. 43).

The process of *objectification* occurs in tandem with anchoring, thereby making the new phenomenon concrete in communication; an iconic aspect is attached to it. Usually the process leads to a number of figurative or symbolic meanings; metaphors play an important role (Moscovici, 1984b; Wagner, Elejabarrieta and Lahnsteiner, 1995). Metaphors are powerful because they allow for the slotting of ideas that are unfamiliar into others that are already known. It is the experiential world of the group that determines which images and metaphors are 'good to think' (Wagner, Duveen et al., 1999, p. 100). More than accuracy, it is the criterion of *plausibility* that determines which images are chosen to objectify the new (Wagner, Kronberger and Seifert, 2002). In his study of the reception of psychoanalysis in different social milieus, Moscovici shows, for example, that the Catholic press saturated its descriptions of psychoanalysis with the familiar image of 'confession', thereby highlighting some aspects of the new while hiding others (such as, for example, sexuality). Connected to social identities and ways of life, images become *socially* true, rather than true in a scientific sense. Symbols, images and metaphors facilitate communication between group members.

Social representations serve the purpose of communicating about and relating to the object in question. The familiarized object is added to the group's belief system – a collective repertoire to which the individual can refer when in discourse. The shared representation reinforces the social identity of the group and fosters the boundaries with other groups. This in turn determines what is thinkable and meaningful in a group when encountering further unfamiliarity. The process of social representation involves a complex interplay between normative elements preserving the status quo and disruptive elements aiming at change and innovation; there is both autonomy and constraint in every environment (Moscovici, 1984b).

'Knowing' in everyday life

The theory of social representations highlights that everyday knowledge serves different purposes than scientific knowledge. Why should everyday people learn and know about science and technology at all (Wagner, 2007)? Of course individuals sometimes will be driven by curiosity and epistemological goals. However, often in everyday life other motives are more predominant. Everyday knowledge not only describes and names phenomena (the *declarative* aspect) but it also makes them intelligible (the *explanative* aspect) and gives instructions on how to deal practically with objects or ideas at hand (the *instrumental* aspect; Wagner and Hayes, 2005). Innovation-*evaluation* is a prime task in dealing with the unknown. People are subject to a 'pragmatic imperative' (Wagner and Hayes, 2005); that is, in contrast to scientific observation, everyday life is characterized by being concerned and by a need to act. In dealing with the unknown, the most important thing to know, therefore, is whether the unknown needs further attention or not (Thompson, 1999). Knowledge in this sense is 'knowledge *to be used*' (Gervais and Jovchelovitch, 1998b, p. 30). Knowledge about an innovation need not cover all scientific detail, but it must allow for an appraisal of what to expect and how to act. The individual in a supermarket, for example, needs quick orientation on whether buying food produced with the help of biotechnology is a good thing or not. Scientific theories may be more or less appealing, depending on whether they offer solutions to the everyday needs and concerns of life (Bangerter and Heath, 2004).

However, not all innovation demands action that is directed at the innovation itself. Rather, the everyday need for acting includes the necessity of holding opinions and taking sides in communication (Wagner, 2007). There are frequent external pressures for sense-making. If an issue receives a certain amount of attention (e.g. in the media), then people are pressured to develop at least a rudimentary idea about the innovation. In social life, it is embarrassing to appear ignorant and as a result people will be pressured to form opinions (Wagner, Kronberger and Seifert, 2002). Hence it is sufficient that interpretations of the innovation are 'good enough' to participate in dialogue (Wagner and Hayes, 2005). Metaphoric and iconic representations may be irritating to experts, but they often suffice to constitute acceptable and legitimate formulations in communication with other laypeople. Sense-making thus functions to reduce feelings of ambivalence, ignorance and uncertainty.

Sense-making activities also tend to occur along the lines of social identities (Duveen, 2001b; Joffe, 2003), which go hand in hand with the emphasis on specific values and agendas. By understanding an object the way they do, individuals pertain to a certain kind of people; they connect to a specific group and distance themselves from others. Shared assumptions about how the world is and should be represent the background against which scientific innovation is interpreted and evaluated. As highlighted by Moscovici's (1961/1976) analysis of the reception of psychoanalysis in different social milieus of 1950s France, the very same information may lead to different interpretations and evaluations, depending on how it is integrated into a group's network of understandings. New information may also be selected and referred to in communication in order to *justify* certain views and practices, thereby strengthening a shared identity (Wagner and Hayes, 2005).

Collective symbolic coping

Reformulations of scientific and technological knowledge in everyday contexts have received a good amount of attention from researchers working within the social representations framework. Science contents that directly impact human experience (such as the body, nature or life) have received particular attention. Examples include representations of health and illness (Flick *et al.*, 2003; Herzlich, 1973; Jovchelovitch and Gervais, 1999), the psyche and mental illness (De Rosa, 1987; Jodelet, 1989/1991; Morant, 2006; Wagner, Duveen *et al.*, 1999), organ transplants (Moloney, Hall and Walker, 2005; Moloney and Walker, 2000), emerging infectious diseases such as Aids, avian flu, MRSA or Ebola (Joffe, 1996; Joffe and Haarhoff, 2002; Joffe and Lee, 2004; Marková and Wilkie, 1987; Páez et al., 1991; Wagner-Egger et al., 2011; Washer and Joffe, 2006), sexuality and conception (Bangerter, 2000; Lavie-Ajayi and Joffe, 2009; Wagner, Elejabarrieta and Lahnsteiner, 1995) and nature, biology and environmental issues (Caillaud, Kalampalikis and Flick, 2012; Castro, 2006; Selge and Fischer, 2011; Smith and Joffe, 2013). Much of this research addresses the question of how bits and pieces of science mix with other sources of everyday knowledge in understanding topics that are proximate to everyday life.

Research on the reception and transformation of specific scientific theories is less frequent. Besides Moscovici's classic study on psychoanalysis, there is a group of studies addressing social representations of biotechnology, a controversial scientific development that fundamentally impacts everyday understandings of nature and life (Bauer and Gaskell, 1999; Castro and Gomes, 2005; Green and Clémence, 2008; Kronberger et al., 2001; Wagner, Kronberger and Seifert, 2002; see also contributions in the edited volumes Bauer and Gaskell, 2002; Gaskell and Bauer, 2002, 2006). Research in this tradition, for example, highlights that a focus on risk perception is too narrow to capture the various concerns of European publics; that prior knowledge and attitudes determine the ways in which the new becomes understood; or that in everyday understandings biotechnology has been saturated with iconic content, such as when captured in the image of Dolly the cloned sheep or in genetically modified tomatoes.

Among other sources of data, this research used data from Eurobarometer surveys (that is, representative surveys fielded in all European member states). Inspired by the social representations framework, these surveys not only included items on textbook knowledge of genetics but also items that capture everyday images associated with biotechnology. Respondents, for example, were presented with items such as 'only genetically modified tomatoes possess genes whereas natural ones do not', 'by ingesting a genetically modified fruit, the person's genes might also become modified' and 'genetically modified organisms are always bigger than natural ones'. The images depicting genes as something foreign to 'natural' organisms, genetic modification as infectious and causing 'monstrous' appearance, had been identified in prior qualitative research. In fact, a considerable portion of the European citizens surveyed indicated agreement to the items, which can, of course, be interpreted as a sign of public ignorance or misunderstanding. Analyses inspired by the social representations framework, however, understand the items as relating to the figurative schema of biotechnology and do not stop at diagnosing a divergence between science and common sense. Wagner and colleagues (2002), for example, suggested a process model of 'collective symbolic coping', addressing why and when collectives are likely to promote such imagination. While experts in politics and public institutions must ensure – by technical action, political decision and law-making – that an innovation does not cause unacceptable harm (*material coping*), everyday people are hard pressed to *symbolically cope* with the unfamiliar (for collective symbolic coping with biotechnology, see also Wagner, 1998; Wagner, Duveen *et al.*, 1999; Wagner and Kronberger, 2001; see Gilles *et al.*, 2013, for collective symbolic coping with disease threat). In this perspective, belief in images is not considered to be faulty individual reasoning but rather a collective effort of sense-making in groups that are hard pressed to form an opinion. The model suggests that collective symbolic coping should occur in contexts of a sudden increase in public controversy, as reflected in policy activity and media reporting. The empirical analyses in the biotechnology context – in line with the model – illustrate that in countries with little debate people did not shy away from admitting ignorance. In countries with a sudden onset of 'hot' debate, however, admitted ignorance decreased while belief in the images increased. It is suggested that everyday people, in order to appear as competent citizens, must develop a rudimentary knowledge that enables participation in everyday communication. Such knowledge, which often takes the form of metaphors and images, need not be correct from a scientific point of view but it must be plausible and allow for evaluation from a social group's perspective. As such, image knowledge is functional in providing judgemental confidence and reducing self-ascribed ignorance in times of public debate over an unfamiliar topic.

Over the years, biotechnology has become more familiar to most people. Nowadays people may even refer to the collective knowledge on biotechnology in order to understand other unfamiliar techno-scientific developments. The social representations approach stresses that there is a tendency for laypeople to establish links between different technological developments and to 'anchor' the unfamiliar in the more familiar. Experts often succumb to an 'empty vessels fallacy' (Rogers, 1995) by ignoring the importance of prior knowledge. From a social representations perspective, in contrast, studying technological innovations in separation from each other appears to be based on a dubious assumption, since people's experience with one innovation influences the perception of other developments; as highlighted above, old ideas and past experiences are the main tools for assessing new ideas.

Synthetic biology represents a newly forming interdisciplinary field that aims at 'programming' standardized biological parts to create functional systems. In recent years the development has received quite a bit of attention in academic and policy circles. The situation, however, is different for laypeople. In 2010 laypeople across Europe were hardly familiar with the development: 83 per cent of respondents had not heard about synthetic biology (Gaskell *et al.*, 2011). Two years earlier, synthetic biology had been singled out to investigate in a natural experiment of how different groups engage in sense-making processes of a new and unfamiliar development (Kronberger *et al.*, 2009; Kronberger, Holtz and Wagner, 2012). Scientists working in the field of synthetic biology were invited to write press releases on their work; the resulting texts were passed on to journalists from major Austrian newspapers and magazines. They in turn wrote articles that were used as stimulus material for group discussions with members of the Austrian public. By adopting this procedure some degree of alertness was created for the participants, pressuring them to engage in sense-making processes. The results showed that biotechnology represented an important anchor for synthetic biology as it moved from the lab via the media to the general public. While in the scientists' press releases references to biotechnology were virtually absent, there was an increase in such linking in the media articles, a tendency that became even more pronounced in the group discussions. Individuals not only compared synthetic biology to biotechnology, but as a collective, moved towards addressing synthetic biology in terms of biotechnology's vocabulary and images. Furthermore and in line with the collective symbolic coping model, participants across all groups gained in judgemental confidence over the course of the discussion. At the same time, however, the groups came to *evaluate* synthetic biology in different ways. Despite reading the very same newspaper articles and having started the discussion being unfamiliar with and neutral towards synthetic biology, groups selectively discussed specific aspects of the technology. Especially if the anchor – biotechnology – was important to a group's worldview and agenda, members of the group collectively elaborated an evaluative stance that was both in line with their prior view of biotechnology and their shared frame of values. For example, members of an environmental NGO and of a religious-developmental organization, both of which held outspoken critical views on biotechnology, considered the media articles 'euphoric' about synthetic biology, while members of an economic interest organization and science students, who held comparatively positive views about biotechnology, criticized aspects of the articles as fear-mongering. Over the course of the discussion the former groups moved towards a clearly negative stance towards synthetic biology, while the latter groups moved towards a positive stance. Other real-world groups with less interest in biotechnology were more likely to consider the articles neutral or of little interest to them; reading about and discussing synthetic biology hardly changed their indifferent position. Social identities channelled information uptake and deliberations and so influenced opinion formation on the new technology. Finally, the study also highlights that none of the groups considered synthetic biology different enough from biotechnology to warrant special attention. It seems that in this case science has caught up with public imagination rather than the other way around. Experts had worried that the engineering aspect of synthetic biology might be met with concern. With labels like genetic *engineering* and *biotechnology*, however, laypeople had anticipated and imagined years ago some of the projects that synthetic biology is about to conduct today. The scientifically new need not always result in new representations; publics may consider an innovation old wine in new bottles. As a consequence, the unfamiliar development is met with no more – but also no less – concern than the more familiar technology.

Challenges for future research

In modern societies science plays an unprecedented role in legtimizing political and public decision-making; at the same time, however, the authority of science is more and more contested. Although science – more than ever – is met with great hopes for providing scientific-technical solutions to all kinds of problems, the suggested solutions are less likely to be accepted without controversy. As Nowotny (2010) says, 'society has learned to "speak back to science"' (p. 319); groups of the public actively participate in negotiations and renegotiations of new developments. This is hardly a surprise from the perspective of a social representations framework, which has always stressed the fact that when science and common sense meet, constructive reformulation must be expected. This is not so much due to error-prone lay thinking, but rather to the various roles and functions that science can have in everyday life. Often, dissemination of scientific knowledge is not uninterested and neutral but involves a strategic and political dimension; bits and pieces of science can be used to justify the status quo or to promote social change. Similarly, much theorizing on the relationship between science and common sense nowadays accepts the notion that a one-way progression of knowledge from science to common sense is hardly realistic. As a consequence, the social representations perspective no longer appears to go against the tide in combatting a deficit model of common sense.

There are, of course, controversies and open questions. For example, Moscovici had suggested that science and common sense represent two different ways of conceiving the world by differentiating a reified from a consensual universe (Moscovici, 1984b). The idea of incompatibility between the two universes has been met with criticism by Bangerter (1995), who suggests conceptualizing the distinction as a relative one (see also Flick, 1998; Foster, 2003; Purkhardt, 1993). Reification and consensual processes can occur as part of knowledge production in both science and everyday life. In fact, research within the social representations framework has focussed on reformulations of science in common sense but has paid less attention to the reverse relationship (Foster, 2003). In what ways can common sense 'speak back' to science and impact expert knowledge? There are many possible ways, ranging from resistance to collaboration. Recent projects assembled under the umbrella term 'citizen science', for example, represent an example of how the boundaries between science and everyday life can become blurred. Citizen science involves networks of laypeople engaged in accomplishing scientific tasks. Although many such projects have a gaming component, they contribute to the production of scientific knowledge (Hand, 2010). A recent article (Eiben *et al.*, 2012) published in *Nature Biotechnology*, for example, has received quite a bit of attention as the author list includes 'Foldit players', that is, the collective of players of an online game called Foldit (http://fold.it). The game invites laypeople to engage in folding proteins in search of low energy configurations. The laypeople's activities had helped researchers to create an improved enzyme and so contributed to the crowd-sourced redesign of a protein that was finally published in an important scientific journal. While many citizen science projects started as attempts at educating or engaging the public, the benefits to science are increasingly acknowledged. The example shows that scientific and common-sense knowledge need not always be incompatible. Following epistemic goals, laypeople and scientists can fruitfully cooperate. However, there are also instances in everyday life where other goals and affordances drive the construction of knowledge. In such situations science is unlikely to replace common sense as it does not respond to important human problems and needs (Jovchelovitch, 2008).

Other open questions, to name a few, include the role of power relations, intergroup relationships and their impact on social representation, the role of the time dimension as introduced in the notion of representational 'projects' (Bauer and Gaskell, 1999), or the role of new forms of communication such as those observable in the internet. Research on social representations must also continue to address the ways in which common-sense knowledge is functional to everyday life and to maintaining the status quo or promoting change. Thus, the framework would also profit from more explicit combination with other theories, for example, from the field of science and technology studies or from the sociology of knowledge (Bauer and Gaskell, 2008; Foster, 2003; Purkhardt, 1993; Riesch, 2010). Despite Moscovici's (1961/1976) early emphasis on group-level sense-making processes, empirical studies addressing real-world groups are surprisingly rare. There clearly is a need for more theorizing and empirical research on the role played by social representations in defining and defending groups and their social identities.

The relationship between science and common sense has received considerable attention, not least because of its political implications. Framing debates on modern technology as risk issues, for example, is useful to political decision-making in that it allows for constructing indifference relations between alternative courses of action. It allows for the comparison of a number of qualitatively different possible outcomes based on a single metric: the riskiness of the options (Jaeger et al., 2001). Translating conflicting values, objectives and goals into measurable risks is of high practical interest (Keeney and Raiffa, 1976). Once options can be ranked according to their riskiness, decision-making becomes straightforward. It is this functional advantage that has given the risk construct its privileged place in expert discourses on innovation and modern technology. Social representations research not only highlights that in everyday life the risk concept is too narrow to capture the range of concerns people direct at techno-scientific developments, but it also suggests that more often than not there are tensions between social groups and their values and agendas. Education and other 'debiasing' strategies are not likely to dissolve such differences. From a practical point of view, it may be disappointing that the social representations framework does not suggest simple rules and guidelines for political decision-making. However, by pointing to the task of modern societies to manage diversity and competing views (Bauer and Gaskell, 2008), the framework contributes to a complex and hardly outdated problem.

25 The self-control ethos

Helene Joffe

This chapter highlights the key role played by self-control in people's social representations of themselves and of others. Self-control is the ability to exercise restraint over one's emotions, desires and actions. An ethos is a fundamental value within a given culture that displays moral character. Thus the self-control ethos is the guiding value within a culture wherein restraint is regarded as demonstrating moral fortitude. This chapter reiterates and develops the theory, proposed by Joffe and Staerklé (2007) that within western cultures the self-control ethos plays a key role in the social construction of certain groups as inferior, and concomitantly, others as superior. Key developments lie in pinpointing the symbolic power held by groups that represent contravention of multiple aspects of the self-control ethos, as well as the inclusion of the concept of the thema underpinning the social representations of out-groups.

The chapter begins by pointing to how mainstream models of social psychology have theorized aspersions concerning out-groups. Following this, a more visceral-emotive model of the content of stereotyping and prejudice is called for. The chapter then proposes an alternative, social representational stance to the content of people's aspersions regarding out-groups. Having suggested the centrality of the self-control ethos in shaping social representations, its instantiation in relation to body, mind and destiny is elaborated. Finally, the chapter discusses how the self-control ethos functions to perpetuate the exclusion and derogation of certain groups, on the one hand, and to buttress the superiority of dominant groups and maintain the social status quo, on the other.

The nature of stereotype content in existing theories of intergroup relations

The *content* of thought underpinning commonly derogated out-groups, and thus stereotyping and prejudice, has not attracted sufficient attention in the social sciences. The more mainstream theories of stereotypes regarding out-groups have tended to theorize the *process* of stereotyping in the hope that the contents of

---

Many of the ideas expressed in this chapter were formed together with Christian Staerklé when we jointly devised the concept of the self-control ethos. My thanks also go to Cliodhna O'Connor, Nick Smith and James Elsey for their invaluable contributions to the ideas expressed herein.

people's aspersions regarding others will take care of themselves (Duveen, 2001b). Tajfel (1969), for example, introduced the idea that the psychological process underpinning stereotypical judgement and prejudice is categorization. People use categorization to make sense of their experiences and to create coherence in their understanding of the world. While within Tajfel's (1979) conceptualization of social identity 'shared constructions of social reality' play a key role in the formation of social categories, and thus content is central, the dominant offshoot of the theory, self-categorization theory (Turner, 1999) has focussed more exclusively on categorization processes. Indeed, what is now termed the Social Identity Approach, which encompasses both traditions, is far more process based.

In recent years psychologists have become interested in studying the content of stereotypes. After several decades of marginalization, stereotype content appears in the Structural Theory of Stereotype Content (Fiske et al., 2002). It emphasizes the structural features of a society that shape stereotype content. Above all, status and competition between groups are seen to forge stereotype content. In particular, economic interdependence and power relations between groups determine content. A number of different types of prejudice result from this interrelationship and each is associated with a different emotion. In the North American context, for example, *envious prejudice* tends to be directed at high-status, competitive groups such as business women and Jews, who are perceived to have low warmth levels and high competence levels. *Paternalistic prejudice* is targeted at low status groups who are seen as warm but not competent, including housewives and migrant workers. *Contemptuous prejudice* results when a group is seen as both cold and incompetent, such as welfare beneficiaries and asylum seekers. The last of the three group types attracts the strongest and most stigmatizing prejudice.

The focus on contents that derive from structural features of a given society is undoubtedly important. However, it obscures other possible sources of stereotype content. Certain groups, such as gay people, do not appear to be defined by criteria that relate to economic interdependence and power relations based on material resources. Indeed in Fiske and colleagues' (2002) work homosexuals are consistently located around the centre of the warmth and competence dimensions. Furthermore, other key targets of prejudice, such as drug users, smokers and obese people, are absent from such research. This suggests that factors beyond the structural features of intergroup relations drive stereotype content.

Neglected aspects of stereotype content: visceral and symbolic elements

The first of these neglected factors is visceral emotion. While the structural model includes the envious, pity-based and contemptuous emotions that underpin different types of prejudice, the emotions associated with many out-groups, such as smokers, obese and gay people, are more visceral. Strong forms of prejudice tend to contain extreme hate and disgust. The two extreme emotions are interrelated: all entities that are regarded with disgust are deemed offensive in some way (Rozin,

Haidt and McCauley, 2000). Specifically, a key argument in the disgust literature is that entities are regarded as disgusting if they suggest an affinity between animals and humans. This relates to Douglas' (1966) hypothesis that the violation of the boundary between categories, such as that between animal and human, elicits the visceral emotion of disgust. Humans see themselves as distinct from and superior to animals and accentuate their distance from animals by way of disgust (ibid.). This 'animal reminder' theory has been challenged (see Royzman and Sabini, 2001), with some arguing that it is, rather, 'disease reminders' that elicit disgust (Curtis and Biran, 2001). Either way, groups tainted with being disgusting, such as smokers in contemporary western society, elicit recoil. Hatred then springs from the strong sense of offense that the disgust-inducing group evokes. These visceral emotions do not appear to stem from structural dynamics between groups.

The second factor driving stereotype content, which is not necessarily tied to structural intergroup relations, is symbolization. Beyond lacking the visceral element, structural models do not incorporate the symbolic components of stereotype content. This is an important oversight, as some of the most extreme forms of prejudice in modern history have used symbols to portray derogated groups as animalistic, with implications of danger and disgust. For example, Nazi propaganda presented Jews as maggots, vermin and bacteria (Bar-Tal, 1990). In the history of western writing about Africa, black people have been symbolized as animal-like (see Joffe, 1999, for an overview) and gypsies have been similarly associated with wild animals in contemporary Europe (Pérez, Moscovici and Chulvi, 2007). Such symbolism forms a key component of stereotype content. The symbols may be invoked, such as in the Nazi example, to actively derogate a group that is structurally and economically of high status and competitive, as a consequence of Fiske and colleagues' (2002) envious type of prejudice. However, the gypsy, who may attract either the contemptuous or paternalistic type of prejudice, seems, more pertinently, to attract complete recoil without clear aspersions concerning the competence and warmth dimension.

Symbolic content and visceral responses are often intertwined: disgust and animalism connect in that the symbolization of a group as animal-like occasions disgust, a defensive emotion guarding against recognition of human animality (Haidt, McCauley and Rozin, 1994). The disgusting animalism associated with Jews, Africans and gypsies positions members of these groups as the very antithesis of self-controlled individuals who symbolize containment in their hygiene, sexuality and civility.

A social representational theory of how groups regard one another

The theory of social representations emphasizes the complex content of human representational systems, as well as the processes that forge them. It is therefore an appropriate theory with which to explore how people regard one another, and themselves, with particular reference to the key values that drive these visions.

The theory conceptualizes how ideas and values that circulate in the social environment get internalized by individuals, thereby becoming a part of how individuals 'see' or represent their social worlds. This puts the theory in a unique position to explore widespread thinking about out-groups. The social representations framework is distinctive among psychological theories in its focus on the link between individuals' thought content and the ideas that circulate in the history and public sphere of a given culture. It is also unusual as a psychological theory in its focus on how material that lies in people's common sense comes to be there, the form it takes and its consequences.

A key driver of the form taken by social representations is the thema. Marková (2000) argues that themata are 'the culturally shared primitive pre-conceptions, images and pre-categorizations [that] not only show the sociocultural embeddedness of social thinking, but also provide a basic starting point for generating social representations' (p. 442). These preconceptions are structured as antimonies, such as good/bad, certain/uncertain, nature/culture and self/other. They underpin common-sense thinking about issues, forming the bedrock used by people to think about issues ranging from climate change to earthquakes, from infectious disease to quality of life. Thinking in antinomies is an inherent part of cultural socialization. How people understand the world and interact with it is structured by the dualities that reflect their cultures' values. The two qualities within the antimony are hierarchically valued. This chapter adds to the themata known to underpin common sense by hypothesizing that within western cultures self-control/lack of self-control forms a further key thema. Self-control gains its meaning by way of contrast to a lack thereof in western societies. It lies latent in people's representations of themselves and of others and thereby structures the way that they discern respectable from disreputable fellow citizens.

How are social representations, stereotypes and the self-control ethos linked?

This chapter argues that stereotype content is a manifestation of an underlying social representation. Thus stereotype content expresses what lies in the social representations of a given culture, and also perpetuates and promotes these representations. The core values of a given culture, in turn, underpin the representations that circulate. The self-control ethos is one key value that gets internalized into people's system of representations. Thus stereotypes about groups express, purvey and promote an ethos of self-control. The social representations that underpin them offer insight into the factors that motivate the stereotypes.

The self-control value and individualism

Each era produces values that define the ways of thinking and behaving that are desirable in a given culture. A body of social psychological writing shows that while self-control is valued across cultures, its form and cultural importance is distinctive in the West. Self-control acts as a master value in societies rooted in an individualist ideology (Oyserman and Markus, 1998), where it is essentialized as a core feature of positive identity. It serves as a standard against which people are judged and judge themselves. This is neatly encapsulated in the finding that high status individuals are perceived as more self-controlled than their low-status counterparts (Lorenzi-Cioldi, 1998).

The reason for its status as a master value in individualist cultures relates to the very core of individualism. Individualist cultures represent the individual, rather than the collective, as the unit of agency, the entity that determines outcomes (Morris, Menon and Ames, 2001). Thus, while individualist cultures conceptualize agency as a property of autonomous individuals, collectivist cultures see agency as operating at the level of the group. Western representations of the person as autonomous and agentic promote the explanation of events in terms of the individuating characteristics of their actors – like self-control – rather than the sociostructural features of the situation.

A culture's individualist ideology structures its members' everyday reality and their understandings of the world, making individual agency the default mode of explaining social events. Cultural values produce a set of common reference points – social representations – through which social groups are conceived at certain points in time. They provide people with the 'raw material' on which they can rely to judge and evaluate their social worlds (see Billig *et al.*, 1988), and tend to appear necessary and natural (Oyserman and Markus, 1998). Thus for westerners, being a socially respected person requires that individuals demonstrate active control over their desires, emotions and actions (Joffe and Staerklé, 2007).

The process of stereotype content formation

While existing literature explains why self-control is so highly valued within individualist cultures, it does not explain how particular values get linked to particular groups in people's minds. From a social representational perspective, the mass media play a crucial role in constructing common sense by disseminating the representations on which laypeople draw in constructing their understandings of the world. In particular, visual images in the media convey forceful symbolic messages (Boholm, 1998; Smith and Joffe, 2013). However, individuals do not absorb media representations uncritically. People form their social representations within communications, which they internalize in accordance with their own interests. The over-representations of black people in the North American media with respect to poverty and welfare (Gilens, 1999) and mentally ill people in relation to violence and crime (Philo, 1996), for example, feed representations in which these groups lack control over their destinies and minds. Since antimonies underpin the way that common sense is structured (see Marková, 2003), if some groups symbolize high levels of self-control, others represent a deficit thereof. The media emit representations of such groups that fit with the ideologies of their audiences.

The theory of social representations ascribes a major role to how people symbolize abstract ideas and values in more figurative entities. To objectify or symbolize is 'to reproduce a concept in an image' (Moscovici, 1984b, p. 49). Thus objectification or symbolization is the process of ascribing a tangible entity to the contents of a representation. Certain groups, such as drug addicts, alcoholics, obese and gay people, become icons of the contravention of the self-control ethos. I will go on to detail how this contravention plays out in aspersions about a given group's body, mind and destiny-control. This is the phenomenon that lies at the heart of this chapter: how and why groups are constructed as lacking or embodying self-control.

A conceptual framework for what underpins stereotype content

The self-control ethos, presented by Joffe and Staerklé (2007), offers an integrative conceptual framework in which ostensibly disparate stereotypic content can be understood as expressing a violation of self-control. Supposed failures of self-control unite aspersions cast upon people who are gay (as lacking sexual restraint; Herek, 1998), obese (as lacking control over their urges; Crandall, 1994), addicted to drugs (as lacking will-power; Echebarria Echabe, Guede and Castro, 1994) or poor (as lacking control over their destiny; Gilens, 1999). Similarly, those from non-western contexts are often seen by westerners as lacking individual autonomy (Said, 1978). Related aspersions are attributed to women, children and mentally ill people. Three domains of self-control feature prominently in this content: lacking self-control over body, mind and destiny. Each domain will be elaborated in turn in a vein that develops and updates ideas offered in the original Joffe and Staerklé (2007) paper.

Self-control of the body

Contemporary standards of civility and 'decency' necessitate the strict regulation of bodily urges and actions. Self-control over the body refers to 'instinctive' urges such as hunger and sex, as well as to acquired urges such as those associated with addictions to legal and illegal substances. Societal preoccupations with health, sexuality and sport convey the value placed on this type of control. Whereas moral virtue and respect are associated with self-controlled bodies, condemnation and denigration are the fate of those seen to be out of control.

Concern with body control in the West can be traced at least as far back as Catholic ideas concerning the vilification of the flesh and to the later Protestant ethic, which valorized self-discipline and abnegation of bodily excess (Weber, 1904–5/1976). Over time these values have been largely divorced from their religious connotations. In addition, Elias (1939/2000) proposed a growing tendency towards self-control over the body in Europe since the early Middle Ages. This largely secular 'civilizing process' has worked in tandem with more religiously shaped forces to increasingly regulate behaviours linked to the body. People assimilate and internalize the rules and conventions of their milieu to arrive at accepted standards of behaviour. Many such standards are culturally contingent and change through the ages. Progressively tighter regulation of behaviours linked to the body, such as when, where and how one blows one's nose, has sex, urinates, has characterized European culture. People thus become increasingly inhibited through the civilizing process, yielding greater revulsion at smaller violations of bodily control, and concomitant feelings of shame and disgust with the body. Countercultural movements in the second half of the twentieth century have challenged these ideals, but many dictates of the civilizing process emerge unscathed. In everyday society, the 'out of control' self is restrained and one's animalistic side veiled in what is considered common courtesy (Joffe and Staerklé, 2007).

Health, in particular, has become a symbol, indeed a metaphor, for bodily self-control in western societies (Crawford, 1985). Health is a state that must be achieved by way of an individual's health-directed behaviours. Its links to heredity and environmental factors are largely occluded. Like the operation of the Protestant ethic in relation to work (see below), the health ethic is linked primarily with self-control but also with the set of related qualities of self-discipline, perseverance, self-denial and will-power. If health results from self-control, then the unhealthy are seen to have an inability to exercise it. In accord with the moralization of healthy behaviour, ill health has come to signify an individual's moral failure. Through the development of a healthy body, one's self-control and personal discipline are seen to be physically expressed. Particularly in middle-class networks, bodily self-control, communicated through health-promoting behaviours, can be the means by which a positive, healthy identity is forged and the derision and derogation of the unhealthy justified. The body thus becomes a crucial focus for the desire for and display of self-control (Crawford, 1985).

Just as the healthy body serves to symbolize the virtuous mastery of bodily urges, so the body of the obese person serves as a palpable demonstration of their moral failing. Importantly, it has been found that anti-fat attitudes in the United States are accounted for not merely by a cultural preference for a slim appearance, but also by the belief that one's weight is necessarily under volitional control (Crandall, 1994). Hence, in addition to providing an instant assessment of a person's health, judgements of someone's weight further imply a judgement of character with regards to a lack of self-control.

Of course, in some contexts bodily expression and release from inhibition are valued. Some bodily conditions, such as cancer, have been associated in popular thought with an excess of control and a build-up of stress (Sontag, 1978). Such notions are reminiscent of the classical psychoanalytic framework, wherein a variety of bodily problems and psychoneuroses are thought to arise due to the pathogenic inhibition of bodily urges, often accounted for by the overwhelming demands of civil society (Freud, 1930). The case of anorexia furnishes a further example wherein bodily control may be deemed excessive. In anorexia, severe dietary restraint leads to detrimental health outcomes. However, it might also be argued that anorexia represents a pathological compulsion – that is, a *loss* of control – as opposed to rigid self-discipline. The image of the anorexic, and indeed the workaholic, is not of a person in control of their body and mind, but of a victim compelled by an irrational ideal.

The contemporary culture of consumption also provides opportunities for clashes between bodily discipline and indulgence (Crawford, 1994; Jodelet, 1984b). However, such indulgences are often presented as rewards for previous self-discipline: gratuitous or 'unearned' self-indulgence is typically frowned upon. Culturally sanctioned bodily expression and indulgence, such as via drinking and dancing, must also take place within proscribed boundaries of time, place and degree, if they are to remain acceptable. The socially acceptable weekend clubber, for example, reapplies his suit and tie the coming Monday. His unacceptable counterpart is stigmatized and associated with lower-status groups. Obesity and smoking addiction, as opposed to 'treat meals' and 'social smoking', are increasingly associated with lower socioeconomic groups (Jarvis and Wardle, 1999; Farrimond and Joffe, 2006).

Disciplined and healthy bodies not only designate self-control at the individual and group levels. They have also been used to demonstrate cultural superiority. This is most perniciously evident in the Nazi glorification of the Aryan physique. Concomitantly, those seen to exemplify 'uncivilized' and unrestrained bodily excesses or aberrations, such as cannibals (Jahoda, 1999), are construed as culturally inferior, justifying oppression and the withholding of rights. Hence, in contemporary social representations of groups, control of the body, moral rectitude, and social and cultural status have become inextricably linked.

Self-control of the mind

The second domain that underpins out-group derogation is self-control over the mind. Here, self-control is characterized by a predominance of rational over emotive thinking. Competence is exemplified in 'scientific thinking', construed as logical and unbiased, in comparison to 'lay' thinking, seen to be replete with biases and unwarranted emotions. Science is also seen to yield modern technology and hence enhanced mastery of the natural world (Moghaddam and Studer, 1998). Scientific expertise is further esteemed as a voice of reason and 'objectivity' in contemporary debates, upholding the stringent standards of truth in the face of distortion, irrationality and superstitious belief. The 'reflexive turn' in modern and postmodern society has somewhat tempered the enthusiasm for scientific progress and a number of high-profile scandals involving scientists (e.g. 'climate gate') have reduced trust in such experts (see Beck, 1986/1992). Nevertheless, the ideal of value-free knowledge derived from objective evidence holds sway.

The social representation of the 'democratic citizen' is another symbol of self-control over the mind, a representation that can bolster a sense of western political superiority. Such a citizen is conceived of as dutifully working to understand political issues and make informed and rational choices via the ballot box (Staerklé,

2005; Staerklé, Clémence and Doise, 1998). Conversely, colonialists construed Orientals as deficient in rationality and autonomy, necessitating subservience under colonial authority (Said, 1978). Indeed, the white ruling class of the nineteenth century was seen to possess great powers of intellect, in contrast to the feeble-minded races that they dominated (Gobineau, 1859). Such judgements have also been levelled at women (Glick and Fiske, 1996), children (Chombart de Lauwe, 1984) and the mentally ill (Jodelet, 1989/1991). Lack of rationality and an overly emotional nature were held as justifications for denying political rights to women in very recent history in the West (see Voet, 1998), and similar arguments (not necessarily unjustifiably) preclude universal suffrage with regards to particular ages of voting.

For children, the supposed deficit of self-control over the mind is tempered by it being a mutable phase, one that will be left behind at the onset of adulthood. In the case of women, many western societies do not formally reinforce this representation, though it lives on in stereotypes, often in a fairly benign manner. Representations of other groups seen to be more severely impaired – such as the mentally ill – can foster stereotypes of dangerous and frightening individuals who have no control of their minds. The role played by the popularization of neuroscience is particularly interesting in this regard. Mental health advocates have embraced neuroscientific explanations of psychiatric disorders, believing that since such explanations demonstrate that the symptoms of mental illness are not under personal control, the stigma that mental illness attracts will be abated. However, research shows that although attribution of erratic behaviour to neurobiological factors does indeed reduce blame for that behaviour, it simultaneously increases fear, social distance, perceived dangerousness and harsh treatment (O'Connor and Joffe, 2013). In line with the workings of the self-control ethos, if neuroscientific understandings of mental illness engender an understanding of psychiatric symptoms as outside of intentional control, then this may incite, rather than subdue, the stigma directed towards mentally ill populations.

Like the dialogical quality found in the body control ethos, where the value of self-control clashes with consumerist culture's drive for indulgence, so the rationalist mind is not always seen as 'in the know'. Within the discipline of psychology itself there has been a recent interrogation of the role that self-controlled, intentional cognitive systems play in driving behaviour. Some of the most prominent academics of the day (e.g. Kahneman, 2011) suggest that more intuitive, associative, automatic, impressionistic systems dominate much of our thinking, perhaps even yielding our best decisions (e.g. Gladwell, 2005). In neuroscience, a burgeoning literature surrounds the idea that emotional input might be essential for optimal, rational decision-making (see Damasio, 1994). The question is whether such findings from the more reified scientific universe percolate into the mass media and thereby impact on lay thinking. Books such as Kahneman's *Thinking, Fast and Slow*, and Gladwell's more populist *Blink* have certainly been major best sellers that permeate lay circles. In addition, the percolation process would be influenced by the debate raging within psychology concerning whether this more non-volitional mind hypothesis has validity (see Shanks *et al.*, 2013). Scientific debate and discord are likely to amplify the media's uptake of such an issue (see Pidgeon, Kasperson and Slovic, 2003). However, it is as yet unclear as to whether the valuing of self-control over the mind will be affected by the putative changes in scientific thinking.

Self-control of destiny

Self-control of one's destiny is the third facet of the self-control ethos linked to aspersions cast upon out-groups. Destiny-control prescribes that individuals should be independent drivers of their own destinies. This is exemplified in Weber's (1904–5/1976) concept of the Protestant ethic, which places great emphasis on self-reliance and the virtue of work in the acquisition of wealth. To accumulate such wealth is taken to be evidence of one's merit in terms of autonomy, work ethic and ultimately self-control of one's destiny.

Destiny self-control is felt to be violated in those seen to be lazy or lacking motivation. Such people fail to plan ahead, to master momentary wants at the expense of long-term sustainability and hence consume beyond their means, becoming dependent upon others. They are thus tinged with associations of being parasitic free-riders, reaping the benefits provided by the society yet contributing nothing themselves. Typical representatives of self-control failure in this regard are the poor, the unemployed, refugees and users of state welfare. As able-bodied individuals are seen to be unimpeded in the pursuit of wealth and self-sufficiency where the self-control ethos holds currency (most notably in North America), able-bodied recipients of state benefits tend to be the most stigmatized of these groups (Fiske *et al.*, 2002; Gilens, 1999). That an individual who might easily work is seen to choose to prey upon the labour of others represents a profound violation of destiny-control.

As with the body and mind facets of the self-control ethos, media coverage plays a central role in the construction, or at least perpetuation, of social representations concerning destiny-control. Research has demonstrated that news reports presenting stereotypical images of the poor shape public understanding of poverty (Gilens, 1999; Iyengar, 1991). Beyond linking a range of negative and out-of-control states to the poor – being criminals, alcoholics and drug addicts, lazy and sexually irresponsible – one particular category has been singled out for reprobation. The poor single mother is portrayed as neglectful, immoral and responsible for her lot (De Goede, 1996; Thomas, 1998). Poor mothers are also depicted as having many children in order to maximize their welfare benefits (Clawson and Trice, 2000). The theory of social representations proposes that people utilize concrete examples to represent abstract, conceptual information (Moscovici and Hewstone, 1984), so vivid illustrations of perceived self-control ethos violations in the media are likely to play a central role in the formation of stereotypes. Tangible figures such as the 'poor single mother' provide media audiences with the opportunity to approach a complex phenomenon such as poverty with a simplified, figurative representation.

The process of objectification thus underpins stereotypic content regarding poor people, media portrayals of whom come to symbolize a failure of destiny-control. Far from viewing such individuals as having been failed by society, poverty is conceptualized as a personal failing and mark of disgrace. It is difficult to think of instances where lack of destiny-control is regarded positively in the vein of lack of body and mind control in contemporary western cultures. Perhaps the happy-go-lucky person would represent this antimony in some way.

To summarize, a substantial portion of derogatory stereotype content can be understood within the framework of the self-control ethos and violations of its three principal dimensions: the body, mind and destiny. A person in control of their body displays the qualities deemed integral to orderly society, valuing civility and discipline. Conversely, immorality, decadence and dirtiness feature prominently in stereotypes of those who fail in bodily control. Control of the mind is characterized by competence, logic and rationality. Conversely, those lacking this ideal are seen to be irrational, emotionally driven and inept, qualities typically associated with low-status positions. Finally, masters of their own destinies are seen to be enterprising, self-sufficient and successful, whereas violators of destiny-control are represented as lazy, undeserving free-riders.

Before exploring the functions that the self-control ethos serves for the society, the chapter now explores some of the empirical research that has developed the original self-control ethos theory (Joffe and Staerklé, 2007).

The chav: multiple violations of the self-control ethos with strong visceral and symbolic aspects

'Chav' is a term of abuse in Britain for the white working class. Adams and Raisborough (2011) apply the self-control ethos (Joffe and Staerklé, 2007) to cultural representations of the chav in popular culture. The chav contravenes all three facets of the self-control ethos: bodily, the chav is associated with drug abuse, obesity, uncontained physical aggression, ostentatious appearance and consumption patterns; in terms of mind, the chav is regarded as lacking in reasoning capacities and intelligence; in terms of destiny, the chav lacks ambition and is lazy and parasitic. Thus this study provides an excellent example of a group constructed as lacking self-control in terms of all three dimensions.

In exploring the self-control ethos via the empirical example of the chav, the Adams and Raisborough paper highlights avenues for advancement of the theory. The most significant development offered to the original self-control ethos theory is that the three dimensions of the self-control ethos rarely exist in isolation. Like the chav, many of the most vilified groups in society *contravene multiple aspects of the self-control ethos*. Adams and Raisborough show that it is the very overlaying of the body, mind and destiny facets of the aspersions levelled at out-groups that provide them with their symbolic and affective significance: the transgression of multiple facets of the self-control ethos, in representations of out-groups, lends the representations of these groups their visceral and symbolic power.

Furthermore, the empirical study of the chav highlights the way that gender plays out in social representations of out-groups. The teenage single mother, who represents a particular stereotype of the chav woman, typifies a blended value violation. While figurative entities exist for each of the violations – the obese, the mad, the poor – they are not independent in that each figure tends to violate in all three categories. Indeed, it may be the violation of all three dimensions that characterizes the key out-groups of the day. Not only is the teenage single mother out of control of her body, as shown above; she simultaneously spoils her destiny by way of the early pregnancy and is depicted as cognitively limited. She typifies the 'bad' woman in the age-old ideological angel–whore dichotomy.

Related to this, the empirical work on the chav develops the affective dimension of denigrating 'the other'. Disgust and contempt motivate the low ranking of certain people (Miller, 1997) and contravention of the self-control ethos provides a particularly powerful stimulus for such visceral responses. The teenage single mum, for example, represents a leaky body in terms of sexual promiscuity, binge drinking and bad diet, the very antithesis of the containment ascribed to civilized western men. Since disgust in relation to such groups is *felt* viscerally, their presence *feels* like proof of their moral degeneracy, and concomitantly, of the righteousness of the in-group.

The final contribution that the empirical study of the chav makes to the self-control ethos theory is in interrogating whether the ascription of vulgar consumption to the chav can add to the theory. The chav's consumption patterns are represented as excessive (e.g. excessive visible brand names, too many tattoos and 'bling'), impulsive and tasteless. This contrasts with the rational choices that mark out the 'good citizen' who is expected to participate in economic life responsibly (Galvin, 2002). This addition to the theory provides food for thought in that it melds bodily and mind excesses and steers the theory into including consumption patterns.

In sum, contravention of the self-control ethos is condensed into certain figurative forms, with the 'chav' being a prototypical example. People form their identities in relation to such white working-class figures, of which there are a number of variations globally. These include 'trailer-trash' (USA), 'bogan' (Australia), 'skanger' (Ireland), 'ned' (Scotland) and regional variants within England such as the 'hoodie' (see Adams and Raisborough, 2011).

The Joffe and Staerklé (2007) self-control ethos has been used in a variety of further contexts. It has been applied to fair-trade farmers (Adams and Raisborough, 2011), to smokers (Farrimond, Joffe and Stenner, 2010), to alcoholism (Young, 2011), to media representations of neuroscience (O'Connor, Rees and Joffe, 2012), to the Chinese ethos of forbearance (Wang and Dai, 2011) and to female orgasm (Lavie-Ajayi and Joffe, 2009), among a number of applications. The particular developments that have been highlighted are those pertaining to the othering of the chav or cultural representation of the white working class. Adams and Raisborough see the self-control ethos as a creative foundation for the psychological analysis of contemporary class relations. Such relations are reflected and maintained in social representations of in-groups and out-groups.

The function of the self-control ethos

The self-control ethos serves a number of key functions. In the main, it justifies the status quo in that groups that conform to it form the dominant groups in western societies, whereas those that violate it form the more subordinate groups. Thus it serves to justify existing social arrangements. In a rather circular manner, such justificatory representations are likely to be endorsed by dominant groups, as it is in their interest to maintain the status quo (Jost and Hunyady, 2002). These dominant groups can disseminate and impose such self-serving representations through control of, and access to, media outlets (Gitlin, 2000).

In a related vein, multiple contraventions of the self-control ethos, in particular, consolidate the position of dominant groups. Just as western psychiatrists working in Africa during the nineteenth and twentieth centuries portrayed the African as the polar opposite of the orderly, logical, morally upright and disciplined European (see McCulloch, 1995; Joffe and Staerklé, 2007), the modern day 'chav' represents a 'sin cocktail' (see Joffe, 1999) of self-control ethos violations (Raisborough and Adams, 2011; see above). Attached to their low status is poverty, stupidity and unhealthiness, the very antithesis of what is valued in western cultures. 'Gypsies' (Pérez, Moscovici and Chulvi, 2007) and Australian aboriginals (Augoustinos, 2001) are targets of similar aspersions.

By maximizing perceived differences between groups through the amplification of multiple value violations, the symbolic distance between the in- and out-groups is enlarged. This justifies exclusion and segregation. Far from viewing such groups as having been failed by society, their problems are conceptualized as personal failings. This corroborates the Just World Hypothesis, which states that people have a need to believe that their environment is a just and orderly one in which people get what they deserve (Lerner and Miller, 1978). The self-control ethos serves this need; it allows a group's failings to be viewed as self-imposed.

The very construction of a polarization between good, upright citizens and an 'other' is rooted in anxiety (Joffe, 1999, 2007). Anxiety is present from the earliest moments of life. Its subjective management springs from a relational process in which the self continually strives for protection from negative feelings evoked in it, by projecting unwanted material on to 'others' at the level of representation. To accomplish this, 'the other' becomes the repository of material that the individual seeks to push out from its own space, to locate externally. Unconsciously people organize their representations in accordance with the struggle for a sense of a boundary between a pure inner space and a polluted other. The purity of the inner space gets conferred on the person's in-groups and the pollution is construed as lying within 'others'. The social representations of out-groups thus provide a sense of comfort and safety since they contain what the self does not want to be affiliated with. Yet, paradoxically, those casting the negative aspersions come to experience 'the other' as a threat by way of its association with polluting, contaminating qualities.

Gaining a positive sense of identity through comparison with negatively valued groups is common in contemporary and earlier western societies alike (Said, 1978). A nineteenth-century Bourgeois continually defined the self through the exclusion of what (and who) was marked out as 'low' in terms of being dirty, repulsive, noisy or contaminating. This exclusion, which still prevails, is constitutive of identity (Stallybrass and White, 1986). Westerners do their 'identity work' (Crawford, 1994), they mark out what it is to be a 'good' and upright citizen precisely by way of devaluing certain qualities. Groups think of themselves in terms not only of antimonies but of hierarchies in which some elements are 'high' and others 'low'. The 'low' elements, many of which revolve around lacking self-control, are associated with 'the other', the 'high' with dominant groups.

Discussion

This chapter has aimed to highlight the nature of the content of the representations people hold in relation to out-groups. In particular, it has brought to light the emotional, visceral and symbolic facets that underpin thought content concerning out-groups. These facets are not well captured by mainstream theories of stereotyping and prejudice. Aspersions cast concerning the dirt, perversity and ugliness of certain groups, and the morals and symbols that surround these qualities, are difficult to access methodologically yet lie at the heart of lay notions of which groups are reviled. Widely circulating thinking about the paedophile, the obese person and the gay man, to name but a few of the major contemporary out-groups, exemplify this. While aspersions made about these seemingly different groups vary, they have in common accusations of lacking self-control. This accusation constructs these groups as less valued than those seen to embody self-control.

A potential contradiction lies at the heart of the argument. While these out-groups are all seen to lack the righteous form of self-control, some are nevertheless seen as self-controlling in that they are calculating, cunning and maximizing of self-interest. The teenage mum who maximizes her receipt of benefits by way of having multiple children is a case in point. This reflects the roots of the self-control ethos in an individualist culture built on the Protestant ethic. The emphasis is on self-reliance. The 'good' citizen is economically productive and the spirits of capitalism and Protestantism converge to form the moral codes expected of this citizen. Thus, taking control of one's destiny by squeezing benefits out of the state is not respectable in western cultures, despite it being a form of self-control, because it is not a self-reliant way of controlling destiny.

The study of what Wang and Dai (2011) call the counterpart of the self-control ethos in China, the 'forbearance ethos', points to how culturally embedded the individualist/Protestant self-control ethos is. While all cultures are likely to instil norms of self-control to some extent, the Chinese 'master value' of forbearance is fundamentally different to that of self-control. Forbearance relates to doing something despite not really wanting to or stopping to do something that one really wants to do. It is characterized by firmness of resolve. Upholding one's own integrity is part of this ethos, as is refraining from harmful emotions, not being too ambitious, conquering one's mishaps, enduring adversity, avoiding non-lucrative hobbies, avoiding physical enjoyment and performing one's duties. Even though some of the nuances of the forbearance ethos are lost in translation, one can gauge a very different orientation to that found in the self-control ethos. Thus the self-control ethos is a product of the culture in which it operates and also shapes cultural mores, particularly in relation to how out-groups are regarded.

One interesting out-group that requires extensive empirical investigation is the elderly. The elderly are certainly stereotyped in terms of multiple violations of the self-control ethos. Dementia and even more gradual forms of memory loss, often seen as an inevitable aspects of getting older, fundamentally alter self-control over mind and destiny. Similarly, the elderly body is perceived as an increasingly unhealthy one that others, rather than the self, have to take care and control of. However, regard for this group may contain aspects of sympathy not found in relation to many other out-groups. This is perhaps because this is a mutable out-group (most people will become elderly and so cannot distance themselves from this group as they do to 'the gypsy' and other racial groups). Why, then, is the same sympathy not extended to those groups that humans may all potentially become, such as obese people, alcoholics, drug users and smokers? Perhaps individuals feel that they can control whether they become addicted to these substances. These are empirical questions. Among them, the issue is to what degree does the blame dynamic, expressed by the just world hypothesis ('people get what they deserve'), affect the construal of self-control violations.

Concluding remarks

This chapter has proposed that the self-control value provides a lens for understanding social representations of in-groups and out-groups and of stereotype content. It has aimed to demonstrate that a range of such contents taint derogated out-groups with qualities that justify their low status and social exclusion, while simultaneously bolstering cultural values and dominant groups' sense of superiority. By analyzing the contents of out-group derogation from a social representational perspective, I have endeavoured to complement and extend existing approaches to stereotype content in a number of ways. Firstly, as the original Joffe and Staerklé (2007) paper did, this chapter establishes a link between cultural values and out-group derogation. Secondly, it adds a dimension to more mainstream psychological theories of stereotype content by paying heed to the visceral, emotive and symbolic aspects that underpin many stereotypes.

Furthermore, and developing the original Joffe and Staerklé thesis, the chapter highlights that the three dimensions of the self-control ethos rarely exist in isolation. Like the chav, many of the most vilified groups in society contravene multiple aspects of the self-control ethos. A further development within this chapter is that themata – the antimonies that lie latent in common-sense thinking – are brought centre stage in theorizing the self-control ethos. They facilitate understanding of the duality upon which many stereotypes are based. This duality – such as self-control and the lack thereof – always contains hierarchical elements in that the culture values one aspect of it and does not value the other. Self-control is a key thema in the latent content of many stereotypes in western societies.

Not only does the highlighting of the content of stereotypes complement the more mainstream social identity and structural approaches to theorizing stereotypes, it also redresses a gap within the social representations approach. Power dynamics continue to be underplayed in approaches concerned with the content of common-sense understandings (Joffe, 1995; Jovchelovitch, 1995). Yet the analysis presented in this chapter suggests that the interests of dominant groups become seamlessly incorporated into a set of latent assumptions concerning derogated groups. In a rather circular process, social representations not only perpetuate themselves, but also endorse the power of the groups that embody the values that underpin them.

26 Social representations of infectious diseases

Véronique Eicher and Adrian Bangerter

Infectious diseases have threatened humankind throughout history, possibly since human societies evolved from hunter-gatherer groups to large-scale sedentary agricultural forms (Diamond, 1999). Today, they remain a threat, accounting for more than a quarter of all deaths worldwide (Morens, Folkers and Fauci, 2004). Human groups have adapted to disease by evolving patterns of behaviour like avoidance of out-groups (Schaller and Park, 2011). But they have also elaborated symbolic representations of the origins of diseases, their transmission, and means of prevention and cure. These behaviours and representations serve two protective functions. First, they may protect the physical integrity of the members of the groups that sustain them by potentially reducing the risk of infection. Second, they protect the symbolic or ideological integrity of the group (Bangerter and Eicher, 2013; Wagner, Kronberger and Seifert, 2002) by enabling it to explain or cope with the breach of meaning that a suddenly occurring social change like an infectious disease outbreak can provoke.

This chapter reviews work on social representations of infectious diseases. In doing so, it builds on pioneering work in social representations of health and illness (Herzlich, 1973) showing how illness is represented as coming from outside the individual and is linked with dysfunctional aspects of society. Infectious diseases are transmitted via contact; as such, the concept of contagion is key, and an analysis inspired by the social representations approach will focus on how contagion is symbolized in common sense. In focussing on symbolic processes of sense-making, such an approach differs from more mainstream psychological approaches that try to understand health-related behaviours by relating them to cognitive constructs like knowledge, attitudes or beliefs (Glanz, Rimer and Viswanath, 2008). The social representations approach is also different in that popular beliefs are not derogated as being deficient (see the deficit model of public understanding, Wynne, 1991) but, quite the contrary, are studied regarding their *functions* for the group that sustains them.

In this chapter we adopt the *collective symbolic coping* model (proposed by Wagner, Kronberger and Seifert, 2002), which addresses the question of the functionality of social representations. Collective symbolic coping describes the sense-making processes by which social groups interpret novel or unexpected events that threaten their worldviews. It is accomplished via the communication that arises around the event, for instance conversations between individuals or mass-media communication. In these processes, representations of the event are constructed and diffused. These representations often appeal to traditional belief systems or patterns of thought that are used as conceptual anchors for the novel event. Collective symbolic coping is postulated to occur in four stages: awareness, divergence, convergence and normalization. Awareness is when an issue emerges as a public concern (for example via media reporting and agenda-setting). In the divergence stage, multiple and often incompatible discourses emerge, creating ambiguity about the situation. For example, in the case of AIDS, many concurrent explanations coexisted at one point (for example AIDS as the 'gay plague', AIDS as transmitted by mosquito bites). In the convergence stage, a single dominant discourse emerges, suppressing the others and reducing uncertainty about the event. To take the example of AIDS again, a dominant medical science narrative of AIDS focussed on explaining the disease as being caused by HIV emerged as part of the convergence stage. Finally, in the normalization stage the event has been integrated into common sense and everyday life. For AIDS, the normalization stage occurred after several decades (Rosenbrock et al., 2000), when infection with HIV ceased to be perceived as a death sentence and more as a serious but chronic condition. It should be noted that the progression of the four stages of the model is not necessarily linear and that individuals may go back and forth between different stages if new information is upcoming. From the normalization stage, for instance, individuals may go back to the divergence stage if new controversy about the disease emerges (Wagner, Kronberger and Seifert, 2002). Or, as Gilles and colleagues (2013) have shown, media coverage of the 2005/6 avian flu outbreak moved from awareness to convergence but then decreased sharply when the disease was no longer an issue.

To show how infectious disease outbreaks indeed constitute threatening events that require collective symbolic coping, in the next section we describe some aspects of the social history of infectious diseases and their effects on society. Then we focus on a key aspect of how diseases are represented, namely the explanation of their origin. We describe three recurrent common-sense explanatory patterns: divine punishment, immoral or unhygienic actions of out-groups, and malevolent actions of powerful groups. These patterns interact with patterns of expert knowledge (various scientific or religious explanations) that have also evolved over time (Bangerter and Eicher, 2013).

Beyond documenting these explanatory patterns, current trends in the analysis of disease representations focus on their temporal nature. As disease outbreaks are often highly dynamic events, groups must adapt their representations. Results from recent studies of emerging infectious diseases like avian influenza and swine flu will be reviewed. Finally, we comment on the implications of a social representations approach to infectious disease for the theory of social representations but also for practical disease prevention, as for instance the design of health campaigns and the issue of public distrust.

Aspects of the social history of infectious diseases

Infectious diseases have affected and transformed human societies throughout history in myriad ways. Disease accompanies war, and is thus associated with the upheavals caused by war. Diseases have even been used as weapons of war. During the Black Death, Mongol armies catapulted plague-infected corpses into a city they were besieging (Wheelis, 2002); during the French and Indian war, British Army officers allegedly attempted to infect native Americans with smallpox by giving them infected blankets (Fenn, 2000). These examples are by no means outdated. On the contrary, as medical science has advanced, so has the potential for deploying diseases intentionally as weaponry, as shown by preoccupations with bioterrorism in the twentieth century (Washer, 2010). More generally, disease outbreaks have often led to intergroup conflict. During the Black Death, for instance, many pogroms against Jews and other acts of violence led to the extermination of entire Jewish communities in many European cities and changed the demographic profile of western Europe (Kelly, 2005).

Infectious diseases transform social structure and social relations, entailing the need for symbolic coping. The fact that the Black Death killed so many people in Europe led to a shortage of cheap manual labour, thereby indirectly increasing the power of peasants, workers and women. This indirectly led to social conflict and insurrections as the newly powerful asserted their rights, but also gave an impetus to the development of technologies to replace human labour. Infectious diseases have also affected intellectual enquiry – a relevant fact for social representations research, which studies expert knowledge and lay mentalities. From antiquity, throughout the Middle Ages and up to the nineteenth century the dominant scientific account of disease in western society was the miasmatic theory. By this theory, diseases were caused by miasmas, or 'bad air', that could disrupt the balance of humours in the body (Kelly, 2005). This theory, anchored in the ancient medical theory of humours, differs notably from contagion or germ theories of disease, which presuppose some form of contact between organisms. Miasmatic theory was eventually eliminated by the germ theory of disease. By this theory, diseases are caused by micro-organisms that are transmitted from one individual to the next via physical contact or airborne or waterborne or other means. Germ theory received notable support through the work of scientists like Pasteur and Koch and through technological innovations like microscopes that allowed actually seeing bacteria (Thagard, 1999).

The development of the germ theory of disease and related developments in technology for manufacturing vaccines on a large scale paved the way in the twentieth century for the elimination of many previously deadly infectious diseases such as tuberculosis and smallpox. This period has been referred to as the golden age of medicine (Washer, 2010). However, in the later twentieth century new diseases emerged (AIDS is a prime example) and some, thought to be eradicated, re-emerged (e.g. tuberculosis), partly as a result of a decline in vaccination rates. In the twenty-first century many 'exotic' diseases now populate the public imagination, including bovine spongiform encephalopathy, Ebola, SARS, avian influenza (H5N1) and swine flu (H1N1). They are characterized by a high degree of uncertainty and risk, both regarding their epidemiological features as well as their unfamiliarity to the public. Therefore, they are interesting candidates for an analysis of how social representations of infectious disease get created and diffused, and what functions these representations serve for social groups.

The next sections will look at the three classic lay explanatory patterns of infection: divine punishment, immoral or unhygienic actions of out-groups, and malevolent actions of evil elites.

Infectious disease as divine punishment

A frequent explanation for disease outbreaks, at least in western history, is divine punishment. This explanation is based on the biblical narratives of plagues. During the Black Death that swept over Europe in the fourteenth century many experts of the time attributed the disease to 'the configuration of the planets, monstrous events in the East, earthquakes across the world, and God' (Cohn, 2002, p. 226). Both experts (church authorities) and laypersons promoted this explanation. A popular movement called the Flagellants emerged, whose practitioners moved in itinerant groups from one settlement to the next, half-naked and whipping themselves as a form of penitence for their sins. Divine punishment explanations may seem primitive to the modern mentality, but they have not disappeared with the rise of secular society. When AIDS emerged in the 1980s, it was initially believed to be related to homosexual practices and was referred to as the 'gay plague'. Such a term metaphorically relates to fundamentalist Christian ideas that homosexuality is a sin and that gays had brought the disease upon themselves by their immoral practices (Washer, 2010). Explaining disease as a form of divine punishment gives meaning to an otherwise inexplicable occurrence, and allows for the maintenance of a particular worldview while at the same time scapegoating deviant groups (e.g. 'sinners' like gays; see also Girard, 1987). This explanation is particularly useful for religious individuals as it supports their beliefs and practices and makes them feel less vulnerable to the disease. If the disease is a divine punishment, then only 'sinners' will be punished while those showing morally upright behaviour are safe.

Infectious disease as caused by immoral or unhygienic actions of out-groups

One of the most common patterns of explanation for disease is the attribution to actions of out-groups. As famously noted by Susan Sontag (1978), this tendency is reflected in references linking diseases to specific groups (e.g. 'Chinese disease', *morbus Germanicus*, Spanish flu). This pattern has been extensively documented in the social representations tradition through the work of Helene Joffe and colleagues. Joffe (1999) describes how risks are often projected on to groups other than one's own. In particular, many illnesses in western societies have been viewed as being caused by a range of moral failings on the part of stigmatized groups. For example, syphilis was attributed to the promiscuity of prostitutes, cholera to the excesses and passions of the poor, and typhus to the filthiness of the Irish. Many of these failings can be seen as an inversion of the western ethos of self-control, and a purported lack of self-control in the stereotypes of non-western cultural groups (or stigmatized groups within western society) serves as a justification for their inferiority (Joffe and Staerklé, 2007; Chapter 25 in this volume). These phenomena constitute the process of *othering* of the disease threat – constructing a representation of a particular characteristic of an out-group and linking that representation to the cause of a disease. Joffe (1999) claimed that othering, via such representations, can serve as a defence mechanism to control anxiety and protect worldviews.

Much research has supported these claims. History documents how Jews (already stigmatized because of their different cultural practices and religious views) were blamed for causing the Black Death plague in medieval Europe. Many Jews across Europe were accused of plotting with Satan against Christianity and poisoning wells with the disease to attain their goals. In the twentieth century, Joffe and Haarhoff (2002) studied British media and laypersons' representations of the Ebola virus. In both cases, the disease was viewed as being African and associated with African cultural practices (like the alleged practice of consuming monkey flesh, or 'bushmeat'). It was depicted as not being a threat to Britain. Laypersons described images of scientists in decontamination suits using such images to compare Ebola to a science fiction story (and not a real event). In a study of social representations of AIDS in Zambian teenagers, Joffe and Bettega (2003) found that AIDS was perceived as originating in the West and as being spread by teenage girls. This explanation allowed boys and men to downplay their own potential role in transmitting HIV. Likewise, in another study (Joffe and Lee, 2004), Hong Kong Chinese women explained the causes of avian flu by attributing it to the unhygienic practices of mainland Chinese chicken rearers and sellers. Washer (2004) documented how the British news media reporting of SARS tended to explain its emergence in China by appealing to Chinese hygienic and culinary habits, highlighting idiosyncrasies such as preferences for eating 'exotic' animals and the tendency to hawk and spit on the ground. More recently, Swiss laypersons interviewed during the 2009 H1N1 (swine flu) pandemic attributed diseases to a range of poor countries, for example viewing AIDS as having originated in Africa (Wagner-Egger et al., 2011). Many were unconcerned that the H1N1 virus might affect them, feeling safe because of Switzerland's wealth and its well-educated citizenry.

Finally, the seminal work by Jodelet (1989/1991) on representations of mental illness has well shown the phenomenon of othering in a village where psychiatric patients were living together with their families. Here, the othering phenomenon was not directly related to the origin of the mental illness, but to the fact that the patients were clearly recognizable and different, thus drawing a clear boundary between the patients and the own group of healthy individuals.

These studies show how widespread othering constitutes an interpretive pattern for making sense of suddenly occurring disease outbreaks, both across different cultures and different diseases. They also show how both media and laypersons exhibit this pattern, albeit in somewhat different ways. Othering often functions as a mechanism to distance disease risk from oneself. By attributing disease to far-flung and 'exotic' places or to people with customs different from one's own, or by characterizing it as 'science fiction', it is possible to construe an otherwise lethal outbreak as something harmless and not relevant to one's own safety or to the safety of one's group. Othering thus constitutes the symbolic counterpart of the optimistic bias that has been documented in risk perception research (Weinstein, 1989).

Infectious disease as caused by evil elites

The symbolic function of disease representations for protecting worldviews is particularly evident in how stigmatized minorities represent the causes of disease. Many such groups adhere to conspiracy theories implicating powerful, malevolent elites (Thorburn Bird and Bogart, 2005).

Typical correlates of conspiracy beliefs include lack of control (Wagner-Egger and Bangerter, 2007; Whitson and Galinsky, 2008), employment insecurity (Goertzel, 1994), anomia and distrust (Goertzel, 1994; Wagner-Egger and Bangerter, 2007) and discrimination (Wagner-Egger and Bangerter, 2007). All of these characteristics can be linked to minorities and low-status groups, suggesting that members of such groups may be more likely to believe in conspiracies than others. For instance, Goertzel (1994) showed that African and Hispanic Americans were more likely to believe in conspiracy theories than white Americans. Additionally, African-Americans were more likely to believe in conspiracies against their group (e.g. the FBI was involved in the assassination of Martin Luther King) than were white and Hispanic Americans, suggesting that people may believe more readily in conspiracies against themselves than in conspiracies against others.

The origins of many diseases, AIDS and influenza for instance, have also been linked to conspiracy theories. We will focus on the case of AIDS here, as it is one of the most researched diseases with regards to conspiracies. Although conspiracy beliefs regarding AIDS are not uncommon among the general population, these beliefs are more frequent among stigmatized minorities than they are among others. African-Americans and Hispanics, for instance, are more likely than white Americans to believe in AIDS conspiracy theories (e.g. AIDS is an agent of genocide created by the US government to kill off minority populations; Ross, Essien and Torres, 2006). Approximately 25 per cent of African-Americans believe that the government uses AIDS to kill African-Americans and minorities in general (Bogart and Thorburn Bird, 2003; Bohnert and Latkin, 2009; Klonoff and Landrine, 1999). These conspiracy beliefs are associated with less prevention behaviour (e.g. less condom use, Ross et al., 2006) and less treatment adherence (Bogart et al., 2010).

Besides ethnic minorities, gay men also tend to believe in conspiracies: Hutchinson and colleagues (2007) showed that 86 per cent believed in at least one conspiracy theory regarding AIDS, most frequently that pharmaceutical companies were hiding the cure for AIDS due to economic reasons. Among this population, African-American and Hispanic respondents were more likely to believe in conspiracies than were white respondents, with more than 50 per cent of African-Americans believing in four out of five conspiracies.

Another strand of research focusses on the conspiracy beliefs of HIV-positive people. In Hutchinson and colleagues' (2007) study, 41 per cent of HIV-positive men believed that HIV does not cause AIDS. This belief, labelled 'AIDS denial', is based on research from the rogue biologist Peter Duesberg (1987), stating that AIDS is caused by drug abuse and anti-retroviral medication. In a community sample of mostly African-American and homosexual HIV-positive people, Kalichman, Eaton and Cherry (2010) showed that more than 20 per cent believed in at least one statement referring to AIDS denialism. This belief had serious consequences, as those who believed that there was a debate among scientists regarding the HIV-AIDS link were less likely to adhere to treatment because they did not trust HIV medication. Likewise, Wald, Synowski and Temosjok (2009) found that 17 per cent of HIV-positive patients held AIDS-denialist beliefs and were less likely than others to be treated with anti-retroviral medications. Finally, Bogart and colleagues (Bogart et al., 2010) showed that a high percentage of African-American men with HIV believed in additional conspiracy theories other than AIDS denialism. For instance, one-third of this population believed that AIDS was produced in a government laboratory, a belief which was again associated with less treatment adherence.

Overall, endorsement of conspiracy beliefs is frequent in stigmatized minorities and may be associated with less prevention and treatment behaviour. Why do these disadvantaged groups believe more frequently in conspiracies? A reason may be that all of these groups have a higher rate of HIV-positivity or have a higher likelihood of being HIV-positive in the future. Indeed, in the United States 29 per cent of reported AIDS cases are African-Americans, although they only represent 12 per cent of the population. African-American women and children represent more than 50 per cent of HIV infections in women and children (Thomas and Quinn, 1993). Similarly, gay and bisexual men represent 51 per cent of reported AIDS cases.[1] The exposure to HIV and the higher likelihood of getting infected may thus make conspiracy beliefs regarding the origin of HIV/AIDS more compelling. Indeed, members of such groups may need to make sense of the negative things that are happening to them. Blaming powerful others who are plotting against them both explains the

---

1 Centers for Disease Control and Prevention (CDC), HIV among gay and bisexual men, 2012, retrieved 11.12.2014 from www.cdc.gov/hiv/topics/msm/index.htm

higher rates of HIV positivity as well as the social stigma and discrimination these groups are exposed to. Conspiracy beliefs of African-Americans may additionally be fuelled by the Tuskegee Syphilis Study, which had lasting consequences on African-Americans' (dis)trust in the US health care system (Brandon, Isaac and LaVeist, 2005). In this study, conducted between 1932 and 1972 by the US Public Health Service, African-American men with syphilis were followed over many years to study the effects of the untreated disease. Participants were neither educated regarding the disease nor treated adequately. Brandon and colleagues showed that more than 75 per cent of their African-American participants believed such a study could happen again, indicating their distrust in the health care system.

As we have seen before, a high percentage of HIV-positive individuals endorse AIDS denialism. AIDS denialists state that HIV does not cause AIDS and is actually a harmless passenger virus. As these statements deny the dangerous nature of HIV, their endorsement protects HIV-positive people from the knowledge that the virus will eventually lead to AIDS. Although this belief may actually be harmful (e.g. when HIV-positive patients refuse anti-retroviral treatment), it also functions as a coping mechanism as it allows them to avoid facing the fact that they will eventually develop AIDS (Kalichman, Eaton and Cherry, 2010).

Conspiracy theories thus have the function of protecting the beliefs and worldviews of the people endorsing them. As stigmatized minorities are often among the disadvantaged members of a society, conspiracies involving powerful others help them to explain and symbolize their condition and thus allow them to cope more effectively with them. The conspiracies thus make the disease seem less mysterious as they explain its origin as well as why it targets some groups of individuals more than others. The conspiracies also reflect the lack of trust of minorities towards authorities, resulting from the experience of disadvantages in general (Goertzel, 1994).

The studies presented in this section are mostly based on cross-sectional quantitative data, although representations of diseases (their origin, transmission, and so on) may change over the course of a disease outbreak. We now turn to some studies that investigate representations in different stages of a disease outbreak, focusing on avian (H5N1) and swine flu (H1N1).

Dynamic social representations of emerging infectious diseases

Research on social representations of infectious diseases is abundant. Studies describe representations of the origin, transmission and protection measures regarding infectious diseases. Many are, however, based on cross-sectional data and are thus unable to capture potential evolutions of representations over time as a disease outbreak evolves. Notable exceptions are longitudinal studies of media (e.g. Ungar, 1998; Washer and Joffe, 2006), which showed changes in reporting over time: for instance, Ungar (1998) showed a shift from panic-inducing 'mutation-contagion' rhetoric to fear-relieving 'containment' rhetoric as the Ebola outbreak progressed. To detect potential shifts in representations of diseases, assessing these representations over time, as the disease emerges, progresses and disappears, seems necessary. In what follows we will describe several studies which have analyzed social representations of avian and swine flu over time.

Wagner-Egger and colleagues (2011) interviewed Swiss adults as to how they viewed collectives (e.g. nations, organizations, social categories) during the H1N1 influenza pandemic. Drawing on Propp's (1968) classification of characters in folk-tales, they defined three basic roles: heroes, villains and victims. During the outbreak of the disease people viewed physicians and researchers as heroes, who they trusted and saw as combatting the disease. The media and private corporations such as the pharmaceutical industries, on the other hand, were seen as villains, who were distrusted and associated with fear-mongering, conspiracies and economic profit (in the case of the pharmaceutical companies). Finally, poor and less developed countries were seen as victims, who suffered the most but were also seen as partly responsible for their plight due to a lack of hygiene and discipline. Mayor and colleagues (2013) extended this study with interviews conducted when H1N1 was epidemic in Switzerland and after the end of the pandemic, using the same characters to analyze the collectives' role. The perception of the media and private corporations as villains remained stable throughout all stages of the disease, as did the image of physicians as heroes. Authorities, however, were seen as heroes at the beginning and during the epidemic, but once it was over, they were distrusted and associated with the pharmaceutical industries. Generally, mentions of distant collectives, like far-flung countries (i.e. othering), decreased sharply after the outbreak of the disease, while local collectives, such as risk groups, became more frequent during the pandemic but declined again after it was over. Interviews at different stages of the pandemic thus show that, although representations as heroes, villains and victims are mostly stable, othering is most prominent when the disease is far away. When the disease comes closer to one's country, however, othering may not be as effective as an interpretive device.

Gilles and colleagues (2013) analyzed the *othering* phenomenon (Ungar, 1998) during the peak in media reports of the 2005–2007 avian influenza (H5N1) outbreak and after media coverage had declined. The peak of media reports was identified as the divergence stage of the collective symbolic coping model, in which different – often competing – explanations were discussed. In this stage more than in the remaining stages, *othering* occurred more often. The same was true for Middle Eastern countries, but only for people who had a strong hierarchical view of society and felt vulnerable to diseases in general. These results show again that *othering* does not occur throughout all stages of a disease outbreak, but is specific to stages in which uncertainty is highest.

In a two-wave study on H5N1 and H1N1, Eicher and colleagues (2014) analyzed the stability and change of chains of reasoning linking fundamental beliefs (i.e. belief in a dangerous world, Duckitt *et al.*, 2002) with explanations of the origin of diseases and perceived effectiveness of different protection measures. People who believed the world to be a dangerous place endorsed conspiracy and unhygienic outgroup origins to a stronger degree, while they did not perceive the origin to be natural (e.g. a different strain of an earlier type of influenza). These origin explanations were linked to perceptions of effectiveness of different protection measures: the unhygienic out-group origin was linked to discrimination measures, while the natural explanation was associated with expert-recommended protection measures. Additionally, the conspiracy origin was linked to less perceived effectiveness of aid interventions. These results were stable after one year and could be shown both for the H5N1 and the H1N1 influenza. This suggests that there are several chains of reasoning that people may follow when trying to understand a disease, and explains why different people endorse different origin explanations and protection measures. The chains of reasoning seem to be relatively stable as they were shown to be similar over two time points and two strains of influenza, which supports the assumption that fundamental beliefs play an important role in people's representations and act as anchors to new information (Moscovici, 2000; Wagner and Hayes, 2005). The endorsement of the different types of origin explanations and protection measures did, however, also vary over time, such that the expert-recommended protection measures, for instance, were seen as more effective in the second wave (when neither influenza was a direct threat anymore) than in the first wave (when H1N1 was just emerging). These changes thus reflect the adaptation of people's beliefs to different stages of the disease, but the antecedents and consequences of the beliefs remain the same. While perceived efficacy of expert-recommended protection increased for everyone in the second wave (because influenza did not seem as threatening anymore), it was still higher for those endorsing a natural origin explanation than for those endorsing conspiracy or unhygienic out-group explanations.

These studies show that social representations of diseases are both flexible and stable over time. The studies by Mayor and colleagues (2013) and Gilles and colleagues (2013) confirm the adaptation of representations to different stages of an outbreak: when ambiguity is high (e.g. at the beginning of a disease), *othering* – by attributing disease to far-flung countries – is prominent but declines once the disease comes closer. As soon as the disease enters the country, it is no longer possible to attribute the disease to far-flung countries and new forms of othering (e.g. focusing on specific risk groups within the own society) have to be used. The focus of othering thus changes from 'exotic' and far-flung others to particular subgroups within the society. These results confirm the importance of analyzing representations over the course of a disease, as they may shift.

Eicher and colleagues (2014), on the other hand, show that representations of diseases stay stable over time and different strains of disease, in the sense that the consequences linked to different origin explanations do not change. Social representations may thus evolve with specific stages of diseases. Different explanations may be favoured at one time over another, but the structure within the representation (e.g. causes linked to consequences) is stable. Future research should focus more on longitudinal investigations of disease representations, which may promote a better understanding of the underlying processes of changes and stability over the course of time and diseases.

Implications of research on social representations of infectious diseases

Research on the social representations of infectious diseases has led to a better understanding of the processes of social representations. The emergence of new infectious diseases represents a novel and threatening event, which is often broadly discussed in societies and the media. Additionally, disease outbreaks are dynamic, as they appear and often disappear relatively quickly. As such, they represent ideal opportunities to study the emergence and evolution of social representations, for instance in the form of the collective symbolic coping model, which has been successfully applied to infectious diseases (Gilles *et al.*, 2013). When diseases are still far away, social representations are mainly based on the discourse present in the media and society. When the disease comes closer and people need to act or adapt their practices (e.g. get vaccinated), social representations are also influenced by the experience of the disease and its consequences. The dynamic nature of disease outbreaks makes them particularly adequate study topics for the longitudinal patterns of representations.

Next to these theoretical advances, studying social representations of diseases has also led to a better understanding of people's reasoning about diseases. Mainstream theories of health behaviour like the Health Belief Model (Janz and Becker, 1984; Rosenstock, 1966) include risk perception and rational threat assessment as major components. Consequently, public health and prevention campaigns are often guided by a rational risk perception approach, and when people do not comply with official recommendations, they are seen as irrational and ignorant (i.e. the deficit model, Weigold, 2001; Wynne, 1991). The studies reviewed in this chapter, however, show that people do follow coherent (even if normatively incorrect) chains of reasoning and determine the effectiveness of different protection measures based on their explanations of the origins of diseases and more fundamental beliefs of the nature of the world (as a basically safe vs. dangerous place) (Eicher *et al.*, 2014). Their reasoning is therefore functional for maintaining their worldviews, although it does not necessarily lead to the same protection measures that health experts recommend. These results need to be taken into account when planning public health campaigns: instead of focussing solely on 'objective' risk assessment and effective protection measures, official communications should take people's everyday thinking about diseases into account. If people can integrate information on origins and protection measures within their prevailing worldviews, then they may be more willing to follow these recommended protection measures. The studies of Wagner-Egger and colleagues (2011) and Mayor and colleagues (2013) additionally show that people do not always trust authorities and can be suspicious of the media, which is supposed to inform them about the disease. This distrust of authorities and the media can have far-reaching consequences. For example, in a study on the H1N1 pandemic, Gilles and colleagues (2011) found that trust in medical authorities was the sole predictor of actual vaccination behaviour six months later. Additionally, trust influenced the perceived effectiveness of officially recommended protection measures such as washing hands or sneezing into the elbow. It is therefore worrying that trust in institutions (e.g. government, medical authorities) decreased over the course of the swine flu pandemic (Bangerter *et al.*, 2012). This may be particularly problematic for future diseases, which may prove to be more virulent. Public distrust therefore needs to be addressed explicitly and taken into account in public health campaigns, to ensure people's adherence to medical recommendations. The social representational approach to infectious diseases research has been very useful in showing people's reasoning about the origin, transmission process and effective protection measures for different diseases. These findings should be taken into account when planning public health campaigns and communicating about newly emerging diseases.

27 Social change, social marketing and social representations

Mary Anne Lauri

The term *social marketing* was introduced by Philip Kotler and Gerald Zaltman in an article published in 1971. Since then much has been written about it and the concept has become an established tool used by agents of change. One of the first definitions states that social marketing is the design and implementation of a programme 'to influence the acceptability of social ideas' (Kotler and Zaltman, 1973, p. 56). The concept has been put into practice and used extensively to change public behaviours and promote social change. Literature reports its effective use in promoting, among many other things, environmental awareness (e.g. Maibach, 1993), sustainable behaviour (e.g. McKenzie-Mohr and Smith, 1999), health improvement (e.g. Gordon *et al.*, 2006), reduction in alcohol consumption (e.g. Rothschild, 2006), condom use and reproductive health (e.g. Van Rossem and Meekers, 2007) and breastfeeding (e.g. Lomas, 2009). Although social marketing borrows concepts from advertising, the task which has to be achieved by its users is more difficult. Change agents are targeting society with the aim of bringing about a widespread change in behaviour. Such changes, like using seat belts, separating rubbish and reducing the amount of alcohol and food consumed, are often not ones that a person would necessarily enjoy. As opposed to advertisers, social marketers must not only know one particular group very well but must know society very well. In this context, the theory of social representations, as will be argued in this chapter, can provide change agents with a theoretical framework which can help them understand the complex interplay of beliefs and values within a society and how these influence behaviours.

Despite the successes the social marketing model has achieved, it does have some limitations, which if addressed could increase its effectiveness. Most of the literature on social marketing regards change of public opinion and change of attitudes as being governed by the same processes. In this chapter I will argue that this assumption may be incorrect and that the kind of social change which social marketing is expected to bring about cannot be equated with a sum of individual attitude changes. Social change not only involves a change in the privately held attitudes of individuals, but also involves a change in societal beliefs and public opinion (Gaskell and Frazer, 1990). Himmelweit (1990) reiterates that public opinion differs from privately held opinion in that 'attitudes derive from society and are reworked by individuals as part and parcel of their own experiences and as a function of their correspondence with existing social representations' (p. 41). In the same vein, Farr (1990, 1993) explains, how, for example, Herzlich's study on health and illness sheds light on why campaigns designed to increase the fluoride levels in local water supplies had failed when this issue was put to the vote at a community level. On one hand, scientists claimed that an excess of fluoride was bad for one's health. On the other hand, campaigners were proposing an increase in the fluoride level of water as a measure to reduce the incidence of dental caries. The public could not understand why one should add a 'bad' chemical to water which was considered 'pure' and 'natural', and therefore they voted against the initiative. Farr (1993) concludes that health professionals ought to have taken into account people's conceptions of health and illness before devising their campaigns.

It is essential that before applying social marketing principles, change agents should study and understand how the public makes sense of the proposed change on two levels: (1) on an individual level, that is, how the proposed change will influence the private lives of individuals; and (2) on a societal level, that is, how this will challenge or fit in with the social representations the public has of proposed change. For example, as will be explained in more detail below, the promotion of donating organs after one's death has implications on two levels: public opinion and personal attitudes. If public opinion is against organ donation, the attitudes of potential donors are influenced negatively and the next of kin of potential donors may refuse to give permission for the organs of the family member to be donated. On the other hand, if public opinion is in favour of organ donation but individuals do not have positive attitudes towards donating organs, they will not carry a donor card and will not discuss it with their next of kin. I shall use the organ donation campaign held in Malta to illustrate some of the arguments put forward in this chapter.

The theories in the area of changing public opinion have important implications for the theoretical underpinnings of social marketing. Much of the literature on campaign research, including that of social marketing, is very much influenced by the research on attitudes. Farr (1996) points out that the study of attitude and attitude change has developed in two different directions following trends established by two different models of social psychology: the European, which is more sociological in nature, and the American, which is more psychological (p. 9). These different approaches have resulted in different definitions of attitude. Some perceive attitudes to be shared constructs while others see them as being idiosyncratic and individualistic. The theory behind social marketing is very much influenced by the psychological literature on attitudes and attitude change and hence sees attitudes as individual tendencies. I argue that social marketing may become more effective if it incorporates the sociological trend in attitude research. In the next section I will discuss the implications of adopting a more social approach towards social marketing by suggesting the use of the theory of social representations as the theoretical framework within which to design social marketing campaigns. The theory of social representations explains the nature of public opinion and widespread beliefs, the functions they serve and also the processes of how they work (Moscovici, 1984b).

It provides a framework for the model of social change which Philip Kotler and Eduardo Roberto put forward in 1989 when they described the Social Marketing Model in detail.

Understanding the social marketing environment: the role of social representations

Kotler and Roberto (1989) argued that the first step in any plan for social change should be the understanding of the social marketing environment. In the framework of the theory of social representations this means that any plan for social change should start by discovering the social representations which the various target groups within society have of the issue being promoted. Social representations should be the point of departure. Kotler *et al.* argue that change agents must know target groups inside-out (p. 29). A successful public campaign, they claim, depends on a society's readiness to adopt a particular objective or change (p. 13). This readiness to adopt can be evaluated and understood by conducting formative research which identifies the social representations circulating within society, the functions they serve and how these can help or hinder the planned change.

Himmelweit (1990) argues that the study of a social phenomenon requires a multi-level approach at the macro level as well as the micro level. If one is to understand and change behaviour on a societal scale, then one needs to draw on a diversity of sources and gain knowledge from different sources such as experts on the subject, epidemiological statistics, trend analysis, comparative analysis about the uptake of new ideas and practices by professionals, but most of all public opinion (p. 27). Himmelweit postulates that public opinion, in the context of understanding and bringing about change, becomes similar to Moscovici's social representations, which enter and influence the mind of each individual but are not thought out by them. Instead, they are rethought, recited and re-presented (p. 80). Since social marketing involves changing public opinion and the behaviour of a large group of people, the theory of social representations presents an ideal framework. The point of view advocated here is not merely a slight shift in emphasis. Rather, it impacts upon every step of the social marketing process: the type of formative research, the segmentation of the target audience, the encoding of campaign messages, and the way feedback is obtained and evaluated.

Below, I shall suggest four developments to the social marketing model based on the theory of social representations. These propositions address the social dimension of social marketing, and can make social campaigns more effective. The modifications to the social marketing model were put into practice in an organ donation campaign that was carried out and documented in Malta between 1996 and 2000, and I shall briefly discuss this. A more detailed description of this campaign and its short-term and long-term effects is given in Lauri (2008). Other successful campaigns have been carried out using the proposed developments but the reports cannot be accessed.

Social representations should be at the foundation of planned social change

Kotler and Roberto (1989) claim that success in marketing social ideas or practices 'requires being able to predict how the target adopters will behave. Prediction, in turn, requires knowing the processes that guide and determine the behaviour of target adopters' (p. 91). In order to understand these processes, Kotler and Roberto propose two major tasks: the analysis of the social marketing environment, and researching the target adopter population. The former involves the study of macro-social factors such as political decisions, laws and physical and economic conditions of the country, which could affect the behaviour of target adopters. The latter, on the other hand, involves the study of attitudes and behavioural styles of the target adopters. The model put forward by Kotler and Roberto considers these two tasks to form the foundation on which social marketers can design social marketing strategies and plan the marketing mix.

The study of macro-social factors in Kotler's model is carried out by experts. Change agents need a framework for mapping the environment to understand what forces to map and how to map and read the results (p. 79). The analysis of the political, religious, legal, economic, demographic and sociocultural environments is carried out by professionals consulted by the change agents. This is what Moscovici (1984b) calls the reified universe. However, there is another side of the coin. These macro-social elements must also be analyzed from the point of view of the target adopters, that is, how target adopters view the political situation of the country, how *they* understand the teachings of the church, how *they* look upon laws and the legal system of the country, how *they* experience the culture and traditions of their country. Moscovici calls this the consensual universe. He also points out that while the sciences are the means by which we understand the reified universe, social representations are the way we understand the consensual universe (Moscovici, 1984b, p. 22).

Moscovici argues that in order to understand how ordinary people create and use meanings to make sense of their world, social scientists must understand the consensual universe. When Kotler and Roberto (1989) advocate the analysis of the social marketing environment, they are advocating the analysis and understanding of the reified universe, the social marketing environment as studied and understood by experts, and how experts believe these processes are influencing the target audience. However, the understanding of the consensual universe, the way target adopters make sense of the macro-social aspects of the environment in which they live, is equally important. This analysis could yield a totally different picture from that which is obtained by an analysis of statistics and legislative trends and records. The study of the reified universe is an analysis of data as perceived by experts in the field, while the study of the consensual universe is an analysis of the environment as perceived by target adopters. The latter is separate and different from the former and is equally essential in order to predict as accurately as possible the future behaviour of the target adopters. Ignoring this crucial part of the total picture can result in a less effective campaign.

An example of this important distinction was encountered in the organ donation campaign carried out in Malta. Malta is a small island in the Mediterranean with a population of 440,000 people. The main religion is Roman Catholic and the two official languages are Maltese and English. During the pre-campaign research carried out with both the experts and the public, one major finding was that there was a mistaken perception by the public that the church, as an institution, was against organ donation and that the Catholic religion condemned it because it was desecrating the human body. The teachings of the church in fact promoted organ donation. Had only the opinion of the religious experts been sought, the researchers would have been told that the Catholic Church supports organ donation and they would perhaps not have become aware of the misconception held by the public. Since the church in Malta is a very influential social structure, the change agents asked the bishops to issue a pastoral letter as part of the campaign. This was read in every parish and explained that not only did the teachings of the church not condemn organ donation, but in fact that it was considered a noble act.

The methodology employed during formative research should be social in nature

One of the major innovations which made the concept of social marketing different from other earlier forms of promoting a product or idea was the use of consumer research to understand the attitudes and behaviours of target groups and the social marketing environment. When Kotler and Zaltman (1973) first proposed the model of social marketing, they highlighted the importance of research as the basis for all major decisions. Research was proposed at every stage of the social marketing process.

Kotler and Roberto (1989) suggested various methods to collect data. However, they considered the survey to be one of the major tools, and proposed that in implementing marketing research techniques, the following questions had to be answered: Who should be surveyed? How many should be surveyed? How should the respondents be selected? How should their responses be gathered? How should their responses be interpreted? (p. 73). Such an approach to consumer research is a result of an individualist orientation to understanding and implementing social change. Survey research methods, while being highly efficient at collecting a large volume of data, which can be analyzed quantitatively and at a relatively low cost in terms of time and effort, often neglects the social context and the dynamics of public opinion. To understand public opinion, surveys must be accompanied by other research tools. The scope of public opinion goes beyond the results of systematic questioning of a representative sample. Jaspars and Fraser (1984) suggest that understanding attitudes through surveys ignores the socially shared aspects of beliefs. They argue that within a population, people might hold different attitudes about a particular issue or subject, yet they might share the same social representations of the topic or issue on which they are holding the attitude. Traditional attitude research, which concentrates on finding differences between subjects, sometimes ignores such socially shared aspects. Some researchers, like for example Doise,

Clémence and Lorenzi-Cioldi (1992), have used surveys to study social representations. However, a much better understanding can be achieved if we go beyond the manifest responses which participants provide in many attitude surveys and 'concern ourselves with the representations which are implicit in these responses' (Jaspars and Fraser, 1984, p. 122).

Similarly, Billig (1993) argues that fixed instruments of measurement, such as the questionnaire, cannot tap social representations, which are in themselves fluid phenomena. Public opinion research is very often a descriptive snapshot. It is not enough for researchers to know the percentage of people favouring this or that position; they must also seek to understand how social representations are created and how they are transformed through usage. Billig (1993) postulates that such transformations of meanings, and the way they are transformed, cannot be captured in the thick netting of the standard opinion questionnaire. He argues that 'to use the pollster's measuring devices to understand these meanings would be like trying to entrap the morning mist in an elephant net' (p. 44).

Farr (1993) argues that 'we need the theory of social representations to account for the dynamics of the change in public opinion and why the distribution of opinion takes the particular form it does' (p. 35). He points out that one of the great virtues of the theory of social representations is that it does not privilege a particular method of research. Researchers using social representations as the framework for their research have used various methodologies to collect and analyze data, such as surveys, participant observation, in-depth interviews, focus groups, drawings, media analysis and even experimental studies. However, because social representations are constructed through a process of interaction and communication with other people, and because these interactions and conversations are themselves shaped by people's social representations, the tools used to uncover them must be social in nature. Farr, Trutkowski and Holzl (1996) argue that attitude theory and opinion polling are based upon a strong individualistic notion of the person, and advocate the use of discussion groups in the study of social representations and public opinion, thus restoring the social context in which individuals form opinions and express attitudes. 'The shaping of public opinion is a genuinely innovative and social process i.e. it is a public matter rather than a private affair. The method of investigation should reflect the theory' (p. 23).

The theory of social representations, as proposed by Moscovici, gives importance to the information that circulates in society concerning the object of study. This is why he suggests listening to people in various settings, in pubs and cafés, in academic institutions and work places, in churches and village halls, in other places where people meet and talk in an informal atmosphere about the issues that are of importance to them.

This line of thinking is reflected in the arguments put forward by Farr and colleagues (1996) when they claim that focus groups are the ideal tools to study social representations because there is equivalence between Moscovici's conception of 'the thinking society' and the discussion group. They propose that the discussion group is the thinking society in miniature. When people talk in a group, they generate as well as transmit opinions. This reflects the proposition put forward by Lahlou (2001), who argues that the theory of social representations is especially relevant for describing and understanding important issues because it takes into account the feedback loop between social constructionism and individual thought and practice (p. 162). An important tenet of the theory employed to justify the focus group as a principal method of investigation in social science, is that the researcher may have no prior knowledge of how the participants will represent the object of study. In a focus group it is possible to explore 'local knowledge and understandings' more successfully than for example in the one-to-one interview or questionnaire. Discussions involve an exchange of ideas and images, enabling the researcher to see things through the eyes of participants. Sometimes photos or pictures are used as cues for discussion since these could yield rich sources of data. They reveal perceptions, attitudes and beliefs. A second important advantage of focus groups, from the point of view of an investigation of social representations, is the context in which this exercise takes place. Since it is carried out in a group setting and at the end of a long discussion, the explanations participants voice on particular issues are influenced by both 'personal' and 'group' beliefs aired during the focus groups. Whether the discussion is among a group of friends having a drink in the pub, a group of people having a conversation at work, or a discussion in a focus group, people are influenced by each other in their understanding of issues and concepts and in the production of knowledge.

The debate on the social nature of research has direct implications for social marketing research. As discussed above, in social marketing, the research tool most often used to assess attitudes, behaviours and needs is the survey. It is being suggested here that a more accurate representation of social reality can be obtained if social marketers study social representations as well as attitudes. This can be done by complementing the survey with such techniques as organized focus group discussions, informal conversations, interviews, images and mass-media analysis. Such an approach would take into consideration not only the occurrence and frequency of particular beliefs, but also how these change, develop and influence social change.

In the case of the social marketing campaign carried out in Malta to increase the number of organ donors, the formative research included focus groups together with a survey of the attitudes towards organ donation of a random sample of 400 people as well as interviews with donor families, recipients and hospital staff. During the focus groups, photos were used to help elicit the social representations participants had of donors and non-donors by asking them to choose from a pool of photographs placed in front of them, one photo which to them represented somebody who would donate and another photo which represented somebody who would not donate his or her organs. They were also asked to explain why they had chosen those photos and their answers were analyzed. The adjectives used to describe organ donors and non-donors were then subjected to correspondence analysis and a two-dimensional solution was extracted. Figure 27.1 shows the adjectives used by participants to describe donors and non-donors before the campaign plotted against these two dimensions. The first, and stronger, dimension clearly differentiated

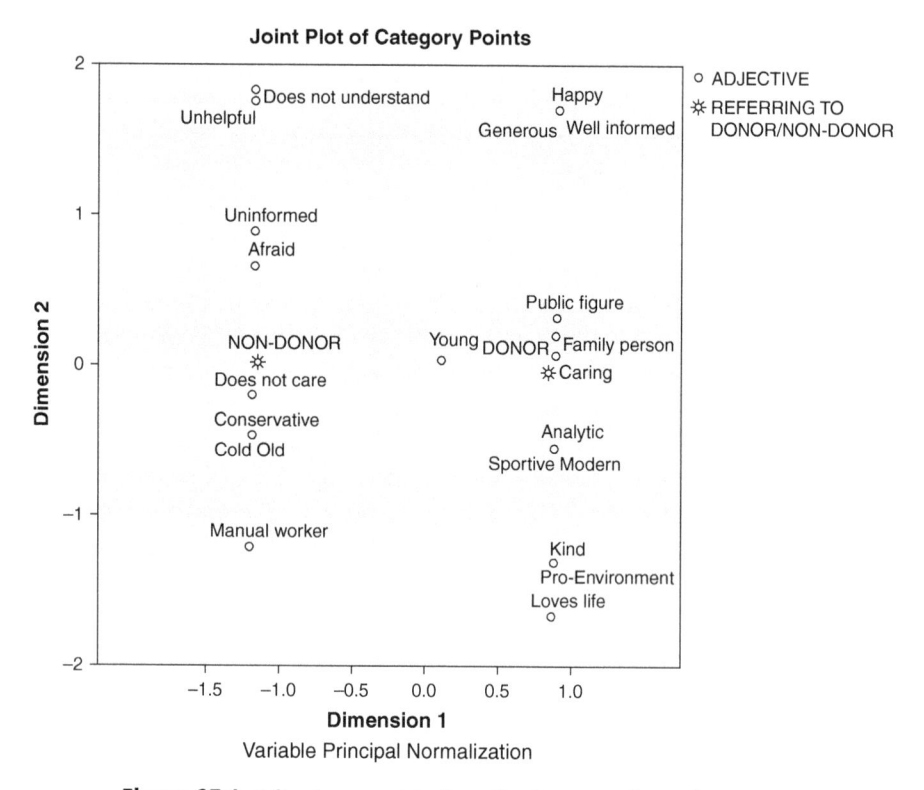

Figure 27.1 *Adjectives used to describe donors and non-donors.*

between adjectives describing donors and non-donors. The second dimension was more complex to interpret. For adjectives describing non-donors, it seemed to discriminate between those who are old or conservative in nature, on one hand, and those who are uninformed, unhelpful or do not understand the plight of others, on the other. For adjectives describing donors, this second dimension seems to discriminate between those who are modern, pro-environment and active in public life, on the one hand, and those who are in general happy, generous and well informed, on the other. In Lauri (2005) a third dimension was extracted to understand better how these adjectives were explained along this dimension and how the adjectives used in focus groups held after the campaign changed from those used before the campaign.

The same focus group text was also analyzed using thematic analysis. A comparison of the two analyses yielded important information in that the researchers became aware of the metaphors used to describe organ donation (Lauri, 2009). These findings, together with the analysis of the data collected through the survey and the interviews, gave a reasonably similar picture of public opinion regarding organ donation, and provided a basis on which to design the campaign. These metaphors brought to light the social representations participants had of organ donation. Some of the metaphors used by participants to describe organ donation

```
              Social
          Representations
             of Body
```

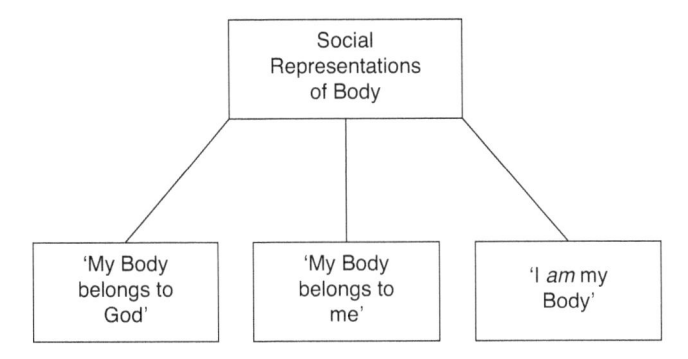

- 'My Body belongs to God'
- 'My Body belongs to me'
- 'I *am* my Body'

Figure 27.2 *Representations of the human body.*

were 'giving a gift', 'giving charity', 'giving a new life', 'recycling of body parts' and 'an insurance policy', among others. While it was found that there was good support for organ donation, it also became clear that participants lacked knowledge and had misconceptions. These were addressed in the campaign by choosing messages which used the same words and metaphors as the ones used by participants.

Target groups should be defined in terms of social representations

Segmenting the target adopter population into homogeneous groups is another phase of the social marketing process proposed by Kotler and Roberto (1989). Marketers employ various criteria for segmentation. These include demographics, psychographics, values and lifestyles, geographic regions, product benefits and purchase situations.

Which variables should social marketers use in segmenting their market? Kotler and Roberto's (1989) answer is that the 'most appropriate segmentation variables are those that best capture differences in the behaviour of target adopters' (p. 149). They explain that, in some cases, the differences in behaviour are a function of demographics. In other cases, geographic or psychographic characteristics are the primary segmentation variables. I argue that the variable most suitable for segmenting the target audience is often the social representations which the target groups hold on the issue in question.

In such cases, segmenting the target adopter audience according to their social representations may be more relevant than segmenting them according to demographics, lifestyles or attitudes. Members of the same target group may have similar attitudes and different social representations, or they may have different attitudes and the same social representations. Again, an example is provided by the organ donation campaign held in Malta. As a result of thematic analysis of the focus group discussion, the researcher found that while the participants used different metaphors to describe organ donation, all of these metaphors stemmed from the representations participants had of their body. Figure 27.2 shows the three representations. One group believed that one's body belonged to God or a higher

Table 27.1 *Campaign messages for groups with different social representations of the body*

Social representations of the body	Metaphors used to describe the body	Metaphors used to describe organ donation	Messages addressed to the target audience
Body belongs to God	Body is a sacred temple Body is a gift from God Body is a tool in God's hands	Doing one's duty Giving life Giving a gift Giving charity Butchering Desecrating body Playing God	Organ donation is an altruistic and noble act supported by the teachings of the church
I own my body	Body is a machine Body is a treasured possession Body is a commodity	Recycling A gift Insurance policy	Let your family know of your wishes; carry a donor card
I am my body	Body is whole Body is unique Body is eternal	Destruction of person's identity Destruction of person's immortality Butchery Desecration Living on, in another person	Organ donation gives a new life to recipients

being, who created it. Another group believed that a person owned his or her body and therefore was responsible for it, had to take care of it and enjoy it. A third group of people had a monistic view of the human person and did not distinguish between their physical body, their spiritual and psychological self and their identity.

Segmentation was carried out according to these three representations and messages were targeted accordingly (Table 27.1). For the first group who saw their body as the 'temple of God', the main message was that the church encouraged organ donation and considered it a noble act. For the second group who believed that individuals owned their body, the main message was that they should make their wishes clear about whether or not they wanted to donate their organs after their death. For the third group who believed that their body was not a possession but was the actual being of the person, the main message was that removing parts of the body after death does not destroy the dignity and identity of the person.

Change agents must use group strategies to effect change

It was recognized in the 1950s by several researchers that when planning social change there was a problem of focussing on individual behaviour without giving due consideration to group behaviour. For example, Dorwin Cartwright (1951) insisted that problems in understanding whether people changed their behaviour or resisted such change had their roots in taking the individual as 'the unit of observation'. Cartwright believed that it was difficult to change individuals in isolation because the pressure to conform makes it difficult for the individual to depart from the norm. Hence, he believed that planned social change or, as he called it, 'social management', should target groups rather than individuals.

Although Cartwright's work was carried out more than half a century ago, there are various other theories in social psychology that support his claim and that could explain why group strategies could be more effective in bringing about a change in attitudes more than other strategies directed at individuals. Several studies carried out by researchers which formed part of the Research Centre for Group Dynamics in Michigan in the 1950s can throw light on the issue of social influence in groups.

This tradition of the 1950s, which predated notions of social marketing and stressed the importance of societal attitudes and behaviour in bringing about social change, is best illustrated by a seminal study by Kurt Lewin and colleagues as part of a project to change the attitudes of the American people towards certain types of food. It is perhaps one of the very first studies of social marketing. Lewin (1958) as well as his colleagues used a number of methods to understand and change the behaviour of the American people. One of his interventions to understand the target audience was to conduct a series of experiments with the aim of investigating the effectiveness of individual instruction versus group discussion in bringing about a change in attitudes and behaviour. These experiments were later repeated under more carefully controlled conditions by Pennington, Harary and Bass (1958), who found that opinion change was greater when group discussion was allowed than when no discussion took place. Group decision-making, they argued, was effective in causing opinion change. It was the opportunity to discuss one's beliefs and come to a decision which helped group members change their attitude and behaviour. The advantages of the group decision method result primarily from the fact that group discussion facilitates decision-making and perception of consensus.

Lewin believed that it is very difficult to change individual conduct and attitudes that are rooted in groups by efforts which are directed at the individual. He claimed that 'many social habits are anchored in the relation between the individuals and certain group standards... If the individual should try to diverge "too much" from group standards, he would find himself in increasing difficulties... Most individuals, therefore stay pretty close to the groups they belong or wish to belong' (Lewin, 1958, p. 209). Planned social change which is aimed at individuals and which uses individual change strategies is bound to be less effective than one based on group strategies. The classic studies by Cartwright and Lewin indicate that, in the 1940s and 1950s, social psychologists had a more collective notion of attitudes. It is perhaps pertinent to reconsider these studies in a new light and apply them to changing public opinion and to social marketing.

Campaigns very often emphasize the use of television, magazines and the internet with the aim of reaching many people. However, most of the time people use these media when they are alone. In such situations, the isolated individual is more likely to reject the message. Media campaigns based on the faulty assumptions of the magic bullet theory or the hypodermic needle model (Lasswell, 1948) may fail to bring about the desired effect. Therefore, the campaign design should, as much as possible, include group strategies which encourage and facilitate group discussion and decision-making. This can be done by targeting groups through social media and interpersonal contact rather than through the traditional mass media. Talks, online chat groups, online social networks, discussions, participation in projects and other such initiatives help to encourage group members to take collective action, thus reducing the perceived risk of taking a particular decision on one's own.

The organ donation campaign in Malta aimed mainly at targeting groups as opposed to individuals. Meetings were held with groups of media personalities rather than individual journalists and anchor persons. Discussion among these opinion leaders as well as media owners helped to persuade them to help put organ donation on the public agenda. The new media were still in their infancy then, and could not be used as much as one would today. Another group strategy was outreach work mainly in schools and work places. Campaign volunteers with the right skills were given training on how to conduct group discussions. The main targets for these discussions were students, employees in work places and church groups. Various talks and discussions were held with post-secondary school children, university students, parent–teacher associations, NGOs, departments in the public sector, factory workers and parish church groups. These events normally involved an information-giving session followed by a discussion among participants, very much like Lewin's method. At the end of a talk and discussion, group members were encouraged to register for the organ donor card as a group initiative. Group techniques also included seminars by trained facilitators for specially targeted groups like family doctors and parish priests, who were considered gatekeepers who could influence the families they came in contact with. There are indications that the messages worked. There were some changes in participants' perceptions of organ donation registered in the focus group discussions after the campaigns as seen in Table 27.2.

This change in attitudes and social representations had tangible results. There was an increase in the number or organs donated in the years subsequent to the campaign as can be seen in the number of organ transplants registered after 1996.

Figure 27.3 shows the number of organs transplanted in Malta in the years before the national campaign was launched and the years during and following the campaign. Some more organs were donated to an Italian hospital when the tissue

Table 27.2 *Perceptions of organ donation after the campaign*

	Organ donation perceived less of this after campaign	Organ donation perceived more of this after campaign
My body belongs to God	Desecration and disrespect Playing God Butchery and disfigurement	Giving life Doing God's wish Doing one's duty
My body belongs to me	Giving a gift Recycling	Investment
I am my body	Disfigurement Destruction of identity	Living on

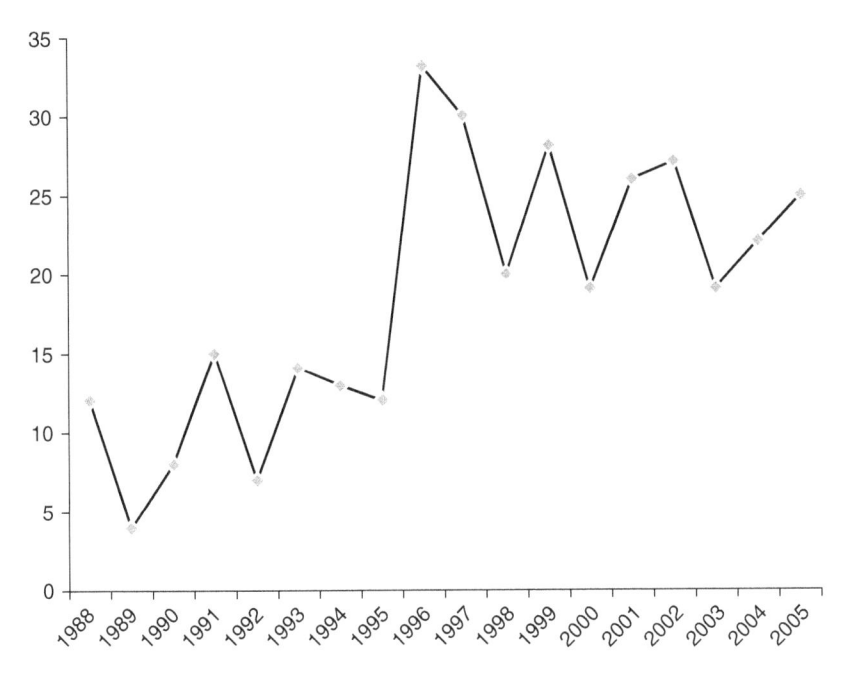

Figure 27.3 *Number of organs transplanted from 1988 to 2005 (source: A. Bugeja, Transplant Coordinator, Malta, personal communication, 12.05.2007).*

typing indicated that there was no match for a Maltese person. The increase in the number of donations cannot be solely attributed to the campaign; however it is reasonable to believe that the social marketing campaign was a major instigator of the increase in the donations of organs. Recent statistics show that rate of donations has been sustained, thanks to NGOs like Lifecycle who strive to increase awareness about organ donation.

Conclusion

In this chapter I have argued how the theory of social representations can inform social marketing campaigns. I have suggested that this theory brings about a paradigm shift in communications campaign research. It provides the theoretical framework for both the design as well as the execution of a social marketing campaign. Understanding the social representations surrounding the behavioural change being advocated is important for the different stages that follow in the campaign. Using social data collecting tools such as focus groups, together with traditional surveys and interviews, enables the change agent to understand the complexity of the issues involved. This would then enable the production of effective messages targeting specific groups holding specific social representations. Group strategies, such as seminars followed by discussions and organizing group initiatives, increase the effectiveness of the social marketing campaigns.

In 1947 Herbert Hyman and Paul Sheatsley published a paper with the title 'Some Reasons Why Information Campaigns Fail' in *Public Opinion Quarterly*. If a similar paper had to be written with the same title today, it would discuss how one major reason why campaigns fail is because the designers of the campaign either are not aware of the social representations of the issue being marketed by the campaign, or, that if they are, they failed to address them adequately.

In this discussion I have attempted to contribute to the literature on social marketing by suggesting that the model should be understood within the theoretical background of the theory of social representations. Does this theory help us find out how to make campaigns work or why campaigns fail? I believe it does. To quote Kevin Roberts from Saatchi and Saatchi, 'if you want to understand how a lion hunts, don't go to the zoo. Go to the jungle'. That is the place where one can learn more about lions, lionesses and cubs (Lefebvre, 2011). If we want to understand people and bring about a change in their behaviour, then we have to go into the field and seek to understand society through understanding social representations. It is only then that one can strive to change them.

References

Abell, J., and Stokoe, E. H. (2001). Broadcasting the royal role: constructing culturally situated identities in the Princess Diana *Panorama interview*. British Journal of Social Psychology, 40, 417–435.

Abrams, D. (1992). Processes of social identification. In G. M. Breakwell (ed.), *The social psychology of identity and the self concept*. London: Academic Press/Surrey University Press.

Abric, J.-C. (2001). A structural approach to social representations. In Deaux and Philogène (eds.), pp. 42–47.

  (1976). Jeux, conflits et représentations sociales. Ph.D. thesis, Université de Provence.

  (1987). *Coopération, compétition et représentations sociales*. Cousset-Fribourg: DelVal.

  (1993). Central system, peripheral system: their functions and roles in the dynamics of social representation. *Papers on Social Representations*, 2(2), 75–78.

  (1994a). *Pratiques sociales et représentations*. Paris: Presses Universitaires de France.

  (1994b). Les représentations sociales: aspects théoriques. In J. C. Abric (ed.), *Pratiques Sociales et Représentations*. Paris: Presses Universitaires de France.

  (2002). L'approche structurale des représentations sociales: dévelopements récents. *Psychologie et Société*, 2(4), 81–103.

  (2003a). L'analyse structurale des représentations sociales. In S. Moscovici and F. Buschini (eds.), *Les méthodes des sciences humaines* (pp. 375–392). Paris: Presses Universitaires de France.

  (2003b). *Méthodes d'étude des représentations sociales*. Ramonville Saint-Agne: Erès.

Adamopoulos, J. (2008). On the entanglement of culture and individual behavior. In F. J. Vijver, D. A. Hemer and Y. H. Poortinga (eds.), *Multilevel analysis of individuals and culture*. New York: Lawrence Erlbaum.

Adams, M., and Raisborough, J. (2011). The self-control ethos and the 'chav'. *Culture and Psychology*, 17(1), 81–97.

Ahmed, N. (2005). Tower Hamlets: insulation in isolation. In T. Abbas (ed.), *Muslim Britain: communities under pressure* (pp. 194–207). London: Zed Books.

Ajzen, I. (1991). The theory of planned behavior. *Organizational Behavior and Human Decision Processes*, 50, 179–211.

Akrich, M., Callon, M., and Latour, B. (2006). *Sociologie de la traduction: textes fondateurs*. « Sciences sociales ». Paris: Presses des Mines.

Alexander, C. (2007). Cohesive identities: the distance between meaning and understanding. In M. Wetherell, M. Laflèche and R. Berkeley (eds.), *Identity, ethnic diversity and community cohesion*. London: Sage.

Allansdottir, A., Jovchelovitch, S., and Stathopoulou, A. (1993). Social Representations: the versatility of a concept. *Papers on Social Representations*, 2. Retrieved 26.09.2008. www.psr.jku.at/PSR1993/2_1993Alla1.pdf

Allgaier, J. (2012). Networking expertise: discursive coalitions and collaborative networks of experts in a public creationism controversy in the UK. *Public Understanding of Science*, 21(3), 299–313. doi: 10.1177/0963662510383385

Allport, G. (1954a). The historical background of modern social psychology. In G. Lindzey (ed.), *Handbook of social psychology*, vol. I (pp. 3–56). Reading, MA: Addison-Wesley.

(1954b). *The nature of prejudice*. Reading, MA: Addison-Wesley.

(1967). Attitudes. In M. Fishbein (ed.), *Readings in attitude theory and measurement* (pp. 1–13). New York: John Wiley.

(1968). The historical background of modern social psychology. In G. Lindzey and E. Aronson (eds.), *The handbook of social psychology*, vol. I (2nd edn) (pp. 1–80). Reading, MA: Addison-Wesley.

Allport, G. W., and Ross, J. M. (1967). Personal religious orientation and prejudice. *Journal of Personality and Social Psychology*, 5(4), 432–443.

Alves, H., and Correia, I. (2008). On the normativity of expressing the belief in a just world: empirical evidence. *Social Justice Research*, 21(1), 106–118.

Amancio, T. (2007). Imaginarios cinematográficos sobre Brasil. In A. Arruda and M. de Alba (eds.), *Espacios imaginarios y representaciones sociales. Aportes desde Latinoamérica* (pp. 129–161). Barcelona: UAM-Anthropos.

Ameli, S. R., and Islamic Human Rights Commission (Great Britain) (2007). *The British media and Muslim representation: ideology of demonisation*. London: Islamic Human Rights Commission.

Anderson, B. (1983). *Imagined communities: reflections on the origin and spread of nationalism*. London: Verso.

Andreouli, E. (2010). Identity, positioning and self other relations. *Papers on Social Representations*, 19(1), 14.1–14.13.

(2013). Identity and acculturation: the case of naturalised citizens in Britain. *Culture and Psychology*, 19(2), 165–183.

Andreouli, E., and Dashtipour, P. (2013). British citizenship and the 'other': an analysis of the earned citizenship discourse. *Journal of Community and Applied Social Psychology*. doi: 10.1002/casp.2154

Andreouli, E., and Howarth. C. (2013). National identity, citizenship and immigration: putting identity in context. *Journal for the Theory of Social Behaviour*, 43(3), 361–382. doi: 10.1111/j.1468–5914.2012.00501.x

Anwar, M. (2005). Muslims in Britain: issues, policy and practice. In T. Abbas (ed.), *Muslims in Britain: communities under pressure* (pp. 31–46). London: Zed Books.

Arendt, H. (1958). *The human condition*. University of Chicago Press.

Arnett, J. J. (2008). The neglected 95%: why American psychology needs to be less American, *American Psychologist*, 63(7), 602–14.

Aronson, E., Wilson, T. D., and Akert, A. M. (2005). *Social Psychology* (5th edn). Upper Saddle River, NJ: Prentice Hall.

Arruda, A. (1993). Representaciones y opiniones, o jugando con la muñeca rusa. *Revista AVEPSO* 16(1, 2, 3).

(1998). O ambiente natural e seus habitants no imaginário brasileiro. In A. Arruda (ed.), *Representando a alteridade* (pp. 17–46). Petrópolis: Vozes.

(2003). Living is dangerous: research challenges in social representations. *Culture and Psychology*, 9(4), 339–359.

(2005). Durkheim e o imaginário. In C. P. de Sá (ed.), *Imaginário e representações sociais* (pp. 209–232). Rio de Janeiro: Museu da República.

(2007). Dimensões do imaginário. In A. S. P. Moreira and B. V. Camargo (eds.), *Contribuições para a teoria e o método de estudo das representações sociais* (pp. 113–129). João Pessoa: Editora UFPb.

(forthcoming). Social imaginary and social representations of Brazil. Special issue, *Papers on Social Representations*.

Arruda, A., and de Alba, M. (Eds.) (2007). *Espacios imaginarios y representaciones sociales. Aportes desde Latinoamérica*. Barcelona: UAM-Anthropos.

Arruda, A., Jamur, M., Melicio, T., and Barroso, F. (2010). De pivete a funqueiro: genealogia de uma alteridade. *Cadernos de. Pesquisa Fundação Carlos Chagas.*, 40(140), 407–425.

Arthi (2012). Representing mental illness: a case of polyphasias. *Papers on Social Representations* 21, 5.1–5.26.

Arthi, Provencher, C., and Wagner, W. (Eds.) (2012). Cognitive Polyphasia. *Papers on Social Representations* (special issue), 21(1).

Asad, T. (1993). *Genealogies of religion: discipline and reasons of power in Christianity and Islam*. Baltimore, MD: Johns Hopkins University Press.

Asch, S. E. (1946). Forming impressions of personality. *Journal of Abnormal and Social Psychology*, 41, 258–292.

(1952/1987). *Social psychology*. Oxford University Press.

Assman, J. (2011). *Cultural memory and early civilization*. Cambridge University Press.

Astuti, R., and Harris, P. L. (2008). Understanding mortality and the life of the ancestors in Madagascar. *Cognitive Science*, 32, 713–740.

Atsumi, T., and Suwa, K. (2009). Toward reconciliation of historical conflict between Japan and China: design science for peace in Asia. In C. Montiel and N. Noor (eds.), *Peace psychology in Asia*. New York: Springer.

Attride-Stirling, J. (2001). Thematic networks: an analytic tool for qualitative research. *Qualitative Research*, 1(3), 385–405.

Augoustinos, M. (1990). The mediating role of social representations on causal attributions in the social world. *Social Behaviour*, 5, 49–62.

(1998). Social representations and ideology: towards the study of ideological representations. In Flick (ed.), pp. 156–169.

(2001). Social categorization: towards theoretical integration. In Deaux and Philogène (eds.), pp. 201–216.

Augoustinos, M., and Innes, J. M. (1990). Towards an integration of social representations and social schema theory. *British Journal of Social Psychology*, 29(3), 213–231.

Augoustinos, M., and Riggs, D. (2007). Representing 'us' and 'them': constructing white identities in everyday talk. In Moloney and Walker (eds.), pp. 109–130.

Augoustinos, M, Walker, I., and Donaghue, N. (2005). *Social cognition: an integrated introduction*. London: Sage.

Augras, M. (2000). Mil janelas: teóricos do imaginário. *Psicologia Clínica*, 12(1), 107–131.

Austin, J. L. (1961). *How to do things with words*. Oxford: Clarendon Press.

Aveling, E.-L. (2011). Mediating between international knowledge and local knowledge: the critical role of local field officers in an HIV prevention intervention. *Journal of Community and Applied Social Psychology*, 21(2), 95–110.

Aveling, E.-L., and Gillespie, A. (2008). Negotiating multiplicity: adaptive asymmetries within second-generation Turks 'society of mind'. *Journal of Constructivist Psychology*, 21(3), 200–222.

Bachelard, G. (1949/2002). *La psychanalyse du feu*. Paris: Éditions du Seuil.

Baczko, B. (1991). *Los imaginários sociales. Memorias y esperanzas colectivas*. Buenos Aires: Ediciones Nueva Visión.

Baeza, M. A. (2008). *Mundo real, mundo imaginario social. Teoría y práctica de sociología profunda*. Santiago de Chile: RIL Editores.

Bahn, C. (2003). Gewalt und Gegengewalt im 'Deutschen Herbst' 1977. Eine Untersuchung der staatlichen Reaktionen auf den Terrorismus in der Bundesrepublik Deutschand. Masters thesis, Freie Universität Berlin.

Baker, S. (2007). Sustainable development as symbolic commitment: declaratory politics and the seductive appeal of ecological modernization in the European Union. *Environmental Politics*, 16, 297–317.

Bakhtin, M. (1984). *Problems of Dostoyevsky's poetics*. Trans. C. Emerson. Minneapolis: University of Minnesota Press.

Bakhurst, D. (1990). Social memory in soviet thought. In D. Middleton and D. Edwards (eds.), *Collective remembering* (pp. 203–226). London: Sage.

Banchs, M. A. (1996). El papel de la emoción en la construcción de representaciones sociales: Invitación para una reflexion teorica. *Textes Sur les Représentations Sociales*, 5(2), 113–125.

Banchs, M. A., Agudo, A., and Astorga, L. (2007). Imaginarios, representaciones y memoria social. In Arruda and de Alba (eds.), pp. 47–95.

Bandura, A. (1977). Self-efficacy: toward a unifying theory of behavioral change. *Psychological Review*, 84(2), 191–215.

  (1986). *Social foundations of thought and action: a social cognitive theory*. Englewood Cliffs, NJ: Prentice Hall.

  (1997). *Self-efficacy: the exercise of control*. New York: Freeman.

Bangerter, A. (1995). Rethinking the relation between science and common sense: a comment on the current state of SR theory. *Papers on Social Representations*, 4(1), 61–78.

  (2000). Transformation between scientific and social representations of conception: the method of serial reproduction. *British Journal of Social Psychology*, 39, 521–535.

Bangerter, A., and Eicher, V. (2013). The role of a cultural immune system in resisting expert explanations of infectious disease. In M. Bauer, R. Harré, and C. Jensen (eds.), *Beyond rationality: resistance and the practice of rationality* (pp. 101–123). Cambridge: Cambridge Scholars Publishing.

Bangerter, A., and Heath, C. (2004). The Mozart effect: tracking the evolution of a scientific legend. *British Journal of Social Psychology*, 43(4), 605–623.

Bangerter, A., Krings, F., Mouton, A., Gilles, I., Green, E., and Clémence, A. (2012). Longitudinal investigation of public trust in institutions relative to the 2009 H1N1 pandemic in Switzerland. *PLoS ONE*, 7(11), e49806.

Barbier, R. (1994). Sobre o imaginário. *Em aberto*, 14(61), 15–25.

Barbour, R. (2014). Analyzing focus groups. In U. Flick (ed.), *The Sage handbook of qualitative data analysis*. London: Sage.
Barker, R. G. (1968). *Ecological psychology: concepts and methods for studying the environment of human behavior*. Stanford University Press.
Barsalou, L. W. (2009). Simulation, situated conceptualization, and prediction. *Philosophical transactions of the Royal Society of London. Series B, Biological sciences*, 364(1521), 1281–1289. doi: 10.1098/rstb.2008.0319
Bar-Tal, D. (1990). *Group beliefs*. New York: Springer.
Barthes, R. (1957). *Mythologies*. Paris: Éditions du Seuil.
  (1968). *Elements of semiology*. New York: Hill & Wang.
Bartlett, F. C. (1923). *Psychology and primitive culture*. Cambridge University Press.
  (1925). The social functions of symbols. *Australasian Journal of Psychology and Philosophy*, 3, 1–11.
  (1932). *Remembering: a study in experimental and social psychology*. Cambridge University Press.
  (1935). Remembering. *Scientia*, 57, 221–226.
Bataille, M. (2002). Un noyau peut-il ne pas être central. In C. Garnier and W. Doise (eds.), *Les représentations sociales, balisage du Domaine d'Etude*. Montreal: Éditions Nouvelles.
Batel, S., and Castro, P. (2009). A social representations approach to the communication between different spheres: an analysis of the impacts of two discursive formats. *Journal for the Theory of Social Behaviour*, 39(4), 415–433.
Bauer, M. W. (1994). Popular science as 'cultural immunisation': the resistance function of social representations. In P. A. Guareshi and S. Jovchelovitch (eds.), *Texts on social representations*. Petropolis-Brazil: Vozes.
  (2000). Science in the media as cultural indicator: contextualizing surveys with media analysis. In M. Dierkes and C. V. Grote (eds.), *Between understanding and trust: the public, science and technology*. London: Routledge.
  (2005). Distinguishing RED and GREEN biotechnology – cultivation effects of the elite press. *International journal of public opinion research*, 17(1), 63–89.
  (2009). Editorial. *Public Understanding of Science*, 18, 378–382.
  (2013). New technology: a social psychology of dis-inhibition and constraint. In M. W. Bauer, R Harré and C. Jensen (eds.), *Rationality and the practice of resistance* (pp. 79–100). Cambridge: Cambridge Scholars Publishers.
  (2015). *Atom, bytes and genes – public resistance and techno-scientific responses*. London and New York: Routledge.
Bauer, M. W., and Gaskell, G. (1999). Towards a paradigm for research on social representations. *Journal for the Theory of Social Behaviour*, 29(2), 163–186.
  (2002). *Biotechnology – the making of a global controversy*. Cambridge University Press.
  (2008). Social representations theory: a progressive research programme for social psychology. *Journal for the Theory of Social Behaviour*, 38(4), 335–354.
Bauer, M. W., Allum, N. C., and Miller, S. (2007). What can we learn from 25 years of PUS survey research? Liberating and expanding the agenda. *Public Understanding of Science*, 16, 79–95.
Bauer, M. W., Gaskell, G., and Allum, N. A. (2000). Quality, quantity and knowledge interests: avoiding confusion. In M. W. Bauer and G. Gaskell (eds.), *Qualitative researching with text, images and sound* (pp. 3–17). London: Sage.

Baumeister, R. F., Vobs, K. D., and and Funder, D. C. (2008). Psychology as the science of self-report and finger movements. *Perspectives on Psychological Science*, 2(4), 396–403.

Beauvois, J.-L. (1994). *Traité de la servitude libérale: analyse de la soumission*. Paris: Dunod.

Beck, L., and Ajzen, I. (1991). Predicting dishonest actions using the theory of planned behavior. *Journal of Research in Personality*, 25(3), 285–301.

Beck, U. (1986/1992). *The risk society: towards a new modernity*. London: Sage.
  (2006). *Cosmopolitan vision*. Cambridge: Polity Press.
  (2009). *World at risk*. Cambridge: Polity Press.

Behnke, K. (1992). Krise der repraesentation. In J. Ritter and K. F. Grunder (eds.), *Historisches Worterbuch der Philosophie*, vol. VIII (pp. 846–853). Basel: Schwabe.

Belzen, J. A. (1997). The Historiocultural approach in the psychology of religion: perspectives for interdisciplinary research. *Journal for the Scientific Study of Religion*, 36(3), 358–371.
  (1999a). The cultural psychological approach to religion: contemporary debates on the object of the discipline. *Theory and Psychology*, 9(2), 229–255.
  (1999b). Religion as embodiment: cultural-psychological concepts and methods in the study of conversion among 'Bevindelijken'. *Journal for the Scientific Study of Religion*, 38(2), 236–253.
  (2005). In defense of the object: on trends and directions in the psychology of religion. *International Journal for the Psychology of Religion*, 15(1), 1–16.
  (2010). *Towards cultural psychology of religion: principles, approaches, applications*. New York: Springer.

Benford, T. D., and Snow, D. A. (2000). Framing processes and social movements: an overview and assessment. *Annual Review of Sociology*, 26, 611–639.

Benhabib, S. (2002). *The claims of culture: equality and diversity in the global era*. Princeton University Press.

Bennett, M. R., and Hacker, P. M. S. (2003). *Philosophical foundations of neuroscience*. Oxford: Blackwell.

Berger, P., and Luckmann, T. (1966). *The social construction of reality*. Harmondsworth: Penguin.

Berry, J. W. (2011). Integration and multiculturalism: ways towards social solidarity. *Papers on Social Representations*, 20, 2.1–2.21.

Bertalanffy, L. von (1968). *General system theory: foundations, development, applications* (revised edn). New York: George Braziller.

Bertoldo, R., Castro, P., and Bousfield, B. (2013). Pro-environmental beliefs and behaviors: two levels of response to environmental social norms. *Revista Latinoamericana de Psicologia*, 45, 435–446.

Bevan, R. (2006). *The destruction of memory: architecture at war*. London: Reaktion Books.

Bhatia, S. (2002). Acculturation, dialogical voices and the construction of the diasporic self. *Theory and Psychology*, 12(1), 55–77.

Billig, M. (1985). Prejudice, categorization and particularization: from a perceptual to a rhetorical approach. *European Journal of Social Psychology*, 15, 79–103.

(1987). *Arguing and thinking: a rhetorical approach to social psychology*. Cambridge University Press.
  (1988). Social representations, objectification and anchoring: a rhetorical analysis. *Social Behaviour*, 3, 1–16.
  (1991). *Ideologies and beliefs*. London: Sage.
  (1993). Studying the thinking society: social representations, rhetoric, and attitudes. In Breakwell and Canter (eds.), pp. 39–62.
  (1995). *Banal nationalism*. London: Sage.
  (1996). *Arguing and thinking: a rhetorical approach to social psychology* (2nd edn). Cambridge University Press.
  (2008a). The language of critical discourse analysis: the case of nominalization. *Discourse and Society*, 19, 783–800.
  (2008b). Social representations and repression: examining the first formulations of Freud and Moscovici. *Journal for the Theory of Social Behaviour*, 38, 355–368.
  (2011). Writing social psychology: fictional things and unpopulated texts. *British Journal of Social Psychology*, 50, 4–20.
  (2013). *Learn to write badly: how to succeed in the social sciences*. Cambridge University Press.
Billig, M., Condor, S., Edwards, D., Gane, M., Middleton, D., and Padley, A. (1988). *Ideological dilemmas: a social psychology of everyday thinking*. London: Sage.
Bloch, E. (1953/1986). *The principle of hope*. Trans. N. Plaice, S. Plaice and P. Knight. Oxford: Basil Blackwell.
Bloomfield, L. (1933). *Language*. New York: Henry Holt.
Bodey, M. (2007). Four decades of 'God's Great Equaliser'. *The Australian*, 19 April. Retrieved 27.08.2010. www.theaustralian.com.au/media/four-decades-of-gods-great-equaliser/story-e6frg996-1111113367351
Boehme, H. (2006). *Fetischismus und Kultur – eine andere Moderne*. Hamburg: Rowolts Enzyklopaedie.
Bogart, L. M., and Thorburn Bird, S. (2003). Exploring the relationship of conspiracy beliefs about HIV/AIDS to sexual behaviors and attitudes among African-American adults. *Journal of the National Medical Association*, 95, 1–10.
Bogart, L. M., Wagner, G., Galvan, F. H., and Banks, D. (2010). Conspiracy beliefs about HIV are related to antiretroviral treatment: nonadherence among African American men with HIV. *Journal of Acquired Immune Deficiency Syndromes*, 53, 648–655.
Bohnert, A. S. B., and Latkin, C. A. (2009). HIV testing and conspiracy beliefs regarding the origins of HIV among African Americans. *AIDS Patient Care and STDs*, 23, 759–763.
Boholm, A. (1998). Visual images and risk messages: commemorating Chernobyl. *Risk, Decision and Policy*, 3(2), 125–43.
Bonaiuto, M., Breakwell, G. M. and Cano, I. (1996). Identity processes and environmental threat : the effects of nationalism and local identity upon perception of beach pollution. *Journal of Community and Applied Social Psychology*, 6, 157–175.
Bonfantini, M. A. (1987). *La semiosi e l'abduzione* (*The semiosis and the abduction*). Milan: Bompiani.
Boukydis, C. F. Z., and Burgess, R. L. (1982). Adult physiological response to infant cries: effects of temperament of infant, parental status, and gender. *Child Development*, 53, 1291–1298.

Bourdieu, P. (1979/1984). *Distinction: a social critique of the judgement of taste*. Trans. R. Nice. Cambridge, MA: Harvard University Press.
  (1990). *The logic of practice*. Cambridge: Polity Press.
Bourdieu, P., and Nice, R. (1977). *Outline of a theory of practice*. Cambridge University Press.
Bourdieu, P., and Passeron, J.-C. (1990). *Reproduction in education, society and culture*. London: Sage.
Boyes, R. M. D. (2000). Fallacies in interpreting historical and social data. In M. W. Bauer and G. Gaskell (eds.), *Qualitative researching with text, image and sound – a practical handbook* (pp. 318–335). London: Sage.
Bradbury, M. A. I. (1999). *Representations of death: a social psychological perspective*. London and New York: Routledge.
Branco, A. U., and Valsiner, J. (1997). Changing methodologies: a co-constructivist study of goal orientations in social interactions. *Psychology and Developing Societies*, 9(1), 35–64.
Brandon, D. T., Isaac, L. A., and LaVeist, T. A. (2005). The legacy of Tuskegee and trust in medical care: is Tuskegee responsible for race differences in mistrust of medical care? *Journal of the National Medical Association*, 97, 951–956.
Brandtstädter, J. (1982). Apriorische Elemente in psychologischen Forschungsprogrammen. *Zeitschrift Für Sozialpsychologie*, 13, 267–277.
Branscombe, N. R., Slugoski, B., and Kappen, D. M. (2004). The measurement of collective guilt: what it is and what it is not. In N. R. Branscombe and B. Doosje (eds.), *Collective guilt: international perspectives* (pp. 16–34). Cambridge University Press.
Braun, V., and Clarke, V. (2006). Using thematic analysis in psychology. *Qualitative Research in Psychology*, 3(2), 77–101.
Breakwell, G. M. (1978). Some effects of marginal social identity. In H. Tajfel (ed.), *Differentiation between social groups* (pp. 301–336). London: Academic Press.
  (1979). Illegitimate group membership and inter-group differentiation. *British Journal of Social and Clinical Psychology*, 18, 141–149.
  (1986). *Coping with threatened identities*. London and New York: Methuen.
  (1988). Strategies adopted when identity is threatened. *Revue Internationale de Psychologie Sociale*, 1(2), 189–204.
  (1990). Social beliefs about gender differences. In Fraser and Gaskell (eds.), pp. 210–225.
  (1992). L'efficacité auto-imputée et l'éloignement: aspects de l'identité. *Cahiers Internationaux de Psychologie Sociale*, 15, 9–29.
  (1993). Social representations and social identity. *Papers on Social Representations*, 2(3), 198–217.
  (2001a). Social representational constraints upon identity processes. In Deaux and Philogene (eds.), pp. 271–284.
  (2001b). Promoting individual and social change. In F. Butera and G. Mugny (eds.), *Social influence in social reality*. Goettingen: Hogrefe & Huber.
  (2001c). Mental models and social representations of hazards: the significance of identity processes. *Journal of Risk Research*, 4(4), 341–351.
  (2004). Identity change in the context of the growing influence of European Union institutions. In R. Hermann, T. Risse and M. B. Brewer (eds.), *Transnational*

identities: becoming European in the EU (pp. 25–39). New York: Rowman & Littlefield.
  (2007). *The psychology of risk*. Cambridge University Press.
  (2010). Resisting representations and identity processes. *Papers on Social Representations*, 19, 6.1–6.11.
  (2011). Empirical approaches to social representations and identity processes: 20 years on. *Papers on Social Representations*, 20, 17.1–17.4.
  (2014). Identity and social representations. In R. Jaspal and G. M. Breakwell (eds.), *Identity process theory: identity, social action and social change*. Cambridge University Press.
  (Ed.) (1983). *Threatened identities*. Chichester: John Wiley.
Breakwell, G. M. and Canter, D. (Eds.) (1993). *Empirical approaches to social representations*. Oxford: Clarendon Press.
Breakwell, G. M., and Lyons, E. (Eds.) (1996). *Changing European identities: social psychological analyses of change*. Oxford: Butterworth-Heinemann.
Breakwell, G. M., Fife-Schaw, C., and Devereux, J. D. (1989). Political activity and political attitudes in teenagers: is there any correspondence? *Political Psychology*, 10(4), 745–755.
Breakwell, G. M., Smith, J., and Wright, D. (Eds.) (2012). *Research methods in psychology*. London: Sage.
Brockmeier, M. (2010). After the archive: remapping memory. *Culture and Psychology*, 16(1), 5–35.
Bröder, A. (2011). *Versuchplanung und experimentelles Praktikum*. Goettingen: Hogrefe.
Brondi, S., Sarrica, M., Cibin, R., Neresini, F., and Contarello, A. (2012). The Chiampo river 30 years later: long-term effects of environmental regulations on social representations. *Journal of Community and Applied Social Psychology*, 22(4), 283–299.
Brubaker, R., and Cooper, F. (2000). Beyond identity. *Theory and Society*, 29, 1–47.
Buijs, A., Hovardas, T., Figari, H., Castro, P., Devine-Wright, P., Fischer, A., Mouro, C., *et al.* (2012). Understanding people's ideas on natural resource management: Research on social representations of nature. *Society and Natural Resources*, 25, 1167–1181.
Bulgakov, S. (1931/2012). *Icons and the name of God*. Trans. B. Jakim. Grand Rapids, MI: Eerdmans.
Burridge, J. D. (2005). The construction of discursive difficulty: the circulation of, and resistance to, moral asymmetries in the public debate over the invasion of Iraq in 2003. Doctoral thesis, University of Nottingham.
Caillaud, S., and Kalampalikis, N. (2013). Focus groups and ecological practices: a psychosocial approach. *Qualitative Research in Psychology*, 10(4), 382–401. doi: 10.1080/14780887.2012.674176
Caillaud, S., Kalampalikis, N., and Flick, U. (2012). The social representations of the Bali Climate Conference in the French and German media. *Journal of Community and Applied Social Psychology*, 22(4), 363–378. doi: 10.1002/casp
Calhoun, C. (2002). Imagining solidarity: cosmopolitanism, constitutional patriotism and the public sphere. *Public Culture*, 14(1), 147–171.
  (Ed.) (1992). *Habermas and the public sphere*. Cambridge, MA: MIT Press.

Callaghan, P., Moloney, G., and Blair, D. (2012). Contagion in the representational field of water recycling: informing new environment practice through social representation theory. *Journal of Community and Applied Social Psychology*, 37, 20–37.

Campbell, A., Muncer, S., and Coyle, E. (1992). Social representations of aggression as an explanation of gender differences: a preliminary study. *Aggressive Behavior*, 18, 92–108.

Campbell, C. M. (2003). *'Letting them die': why HIV/AIDS prevention programs fail*. Oxford: International African Institute.

Campbell, C., and Jovchelovitch, S. J. (2000). Health, community and development: towards a social psychology of participation. *Journal of Community and Applied Social Psychology*, 10(4), 255–270.

Campbell, D. T., and Stanley, J. C. (1963). *Experimental and quasi-experimental designs for research*. Chicago: Rand McNally.

Campos, P. H. F., and Rouquette, M. L. (2003). Abordagem estrutural e componente afetivo das representações sociais. *Psicologia: Reflexão e Crítica*, 16(3).

Canclini, N. (1997). *Imaginarios urbanos*. Editorial Universitaria de Buenos Aires.

Cantor, G. (1874). Ueber eine Eigenschaft des Inbegriffs aller reellen algebraischen Zahlen. *Journal für die Reine und Angewandte Mathematik*, 77, 258–26.

Cardena, E., Lynn, S. J., and Krippner, S. (Eds.) (2000). *Varieties of anomalous experience*. Washington DC: American Psychological Association.

Cartwright, D. (1951). Achieving change in people: some applications of group dynamics theory. *Human Relations*, 4, 381–392.

Carugati, F., Selleri, P., and Scappini, E. (1994). Are social representations an architecture of cognitions? A tentative model for extending the dialog. *Papers on Social Representations*, 3(2), 1–18.

Carvalho, J. M. (1990). *A formação das almas. O imaginário da República no Brasil*. São Paulo: Companhia das Letras.

Castells, M. (2002). Local and global: cities in the network society. *Tijdschrift voor Economische en Sociale Geografie*, 93(5), 548–558.

(2004). *The network society: a cross-cultural perspective*. Oxford: Blackwell.

(2008). The new public sphere: Global civil society, communication networks and global governance. *Annals of the American Academy of Political ans Social Science*, 616, 78–93.

Castoriadis, C. (1975). *The imaginary institution of society*. Cambridge: Polity Press.

(1997). *World in fragments*. Stanford University Press.

Castorina, J. A. (2010). The ontogenesis of social representations: a dialectic perspective. *Papers on Social Representations*, 19, 18.1–18.19.

Castro, P. (2006). Applying social psychology to the study of environmental concern and environmental worldviews: contributions from the social representations approach. *Journal of Community and Applied Social Psychology*, 16(4), 247–266.

(2012). Legal innovation for social change: exploring change and resistance to different types of sustainability laws. *Political Psychology*, 33, 105–121.

Castro, P., and Batel, S. (2008). Social representation, change and resistance: on the difficulties of generalizing new norms. *Culture and Psychology*, 14(4), 475–497.

Castro, P., and Gomes, I. (2005). Genetically modified organisms in the Portuguese press: thematization and anchoring. *Journal for the Theory of Social Behaviour*, 35(1), 1–17.

Castro, P., and Mouro, C. (2011). Psycho-social processes in dealing with legal innovation in the community: insights from biodiversity conservation. *American Journal of Community Psychology*, 47, 362–373.

Castro, P., Garrido, M., Reis, E., and Menezes, J. (2009). Ambivalence and conservation behaviour: an exploratory study on the recycling of metal cans. *Journal of Environmental Psychology*, 29, 24–33.

Castro, P., Mouro. C., and Gouveia, R. (2012). The conservation of biodiversity in protected areas: comparing the presentation of legal innovations in the national and the regional press. *Society and Natural Resources*, 25, 539–555.

Catán, L. (1986). The dynamic display of process: historical development and contemporary uses of the microgenetic method. *Human Development*, 29, 252–263.

Chombart de Lauwe, M. J. (1984). Changes in the representation of the child in the course of social transmission. In Farr and Moscovici (eds.), pp. 185–209.

Chryssides, I., Dashtipour, P., Keshet, S., Righi, C., Sammut, G., and Sartawi, M. (2009). Commentary. We don't share! The social representation approach, enactivism and the fundamental incompatibilities between the two. *Culture and Psychology*, 15(1), 83–95.

Chryssochoou, X. (2003). Studying identity in social psychology: some thoughts on the definition of identity and its relation to action. *Language and Politics*, 22, 225–242.

(2004). *Cultural diversity: its social psychology*. Oxford: Blackwell.

(2009a). Identity projects in multicultural nation-states. In I. Jasinskaja-Lahti and T. A. Mahonen (eds.), *Identities, intergroup relations and acculturation: the cornerstones of intercultural encounters*. Gaudeamus Helsinki University Press.

(2009b). Strategies of immigrants' inclusion: the views of Greeks, of Voreioipirotes and of Albanians in Athens. In M. Pavlou and A. Skoulariki (eds.), *Immigrants and minorities: discourses and politics*. Athens: Vivliorama.

(2010). Representations of the social and of the cultural in the meaning making of the co-existence in multicultural environments: a social psychological analysis of ideological opposition to migration. In S. Papastamou, G. Prodromitis and V. Pavlopoulos (eds.), *Social thought, cognition and behavior* (pp. 491–523). Athens: Pedio.

(2014). Identity processes in culturally diverse societies: how cultural diversity is reflected in the self? In R. Jaspal and G. M. Breakwell (eds.), *Identity process theory: identity, social action and social change*. Cambridge University Press.

Chryssochoou, X., and Dede, E. (2013). Albanians in Greece: identity, strategies of social mobility and attitudes towards acculturation. Unpublished manuscript, Panteion University of Social and Political Sciences.

Chryssochoou, X., and Lyons, E. (2011). Perceptions of (in)compatibility between identities and participation in the national polity of people belonging to ethnic minorities. In A. E. Azzi, X. Chryssochoou, B. Klandermans and B. Simon (eds.), *Identity and participation in culturally diverse societies* (pp. 69–88). Chichester: Wiley-Blackwell.

Cialdini, R. B., and Trost, M. R. (1998). Social influence: social norms, conformity, and compliance. In D. T. Gilibert, S. T. Fiske and G. Lindzey (eds.), *The Handbook of Social Psychology*, vol. II (4th edn) (pp. 151–192). New York: McGraw-Hill.

Clawson, R. A., and Trice, R. (2000). Poverty as we know it: media portrayals of the poor. *Public Opinion Quarterly*, 64, 53–64.

Clémence, A. (2001). Social positioning and social representations. In Deaux and Philogène (eds.), pp. 83–95.

Coase, R. (1960). The problem of social cost. *Journal of Law and Economics*, 3, 1–44.

Cohen, A. P. (1995). *The symbolic construction of community*. London: Routledge.

Cohen, R. (1994). *Frontiers of identity. The British and others*. London: Longman.

Cohn, S. K., Jr. (2002). *The Black Death transformed: disease and culture in early Renaissance Europe*. London: Edward Arnold.

Cole, M. (1996). *Cultural psychology: a once and future discipline*. Cambridge, MA: Belknap Press.

Cole, M., Engestrom, Y., and Vasquez, O. (1997). *Mind, culture and activity: seminal papers from the Laboratory of Comparative Human Cognition*. Cambridge University Press.

Coleman, J. W. (1986). *Individual interests and collective action*. Cambridge University Press in collaboration with Maison des Sciences del' Homme.

Communities and Local Government and National Centre for Social Research (2010). *Citizenship Survey 2008–2009*. Colshester: UK Data Archive.

Condor, S. (1996). Social identity and time. In W. P. Robinson (ed.), *Social groups and identities: developing the legacy of Henri Tajfel* (pp. 285–315). Oxford: Butterworth Heinemann.

  (1997). 'And so say all of us?': some thoughts on 'experiential democratization' as an aim for critical social psychologists. In T. Ibáñez and L. Iñiguez (eds.), *Critical social psychology* (pp. 111–146). London: Sage.

  (2000). Pride and prejudice: identity management in English people's talk about 'this country'. *Discourse and Society*, 11(2), 175–205.

  (2006). Temporality and collectivity: diversity, history and the rhetorical construction of national entitativity. *British Journal of Social Psychology*, 45, 657–682.

Connerton, P. (1989). *How societies remember*. Cambridge University Press.

Cornish, F., and Ghosh, R. (2007). The necessary contradictions of 'community-led' health promotion: a case study of HIV prevention in an Indian red light district. *Social Science and Medicine*, 64, 496–507.

Cornish, F., Montenegro, C. R., van Reisen, K., Zaka, F., and Sevitt, J. (2014). Trust the process: Community health psychology after Occupy. *Journal of Health Psychology*, 19(1), 60–71.

Crandall, C. S. (1994). Prejudice against fat people: ideology and self-interest. *Journal of Personality and Social Psychology*, 66, 882–894.

Crawford, R. (1985). A cultural account of health – control, release and the social body. In J. B. McKinlay (ed.), *Issues in the political economy of health care* (pp. 60–103). London: Tavistock Press.

  (1994). The boundaries of the self and the unhealthy other: reflections on health, culture and AIDS. *Social Science and Medicine*, 38, 1347–1365.

Creswell, J., and Piano Clark, V. (2010). *Designing and conducting mixed methods research*. London: Sage.

Crossley, N. (1996). *Intersubjectivity: the fabric of social becoming*. London: Sage.
Curtis, V. A., and Biran, A. (2001). Dirt, disgust and disease: is hygiene in our genes? *Perspectives in Biology and Medicine*, 44(1), 7–31.
Dake, P. (1992). Myths of nature: culture and the social construction of risk. *Journal of Social Issues*, 48, 21–37.
Damasio, A. (1994). *Descartes error: emotion, rationality and the human brain*. New York: Putnam.
Danzelman, P. (2010). British citizenship statistics. www.homeoffice.gov.uk/publications/science-research-statistics/research-statistics/immigration-asylum-research/hosb0910/hosb0910?view=Binary (06/11/2012)
Danziger, K. (1997). *Naming the mind: how psychology found its language*. London: Sage.
Darwin, C. (1859). *On the Origin of Species by Means of Natural Selection, or the Preservation of Favoured Races in the Struggle for Life*. London: John Murray.
Davies, B., and Harré, R. (1990). Positioning: the discursive production of selves. *Journal for the Theory of Social Behaviour*, 20, 43–63.
Dawkins, R. (1976). *The selfish gene*. Oxford University Press.
De Alba, M. (2002). Sémiologie urbaine et mémoire collective des monuments historiques de Mexico. In S. Laurens and N. Roussiau (eds.), *La mémoire sociale: identités et representations sociales* (pp. 233–242). Presses Universitaires de Rennes.
  (2004). Mapas mentales de la Ciudad de México: una aproximación psicosocial al estudio de las representaciones espaciales. *Estudios Demográficos y Urbanos*, 19(1), 115–143.
  (2006). Experiencia urbana e imágenes colectivas de la Ciudad de México. *Estudios Demográficos*, 21,3(63), 663–700.
  (2007). Mapas imaginarios del Centro Histórico de la Ciudad de México: de la experiencia al imaginario urbano. In Arruda and de Alba (eds.), pp. 285–319.
  (2011). Social representations of urban spaces: a comment on mental maps of Paris. *Papers on Social Representations*, 20, 29.1–29.14.
De Goede, M. (1996). Ideology in the US welfare debate: neo-liberal representations of poverty. *Discourse and Society*, 7(3), 317–357.
De Rosa, A. S. (1987). The social representations of mental illness in children and adults. In W. Doise and S. Moscovici (eds.), *Current issues in European social psychology*, vol. II (pp. 47–138). Cambridge University Press.
  (1993). Social representations and attitudes: problems of coherence between the theoretical definition and procedure of research. *Papers on Social Representations*, 2(3). www.psr.jku.at/PSR1993/2_1993deRos.pdf
  (1994). La società e il malato mentale: opinioni, atteggiamenti, stigmatizzazioni e pregiudizzi. In Guglielmo Bellelli (ed.), *L'altra malattia. Come la società pensa la malattia mentale* (pp. 43–131). Naples: Signori Editore.
  (2000). The king is naked. Critical advertisement and fashion. The Benetton phenomenon. In Deaux and Philogène (eds.), pp. 48–82.
  (2006). The 'boomerang' effect of radicalism in discursive psychology: a critical overview of the controversy with the social representations theory. *Journal for the Theory of Social Behaviour*, 36, 161–201.
  (2011). Mito, ciência e representações sociais. In E. C. Paredes and D. Jodelet (eds.), *Pensamento mítico e representações sociais* (pp. 123–179). Cuiabá: EdUFMG/FAPEMAT/EdIUNI.

De Rosa, A. S., and Farr, R. (2001). Icon and symbol: two sides of the same coin in the investigation of social representationsocial representation. In F. Buschini and N. Kalampalikis (Eds.), *Penser la vie, le social, la nature. Mélanges en honneur de Serge Moscovici* (pp. 237–256). Paris: Maison de Sciences de l'Homme.

De Rosa, A. S., and Mormino, C. (2002). Au confluent de la mémoire sociale: étude sur l'identité nationale et européene. In S. Laurens and N. Roussiau (eds.), *La mémoire sociale: identités et representations sociales* (pp. 119–137). Presses Universitaires de Rennes.

Deaux, K. (2006). *To be an immigrant*. New York: Russell Sage Foundation.

Deaux, K., and Philogène, G. (2001). *Representations of the social: Bridging theoretical traditions*. Oxford: Blackwell.

Deconchy, J.-P. (1990). Sociocultural context and psychological meachanisms. In Himmelweit and Gaskell (eds.), *Societal Psychology* (pp. 177–192). London: Sage.

de-Graft Aikins, A. (2002). Exploring biomedical and ethnomedical representations of diabetes in Ghana and the scope for cross-professional collaboration: a social psychological approach to health policy. *Social Science Information*, 41(4), 603–630.

(2003). Living with diabetes in rural and urban Ghana: a critical social psychological examination of illness action and scope for intervention. *Journal of Health Psychology*, 8(5), 557–72.

(2005). Healer shopping in Africa: New evidence from rural-urban qualitative study of Ghanaian diabetes experiences. *British Medical Journal*, 331(7519), 737.

(2012). Familiarising the unfamiliar: cognitive polyphasia, emotions and the creation of social representations. *Papers on Social Representations*, 21, 7.1–7.28.

Demeulenaere, P. (2011). *Analytical sociology and social mechanisms*. Cambridge University Press.

den Boer, P. (2010). Loci memoriae – Lieux de mémoire. In A. Eril and A. Nünning (eds.), *A companion to cultural memory studies* (pp. 19–26). Berlin: De Gruyter.

Dennett, D. C. (1996). *Darwin's dangerous idea: evolution and the meanings of life*. Harmondsworth: Penguin.

Denzin, N. K. (1978). *The research act*. 2nd edn. Chicago, IL: Aldine.

Deutsch, M. (1985). *Distributive justice*. New Haven, CT: Yale University Press.

Devine-Wright, P. (2009). Rethinking NIMBYism: the role of place attachment and place identity in explaining place-protective action. *Journal of Community & Applied Social Psychology*, 19, 426–441.

Diamond, J. (1999). *Gun, germs and steel: the fate of human societies*. New York: W. W. Norton.

Dietz, T., Stern P. C., and Guagnano, G. A. (1998). Social structural and social psychological bases of environmental concern. *Environment and Behavior*, 30, 450–471.

Doise W., (1980). Levels of explanation. *European Journal of Social Psychology*, 10, 213–231.

(1985). Les représentations sociales: définition d'un concept. *Connexions*, 45, 243–253.

(1986a) *Levels of explanation in social psychology*. Cambridge University Press.

(1986b). Les représentations sociales: définition d'un concept. In W. Doise and A. Palmonari (eds.), *L'étude des représentations sociales. Textes de base en psychologie* (pp. 81–94). Neuchâtel: Delachaux et Niestlé.

(1989). Constructivism in social psychology. *European Journal of Social Psychology*, 19, 389–400.

(1990). Les représentations sociales. In C. Bonnet, R. Ghiglione and T. F. Richard (eds.), *Traité de psychologie cognitive*, vol. III (pp. 111–174). Paris: Dunod.

(2001). Human rights studied as normative social representations. In Deaux and Philogène (eds.), pp. 96–112.

Doise, W., and Hanselmann, C. (1990). Conflict and social marking in the acquisition of operational thinking. *Learning and instruction*, 1, 119–127.

Doise, W., and Mugny, G. (1984). *The social development of the intellect*. Oxford: Pergamon.

Doise, W., and Staerklé, C. (2002). From social to political psychology: the societal approach. In K. Monroe (ed.), *Political psychology* (pp. 151–172). Hillsdale, NJ: Lawrence Erlbaum.

Doise, W., Clémence, A., and Lorenzi-Cioldi, F. (1992). *Représentations sociales et analyses de données*. Presses Universitaires de Grenoble.

(1993). *The quantitative analysis of social representations*. Hemel Hempstead: Harvester Wheatsheaf.

Doise, W., Deschamps, J. C., and Meyers, G. (1978). The accentuation of intercategory similarities. In H. Tajfel (ed.), *Differentiation between social groups* (pp. 159–168). London: Academic Press.

Doise, W., Mugny, G., and Pérez, J. A. (1998). The social construction of knowledge, social marking and sociocognitive conflict. In Flick (ed.), pp. 77–90.

Doise, W., Mugny, G., and Perret-Clermont, A. N. (1975). Social interaction and the development of cognitive operations. *European Journal of Social Psychology*, 5, 367–383.

Doise, W., Spini, D., and Clémence, A. (1999). Human rights studied as social representations in a cross-national context. *European Journal of Social Psychology*, 29, 1–29.

Donald, M. (1991). *Origins of the modern mind*. Cambridge, MA: Harvard University Press.

Donath, J. S. (1998). Identity and deception in the virtual community. In P. Kollock and M. Smith (ed.), *Communities in cyberspace* (pp. 29–59). London: Routledge.

Doosje, B., Branscombe, N. R., Spears, R., and Manstead, A. S. R. (1998). Guilty by association: when one's group has a negative history. *Journal of Personality and Social Psychology*, 75, 872–886.

Douglas, M. (1966). *Purity and danger*. London: Routledge & Kegan Paul.

(1982). *In the active voice*. London: Routledge & Kegan Paul.

Douglas, M., and Wildavsky, A. (1982). *Risk and culture: an essay on the selection of technological and environmental dangers*. Berkeley: University of California Press.

Dovi, S. (2011). Political Representation. In Edward N. Zalta (gen. ed.), *The Stanford encyclopedia of philosophy* (winter edn). http://plato.stanford.edu/archives/win2011/entries/political-representation/

Dresler-Hawke, E., and Liu, J. H. (2006). Collective shame and the positioning of German national identity. *Psicologia Politica*, 32, 131–153.

Dubecki, L. (2007). The pain of a senseless death in a safe suburb. *The Age*, 11 October, 1.

Dubois, N., and Beauvois, J.-L. (2005). Normativeness and individualism. *European Journal of Social Psychology*, 35(1), 123–146. doi: 10.1002/ejsp.236

Duby, G. (1978). *Les trois ordres ou l'imaginaire du féodalisme*. Paris: Gallimard.

Duckitt, J. (2001). A dual-process cognitive-motivational theory of ideology and prejudice. In M. P. Zanna (ed.), *Advances in experimental social psychology*, vol. XXXIII (pp. 41–113). San Diego, CA: Academic Press.

Duckitt, J., Wagner, C., du Plessis, I., and Birum, I. (2002). The psychological bases of ideology and prejudice: testing a dual process model. *Journal of Personality and Social Psychology*, 83, 75–93.

Due, C. (2010). A discursive analysis of media representations of belonging in Australia. Ph.D. thesis, University of Adelaide.

Duesberg, P. H. (1987). Retroviruses as carcinogens and pathogens: expectations and reality. *Cancer Research*, 47, 1199–1220.

Duffy, E. (1992). *The stripping of the altars*. New Haven, CT: Yale University Press.

Dunlap, R. E. (2008). The new environmental paradigm scale: from marginality to worldwide use. *Journal of Environmental Education*, 40, 1–18.

Durand, G. (1992). *Les structures anthropologiques de l'imaginaire*. Paris: Dunod.

  (1998). *O imaginário. Ensaio acerca das ciências e da filosofia da imagem*. Rio de Janeiro: DIFEL.

Durkheim, E. (1893). *The division of labor in society*. New York: Free Press.

  (1894). *Le suicide: étude de sociologie*. Paris: F. Alcan.

  (1895/1992). *Les règles de la méthode sociologique*. Paris: Presses Universitaires de France – Quadrige.

  (1898/1996). Representations individuelles et representations collectives. In E. Durkheim, *Sociologie et philosophic*. Paris: Presses Universitaires de France.

  (1912). *The elementary forms of the religious life*. Oxford University Press.

  (1912/1968). *Les formes élémentaires de la vie religieuse* (5th edn). Collection Bibliothèque de Philosophie Contemporaine. Paris: Presses Universitaires de France.

  (1924/1974). *Sociology and philosophy*. New York: Free Press.

Durkheim, E., and Mauss, M. (1905/1963). *Primitive classification*. University of Chicago Press.

Duveen, G. (1983). From social cognition to the cognition of social life: an essay in decentration. Ph.D. thesis, University of Sussex.

  (1993). The development of social representations of gender. *Papers on Social Representations*, 2, 171–177.

  (1997). Psychological development as a social process. In L. Smith, P. Tomlinson and J. Dockerell (eds.), *Piaget, Vygotsky and beyond*. London: Routledge.

  (2001a). Genesis and structure: Piaget and Moscovici. In F. Buschini and N. Kalampalikis (eds.), *Penser la vie, le social, la nature: mélange en l'honneur de Serge Moscovici* (pp. 163–173). Paris: Éditions de la Maison des Sciences de l'Homme.

  (2001b). Representations, identities, resistance. In Deaux and Philogène (eds.), pp. 257–270.

  (2001c). Social representations. In C. Fraser and B. Burchell (eds.), *Introducing social psychology*. Cambridge: Polity Press.

  (2002). Construction, belief, doubt. *Psychologie et Societé*, 3, 139–155.

  (2007). Culture and social representations. In Valsiner and Rosa (eds.), pp. 543–559.

  (2008). Social actors and social groups: a return to heterogeneity in social psychology. *Journal for the Theory of Social Behaviour*, 38(4), 369–374.

  (2013). Social life and the epistemic subject. In S. Moscovici, S. Jovchelovitch and B. Wagoner (eds.), *Development as social process: selected writings of Gerard Duveen* (pp. 67–89). London: Routledge.

Duveen, G., and De Rosa, A. S. (1992). Two approaches to the origins of development of social knowledge. *Papers on Social Representations*, 1, 94–108.

Duveen, G., and Lloyd, B. (1986). The significance of social identities. *British Journal of Social Psychology*, 25, 219–230.
  (1990). Introduction. In G. Duveen and B. Lloyd (eds.), *Social representations and the development of knowledge* (pp. 1–10). Cambridge University Press.
Duveen, G., and Psaltis, C. (2008). The constructive role of asymmetries in social interaction. In U. Mueller, J. Carpendale, N. Budwig and B. Sokol, *Social life and social knowledge: toward a process account of development* (pp. 183–204). Mahwah, NJ: Lawrence Erlbaum.
Eagle, M. (1967). The effect of learning strategies upon free recall. *American Journal of Psychology*, 80(3), 421–425.
Ebbinghaus, H. (1885/1913). *Memory: a contribution to experimental psychology*. New York: Dover Publications.
Echebarria Echabe, A., Guede, E. F., and Castro, J. L. G. (1994). Social representations and intergroup conflict: who's smoking here? *European Journal of Social Psychology*, 24(3), 339–356.
Eco, U. (1973). *Il segno (The sign)*. Milan: ISEDI.
  (1976). *Einfuehrung in die Semiotik*. Munich: UTB-Fink Verlag.
  (1976). *A theory of semiotics*. Bloomington: Indiana University Press.
  (1984). *Semiotics and the philosophy of language*. Bloomington: Indiana University Press.
  (1985). *Einfuehrung in die semiotik*. 5th edn. Munich: UTB-Fink Verlag.
  (1990). *The limits of interpretation*. Bloomington: Indiana University Press.
  (2000). *Kant and the platypus: essays on language and cognition*. New York: Harcourt Brace.
Edwards, D. (1997). *Discourse and cognition*. London: Sage.
  (2006). Discourse, cognition and social practices: the rich surface of social interaction. *Discourse Studies*, 8, 41–49.
Edwards, D., and Potter, J. (1992). *Discursive psychology*. London: Sage.
Edwards, D., Ashmore, M., and Potter, J. (1995). Death and furniture: the rhetoric, politics and theology of bottom line arguments against relativism. *History of the Human Sciences*, 8, 25–49.
Egan, K. (1997). *The educated mind*. University of Chicago Press.
Eiben, C. B., Siegel, J. B., Bale, J. B., Cooper, S., Khatib, F., Shen, B. W., Foldit Players, Stoddard, B. L., Popovic, Z., and Baker, D. (2012). Increased Diels-Alderase activity through backbone remodeling guided by Foldit players. *Nature Biotechnology*, 30(2), 190–192.
Eicher, V., Clémence, A., Bangerter, A., Mouton, A., Gilles, I., and Green, E. G. T. (2014). Fundamental beliefs, origin explanations, and perceived effectiveness of protection measures: exploring laypersons' chains of reasoning about infectious diseases. *Journal of Community and Applied Social Psychology*, 24, 359–375.
Eire, M. N. C. (1986). *War against the idols – the reformation of worship from Erasmus to Calvin*. Cambridge University Press.
Elcheroth, G., Doise, W., and Reicher, S. (2011). On the knowledge of politic and the politics of knowledge: how a social representations approach helps us rethink the subject of political psychology. *Political Psychology*, 32, 729–758.
Elias, N. (1939/2000). *The civilising process*. Oxford: Blackwell.
Ellen, R. (1988). Fetishism. *Man, n.s*, 23(2), 213–235.

Emmons, R. A., and McCullough, M. E. (Eds.) (1999). Religion in the psychology of personality. *Journal of Personality* 67(6).
  (2003). The psychology of religion. *Annual Review of Psychology*, 54, 377–402.
Esposito, J. L. (1984). *Islam and politics* (3rd edn). Syracuse University Press.
Evans, E. M., and Lane, J. D. (2011). Contradictory or complementary? Creationist and evolutionist explanations of the origin(s) of species. *Human Development*, 54(3), 144–159.
Fabbri, P. (1998). *La svolta semiotica* (*The semiotic turn*). Rome: Laterza.
Falomir, J. M., Staerklé, C., Depuiset, M.-A., and Butera, F. (2005). Democracy justifies the means: political group structure moderates the perceived legitimacy of intergroup aggression. *Personality and Social Psychology Bulletin*, 31, 1683–1695.
Farr, R. M. (1981). Social representations: a French tradition of research. *Journal for the Theory of Social Behaviour*, 17, 343–370.
  (1990a). Social representations as widespread beliefs. In Fraser and Gaskell (eds.), pp. 47–64.
  (1990b). Waxing and waning of interest in societal psychology: a historical perspective. In Himmelweit and Gaskell (eds.), pp. 46–65.
  (1991). Individualism as a collective representation. In V. Aebischer, J. P. Deconchy and E. M Lipiansky (eds.), *Ideologies et representations sociales* (pp. 129–143). Cousset, Fribourg: Delval.
  (1993). Theory and method in the study of social representations. In Breakwell and Canter (eds.), pp. 15–38.
  (1994). Attitudes, social representations and social attitudes. *Papers on Social Representations*, 3, 33–36.
  (1996). *The roots of modern social psychology*. Oxford: Blackwell.
  (1997). The significance of the skin as a natural boundary in the sub-division of psychology. *Journal for the Theory of Social Behaviour*, 27(2/3), 305–323.
Farr, R. M., and Marková, I. (1995). Professional and lay representations of health, illness and handicap: a theoretical overview. In I. Marková and R. M. Farr (eds.), *Representations of health, illness and handicap* (pp. 93–110). New York: Harwood Academic Publishers.
Farr, R. M., and Moscovici, S. (Eds.) (1984). *Social representations*. Cambridge University Press
Farr, R. M., Trutkowski, C., and Holzl, E. (1996). Public opinion, group discussion and theory of social representations. Research Papers in Psychology 9602. London School of Economics.
Farrimond, H. R., and Joffe, H. (2006). Pollution, peril and poverty: a British study of the stigmatization of smokers. *Journal of Community and Applied Social Psychology*, 16(6), 481–491.
Farrimond, H. R., Joffe, H., and Stenner, P. (2010). A Q-methodological study of smoking identities. *Psychology and Health*, 25(8), 979–998.
Faucheux, C., and Moscovici, S. (1968). Self-esteem and exploitative behavior in a game against chance and nature. *Journal of Personality and Social Psychology*, 8, 83–88.
Favell, A. (2001). *Philosophies of integration. Immigration and the idea of citizenship in France and Britain* (2nd edn). New York: Palgrave in association with Centre for Research in Ethnic Relations, University of Warwick.

Félonneau, M.-L., and Becker, M. (2008). Pro-environmental attitudes and behaviour: revealing perceived social desirability. *Revue Internationale de Psychologie Sociale*, 21, 25–53.
Fenn, E. A. (2000). Biological warfare in eighteenth-century North America: beyond Jeffery Amherst. *Journal of American History*, 86, 1552–1580.
Ferrari, M. (2007). Examining triangle metaphors: utility in developmental theory and scientific application. *Human Development*, 50, 234–240.
Festinger, L. (1957). *A theory of cognitive dissonance*. Stanford University Press.
Fife-Schaw, C., and Breakwell, G. M. (1991). The class basis of late teenage voting preferences. *European Sociological Review*, 7(2), 135–147.
  (1990). Predicting the intention not to vote in late teenage. *Political Psychology*, 11(4), 739–755.
Figari, H., and Skogen, K. (2011). Social representations of the wolf. *Acta Sociologica*, 54, 317–332.
Finkel, N. J., and Moghaddam, F. M. (2005). *The psychology of rights and duties: empirical contributions and normative commentaries*. Washington DC: American Psychological Association.
Finney, P. (2011). *Remembering the road to World War Two: international history, national identity, collective memory*. London: Routledge.
Fischer, A., Peters, V., Neebe, M., Vavra, J., Kriel, A., Lapk, M., and Megyesi, B. (2012). Climate change? No, wise resource use is the issue: social representations of energy, climate change and the future. *Environmental Policy and Governance*, 22, 161–176.
Fishbein, M. (Ed.) (1967). *Readings in attitude theory and measurement*. New York: John Wiley.
Fiske, S. T., Cuddy, A. J. C., Glick, P., and Xu, J. (2002). A model of (often mixed) stereotype content: competence and warmth respectively follow from perceived status and competition. *Journal of Personality and Social Psychology*, 82, 878–902.
Flache, A., and Macy, M. (1996). The weakness of strong ties: collective action failure in highly cohesive groups. *Journal of Mathematical Sociology*, 21, 3–28.
Flament, C. (1981). L'analyse de similitude: une technique pour les recherches sur les représentations sociales. *Cahiers de Psychologie Cognitive*, 1(4), 375–396.
  (1989). Structure et dynamique des représentations sociales. In D. Jodelet (ed.), *Les représentations sociales*. Paris: Presses Universitaires de France.
  (1994). Structure, dynamique et transformation des représentations sociales. In J.-C. Abric (ed.), *Pratiques sociales et représentations* (pp. 37–57). Paris: Presses Universitaires de France.
  (1996). Les valeurs du travail, la psychologie des représentations sociales comme observatoire d'un changement historique. In J. C. Abric (ed.), *Exclusion sociale, insertion et prévention*. Ramonville Saint-Agne: Erès.
  (1999). La représentation sociale comme système normatif. *Psychologie et Société*, 1, 29–54.
Flament, C., Guimelli, C., and Abric, J.-C. (2006). Effets de masquage dans l'expression d'une représentations sociale. *Cahiers Internationaux de Psychologie sociale*, 69(1), 15–31.
Flavell, J. H., and Draguns, J. (1957). A microgenetic approach to perception and thought. *Psychological Bulletin*, 54, 197–217.

Flick, U. (1992). Triangulation revisited: strategy of validation or alternative. *Journal for the Theory of Social Behaviour*, 22, 175–198.
  (1998). Everyday knowledge in social psychology. In Flick (ed.), pp. 41–59.
  (2007). *Managing the quality of qualitative research*. London: Sage.
  (2011a). *Introducting to research methodology – a beginner's guide to doing a research project*. London: Sage.
  (2011b). Mixing methods, triangulation and integrated research – challenges for qualitative research in a world of crisis. In N. Denzin and M. Giardina (eds.), *Qualitative inquiry and global crisis* (pp. 132–152). Walnut Creek: Left Coast Press.
  (2014). *An introduction to qualitative research*. London: Sage.
  (Ed.) (1998). *The psychology of the social*. Cambridge University Press.
Flick, U., and Foster, J. L. H. (2008). Social representations. In C. Willig and W. Stainton-Rogers (eds.), *The Sage handbook of qualitative methods in psychology* (pp. 195–214). London: Sage.
Flick, U., and Röhnsch, G. (2007). Idealization and neglect – health concepts of homeless adolescents. *Journal of Health Psychology*, 12(5), 737–750.
Flick, U., Fischer, C., Neuber, A., Schwartz, F. W., and Walter, U. (2003). Health in the context of growing old: social representations of health. *Journal of Health Psychology*, 8(5), 539–556.
Flick, U., Garms-Homolová, V., Herrmann, W., Kuck, J., and Röhnsch, G. (2012). 'I can't prescribe something just because someone asks for it': using mixed methods in the framework of triangulation. *Journal of Mixed Methods Research*, 6(2), 97–110.
Fornari, F. (1979). *I fondamenti di una teoria psiconalitica del linguaggio* (*Foundations for a psychoanalytic theory of language*). Turin: Boringhieri.
Foster, J. L. H. (2003). Representational projects and interacting forms of knowledge. *Journal for the Theory of Social Behaviour*, 33(3), 231–244.
  (2007). *Journeys through mental illness: client's experiences and understandings of mental distress*. Basingstoke: Palgrave Macmillan.
  (2011). Reflections on Bauer and Gaskell's 'Towards a paradigm for research in social representations'. *Papers on Social Representations*, 20, 23.1–23.12.
Foucault, M. (1975). *Surveiller et punir. Naissance de la prison*. Paris: Gallimard.
  (2006). *History of madness*. London: Routledge.
Franks, B., and Jovchelovitch, S. (in progress). Living with and without contradictions: cultural and evolutionary foundations for knowledge system coexistence.
Fraser, C. (1994). Attitudes, social representations and widespread beliefs. *Papers on Social Representations*, 3, 13–25.
Fraser, C., and Gaskell, G. (Eds.) (1990). *The social psychological study of widespread beliefs*. Oxford University Press.
Freire, P. (1973/2010). *Education for critical consciousness*. Ed. M. Bergman Ramos. London: Continuum.
Freud, S. (1923/1962). *Das Ich und das Es* (*The ego and the id*). Trans. J. Strachey. Standard edn, vol. xix. London: Hogarth Press.
  (1930). *Civilization and its discontents*. In *The future of an illusion, Civilization and its discontents, and other works*. Standard edn, vol. xxi (pp. 57–146). London: Hogarth Press.

Friestad, C., Rise, J., and Roysamb, E. (1999). Social representations of smoking and attitudes towards smoking restrictions in the Norwegian Navy. *Scandinavian Journal of Psychology*, 40, 187–196.

Frigg, R. (2002). Models and representations: why structures are not enough. *LSE CPNSS, Technical Report 25/02*.

  (2010). Fiction and Scientific representation. In R. Frigg and M. C. Hunter (eds.), *Beyond mimesis and convention. Representations in arts and science*. Boston Studies of Philosophy 262 (pp. 97–138). New York: Springer.

Friling, D. (2012). 'Having it all': cognitive polyphasia as preserving complex reality; the Israeli case. *Papers on Social Representations*, 21, 2.1–2.24.

Gabor, T. (1994). *'Everybody does it!': crime by the public*. University of Toronto Press.

Galvin, R. (2002). Disturbing notions of chronic illness and individual responsibility: towards a genealogy of morals. *Health*, 6, 107–137.

García Canclini, N. (1995/2001). *Hybrid cultures: strategies for entering and leaving modernity*. Trans. C. L. Chiappari and S. L. López. Minneapolis: Univesity of Minnesota Press.

Garfinkel, H. (1984). Passing and the managed achievement of sex status in an intersexed person, part I. In H. Garfinkel (ed.), *Studies in ethnomethodology* (pp. 116–185). Cambridge: Polity Press.

Garland, D. (2001). *The culture of control: crime and order in contemporary society*. Oxford University Press.

Garza-Cuarón, B. (1991). *Connotation and meaning*. Berlin: Mouton de Guyter.

Gaskell, G. (2001). Attitudes, social representations and beyond. In Deaux and Philogène (eds.), pp. 228–241.

Gaskell, G., and Bauer, M. W. (Eds.) (2002). *Biotechnology 1996–2000: the years of controversy*. London: Science Museum Press.

  (Eds.) (2006). *Genomics and society: legal, ethical and social dimensions*. London: Earthscan.

Gaskell, G., and Frazer, C. (1990). The social psychological study of widespread beliefs. In C. Frazer and G. Gaskell (eds.), *The social psychological study of widespread beliefs*. Oxford University Press.

Gaskell, G., Ten Eyck, T., Jackson, J., and Veltri, G. (2005). Imagining nanotechnology: cultural support for innovation in Europe and the United States. *Public Understanding of Science*, 14, 81–90.

Gaskell, G., Allansdottir, A., Allum, N., Castro, P., Esmer, Y., Fischler, C., et al. (2011). The 2010 Eurobarometer on the life sciences. *Nature Biotechnology*, 29(2), 113–114.

Gaskell, G., Allum, N., Wagner, W., Nielsen, T. H., Jelsø, E., Kohring, M., et al. (2001). In the public eye: Representations of biotechnology in Europe. In Gaskell and Bauer (eds.), pp. 53–79.

Geertz, C. (1968). *Islam observed: religious development in Morocco and Indonesia*. New Haven, CT: Yale University Press.

  (1976). *The religion of Java*. University of Chicago Press.

  (1980). *Negara: the theater state in nineteenth-century Bali*. Princeton University Press.

Gellner, E. (1983). *Nations and nationalism*. Oxford: Blackwell.

  (1997). *Nationalism*. London: Weidenfeld & Nicolson.

Gelman, S. A., and Wellman, H. M. (1991). Insides and essences: early understandings of the nonobvious. *Cognition*, 38, 213–244.

Gentner, D., and Clement, C. (1988). Evidence for relational selectivity in the interpretation of analogy and metaphor. In G. H. Bower (ed.), *The psychology of learning and motivation, advances in research and theory*. New York: Academic Press.

Gergen, K. (1991). *The saturated self. Dilemmas of identity in contemporary life*. New York: Basic Books.

(2009). *Relational being: beyond self and community*. Oxford University press.

Gervais, M.-C. (1997). Social representations of nature: the case of the 'Braer' oil spill in Shetland. Ph.D. thesis, London School of Economics and Political Science.

Gervais, M.-C., and Jovchelovitch, S. (1998a). Health and identity: the case of the Chinese community in England. *Social Science Information*, 37(4), 709–729.

(1998b). *The health beliefs of the Chinese community in England: a qualitative research study*. London: Health Education Authority.

Gervais, M.-C., Morant, N., and Penn, G. (1999). Making sense of 'absence': towards a typology of absence in social representations theory and research. *Journal for the Theory of Social Behaviour*, 29(4), 419–444.

Gezenstvey-Lamy, M. A., Ward, C., and Liu, J. H. (2013). Motivation for ethno-cultural continuity. *Journal of Cross-Cultural Psychology*, 44(7), 1047–1066.

Giami, A. (2001). Counter-transference in social research: Georges Devereux and beyond. London School of Economics–Methodology Institute Discussion Papers, qualitative series.

Gibson, J. J. (1966). *The senses considered as perceptual systems*. Boston, MA: Houghton Mifflin Harcourt.

(1982). Notes on affordances. In E. Reed and R. Jones (eds.), *Reasons for realism. Selected essays of James J. Gibson* (pp. 401–418). London: Lawrence Erlbaum.

(1986). *The ecological approach to visual perception*. London: Lawrence Erlbaum.

Gibson, S. (2011). Social psychology, war and peace: towards a critical discursive peace psychology. *Social and Personality Psychology Compass*, 5, 239–250.

(2012a). History in action: the construction of historical analogies in televised debates concerning the Iraq War. *Papers on Social Representations*, 21, 13.1–13.35.

(2012b). 'I'm not a war monger but...': discourse analysis and social psychological peace research. *Journal of Community and Applied Social Psychology*, 22, 159–173.

(2012c). Supporting the troops, serving the country: rhetorical commonplaces in the representation of military service. In S. Gibson and S. Mollan (eds.), *Representations of peace and conflict*. Basingstoke: Palgrave Macmillan.

Gibson, S., and Condor, S. (2009). State institutions and social identity: national representation in soldiers' and civilians' interview talk concerning military service. *British Journal of Social Psychology*, 48, 313–336.

Gibson, S., and Noret, N. (2010). Historical experiences, collective memory, and willingness to fight for one's country: comments on Paez *et al.* (2008). *Journal of Cross-Cultural Psychology*, 41, 445–450.

Giddens, A. (1984). *The constitution of society: outline of the theory of structuration*. Cambridge: Polity Press.

(1991). *Modernity and self-identity: self and society in the late modern age*. Cambridge: Polity Press.

Gilens, M. (1999). *Why Americans hate welfare*. University of Chicago Press.

Gilles, I., Bangerter, A., Clémence, A., Green, E. G. T., Krings, F., Staerklé, C., and Wagner-Egger, P. (2011). Trust in medical organizations predicts pandemic (H1N1) 2009 vaccination behavior and perceived efficacy of protection measures in the Swiss public. *European Journal of Epidemiology*, 26, 203–210.

Gilles, I., Bangerter, A., Clémence, A., Green, E. G. T., Krings, F., Mouton, A., Rigaud, D., Staerklé, C., and Wagner-Egger, P. (2013). Dynamic collective symbolic coping with disease threat and othering: a case study of avian influenza. *British Journal of Social Psychology*, 52, 83–102.

Gillespie, A. (2006). *Becoming other: from social interaction to self-reflection*. Charlotte, NC: Information Age Publishing.

  (2008). Social representations, alternative representations and semantic barriers. *Journal for the Theory of Social Behaviour*, 38(4), 375–391.

  (2013). Conceptualizing the individual and the community. In F. Dervin and M. Korpela (eds.), *Cocoon communities*. Cambridge: Cambridge Scholars Publishing.

Gillespie, A., and Richardson, B. (2011). Exchanging social positions: enhancing perspective taking within a cooperative problem solving task. *European Journal of Social Psychology*, 41(5), 608–616.

Gillespie, A., Howarth, C., and Cornish, F. (2012). Four problems for researchers using social categories. *Culture and Psychology*, 18(3), 391–402.

Gillespie, A., Kadianaki, I., and O'Sullivan-Lago, R. (2012). Encountering alterity: geographic and semantic movements. In J. Valsiner (ed.), *The Oxford handook of culture and psychology*. Oxford University Press.

Gillibert, D., and Cambon, L. (2003). Paradigms of the sociocognitive approach. In N. Dubois, *A sociocognitive approach to social norms* (pp. 38–69). London: Routledge.

Gilroy, P. (2004). *After empire: melancholia or convivial culture?* London: Routledge.

Girard, R. (1987). Generative scapegoating. In R. Hamerton-Kelly (ed.), *Violent origins: ritual killing and cultural foundation* (pp. 73–105). Stanford University Press.

Gitlin, T. (2000). *Inside prime time*. Berkeley: University of California Press.

Gladwell, M. (2005). *Blink: the power of thinking without thinking*. New York: Little, Brown.

Glanz, K., Rimer, B. K., and Viswanath, K. (Eds.) (2008). *Health behavior and health education: theory, research, and practice*. San Francisco: Jossey-Bass.

Glasser, T. L., and Salmon, C. T. (Eds.) (1995). *Public opinion and the communication of consent*. New York: Guilford Press.

Gleason, P. (1983). Identifying identity: a semantic history. *Journal of American History*, 69(4), 910–932.

Glick, P., and Fiske, S. T. (1996). The ambivalent sexism inventory: differentiating hostile and benevolent sexism. *Journal of Personality and Social Psychology*, 70, 491–512.

Gobineau, J. A. de (1859). *The moral and intellectual diversity of races, with particular reference to their respective influence in the civil and political history of mankind*. Philadelphia, PA: Lippincott.

Goertzel, T. (1994). Belief in conspiracy theories. *Political Psychology*, 15, 731–742.

Gonzales, M. H., Davis, J. M., Loney, G. L., Lukens, C. K., and Junghans, C. M. (1983). Interactional approach to interpersonal attraction. *Journal of Personality and Social Psychology*, 44(6), 1192–1197.

Goodman, N. (1976). *Languages of art*. Indiana: Hackett.

Goody, J. (1986). *The domestication of the savage mind*. Cambridge University Press.
Gordon, R., McDermott, L., Stead, M., and Angus, K. (2006). The effectiveness of social marketing interventions for health improvement: what's the evidence? *Public Health*, 120(12), 1133–1139.
Granovetter, M. S. (1973). The strength of weak ties. *American Journal of Sociology*, 78(6), 1360–1380.
Graumann, C. F. (1986). The individualization of the social and the desocialization of the individual: Floyd H. Allport's contribution to social psychology. In C. F. Graumann and S. Moscovici (eds.), *Changing conceptions of crowd, mind and behavior* (pp. 97–116). New York: Springer.
Green, E. G. T., and Clémence, A. (2008). Discovery of the faithfulness gene: a model of transmission and transformation of scientific information. *British Journal of Social Psychology*, 47(3), 497–517.
Greimas, A. J. (1970). *Sign, language, culture*. Paris: Mouton.
  (1990). *The social sciences: a semiotic view*. Minneapolis: University of Minnesota Press.
Greimas, J., and Cortes, J. (1979). *Sémiotique. Dictionnaire raisonne de la théorie du langage*. Paris: Hachette.
Greve, W. (2001). Traps and gaps in action explanation: theoretical problems of a psychology of human action. *Psychological Review*, 108(2), 435–451.
Gries, P. (2004). *China's new nationalism: pride, politics, and diplomacy*. Berkeley: University of California Press.
Griffitt, W., and Veitch, R. (1974). Preacquaintance attitude similarity and attraction revisited: ten days in a fallout shelter. *Sociometry*, 37(2), 163–173.
Grigoropoulou, N., and Chryssochoou, X. (2011). Are religious minorities in Greece better accepted if they assimilate? The effects of acculturation strategy and group membership on religious minority perceptions. *Journal of Community and Applied Social Psychology*, 21, 499–514.
Guerrero, A. (2007). Imágenes de América Latina y México a través de los mapas mentales. In Arruda and de Alba (eds.), pp. 235–284.
Guimelli, C. (1988). Agression idéologique, pratiques nouvelles et transformation progressive d'une représentation sociale. Ph.D. thesis, Université de Provence.
  (1993). Locating the central core of social representations: towards a method. *European Journal of Social Psychology*, 23(5), 555–559.
  (1994). Transformation des représentations sociales, pratiques nouvelles et schèmes cognitifs de base. In Guimelli (ed.), pp. 171–198.
  (1998). Differentiation between the central core elements of social representations: normative and functional elements. *Swiss Journal of Psychology*, 57(4), 209–224.
  (Ed.) (1994). *Structures et transformations des représentations sociales*. Neuchâtel: Delachaux et Niestlé.
Haas, V. (2002). Approche psychosociale d'une reconstruction historique. Le cas vichyssois. *Cahiers Internationaux de Psychologie Sociale*, 53, 32–45.
  (2004). Les cartes cognitives: un outil pour étudier la ville sous ses dimensions sociohistoriques et affectives. *Bulletin de Psychologie*, 57(6), 474, 621–633.
Habermas, J. (1985). *Theorie des kommunikativen Handelns*, vol. II, *Zur Kritik der funktionalistischen Vernunft*. Frankfurt-on-Main: Suhrkamp.

(1989). *The structural transformation of the public sphere: an inquiry into a category of bourgeois society*. Cambridge: Polity Press.
Hagenaars, J. A., and McCutcheon, A. L. (2002). *Applied latent class analysis*. Cambridge University Press.
Haidt, J., McCauley, C. R., and Rozin, P. (1994). Individual differences in sensitivity to disgust: a scale sampling seven domains of disgust elicitors. *Personality and Individual Differences*, 16, 701–713.
Halbertal, M., and Magarlit, A. (1992). *Idolatry*. Cambridge, MA: Harvard University Press.
Halbwachs, M. (1925/1992). *On collective memory*. University of Chicago Press.
  (1950/1980). *The collective memory*. New York: Harper & Row.
Halkier, B. (2010). Focus groups as social enactments: integrating interaction and content in the analysis of focus group data. *Qualitative Research*, 10(1), 71–89.
Hall, S. (1997). Introduction. In S. Hall (ed.), *Representation: cultural representations and signifying practices* (pp. 1–11). London: Sage.
Halmos, P. R. (1960). *Naive set theory*. Princeton, NJ: D. Van Nostrand.
Hammack, P. (2008). Narrative and the cultural psychology of identity. *Personality and Social Psychology Review*, 12, 222–247.
Hand, E. (2010). People power. *Nature*, 466(5), 685–687.
Hanke, K., Liu, J. H., Sibley, C., Paez, D., Gaines, S. P. Jr, Moloney, G., et al. (in press). 'Heroes' and 'villians' of world history across cultures. *PloS-ONE*.
Hanke, K., Liu, J. H., Hilton, D. J., Milewicz, M., Garber, I., Huang, L. L., Gastardo-Conaco, C., Wang, F. X. (2013). When the past haunts the present: intergroup forgiveness and historical closure in post-World War II societies in Asia and in Europe. *International Journal of Intercultural Relations*, 37(3), 287–301.
Hanson-Easey, S., and Augoustinos, M. (2010). Out of Africa: accounting for refugee policy and the language of causal attribution. *Discourse and Society*, 21(3), 295–323.
Harré, R. (1984). Some reflections on the concept of 'social representations'. *Social Research*, 51, 927–938.
  (1998). The epistemology of social representations. In Flick (ed.), pp. 129–137.
Harré, R, and Moghaddam, F. M. (Eds.) (2003a). *Friends and enemies*. Santa Barbara, CA: Praeger.
  (2003b). *The self and others: positioning individuals and groups in personal, political, and cultural contexts*. Westport, CT: Praeger.
  (Eds.) (2012). *Psychology for the third millennium: integrating cultural and neuroscience perspectives*. Thousand Oaks, CA: Sage.
Harré, R., and Sammut G. (2013). 'What lies between?' In Sammut, Daanen and Moghaddam (eds.), pp. 15–30.
Harré, R., and Secord, P. F. (1972). *The explanation of social behaviour*. Oxford: Basil Blackwell.
Harré, R., Brockmeier, J., and Muhlhausler, P. (1999). *Greenspeak: a study of environmental discourse*. London: Sage.
Harré, R., and Moghaddam, F. M., Likerton Cairnie, T., Rothbart, D., and Sabat, S. (2009). Recent advances in positioning theory. *Theory and Psychology*, 19, 5–31.
Harris, P. (2011). Conflicting thoughts about death. *Human Development*, 54(3), 160–168.
  (1987). *Reading Saussure*. La Salle, IL: Open Court.
Haslam, N., Rothschild, L., and Ernst, D. (2000). Essentialist beliefs about social categories. *British Journal of Social Psychology*, 39(1), 113–127.

(2002). Are essentialist beliefs associated with prejudice? *British Journal of Social Psychology*, 41, 87–100.

Hawk, B. (1992). Introduction: Metaphors of African coverage. In B. Hawk (ed.), *Africa's media image* (pp. 3–14). New York: Praeger.

He, Y. (2007). History, Chinese nationalism and the emerging Sino-Japanese Conflict. *Journal of Contemporary China*, 16(50), 1–24.

Hedström, P., and Bearman, P. (2009). *The Oxford handbook of analytical sociology*. Oxford University Press.

Hedström, P., and Swedberg, R. (1998). *Social mechanisms: an analytical approach to social theory*. Cambridge University Press.

Hedström, P., and Ylikoski, P. (2010). Causal mechanisms in the social sciences. *Annual Review of Sociology*, 36, 49–67.

Heider, F. (1946). Attitudes and cognitive organization. *Journal of Psychology*, 21, 107–112.

(1958). *The psychology of interpersonal relations*. New York: John Wiley.

Hein, L., and Selden, M. (Eds.) (2000). *Censoring history: citizenship and memory in Japan, Germany, and the United States*. Armonk, NY: East Gate.

Hendy, J., Lyons, E., and Breakwell, G. M. (2006). Genetic testing and the relationship between specific and general self-efficacy. *British Journal of Health Psychology*, 11, 221–233.

Herek, G. M. (Ed.) (1998). *Stigma and sexual orientation: understanding prejudice against lesbians, gay men, and bisexuals*. Thousand Oaks, CA: Sage.

Hermans, H. J. M., and Kempen, H. J. G. (1993). *The dialogical self. Meaning as movement*. San Diego, CA: Academic Press.

Herriot, P. (2007). *Religious fundamentalism and social identity*. New York: Routledge.

Herzlich, C. (1973). *Health and illness. A social psychological analysis*. London: Academic Press.

Hewit, J. P., and Stokes, R. (1975). Disclaimers. *American Sociological Review*, 40, 1–11.

Hill, P. C., and Gibson, N. J. S. (2008). Whither the roots? Achieving conceptual depth in the psychology of religion. *Archiv für Religionspsychologie*, 30, 19–35.

Hill, P. C., and Hood, R. W. J. (1999). *Measures of religiosity*. Birmingham, AL: Religious Education Press.

Hilton, D. J., and Liu, J. H. (2008). Culture and inter-group relations: the role of social representations of history. In R. Sorrentino and S. Yamaguchi (eds.), *The handbook of motivation and cognition: the cultural context* (pp. 343–368). New York: Guilford.

Hilton, D. J., Erb, H.-P., McDermott, M., and Molian, D. J. (1996). Social representations of history and attitudes to European unification in Britain, France and Germany. In Breakwell and Lyons (eds.), pp. 275–295.

Himmelweit, H. T. (1990). Societal psychology: implications and scope. In Himmelweit and Gaskell (eds.), pp. 17–45.

Himmelweit, H., and Gaskell, G. (1990). *Societal psychology*. London: Sage.

Hirschfeld, L. A. (1996). *Race in the making: cognition, culture, and the child's construction of human kinds*. Cambridge, MA: MIT Press.

Hjelmslev, L. (1943). *Omkring Sprogteoriens Grundlaeggelse: Festskrift udgivet af Koebenhavns Universitet i Anledning af Universitetets Aarsfest November 1943*. Koebenhavns Universitet Presse.

Hobsbawm, E. J. (1990a). *Nations and nationalism since 1780: programme, myth, reality*. Cambridge University Press.
  (1990b). *Nations et nationalisme depuis 1780*. Paris: Gallimard.
Hobsbawm, E. J., and Kertzer, D. J. (1992). Ethnicity and nationalism in Europe today. *Anthropology Today*, 8(1), 3–8.
Hobsbawm, E. J., and Ranger, T. (Eds.) (1983/2010). *The invention of tradition*. Cambridge University Press.
Hodge, B., and Kress, G. R. (1988). *Social semiotics*. Ithaca, NY: Cornell University Press.
Hodgetts, D., Sonn, C., Curtis, C., Nikora, L., and Drew, N. (2010). *Social psychology and everyday life*. Basingstoke: Palgrave Macmillan.
Hodgson, G. M. (2006). What are institutions? *Journal of Economic Issues* (Association for Evolutionary Economics), 40(1), 1–25.
Hogg, M. A. (2006). Social identity theory. In P. J. Burke (ed.), *Contemporary Social Psychological Theories* (pp. 111–128). Stanford University Press.
Hoijer, B. (2010). Emotional anchoring and objectification in the media reporting on climate change. *Public Understanding of Science*, 19, 717–731.
Holanda, S. B. (1994). *Visão do paraiso. Os motivos edênicos na colonização do Brasil*. São Paulo: Brasiliense.
Holstein, J. A., and Miller, G. (1993). Social constructionism and social problems work. In G. Miller and J. A. Holstein (eds.), *Reconsidering social constructionism: social problems and social issues* (pp. 131–152). Chicago: Aldine.
Holtz, P., and Wagner, W. (2009). Essentialism and attribution of monstrosity in racist discourse: right-wing Internet postings about Africans and Jews. *Journal of Community and Applied Social Psychology*, 19, 411–425.
Holzkamp, K. (1986). Wie weit können sozialpsychologische Theorien experimentell geprüft werden? *Zeitschrift Für Sozialpsychologie*, 17, 216–238.
Hondrich, T. (1995). Representation. In *Oxford companion to philosophy*. Oxford University Press.
Hovardas, T., and Korfiatis, K. J. (2008). Framing environmental policy by the local press: case study from the Dadia Forest Reserve, Greece. *Forestry Policy and Economics*, 10, 316–325.
Hovardas, T., and Stamou, G. P. (2006). Structural and narrative reconstruction of representations on 'nature', 'environment', and 'ecotourism'. *Society and Natural Resources*, 19, 225–237.
Howard, G. S., and Conway, C. G. (1986). Can there be an empirical science of volitional action? *American Psychologist*, 41(11), 1241–1251.
Howarth, C. (2000). 'So, you're from Brixton?' Towards a social psychology of community. Ph.D. thesis, London School of Economics and Political Science.
  (2001). Towards a social psychology of community: a social representations perspective. *Journal for the Theory of Social Behaviour*, 31(2), 223–238.
  (2002a). Identity in whose eyes? The role of social representations in identity construction. *Journal for the Theory of Social Behaviour*, 32(2), 145–162.
  (2002b). 'So, you're from Brixton?' The struggle for recognition and esteem in a multicultural community. *Ethnicities*, 2(2), 237–260.
  (2006a). How social representations of attitudes have informed attitude theories: the consensual and the reified. *Theory and Psychology*, 16, 691–714.

(2006b). Race as stigma: positioning the stigmatised as agents, not objects. *Journal of Community and Applied Psychology*, 16, 442–451.

(2006c). A social representation is not a quiet thing: exploring the critical potential of social representations theory. *British Journal of Social Psychology*, 45, 65–86.

(2007). 'It's not their fault that they have that colour skin is it?': young British children and the possibilities for contesting racialized representations. In Moloney and Walker (eds.), pp. 131–156.

(2009). 'I hope we won't have to understand racism one day': researching or reproducing 'race' in social psychological research? *British Journal of Social Psychology*, 48(3), 407–426.

(2010). Revisiting gender identities and education: notes for a social psychology of resistant identities in modern culture. *Papers in Social Representations*, 19(1).

Howarth, C., Andreouli, E., and Kessi, S. (2014). Social representations and the politics of participation. In K., Kinnvall, T. Capelos, H. Dekker and P. Nesbitt-Larking (eds.), *Palgrave handbook of global political psychology*. Basingstoke: Palgrave Macmillan.

Howarth, C. S., Foster, J. L. H., and Dorrer, N. (2004). Exploring the potential of the theory of social representations in community-based health research – and vice versa? *Journal for Health Psychology*, 9(2), 229–243.

Howarth, C., Kalampalikis, N., and Castro, P. (2011). 50 years of research on social representations: central debates and challenging questions. *Papers on Social Representations*, 20(2), 9.1–9.11.

Howarth, C., Wagner, W., Magnusson, N., and Sammut, G. (2014). 'It's only other people who make me feel black': acculturation, identity and agency in a multicultural community. *Political Psychology*. doi: 10.1111/pops.12020

Huang, L. L., Liu, J. H., and Chang, M. L. (2004). The double identity of Chinese Taiwanese: a dilemma of politics and identity rooted in history. *Asian Journal of Social Psychology*, 7(2), 149–189.

Huntington, S. P. (1996). *The clash of civilizations and the remaking of world order*. New York: Simon & Schuster.

Hutchby, I., and Wooffitt, R. (1998). *Conversation analysis: principles, practices and applications*. Cambridge: Polity Press.

Hutchinson, A. B., Begley, E. B., Sullivan, P., Clark, H. A., Boyett, B. C., and Kellerman, S. E. (2007). Conspiracy beliefs and trust in information about HIV/AIDS among minority men who have sex with men. *Journal of Acquired Immune Deficiency Syndromes*, 45, 603–605.

Hyman, H., and Sheatsley, P. (1947). Some reasons why information campaigns fail. *Public Opinion Quarterly*, 11(3), 412–423.

Inglehart, R., and Baker, W. E. (2000). Modernization, culture change, and the persistence of traditional values. *American Sociological Review*, 65, 19–51.

Inhelder, B., Sinclair, H., and Bovet, M. (1974). *Learning and the development of cognition*. Cambridge, MA: Harvard University Press.

Irwin, A., and Wynne, B. (1996). *Misunderstanding science? The public reconstruction of science and technology*. Cambridge University Press.

Isin, E. F., and Wood, P. K. (1999). *Citizenship and identity*. London: Sage.

Iyengar, S. (1991). *Is anyone responsible? How television frames political issues*. University of Chicago Press.

Jaeger, C. C., Renn, O., Rosa, E. A., and Webler, T. (2001). *Risk, uncertainty, and rational action*. London: Earthscan.

Jahoda, G. (1977). In pursuit of the emic–etic distinction: can we ever capture it? In Y. H. Poortinga (ed.), *Basic problems in cross-cultural psychology* (pp. 55–63). Amsterdam and Lisse: Swetz and Zeitlinger B.V.

 (1988). Critical notes and reflections on 'social representations'. *European Journal of Social Psychology*, 18, 195–209.

 (1999). *Images of savages: ancient roots of modern prejudice in western culture*. London: Routledge.

James, W. (1890). *The principles of psychology*. Basingstoke: Macmillan.

 (1902/1936). *The varieties of religious experience: a study in human nature*. New York: Modern Library.

Janz, N. K., and Becker, M. H. (1984). The health belief model: a decade later. *Health Education and Behavior*, 11, 1–47.

Jarvis, M. J., and Wardle, J. (1999). Social patterning of individual health behaviours: the case of cigarette smoking. In M. Marmot and R. G. Wilkinson (eds.), *Social determinants of health* (pp. 240–255). Oxford University Press.

Jaspal, R., and Cinnirella, M. (2010). Coping with potentially incompatible identities: accounts of religious, ethnic and sexual identities from British Pakistani men who identify as Muslim and gay. *British Journal of Social Psychology*, 49, 849–870.

Jaspars, J., and Fraser, C. (1984). Attitudes and social representations. In Farr and Moscovici (eds.), pp. 101–123.

Jefferson, G. (2004). Glossary of transcript symbols with an introduction. In G. H. Lerner (ed.), *Conversation analysis: studies from the first generation* (pp. 13–31). Amsterdam: John Benjamins.

Jensen, E., and Wagoner, B. (2009). Continuing commentary: a cyclical model of social change. *Culture and Psychology*, 15(2), 217–228.

Jodelet, D. (1989/1991). *Madness and social representations: living with the mad in one French community*. Hemel Hempstead: Harvester Wheatsheaf.

 (1982). Les représentations socio-spatiales de la ville. In P. H. Derycke (ed.), *Conceptions de l'espace. Recherches pluridisciplinaires de l'Université Paris X* (pp. 145–177). Nanterre: Université Paris X.

 (1983). *Civils et brédins. Rapport à la folie et représentations sociales de la maladie mentale en milieu rural*. Paris: EHESS.

 (1984a). Représentation sociale: phénomènes, concept et théorie. In S. Moscovici (ed.), *Psychologie sociale* (pp. 357–378). Paris: Presses Universitaires de France.

 (1984b). The representations of the body and its transformation. In Farr and Moscovici (eds.), *Social representations*. Cambridge: Cambridge University Press.

 (1989a). *Les représentations sociales*. Paris: Presses Universitaires de France.

 (1989b). *Folie et représentations sociales*. Paris: Presses Universitaires de France.

 (2007). Travesías latinoamericanas: dos miradas francesas sobre Brasil y México. In A. Arruda and M. de Alba (eds.), *Espacios imaginarios y representaciones sociales. Aportes desde Latinoamérica* (pp. 99–128). Barcelona: UAM-Anthropos.

 (2008). Social representations: the beautiful invention. *Journal for the Theory of Social Behaviour*, 38(4), 411–430.

 (2010). La memoria de los lugares urbanos. *Alteridades*, 39, 81–89.

(2011). O lobo, nova figura do imaginário feminino. In E. C. Paredes and D. Jodelet (eds.), *Pensamento mítico e representações sociais* (pp. 33–84). Cuiabá: EdUFMG/FAPEMAT/EdIUNI.

Jodelet, D., and Milgram, S. (1977). *Cartes mentales et images sociales de Paris*. Paris: DGRST.

Joffe, H. (1995). Social representations of AIDS: towards encompassing issues of power. *Papers on Social Representations*, 4, 29–40.

(1996). AIDS research and prevention: a social representational approach. *British Journal of Medical Psychology*, 69(3), 169–190.

(1999). *Risk and 'the Other'*. Cambridge University Press.

(2003). Risk: from perception to social representation. *British Journal of Social Psychology*, 42, 55–73.

(2007). Identity, self-control and risk. In G. Maloney and I. Walker (eds.), *Social representations and identity: content, process and power*. Basingstoke: Palgrave Macmillan.

Joffe, H., and Bettega, N. (2003). Social representation of AIDS among Zambian adolescents. *Journal of Health Psychology*, 8, 616–631.

Joffe, H., and Haarhoff, G. (2002). Representations of far-flung illnesses: the case of Ebola in Britain. *Social Science and Medicine*, 54(6), 955–969.

Joffe, H., and Lee, N. Y. (2004). Social representation of a food risk: the Hong Kong avian bird flu epidemic. *Journal of Health Psychology*, 9, 517–533.

Joffe, H., and Staerklé, C. (2007). The centrality of the self-control ethos in western aspersions regarding outgroups: a social representational analysis of common stereotype content. *Culture and Psychology*, 13(4), 395–418.

Joffe, H., Washer, P., and Solberg, C. (2011). Public engagement with emerging infectious disease: the case of MRSA in Britain. *Psychology and Health*, 26(6), 667–683.

Jonas, H. (1934/2001). *The Gnostic religion* (3rd edn). Trans. H. Jonas. Boston, MA: Beacon Press.

Jost, J. T., and Ignatow, G. (2001). What we do and don't know about the functions of social representations. In Deaux and Philogène (eds.), pp. 190–198.

Jost, J., and Banaji, M. (1994). The role of stereotyping in system-justification and production of false consciousness. *British Journal of Social Psychology*, 33, 1–27.

Jost, J., and Hunyady, O. (2002). The psychology of system justification and the palliative function of ideology. *European Review of Social Psychology*, 13, 111–153.

Jovchelovitch, S. (1995). Social representations in and of the public sphere: towards a theoretical articulation. *Journal for the Theory of Social Behaviour*, 25(1), 81–102.

(1996). In defence of representations. *Journal for the Theory of Social Behaviour*, 26(2), 121–136.

(2000). *Representações Sociais e Esfera Pública: Um Estudo Sobre a Construção Simbólica dos Espaços Públicos no Brasil*. Rio de Janeiro: Petrópolis.

(2007). *Knowledge in context: representations, community and culture*. London: Routledge.

(2008). The rehabilitation of common sense: social representations, science and cognitive polyphasia. *Journal for the Theory of Social Behaviour*, 38(4), 431–448.

(2010). From social cognition to the cognition of social life. *Papers on Social Representations*, 19, 3.1–3.10.

(2012). Narrative, memory and social representations: a conversation between history and social psychology. *Integrative Psychological and Behavioral Science*, 46(4), 440–456.

Jovchelovitch, S., and Bauer, M. (2000). Narrative interviewing. In M. Bauer and G. Gaskell (eds.), *Qualitative researching with text, image and sound* (pp. 55–74). London: Sage.

Jovchelovitch, S., and Gervais, M.-C. (1999). Social representations of health and illness: the case of the Chinese community in England. *Journal of Community and Applied Social Psychology*, 9(4), 247–260.

Jovchelovitch, S., and Priego-Hernández, J. (2013). *Underground sociabilities: identity, culture and resistance in Rio de Janeiro's favelas*. Brasilia: UNESCO.

Julius, A. (2001). *Idolizing pictures: idolatry, iconoclasm and Jewish art (Walter Neurath Memorial Lectures)*. London: Thames & Hudson.

Kadianaki, I. (2010). Commentary: making sense of immigrant identity dialogues. *Culture and Psychology*, 16(3), 437–448.

Kahneman, D. (2011). *Thinking, fast and slow*. New York: Farrar, Straus & Giroux.

Kalampalikis, N. (2003). L'approche de la méthode Alceste dans l'analyse des représentations sociales. In J.-C. Abric (ed.), *Méthodes d'études des représentations sociales* (pp. 147–163). Ramonville Saint-Agne: Erès.

Kalampalikis, N., and Moscovici, S. (2005). Une approche pragmatique de l'analyse Alceste. *Cahiers Internationaux de Psychologie Sociale*, 66, 15–24.

Kalichman, S. C., Eaton, L., and Cherry, C. (2010). There is no proof that HIV causes AIDS: AIDS denialism beliefs among people living with HIV/AIDS. *Journal of Behavioral Medicine*, 33, 432–440.

Karstedt, S., and Farrall, S. (2006). The moral economy of everyday crime. *British Journal of Criminology*, 46(6), 1011–1037.

(2007). *Law-abiding majority? The everyday crimes of the middle classes*. London: Centre for Crime and Justice Studies.

Kasanen, K., Räty, H., and Snellman, L. (2001). Seating order as a symbolic arrangement. *European Journal of Psychology of Education*, 16(2), 209–222.

Kashima, Y. (2004). Culture, communication, and entitativity: a social psychological investigation of social reality. In V. Yzerbyt, C. Judd and O. Corneille (eds.), *The psychology of group perception* (pp. 257–273). Hove: Psychology Press.

Kashima, Y., Kashima, E., Bain, P., Lyons, A., Scott Tindale, R., Scott, Robins, G., *et al.* (2010). Communication and essentialism: grounding the shared reality of a social category. *Social Cognition*, 28, 306–328.

Kasimis, C., and Papadopoulos, A. G. (2005). The multifunctional role of migrants in the Greek countryside: implications for the rural economy and society. *Journal of Ethnic and Migration Studies*, 31(1), 99–127.

Katona, G. (1975). *Psychological economics*. New York: Elsevier.

Kaufman, D. (2004). Corruption, governance and security: challenges for the rich countries and the world. World Bank Global Competitiveness Report.

Keeney, R. L., and Raiffa, H. (1976). *Decisions with multiple objectives: preferences and value tradeoffs*. New York: John Wiley.

Kelly, J. (2005). *The great mortality: an intimate history of the Black Death, the most devastating plague of all time*. New York: HarperCollins.

Kempton, W. (1986). Two theories for home heat control. *Cognitive Science*, 10, 75–90.

Kepel, G. (2006). *Jihad: the trail of political Islam*. London: I. B. Tuaris.
Kiely, R., McCrone, D., and Bechhofer, F. (2005). Whither Britishness? English and Scottish people in Scotland. *Nations and Nationalism*, 11(1), 65–82.
Kinnvall, C., and Nesbitt-Larking, P. (2011). Citizenship regimes and identity strategies among young Muslims in Europe. In A. E. Azzi, X. Chryssochoou, B. Klandermans, and B. Simon (eds.), *Identity and participation in culturally diverse societies: a multidisciplinary perspective* (pp. 195–219). New York: Wiley-Blackwell.
Kish, L. (1965). *Survey sampling*. New York: John Wiley.
Klein, O., and Licata, L. (2003). When group representations serve social change: the speeches of Patrice Lumumba during the Congolese decolonization. *British Journal of Social Psychology*, 42, 571–593.
Klein, O., Spears, R., and Reicher, S. (2007). Social identity performance: extending the strategic side of SIDE. *Personality and Social Psychology Review*, 11, 28–45.
Klonoff, E. A., and Landrine, H. (1999). Do Blacks believe that HIV/AIDS is a government conspiracy against them? *Preventive Medicine*, 28, 451–457.
Kohl, P. L., and Fawcett, C. (1996). *Nationalism, politics, and the practice of archaeology*. Cambridge University Press.
Kotler, P., and Roberto, E. (1989). *Social marketing: strategies for changing public behaviour*. New York: Free Press.
Kotler, P., and Zaltman, G. (1973). Social marketing: an approach to planned social change. In W. Lazer, and E. Kelley (eds.), *Social marketing: perspectives and viewpoints* (pp. 52–69). Homewood, IL: Richard D. Erwin.
Kronberger, N., and Wagner, W. (2003). Keywords in context: statistical analysis of text features. In M. Bauer and G. Gaskell (eds.), *Qualitative researching with text, image and sound. A practical handbook* (pp. 299–317). London: Sage.
  (2007). Inviolable versus alterable identities: culture, biotechnology, and resistance. In Moloney and Walker (eds.), pp. 176–196.
Kronberger, N., Holtz, P., and Wagner, W. (2012). Consequences of media information uptake and deliberation: focus groups' symbolic coping with synthetic biology. *Public Understanding of Science*, 21(2), 174–187.
Kronberger, N., Holtz, P., Kerbe, W., Strasser, E., and Wagner, W. (2009). Communicating synthetic biology: from the lab via the media to the broader public. *Systems and Synthetic Biology*, 3(1), 19–26.
Kronberger, N., Dahinden, U., Allansdottir, A., Seger, N., Pfenning, U., Gaskell, G., *et al.* (2001). 'The train departed without us'. Public perceptions of biotechnology in ten European countries. *Notizie di Politeia*, 17(63), 26–36.
Kruglanski, A. W. (1989). *Lay epistemics and human knowledge: cognitive and motivational bases*. New York: Plenum.
Kruglanski, A. W., Pierro, A., Mannetti, L., and De Grada, E. (2006). Groups as epistemic providers: need for closure and the unfolding of group-centrism. *Psychological Review*, 113(1), 84.
Kuhn, T. S. (1962). *The structure of scientific revolutions*. University of Chicago Press.
Kung, G. (1993). Ontology and the construction of systems. *Synthese*, 95, 29–53.
Kuttner, H., and Moore, C. L. (1945). *The piper's son*. New York: Ballantine.
Kyle, K. (2011). *Suez: Britain's end of empire in the Middle East* (new edn). London: I. B. Tauris.

Lacan, J. (1973/2005). O simbólico, o imaginário e o real (pp. 11–53) In J. Lacan, *Nomes.do.pai*. Rio de Janeiro: Jorge Zahar.

Lahlou, S. (1995). Penser Manger. Les représentations sociales de l'alimentation. Doctoral thesis. Paris: École des Hautes Études en Sciences Sociales.

  (1998). *Penser manger: alimentation et représentations sociales*. Paris: Presses Universitaires de France.

  (2000). Attracteurs cognitifs et travail de bureau. *Intellectica*, 30, 75–113.

  (2001). Functional aspects of social representations. In Deaux and Philogène (eds.), pp. 131–146.

  (2008). *L'installation du monde. De la représentation à l'activité en situation*. Aix-en-Provence: Presses de l'Université de Provence.

  (2010). Individual representations and social representations: a clarification. Paper presented at the 10th International Conference on Social Representations. Tunis, Tunisia.

  (2011a). Socio-cognitive issues in human-centred design for the real world. In G. Boy (ed.), *The handbook of human–machine interaction* (pp. 165–188). Farnham: Ashgate.

  (2011b). Difusão de representações e inteligência coletiva distribuída. In A. M. de Oliveira Almeida, M. de Fatima Souza Santos and L. A. Trindade (ed.), *Teoria Das Representações Sociais – 50 Anos* (pp. 59–97). Brasilia: TechnoPolitik Editora.

Lakoff, G., and Johnson, M. (1980). *Metaphors we live by*. University of Chicago Press.

Laland, K. N., Odling-Smee, J., and Feldman, M. W. (2001). Cultural niche construction and human evolution. *Journal of Evolutionary Biology*, 14(1), 22–33. doi:10.1046/j.1420–9101.2001.00262.x

Lamont, M., and Molnar, V. (2002). The study of boundaries in the social sciences. *Annual Review of Sociology*, 28, 167–195.

Lasswell, H. D. (1948). The structure and function of communication in society. In E. Bryson (ed.), *The communication of ideas* (pp. 37–51). New York: Harper & Bros.

László, J. (2008). *The science of stories: an introduction to narrative psychology*. London: Routledge.

László J., Ehmann, B., and Imre, O. (2002). Les représentations sociales de l'histoire: La narration populaire historique et l'identité nationale. In S. Laurens and N. Roussiau (eds.), *La mémoire sociale. Identités et représentations sociales*. Université Presse de Rennes.

Latour, B. (1996). On interobjectivity. *Mind, Culture, and Activity: An International Journal*, 3, 228–245.

Latour, B., and Weibel, P. (Eds.) (2002). *Iconoclash – beyond the image: wars in science, religion and art*. Karlsruhe and Cambridge, MA: ZKM and MIT Press.

Lauri, M. A. (2005). Social representations of organ donors and non-donors. *Journal of Community and Applied Social Psychology*, 15, 108–119.

  (2008). Changing public opinion towards organ donation. A social psychological approach to social marketing. In L. O. Pietrieff and R. V. Miller (eds.), *Public opinion research focus* (pp. 9–36). New York: Nova Science Publishers.

  (2009). Metaphors of organ donation, social representations of the body and the opt-out system. *British Journal of Health Psychology*, 14, 647–666.

Lavie-Ajayi, M., and Joffe, H. (2009). Social representations of female orgasm. *Journal of Health Psychology*, 14(1), 98–107.

Le Goff, J. (1988). *The medieval imagination*. University of Chicago Press.
  (2005). *Héros et merveilles du moyen âge*. Paris: Éditions du Seuil.
Lefebvre, R. (2011). *On social marketing and social change: selected readings 2005–2009*. Seattle, IL: CreateSpace Independent Publishing Platform.
Legare, C. H., and Gelman, S. A. (2008). Bewitchment, biology, or both: the co-existence of natural and supernatural explanatory frameworks across development. *Cognitive Science*, 32(4), 607–642.
Legare, C. H., Evans, E. M., Rosengren, K. S., and Harris, P. L. (2012). The coexistence of natural and supernatural explanations across cultures and development. *Child Development*, 83(3), 779–793.
Leman, P. (2010). Social psychology and developmental psychology: conversation or collaboration? Commentary on J. A. Castorina, 'The Ontogenesis of Social Representations: A Dialectic Perspective'. *Papers on Social Representations*, 19, 19.1–19.8.
Leman, P. J., and Duveen, G. (1999). Representations of authority and children's moral reasoning. *European Journal of Social Psychology*, 29, 557–575.
Lepenies, W. (1969/1972). *Melancholie und Gesellschaft*. Frankfurt-on-Main: Suhrkamp.
Lerner, M. J. (1980). *The belief in a just world: a fundamental delusion*. New York: Plenum Press.
Lerner, M. J., and Miller, D. T. (1978). Just world research and the attribution process: looking back and ahead. *Psychological Bulletin*, 85(5), 1030–1051.
Leuba, J. H. (1916). *The belief in God and immortality: a psychological, anthropological and statistical study*. Boston, MA: Sherman, French.
Lewin, K. (1936). *Principles of topological psychology*. New York: McGraw-Hill.
  (1952). *Field theory in social science: selected theoretical papers by Kurt Lewin*. London: Tavistock.
  (1958). Group decision and social change. In E. E. Maccoby, T. M. Newcombe and E. L. Hartley (eds.), *Readings in social psychology*. New York: Henry Holt.
Lewontin, R. C. (2001). *The triple helix: gene, organism, and environment*. Cambridge, MA: Harvard University Press.
Leyens, P., Rodriguez-Perez, A., Rodriguez-Torres, R., Gaunt, R., Paladino, M., Vaes, J. *et al.* (2001). Psychological essentialism and the differential attribution of uniquely human emotions to ingroups and outgroups. *European Journal of Social Psychology*, 31, 395–411.
Lheureux, F., Rateau, P., and Guimelli, C. (2008). Hiérarchie structurale, conditionnalité et normativité des représentations sociales. *Cahiers Internationaux de Psychologie Sociale*, 77, 41–55.
Likert, R. (1967). The method of constructing an attitude scale. In Fishbein (ed.), pp. 90–95.
Lima, M. L., and Castro, P. (2005). Cultural theory meets the community: worldviews and local issues. *Journal of Environmental Psychology*, 25, 23–35.
Linell, P. (2009). *Rethinking language, mind, and world dialogically. Interactional and contextual theories of human sense-making*. Charlotte, NC: Information Age Publishing.
Litton, I., and Potter, J. (1985). Social representations in the ordinary explanation of a 'riot'. *European Journal of Social Psychology*, 15, 371–388.
Liu, J. H. (1999). Social representations of history: preliminary notes on content and consequences around the Pacific Rim. *International Journal of Intercultural Relations*, 23, 215–236.

Liu, J. H., and Atsumi, T. (2008). Historical conflict and resolution between Japan and China: seveloping and applying a narrative theory of history and identity. In T. Sugiman, K. J. Gergen, W. Wagner and Y. Yamada (eds.), *Meaning in action: constructions, narratives, and representations* (pp 327–344). New York and Tokyo: Springer.

Liu, J. H., and Gastardo-Conaco, C. (2011). Theory and methods of a representational approach to understanding social movements: the role of the EDSA revolution in a national psychology of the Philippines. *Social Justice Research*, 24, 168–190.

Liu, J. H., and Hilton D. J. (2005). How the past weighs on the present: social representations of history and their role in identity politics. *British Journal of Social Psychology*, 44(4), 537–556.

Liu, J. H., and Khan, S. S. (2014). Nation building through historical narratives in pre-independence India: Gandhi, Nehru, Savarkar, and Golwarkar as entrepreneurs of identity. In M. Hanne, W. D. Crano and J. S. Mio (ed.), *Warring with words: narrative and metaphor in domestic and international politics* (pp. 211–237). New York: Psychology Press.

Liu, J. H., and László, J. (2007). A narrative theory of history and identity: social identity, social representations and the individual. In Moloney and Walker (eds.), pp. 85–107.

Liu, J. H., and Sibley, C. G. (2004). Attitudes and behavior in social space: public good interventions based on shared representations and environmental influences. *Journal of Environmental Psychology*, 24(3), 373–384.

  (2009). Culture, social representations, and peacemaking: a symbolic theory of history and identity. In C. J. Montiel and N. M. Noor (eds.), *Peace psychology in Asia* (pp. 21–39). New York: Springer.

  (2013). From ordinal representations to representational profiles: a primer for describing and modelling social representations of history. *Papers on Social Representations*, 22, 5.1–5.30.

Liu, J. H., and Sibley, C. G., and Huang, L. L. (2014). History matters: effects of culture specific symbols on political attitudes and intergroup relations. *Political Psychology*, 35(1), 57–79.

Liu, J. H., Lawrence, B., Ward, C., and Abraham, S. (2002). Social representations of history in Malaysia and Singapore: on the relationship between national and ethnic identity. *Asian Journal of Social Psychology*, 5(1), 3–20.

Liu, J. H., Wilson, M. W., McClure, J., Higgins, T. R. (1999). Social identity and the perception of history: cultural representations of Aotearoa/New Zealand. *European Journal of Social Psychology*, 29, 1021–1047.

Liu, J. H., Páez, D., Slawuta, P., Cabecinhas, R., Techio, E., Kokdemir, D., Sen, R., Vincze, O., Muluk, H., Wang, F., and Zlobina, A. (2009). Representing world history in the 21st century: the impact of 9/11, the Iraq War, and the nation-state on dynamics of collective remembering. *Journal of Cross-Cultural Psychology*, 40, 667–692.

Liu, J. H., Paez, D., Techio, E., Slawuta, P., Zlobina, A., and Cabecinhas, R. (2010). From gist of a wink to structural equivalence of meaning: towards a cross-cultural psychology of the collective remembering of world history. *Journal of Cross-Cultural Psychology*, 41, 451–456.

Liu, J. H., Yamagishi, T., Wang, F. X., Schug, J., Lin, Y. C., Huang, L. L., and Yu, S. H. (2011). Unbalanced triangle in the social dilemma of trust: Internet studies of real-time real money social exchange between China, Japan, and Taiwan. *Asian Journal of Social Psychology*, 14(4), 246–257.

Liu, J. H., Goldstein-Hawes, R., Hilton, D. J., Huang, L. L., Gastardo-Conaco, C., Dresler-Hawke, E., Pittolo, F., Hong, Y. Y., Ward, C., Abraham, S., Kashima, Y., Kashima, E., Ohashi, M., Yuki, M., and Hidaka, Y. (2005). Social representations of events and people in world history across twelve cultures. *Journal of Cross-Cultural Psychology*, 36(2), 171–191.

Liu, J. H., Paez, D., Hanke, K., Rosa, A., Hilton, D. J., Sibley, C., *et al.* (2012). Cross cultural dimensions of meaning in the evaluation of events in world history? Perceptions of historical calamities and progress in cross-cultural data from 30 societies. *Journal of Cross-Cultural Psychology*, 43(2), 251–272.

Lloyd, B., and Duveen, G. (1990). A semiotic analysis of the development of social representations of gender. In B. Lloyd and G. Duveen (eds.), *Social representations and the development of knowledge*. Cambridge University Press.

(1992). *Gender identities and education*. Hemel Hempstead: Harvester-Wheatsheaf.

Lo Monaco, G., and Guimelli, C. (2011). Hegemonic and polemical beliefs: culture and consumption in the social representation of Wine. *Spanish Journal of Psychology*, 14(1), 237–250.

Lo Monaco, G., Lheureux, F., and Halimi-Falkowicz, S. (2008). Test d'indépendance au contexte (TIC) et structure des représentations sociales. *Swiss Journal of Psychology*, 67(2), 119–123.

Lomas, C. (2009). Beyond getting the message – why the NMS is adopting social marketing – breast feeding. *NursingTimes.net*, 9 June. www.nursingtimes.net/whats-new-in-nursing/primary-care/beyond-getting-the-message-why-the-nhs-is-adopting-social-marketing/5002452.article

Lopes, C. A. (2012). From description to explanation in cross-national research: the case of economic morality. Doctoral thesis, London School of Economics and Political Science.

Lorenz, K. (1935). Der Kumpan in der Umwelt des Vogels: der Artgenosse als auslösendes Moment sozialer Verhaltungsweisen. *Lorenz. Journal für Ornithologie*, 83(37–215), 289–413. (Translated as Companions as factors in the bird's environment: the conspecific as the eliciting factor for social behaviour patterns (1970)).

Lorenzi-Cioldi, F. (1998). Group status and perceptions of homogeneity. *European Review of Social Psychology*, 9, 31–75.

Lorenzi-Cioldi, F., and Clémence, A. (2001). Group processes and the construction of social representations. In M. A. Hogg and S. Tindale (eds.), *Blackwell handbook of social psychology: group processes* (pp. 311–333). Oxford: Blackwell.

Lotman, I. U. M. (1990). *Universe of the mind: a semiotic theory of culture*. Bloomington: Indiana University Press.

Lowe, R. D. (2012). Temporality and identity: the role of time in the representation of social identities at political demonstrations. *Papers on Social Representations*, 21, 14.1–14.29.

Lozada, M. (2007). 'El otro es el enemigo': Representaciones e imaginarios socials en tiempos de polarización: el caso de Venezuela. In A. Arruda and M. de Alba (eds.), *Espacios imaginarios y representaciones sociales. Aportes desde Latinoamérica* (pp. 381–406). Barcelona: Anthropos/UAM.

Luhmann, N. (1984). *Soziale Systeme – Grundiss einer allgemeinen Theorie*. Frankfurt-on-Main: Suhrkamp.
Lunt, P., and Livingstone, S. (1996). Rethinking the focus group in media and communications research. *Journal of Communication*, 46, 79–98.
Luria, A. R. (1976). *Cognitive development: its cultural and social foundations*. Cambridge, MA: Harvard University Press.
Lyens, P., Rodriguez-Perez, A., Rodriguez-Torres, R., Gaunt, R., Paladino, M., Vaes, J., *et al.* (2001). Psychological essentialism and the differential attribution of uniquely human emotions to ingroups and outgroups. *European Journal of Social Psychology*, 31, 395–411.
Lyons, E. (1996). Coping with social change: processes of social memory in the reconstruction of identities. In Breakwell and Lyons (eds.), pp. 31–40.
McCann, P., Augoustinos, M., and LeCouteur, A. (2004). 'Race' and the Human Genome Project: constructions of scientific legitimacy. *Discourse and Society*, 15, 409–432.
MacCulloch, D. (2003). *Reformation – Europe's house devided, 1490–1700*. London: Allen Lane.
  (2013). *Silence – a Christian history*. London: Allen Lane.
McCulloch, J. (1995). *Colonial psychiatry and 'the African mind'*. Cambridge University Press.
Macdonald, S. (2006). Words in stone? Agency and identity in a Nazi landscape. *Journal of Material Culture*, 11, 105–126.
McGhee, D. (2005). *Intolerant Britain? Hate, citizenship and difference*. Milton Keynes: Open University Press.
McGuire, W. J. (1985). Attitudes and attitude change. In G. Lindzey and E. Aronson (eds.), *The handbook of social psychology*, vol. II (3rd edn) (pp. 233–346). New York: Random House.
  (1986). The vicissitudes of attitudes and similar representational constructs in twentieth century psychology. *European Journal of Social Psychology*, 16, 89–130.
McKenzie-Mohr, D., and Smith, W. (1999). *Fostering sustainable behaviour: an introduction to community-based social marketing*. Canada: New Society Publishers.
McKinlay, A., and Potter, J. (1987). Social representations: a conceptual critique. *Journal for the Theory of Social Behaviour*, 17(4), 471–487. doi: 10.1111/j.1468-5914.1987.tb00109.x
McQuail, D., and Windahl, S. (1993). *Communication models for the study of mass communication* (2nd edn). London: Longman.
Madoglou, A., Melista, A., and Liaris-Hochhaus, S. (2010). Greeks' and Germans' representations of world events: selective memory and voluntary oblivion. *Papers on Social Representations*, 19, 22.1–22.40.
Maffesoli, M. (1993). *La contemplation du monde*. Paris: Grasset.
Maibach, E. (1993). Social marketing for the environment: using information campaigns to promote environmental awareness and behaviour change. *Health Promotion International*, 8(3), 209–224.
Makriyianni, C. and Psaltis, C. (2007). History teaching and reconciliation. *Cyprus Review*, 19, 43–69.
Malinowski, B. (1926). *Myth in primitive psychology*. London: Kegan Paul, Trench, Trubner.

(1948). *Magic, science and religion and other essays*. Glencoe, IL: Free Press.
Mandelblit, N., and Zachar, O. (1998). The notion of dynamic unit: conceptual developments in cognitive science. *Cognitive Science*, 22, 229–268.
Marková, I. (1982). *Paradigms, thought and language*. New York: John Wiley.
  (1992). Scientific and public knowledge of AIDS: the problem of their integration. In M. von Cranach, W. Doise and G. Mugny (eds.), *Social representations and the social bases of knowledge*. Goettingen: Hogrefe & Huber.
  (1996). Towards an epistemology of social representations. *Journal for the Theory of Social Behaviour*, 26(2), 177–193.
  (2000). Amédèe or how to get rid of it: social representations from a dialogical perspective. *Culture and Psychology*, 6, 419–460.
  (2003). *Dialogicality and social representations: the dynamics of mind*. Cambridge University Press.
  (2007a). Knowledge and interaction through diverse lenses. *Interacções*, 7, 7–29.
  (2007b). Social identities and social representations. How are they related? In Moloney and Walker (eds.), pp. 215–236.
  (2008a). The epistemological significance of the theory of social representations. *Journal for the Theory of Social Behaviour*, 38(4), 461–487.
  (2008b). Persuasion and propaganda. *Diogenes*, 217, 37–51.
  (2010). Gerard Duveen on the epistemology of social representations. *Papers on Social Representations*, 19, 4.1–4.9.
  (2012). Confession as a communicative genre. In Marková and Gillespie (eds.), pp. 181–200.
Marková, I., and Gillespie, A. (2008). *Trust and distrust: sociocultural perspectives*. Charlotte, NC: Information Age Publishing.
  (Eds.) (2012). *Trust and conflict: representation, culture and dialogue*. London: Routledge.
Marková, I., and Jovchelovitch, S. (2008). Introduction. *Journal for the Theory of Social Behaviour* (special issue on *Psychoanalysis: its image and its public* (1961)), 38(4), 327–334.
Marková, I., and Wilkie, P. (1987). Representations, concepts and social change: the phenomenon of AIDS. *Journal for the Theory of Social Behaviour*, 17(4), 389–409.
Marková, I., Linell, P., Grossen, M., Salazar-Orvig, A. (2007). *Dialogue in focus groups: exploring socially shared knowledge*. London: Equinox.
Markowe, L. A. (1996). *Redefining the self: coming out as lesbian*. Cambridge: Polity Press.
Marlowe, J. M. (2010). Beyond the discourse of trauma: shifting the focus on Sudanese refugees. *Journal of Refugee Studies*, 23(2), 183–198.
Marranci, G. (2009). *Understanding Muslim identity: rethinking fundamentalism*. Basingstoke: Palgrave Macmillan.
Martin, J. (2007). Triangles in context: a comment on Zittoun, Gillespie, Cornish, and Psaltis. *Human Development*, 50, 230–233.
Massey, D. (2007). *World city*. Cambidge: Polity Press.
Matte Blanco, I. (1975). *The unconscious as infinite sets. An essay in bi-logic*. London: Duckworth.
Mauss, M. (1934). Les techniques du corps. *Journal de Psychologie*, 32(3–4). (Reprinted in M. Mauss, *Sociologie et anthropologie*, Paris: Presses Universitaires de France, 1936.)

Maynard, A. E. (2009). Context and structure in social interaction and cognitive development. *Human Development*, 52, 313–319.
Mayo, M. (2000). *Cultures, communities, identities: cultural strategies for participation and empowerment*. Basingstoke: Palgrave Macmillan.
Mayor, E., Eicher, V., Bangerter, A., Gilles, I., Clémence, A., and Green, E. G. T. (2013). Dynamic social representations of the 2009 H1N1 pandemic: shifting patterns of sense-making and blame. *Public Understanding of Science*, 22(8), 1011–1024.
Mead, G. H. (1934). *Mind, self, and society from the standpoint of a social behaviorist*. University of Chicago Press.
Medin, D. L. (1989). Concepts and conceptual structure. *American Psychologist*, 44, 1469–1481.
Medin, D. L., and Ortony, A. (1989). Psychological essentialism. In S. Vosniadou and A. Ortony (eds.), *Similarity and analogical reasoning* (pp. 179–195). Cambridge University Press.
Merton, R. K. (1938). Social structure and anomie. *American Sociological Review*, 3(5), 672–682.
 (1957). *Social theory and social structure*. Glencoe, IL: Free Press.
Messner, S. (1988). Merton's anomie: the road not taken. *Deviant Behavior*, 9, 33–53.
Messner, S., and Rosenfeld, R. (2010). Institutional-anomie theory: a macro-sociological explanation of crime. In A. J. L. Krohn, A. J. Lizzotte, and G. P. Hall (eds.), *Handbook on crime and deviance* (pp. 209–224). New York: Springer Science, Business Media.
Michel-Guillou, E. (2012). Développement durable et agriculture durable: appropriation des concepts et expression des résistances. *Cahiers Psychologie Politique*, 21 (Juillet). http://lodel.irevues.inist.fr/cahierspsychologiepolitique/index.php?id=2167
Milgram, S. (1984). Cities as social representations. In Farr and Moscovici (eds.), *Social Representations*. Cambridge: Cambridge University Press.
Milgram. S. (1963). Behavioural study of obedience. *Journal of Abnormal and Social Psychology*, 67, 371–78.
 (1974). *Obedience to authority: an experimental view*. London: Tavistock.
 (1977). *The individual in a social world: essays and experiments*. New York: Longman Higher Education.
Milgram, S., and Jodelet, D. (1976). Psychological maps of Paris. In I. Proshansky and E. Rivlin (eds.), *Environmental psychology: people and their physical settings* (pp. 104–124). New York: Holt Rinehart & Winston.
Milland, L. (2001). De la dynamique des rapports entre représentations sociales du travail et du chômage. Ph.D. thesis, Université de Provence.
Miller, D. (2002). Opinion polls and the misrepresentation of public opinion on the war with Afghanistan. *Television and New Media*, 3, 153–161.
Miller, W. (1997). *The anatomy of disgust*. Cambridge, MA: Harvard University Press.
Moghaddam, F. M. (2003). Interobjectivity and culture. *Culture and Psychology*, 9(3), 221–232. doi: 10.1177/1354067X030093004
 (2006a). *From the terrorists' point of view: what they experience and why they come to destroy*. Westport, CT: Praeger.
 (2006b). Interobjectivity: the collective roots of individual consciousness and social identity. In T. Postmes and J. Jetten (eds.), *Individuality and the group: advances in social identity* (pp. 155–174). London: Sage.
 (2008a). *Multiculturalism and intergroup relations: psychological implications for democracy in global context*. Washington DC: American Psychological Association.

(2008b). The psychological citizen and the two concepts of social contract: a preliminary analysis. *Political Psychology*, 29, 881–901.
  (2012). The omnicultural imperative. *Culture and Psychology*, 18(3), 304–330.
Moghaddam, F. M., and Ginsberg, S. (2003b). Culture clash and patents: positioning and intellectual property rights. In Harre and Moghaddam (eds.), pp. 235–249.
Moghaddam, F. M., and Harré, R. (Eds.) (2010). *Words of conflict, words of war: how the language we use in political discourse sparks fighting*. Santa Barbara, CA: Praeger.
Moghaddam, F. M., and Studer, C. (1998). *Illusions of control: striving for control in our personal and professional lives*. Westport, CT: Praeger.
Moghaddam, F. M., Hanley, E., and Harré, R. (2003b). Sustaining intergroup harmony: an analysis of the Kissinger papers through positioning analysis. In Harré and Moghaddam (eds.), pp. 137–155.
Moliner, P. (1988). La représentation sociale comme grille de lecture. Ph.D. thesis, Université de Provence.
  (1989). Validation expérimentale de l'hypothèse du noyau central des représentations sociales. *Bulletin de Psychologie*, 42, 759–762.
  (1993). ISA: l'induction par scénario ambigu. Une méthode pour l'étude des représentations sociales. *Revue Internationale de Psychologie Sociale*, 2, 7–21.
  (1994). Les méthodes de repérage et d'identification du noyau des représentations. In Guimelli (ed.), pp. 199–232.
  (1996). *Images et représentations sociales*. Presses Universitaires de Grenoble.
  (2001). *La dynamique des représentations sociales*. Presses Universitaires de Grenoble.
  (2007). La teoria del nucleo matriz de las representaciones sociales. In T. Rodriguez Salazar and M. L. Garcia Curiel (eds.), *Representaciones sociales. Teoria e investigacion* (pp. 137–155). Guadalajara: CUCHS-UDG.
Moliner, P., and Martos, A. (2005). La fonction génératrice de sens du noyau des représentations sociales. Une remise en cause? *Papers on Social Representations*, 14, 1–9.
Moliner, P., Rateau, P., and Cohen-Scali, V. (2002). *Les représentations sociales. Pratique des études de terrain*. Presses Universitaires de Rennes.
Moloney, G., and Walker, I. (2000). Messiahs, pariahs, and donors: the development of social representations of organ transplants. *Journal for the Theory of Social Behaviour*, 30(2), 203–227.
  (2002). Talking about transplants: social representations and the dialectical, dilemmatic nature of organ donation and transplantation. *British Journal of Social Psychology*, 41, 299–320.
  (Eds.) (2007). *Social representations and identity: content, process and power*. Basingstoke: Palgrave Macmillan.
Moloney, G., Hall, R., and Walker, I. (2005). Social representations and themata: the construction and functioning of social knowledge about donation and transplantation. *British Journal of Social Psychology*, 44, 415–441.
Morant, N. (2006). Social representations and professional knowledge: the representation of mental illness among mental health practitioners. *British Journal of Social Psychology*, 45(4), 817–838.
Morens, D. M., Folkers, G. K., and Fauci, A. S. (2004). The challenge of emerging and re-emerging infectious diseases. *Nature*, 430, 242–249.
Morin, E. (1956/1985). *Le cinéma ou l'homme imaginaire*. Paris: Éditions de Minuit.

Morris, M. W., Menon, T., and Ames, D. R. (2001). Culturally conferred conceptions of agency: a key to social perception of persons, groups, and other actors. *Personality and Social Psychology Review*, 5(2), 169–182.

Moscovici, S. (1961/1976). *La psychanalyse, son image et son public*. Paris: Presses Universitaires de France.

　(1961/2008). *Psychoanalysis: its image and its public*. Edited by G. Duveen, trans. D. Macey. Cambridge: Polity Press.

　(1963). Attitudes and opinions. *Annual Review of Psychology*, 14, 231–260.

　(1972). Society and theory in social psychology. In J. Israel and H. Tajfel (eds.), *The context of social psychology* (pp. 17–68). London: Academic Press.

　(1973). Foreword to C. Herzlich, *Health and Illness*. London: Academic Press.

　(1976). *Social influence and social change*. London: Academic Press.

　(1980). Towards a theory of conversion behavior. In L. Berkowitz (ed.), *Advances in experimental social psychology*, vol. XIII (pp. 209–239). New York: Academic Press.

　(1981a). *L'âge des foules*. Paris: Fayard.

　(1981b). On social representations. In J. Forgas (ed.), *Social cognition: perspectives on everyday understanding* (pp. 181–210). New York: Academic Press.

　(1984a). Introduction: le domaine de la psychologie sociale. In S. Moscovici (ed.), *Psychologie sociale* (pp. 5–22). Paris: Presses Universitaires de France.

　(1984b). The phenomenon of social representations. In Farr and Moscovici (eds.), pp. 3–68.

　(1985a). *The age of the crowd: a historical treatise on mass psychology*. Cambridge University Press.

　(1985b). Comment on Potter and Litton. *British Journal of Social Psychology*, 24, 91–92.

　(1985c). Social influence and conformity. In G. Lindzey and E. Aronson (eds.), *The handbook of social psychology*, vol. II (3rd edn) (pp. 347–412). New York: Random House.

　(1988). Notes towards a description of social representations. *European Journal of Social Psychology*, 18(3), 211–250.

　(1989). Des representations collectives aux representations sociales: elements pour une histoire. In D. Jodelet (ed.), *Les representations sociales*. Paris: Presses Universitaires de France.

　(1990a). The generalised self in mass society. In Himmelweit and Gaskell (eds.), ...

　(1990b). Social psychology and developmental psychology: extending the conversation. In G. Duveen and B. Lloyd (eds.), *Social representations and the development of knowledge*. Cambridge University Press.

　(1992). La nouvelle pensée magique. *Bulletin de Psychologie*, 405, 301–324.

　(1993a). Introductory address. *Papers on Social Representations*, 2, 160–170.

　(1993b). The return of the unconscious. *Social Research*, 60(1), 39–94.

　(1994). Social representations and pragmatic communication. *Social Science Information*, 33(2), 163–177.

　(1998). The history and actuality of social representations. In Flick (ed.), pp. 209–247.

　(1998/2000). The history and actuality of social representations. In G. Duveen (ed.), *Social representations: explorations in social psychology* (pp. 120–154). Cambridge: Polity Press.

(2000). *Social representations. Explorations in social psychology*. Cambridge: Polity Press.
(2001). Why a theory of social representations? In Deaux and Philogène (eds.), pp. 8–36.
(2005). Le regard psychosocial: Entretien avec Birgitta Orfali. http://documents.irevues. inist.fr/bitstream/handle/2042/8947/HERMES_2005_41_17.pdf?sequence=1
(2010). Let us not forget to think, nor the thinkers! *Papers on Social Representations*, 19, 1.1–2.4.

Moscovici, S., and Duveen, G. (2000). *Social representations*. Cambridge: Polity Press.

Moscovici, S., and Hewstone, M. (1983). Social representations and social explanation: from the 'naive' to the 'amateur' scientist. In M. Hewstone (ed.), *Attribution theory: social and functional extensions* (pp. 98–125). Oxford: Blackwell.
(1984). De la science au sens commun. In S. Moscovici (ed.), *Psychologie sociale* (pp. 539–566). Paris: Presses Universitaires de France.

Moscovici, S., and Kalampalikis, N. (2005). Une approche pragmatique de analyse Alceste. *Cahiers Internationaux de Psychologie Sociale*, 66, 15–24.

Moscovici, S., and Marková, I. (1996). Presenting social representations: a conversation. *Culture and Psychology*, 4, 371–410.
(2000). Ideas and their development: a dialogue between Serge Moscovici and Ivana Marková. In G. Duveen (ed.), *Social representations: explorations in social psychology* (pp. 224–286). Cambridge: Polity Press.
(2006). *The making of modern social psychology. The hidden story of how an international social science was created*. Cambridge: Polity Press.

Moscovici, S., Jovchelovitch, S., and Wagoner, B. (Eds.) (2013). *Development as a social process: contributions of Gerard Duveen*. London: Routledge.

Mouffe, C. (1993). *The return of the political*. London: Verso.

Mouro, C. (2011). Perspectivas locais sobre a conservação da biodiversidade: representações e dinâmicas identitárias associadas a inovações legais (Local perspectives on biodiversity conservation: representations and identity dynamics associated to legal innovations). Ph.D. thesis, Lisbon, ISCTE-IUL.

Mouro, C., and Castro, P. (2010). Local communities responding to ecological challenges – a psycho-social approach to the Natura 2000 network. *Journal of Community and Applied Social Psychology*, 20, 139–155.
(2012). Cognitive polyphasia in the reception of legal innovations for biodiversity conservation. *Papers on Social Representations*, 21, 3.1–3.21.

Mugny, G., and Pérez, J. A. (1991). *The social psychology of minority influence*. Cambridge University Press.

Muncy, J. A., and Vitell, S. J. (1992). Consumer ethics: an investigation of the ethical beliefs of the final consumer. *Journal of Business Research*, 24(4), 297–311.

Nakicenovic, N. (1995). Overland transportation networks: history of development and future prospects. In D. F. Batten, J. L. Casti and R. Thord (eds.), *Networks in action: communication, economics and human knowledge*. Berlin: Springer.

Nehru, J. (1946). *The discovery of India*. Oxford University Press.

Newcomb, T. M. (1946). The influence of attitude climate upon some determinants of information. *Journal of Abnormal and Social Psychology*, 41, 291–302.

Nicolopoulou, A., and Weintraub, J. (2009). Why operativity-in-context is not quite a sociocultural model. *Human Development*, 52, 320–328.

Nisbett, R., and Ross, L. (1980). *Human inference: strategies and shortcomings of social judgement*. Englewood Cliffs, NJ: Prentice Hall.

Noelle-Neumann, E. (1993). *The spiral of silence*. University of Chicago Press.
Noon, D. H. (2004). Operation enduring analogy: World War II, the war on terror, and the uses of historical memory. *Rhetoric and Public Affairs*, 7, 339–364.
Nora, P. (1989). Between memory and history: les lieux de mémoire. *Representations*, 26, 7–25.
Nowotny, H. (2010). Out of science – out of sync? In *World Social Science Report* (pp. 319–322). Paris: UNESCO and International Social Science Council.
O'Connor, C., and Joffe, H. (2013). Media representations of early human development: protecting, feeding and loving the developing brain. *Social Science and Medicine*, 97, 297–306.
O'Connor, C., Rees, G., and Joffe, H. (2012). Neuroscience in the public sphere. *Neuron*, 74, 220–226.
O'Gorman, E. (1992) *A invenção da América*. São Paulo: Universidade Estadual Paulista Júlio de Mesquita Filho (UNESP).
Olick, J., and Robbins, J. (1998). Social memory studies: from 'collective memory' to the historical sociology of mnemonic practices. *Annual Review of Sociology*, 24, 105–140.
Opp, K.-D. (2011). Modeling micro–macro relationships: problems and solutions. *Journal of Mathematical Sociology*, 35, 209–234.
Orecchioni-Kerbrat, C. (1983). *La connotation*. Presses Universitaires de Lyon.
Oren, N., and Bar-Tal, D. (2014). Collective identity and intractable conflict. In R. Jaspal and G. M. Breakwell (eds.), *Identity process theory: identity, social action and social change*. Cambridge University Press.
Orne, M. (1962). On the social psychology of the psychological experiment: with particular reference to demand characteristics and their implications. *American Psychologist*, 17, 776–83.
Ortony, A. (1979). Metaphor, language and thought. In A. Ortony (ed.), *Metaphor and thought* (pp. 1–19). Cambridge University Press.
Oyserman, D., and Markus, H. R. (1998). Self as a social representation. In Flick (ed.), pp. 107–125.
Páez, D., and Liu, J. H. (2011). Collective memory of conflicts. In D. Bar-Tal (ed.), *Intergroup conflicts and their resolution: social psychological perspectives* (pp. 105–124). New York: Psychology Press.
Páez, D., Echebarria, A., Valencia, J., Romo, I., San Juan, C., and Vergara, A. (1991). AIDS social representations: contents and processes. *Journal of Community and Applied Social Psychology*, 1(2), 89–104.
Páez, D., Liu, J. H., Techio, E., Slawuta, P., Zlobina, A., and Cabecinha, R. (2008). 'Remembering' World War II and willingness to fight: sociocultural factors in the social representation of historical warfare across 22 societies. *Journal of Cross-Cultural Psychology*, 39, 373–380.
Paloutzian, R. F., and Park, C. L. (2005). *Handbook of the psychology of religion and spirituality*. New York: Guilford Press.
Papastamou, S. (1983). Strategies of minority and majority influence. In W. Doise and S. Moscovici (eds.), *Current issues in European social psychology*, vol. I (pp. 33–83). Cambridge University Press.
Paris, M. (2000). *Warrior nation: images of war in British popular culture, 1850–2000*. London: Reaktion Books.

Parker, I. (1987). Social representations: social psychology's (mis)use of sociology. *Journal for the Theory of Social Behaviour*, 17(4), 447–470.
  (1992). *Discourse dynamics: critical analysis for social and individual psychology.* London: Routledge.
Parsons, T. (1951). *The social system.* Glencoe, IL: Free Press.
Patterson, A., Cromby, J., Brown, S. D., Gross, H., and Locke, A. (2011). 'It all boils down to respect doesn't it?': enacting a sense of community in a deprived inner-city area. *Journal of Community and Applied Social Psychology*, 21, 342–357.
Pehrson, S., Vignoles, V. L., and Brown, R. (2009). National identification and anti-immigrant prejudice: individual and contextual effects of national definitions. *Social Psychology Quarterly*, 72, 24–38.
Peirce, C. S. (1955). Logic as semiotic: the theory of signs. In J. Buchler (ed.), *Philosophical writings of Peirce*. New York: Dover Publications.
  (1960). *Collected papers of Charles Sanders Peirce.* Ed. C. Hartshorne, with P. Weiss and A. W. Burks. Vol. IV. Cambridge, MA: Belknap Press.
Penne, J. W. (Ed.) (1997). *Collective memory of political events: a social psychological perspective.* Mahwah, NJ: Lawrence Erlbaum.
Pennebaker, J. W., Rentfrow, J., Davis, M., Paez, D., Techio, E., Slawuta, P., Zlobina, A., Deschamps, J., and Bellelli, G. (2006). The social psychology of history: defining the most important events of world history. *Psicología Política*, 32, 15–32.
Pennington, D. F., Harary, F., and Bass, B. M. (1958). Some effects of decision and discussion on coalescence, change, and effectiveness. *Journal of Applied Psychology*, 42(6), 404–408.
Pérez, J. A., and Mugny, G. (1996). The conflict elaboration theory of social influence. In E. Witte and J. Davis (eds.), *Understanding group behavior*, vol. II, *Small group processes and interpersonal relations*. Hillsdale, NJ: Lawrence Erlbaum.
Pérez, J. A., Moscovici, S., and Chulvi, B. (2007). The taboo against group contact: hypothesis of gypsy ontologization. *British Journal of Social Psychology*, 46, 249–272.
Perret-Clermont, A.-N. (1980). *Social interaction and cognitive development in children.* London: Academic Press.
  (1994). Articuler l'individuel et le collectif. *New Review of Social Psychology*, 3, 94–102.
Perret-Clermont, A.-N., and Schubauer-Leoni, M.-L. (1981). Conflict and cooperation as opportunites for learning. In P. Robinson (ed.), *Communication in development*. London: Academic Press.
Perret-Clermont, A.-N., Perret, J. A., and Bell, N. (1991). The social construction of meaning and cognitive activity in elementary school children. In L. B. Resnick, J. M. Levine and S. D. Teasley (eds.), *Perspectives on socially-shared cognition* (pp. 41–62). Washington, DC: American Psychological Association.
Perrot, M. (1998). Georges Duby et l'imaginaire-écran de la féminilité. *Clio. Histoire, femmes et sociétés* 8. doi: 10.4000/clio.312, on 08/23/2013
Philo, G. (Ed.) (1996). *Media and mental distress.* London: Longman.
Philogène, G. (1999). *From Black to African American: a new social representation.* Westport, CT: Greenwood-Praeger.
Phinney, J. S. (2003). Ethnic identity and acculturation. In K. M. Chun, P. Balls-Organista and G. Marin (eds.), *Acculturation: advances in theory, measurement, and applied research* (pp. 63–81). Washington, DC: American Psychological Association.

Piaget, J. (1932). *The moral judgement of the child*. London: Routledge & Kegan Paul.
  (1941/1952). *The child's conception of number*. London: Routledge & Kegan Paul.
  (1954). *The construction of reality in the child*. New York: Basic Books.
  (1995a). Logical operations and social life. In *Sociological Studies*, pp. 134–157.
  (1995b). *Sociological studies*. London: Routledge.
Piaget, J., and Inhelder, B. (1969). *The psychology of the child*. London: Routledge & Kegan Paul.
Pidgeon, N., Kasperson, R. E., and Slovic, P. (Eds.) (2003). *The social amplification of risk*. Cambridge University Press.
Pigg, S. L. (1996). The credible and the credulous: the question of 'villagers' beliefs' in Nepal. *Cultural Anthropology*, 11(2), 160–201.
Pitkin, H. F. (1967). *The concept of representation*. Berkeley, MA: University of California Press.
Pitt, D. (2013). Mental representation. In Edward N. Zalta (gen. ed.), *The Stanford encyclopedia of philosophy* (Fall edn). http://plato.stanford.edu/archives/fall2013/entries/mental-representation/
Pomerantz, A. M. (1986). Extreme case formulations: a way of legitimizing claims. *Human Studies*, 9, 219–229.
Potter, A., and Hepburn, A. (2005). Qualitative interviews in psychology: problems and possibilities. *Qualitative Research in Psychology*, 2, 281–307.
Potter, J. (1996a). Attitudes, social representations and discursive psychology. In M. Wetherell (ed.), *Identities, groups and social issues*. London: Sage.
  (1996b). *Representing reality: discourse, rhetoric and social construction*. London: Sage.
Potter, J., and Billig, M. (1992). Re-representing representations – discussion of Räty and Snellman. *Ongoing Production on Social Representations*, 1, 15–20.
Potter, J., and Edwards, D. (1999). Social representations and discursive psychology: from cognition to action. *Culture and Psychology*, 5(4), 447–458. doi:10.1177/1354067X9954004
Potter, J., and Litton, I. (1985). Some problems underlying the theory of social representations. *British Journal of Social Psychology*, 24, 81–90.
Potter, J., and Wetherell, M. (1987). *Discourse and social psychology: beyond attitudes and behaviour*. London: Sage.
  (1998). Social representations, discourse analysis, and racism. In Flick (ed.), pp. 138–155.
Poumadère, M., and Bertoldo, R. (2010). Risk information and minority identity in the neighbourhood of industrial facilities. *Catalan Journal of Communication and Cultural Studies*, 2, 213–229.
Prado de Sousa, C. (2007). Representaciones sociales y el imaginario de la escuela. In A. Arruda and M. de Alba (eds.), *Espacios imaginarios y representaciones sociales. Aportes desde Latinoamérica* (pp. 199–231). Barcelona: Anthropos/UAM.
Priego-Hernández, J. (2011). Sexual and reproductive health among indigenous Mexican adolescents: a socio-representational perspective. Ph.D. thesis, London School of Economics and Political Science.
Propp, V. (1968). *Morphology of the folk tale*. Austin: University of Texas Press.
Provencher, C. (2011a). Lauri on organ donation or how to teach the theory of social representations using a quality empirical study. *Papers on Social Representations*, 20, 35.1–35.10.

Provencher, C. (2011b). Towards a better understanding of cognitive polyphasia. *Journal for the Theory of Social Behaviour*, 41(4), 377–395.

Psaltis, C. (2005a). Communication and the construction of knowledge or transmission of belief: the role of conversation type, behavioural style and social recognition. *Studies in Communication Science*, 5, 209–228.

(2005b). Social relations and cognitive development: the influence of conversation types and representations of gender. Ph.D. thesis, University of Cambridge.

(2007). International collaboration as construction of knowledge and its constraints. *Integrative Psychological and Behavioral Science*, 41, 187–197.

(2011a). The constructive role of gender asymmetry in social interaction: further evidence. *British Journal of Developmental Psychology*, 29(2), 305–312.

(2011b). From the epistemic to the social-psychological subject: the missing role of social identities, asymmetries of status, and social representations. *Human Development*, 54, 234–240.

(2012a). Culture and social representations: a continuing dialogue in search for heterogeneity in social developmental psychology. *Culture and Psychology*, 18(3), 375–390.

(2012b). Intergroup trust and contact in transition: a social representations perspective on the Cyprus conflict. In Markova and Gillespie (eds.), pp. 83–104.

(2012c). Social representations of gender in peer interaction and cognitive development. *Social and Personality Psychology Compass*, 6(11), 840–851.

Psaltis, C., and Duveen, G. (2006). Social relations and cognitive development: the influence of conversation type and representations of gender. *European Journal of Social Psychology*, 36, 407–430.

(2007). Conservation and conversation types: forms of recognition and cognitive development. *British Journal of Developmental Psychology*, 25, 79–102.

Psaltis, C., and Zapiti, A. (2014). *Interaction, communication and development: psychological development as a social process*. London: Routledge.

Psaltis, C., Duveen, G., and Perret-Clermont, A. N. (2009). The social and the psychological: structure and context in intellectual development. *Human Development*, 52, 291–312.

Purkhardt, S. C. (1993). *Transforming social representation: a social psychology of common sense and science*. London: Routledge.

Rateau, P., Moliner, P., Guimelli, C., and Abric, J. C. (2011). Social representations theory. In P. A. M. Van Lange, A. W. Kruglanski and E. Tory Higgins (eds.), *Handbook of theories of social psychology* (pp. 477–497). London: Sage.

Räty, H., and Snellman, L. (1992a). Making the unfamiliar familiar – some notes on the criticism of the theory of social representations. *Ongoing Production on Social Representations*, 1, 3–13.

(1992b). Some further notes: replies to Ibañez and Potter and Billig. *Ongoing Production on Social Representations*, 1, 27–28.

Raudsepp, M. (2005). Why is it so difficult to understand the theory of social representations? *Culture and Psychology*, 11(4), 455–468.

Raudsepp, M., and Wagner, W. (2012). The essentially Other – representational processes that divide groups. In Marková and Gillespie (eds.), pp. 105–122.

Raven, B. (1993). The bases of power: origins and recent developments. *Journal of Social Issues*, 49, 227–251.

Reader, T., Flin, R., and Cuthbertson, B. (2007). Communication skills and error in the intensive care unit. *Current Opinions in Critical Care*, 13, 732–736.

Redner, H. (1994). *A new science of representation*. Boulder, CO: Westview Press.

Reicher, S. (2004). The context of social identity: domination, resistance and change. *Political Psychology*, 26(6), 921–945.

Reicher, S. D. (1984). The St Pauls' riot: an explanation of the limits of crowd action in terms of a social identity model. *European Journal of Social Psychology*, 14(1), 1–21.

  (1996). 'The battle of Westminster': developing the social identity model of crowd behaviour in order to explain the initiation and development of collective conflict. *European Journal of Social Psychology*, 26(1), 115–134.

Reicher, S., and Hopkins, N. (2001). *Self and nation*. London: Sage.

Reicher, S. D., Haslam, S. A., and Hopkins, N. (2005). Social identity and the dynamics of leadership: leaders and followers as collaborative agents in the transformation of social reality. *Leadership Quarterly*, 16, 547–568.

Reicher, S., Hopkins, N., Levine, M., and Rath, R. (2005). Entrepreneurs of hate and entrepreneurs of solidarity: social identity as a basis for mass communication. *International Review of the Red Cross*, 87(860), 621–637.

Renard, E., Bonardi, C., Roussiau, N., and Girandola, F. (2007). Forced compliance, double forced compliance and experimental dynamics in social representations. *Revue Internationale de Psychologie Sociale*, 20(2), 79–130.

Renedo, A. (2010). Polyphony and polyphasia in self and knowledge. *Papers on Social Representations*, 19, 12.1–12.21.

Renedo, A., and Jovchelovitch, S. (2007). Expert knowledge, cognitive polyphasia and health – a study on social representations of homelessness among professionals working in the voluntary sector in London. *Journal of Health Psychology*, 12(5), 779–790.

Richards (1997). *'Race', racism and psychology: towards a reflexive history*. New York: Routledge.

Ridgeway, C. (2001). The emergence of status beliefs. From structural inequality to legitimizing ideology. In J. T. Jost and B. Major (eds.), *The psychology of legitimacy. Emerging perspectives on ideology, justice and intergroup relations* (pp. 257–277). Cambridge University Press.

Riesch, H. (2010). Theorising boundary work as representation and identity. *Journal for the Theory of Social Behaviour*, 40(4), 452–473.

Rimé, B. (1997). How individual emotional episodes feed collective memory. In J. W. Pennebaker, D. Paez and B. Rimé (eds.), *Collective memory of political events* (pp. 131–146). Mahwah, NJ: Lawrence Erlbaum.

Ring, K. (1967). Experimental social psychology: some sober questions about some frivolous values. *Journal of Experimental Social Psychology*, 3(2), 113–123.

Rogers, E. (1962). *Diffusion of innovations*. London: Collier Macmillan.

Rogers, E. M. (1995). *Diffusion of innovations* (4th edn). New York: Free Press.

Roland, G. R. (2004). Understanding institutional change: fast-moving and slow-moving institutions. *Studies in Comparative International Development*, 38(4), 109–131.

Rommetveit, R. (1984). The role of language in the creation and transmission of social representations. In Farr and Moscovici (eds.), *Social representations*. Cambridge: Cambridge University Press.

Roqueplo, P. (1990). Le savoir décalé. In L. Sfez, G. Coutlée, and P. Musso (eds.), *Technologies et symboliques de la communication. Colloque de Cerisy* (pp. 75–80). Presses Universitaires de Grenoble.

Rosa, A. (2007). Acts of psyche, actuations as synthesis of semiosis and action. In J. Valsiner and A. Rosa (eds.), *The Cambridge handbook of sociocultural psychology*. New York: Cambridge University Press.

Rosa, A., and Blanco, F. (2007). Actuations of identification in the games of identity. *Social Practice/Psychological Theorizing*. Retrieved 10.10.2007. www.spptgulerce.boun.edu.tr/

Rose, D. (1997). Television, madness and community care. *Journal of Community and Applied Social Psychology*, 8(3), 213–228.

(2000). Analysis of moving images. In M. Bauer and G. Gaskell (eds.), *Qualitative researching with text, image and sound*. London: Sage.

(2003). Patients' perspectives on Electro-Convulsive Therapy: systematic review. *BMJ*, 326, 1363.

Rose, D., Efraim, D., Gervais, M.-C., Joffe, H., Jovchelovitch, S., and Morant, N. (1995). Questioning consensus in social representations theory. *Papers on Social Representations*, 4(2), 150–176.

Rosenberg, M. J., and Hovland, C. I. (1960). Cognitive, affective and behavioral components of attitudes. In C. I. Hovland and M. J. Rosenberg (eds.), *Attitude organization and change*. New Haven, CT: Yale University Press.

Rosenbrock, R., Dubois-Arber, F., Moers, M., Pinell, P., Schaeffer, D., and Setbon, M. (2000). The normalization of AIDS in Western European countries. *Social Science and Medicine*, 50, 1607–1629.

Rosengren, K. S., and Gutiérrez, I. T. (2011). Searching for coherence in a complex world: introduction to the special issue on explanatory coexistence. *Human Development*, 54(3), 123–125.

Rosenstock, I. M. (1966). Why people use health services. *Milbank Memorial Fund Quarterly*, 44, 94–127.

Ross, L., and Nisbett, R. E. (1991). *The person and the situation*. New York: McGraw-Hill.

Ross, M. W., Essien, E. J., and Torres, I. (2006). Conspiracy beliefs about the origin of HIV/AIDS in four racial/ethnic groups. *Journal of Acquired Immune Deficiency Syndromes*, 41, 342–344.

Rothbart, M., and Taylor, M. (1992). Category and social reality: do we view social categories as natural kinds? In G. R. Semin and K. Fieder (eds.), *Language and social cognition* (pp. 11–36). London: Sage.

Rothschild, M. L., Mastin, B., and Miller, T. W. (2006). Reducing alcohol-impaired driving crashes through the use of social marketing. *Accident Analysis and Prevention*, 38(6), 1218–1230.

Rouquette, M.-L. (1994). *Sur la connaissance des masses, essai de psychologie politique*. Presses Universitaires de Grenoble.

Rouquette, M. L., and Rateau, P. (1998). *Introduction à l'étude des représentations sociales*. Presses Universitaires de Grenoble.

Roy, O. (2004). *Globalized Islam: the search for a new ummah*. New York: Columbia University Press.

Royzman, E. B., and Sabini, J. (2001). Something it takes to be an emotion: the interesting case of Disgust. *Journal for the Theory of Social Behaviour*, 31(1), 29–59.

Rozin, P., Haidt, J., and McCauley, C. R. (2000). Disgust. In M. Lewis and J. Haviland (eds.), *Handbook of emotions* (2nd edn) (pp. 637–653). New York: Guilford Press.

Runciman, W. G. (1966). *Relative deprivation and social justice: a study of attitudes to social inequality in twentieth-century England*. London: Routledge & Kegan Paul.

Runde, V. (2005). Set theory. In V. Runde, *A taste of topology* (pp. 5–22). Berlin: Springer.

Russell, B. (1908). Mathematical logic as based on the theory of types. *American Journal of Mathematics*, 30(3), 222–262. doi:10.2307/2369948

Said, E. W. (1978). *Orientalism: Western conceptions of the orient*. Harmondsworth: Penguin.

Salvatore, S., and Venuleo, C. (2008). Understanding the role of emotion in sense-making. A semiotic psychoanalytic oriented perspective. *Integrative Psychological and Behavioral Science*, 42(1), 32–36.

Salzman, C. D., and Fusi, S. (2010). Emotion, cognition, and mental state representation in amygdala and prefrontal cortex. *Annual Review of Neuroscience*, 33(March), 173–202. Retrieved from http://www.ncbi.nlm.nih.gov/pubmed/20331363

Sammut, G. (2010). The point of view: towards a social psychology of relativity. Doctoral thesis, London School of Economics and Political Science.

(2011). Civic solidarity: the negotiation of identity in modern societies. *Papers on Social Representations*, 20, 4.1–4.24.

(2012). The immigrants' point of view: acculturation, social judgment, and the relative propensity to take the perspective of the other. *Culture and Psychology*, 18(2), 184–197.

(2013). Measuring attitudes and points of view: social judgment of proposals for the evision of student stipends in higher education. *Psychology and Society*, 5(1), 54–66.

Sammut, G., and Bauer, M. W. (2011). Social influence: modes and modalities. In D. Hook, B. Franks and M. W. Bauer (eds.), *The social psychology of communication* (pp. 87–106). Basingstoke: Palgrave Macmillan.

Sammut, G., and Gaskell, G. (2010). Points of view, social positioning and intercultural relations. *Journal for the Theory of Social Behaviour*, 40, 47–64.

(2012). Explaining social behavior in situ: the study of points of view. In S. Salvatore, A. Gennaro and J. Valsiner (eds.), *Yearbook of idiographic science*, vol. IV, *Making sense of infinite uniqueness: the emerging system of idiographic science* (pp. 45–54). Charlotte, NC: Information Age Publishing.

Sammut, G., and Howarth, C. (2014). Social representations. In T. Teo (ed.), *Encyclopedia of critical psychology* (pp. 1799–1802). New York: Springer.

Sammut, G., and Sartawi, M. (2012). Perspective-taking and the attribution of ignorance. *Journal for the Theory of Social Behaviour*, 42(2), 181–200.

Sammut, G., Andreouli, E., and Sartawi, M. (2012). Social influence and social change: states and strategies of social capital. In B. Wagoner, E. Jensen and J. Oldmeadow (eds.), *Culture and social change: transforming society through the power of ideas* (pp. 263–274). Charlotte, NC: Information Age Publishing.

Sammut, G., Daanen, P., and Moghaddam, F. M. (2013). *Understanding self and others: explorations in intersubjectivity and interobjectivity*. London: Routledge.

Sammut, G., Daanen, P., and Sartawi, M. (2010). Interobjectivity: representations and artefacts in cultural psychology. *Culture and Psychology*, 16(4), 451–463. doi: 10.1177/1354067X10380158

Sammut, G., Tsirogianni, S., and Wagoner, B. (2012). Representations from the past: social relations and the devolution of social representations. *Integrative Psychological and Behavioral Science*. doi: 10.1007/s12124-012-9212-0

Sani, F., Bowe, M., and Herrera., M. (2008). Perceived collective continuity and social well-being: exploring the connections. *European Journal of Social Psychology*, 38, 365–374.

Sani, F., Bowe, M., Herrera, M., Manna, C., Cossa, T., Miao, X., *et al.* (2007). Perceived collective continuity: seeing groups as entities that move through time. *European Journal of Social Psychology*, 37, 1118–1134.

Sapir, E. (1921/1970). *Language*. London: Rupert Hart-Davis.

Sarrasin, O., Green, E. G. T., Fasel, N., Christ, O., Staerklé, C., and Clémence, A. (2012). Opposition to anti-racism laws across Swiss municipalities: a multilevel analysis. *Political Psychology*, 33(5), 659–681.

Sartawi, M., and Sammut, G. (2012). Negotiating British Muslim identity: everyday concerns of practicing Muslims in London. *Culture and Psychology*, 18(4), 559–567.

Sartre, J.-P. (1943/2003). *Being and nothingness*. London: Routledge.

Saussure, F. (1959). *Course in general linguistics*. New York: Philosophical Library.

Saussure, F. de (1916/1960). The nature of the linguistic sign. Trans. W. Baskin. In *Course in general linguistic* (pp. 65–71). London: Peter Owen.

Savarkar, V. D. (1921–22). *The essentials of Hindutva*. Retrieved 30.08.2012. www.savarkar.org/en/hindutva-hindu-nationalism/essentials-hindutva

Schaller, M., and Park, J. H. (2011). The behavioral immune system (and why it matters). *Current Directions in Psychological Science*, 20, 99–103.

Scheidegger, R., and Staerklé, C. (2011). Political trust and distrust in Switzerland: a normative analysis. *Swiss Political Science Review*, 17, 164–187.

Scheidegger, R., and Tuescher, T. (2010). Does orthodoxy of knowledge polarize social anchoring? Representations of the market as a function of academic major and subjective knowledge in economics. *Papers on Social Representations*, 19, 25.1–25.22.

Schelling, T. (1971). Dynamic models of segregation. *Journal of Mathematical Sociology*, 1, 143–186.

(1978). *Micromotives and macrobehavior*. New York: W. W. Norton.

Schubauer-Leoni, M.-L., and Grossen, M. (1993). Negotiating the meaning of questions in didactic and experimental contracts. *European Journal of Psychology of Education*, 8, 451–471.

Schuman, H., and Rieger, C. (1992). Historical analogies, generational effects and attitudes towards war. *American Sociologist*, 57, 315–326.

Schuman, H., and Rodgers, W. L. (2000). Cohorts, chronology, and collective memories. *Public Opinion Quarterly*, 68, 217–254.

Schwartz, B. (1996). Memory as a cultural system: Abraham Lincoln in World War II. *American Sociological Review*, 61, 908–27.

(1997). Collective memory and history: how Abraham Lincoln became a symbol of racial equality. *Sociological Quarterly*, 38, 469–496.

Schwartz, S. H. (1992). Universals in the content and structure of values: theory and empirical tests in 20 countries. *Advances in Experimental Social Psychology*, 25, 1–65.

Selge, S., and Fischer, A. (2011). How people familiarize themselves with complex ecological concepts-anchoring of social representations of invasive non-native species. *Journal of Community and Applied Social Psychology*, 21(4), 297–311.

Selge, S., Fischer, A., and van der Wal, R. (2011). Public and professional views on invasive non-native species – a qualitative social scientific investigation. *Biological Conservation*, 144, 3089–3097.

Semin, G. R. (1985). The 'phenomenon of social representations': a comment on Potter and Litton. *British Journal of Social Psychology*, 24, 93–94.

Sen, R. (2012). Hetero-referentiality and divided societies. In D. J. Christie (ed.), *The encyclopedia of peace psychology*. Chichester: Wiley-Blackwell.

Sen, R., and Wagner, W. (2005). History, emotion and hetero-referential representations in inter-group conflict: the example of Hindu–Muslim relation in India. *Papers on Social Representations*, 14, 2.1–2.3.

Sen, R., Wagner, W., and Howarth, C. (2014). *Transcending boundaries: fundamentalism, secularism and social capital in multifaith societies*. New York: Springer.

Shanks, D. R., Newell, B. R., Lee, E. H., Balakrishnan, D., Ekelund, L., Cenac, Z., Kawadia, F., and Moore, C. (2013). Priming intelligent behaviour: an elusive phenomenon. *PLoS ONE*, 8(4), e56515. doi: 10.1371/journal.pone.0056515

Shaw, A. (1988). *A Pakistani community in Britain*. London: Blackwell.

Sherif, M. (1936). *The psychology of social norms*. New York: HarperCollins.

Sherif, M., and Hovland, C. I. (1961). *Social judgment: assimilation and contrast effects in communication and attitude change*. New Haven, CT: Yale University Press.

Sherif, M., and Sherif, C. (1956). *An outline of social psychology*. New York: Harper & Row.

Sherif, M., and Sherif, C. W. (1964). *Reference groups*. New York: Harper & Row.

Sherif, C. W., Sherif, M., and Nebergall, R. E. (1965). *Attitude and attitude change: the social judgment-involvement approach*. Philadelphia: Saunders.

Shotter, J. (1993). *Conversational realities: constructing life through language*. London: Sage.

Shuman, H., and Rieger, C. (1992). Historical analogies, generational effects, and attitudes towards war. *American Sociological Review*, 54, 359–81.

Sibley, C. G., and Liu, J. H. (2004). Attitudes towards biculturalism in New Zealand: social dominance and Pakeha attitudes towards the general principles and resource-specific aspects of bicultural policy. *New Zealand Journal of Psychology*, 33, 88–99.

　(2012). Social representations of history and the legitimation of social inequality: the causes and consequences of historical negation. *Journal of Applied Social Psychology*, 42, 598–623.

　(2013). Relocating attitudes as components of representational profiles: mapping the epidemiology of intergroup policy attitudes using Latent Class Analysis. *European Journal of Social Psychology*, 43(2), 160–174.

Sibley, C. G., Liu, J. H., Duckitt, J., and Khan, S. S. (2008). Social representations of history and the legitimation of social inequality: the form and function of historical negation. *European Journal of Social Psychology*, 38, 542–565.

Siegler, R. S. (1995). How does change occur?: a microgenetic study of number conservation. *Cognitive Psychology*, 25, 225–273.

Siegler, R. S., and Crowley, K. (1991). The microgenetic method: a direct means for studying cognitive development. *American Psychologist*, 46, 606–620.

Silva, A. (2007). *Imaginarios urbanos desde América Latina: Archivos*. Barcelona: Fundación Antonio Tapiès.

Simao, L. M. (2003). Beside rupture – disquiet; beyond the other – alterity. *Culture and Psychology*, 9(4), 449–459.

Simon, B., and Klandermans, B. (2001). Politicized collective identity: a social psychological analysis. *American Psychologist*, 56, 319–331.

Sloterdijk, P. (2012). *You have to change your life*. Cambridge: Polity Press.

Smedslund, J. (1978). Bandura's theory of self-efficacy: a set of common sense theorems. *Scandinavian Journal of Psychology*, 19, 1–14.

  (1985). Necessarily true cultural psychologies. In K. J. Gergen and K. E. Davis (eds.), *The social construction of the person*. New York: Springer.

Smith, A. (1776). *An inquiry into the nature and causes of the wealth of nations*. London: W. Strahan and T. Cadell.

Smith, L. (1993). *Necessary knowledge: Piagetian perspectives on constructivism*. Hove: Lawrence Erlbaum.

Smith, N., and Joffe, H. (2013). How the public engages with global warming: a social representations approach. *Public Understanding of Science*, 22(1), 16–32.

Sonesson, G. (1989). *Pictorial concepts. Inquiries into the semiotic heritage and its relevance for the analysis of the visual world*. Lund University Press.

Sontag, S. (1978). *Illness as metaphor*. New York: Farrar, Straus & Giroux.

Sorsana, C., and Trognon, A. (2011). Contextual determination of human thinking: about some conceptual and methodological obstacles in psychology studies. *Human Development*, 54, 204–233.

Souza, L. M. (1986). *O diabo e a Terra de Santa Cruz; feitiçaria e religiosidade popular no Brasil colonial*. São Paulo: Companhia das Letras.

Soyland, A. J. (1994). *Psychology as metaphor*. London: Sage.

Spears, R. (1997). Introduction. In T. Ibáñez and L. Íñiguez (eds.), *Critical social psychology* (pp. 1–26). London: Sage.

Spellman, B. A., and Holyoak, K. J. (1993). If Saddam is Hitler then who is George Bush? Analogical mapping between systems of social roles. *Journal of Personality and Social Psychology*, 62, 913–933.

Spence, A., and Pidgeon, N. (2010). Framing and communicating climate change: the effects of distance and outcome frame manipulations. *Global Environmental Change*, 20, 656–667.

Sperber, D. (1990). The epidemiology of beliefs. In Fraser and Gaskell (eds.), pp. 25–44.

  (1996). *La Contagion des idées*. Paris: Odile Jacob.

Spilka, B., and Schmidt, G. (1983). Stylistic factors in attributions: the role of religion and locus of control. Paper presented at the Annual Convention of the Rocky Mountain Psychological Association.

Spini, D., and Doise, W. (1998). Organizing principles of involvement in human rights and their social anchoring in value priorities. *European Journal of Social Psychology*, 28, 603–622.

Staerklé, C. (2005). L'idéal démocratique perverti: représentations antagonistes dans la mise en altérité du non-Occident. In M. Sanchez-Mazas and L. Licata (eds.), *L'autre. Regards psychosociaux* (pp. 117–148). Presses Universitaires de Grenoble.

(2009). Policy attitudes, ideological values and social representations. *Social and Personality Psychology Compass*, 3, 1096–1112.

(2011). Back to new roots: societal psychology and social representations. In J. P. Valentim (ed.), *Societal approaches in social psychology*. Bern: Peter Lang.

Staerklé, C., Clémence, A., and Doise, W. (1998). Representation of human rights across different national contexts: the role of democratic and non-democratic populations and governments. *European Journal of Social Psychology*, 28, 207–226.

Staerklé, C., Clémence, A., and Spini, D. (2011). Social representations: a normative and dynamic intergroup approach. *Political Psychology*, 32, 759–768.

Staerklé, C., Likki, T., and Scheidegger, R. (2012). A normative approach to welfare attitudes. In S. Svallfors (ed.), *Contested welfare states: welfare attitudes in Europe and beyond* (pp. 81–118). Stanford University Press.

Stallybrass, P., and White, A. (1986). *The poetics and politics of transgression*. London: Methuen.

Stephens, C. (2007). Participation in different fields of practice: using social theory to understand participation in community health promotion. *Journal of Health Psychology*, 12(6), 949–960.

Stevenson, C., Condor, S., and Abell, J. (2007). The majority–minority conundrum in Northern Ireland: an Orange Order perspective. *Political Psychology*, 28, 107–125.

Stone, L., and Muir, R. (2007). *Who are we? Identities in Britain, 2007*. London: Institute for Public Policy Research.

Sullivan, C., Gibson, S., and Riley, S. (2012). *Doing your qualitative psychology project*. London: Sage.

Symons, D. (1979). *The evolution of human sexuality*. Oxford University Press.

Tajfel, H. (1969). Cognitive aspects of prejudice. *Journal of Social Issues*, 25, 79–97.

(1974). Social identity and intergroup behavior. *Social Science Information*, 13(2), 65–93.

(1978). *Differentiation between social groups: studies in the social psychology of intergroup relations*. London: Academic Press.

(1979). Individuals and groups in social psychology. *British Journal of Social and Clinical Psychology*, 18, 183–190.

(1981). *Human groups and social categories: studies in social psychology*. Cambridge University Press.

Tajfel, H., and Turner, J. C. (1986). The social identity theory of intergroup behaviour. In S. Worchel and W. C. Austin (eds.), *Psychology of intergroup relations* (pp. 7–24). Chicago: Nelson-Hall.

Tajfel, H., and Turner, J. C. (1979). An integrative theory of intergroup conflict. In W. G. Austin and S. Worchel (eds.), *The social psychology of intergroup relations*. Monterey, CA: Brooks-Cole.

Tan, S., and Moghaddam, F. M. (1995). Reflexive positioning and culture. *Journal for the Theory of Social Behavior*, 25, 387–400.

Tate, C., and Audette, D. (2001). Theory and research on 'Race' as a natural kind variable in psychology. *Theory and Psychology*, 11, 495–520.

Taves, A. (2009). *Religious experience reconsidered: a building block approach to the study of religion and other special things*. Princeton University Press.

Taylor, A. J., and Rourke, J. T. (1995). Historical analogies in the Congressional foreign policy process. *Journal of Politics*, 57, 460–468.

Taylor, C. (1992). *Multiculturalism and 'the politics of recognition'*. Princeton University Press.
  (2004). *Modern social imaginaries*. Durham: Duke University Press.
Terkel, S. (1984). *The good war: an oral history of World War II*. New York: New Press.
Terry, D. J., and Hogg, M. A. (1996). Group norms and the attitude–behaviour relationship: a role for ingroup norms. *Personality and Social Psychology Bulletin*, 22(8), 776–793.
Tesser, A. (1993). On the Importance of heritability in psychological research: the case of attitudes. *Psychological Review*, 100, 129–142.
Thagard, P. (1999). *How scientists explain disease*. Princeton University Press.
Thaler, R. H., and Sunstein, C. R. (2008). *Nudge: improving decisions about health, wealth, and happiness*. New Haven, CT: Yale University Press.
Thiesse, A. M. (1999). *La création des identités nationales. Europe XVIIIe–XXe siècle*. Paris: Éditions du Seuil.
Thomas, S. (1998). Race, gender, and welfare reform: the antinationalist response. *Journal of Black Studies*, 28, 419–446.
Thomas, S. B., and Quinn, S. C. (1993). The burdens of race and history on Black Americans' attitudes toward needle exchange policy to prevent HIV disease. *Journal of Public Health Policy*, 14, 320–347.
Thommen, B., Amann, R., and von Cranach, M. (1988). *Handlungsorganisation durch soziale Repräsentationen – Welchen Einfluß haben therapeutische Schulen auf das Handeln ihrer Mitglieder?* Bern: Huber.
Thompson, P. B. (1999). The ethics of truth-telling and the problem of risk. *Science and Engineering Ethics*, 5(4), 489–510.
Thorburn Bird, S., and Bogart, L. M. (2005). Conspiracy beliefs about HIV/AIDS and birth control among African Americans: implications for the prevention of HIV, other STIs, and unintended pregnancy. *Journal of Social Issues*, 61, 109–126.
Thrush, D., Fife-Schaw, C., and Breakwell, G. M. (1997). Young people's representations of others' views of smoking: is there a link with smoking behaviour? *Journal of Adolescence*, 20, 57–70.
Thurstone, L. L. (1967a). Attitudes can be measured. In Fishbein (ed.), pp. 77–89.
  (1967b). The measurement of social attitudes. In Fishbein (ed.), pp. 14–25.
Tileagă, C. (2009). The social organization of representations of history: the textual accomplishment of coming to terms with the past. *British Journal of Social Psychology*, 48, 337–355.
Timotijevic, L., and Breakwell, G. M. (2000). Migration and threats to identity. *Journal of Community and Social Psychology*, 10, 355–372.
Tolman, E. C. (1948). Cognitive maps in rats and men. *Psychological Review*, 55(4), 189–208.
Tomasello, M. (1999). *The cultural origins of human cognition*. Cambridge, MA: Harvard University Press.
Tomasello, M., Carpenter, M., Call, J., Behne, T., and Moll, H. (2005). Understanding and sharing intentions: the origins of cultural cognition. *Behavioral and Brain Sciences*, 28, 675–735.
Tourangeau, R., and Sternberg, R. (1981). Aptness in metaphor. *Cognitive Psychology*, 13, 27–55.
  (1982). Understanding and appreciating metaphors. *Cognition*, 11, 203–244.

Tsirogianni, S., and Andreouli, E. (2011). Beyond social cohesion: the role of 'Fusion of Horizons' in inter-group solidarities. *Papers on Social Representations*, 20(1), 5.1–5.25.

Turner, G. (2009). Politics, radio and journalism in Australia: the influence of 'talkback'. *Journalism*, 10, 411–430.

Turner, J. C. (1999). Some current issues in research on social identity and self-categorization theories. In N. Ellemers, R. Spears and B. Doosje (eds.), *Social identity* (pp. 6–34). Oxford: Blackwell.

Turner, J. C., Hogg, M. A., Oakes, P. J., Reicher, S. D., and Wetherell, M. (1987). *Rediscovering the social group*. Oxford: Blackwell.

Tyler, T. (2001). Public trust and confidence in legal authorities: what do majority and minority group members want from the law and legal institutions? *Behavioral Sciences and the Law*, 19, 215–235.

Uexküll, J. von (1965). Mondes animaux et monde humain. In J. von Uexküll (ed.), *Mondes animaux et monde humain, suivi de théorie de la signification* (pp. 1–90). Paris: Denoël.

UK Office for National Statistics (2004). *Focus on Religion*. London: ONS.

Ungar, S. (1998). Hot crises and media reassurance. *British Journal of Sociology*, 49, 36–56.

Urry, J. (2007). *Mobilities*. Cambridge: Polity Press.

Uslaner, E. (2008). *Corruption, inequality and the rule of law*. Cambridge University Press.

Uzelgun, M., and Castro, P. (2014). The voice of science in the mainstream Turkish press. *Environmental Communication: a journal of nature and culture*, 8(3), 326–344.

Uzzell, D., and Räthzel, N. (2009). Transforming environmental psychology. *Journal of Environmental Psychology*, 29, 340–350.

Vala, J., and Castro, P. (2013). Pensamento social e representações sociais. In J. Vala and M. B. Monteiro (eds.), *Psicologia social* (9th edn, revised) (pp. 569–602). Lisbon: Fundação Calouste Gulbenkian.

Vala, J., Garcia-Marques, L., Gouveia-Pereira, M., and Lopes, D. (1998). Validation of polemical social representations: introducing the intergroup differentiation of heterogeneity. *Social Science Information*, 37, 469–492.

Valladares, L. (2000). A gênese da favela carioca. A produção anterior às ciências sociais. *Revista Brasileira de Ciências Sociais*, 15(44), 5–34.

Valsiner, J. (2000). *Culture and human development*. London: Sage.

 (2007). *Culture in minds and societies: foundations of cultural psychology*. London: Sage.

 (Ed.) (2012). *The Oxford handbook of culture and psychology*. Oxford University Press.

 (2014). Needed for cultural psychology: methodology in a new key. *Culture and Psychology*, 20(1), 3–30.

Valsiner, J., and Rosa, A. (Eds.) (2007). *The Cambridge handbook of sociocultural psychology*. Cambridge University Press.

Valsiner, J., and Van der Veer, R. (2000). *The social mind: construction of the idea*. Cambridge University Press.

Van der Veer, R., and Valsiner, J. (1991). *Understanding Vygotsky. A quest for synthesis*. Oxford: Basil Blackwell.

van Dijk, T. A. (1992). Discourse and the denial of racism. *Discourse and Society*, 3, 87–118.

van Oorschot, W. (2006). Making the difference in social Europe: deservingness perceptions among citizens of European welfare states. *Journal of European Social Policy*, 16(1), 23–42.

Van Rossem, R., and Meekers, D. (2007). The search and impact of social marketing and reproductive health communication campaigns in Zambia. *BMC Public Health*, 7(352). doi: 10.1186/1471-2458-7-352

Vergès, P. (1992). L'évocation de l'argent: une méthode pour la définition du noyau central d'une représentation. *Bulletin de Psychologie*, 405, 203–209.

Verheggen, T., and Baerveldt, C. (2007). We don't share! The social representation approach, enactivism and the ground for an intrinsically social psychology. *Culture and Psychology*, 13(1), 5–27.

Verkuyten, M. (2003). Discourses about ethnic group (de-)essentailism: oppressive and progressive aspects. *British Journal of Social Psychology*, 42, 371–391.

Vignoles, V. L., Chryssochoou, X., and Breakwell, G. M. (2000). The distinctiveness principle: motivation, identity and the bounds of cultural relativity. *Personality and Social Psychology Review*, 4(4), 337–354.

  (2002a). Evaluating models of identity motivation: self-esteem is not the whole story. *Self and Identity*, 1, 201–218.

  (2002b). Sources of distinctiveness: position, difference and separateness in the identities of Anglican parish priests. *European Journal of Social Psychology*, 32(6), 761–781.

  (2004). Combining individuality and relatedness: representations of the person among the Anglican clergy. *British Journal of Social Psychology*, 43(1), 113–132.

Vijver, F. J., and Leung, K. (2000). Methodological issues in psychological research on culture. *Journal of Cross-Cultural Psychology*, 31(1), 33–51.

Vincze, O., Toth, J., and László, J. (2007). Representations of the Austro-Hungarian monarchy in the history books of the two nations. *ETC – Empirical Text and Culture Research*, 3, 62–71.

Vitebsky, P. (1993). *Dialogues with the dead*. Cambridge University Press.

Voelklein, C., and Howarth, C. (2005). A review of controversies about social representations theory: a British debate. *Culture and Psychology*, 11(4), 431–454.

Voet, R. (1998). *Feminism and citizenship*. London: Sage.

Vygotsky, L. S. (1962). *Thought and language*. Cambridge, MA: MIT Press.

  (1978). *Mind in society: the development of the higher psychological processes*. Cambridge, MA: Harvard University Press.

  (1987). *The collected works of L. S. Vygotsky*, vol. IV, *The history of the development of higher mental functions*. New York: Plenum Press.

Vygotsky, L., and Luria, A. (1994). Tool and symbol in child development. In J. Valsiner and R. van der Veer (eds.), *The Vygotsky reader* (pp. 99–172). Oxford: Blackwell.

Wacquant, L. (2002). From slavery to mass incarceration: rethinking the race question in the US. In M. Tonry (ed.), *Why punish? How much?* (pp. 387–402). Oxford University Press.

Wagner, W. (1993). Can representations explain social behaviour? A discussion of social representations as rational systems. *Papers on Social Representations*, 2, 236–249.

  (1994a). The fallacy of misplaced intentionality in social representation research. *Journal for the Theory of Social Behaviour*, 24, 243–266.

  (1994b). Fields of research and socio-genesis of social representations: a discussion of criteria and diagnostics. *Social Science Information*, 33(2), 199–228.

  (1995). Social representations, group affiliation, and projection: knowing the limits of validity. *European Journal of Social Psychology*, 25(2), 125–139.

(1996). Queries about social representations and construction. *Journal for the Theory of Social Behaviour*, 26(2), 95–120.

(1998). Social representations and beyond: brute facts, symbolic coping and domesticated worlds. *Culture and Society*, 4(3), 297–329.

(2007). Vernacular science knowledge: its role in everyday life communication. *Public Understanding of Science*, 16(1), 7–22.

Wagner, W., and Hayes, N. (2005). *Everyday discourse and common sense*. Basingstoke: Palgrave Macmillan.

Wagner, W., and Kronberger, N. (2001). Killer tomatoes! Collective symbolic coping with biotechnology. In Deaux and Philogène (eds.), pp. 147–164.

Wagner, W., Elejabarrieta, F., and Lahnsteiner, I. (1995). How the sperm dominates the ovum – objectification by metaphor in the social representation of conception. *European Journal of Social Psychology*, 25, 671–688.

Wagner, W., Holtz, P., and Kashima, Y. (2009). Construction and deconstruction of essence in representating social groups: identity projects, stereotyping, and racism. *Journal for the Theory of Social Behaviour*, 39(3), 363–383.

Wagner, W., Kronberger, N., and Seifert, F. (2002). Collective symbolic coping with new technology: knowledge, images and public discourse. *British Journal of Social Psychology*, 41, 323–343.

Wagner, W., Mecha, A., and Carvalho, M. R. (2008). Discourse and representation in the construction of witchcraft. In T. Sugiman, K. J. Gergen, W. Wagner and Y. Yamada (eds.), *Meaning in action: constructions, narratives and representations* (pp. 37–48). New York: Springer.

Wagner, W., Duveen, G., Temel, M., and Verma, J., (1999). The modernization of tradition: thinking about madness in Patna, India. *Culture and Psychology*, 5(4), 413–445.

(2000). 'I have some faith and at the same time I don't believe': cognitive polyphasia and cultural change in India. *Journal of Community and Applied Social Psychology*, 10(4), 301–314.

Wagner, W., Sen, R., Permanadeli, R., and Howarth, C. S. (2012). The veil and Muslim women's identity: cultural pressures and resistance to stereotyping. *Culture and Psychology*, 18(4), 521–541.

Wagner, W., Kronberger, N., Nagata, M., Sen, R., Holtz, P., and Palacios, F. (2010). Essentialist theory of 'hybrids': from animal kinds to ethnic categories and race. *Asian Journal of Social Psychology*, 13, 232–246.

Wagner, W., Duveen, G., Farr, R., Jovchelovitch, S., Lorenzi-Cioldi, F., Marková, I., and Rose, D. (1999). Theory and method of social representations. *Asian Journal of Social Psychology*, 2, 95–125.

Wagner-Egger, P., and Bangerter, A. (2007). La vérité est ailleurs: corrélats de l'adhésion aux théories du complot (The truth lies elsewhere: correlates of belief in conspiracy theories). *Revue Internationale de Psychologie Sociale*, 20, 31–61.

Wagner-Egger, P., Bangerter, A., Gilles, I., Green, E., Rigaud, D., Krings, F., Staerklé, C., and Clémence, A. (2011). Lay perceptions of collectives at the outbreak of the H1N1 epidemic: heroes, villains and victims. *Public Understanding of Science*, 20, 461–476.

Wagoner, B. (2009a). The experimental methodology of constructive microgenesis. In J. Valsiner, P. C. M. Molenaar, M. C. D. P. Lyra and N. Chaudhary (eds.), *Dynamic process methodology in social and developmental sciences* (pp. 99–121). New York: Springer.

(2009b). Remembering methodology: experimenting with Bartlett. In A. Toomela and J. Valsiner (eds.), *Methodological thinking in psychology: 60 years gone astray?* (pp. 145–188). Charlotte, NC : Info Age Publishing.

(2012). Culture in constructive remembering. In J. Valsiner (ed.), *Oxford handbook of culture and psychology* (pp. 1034–1055). Oxford University Press.

(2013a). Bartlett's concept of schema in reconstruction. *Theory and Psychology*, 23(5), 553–575.

(2013b). Culture and mind in reconstruction: Bartlett's analogy between individual and group processes. In A. Marvakis, J. Motzkau, D. Painter, R. Ruto-Korir, G. Sullivan, S. Triliva and M. Wieser (eds.), *Doing psychology under new conditions* (pp. 273–278). Concord, ON: Captus Press.

Wakefield, J. R. H., Hopkins, N., Cockburn, C., Shek, K. M., Muirhead, A., Reicher, S., and van Rijswijk, W. (2011). The impact of adopting ethnic or civic conceptions of national belonging for others' treatment. *Personality and Social Psychology Bulletin*, 37(12), 1599–1610.

Wald, R., Synowski, S., and Temosjok, L. (2009). Conspiracy beliefs are related to antiretroviral therapy use. Paper presented at the Society for Behavioral Medicine.

Wandel, L. P. (1994). *Voracious idols and violent hands – iconoclasm in Reformation Zurich, Strasbourg and Basel*. Cambridge University Press.

Wang, M., and Dai, J. (2011). Chinese forbearance ethos disclosing selfing and othering in stereotyping modelling. *Culture and Psychology*, 17(3), 398–417.

Washer, P. (2004). Representations of SARS in the British newspapers. *Social Science and Medicine*, 59, 2561–2571.

(2010). *Emerging infectious diseases and society*. Basingstoke: Palgrave Macmillan.

Washer, P., and Joffe, H. (2006). The 'hospital superbug': social representations of MRSA. *Social Science and Medicine*, 63(8), 2141–2152.

Weber, M. (1904–5/1976). *The Protestant ethic and the spirit of capitalism* (2nd edn). Trans. T. Parsons. London: Allen & Unwin.

(1922). *Economy and society: an outline of interpretive sociology*. Berkeley, CA: University of California Press.

(1963). *The sociology of religion*. Boston, MA: Beacon Press.

Webster, D. M., and Kruglanski, A. W. (1997). Cognitive and social consequences of the need for cognitive closure. *European Review of Social Psychology*, 8(1), 133–173.

Weigold, M. F. (2001). Communicating science. *Science Communication*, 23, 164–193.

Weinstein, N. D. (1989). Optimistic biases about personal risks. *Science*, 246, 1232–1233.

Werner, H. (1956). Microgenesis and aphasia. *Journal of Abnormal Social Psychology*, 52, 347–353.

Wertsch, J. (2002). *Voices of collective remembering*. Cambridge University Press.

Wetherell, M. (1998). Positioning and interpretative repertoires: conversation analysis and post-structuralism in dialogue. *Discourse and Society*, 9, 387–412.

(Ed.) (2009). *Identity in the 21st century: new trends in changing times*. Basingstoke: Palgrave Macmillan.

Wheelis, M. (2002). Biological warfare at the 1346 siege of Caffa. *Emerging Infectious Diseases*, 8, 971–975.

White, H. (1987). *The content of the form: narrative discourse and historical representation.* Baltimore, MD: Johns Hopkins University Press.
Whitehead, A. N., and Russell, B. (1962). *Principia mathematica* (2nd edn). Cambridge University Press.
Whitson, J. A., and Galinsky, A. D. (2008). Lacking control increases illusory pattern perception. *Science*, 322, 115–117.
Wiktorowicz, Q. (2005). *Radical Islam rising: Muslim extremism in the West.* Lanham, MD: Rowman & Littlefield.
Wildavsky, A. B. (1987). Choosing preferences by constructing institutions: cultural theory of preference formation. *American Political Science Review*, 81, 3–21.
Wittgenstein, L. (1994). *Über Gewißheit (On certainty).* Frankfurt-on-Main: Suhrkamp.
Wohl, M. J. A., and Branscombe, N. R. (2005). Forgiveness and collective guilt assignment to historical perpetrator groups depend on level of social category inclusiveness. *Journal of Personality and Social Psychology*, 88, 288–303.
Wooffitt, R. (2005). *Conversation analysis and discourse analysis: a comparative and critical introduction.* London: Sage.
Woolgar, S. (1989). The ideology of representation and the role of the agent. In H. Lawson and L. Appignanesi (eds.), *Dismantling truth. Reality in the post-modern world* (pp. 131–144). London: Weidenfeld & Nicolson.
Wulff, D. (1991). *Psychology of religion: classic and contemporary views.* New York: John Wiley.
Wundt, W. (1916). *Elements of folk psychology: outlines of a psychological history of the development of mankind.* London: Allen & Unwin.
Wunenburger, J. J. (2003). *L'imaginaire.* Paris: Presses Universitaires de France.
Wunenburger, J. J., and Araujo, A. F. (2006). *Educação e imaginário.* São Paulo: Cortez.
Wynne, B. (1982). *Rationality and ritual: the Windscale inquiry and nuclear decisions in Britain.* British Society for the History of Science.
  (1991). Knowledges in context. *Science, Technology and Human Values*, 16, 111–121.
  (1995). Public understanding of science. In S. Jasanoff, G. E. Markle, J. C. Petersen and T. Pinch (eds.), *Handbook of science and technology studies* (pp. 361–391). London: Sage.
  (2002). Risk and environment as legitimatory discourses of technology: reflexivity inside out? *Current Sociology*, 50, 459–477.
Yates, F. (1966). *The art of memory.* University of Chicago Press.
Young, J. (1999). *The exclusive society: social exclusion, crime and difference in late modernity.* London: Sage.
Young, L.B. (2011). Joe Sixpack: normality, deviance, and the disease model of alcoholism. *Culture and Psychology*, 17(3), 378–397.
Yzerbyt, V. Y., Rocher, S. J., and Schadron, G. (1997). Stereotypes as explanations: a subjective essentialistic view of group perception. In R. Spears, P. J. Oakes, N. Ellemers an S. A. Haslam (eds.), *The social psychology of stereotyping and group life* (pp. 20–50). Oxford: Blackwell.
Zaller, J., and Feldman, S. (1992). A simple theory of the survey response. *American Journal of Political Science*, 36, 579–616.
Zapiti, A. (2012). Peer interaction and cognitive development: the role of gender at 6–7 and 10–11 years olds. Ph.D. thesis, Univeristy of Cyprus.

Zapiti, A., and Psaltis, C. (2012). Asymmetries in peer interaction: the effect of social representations of gender and knowledge asymmetry on children's cognitive development. *European Journal of Social Psychology*, 42(5), 578–588.

Zelditch, M. (2001). Theories of legitimacy. In J. T. Jost and B. Major (eds.), *The psychology of legitimacy. Emerging perspectives on ideology, justice and intergroup relations* (pp. 33–53). Cambridge University Press.

Zinnbauer, B. J., and Pargament, K. I. (2005). Religion and spirituality. In R. F. Paloutzian and C. L. Park (eds.), *Handbook of the psychology of religion*. New York: Guilford Press.

Zittoun, T., Cornish, F., Gillespie, A., and Psaltis, C. (2007). The metaphor of the triangle in theories of human development. *Human Development*, 50, 208–229.

Zittoun, T., Duveen, G., Gillespie, A., Ivinson, G., and Psaltis, C. (2003). The use of symbolic resources in developmental transitions. *Culture and Psychology*, 9(4), 415–448.

Zittoun, T., Perret-Clermont, A.-N., and Barrelet, J.-M. (2008). The socio-intellectual genealogy of Jean Piaget. In A.-N. Perret-Clermont and J.-M. Barrelet (eds.), *Jean Piaget and Neuchâtel. The learner and the scholar* (pp. 109–118). Hove and New York: Psychology Press.

Index

Abric, J.-C. 202, 210
acculturation 355
action
   communicative 344, 350–352
   representations as 25–27
Adams, M. 379–380
affiliative bonds 126–127
African Muslims 351
African-Americans 158
   belief in conspiracy theories 390–392
aggregation 94
aggression 73
AIDS/HIV 388, 389
   conspiracy theories 390–392
Ajzen, I. 14–15, 17
Allport, G. W. 31, 98, 347
   Nature of Prejudice, The (1954) 324
Allum, N. C. 359
alternative representations 10, 125, 153–154, 173, 174, 291
anchoring 9, 118, 310, 361–362, 365–366
   and analysis of mediated communication 304, 306
   beliefs 289
   and meaning 131, 259
   re-anchoring 264
   semiotic process 243–244
   social imaginary 129, 133–134, 135, 137–138, 141
   social objects 193
   social signification 234, 235–236
Anderson, Benedict 314
Andreouli, E. 317
Andrews, Kevin 326–330, 331–332, 337
animal reminder theory 371
anomie theory 33, 36–37, 38
anorexia 375–376
antimonies 372, 373, 384
anxiety 381
Arendt, H. 165
Arthi, P. C. 67
Asad, T. 348–349
Asch, Solomon 84, 86, 96–97, 101–103, 104, 106, 108, 110

assimilation-accommodation process 253, 258
attitude(s) 96–100, 108–110, 398
   anti-fat 375
   change 407–409
   melancholic 61–63
   research methods 401–402
   scales 98–99
   social nature of 100–103
   tri-component model 84
attitude theory vs. social representation theory 30
attribution theory 84
Augoustinos, M. 255
autobiographical self 227
avian flu (H5N1 virus) 389
Awak, Daniel 336

Bachelard, G. 134
Baczko, B. 134
Bakhtin, M. 182
Bandura, A. 14, 17
Bangerter, A. 367
Barbour, R. 70
Barker, R. G. 13, 196
Barthes, R. 238–239
Bartlett, Frederic 143–162
   reconstructive remembering 146–148, 149
   signs and symbols 234, 244
   social constructiveness 153
Bass, B. M. 407
Bataille, M. 93
Batel, S. 305
Bauer, M. W. 7–8, 29, 66, 67, 68, 106, 180, 186, 247, 310, 359
Becker, M. 302
behaviour 4–6
   and action 12–13
   attitudes causing 14–15
   collective 37–38
   crowd 24–25
   cultural 22–24
   deviant 33, 36
   ecological 16–17
   effect of belief 17–19, 20–22
   littering 17

471

behaviour (cont.)
  mutual representational 24–25
  mutually hurting 25
  observation of 13–14
  overt 13–14, 19–20
  social representations theory 15–17
  social vs. individual 99
  verbal 13
  volitional 18–19
behavioural settings 196
belief-behaviour 17–19
Belzen, J. A. 347, 348
Berger, P. 193
Bertoldo, R. 302, 305
Bettega, N. 389
Billig, Michael 3–4, 101, 210, 213, 215, 315, 402
Bin Laden, Osama 278
biotechnology 8, 54, 67, 137, 363, 364–366
Black Death 387, 388, 389
Blanco, Matte 235
Bloomfield, L. 237–238
body control 374
Bogart, L. M. 391
Bonfantini, M. A. 240–241, 242
boundary object 49–50
Bourdieu, P. 150, 343
Bowe, M. 272
Brandon, D. T. 392
Brazil 137–138
Breakwell, G. M. 80, 254, 259, 260
British Muslims 345–346, 349
Britishness 315–318, 322, 345
Brondi, S. 301, 303
Buback, Siegfied 26
Buijs, A. 299–300, 304
Bush, George, Jr 276, 278

Caillaud, S. 75, 306
Callaghan, P. 305
Campbell, A. 72
Campbell, D. T. 32
Canter, D. 80
Cartwright, D. 407
Carugati, F. 76
Castells, M. 166
Castoriadis, C. 129, 133, 135, 141
Castro, P. 16, 302, 305
categorization 36, 184, 284, 290, 312, 370, *see also* social categories
central core (nucleus) theory 9, 83–84, 95
  central elements 83, 85–90, 91–94, 95
  corroborative methods 90, 91–92
  exploratory methods 90–91
  matrix core 93–95
  peripheral elements 83, 85–90, 91–92, 93, 94

Chalcedonian creed 46
Challenging (Mise en Cause) technique 91–92, 93
'chav' 379–381
Cherry, C. 391
cholera 389
Christianity 44, 388, 389
Chryssides, I. 8
Churchill, Winston 274
Cinnirella, M. 254
citizen science 367–368
Clarke, Philip 327
Clémence, A. 33, 72, 74, 401
Clement, C. 235
climate change 297
cognitive balance theory 84
cognitive development 114–115, 118–123, 168
cognitive dissonance 56, 84, 177
cognitive maps 135–136, 139–140
cognitive polyphasia 6, 56, 158, 163–164, 167–169, 177–178, 303
  displacement 174, 177
  and emancipated representations 302
  hybridization 174–177
  mobility and 184–185
  selective prevalence 174
  self and community 169–171
  and social relations 125–126
  varieties 172–177
cognitive processing 4–5
Coleman boat 34, 40
Coleman, J. W. 34, 36
collective remembering/memory 9, 143, 151–158, 225–226
  Bartlett's reconstructive remembering 146–148
  changes in communication technology 152–154
  Durkheim's approach 143–145
  and environment 154–156
  Halbwachs' contribution 144–146
  of historical events 273–274
  language and 152–154
  narratives and 275
  and social representations of history 276
  Vygotsky's contribution 148–150
collective representations 6, 29, 166, 179, 224, 282, 283, 344
collective symbolic coping 137, 363–366, 385–386, 387, 393, 395
collective/common consciousness 29
common sense xiii, 6–8, 11, 14, 20, 27, 41, 50, 66, 100, 107, 239, 247, 340
  everyday 323, 324, 356
  explanatory patterns 386
  global warming 306

identity as 312
knowledge 310, 311
local 167, 169
mass media's role in 373
Moscovici 115, 167, 325, 342, 360
science and 359–361, 364, 367–368
social functions 52
social order beliefs and 288, 292–294
themata 372, 384
communication 8–10
conflict and 303–306
diffusion model 51
high-fidelity model 51, 62
intergroup and interpersonal relations 10
mediated 304, 306
Moscovici 113, 117–118, 166, 280, 285–286, 360
pragmatic aspects 117
public spheres 164–165
self–alter–object 165–166, 178
and social change 283
socialization 10
strategies 9
technology 152–154
see also diffusion; language; microgenesis; propagation; propaganda
communicative games 51, 241, 243, 247
community 179
diversity 179–180, 181–184, 188–189
social representations theory and 180–181, 188–190
conflict 24–25, 299
collective remembering of 273–274
and communication 299–300, 303–306
of connotative meanings 246–247
resolution 120
language and 231
intragroup 335–338
Connerton, P. 151
connotation 234, 236–238
cultural objects 239
encyclopedic 238, 241–243
ideological 239
interpretative approach 239–243
pragmatic approach 240–241
structuralist approach 238–239, 240, 241
consensual universe 400
consent, production of 288–291
conspiracy theories 390–394
contemptuous prejudice 370
contractual realism 29
conventionalization 146–148
conversation types 122–123
conversion theory of minority influence 280
cooperation
aggregation rules 37–38
meaning in interaction 22–24

coping strategies 257–259, 263
Cortes, J. 242
Coyle, E. 73
critical mass (mechanism/models) 39–40
cultural borrowings 163
cultural development 196
cultural theory 304
culture 126

Dai, J. 382
Danziger, I. 213
De Rosa, A. S. 136
Deconchy, J.-P. 289
Dennett, D. C. 204
denotation 94, 234, 236–238, 243–244
ideological 239
interpretative approach 239–243
structuralist approach 238–239
Denzin, N. 77
Devereux, J. D. 254
differentiation 8, 58–59, 60, 107, 156, 190, 261, 323, 324
categorical 288, 292–294
normative 290–291, 293
social 284–285
diffusion 9, 10, 62, 126, 180, 285–288, 293, 360
discourse 214–215
essentialist and de-essentialist 340
out-group representation 323, 324, 325, 326–338
political 325, 326–330, 338
private 231–232
truth 23
discourse analysis 100, 210, 211, 216–222
sedimentation 212–214
disgust 370–371, 380
distributive justice 281
Doise, W. 30, 31–32, 33, 42, 72, 74, 114, 119–120, 213, 401
dominant ideology hypothesis 289
double stimulation 114
Douglas, M. 371
Draguns, J. 114
Duesberg, Peter 391
Durkheim, Emile 146, 156
body's role in remembering 151
cognitive development 168
collective representations 6, 29, 166, 179, 282, 283, 344
concepts 148
Elementary Forms of Religious Life (1912) 144, 149
figuration 131
mechanistic and organic solidarity 187
memory 143–145
shared cultural symbols 234
on suicide 31

Duveen, G.
  culture 126
  group solidarity 10, 285–293
  levels of representations 64
  microgenesis 10, 29, 113, 116–117, 118–119, 120–127, 253

Eagle, M. 18
Eaton, L. 391
Ebbinghaus, H. 146
Ebola 389, 393
Eco, U. 29, 237, 238, 241–243, 244, 248
economics 35
Edwards, D. 210, 215, 221
Eicher, V. 393, 394
Einstein, Albert 277
Elcheroth, G. 213
Elias, N. 374
emancipated representations 6, 302
embodied self 227
Emmons, R. A. 346
emotion, visceral 370–371, 380
envious prejudice 370
environment 154–156
  modification of 196
environmentalism 295–297, 308
episodic interview 67
Erikson, E. 309
essentialism 323–325, 339–340
  subjective 339
ethnic minorities 315, 390–392
ethos 369
European Association of Social Psychology 31
European Committee for Social Cohesion 188
evaluation process 253

Fabbri, P. 242
factor analysis 72, 73–74
  Correspondence Factor Analysis 72
  Latent Class Analysis (LCA) 278
  Multiple Factor Analysis 72
  Structural Equation Modeling (SEM) 76
  Principle Component Analysis 72
Farr, Robert 101, 398, 402
  'individualization of the social' 31
  theory of social representation 11
Faucheux, C. 15–16, 21
Felonneau, M.-L. 302
Festinger, L. 84
fetishism 46, 70
Fife-Schaw, C. 254
figuration 131–133
Finney, P. 221–222
Fiske, S. T. 370, 371
Flache, A. 37
Flament, Claude 87–88, 93

Flavell, J. H. 114
Flick, U. 67, 75, 306
floating representations 117
'Fm effect' 122
focus groups 67, 70–71, 402
Foot, Michael 221
Fornari, F. 235
Foster, J. L. H. 69
Foucault, M. 242
Francis, Bob 336–338
Fraser, C. 401
Fraser, Gilles 46
free market 284
Freire, Paulo 177
Freud, S. 234
Friestad, C. 76
Frigg, R. 48

Garrido, M. 16
Gaskell, G. 7–8, 29, 67, 68, 98, 106, 180, 186, 247, 310, 359
Geertz, C. 129, 348, 351
gender
  asymmetry 131
  categories 324
  differences 73
  identities 29, 121–122
  representations 20, 65, 119, 151–158, 160, 312, 380
gender role beliefs 20
Gentner, D. 235
Geortzel, T. 390
Gergen, K. 188
Gervais, M. C. 182
Gestalt, critique of behaviourism 4–6
Giddens, A. 193
Gilens, M. 374
Gilles, I. 393, 394, 396
Gillespie, A. 291, 345
Gladwell, M. 377
globalization 315
Gnostics 46–47
Gony, Leip 332–335
Greimas, A. J. 238–239, 242
group essence 324, 339
group interview 67
groups
  belongingness 120
  commonalities 24–25
  coping strategies 258
  decision making 407
  friendship ties 353
  focus 67, 70–71, 402
  hetero-referential relationships 24, 27
  identification 15
  identity 343–344, 345–346
  interdependence 36

majority influence 285, 288–291
minority influence 285, 291–293
norms 344
orthodox 289
own vs. alternative representations 153–154
segmentation 58–59
understanding of reality 6
see also ingroups; intergroup relations; out-groups
Guimelli, C. 73, 89

H1N1 virus (swine flu) 389, 393–394, 396
H5N1 virus (avian flu) 389
Haarhoff, G. 389
Habermas, H. 23, 165
Haddon, Alfred Cort 147
Hakeem, Hakeem 331–332
Halbertal, M. 45
Halbwachs, Maurice 143–146, 149, 155, 158, 162
Halkier, B. 70
Hanke, K. 278
Hanley, E. 231
Harary, F. 407
Harré, R. 51, 99, 156, 203, 231
Haslam, N. 324
hatred 371
Hawk, B. 334
Hayes, N. 8, 32–33, 131–132
Health Belief Model 395
health ethic (as symbol/metaphor) 375
hegemonic representations 6, 302
Heider, F. 84, 106
Hepburn, A. 212
Hermans, H. J. M. 182
Herrera, M. 272
Herzlich, Claudine 66, 225, 398
Hewstone, M. 338
Hill, P. C. 347
Hilton, D. J. 216, 270, 276
Himmelweit, H. T. 5, 18, 397, 399
Hispanic Americans, belief in conspiracy theories 390–391
history 269–270
  measuring and modelling 275–279
  social representations of 215–217, 271–275
  textual analysis 275
  uses of representations of 217–222
Hitler, Adolf 231, 274, 275, 276, 277, 278
Hjelmslev, L. 238–239, 240
Hodge, B. 242
Holzl, E. 402
homosexuality 292, 370, 388, 391
Hood, R. W. J. 347
Hovland, C. I. 83, 84, 96
Howard, Peter 221

Howarth, C. 138, 183, 211, 215, 220, 250, 255, 317, 340
Huang, L.-L. 279
Hussein, Saddam 278
Hutchinson, A. B. 391
Hyman, H. 410

I and *Me* 343–344
iconoclasm, 43–50, 56, 57, 62, 63
identity content configuration (ICC) 253
identity process theory 250–266
  coping/change strategies 257–259, 263
  social context 255–256
  and social representations theory 263–265
identity 24
  and action 24, 313
  processes 253
  principles 254–255
  threat 256–257
  structure 251–253
  concept 309
  and social representation 259–265, 311–314
  see also national identity; social identity
images
  moving 140–141
  religious 43–47, 57
  see also imaginary; social imaginary
imaginary 128–130, 133
  iconic 135–136
  as knowledge 134–135
  Latin American 138–139
  power of 133–134
  research methods 139–141
  social representations and 135–139
  see also social imaginary
Imiaslavic controversy 43
immigrants 185–186
individual differences, organizing principles 72–73
individual vs. collective representations 6
individualism 30, 31
individualist cultures 372–373
infectious disease 385–386
  conspiracy theories 390–392, 394
  caused by out-groups 388–390, 394
  as divine punishment 388
  germ theory 387
  miasmatic theory 387
  othering of threat 389
  social history 387–388
  social representations 392–395
  as weapons of war 387
in-groups
  and out-groups 25
  identities 180
  norms 15, 24–25
  over-evaluation 36

Inhelder, B. *et al.* 114
Innes, J. M. 255
installation theory 193–196, 207, 208
  institutional layer 197–198
  physical layer 197
  psychological layer 197–198
institutions, evolutionary role 206–208
intergroup relations 10
  attitudes 36
  conflict 35–36, 305, 387
  positioning analysis 232
  stereotype content 369–370
internalization 120
International Union for the Preservation of Nature 296
interobjectivity 160, 199
interpersonal relations 10
interview methods 66–68, 212
Iramuteq 90
Isaac, L. A. 392
Islam
  communal transformation 352–354
  icons 44, 45, 348
  prescriptions 350–352

James, William 343, 346
Japanese (language) 228
Jaspal, R. 254
Jaspars, J. 401
Jews, and disease threat 387, 389
Jodelet, Denise 22, 52, 69, 135–136, 143, 158–160, 224, 389
  Madness and Social Representations 156, 183
Joffe, H. 69, 369, 374, 380, 383, 389
Johnson, M. 131
Jovchelovitch, S. 66, 124, 165, 171, 182
Just World Hypothesis 31, 32, 381, 383
justice perceptions 281

Kahneman, D. 377
Kalampalikis, N. 75, 306
Kalichman, S. C. 391
Kant, Immanual 281
Kasanen, K. 19
Katona, G. 35
Kelly, Fran 329–330
Kempton, W. 20–21
Kinnvall, C. 318
knowledge
  common sense 311
  distributed 201
  encounters 171–177
  everyday 362–363
  the imaginary as 134–135
  innovation-evaluation 362–363
  loci of production 243–244
  microgenesis of 113–127
  necessary 121
  scientific 358–368
  see also social knowledge
Kotler, P. 397, 399–400, 401, 405
Kress, G. R. 242
Krueger, F. 113
Kuhn, Thomas 3, 41

labour, social division of 201
Lahlou, S. 403
Lakoff, G. 131
Lakotas, 3
language 117, 228–229
  and conflict 231
  connotative 238, 241, 242
  context 229
  cultural variation 228
  denotative 238
  multiple signification and connotative meanings 235
  orality to literacy 152–154
László, J. 274, 275
Lauri, M. A. 399, 404
LaVeist, T. A. 392
Le Goff, J. 128, 130
legitimacy 269–270, 279, 280–282, 284, 288, 290, 291–292, 293–294
Lenin, V. 3
Leontiev, A. N. 149
Lepenies, W. 62, 63
Lerner, M. J. 31, 32
Lewin, Kurt 7, 30, 31, 54, 407–408
Lewinian life space 7
Likert, R. 98–99
Liu, J. H. 215–216, 270, 271, 274, 276, 277, 279
Livingstone, L. 71
Lloyd, B. 10, 64, 113, 116–117
Lo Monaco, G. 73
Lorenzi-Cioldi, F. 72, 401
Lorenz, K. 200
Lotman, I. U. M. 242, 246
Luckmann, T. 193
Lunt, P. 71
Luria, A. R. 114

Macy, M. 37
madness 158–160, 183
Margalit, A. 45
Marková, I. 145, 173, 210, 372
Markowe, L. A. 254
Marx, Karl 3
Matrix Core Theory (théorie du Noyau Matrice) 84, 93–95
Mauss, Marcel 151
Mayor, E. 393, 394, 395

Mead, G. H. 165, 343–344
melancholia 61–63
memes 203
memory *see* collective remembering/memory; remembering
Menezes, J. 16
mental illness 158–160, 183
mental maps 135–136, 139–140
mental representation 49, 106, 139–140, 204, 207
Merton, R. K. 33, 36–37, 38
Messner, S. 38
metaphors 235, 362, 375
  construction of 131–138
methodological individualism 30, 31, 33
methodological intersubjectivism 30
Miaphysitism 46
Michel-Guillou, E. 304
microgenesis 10, 19–20, 29, 113–115
  social interaction and cognitive development 118–123
  and social representations theory 116–118
Milgram, S. 31, 196
Mill, John Stuart 237
Miller, S. 359
minority groups 161, 285, 295, 340, 390–392
mnemonic technologies 148–150
Moghaddam, F. M. 112, 231
Moliner, P. 132
Moloney, G. 138
monuments 155–156
moral order 284
mores 101
Moscovici, Serge
  anchoring 9, 118, 193, 310
  attitudes 97
  cause of behaviour 15–16, 21, 108
  closed-mindedness 111
  cognitive polyphasia 145, 167–168
  collective representations 29
  communication 113, 117–118, 166, 280, 285–286, 360
  consensual universe 400
  conversion theory 291
  on Duveen 123–124
  figurative nucleus 85
  I and *Me* 343
  knowledge construction 361
  knowledge production 243
  Psychanalyse, La: son image et son public (1961) 59, 111, 143, 156, 359–360
  logical system vs. normative metasystem 119
  model of social influence 115
  objectification 9, 147, 248, 310
  organization of the mind 97
  propaganda 173

psychoanalysis 8, 11, 104, 126, 156–158, 163, 166, 180, 235, 342, 359–360, 362
race 324
reified universe 400
representations 153
research methods 66, 402
science and common sense 367
sense-making 368
social psychology 3–4, 31, 42, 96, 126, 147, 149, 349
social representations 5, 84, 130, 145, 147, 178, 181, 260, 283, 309–310, 323, 325, 335, 338, 344–345, 349
structures 83, 84
types of representations 6, 262
on Vygotsky 149
Mugny, G. 114, 119
Muncer, S. 72
Mussolini, Benito 231

Napoleon 275, 276
narrative 265
  historical 270–271, 275–277
narrative interview 66–67
national identity 135, 271, 305, 309, 313–316
  British 315–318
  Japanese 274–275
  Greek 319–321
  Hungarian 275
nationalism 314–315
nationhood 314
Nazis 161, 274, 371, 376
necessary knowledge 121
Nehru, Jawaharlal, *Discovery of India* (1944) 272–273
neoconservativism 287
neoliberalism 287
Nesbitt-Larking, P. 318
Noelle-Neumann, E. 290
Nora, P. 155, 270
norms
  formation 31
  hegemonic 302
  in-group 15, 24–25
  internality 302
  social 15
Nowotny, H. 367

obedience 31
obesity 375
objectification 9, 72, 85, 129, 135, 147, 310, 362, 374, 379
  alterations to 264
  and meaning 259
  and metaphors 131–138
  semiotic process 243–244
  and social signification 234, 235–236

objects
  dual selection process 206
  representations and 200–202
  sets 205
ontogenesis 116, 118
orientalism 288
Orne, M. 31
orthodoxy 289
Ortony, A. 235
othering 389–390, 393, 394
otherness 158, 183
out-groups 10
  derogation of 36, 369–370, 376–378, 383
  gender 380
  identities 180
  infectious disease and 388–390
  representations of 323, 324, 325, 326–338
  prejudice 369–371, 384
Owen, Frank 221

Paez, D. 274
Paloutzian, R. F. 346
Pargament, K. I. 347
Paris, Michael 221
Parker, I. 210
Parsons, Talcott 194, 282
paternalistic prejudice 370, 371
Pennebaker, J. W. 277
Pennington, D. F. 407
perception 132, 147
  central traits 86
Perez, J. A. 120
Perret-Clermont, A.-N. 114, 117
personal representations vs. social representations 259–263
perspective 100
Piaget, J. 41, 114–115, 121, 124, 127, 168
  Child's Conception of the World (1926/29) 115
Piagetian theory 114–115, 124
Pierce, Charles Sanders 235, 236, 239–243
points of view 96–97, 100, 103, 104, 105–112
polemical representations 6
political representation 48
positioning theory 228, 229–233
  analysis 224–225, 231–232
  conditions of meaningfulness 229–230
  positioning triangle 230–231
Potter, A. 212
Potter, J. 210, 215, 217
Poumadère, M. 305
pragmatic imperative 14
prejudice 324, 369
  reduction of 125
  symbolization and 371
  syndrome 339, 371
  types 370, 371

procedural justice 281
projects 186–187, 190
propaganda 9, 10, 127, 134, 173, 285–286, 291–293, 360
  Nazi 371
propagation 9, 10, 127, 180, 285–286, 288–291, 293, 360
Propp, V. 275, 393
Protestant work ethic 375, 378, 382
Provencher, C. 70
Psaltis, C. 125
psychoanalysis 9, 11, 342, 359–360, 362
  communication 166, 180
  community 180–181
  in the public sphere 163
  representation 93, 104, 111
public opinion 96, 98, 398, 399
  research methods 401–405
public sphere 29, 164–165
  social representations and 165–167
Purkhardt, S. C. 339

questionnaire 402

race 324–325, 340
racialized representations 323
racism 328
radical imaginary 129
Raisborough, J. 379–381
Räty, H. 19
Raudsepp, M. 246–247
realistic group conflict theory 35–36
reciprocity, balance of 106
Red Army Faction 26
Reicher, S. 213
reified universe 400
Reis, E. 16
relative deprivation theory 33, 39–40
religion 346–349
religious orientation scale 347
remembering
  the body and 150–152
  reconstructive 146–148
  see also collective remembering
representations
  as actions 25–27
  alternative 10, 125, 153–154, 173, 174, 291
  collective 6, 29, 166, 179, 224, 282, 283, 344
  emancipated 6, 302
  floating 117
  gender 20, 65, 119, 151–158, 160, 312, 380
  hegemonic 6, 302
  individual sets 202–204, 208
  meanings 47–48
  and objects 200–202
  of out-groups 323, 324, 325, 326–338
  personal 259–263

polemical 6
political 48
racialized 323
of risk 305
'shared' 203
stability and dynamics 87–90
types 6, 262
see also social representations
reproduction (of society) 193, 194, 199
research methodology 57–63, 64
    attitude towards 61–63
    content 60
    cross-overs of cultural trajectories 61
    levels of analysis 64–65
    longitudinal-sequential data 60–61
    mixed methods 78–79
    multi-level analysis 57–58
    multi-method analysis 58
    qualitative 66–71
        conversation analysis 70
        documentary analysis 70
        ethnographic approach 69–70
        interviews 66–68, 212
        longitudinal studies 65
        questionnaire 402
        surveys 391, 401–402
        thematic analysis 70–71
    quantitative 71–77
        Alceste method 74–77
        factor analysis 72, 73–74
        hierarchical cluster analysis 74
        horseshoe phenomenon (Guttman effect) 73–74
    researcher's role 68
    segmentation 58–59, 67
    sender–reception studies 59–60
    time-structures 60–61
    triangulation 77–78
retributive justice 281
Rilke, Rainer Maria 45
Rise, J. 76
risk, conflicting representations of 305
ritual 151–152
Rivers, W. H. R. 147
Roberto, E. 399–400, 401, 405
Roberts, Kevin 410
Rocher, S. J. 339
Rogers, W. L. 273
Roland, G. R. 38
role theory 229
Rommetveit, R. 123
Roqueplo, P. 201
Rosa, A. 235
Rose, D. 68
Rosenberg, M. J. 83, 84
Rosenfeld, R. 38
Ross, J. M. 347

Rothbart, M. 324
Rousseau, Jean-Jacques 281
Roysamb, E. 76

Sammut, G. 9
sampling theory 48
Sander, F. 113
Sani, F. 272
Sapir, E. 237
SARS 389
Sartre, Jean-Paul 104, 105, 107
Saussure, Ferdinand de 43, 235–236, 238
Savarkar, Vinayak 273
Scappini, E. 76
Schadron, G. 339
Schelling, Thomas 37–40
Schuman, H. 273
science and technology 358–368
    and self-control 376
    and society, paradigms 359
scientific racism 324
scientific representation 48
selective forgetting 274–275
self/selves 182, 227–228
    cultural variations 228
    positioning analysis 231–232
self-categorization 15, 111, 293, 370
self-control ethos 369
    body 374–376, 379
    'the chav' 379–381
    destiny 378–379
    function of 381–382
    and individualism 372–373
    and infectious diseases 389
    mind 376–378, 379
    social representations and stereotypes 372
self-efficacy theory 14, 17
self-fulfilling prophecy 33–34
self-identity 16
self-indulgence 376
Selleri, P. 76
semantic barriers 10
sense-making 361, 363, 365, 368
    processes 385–386
sexual roles 131
Sheatsley, P. 410
Sherif, M. 31, 35–36
Sibley, C. G. 271, 278, 279
Siegler, R. S. 114
signification
    asymmetrical/symmetrical 234
    counter-signification 247–248
    designification 248
    multiple levels 234
    recursive semiosis 244–248
    resignification 247–248
    social 235–236

single mothers 378, 380
Sloterdijk, P. 45
smallpox 387
Smedslund, J. 17–18
Smith, Adam 35
Smith, L. 121
Snellman, L. 19
social behaviour, nested model 108–110
social categories 324
  of belonging 182
  gender 324
  racial 326, 327–328, 329, 334
social change
  group strategies 407–409
  and social marketing 397–399
  and social representations 400–401
social cognition 84–85, 95, 170
social cohesion 188–189
social conformism 39–40
social construction 100, 153, 194, 199, 207–208
Social Darwinism 324
social diversity 284
social exclusion 284, 291, 318, 323, 328, 330, 335, 340, 356, 369, 381–382, 383
social gender identities 121–122
  formation 29
Social Genevans 114, 116, 119
social identity 10, 24, 35, 36, 116–117, 251–252, 370
  history and the construction of 271
  and Self-categorization Theory 15
  and social representations 138
social imaginary 128–130, 133–134
  significations 139, 140
social knowledge 96, 101, 179–180, 341, 343, 358
  expressions of 344
  and identity 183–184
  as interdependence 186–188
  intersecting 184, 190
  movement in 184–186
  projects 186–187, 190
  transformative aspects 355, 356
social marketing 397–399
  media campaigns 408
  organ donation campaign 401, 403–406, 408–409
  research methods 401–405
  role of social representations 399
  segmentation of target groups 405–406
  and social change 400–401
social marking 119–120
social mechanisms 33
  and economic morality 38–40
  macro-level 40–41
  contextual 41

micro-level 41
  in social psychology and sociology 35–38
  transformational 35, 41–42
social object 21–22
social order 280
  conflict theories 282, 283
  consensus 280–282
  diffusion 285–288
  propagation 288–291
  social representations approach 282–286
Social Order Representations Model 284
social organization, theory of 36–37
social positioning 104–105
social psychology
  genetic 156
  levels of analysis 30
  social mechanisms 35–38
social regulations 119–120
social remembering 151–158, see also collective remembering
social re-presentation 8, 107, 352–354
social representations
  dual nature/functions of 341–343, 355–356
  emotional content 265
  evolution of 204–206, 208
  and identity process theory 263–265
  imaging dimension 130–131, 135–142
  as a logical function 51–53
  macro/micro analysis 29–40
  methodological considerations 57–63
  models 7–8, 31, 54, 61, 63, 106, 107
  paradigmatic definition 52–53, 63
  vs. personal 259–263
  and points of view 104–112
  prescriptive function 343–344
  processes 360–362
  stereotypes and self-control ethos 372
  stickiness 60, 262–263
  transformative functions 344–346, 349, 354, 355, 356
  types 262–263
social representations theory 24, 27, 309–311
  analysis of communication systems 53–54
  attitude of 61–63
  formulation 50–51
  intensional approach 202–203
  and intergroup regard 371–372
  and semiotics 235–236
  structural features and functions 54
social self 227
social structure 36–37
social memory see collective remembering/memory
socialization 10
sociocognitive conflict 115
sociogenesis 116, 118

sociological imagination 70–71
sociology
  social mechanisms 35–38
  transformational mechanisms 35
Sontag, Susan 388
Soyland, A. J. 213
Sperber, Dan 204
Spini, D. 74
S-R responses 5–6
Staerklé, C. 369, 374, 380, 383
Stalin, Josef 276
Stanley, J. C. 32
statistical representation 48
Stephens, C. 182, 184
stereotype content
  conceptual framework 374–379
  formation process 373–374
  social representations and self-control ethos 372
  symbolization 371, 374
  visceral emotion 370–371, 380
stereotyping 369
Sternberg, R. 235
structural approach 211
structural inequality 284
Structural Theory of Stereotype Content 370
structuration theory 193
Sudanese refugees 323, 325–326
  newsprint representations 330–335
  political discourse, representations in 326–330
  radio representations 335–338
suicide 31
Sumner, W. G. 101
survey research methods 391, 401–402
sustainability
  illustrations of conflict and communication 303–306
  illustrations of time and institution 300–303
  social study of 295
  and theory of social representations 298–300
swine flu (H1N1 virus) 389, 393–394, 396
symbolic coping *see* collective symbolic coping
Synowski, S. 391
synthetic biology 365–366
syphilis 389, 392

Tajfel, H. 25, 31, 35, 370
Tan, S. 232
Taylor, Charles 47
Taylor, M. 324
Temosjok, L. 391
Terkel, S. 221
themata 306, 372, 384
Theory of Planned Behaviour 14–15
Theory of Self-Efficacy 14, 17
thought
  and action 225–226
  and language 228–229
Thurstone, L. L. 98
Tileagă, C. 217
Toblerone model of social representations 7–8, 29, 54, 57, 61, 63, 106
Toblerone pack model of social representations 107
Tolman, E. C. 136
Toth, J. 275
Tourangeau, R. 235
tribalism 335–338
trust/distrust 386, 390–393, 395–396
Trutkowski, C. 402
Tsirogianni, S. 9
Tuskegee Syphilis Study 392

Uexküll, J. von 195, 196
Ungar, S. 393
Urry, J. 184
utterances, significance of 229

Valsiner, J. 235
Vergès, P. 90
Verkuyten, M. 340
Vignoles, V. L. 254
Vincze, O. 275
Voelklein, C. 215
Vygotsky, L. S. 113, 127, 143–162
  development principle 226–227, 232
  double stimulation 114
  internalization 120
  mediated memory 148–150, 155, 156
  semiotic position 244

Wagner, W. 8, 32–33, 131–132, 137, 185, 364
Wagner-Egger, P. 393, 395
Wagoner, B. 9
Wald, R. 391
Wang, M. 382
waterwheel model of social representations 54, 56, 61, 63, 107
Weber, Max 30, 378
Werner, H. 113
Wertsch, J. 154, 275
Wetherell, M. 217
White, Hayden 270
wind rose model of social representations 8, 54, 55–56, 107
Wittgenstein, L. 51
writing 215
Wunenburger, J. J. 134

Yzerbyt, V. Y. 339

Zaltman, E. 397, 401
Zinnbauer, B. J. 347